# INTRODUCTION TO BUSINESS LAW

**3**

## Jeffrey F. Beatty
*Boston University*

## Susan S. Samuelson
*Boston University*

SOUTH-WESTERN
CENGAGE Learning™

Australia • Brazil • Japan • Korea • Mexico • Singapore • Spain • United Kingdom • United States

SOUTH-WESTERN
CENGAGE Learning™

**Introduction to Business Law,
Third Edition**

Jeffrey F. Beatty and Susan S. Samuelson

Editorial Director: Jack W. Calhoun

Editor-in-Chief: Rob Dewey

Acquisitions Editor: Vicky True

Senior Developmental Editor: Laura Bofinger

Executive Marketing Manager: Lisa Lysne

Marketing Manager: Jennifer Garamy

Content Project Manager:
Jacquelyn K Featherly

Media Editor: Kristen Meere

Manufacturing Coordinator: Kevin Kluck

Production House/Compositor:
Macmillan Publishing Solutions

Senior Art Director: Michelle Kunkler

Cover and Internal Designer:
Design Matters, Cincinnati, OH

Cover Images:
© Larry Lee Photography/CORBIS

Photo Manager: John Hill

Photo Researcher: Darren Wright

For product information and technology assistance, contact us at
**Cengage Learning Customer & Sales Support, 1-800-354-9706**

For permission to use material from this text or product,
submit all requests online at **www.cengage.com/permissions**.
Further permissions questions can be emailed to
**permissionrequest@cengage.com**.

ExamView® and ExamView Pro® are registered trademarks of FSCreations, Inc. Windows® is a registered trademark of the Microsoft Corporation used herein under license. Macintosh® and Power Macintosh® are registered trademarks of Apple Computer, Inc., used herein under license.

Library of Congress Control Number: 2009921772

Student Edition ISBN 13: 978-0-324-82699-9

Student Edition ISBN 10: 0-324-82699-0

**South-Western Cengage Learning**
5191 Natorp Boulevard
Mason, OH 45040
USA

Cengage Learning products are represented in Canada by Nelson Education, Ltd.

For your course and learning solutions, visit **academic.cengage.com**.

Purchase any of our products at your local college store or at our preferred online store, **www.ichapters.com**.

Printed in the United States of America
2 3 4 5 6 7 13 12 11 10 09

# CONTENTS: OVERVIEW

**Preface**                                        xii

## UNIT 1

### THE LEGAL ENVIRONMENT                          1

1   Introduction to Law                            2
2   Business Ethics and Social Responsibility      15
3   Courts, Litigation, and
    Alternative Dispute Resolution                 27
4   Constitutional, Statutory,
    Administrative, and Common Law                 47
5   Intentional Torts and Business Torts           66
6   Negligence and Strict Liability                80
7   Criminal Law and Procedure                     94
8   International Law                              111

## UNIT 2

### CONTRACTS                                      127

9   Introduction to Contracts                     128
10  Legality, Consent, and Writing                148
11  Conclusion to Contracts                       170
12  Sales and Product Liability                   191
13  Negotiable Instruments                        211
14  Secured Transactions                          226
15  Bankruptcy                                    244

## UNIT 3

### AGENCY AND EMPLOYMENT LAW                      261

16  Agency                                        262
17  Employment Law                                279
18  Employment Discrimination                     294
19  Labor Law                                     309

## UNIT 4

### BUSINESS ORGANIZATIONS                         325

20  Starting a Business:
    LLCs and Other Options                        326
21  Corporations                                  344
22  Government Regulation:
    Securities and Antitrust                      360
23  Accountants' Liability                        375

## UNIT 5

### PROPERTY AND CONSUMER LAW                      391

24  Consumer Law                                  392
25  Environmental Law                             408
26  Cyberlaw                                      422
27  Intellectual Property                         437
28  Real Property                                 451
29  Landlord-Tenant Law                           465
30  Personal Property and Bailment                479
31  Estate Planning                               492
32  Insurance                                     507

**Appendix A**
The Constitution of the United States             A1

**Appendix B**
Uniform Commercial Code                           B1

**Glossary**                                      G1
**Table of Cases**                                T1
**Index**                                         I1

iii

# CONTENTS

**Preface**     xii

## UNIT 1

### THE LEGAL ENVIRONMENT     1

## Chapter 1
### Introduction to Law     2
Three Important Ideas about Law     3
   Power     3
   Importance     4
   Fascination     4
Sources of Contemporary Law     4
   Constitutions     4
   Statutes     5
   Common Law and Equity     5
   Administrative Law     7
Criminal and Civil Law     7
   Law and Morality     7
Working with the Book's Features     8
   Analyzing a Case     8
   *Kuehn v. Pub Zone*     8
   "You Be the Judge"     10
YOU BE THE JUDGE *James v. Meow Media*     10

## Chapter 2
### Business Ethics and
### Social Responsibility     15
Why Bother with Ethics?     17
   Society as a Whole Benefits from
      Ethical Behavior     17
   Money Does Not Buy Happiness     17
   People Feel Better when
      They Behave Ethically     18
   Unethical Behavior Can Be Very Costly     18
What Is Ethical Behavior?     18
   Analyzing the Ethics Checklist     19
   Applying the Ethics Checklist:
      Making Decisions     20

## Chapter 3
### Courts, Litigation, and
### Alternative Dispute Resolution     27
Three Fundamental Areas of Law     28
   Litigation versus Alternative
      Dispute Resolution     28
Alternative Dispute Resolution     28
   Mediation     29
   Arbitration     29
Court Systems     29
   State Courts     29
   Federal Courts     31
Litigation     33
   Pleadings     33
   *Stinton v. Robin's Wood, Inc.*     37
   *Jones v. Clinton*     38
Trial     39
   Adversary System     39
   Right to Jury Trial     39
   Opening Statements     40
   Burden of Proof     40
   Plaintiff's Case     40
   Defendant's Case     41
   Closing Argument     41
   Verdict     41
Appeals     42
   Appeal Court Options     42

## Chapter 4
### Constitutional, Statutory,
### Administrative, and Common Law     47
Constitutional Law     48
   Government Power     48
   Power Granted     48
YOU BE THE JUDGE *Kennedy v. Louisiana*     50
   Protected Rights     50
   *Texas v. Johnson*     52
   Fifth Amendment: Due Process
      and the Takings Clause     52
   Fourteenth Amendment: Equal
      Protection Clause     54

Statutory Law                                           54
   Committee Work                         55
Common Law                                              56
   Stare Decisis                          57
   Bystander Cases                        57
   *Tarasoff v. Regents of The University
    of California*                     58
Administrative Law                                      59
   Rule Making                            59
   Adjudication                           60

**Chapter 5**
**Intentional Torts and**
**Business Torts**                                      66
Intentional Torts                                       68
   Defamation                             68
   Opinion                                68
YOU BE THE JUDGE *Yeagle v. Collegiate Times*           69
   Public Personalities                   69
   *Jane Doe and Nancy Roe v. Lynn Mills*  71
Damages                                                 71
   Compensatory Damages                   71
   Punitive Damages                       72
   *Boeken v. Philip Morris, Incorporated* 73
Business Torts                                          74
   Tortious Interference with a Contract  74
   Intrusion                              74
   Commercial Exploitation                75

**Chapter 6**
**Negligence and Strict Liability**                     80
Negligence                                              81
   Duty of Due Care                       81
   *Hernandez v. Arizona Board of Regents* 82
   Landowner's Duty                       82
   Crime and Tort: Landowner's Liability  83
   *Wiener v. Southcoast Childcare Centers, Inc.*  83
   Breach of Duty                         84
   Factual Cause and Foreseeable Harm     84
   Injury                                 86
   *Ra v. Superior Court*                 87
   Damages                                87
Defenses                                                87
   Assumption of the Risk                 87
   Contributory and Comparative
    Negligence                         88
Strict Liability                                        89
   Ultrahazardous Activity                89

YOU BE THE JUDGE *New Jersey Department
of Environmental Protection v. Alden Leeds, Inc.*       89

**Chapter 7**
**Criminal Law and Procedure**                          94
Crime, Society, and Law                                 95
   Civil Law/Criminal Law                 95
   The Prosecution's Case                 96
   Defenses                               97
YOU BE THE JUDGE *Bieber v. People*                     97
Crimes That Harm Business                               98
   Larceny                                98
   Computer Crime                         98
   *United States v. Dragon*              99
   Fraud                                  99
   Embezzlement                           100
Crimes Committed by Business                            101
   *Commonwealth v. Angelo Todesca Corp.*  101
   Compliance Programs                    102
   RICO                                   102
   Money Laundering                       102
   *United States v. Kennard*             103
The Criminal Process                                    104
   Warrant                                105
   Search and Seizure                     105
   Arrest                                 105
   Indictment                             106
   Arraignment                            106
   Trial and Appeal                       106

**Chapter 8**
**International Law**                                    111
MNEs and Power                                          113
Trade Regulation                                        113
   Export Controls                        113
   Import Controls                        114
   *Avenues in Leather, Inc. v. U.S.*      114
   Regional Agreements                    117
International Sales Agreements                           118
   What Law Governs the Sale of Goods?    118
   Choice of Forum                        119
   Final Choices                          119
   Letter of Credit                       119
   *Centrifugal Casting Machine Co., Inc.
    v. American Bank & Trust Co.*      120
YOU BE THE JUDGE *Carnero v. Boston
Scientific Corporation*                                 121
Foreign Corrupt Practices Act                           122

## UNIT 2

### CONTRACTS                                              127

**Chapter 9**

**Introduction to Contracts**                             128

The Purpose of a Contract                                 130
  Judicial Activism versus Judicial Restraint   130
  Issues (and Answers)                           131
  Contracts Defined                              131
Types of Contracts                                        131
  Bilateral and Unilateral Contracts            131
  Express and Implied Contracts                  132
  *Demasse v. ITT Corporation*                   132
  Executory and Executed Contracts               133
  Valid, Unenforceable, Voidable,
    and Void Agreements                 133
Remedies Created by Judicial Activism                     133
  Promissory Estoppel                            134
  Quasi-Contract                                 134
  *Novak v. Credit Bureau Collection Service*    135
Sources of Contract Law                                   135
  Common Law                                     135
  Uniform Commercial Code                        136
  Restatement (Second) of Contracts              136
Agreement                                                 137
  Meeting of the Minds                           137
  Offer                                          137
  Problems with Definiteness                     137
  *Baer v. Chase*                                138
  Termination of Offers                          139
  Acceptance                                     139
  Mirror Image Rule                              139
  UCC and the Battle of Forms                    140
Consideration                                             141
  Illusory Promise                               142
YOU BE THE JUDGE *Culbertson v. Brodsky*                  142

**Chapter 10**

**Legality, Consent, and Writing**                        148

Legality                                                  150
  Restraint of Trade                             150
  Sale of a Business                             150
  Employment                                     150
  *King v. Head Start Family Hair Salons, Inc.*  151
  Exculpatory Clauses                            152
Unconscionable Contracts                                  153
Capacity and Consent                                      154
  Capacity                                       154
  Reality of Consent                             155
  *Fimbel v. DeClark*                            158

Contracts in Writing                                      160
  Written Contracts                              160
  Contracts That Must Be in Writing              161
  *Baker v. Daves*                               161
YOU BE THE JUDGE *Sawyer v. Mills*                        163
  Promise Made in Consideration of Marriage      164
  What the Writing Must Contain                  164

**Chapter 11**

**Conclusion to Contracts**                               170

Third Party Beneficiary                                   171
  *Schauer v. Mandarin Gems of
    California, Inc.*                   173
Assignment and Delegation                                 174
  Assignment                                     174
  Delegation of Duties                           175
Performance and Discharge                                 176
  Performance                                    176
  Good Faith                                     177
  *Brunswick Hills Racquet Club Inc. v.
    Route 18 Shopping Center Associates* 178
  Breach                                         179
  Impossibility                                  179
Remedies                                                  179
  Expectation Interest                           180
YOU BE THE JUDGE *Bi-Economy Market,
Inc. v. Harleysville Ins. Co. of New York*                182
  Reliance Interest                              183
  Restitution Interest                           183
  Other Equitable Interests                      183
  *Milicic v. Basketball Marketing Company, Inc.* 185

**Chapter 12**

**Sales and Product Liability**                           191

Sales                                                     192
  Development of the UCC                         192
  Contract Formation                             194
  *Jannusch v. Naffziger*                        195
  Performance and Remedies                       198
Warranties and Product Liability                          199
  Express Warranties                             200
YOU BE THE JUDGE *Keller v. Inland
Metals All Weather Conditioning, Inc.*                    200
  Implied Warranties                             201
  *Goodman v. Wenco Foods, Inc.*                 202
  Negligence                                     203
  Strict Liability                               203
  *Uniroyal Goodrich Tire Company v.
    Martinez*                           205

**Chapter 13**
   **Negotiable Instruments** 211
Commercial Paper 212
Types of Negotiable Instruments 212
The Fundamental "Rule" of Commercial Paper 213
   Negotiability 214
YOU BE THE JUDGE *Blasco v. Money*
*Services Center* 216
   Negotiation 217
   Holder in Due Course 218
   Consumer Exception 220
   *Scott v. Mayflower Home Improvement Corp.* 220

**Chapter 14**
   **Secured Transactions** 226
Secured Transactions 227
   Revised Article 9 229
Attachment of a Security Interest 229
   Agreement 229
   Possession 230
   Value 230
   Debtor Rights in the Collateral 230
   Attachment to Future Property 230
Perfection 231
   Nothing Less Than Perfection 231
   Perfection by Filing 231
   *Corona Fruits & Veggies, Inc. v. Frozsun*
      *Foods, Inc.* 233
   Perfection by Possession 234
   Perfection of Consumer Goods 234
Protection of Buyers 236
   Buyers in Ordinary Course of Business 236
YOU BE THE JUDGE *Conseco Finance*
*Servicing Corp. v. Lee* 237
Priorities Among Creditors 237
Default and Termination 238
   Default 238
Termination 239

**Chapter 15**
   **Bankruptcy** 244
Overview of Bankruptcy 245
Chapter 7 Liquidation 246
   Filing a Petition 246
   Voluntary Petition 246
   Involuntary Petition 247
   Trustee 247
   Creditors 247
   Automatic Stay 248
   *Jackson v. Holiday Furniture* 248

Bankruptcy Estate 249
Payment of Claims 250
Discharge 251
*In Re: John & Julie Hoffman* 253
Chapter 11 Reorganization 253
   Debtor in Possession 254
   Creditors' Committee 254
   Plan of Reorganization 254
   Confirmation of the Plan 254
   Discharge 254
   Small-Business Bankruptcy 254
Chapter 13 Consumer Reorganizations 255
   Beginning a Chapter 13 Case 255
   Plan of Payment 256
   Discharge 256

# UNIT 3

## AGENCY AND EMPLOYMENT LAW 261

**Chapter 16**
   **Agency** 262
Creating an Agency Relationship 263
   Consent 263
   Control 264
   Fiduciary Relationship 264
Duties of Agents to Principals 264
   Duty of Loyalty 264
   *Otsuka v. Polo Ralph Lauren*
      *Corporation* 264
   Other Duties of an Agent 266
   Principal's Remedies when the Agent
      Breaches a Duty 267
Duties of Principals to Agents 267
Terminating an Agency Relationship 267
Liability 268
   Principal's Liability for Contracts 268
   Agent's Liability for Contracts 269
   Principal's Liability for Torts 270
   *Doe v. Liberatore* 272
   Agent's Liability for Torts 273

**Chapter 17**
   **Employment Law** 279
Introduction 280
Employment Security 280
   National Labor Relations Act 280
   Family and Medical Leave Act 281
   COBRA 281

Common Law Protections 281
*Kozloski v. American Tissue*
   *Services Foundation* 282
Whistleblowing 284
Safety and Privacy in the Workplace 285
Workplace Safety 285
Employee Privacy 286
YOU BE THE JUDGE *Michael A.*
*Smyth v. the Pillsbury Co.* 287
Financial Protection 287
Fair Labor Standards Act 287
Workers' Compensation 288
Social Security 288

**Chapter 18**
   **Employment Discrimination** 294
Equal Pay Act of 1963 295
Title VII 295
Proof of Discrimination 295
YOU BE THE JUDGE *Jespersen v.*
*Harrah's* 296
Color 297
Religion 298
Defenses to Charges of
   Discrimination 298
Affirmative Action 299
Sexual Harassment 299
Procedures and Remedies 300
Pregnancy 300
Age Discrimination 301
*Smith v. City of Jackson* 301
Americans with Disabilities Act 302

**Chapter 19**
   **Labor Law** 309
Unions Develop 311
Labor Unions Today 312
Organizing a Union 312
Exclusivity 312
Organizing 313
What Workers May Do 313
What Employers May Do 314
*Progressive Electric, Inc. v.*
   *National Labor Relations Board* 314
YOU BE THE JUDGE *Hoffman Plastic*
*Compounds, Inc. v. National Labor*
*Relations Board* 315
Collective Bargaining 316
Subjects of Bargaining 316

Duty to Bargain 317
Enforcement 317
*Brentwood Medical Associates v.*
   *United Mine Workers of America* 318
Concerted Action 318
Strikes 319
Replacement Workers 319
Picketing 319
Lockouts 320
Regulating Union Affairs 320

# UNIT 4

## BUSINESS ORGANIZATIONS    325

**Chapter 20**
   **Starting a Business:**
   **LLCs and Other Options** 326
Sole Proprietorships 327
Corporations 328
Corporations in General 328
Close Corporations 329
S Corporations 330
Limited Liability Companies 331
YOU BE THE JUDGE *Ridgaway v. Silk* 331
*Wyoming.com, LLC v. Lieberman* 332
*BLD Products, Ltd. v. Technical Plastics*
   *of Oregon, LLC* 333
General Partnerships 334
Formation 335
Taxes 335
Liability 335
Management 335
Terminating a Partnership 336
Limited Liability Partnerships 337
*Apcar v. Gaus* 337
Limited Partnerships and Limited
Liability Limited Partnerships 338
Professional Corporation 339

**Chapter 21**
   **Corporations** 344
Promoter's Liability 345
Incorporation Process 345
Where to Incorporate? 346
The Charter 346
After Incorporation 347
Directors and Officers 347
Bylaws 348

Death of the Corporation 348
Piercing the Corporate Veil 348
Termination 349
The Role of Corporate Management 349
The Business Judgment Rule 350
Duty of Loyalty 350
*Lippman v. Shaffer* 351
Duty of Care 352
*RSL Communications v. Bildirici* 352
The Role of Shareholders 353
Rights of Shareholders 353
Right to Information 353
Right to Vote 354
Corporate Governance in Publicly
Traded Companies: Sarbanes-Oxley
and Stock Exchange Rules 355

**Chapter 22**
**Government Regulation:**
**Securities and Antitrust** 360
Securities Laws 361
What Is a Security? 361
Securities Act of 1933 361
Securities Exchange Act of 1934 363
Insider Trading 363
*United States v. O'Hagan* 364
Foreign Corrupt Practices Act 365
Blue Sky Laws 365
Antitrust 365
The Sherman Act 366
*Leegin Creative Leather
Products, Inc. v. PSKS, Inc.* 366
The Clayton Act 368
The Robinson-Patman Act 369

**Chapter 23**
**Accountants' Liability** 375
Introduction 376
Audits 376
Opinions 377
Congress Responds to Enron: Sarbanes-Oxley 378
Liability to Clients 379
Contract 379
Negligence 379
YOU BE THE JUDGE *Oregon Steel
Mills, Inc. v. Coopers & Lybrand, LLP* 379
Fraud 380
Breach of Trust 380

Liability to Third Parties 381
Negligence 381
*Ellis v. Grant Thornton* 381
Fraud 382
Securities Act of 1933 382
Securities Exchange Act of 1934 382
Criminal Liability 383
Other Accountant-Client Issues 384
The Accountant-Client Relationship 384
Accountant-Client Privilege 384

**UNIT 5**
**PROPERTY AND CONSUMER LAW 391**

**Chapter 24**
**Consumer Law** 392
Introduction 393
Sales 393
Deceptive Acts or Practices 393
YOU BE THE JUDGE *Federal Trade
Commission v. Business Card Experts, Inc.* 394
Unfair Practices 394
Bait and Switch 395
Mail or Telephone Order Merchandise 395
Telemarketing 396
Unordered Merchandise 396
Door-to-Door Sales 396
Consumer Credit 397
Truth-in-Lending Act 397
Home Mortgage Loans 397
Fair Credit Billing Act 398
Fair Credit Reporting Act 398
Fair and Accurate Credit Transactions Act 398
Fair Debt Collection Practices Act 399
Equal Credit Opportunity Act 400
*Treadway v. Gateway Chevrolet Oldsmobile Inc.* 400
Consumer Leasing Act 401
Magnuson-Moss Warranty Act 401
Consumer Product Safety 402

**Chapter 25**
**Environmental Law** 408
Introduction 409
Air Pollution 409
The Clean Air Act 409

YOU BE THE JUDGE *Central Arizona Water Conservation District v. EPA* 410
New Sources of Pollution 410
Water Pollution 410
The Clean Water Act 411
Wetlands 411
Sewage 412
Waste Disposal 412
Resource Conservation and Recovery Act 413
*United States of America v. Kelly* 413
Superfund 414
Natural Resources 414
National Environmental Policy Act 415
Endangered Species Act 415
*Gibbs v. Babbitt* 416

Chapter 26
**Cyberlaw** 422
Privacy 423
Of Cookies and Caches 423
Government Regulation of Online Privacy 424
*United States of America v. Angevine* 425
YOU BE THE JUDGE *Scott v. Beth Israel Medical Center Inc.* 426
Spam 428
Internet Service Providers and Web Hosts:
Communications Decency Act of 1996 428
*Carafano v. Metrosplash.com, Inc.* 429
Crime on the Internet 430
Hacking 430
Fraud 430

Chapter 27
**Intellectual Property** 437
Introduction 438
Patents 438
Requirements for a Patent 439
Patent Application and Issuance 440
Copyrights 441
Infringement 441
First Sale Doctrine 441
Fair Use 441
YOU BE THE JUDGE *Perfect 10, Inc. v. Google Inc.* 442
Digital Music and Movies 443
*Metro-Goldwyn-Mayer Studios Inc. v. Grokster, Ltd.* 443
International Copyright Treaties 444

Trademarks 444
Ownership and Registration 444
Valid Trademarks 445
Domain Names 445
International Trademark Treaties 446
Trade Secrets 446
*Pollack v. Skinsmart Dermatology and Aesthetic Center P.C.* 447

Chapter 28
**Real Property** 451
Nature of Real Property 452
*Freeman v. Barrs* 453
Estates in Real Property 454
Freehold Estates 454
Fee Simple Absolute 454
Fee Simple Defeasible 454
Life Estate 454
Concurrent Estates 454
Nonpossessory Interests 455
Easements 455
YOU BE THE JUDGE *Carvin v. Arkansas Power and Light* 456
Profit 457
License 457
Mortgage 457
Sale of Real Property 457
Seller's Obligations Concerning the Property 458
Sales Contract and Title Examination 458
Closing and Deeds 458
Recording 459
Adverse Possession 459
Entry and Exclusive Possession 459
Open and Notorious Possession 459
A Claim Adverse to the Owner 459
Continuous Possession for the Statutory Period 459
*Ray v. Beacon Hudson Mountain Corp.* 460
Land Use Regulation 460
Zoning 460
Eminent Domain 461

Chapter 29
**Landlord-Tenant Law** 465
Three Legal Areas Combined 466
Lease 466
Types of Tenancy 467
Tenancy for Years 467
Periodic Tenancy 467

faucet, he received a violent electric shock that shot him through the air, melted his sneakers and glasses, set his clothes on fire, and seriously scalded him. Tom sued, claiming that Jenny had caused the damage when she negligently repaired a second-floor toilet. Water from the steady leak had flooded through the walls, soaking wires and eventually causing the faucet to become electrified. You are Jenny's lawyer. Use one (and only one) element of negligence law to move for summary judgment.

**Strategy:** The four elements of negligence we have examined thus far are duty to this plaintiff, breach, factual cause, and foreseeable type of injury. Which element seems to be most helpful to Jenny's defense? Why?

**Result:** Jenny is entitled to summary judgment because this was not a foreseeable type of injury. Even if she did a bad job of fixing the toilet, she could not possibly have anticipated that her poor workmanship could cause *electrical* injuries—and violent ones—to anybody.[1]

........................................................................................................................

# NEW COVERAGE FOR THIS EDITION

We have rewritten every chapter for this third edition to ensure coverage of rapidly evolving issues. Here are a few representative updates.

Does money buy happiness? Many students believe it does. Chapter 2, on ethics, includes a discussion of the latest research on the relationship between money and happiness. Far from making people happy, purchasing more stuff just puts them on the "hedonic treadmill"—struggling to buy more and more things so they can get that buyer's high, only to discover that they can never buy enough to maintain the thrill.

In Chapter 3, on dispute resolution, we offer an expanded look at the biggest recent change in litigation: the explosive rise of electronic discovery and its consequences to business. In one recent case, a defendant had to pay 31 lawyers full time, for six months, just to wade through the e-ocean of documents and figure out which had to be supplied. In Chapter 4, on constitutional law, we take a new tack on the venerable issue of judicial review by examining the Supreme Court's news-grabbing 2008 decision in *Kennedy v. Louisiana*, on child rape. Chapter 5 explores state efforts at tort reform and brings the issue up to the minute with a discussion of the Supreme Court's ruling in the *Exxon Valdez* case.

One of the hottest topics in international law is extraterritoriality. Does the whistleblower protection of Sarbanes-Oxley apply overseas? We examine both sides of the argument (in Chapter 8) and provide a current Second Circuit case. In Chapter 9, on contracts, we look at a new case concerning the old issue of quasi-contract. If a patient never consented to medical procedures because he was unconscious, is he liable for unjust enrichment?

Chapter 16, on agency law, is now based on the Restatement (Third) of Agency—an update from the Restatement (Second). As a result, there are significant changes in vocabulary. "Master/servant" has become "employer/employee," and a "partially disclosed" principal has become an "unidentified" principal.

Chapter 20, on starting a business, expands coverage on LLCs. The chapter also takes a hard look at the practical differences between an LLC and a corporation and discusses how to decide which form to choose.

Chapter 21, on corporations, uses the charter from Facebook.com as an example. Students will learn what choices Mark Zuckerberg made when he started Facebook in his dorm room.

Chapter 27, on intellectual property, describes the Patent and Trademark Office's new Peer to Patent system, which uses the online community to review patents. It also discusses the first sale doctrine in copyright law to help clarify for students when trading music is, and is not, legal.

---

[1] Based on *Hebert v. Enos*, 60 Mass. App. Ct. 817, 806 N.E.2d 452 (Massachusetts Court of Appeals, 2004).

There are many real-life examples involving iPods, the Rev. Jerry Falwell, and the John Lennon song "Imagine."

In addition to the "Exam Strategy" feature and the coverage of dozens of new issues and cases, here are some existing qualities that make our book different from all others in a crowded field.

## STRONG NARRATIVE

The law is full of great stories, and we use them. Your students and ours should come to class excited. In Chapter 3, on dispute resolution, we explain litigation by tracking a double indemnity lawsuit. An executive is dead. Did he drown accidentally, obligating the insurance company to pay? Or did the businessman commit suicide, voiding the policy? The student follows the action from the discovery of the body, through each step of the lawsuit, to the final appeal. The chapter offers a detailed discussion of dispute resolution, but it does so by exploiting the human drama that underlies litigation.

Students read stories and remember them. Strong narratives provide a rich context for the remarkable quantity of legal material presented. When students care about the material they are reading, they persevere. We have been delighted to find that they also arrive in class eager to question, discuss, and learn.

## AUTHORITATIVE

We insist, as you do, on a law book that is indisputably accurate. A professor must teach with assurance, confident that every paragraph is the result of exhaustive research and meticulous presentation. Dozens of tough-minded people spent thousands of hours reviewing this book, and we are delighted with the stamp of approval we have received from trial and appellate judges, working attorneys, scholars, and teachers.

We reject the cloudy definitions and fuzzy explanations that can invade judicial opinions and legal scholarship. To highlight the most important rules, we use bold print, and then follow with vivacious examples written in clear, forceful English. (See, for example, the description of an automatic stay in Chapter 15, on bankruptcy, p. 248.)

## COMPREHENSIVE

Staying comprehensive means staying current. Look, for example, at the important field of corporate governance. We present a clear path through the thicket of new issues, such as board composition and executive compensation. We want tomorrow's business leaders to anticipate the challenges that await them and then use their knowledge to avert problems.

This book also provides a strong narrative flow. Like you, we are here to teach. We do not use boxes because, in our experience, they disrupt the flow of the text. Students inform us that a box indicates peripheral material, that is, material they routinely skip; we prefer to give them an uncluttered whole.

## A BOOK FOR STUDENTS

We have written this book as if we were speaking directly to our students. We provide black letter law, but we also explain concepts in terms that hook students. Over the years, we have learned how much more successfully we can teach when our students are intrigued. No matter what kind of a show we put on in class, they are only learning when they want to learn.

Every chapter begins with a story, either fictional or real, to illustrate the issues in the chapter and provide context. Chapter 26, on cyberlaw, begins with the true story of a college student who discovers nude pictures of himself online. These photos had been taken in the locker room without his knowledge. What privacy rights do any of us have? Does the Internet jeopardize them? Students want to know—right away.

Most of today's undergraduates were not yet born when Jimmy Carter was president. They come to college with varying levels of preparation; many now arrive from other countries. We have found that to teach business law most effectively we must provide its context. Chapter 23, on accountants, explains how a changing culture within Arthur Andersen led to the firm's downfall during the Enron scandal.

At the same time, we enjoy offering "nuts and bolts" information that grabs students. In Chapter 24, on consumer law, we bring home the issue of credit history by providing phone numbers and Web sites that students can use to check their own credit reports.

Students respond enthusiastically to this approach. One professor asked a student to compare our book with the one that the class was then using. This was the student's reaction: "I really enjoy reading the [Beatty & Samuelson] textbook and I have decided that I will give you this memo ASAP, but I am keeping the book until Wednesday so that I may continue reading. Thanks! :-)"

# HUMOR

Throughout the text, we use humor—judiciously—to lighten and enlighten. Not surprisingly, students have applauded this—but is wit appropriate? How dare we employ levity in this venerable discipline! We offer humor because we take law seriously. We revere the law for its ancient traditions, its dazzling intricacy, its relentless though imperfect attempt to give order and decency to our world. Because we are confident of our respect for the law, we are not afraid to employ some levity. Leaden prose masquerading as legal scholarship does no honor to the field.

Humor also helps retention. We have found that students remember a contract problem described in a fanciful setting, and from that setting recall the underlying principle. By contrast, one widget is hard to distinguish from another.

# FEATURES

We chose the features for our book with great care. As mentioned above, all features are considered an essential part of the text and are woven into its body. Also, each feature responds to an essential pedagogical goal. Here are some of those goals and the matching feature.

### You Be the Judge

GOAL: Get them thinking independently. When reading case opinions, students tend to accept the court's "answer." Judges, of course, try to reach decisions that appear indisputable, when in reality they may be controversial—or wrong. From time to time, we want students to think through the problem and reach their own answer. Most chapters contain a "You Be the Judge" feature, providing the facts of the case and conflicting appellate arguments. The court's decision, however, appears only in the Instructor's Manual. Since students do not know the result, discussions tend to be more free-flowing. Students disagree with the court at least half the time. They are thinking.

### Ethics

GOAL: Make ethics real. We ask ethical questions about cases, legal issues, and commercial practices. Is it fair for one party to void a contract by arguing, months after the fact, that there was no consideration? What is wrong with bribery? We do not have definitive answers but believe that asking the questions and encouraging discussion reminds students that ethics is an essential element of justice and of a satisfying life.

### Cases

GOAL: Bring case law alive. Each case begins with a summary of the facts followed by a statement of both the issue and the decision. Next comes a summary of the court's opinion. We have written this ourselves, to make the judges' reasoning accessible to all readers, while retaining the court's focus and the decision's impact. We cite cases using a modified blue-book form. In the principal cases in each chapter, we provide the state or federal citation, the regional citation, and an appropriate electronic citation. We also give students a brief description of the court.

### Exam Review and Practice Exams

GOAL: Encourage students to practice! At the end of the chapters, we provide a list of review points and several additional "Exam Strategy" exercises. To support students' different learning styles, we provide several types of questions in the Practice Exam: matching, multiple choice, True/False, and short answer. We also include these types of questions:

- Internet Research Problem. This question sends students to the Internet to explore issues from the chapter.
- Ethics. This question highlights the ethical issues of a dispute and calls upon the student to formulate a specific, reasoned response.
- CPA Questions. For topics covered by the CPA exam, administered by the American Institute of Certified Public Accountants, the practice tests include questions from previous CPA exams.
- Role Reversal. Students are asked to formulate their own test questions. Crafting questions is a good way to reinforce what they already understand, and recognize areas that they need to review.

Answers to the odd-numbered questions are available on the Beatty *Introduction to Business Law* Web site at **www.cengage.com/blaw/beatty**. Here is why. Students often ask us how to study for exams. Reviewing the problems in the end-of-chapter practice tests is helpful, but without the answers, students have no way of being sure they are on the right track. The answers to the even-numbered questions appear only in the Instructor's Manual so that faculty can assign them for written or oral presentation.

# TEACHING MATERIALS

For more information about any of these ancillaries, contact your Cengage/South-Western Legal Studies in Business Sales Representative for more details, or visit the Beatty *Introduction to Business Law* Web site at **www.cengage.com/blaw/beatty**.

### Instructor's Manual

We have included special features to enhance class discussion and student progress:

- Dialogues. These are a series of questions and answers on pivotal cases and topics. The questions provide enough material to teach a full session. In a pinch, you could walk into class with nothing but the manual and use the Dialogues to conduct an exciting class.
- Action learning ideas. These are interviews, quick research projects, drafting exercises, classroom activities, commercial analyses, and other suggested assignments that get students out of their chairs and into the diverse settings of business law.
- A chapter theme and a quote of the day.
- Updates of text material.
- Additional cases and examples.
- Answers to You Be the Judge cases from the text and to the Practice Exam questions found at the end of each chapter.

The Instructor's Manual can be obtained online at **www.cengage.com/blaw/beatty**, or on the Instructor's Resource CD.

### Test Bank

The test bank offers hundreds of essay, short answer and multiple choice problems, and may be obtained online at **www.cengage.com/blaw/beatty**, or on the Instructor's Resource CD.

### ExamView Testing Software—Computerized Testing Software

This testing software contains all of the questions in the printed test bank. This easy-to-use test creation software program is compatible with Microsoft Windows. Instructors can add or edit questions, instructions, and answers; and select questions by previewing them on the screen, selecting them randomly, or selecting them by number. Instructors can also create and administer quizzes online, whether over the Internet, a local area network (LAN), or a wide area network (WAN). The ExamView testing software is available on the Instructor's Resource CD.

### Instructor's Resource CD (IRCD) (ISBN: 0-324-82959-0)

The IRCD contains the ExamView testing software files, the test bank in Microsoft Word files, the Instructor's Manual in Microsoft Word files, and the Microsoft PowerPoint Lecture Review Slides.

### Microsoft PowerPoint Lecture Review Slides

PowerPoint slides are available for use by instructors for enhancing their lectures. Download these slides at **www.cengage.com/blaw/beatty**. The PowerPoint slides are also available on the IRCD.

### Business Law Digital Video Library

This dynamic online video library features over 60 video clips that spark class discussion and clarify core legal principles. The library is organized into four series:

- *Legal Conflicts in Business* includes specific modern business and e-commerce scenarios.
- *Ask the Instructor* contains straightforward explanations of concepts for student review.
- *Drama of the Law* features classic business scenarios that spark classroom participation.
- *LawFlix* contains clips from many popular films, including *The Money Pit, Midnight Run,* and *Casino.*

Access to the Business Law Digital Video Library is available as an optional package with each new student text at no additional charge. Students with used books can purchase access to the video clips online. For more information about the Business Law Digital Video Library, visit **www.cengage.com/blaw/dvl**.

### A Handbook of Basic Law Terms, Black's Law Dictionary Series

This paperback dictionary, prepared by the editor of the popular *Black's Law Dictionary,* can be packaged for a small additional cost with any new South-Western Legal Studies in Business text.

### Student Guide to the Sarbanes-Oxley Act

This brief overview for business students explains the Sarbanes-Oxley Act, what is required of whom, and how it might affect students in their business life. Available as an optional package with the text.

### WestLaw®

Westlaw® West Group's vast online source of value-added legal and business information contains over 15,000 databases of information spanning a variety of jurisdictions, practice areas, and disciplines. Qualified instructors who adopt South-Western Legal Studies in Business textbooks may receive ten complimentary hours of Westlaw for their course (certain restrictions apply). Contact your sales representative for more information.

## INTERACTION WITH THE AUTHORS

This is our standard: Every professor who adopts this book must have a superior experience. We are available to help in any way we can. Adopters of this text often call us or e-mail us to ask questions, obtain a syllabus, offer suggestions, share pedagogical concerns, or inquire about ancillaries. One of the pleasures of working on this project has been our discovery that the text provides a link to so many colleagues around the country. We value those connections, are eager to respond, and would be happy to hear from you.

## TO THE STUDENT

Each Practice Test contains one Role Reversal feature, in which we challenge you to create your own exam question. Your professor may ask you to submit the questions in writing or electronically, or to prepare an overhead slide. The goal is to think creatively and accurately. The question should be challenging enough that the average student will need to stop and think, but clear enough that there is only one answer. Questions can be formatted as essay, short answer, or multiple choice.

For a multiple-choice question, the first step is to isolate the single issue that you want to test. For example, in the unit on contract law, you do not want to ask a question that concerns five different aspects of forming an agreement. A good question will focus exclusively on one issue—for example, whether a job offer has to be in writing (some do, others do not). Create a realistic fact pattern that raises the issue. Provide one answer that is clearly correct. Add additional answers that might seem plausible but are definitely incorrect.

Some exam questions are very direct and test whether a student knows a definition. Other questions require deeper analysis. Here are two multiple-choice questions. The first is direct.

Question: Which contract is governed by the Uniform Commercial Code?

A. An agreement for an actor to appear in a movie for a $600,000 fee

B. An agreement for an actor to appear in a movie for a fee of $600,000 plus 2 percent of box office

C. An agreement for the sale of a house

D. An agreement for the sale of 22,000 picture frames

E. An agreement for the rental of an apartment

As you will learn later on, the correct answer is (D), because the Code applies to the sale of goods, not to employment contracts or real estate deals.

The next question is more difficult, requiring the student to spot the issue of law involved (product liability), remember how damages are awarded in such cases (generally, without regard to fault), and make a simple calculation.

Question: Lightweight Corp. manufactures strings of Christmas tree lights and sells 3.5 million sets per year. Every year, between 10 and 20 of the company's strings have a manufacturing defect that causes a consumer injury. Maxine receives a severe shock from a Lightweight string of lights. She sues. The evidence at trial is that: (1) Lightweight's safety record is the best in the industry; (2) all competing companies have a higher rate of injuries; (3) the lights that injured Maxine arrived at her house in the factory box, untouched by anyone outside of Lightweight; (4) Maxine operated the lights properly. Maxine's medical bills amount to $200,000; her lost income is $100,000; and her pain and suffering amounts to $600,000. What is the probable outcome at trial?

A. Maxine will win $200,000.

B. Maxine will win $100,000.

C. Maxine will win $900,000.

**D.** Maxine will win nothing.

**E.** Lightweight might win damages for a frivolous lawsuit.

As you will learn, the correct answer is (C). Lightweight is responsible under product liability law regardless of its careful work and excellent record. Maxine is entitled to all of her damages. Notice that the same question could be used in essay format, simply by deleting the multiple-choice answers.

**Jeffrey F. Beatty**
Phone: (617) 353-6397
E-mail: jfbeatty@bu.edu

**Susan S. Samuelson**
Phone: (617) 353-2033
E-mail: ssamuels@bu.edu

*Boston, Massachusetts*

## · ACKNOWLEDGMENTS ·

We are grateful to the following reviewers who gave such helpful comments for the third edition revisions:

Joseph F Adamo
*Cazenovia College*

Joan P. Alexander
*Nassau College*

Victor Alicea
*Normandale College*

Basil N. Apostle
*Purchase College, SUNY*

Theodore R. Bolema,
*Anderson Economic Group, LLC*

Joseph T. Bork
*University of St. Thomas*

Karen E. Bork
*Northwood University*

Beverly Woodall Broman
*Everest Institute—Pittsburgh, PA*

Jeff W. Bruns
*Bacone College*

E. Katy Burnett
*Kentucky Community & Technical College Systems Online*

Bruce W. Byars
*University of North Dakota*

Dianne L. Caron
*The Art Institute of Seattle*

Amy F. Chataginer
*Mississippi Gulf Coast Community College*

Tim Collins
*Kaplan Career Institute—ICM Campus*

Michael Combe
*Eagle Gate College*

Mark DeAngelis
*University of Connecticut*

Laura C. Denton, Professor
*Maysville Community and Technical College*

Julia G. Derrick
*Brevard Community College*

Dr. Joe D. Dillsaver
*Northeastern State University*

Ted Dinges
*Metropolitan Community College—Longview*

Nicki M. Dodd
*Guilford Technical Community College*

Bradley L. Drell
*Louisiana College, Pineville*

Donna N. Dunn
*Beaufort County Community College*

Jameka Ellison
*Everest University—Lakeland*

Traci C. Etheridge
*Richmond Community College*

Gail S.M. Evans
*University of Houston—Downtown*

Alfred E. Fabian
*Ivy Tech Community College*

Jerrold M. Fleisher
*Dominican College—Orangeburg, New York*

Andrea Foster
*John Tyler Community College—Chester Campus*

Daniel F. Gant
*Savannah River College*

Jolena M. Grande
*Cypress College, CA*

Wade T. Graves
*Grayson County College*

John P. Gray
*Faulkner University*

Scott R. Gunderson
*Dakota County Technical College, MN*

Diane A. Hagan
*Ohio Business College—Sandusky*

Ruth Ann Hall
*The University of Alabama*

Robert L. Hamilton
*Columbia College—Orlando Campus*

Jason M. Harris
*Augustana College, SD*

Toni R. Hartley
*Laurel Business Institute*

Tony Hunnicutt
*Ouachita Technical College*

Robert F. Huyck
*Mohawk Valley Community College*

Christopher R. Inama
*Golden Gate University*

Joseph V. Ippolito
*Brevard College*

David I. Kapelner
*Merrimack College*

Jack E. Karns
*East Carolina University*

Mark King
*Indiana Business College*

Hal P. Kingsley
*Trocaire College*

Samuel Kohn
*New York Institute of Technology*

Kimberly S. Lamb
*Stautzenberger College*

Greg Lauer
*North Iowa Area Community College*

Dennis G. Lee
*Southwest Georgia Technical College*

Paulette S. León
*Northwestern Technical College—Rock Spring, GA*

Leslie S. Lukasik
*Skagit Valley College, Whidbey Island Campus*

Jerome P. McCluskey
*Manhattanville College*

Arin S. Miller
*Keiser University*

Ronald K. Minnehan
*California Lutheran University*

Tonia Hap Murphy
*University of Notre Dame*

John J. Nader
*Davenport University*

Terri J. Nix
*Howard College*

Steven C. Palmer
*Eastern New Mexico University*

Nicole Pierone
*Yakima Valley Community College*

Linda E. Plowman
*The Art Institute of Pittsburgh*

Matthew B. Probst
*Ivy Tech Community College of Indiana—Lawrenceburg*

Anne Montgomery Ricketts
*University of Findlay*

Bruce L. Rockwood
*Bloomsburg University of Pennsylvania*

R.J. Ruppenthal
*Evergreen Valley College*

Mark R. Solomon
*Walsh College—Troy, MI*

Harilaos I. Sorovigas
*Michigan State University*

Kim D. Steinmetz
*Everest College—Phoenix, AZ*

Kenneth R. Taurman, Jr., JD
*Indiana University Southeast*

Natalie L. Turner
*Middle Georgia Technical College—Warner Robins*

Marion R. Tuttle
*New Jersey Institute of Technology*

Janet M. Velazquez
*Kansas City Kansas Community College*

William V. Vetter
*Prairie View A&M University*

Jamie S. Waldo
*Chadron State College*

Deborah B. Walsh
*Middlesex Community College, MA*

David B. Washington
*Augsburg College*

Albert B. West
*Providence College School of Continuing Ed.—Providence, R.I.*

Mathew C. Williams
*Clover Park Technical College*

Ira Wilsker
*Lamar Institute of Technology*

Kelly Collins Woodford
*University of South Alabama*

Gilbert Ybarra
*International Business College*

John W. Yeargain
*Southeastern Louisiana University*

Eric D. Yordy
*Northern Arizona University*

# THE LEGAL ENVIRONMENT

# INTRODUCTION TO LAW

**The Pagans** were a motorcycle gang with a reputation for violence. Two of its rougher members, Rhino and Backdraft, entered a tavern called the Pub Zone, shoving their way past the bouncer. The pair wore gang insignia, in violation of the bar's rules. For a while, all was quiet, as the two sipped drinks at the bar. Then they followed an innocent patron toward the men's room, and things happened fast.

> **Law is powerful, essential, and fascinating. We hope this book will persuade you of all three ideas.**

"Wait a moment," you may be thinking. "Are we reading a chapter on business law or one about biker crimes in a roadside tavern?" Both.

Law is powerful, essential, and fascinating. We hope this book will persuade you of all three ideas. Law can also be surprising. Later in the chapter we will return to the Pub Zone (with armed guards) and follow Rhino and Backdraft to the back of the pub. Yes, the pair engaged in street crime, which is hardly a focus of this text. However, their criminal acts will enable us to explore one of the law's basic principles, negligence. Should a pub owner pay money damages to the victim of gang violence? The owner herself did nothing aggressive. Should she have prevented the harm? Does her failure to stop the assault make her liable?

We place great demands on our courts, asking them to make our large, complex, and sometimes violent society into a safer, fairer, more orderly place. The Pub Zone case is a good example of how judges reason their way through the convoluted issues involved. What began as a gang incident ends up as a matter of commercial liability. We will traipse after Rhino and Backdraft because they have a lesson to teach anyone who enters the world of business.

## ▪ THREE IMPORTANT IDEAS ABOUT LAW ▪

### POWER

A driver is seriously injured in an automobile accident and the jury concludes that the car had a design defect. The jurors award her *$29 million*. A senior vice-president congratulates himself on a cagey stock purchase but is horrified to receive, not profits, but a prison sentence. A homeless person, ordered by local police to stop panhandling, ambles into court and walks out with an order permitting him to beg on the city's streets. The strong hand of the law touches us all. To understand something that powerful is itself power.

Suppose, some years after graduation, you are a mid-level manager at Sublime Corp., which manufactures and distributes video games and related hardware and software. You are delighted with this important position in an excellent company—and especially glad you bring legal knowledge to the job. Sarah, an expert at computer-generated imagery, complains that Rob, her boss, is constantly touching her and making lewd comments. That is sexual harassment and your knowledge of *employment law* helps you respond promptly and carefully. You have dinner with Jake, who has his own software company. Jake wants to manufacture an exciting new video game in cooperation with Sublime, but you are careful not to create a binding deal. (*Contract law.*) Jake mentions that a similar game is already on the market. Do you have the right to market one like it? That answer you already know. (*Intellectual property law.*)

The next day, a letter from the Environmental Protection Agency asks how your company disposes of toxic chemicals used to manufacture computer drives. You can discuss it efficiently with in-house counsel because you have a working knowledge of administrative law. LuYu, your personnel manager, reports that a silicon chip worker often seems drowsy; she suspects drug use. Does she have the right to test him? (*Constitutional law* and *employment law*.) On the other hand, if she fails to test him, could Sublime Corp. be liable for any harm the worker does? (*Tort law and agency law.*)

In a mere week, you might use your legal training a dozen times, helping Sublime to steer clear of countless dangers. During the coming year, you encounter many other legal issues, and you and your corporation benefit from your skills.

It is not only as a corporate manager that you will confront the law. As a voter, investor, juror, entrepreneur, and community member, you will influence and be affected by the law. Whenever you take a stance about a legal issue, whether in the corporate office, the voting booth, or as part of local community groups, you help to create the social fabric of our nation. Your views are vital. This book will offer you knowledge and ideas from which to form and continually reassess your legal opinions and values.

# IMPORTANCE

We depend upon laws for safe communities, functioning economies, and personal liberties. An easy way to gauge the importance of law is to glance through any newspaper and read about nations that lack a strong system of justice. Notice that these countries cannot ensure physical safety and personal liberties. They also fail to offer economic opportunity for most citizens. We may not always like the way our legal system works, but we depend on it to keep our society functioning.

# FASCINATION

Law is intriguing. When the jury awarded $29 million against an auto manufacturer for a defective car design, it certainly demonstrated the law's power. But was the jury's decision right? Should a company have to pay that much for one car accident? Maybe the jury was reacting emotionally. Or perhaps the anger caused by terrible trauma *should* be part of a court case. These are not abstract speculations for philosophers. Verdicts such as this may cause each of us to pay more for our next automobile. Then again, we may be driving safer cars.

# · SOURCES OF CONTEMPORARY LAW ·

It would be nice if we could look up "the law" in one book, memorize it, and then apply it. But the law is not that simple. Principles and rules of law actually come from many different sources. Why is this so?

We inherited a complex structure of laws from England. Additionally, ours is a nation born in revolution and created, in large part, to protect the rights of its people from the government. The Founding Fathers created a national government but insisted that the individual states maintain control in many areas. As a result, each state has its own government with exclusive power over many important areas of our lives. What the Founding Fathers created was **federalism**: a double-layered system of government, with the national government and state governments each exercising important but limited powers. To top it off, the Founders guaranteed many rights to the people alone, ordering national and state governments to keep clear. They achieved all of this in one remarkable document, the United States Constitution.

**Federalism**
A double-layered system of government, with the national and state governments each exercising important but limited powers.

# CONSTITUTIONS

## *United States Constitution*

**United States Constitution**
The supreme law of the land.

The **United States Constitution**, adopted in 1788 by the original 13 colonies, is the supreme law of the land.[1] Any law that conflicts with it is void. This federal Constitution, as it is also known, does three basic things. First, it establishes the national government of the United States, with its three branches. The Constitution creates the Congress, with a Senate and a House of Representatives, and prescribes what laws Congress may pass. The same document establishes the office of the president and the duties that go with it. And it creates the third branch of government, the federal courts, describing what cases they may hear.

Second, the Constitution ensures that the states retain all power not given to the national government. This simple idea has meant that state governments play an important role in all our lives. Major issues of family law, criminal law, property law, and many other areas are regulated predominantly by the various states.

---

[1] The complete text of the Constitution appears in Appendix A.

Third, the Constitution guarantees many basic rights to the American people. Most of these rights are found in the amendments to the Constitution. The First Amendment guarantees the rights of free speech, free press, and the free exercise of religion. The Fourth, Fifth, and Sixth Amendments protect the rights of any person accused of a crime. Other amendments ensure that the government treats all people equally and that it pays for any property it takes from a citizen. Merely by creating a limited government of three branches and guaranteeing basic liberties to all citizens, the Constitution became one of the most important documents ever written.

### State Constitutions

In addition to the Federal Constitution, each state has a constitution that establishes its own government. All states have an executive (the governor), a legislature, and a court system. Thus, there are two entire systems of government affecting each of us: a federal government, with power over the entire country, and a state government, exercising those powers that the United States Constitution did not grant to the federal government. This is federalism at work.

## STATUTES

The second important source of law is statutory law. The Constitution gave to the United States Congress the power to pass laws on many subjects. Laws passed by Congress are called **statutes**. For example, the Constitution allows Congress to pass statutes about the military: to appropriate money, reorganize divisions, and close bases. You can find any federal statute, on any subject, at the Web site of the United States House of Representatives, which is **http://www.house.gov/**.

**State legislatures also pass statutes.** Each state constitution allows the legislature to pass laws on a wide variety of subjects. All state legislatures, for example, may pass statutes about family law issues such as divorce and child custody.

## COMMON LAW AND EQUITY

The common law originated in England as lawyers began to record decisions and urge judges to follow earlier cases. As judges started to do that, the earlier cases, called **precedent**, took on steadily greater importance. Eventually, judges were obligated to follow precedent. **The principle that precedent is binding on later cases is *stare decisis*, which means "let the decision stand."** *Stare decisis* makes the law predictable, and this in turn enables businesses and private citizens to plan intelligently. We will see this principle at work later in this chapter. The **common law** is judge-made law; that is, the body of all decisions made by judges in individual cases.

Sometimes a judge refused to hear a case, ruling that no such claims were legal. The injured party might then take his case to the Chancellor, in London, whose status in the king's council gave him unique, flexible powers. This Court of Chancery had no jury. The court's duty was to accomplish what "good conscience" required; that is, an equitable result. This more creative use of a court's power became known as **equity**.

Principles of equity traveled to the colonies along with the common law rules. All states permit courts to use equitable powers. An example of a contemporary equitable power is an **injunction**, a court order that someone stop doing something. Suppose a music company is about to issue a new compact disc by a well-known singer, but a composer claims that the recording artist has stolen his song. The composer, claiming copyright violation, could seek an injunction to prevent the company from issuing the compact disc. Every state has a trial court that can issue injunctions and carry out other equitable relief. There is no jury in an equity case.

**Statute**
A law passed by Congress or by a state legislature.

**Precedent**
An earlier court case used to influence a court decision in a current case.

*Stare Decisis*
The principle that precedent is binding on later cases.

**Common law**
Judge-made law; the body of all decisions made by judges.

**Equity**
The court's use of its power to create an equitable result.

**Injunction**
A court order requiring someone to stop doing something.

> Presidents are reluctant to sit on the dock of the bay, watching the ships come in.

## Sources of Law

### 50 State Governments

**State Constitution**
- establishes the state government
- guarantees the rights of state residents

### One Federal Government

**United States Constitution**
- establishes limited federal government
- protects states' power
- guarantees liberty of citizens

| Legislative Branch | Executive Branch | Judicial Branch |
|---|---|---|
|  |  |  |
| **State Legislature** | **Governor** | **State Courts** |
| • passes statutes on state law<br>• creates state agencies | • proposes statutes<br>• signs or vetoes statutes<br>• oversees state agencies<br>• issues executive orders | • create state common law<br>• interpret statutes<br>• review constitutionality of statutes and other acts |

**Administrative Agencies**
- oversee day-to-day application of law in dozens of commercial and other areas

| Legislative Branch | Executive Branch | Judicial Branch |
|---|---|---|
| |  |  |
| **Congress** | **President** | **Federal Courts** |
| • passes statutes<br>• ratifies treaties<br>• creates administrative agencies | • proposes statutes<br>• signs or vetoes statutes<br>• oversees administrative agencies<br>• issues executive orders | • interpret statutes<br>• create (limited) federal common law<br>• review the constitutionality of statutes and other legal acts |

**Administrative Agencies**
- oversee day-to-day application of law in dozens of commercial and other areas

**Federal Form of Government.** Priniciples and rules of law come from many sources. The government in Washington, D.C., creates and enforces law throughout the nation. But 50 state governments exercise great power in local affairs, and citizens enjoy constitutional protection from both state and federal government. The Founding Fathers wanted this balance of power and rights, but the overlapping authority creates legal complexity.

## ADMINISTRATIVE LAW

In a society as large and diverse as ours, the executive and legislative branches of government cannot oversee all aspects of commerce. Congress passes statutes about air safety, but U.S. senators do not stand around air traffic towers, serving coffee to keep everyone awake. The executive branch establishes rules concerning how foreign nationals enter the United States, but presidents are reluctant to sit on the dock of the bay, watching the ships come in. **Administrative agencies** do this day-to-day work.

Most administrative agencies are created by Congress or by a state legislature. Familiar examples at the federal level are the Federal Communications Commission (FCC), which regulates most telecommunications; the Federal Trade Commission (FTC), which oversees interstate trade; and the Internal Revenue Service (IRS), whose feelings are hurt if it does not hear from you every April 15. At the state level, regulators set insurance rates for all companies in the state, control property development and land use, and regulate many other issues.

## ▪ CRIMINAL AND CIVIL LAW ▪

It is a crime to embezzle money from a bank, to steal a car, to sell cocaine. **Criminal law** concerns behavior so threatening that society outlaws it altogether. Most criminal laws are statutes, passed by Congress or a state legislature. The government itself prosecutes the wrongdoer, regardless of what the bank president or car owner wants. A district attorney, paid by the government, brings the case to court. The injured party, for example the owner of the stolen car, is not in charge of the case, although she may appear as a witness. The government will seek to punish the defendant with a prison sentence, a fine, or both. If there is a fine, the money goes to the state, not to the injured party.

Civil law is different, and most of this book is about civil law. **Civil law** regulates the rights and duties between parties. Tracy agrees in writing to lease you a 30,000-square-foot store in her shopping mall. She now has a legal duty to make the space available. But then another tenant offers her more money, and she refuses to let you move in. Tracy has violated her duty, but she has not committed a crime. The government will not prosecute the case. It is up to you to file a civil lawsuit. Your case will be based on the common law of contract. You will also seek equitable relief, namely, an injunction ordering Tracy not to lease to anyone else. You should win the suit, and you will get your injunction and some money damages. But Tracy will not go to jail.

Some conduct involves both civil and criminal law. Suppose Tracy is so upset over losing the court case that she becomes drunk and causes a serious car accident. She has committed the crime of driving while intoxicated, and the state will prosecute. Tracy may be fined or imprisoned. She has also committed negligence, and the injured party will file a lawsuit against her, seeking money.

**Criminal law**
concerns behavior so threatening that society outlaws it altogether.

**Civil law**
regulates the rights and duties between parties.

## LAW AND MORALITY

Law is different from morality, yet the two are obviously linked. There are many instances when the law duplicates what all of us would regard as a moral position. It is negligence to drive too fast in a school district, and few would dispute the moral value of that law. And similarly with contract law: if the owner of land agrees in writing to sell property to a buyer at a stated price, the seller must go through with the deal, and the legal outcome matches our moral expectations.

On the other hand, we have had laws that we now clearly regard as immoral. Seventy-five years ago, a factory owner could legally fire a worker for any reason at all—including, for example, her religion. Today, we would say it is immoral to fire a worker because of her faith—and the law prohibits it.

Finally, there are legal issues where the morality is not so clear. Suppose you serve alcohol to a guest who becomes intoxicated and then causes an automobile accident, seriously injuring a pedestrian. Should you, the social host, be liable? This is an issue of tort liability, which we examine in Chapter 5. As with many topics in this book, the problem has no easy answer. As you learn the law, you will have an opportunity to re-examine your own moral beliefs. One of the goals of Chapter 2, on ethics, is to offer you some new tools for that task.

## · WORKING WITH THE BOOK'S FEATURES ·

In this section, we introduce a few of the book's features, and discuss how you can use them effectively. We will start with cases.

## ANALYZING A CASE

**Law case**
A law case is the decision a court has made in a civil lawsuit or criminal prosecution.

A **law case** is the decision a court has made in a civil lawsuit or criminal prosecution. Cases are the heart of the law and an important part of this book. Reading them effectively takes practice. Let us return to the Pub Zone tavern, which we visited in the chapter's opener, and see what we can learn about courts and the law.

### KUEHN v. PUB ZONE

364 N.J. SUPER. 301, 835 A.2D 692, SUPERIOR COURT OF NEW JERSEY, APPELLATE DIVISION, 2003

#### CASE SUMMARY

**Facts:** Maria Kerkoulas owned the Pub Zone bar. She knew that several motorcycle gangs frequented the tavern. From her own experience tending bar, and conversations with city police, she knew that some of the gangs, including the Pagans, were dangerous and prone to attack customers for no reason. Kerkoulas posted a sign prohibiting any motorcycle gangs from entering the bar while wearing "colors"; that is, insignia of their gangs. She believed that gangs without their colors were less prone to violence, and experience proved her right.

Rhino, Backdraft, and several other Pagans, all wearing colors, pushed their way past the tavern's bouncer and approached the bar. Although Kerkoulas saw their colors, she allowed them to stay for one drink. They later moved towards the back of the pub, and Kerkoulas believed they were departing. In fact, they followed a customer named Karl Kuehn to the men's room, where, without any provocation, they savagely beat him. Kuehn was knocked unconscious and suffered brain hemorrhaging, disc herniation, and numerous fractures of facial bones. He was forced to undergo various surgeries, including eye reconstruction.

Although the government prosecuted Rhino and Backdraft for their vicious assault, our case does not concern that prosecution. Kuehn sued the Pub Zone, and that is the case we will read. The jury awarded him $300,000 in damages. However, the trial court judge overruled the jury's verdict. He granted

a judgment for the Pub Zone, meaning that the tavern owed nothing. The judge ruled that the pub's owner could not have foreseen the attack on Kuehn and had no duty to protect him from an outlaw motorcycle gang. Kuehn appealed, and the appeals court's decision follows:

**Issue:** *Did the Pub Zone have a duty to protect Kuehn from the Pagans' attack?*

**Decision:** Yes, the Pub Zone had a duty to protect Kuehn. The decision is reversed, and the jury's verdict is reinstated.

**Reasoning:** Whether a duty exists depends on the foreseeability of the harm, its potential severity, and the defendant's ability to prevent the injury. A court should also evaluate society's interest in the dispute.

A business owner generally has no duty to protect a customer from acts of a third party unless experience suggests that there is danger. However, if the owner could in fact foresee injury, she is obligated to take reasonable safety precautions.

Kerkoulas knew that the Pagans engaged in random violence. She realized that when gang members entered the pub, they endangered her customers. That is why she prohibited bikers from wearing their colors—a reasonable rule. Regrettably, the pub failed to enforce the rule. Pagans were allowed to enter wearing their colors, and the pub did not call the police. The pub's behavior was unreasonable and it is liable to Kuehn.

## Analysis

Let's take it from the top. The case is called *Kuehn v. Pub Zone*. Karl Kuehn is the **plaintiff**, the person who is suing. The Pub Zone is being sued, and is called the **defendant**. In this example, the plaintiff's name happens to appear first, but that is not always true. When a defendant loses a trial and files an appeal, *some* courts reverse the names of the parties for the appeal case.

The next line gives the legal citation, which indicates where to find the case in a law library or online.

The *Facts* section provides a background to the lawsuit, written by the authors of this text. The court's own explanation of the facts is often many pages long and may involve complex matters irrelevant to the subject covered in this book, so we relate only what is necessary. This section will usually include some mention of what happened at the trial court. Lawsuits always begin in a trial court. The losing party often appeals to a court of appeals, and it is usually an appeals court decision that we are reading. The trial judge ruled in favor of Pub Zone, but in the appellate decision we are reading, Kuehn won.

The *Issue* section is very important. It tells you what the court had to decide—and why you are reading the case.

The *Decision* section describes the court's answer to the issue posed. A court's decision is often referred to as its **holding**. The court rules that the Pub Zone did have a duty to Kuehn. The court **reverses** the trial court's decision, meaning it declares the lower court's ruling wrong and void. The judges reinstate the jury's verdict. In other cases, an appellate court may **remand** the case; that is, send it back down to the lower court for a new trial or some other action. If this court had agreed with the trial court's decision, the judges would have **affirmed** the lower court's ruling, meaning to uphold it.

The *Reasoning* section explains why the court reached its decision. The actual written decision may be three paragraphs or 75 pages. Some judges offer us lucid prose, while others seem intent on torturing the reader. Judges frequently digress and often discuss matters that are irrelevant to the issue on which this text is focusing. For those reasons, we have taken the court's explanation and cast it in our own words. If you are curious about the full opinion, you can always look it up.

Let us examine the reasoning. The court points out that a defendant is liable only if he has a duty to the plaintiff. Whether there is such a duty depends on the foreseeability of the injury and other factors. The judges are emphasizing that courts do not reach decisions arbitrarily. They attempt to make thoughtful choices, consistent with earlier rulings, which make good sense for the general public.

The court also points out what it is *not* deciding. The court is *not* declaring that all businesses must guarantee the safety of their patrons against acts by third parties. If an owner had no reason to foresee injury from a third party, the owner is probably not be liable for such harm. However, if experience indicated that the third party presented serious danger, the owner was obligated to act reasonably. The judges note that Kerkoulas knew the Pagans could be violent and had taken reasonable precautions by prohibiting gang colors. However, the pub failed to enforce its sensible rule and failed even to telephone the police. By the very standard the pub had created, its conduct was unreasonable. The court therefore concludes that the Pub Zone was liable for the Pagans' injury to Kuehn, and the judges reinstate the jury's verdict for the injured man.

### EXAM *Strategy*

This feature gives you practice analyzing cases the way lawyers do—and the way *you* must, on tests. Law exams are different from most others because you must determine the issue from the facts provided. Too frequently, students faced with a law exam forget that the questions relate to the issues in the text, and those discussed in class. Understandably, students new to law may focus on the wrong information in the problem, or rely on material learned elsewhere. *Exam Strategy* teaches you to figure out exactly what issue is at stake and then analyze it in a logical, consistent manner. Here is an example, relating to the element of "duty," which the court discussed in the Pub Zone case.

---

**Plaintiff**
The person who is suing.

**Defendant**
The person being sued.

**Holding**
A court's decision.

**Reverse**
To declare the lower court's ruling wrong and void.

**Remand**
To send a case back down to a lower court.

**Affirm**
To uphold a lower court's ruling.

**Question:** The Big Red Traveling (BRT) Carnival is in town. Tony arrives at 8:00 P.M., parks in the lot, and is robbed at gunpoint by a man who beats him and escapes with his money. There are several police officers on the carnival grounds, but no officer is in the parking lot at the time of the robbery. Tony sues, claiming that brighter lighting and more police in the lot would have prevented the robbery. There has never before been any violent crime—robbery, beating, or other incident—at any BRT carnival. BRT claims it had no duty to protect Tony from this harm. Who is likely to win?

**Strategy:** Begin by isolating the legal issue. What are the parties disputing? They are debating whether BRT had a duty to protect Tony from an armed robbery committed by a stranger. Now ask yourself: How do courts decide whether a business has a duty to prevent this kind of harm? The Pub Zone case provides our answer. A business owner is not an insurer of the visitor's safety. The owner generally has no duty to protect a customer from the criminal act of a third party unless the owner could foresee it is about to happen. (In the Pub Zone case, the business owner *knew* of the gang's violent history and could have foreseen the assault.) Now apply that rule to the facts of this case.

**Result:** There has never been a violent attack of any kind at a BRT carnival. BRT cannot foresee this robbery, and has no duty to protect against it. The carnival wins.

## "YOU BE THE JUDGE"

Many cases involve difficult decisions for juries and judges. Often both parties have legitimate, opposing arguments. Most chapters in this book will have a feature called "You Be the Judge," in which we present the facts of a case but not the court's holding. We offer you two opposing arguments based on the kinds of claims the lawyers made in court. We leave it up to you to debate and decide which position is stronger or to add your own arguments to those given.

The following case is another negligence lawsuit, with issues that overlap those of the Pub Zone case. This time the court confronts murder in a high school. Distraught parents of the victims sued producers of a violent film and video games, claiming that the companies were partly responsible for the killings. Once again, the defendants asked the court to dismiss the case, claiming that they owed no duty to protect the victims—the same argument made by the Pub Zone. They pointed out, correctly, that a defendant owed a duty to a plaintiff only if it could foresee the harm that occurred. Could these defendants have foreseen what happened? You be the judge.

## YOU *be the* JUDGE

### JAMES v. MEOW MEDIA
300 F.3d 683
Sixth Circuit Court of Appeals, 2002

**Facts:** Michael Carneal was a 14-year-old freshman at Heath High School in Paducah, Kentucky. He carried a .22-caliber pistol and five shotguns into the school's lobby, where he shot into a crowd of students, killing three and wounding five more. He was arrested and convicted of murder.

An investigation revealed that Carneal regularly played violent video games, including *Doom, Quake,* and *Redneck Rampage.* He also owned a copy of the movie *The Basketball Diaries,* in which a character played by Leonardo DiCaprio envisions murdering a teacher and several classmates.

The parents of the victims sued the producers of *Basketball Diaries* and the video games, alleging that when the companies distributed such violent material to young people, they knew or should have known that they were creating an unreasonable risk of harm to innocent people. The parents claimed that such games and movies made young people insensitive to violence and more likely to commit such appalling acts.

The producers of the games and the movie claimed that they owed no duty to the victims. They argued that Carneal's actions were not foreseeable.

*continued*

The trial court dismissed the case, ruling that Carneal's acts were unforeseeable. The producers had no duty to protect the victims. The parents appealed to the Court of Appeals.

**You Be the Judge:  Did the producers have a duty to protect the victims from harm caused by their products?**

**Argument for the parents:** Your honors, the producers had a duty to the victims of this horrible assault because they should have foreseen what happened. In all likelihood, they *did* foresee it. These manufacturers do not merely churn out brutal, vivid material—they profit from it. That proves that they know their market. They do not blindly send this material into the world, hoping for the best. The producers create, advertise, and distribute games and movies, intending to sell them to young people. They know that many of their customers are adolescents, some of whom are going through periods of alienation, anger, and potential violence. They also know that guns are easily available in our society. Into this combustible mix they toss a match—their movie, their games, all celebrating murder, all soaked in blood.

Each of these products depicts a protagonist engaging in gruesome conduct. Anyone can foresee that the movie and games will desensitize young people to violence and make them more likely to act out what they have seen. The producers know that their efforts will cause innocent people to suffer, and some to die. Yet they carry on, contributing to bloodshed, earning a profit.

Because the producers could foresee the harm, they have a duty to protect against it. The producers failed in that duty. They are liable and must pay the price.

**Argument for the producers:** We agree that these shootings were a tragedy. However, while we share in the sympathy, we do not share in the responsibility. The producers manufactured legal, commonplace items—video games and movies. Millions of young people played the games and watched the movie and never did anything violent or criminal.

It is absurd to suggest that we could have foreseen criminal conduct like this. How can a film producer anticipate every viewer's response to a movie? Perhaps a broken-hearted moviegoer will overreact to a painful scene in a love story. Maybe a high school student will empathize with the injustice inflicted on a movie character of his age. Does that mean we must ban movies about adolescence, or love? Are the producers expected to conduct psychological testing on patrons before admitting them to the cinema or selling them a video game?

Businesspeople should expect that their customers are law-abiding citizens. Carneal was the rare exception: a troubled young man, determined upon violence. While his parents may bear some responsibility, and perhaps others close to him, it is preposterous to foist onto film and game producers the duty to control him.

The producers could not foresee that their customers would commit crimes because most do not. The producers owed no duty to the victims or anyone else and cannot be held responsible for these abnormal acts.

## CHAPTER  CONCLUSION

**We depend upon the law to give us a stable nation and economy, a fair society, a safe place to live and work.** But while law is a vital tool for crafting the society we want, there are no easy answers about how to create it. In a democracy, we all participate in the crafting. Legal rules control us, yet we create them. A working knowledge of the law can help build a successful career—and a solid democracy.

## EXAM REVIEW

1. **FEDERALISM** Our federal system of government means that law comes from a national government in Washington, D.C., and from 50 state governments. (p. 4)

**2.**  **SOURCES OF LAW**  The primary sources of contemporary law are:
  - United States Constitution and state constitutions
  - Statutes, which are drafted by legislatures
  - Common law, which is the body of cases decided by judges, as they follow earlier cases, known as precedent; and
  - Administrative law, the rules and decisions made by federal and state administrative agencies. (pp. 5, 7)

.......................................................................................

**3.**  **CRIMINAL AND CIVIL LAW**  Criminal law concerns behavior so threatening to society that it is outlawed altogether. Civil law deals with duties and disputes between parties, not outlawed behavior. (p. 7)

**EXAM Strategy**

**Question:**  Bill and Diane are hiking in the woods. Diane walks down a hill to fetch fresh water. Bill meets a stranger, who introduces herself as Katrina. Bill sells a kilo of cocaine to Katrina, who then flashes a badge and mentions how much she enjoys her job at the Drug Enforcement Agency. Diane, heading back to camp with the water, meets Freddy, a motorist whose car has overheated. Freddy is late for a meeting where he expects to make a $30 million profit; he's desperate for water for his car. He promises to pay Diane $500 tomorrow if she will give him the pail of water, which she does. The next day, Bill is in jail and Freddy refuses to pay for Diane's water. Explain the criminal law/civil law distinction and what it means to Bill and Diane. Who will do what to whom, with what results?

**Strategy:**  You are asked to distinguish between criminal and civil law. What is the difference? Criminal law concerns behavior that threatens society and is therefore outlawed. The government prosecutes the defendant. Civil law deals with the rights and duties between parties. One party files a suit against the other. Apply those different standards to these facts. (See the "Result" at the end of this section.)

**3. Result:**  The government will prosecute Bill for dealing in drugs. If convicted, he will go to prison. The government will take no interest in Diane's dispute. However, if she chooses, she may sue Freddy for $500, the amount he promised her for the water. In that civil lawsuit, a court will decide whether Freddy must pay what he promised; however, even if Freddy loses, he will not go to jail.

# PRACTICE EXAM

## MATCHING QUESTIONS

Match the following terms with their definitions.

___ A. Statute                              1. Law created by judges.

___ B. Administrative agencies    2. Let the decision stand.

___ C. Common law                    3. A law passed by Congress or a state legislature.

___ D. *Stare decisis*                    4. The supreme law of the land.

___ E. United States Constitution   5. The IRS; the FCC; the FTC.

## TRUE/FALSE QUESTIONS

1. T  F  The idea that current cases must be decided based on earlier cases is called legal positivism.

2. T  F  Civil lawsuits are brought to court by the injured party, but criminal cases must be prosecuted by the government.

3. T  F  Congress established the federal government by passing a series of statutes.

4. T  F  The federal government has three branches: executive, legislative, and administrative.

5. T  F  Law is different from morality, but the two are closely linked.

## MULTIPLE CHOICE QUESTIONS

6. More American law comes from one country than from any other. Which country?
   - A. France
   - B. England
   - C. Germany
   - D. Spain
   - E. Canada

7. Under the United States Constitution, power that is not expressly given to the federal government is retained by
   - A. The courts
   - B. The Congress
   - C. The Founding Fathers
   - D. The states and the people
   - E. International treaty

8. The European Union sometimes struggles to create a unified policy that works for all its member countries, while permitting each nation to maintain adequate power over its own affairs. With what legal principle are they struggling?
   - A. Jurisprudence
   - B. Precedent
   - C. Strict construction
   - D. Federalism
   - E. Morality

9. Judges use precedent to create what kind of law?
   - A. Common law
   - B. Statutes
   - C. National law
   - D. Local law
   - E. Empirical law

10. Rebecca leaves a store at night and enters the store's parking lot. Before she can reach her car, she is robbed at gunpoint. Rebecca sues the store. When a court decides whether the store had a *duty* to prevent this harm, what issue will the judges focus on?
    - A. Federalism
    - B. Equity
    - C. Legal realism
    - D. Morality
    - E. Foreseeability

## SHORT-ANSWER QUESTIONS

11. Union organizers at a hospital wanted to distribute leaflets to potential union members, but hospital rules prohibited leafletting in areas of patient care, hallways, cafeterias, and any areas open to the public. The National Labor Relations Board (NLRB) ruled that these restrictions violated the law and ordered the hospital to permit the activities in the cafeteria and coffee shop. The NLRB cannot create common law or statutory law. What kind of law was it creating?

12. The stock market crash of 1929 and the Great Depression that followed were caused in part because so many investors blindly put their money into stocks they knew nothing about. During the 1920s, it was often impossible for an investor to find out what a corporation was planning to do with its money, who was running the corporation, and many other vital facts. Congress responded by passing the Securities Act of 1933, which required a corporation to divulge more information about itself before it could seek money for a new stock issue. What kind of law did Congress create? Explain the relationship between voters, Congress, and the law.

13. ETHICS The greatest of all Chinese lawgivers, Confucius, did not esteem written laws. He believed that good rulers were the best guarantee of justice. Does our legal system rely primarily on the rule of law or the rule of people? Which do you instinctively trust more? Confucius himself was an extraordinarily wise man. How does that fact influence your analysis?

14. ROLE REVERSAL Each Practice Test contains one Role Reversal feature, in which we challenge you to create your own exam question. The goal is to think creatively and accurately. Crafting questions is a good way to reinforce what you understand and recognize the areas that you need to review. Your professor may ask you to submit the questions in writing or electronically, or to prepare an overhead slide.

   The question should be challenging enough that the average student will need to stop and think, but clear enough that there is only one answer. Useful questions can be formatted as essay, short answer, or multiple choice. Notice that some exam questions are very direct, while others require deeper analysis. Here are two examples. The first focuses on a definition.

**Question:** An injunction is:

(a) A decision by an appeals court affirming the trial court

(b) A decision by an appeals court reversing a trial court

(c) A decision by an appeals court sending a decision back down to a lower court

(d) A theory of law requiring that current cases be decided based on earlier decisions

(e) A judge's order that someone stop doing something

As you know, the correct answer is "e."

   The next question demands that the student spot the issue of law involved (foreseeability) and correctly apply it to the facts provided.

**Question:** Marvin asks Sheila, a qualified auto mechanic, to fix his engine, which constantly stalls while driving. When Marvin returns, Sheila informs him that the engine is now "Perfect—runs like a top." Marvin drives home along Lonesome Highway. Suddenly the car stalls because Sheila rushed her service work and failed to fix the problem. Marvin pulls over and begins the long walk to the nearest telephone. A blimp flies overhead, advertising Top brand tires. Tragically, the blimp suddenly plummets to earth and explodes 20 feet from Marvin, seriously injuring him. Marvin sues Sheila. Sheila's best defense is that:

(a) The falling blimp is so bizarre that Sheila could never have foreseen it.

(b) Sheila made reasonable efforts to fix the engine.

(c) Marvin should have checked the engine himself.

(d) Marvin should have carried a cell phone with him in case of emergencies.

(e) Sheila is a qualified mechanic and her work is presumptively sufficient.

The correct answer is "a." Notice that the same facts could be used as an essay question, simply by deleting the multiple-choice answers. Now it is your turn for Role Reversal: draft a multiple-choice question focusing on federalism.

# INTERNET RESEARCH PROBLEM

Online, find two current cases that interest you: one civil, one criminal. Explain the different roles played by each type of law and summarize the issues in the respective cases.

**You can find further practice problems in the Online Quiz at www.cengage.com/blaw/beatty.**

# BUSINESS ETHICS AND SOCIAL RESPONSIBILITY

**Arthur Haupt** is a 79-year-old retired waiter who lives with his black cat, Max, in a tidy 650-square-foot apartment in Chicago's Rienzi Plaza apartment building. He works 20 hours a week, shelving books at Loyola University's law library, earning $6.95 an hour. He also gets social security and two modest pensions. His total income last year was $18,713. His monthly rent in this federally subsidized apartment is $352. Market rent for an equivalent apartment would be as high as $1,644.

Last fall, Haupt's landlord notified him that he might be evicted. Nationally, landlords have taken about 125,000 units out of the federal subsidy program. At the same time, demand for subsidized housing is rising, in part because big cities such as Chicago are tearing down their old public-housing projects and telling residents to find subsidized apartments instead. Where will Arthur Haupt go?

The landlord, Sheldon Baskin, is not a bad guy. Twenty years ago, he and his partners signed a contract with the federal government, promising to build and

> **His monthly rent in this federally subsidized apartment is $352. Market rent for an equivalent apartment would be as high as $1,644.**

maintain an apartment building for low-income Chicagoans. In exchange, the government guaranteed a steady stream of rent. But now the contract on Rienzi Plaza is set to expire. Baskin could make a larger profit on the building by either selling it, converting it to condominiums, or renting to unsubsidized tenants who could pay more. What does Baskin owe to his investors?

The Rienzi tenants and community groups have begun looking for a white knight—someone who could buy the building and preserve its low-income housing—but so far no luck. Meanwhile, Baskin asked government officials how much more rent they would pay if he extended his contract for five years. Officials said they would have to hire an outside consultant to do a market study, a task that would take months—long past the deadline by which federal regulations require Baskin to announce his decision.[1]

**Ethics**
Ethics is the study of how people ought to act.

Business is an enormously powerful tool that corporate managers can use to accomplish many goals. They may wish to earn a good living, even to become wealthy, but they can also use their business skills to cure the ill, feed the hungry, entertain the bored, and in many other ways affect their community, their country, and their world.

This book is primarily about the impact of law on business. But law is only one set of rules that governs business; ethics is another. **Ethics** is the study of how people ought to act. Law and ethics are often in harmony. Most reasonable people agree that murder should be prohibited. But law and ethics are not always compatible. In some cases, it might be *ethical* to commit an *illegal* act; in others, it might be *unethical* to be *legal*. Here are two examples in which law and ethics might conflict: A 75-year-old man confined to a wheelchair robbed a bank in San Diego of $70 so that he could buy heart medicine. That was illegal—was it unethical?

Or what about Martin Luther King, Jr., who was arrested in Birmingham, Alabama, in 1963, for leading illegal sit-ins and marches to protest laws that discriminated against African Americans. When eight local clergymen criticized his activities, King offered this defense:

> [W]hen you suddenly find your tongue twisted as you seek to explain to your six-year-old daughter why she can't go to the public amusement park that has just been advertised on television, and see tears welling up when she is told that Funtown is closed to colored children. . . . [W]hen you take a cross-country drive and find it necessary to sleep night after night in the uncomfortable corners of your automobile because no motel will accept you. . . . How can [we] advocate breaking some laws and obeying others? I agree with St. Augustine that "an unjust law is not law at all."[2]

---

[1] Based on Jonathan Eig, "Landlord's Dilemma: Help Poor Tenants or Seek More Profits," *Wall Street Journal*, July 17, 2001, p. 1.

[2] Martin Luther King, Jr., "Letter from Birmingham Jail," *The Christian Century*, June 12, 1963. Copyright © 1963 Dr. Martin Luther King, Jr.; Copyright © renewed 1991 Coretta Scott King. Reprinted by arrangement with The Heirs to the Estate of Martin Luther King Jr., c/o Writers House as agent for the proprietor, New York, NY.

The other chapters of this book focus on legal issues, but this chapter concentrates on ethics. In all of the examples in this chapter, the activities are *legal,* but are they *ethical?*

## · WHY BOTHER WITH ETHICS? ·

Business schools teach students how to maximize the profitability of an enterprise, large or small. Some people argue that, in the long run, ethical behavior does indeed pay. But they must mean the very long run, because to date there is little evidence that ethical behavior *necessarily* pays financially, either in the short or the long run.

For instance, when a fire destroyed the Malden Mills factory in Lawrence, Massachusetts, its 70-year-old owner, Aaron Feuerstein, could have shut down the business, collected the insurance money, and sailed off into retirement. But a layoff of the factory's 3,000 employees would have been a major economic blow to the region. So instead Feuerstein kept the workers on the payroll, making the company's patented Polartec fabric, while he rebuilt the factory. However, five years after the fire, Malden Mills filed bankruptcy papers. The company was not able to pay off the loans it had incurred to keep the business going.

In contrast, unethical behavior is no bar to financial success. The first antitrust laws in America were designed, at least in part, to restrain John D. Rockefeller's unethical activities. Yet, four generations later, his name is still synonymous with wealth and his numerous heirs can live comfortably on their inheritance from him.

If ethical behavior does not necessarily pay and unethical behavior sometimes does, why bother with ethics?

### SOCIETY AS A WHOLE BENEFITS FROM ETHICAL BEHAVIOR

John Akers, the former chairman of IBM, argues that without ethical behavior, a society cannot be economically competitive. He puts it this way:

> Ethics and competitiveness are inseparable. No society anywhere will compete very long or successfully with people stabbing each other in the back; with people trying to steal from each other; with everything requiring notarized confirmation because you can't trust the other fellow; with every little squabble ending in litigation; and with government writing reams of regulatory legislation, tying business hand and foot to keep it honest. There is no escaping this fact: the greater the measure of mutual trust and confidence in the ethics of a society, the greater its economic strength.[3]

### MONEY DOES NOT BUY HAPPINESS

Researchers who study happiness find that people expect material goods to make them happier than they actually do. Sure, you enjoy driving that snappy new car home from the dealership, but afterwards your happiness quickly returns to its natural base level. People find themselves on the so-called "hedonic treadmill"—struggling to buy more and more things so they can get that buyer's high, only to discover that they can never buy enough to maintain the thrill. Almost no matter how much people earn, they feel they would be happier if their income were just a little bit

---

[3] David Grier, "Confronting Ethical Dilemmas," unpublished manuscript of remarks at the Royal Bank of Canada, Sept. 19, 1989.

higher. So what does make people happy in the long run? Good relationships, satisfying work, ties to the community—all available at no additional cost.

## PEOPLE FEEL BETTER WHEN THEY BEHAVE ETHICALLY

Every businessperson has many opportunities to be dishonest. Consider how one person felt when he resisted temptation:

> Occasionally a customer forgot to send a bill for materials shipped to us for processing. . . . It would have been so easy to rationalize remaining silent. After all, didn't they deserve to lose because of their inefficiency? However, upon instructing our staff to inform the parties of their errors, I found them eager to do so. Our honesty was beneficial in subtle ways. The "inefficient" customer remained loyal for years. . . . [O]ur highly moral policy had a marvelously beneficial effect on our employees. Through the years, many an employee visited my office to let me know that they liked working for a "straight" company.[4]

Profitability is generally not what motivates managers to care about ethics. Managers want to feel good about themselves and the decisions they have made; they want to sleep at night. Their decisions—to lay off employees, install safety devices in cars, burn a cleaner fuel—affect people's lives.

## UNETHICAL BEHAVIOR CAN BE VERY COSTLY

Unethical behavior is a risky business strategy—it may lead to disaster. An engaged couple made a reservation, and put down a $1,500 deposit, to hold their wedding reception at a New Hampshire restaurant. Tragically, the bride died of asthma four months before the wedding. Invoking the terms of the contract, the restaurant owner refused to return the couple's deposit. In a letter to the groom, he admitted, "Morally, I would of course agree that the deposit should be returned." When newspapers reported this story, customers deserted the restaurant and it was forced into bankruptcy—over a $1,500 disagreement.[5] Unethical behavior does not always damage a business, but it certainly has the potential of destroying a company overnight. So why take the risk?

Even if unethical behavior does not devastate a business, it can cause other, subtler damage. In one survey, a majority of those questioned said that they had witnessed unethical behavior in their workplace and that this behavior had reduced productivity, job stability, and profits. Unethical behavior in an organization creates a cynical, resentful, and unproductive workforce.

So why bother with ethics? Because society benefits when managers behave ethically. Because money does not buy happiness. Because ethical managers have happier, more satisfying lives. Because unethical behavior can destroy a business faster than a snake can bite. And because, in the end, ethical behavior is more likely to pay off.

## · WHAT IS ETHICAL BEHAVIOR? ·

It is one thing to decide, in theory, that being ethical is good; in practice, it can be much more difficult to make the right decisions. Supreme Court Justice Potter Stewart once said that he could not define pornography, but he knew it when he saw it. Many people feel the same way about ethics—that somehow, instinctively, they know what is right and wrong. In real life,

---

[4] Hugh Aaron, "Doing the Right Thing in Business," *Wall Street Journal,* June 21, 1993, p. A10.

[5] John Milne, "N.H. Restaurant Goes Bankrupt in Wake of Wedding Refund Flap," *Boston Globe,* Sept. 9, 1994, p. 25.

however, ethical dilemmas are often not black and white, but many shades of gray. The purpose of this section is to analyze the following ethics checklist as an aid to managers in making tough decisions:

- What are the facts?
- What are the critical issues?
- Who are the stakeholders?
- What are the alternatives?
- What are the ethical implications of each alternative?
  - Is it legal?
  - How would it look in the light of day?
  - What are the consequences?
  - Does it violate important values?
  - What kind of world would this be if everyone behaved this way?

## ANALYZING THE ETHICS CHECKLIST

### What Are the Facts?

Although this question seems obvious, people often forget in the heat of battle to listen to (and, more importantly, to *hear*) all the different viewpoints. It is crucial to discover the facts, firsthand, from the people involved.

### What Are the Critical Issues?

In analyzing ethical dilemmas, expand your thinking to include *all* the important issues. Avoid a narrow focus that encompasses only one or two aspects. In the case of the New Hampshire restaurant that refused to refund a deposit, the owner focused on the narrow legal issue. His interpretation of the *contract* was correct. But if the owner had expanded his thinking to include consideration for his customers, he might have reached a different decision.

### Who Are the Stakeholders?

Stakeholders are all the people potentially affected by the decision. That list might include subordinates, bosses, shareholders, suppliers, customers, members of the community in which the business operates, society as a whole, or even more remote stakeholders, such as future generations.

### What Are the Alternatives?

The next step is to list the reasonable alternatives. A creative manager may find a clever solution that is a winner for everyone. What alternatives might be available to Sheldon Baskin, the landlord who faced a dilemma in the opening scenario?

### What Are the Ethical Implications of Each Alternative?

**Is the Alternative Legal?**   Illegal may not always be synonymous with unethical, but, as a general rule, you need to think long and hard about the ethics of any illegal activities.

**How Would the Alternative Look in the Light of Day?**   If your activities were reported on the evening news, how would you feel? Proud? Embarrassed? Horrified? Undoubtedly, sexual harassment would be virtually eliminated if people thought that their parents, spouse, or partner would shortly see a video replay of the offending behavior.

**What Are the Consequences of This Alternative?**   Ask yourself: Am I hurting anyone by this decision? Which alternative will cause the greatest good (or the least harm) to the most people? For example, you would like to fire an incompetent employee. That decision will clearly have adverse consequences for him. But the other employees in your division will benefit and so will the shareholders of your company. You should look with a particularly critical eye if an alternative benefits you while harming others. Suppose that you become CEO of a company whose headquarters are located in a distant suburb. You would like to move the headquarters closer to your home to cut your commuting time. Of course, such a decision would be expensive for shareholders and inconvenient for other employees. Do you simply impose your will on the company or consider the consequences for everyone?

**Does the Alternative Violate Important Values?**    In addition to consequences, consider fundamental values. It is possible to commit an act that does not harm anyone else, but is still the wrong thing to do. Suppose, for instance, that you are away from home and have the opportunity to engage in a one-night stand. You are absolutely certain that your spouse will never find out and your partner for the night will have no regrets or guilt. There would be no negative consequences, but you believe that infidelity is wrong, *regardless of the consequences,* so you resist temptation.

Some people question whether, as a diverse, heterogeneous society (not to mention, world), we have common values. But throughout history, and across many different cultures, common values do appear, such as: compassion, courage, fairness, integrity, responsibility, and self-control. Although reasonable people may disagree about a precise list of important values, most would agree that values matter. Try compiling your own list of values and then check it periodically to see if you are living up to it in your business and personal life.

> An organization has responsibilities to customers, employees, shareholders, and society . . .

**What Kind of World Would This Be if Everyone Behaved This Way?**    Is this the kind of world in which you would want to live? Imagine that you could cheat on an exam without getting caught. You might gain some short-term benefit—a higher grade. But what would happen if everyone cheated? The professor would have to make the exams harder or curve everyone's grade down. If your school developed a reputation for cheating, you might not be able to find a job after graduation. Cheating works only if most people are honest. To take advantage of everyone else's honesty is contemptible.

## APPLYING THE ETHICS CHECKLIST: MAKING DECISIONS

An organization has responsibilities to customers, employees, shareholders, and society generally, both here and overseas. The purpose of this section is to apply the ethics checklist to business dilemmas. The checklist does not lead to one particular solution; rather it is a method to use in thinking through ethics problems. The goal is for you to reach a decision that satisfies you.

### Organization's Responsibility to Society

**Facts**    In the United States, teenagers routinely list alcohol commercials among their favorite advertisements. Adolescents who frequently see ads for alcohol are more likely to believe that drinkers are attractive, athletic, and successful. They are also more likely to drink, drink excessively, and drink in hazardous situations such as driving a car.

While Secretary of Health and Human Services, Louis W. Sullivan publicly denounced the test marketing of Uptown, a high-tar cigarette targeted at African Americans. He called it "contemptible that the tobacco industry has sought to increase their market" among minorities because this population was "already bearing more than its fair share of smoking-related illness and mortality." Comedian Jay Leno joked that R. J. Reynolds named the cigarette Uptown "because the word 'Genocide' was already taken."[6]

---

[6] Richard W. Pollay, Jung S. Lee, and David Carter-Whitney, "Separate, but Not Equal: Racial Segmentation in Cigarette Advertising," *Journal of Advertising,* Mar. 1992, vol. 21, no. 1, p. 45.

At a time when doctors are concerned that too many children are fat, one-third of all advertisements shown during children's television programs are for just the sort of foods that encourage obesity: those high in fat, sugar, and salt but low in nutrition.

**Critical Issues**    What are the obligations of advertising executives and marketing managers to those who see their ads? Is it ethical to entice teenagers into drinking or African Americans into smoking? If these ads sell product, is that justification enough?

**Stakeholders**    Ad designers are primarily responsible to their firms and the firms' clients. After all, designers are paid to sell product, not to make the world a better place. But what about the people who see the advertisements? Do the designers have any responsibility to them? Or to society as a whole?

**Alternatives**    Firms have at least four alternatives in dealing with issues of ethics in advertising. They can

- Ignore ethics and simply strive to create promotions that sell the most product, whatever the underlying message;
- Try, in a general way, to minimize racism, sexism, and other exploitation;
- Include, as part of the development process, a systematic, focused review of the underlying messages contained in their advertisements; or
- Refuse to create any ads that are potentially demeaning, insensitive, or harmful, recognizing that such a stand may lead to a loss of clients.

**Ethical Implications**    All of these alternatives are perfectly legal. And, far from the ad executives being embarrassed if the ads see the light of day, the whole purpose of ads is to be seen. As for the consequences, the ads may help clients sell their products. But the ads may also harm those who see them. A manager might question whether these ads violate fundamental values. Are they showing consideration for others? Do they encourage self-control? Are they creating the kind of world in which the managers want to live?

## EXAM *Strategy*

**Question:** Under Indian custom, many families pay a staggering dowry when their daughters marry. To avoid this burdensome debt, hundreds of thousands of pregnant women each year pay for an ultrasound to determine the gender of their fetus and then abort females. This practice has become such a problem that Indian law prohibits doctors from revealing a fetus's gender, but many doctors violate the law. In some areas of India, fewer than 800 girls are born for every 1,000 boys. General Electric Co. (GE) is the largest seller of ultrasound machines in the Indian market. Indeed, there is some evidence that GE targets doctors in small towns where this problem is most severe. If you were the head of the Ultrasound Division of GE, what would you do?

**Strategy:** Begin by reviewing the ethics checklist. Stakeholders include GE shareholders and citizens of India. Are there alternatives? What could GE do to ensure that its machines are not used improperly? What are the consequences? Thousands of young men without mates could lead to an increase in prostitution and perhaps even to social unrest, with worldwide implications. Is GE being a responsible member of the world community? Do managers want to live in a world in which female fetuses are aborted because of their gender? Are some values in conflict? If so, which values are most important?

**Result:** That is for you to decide.

## Organization's Responsibility to Its Customers

In this chapter's opening scenario, landlord Sheldon Baskin faced a dilemma: his contract with the federal government was set to expire, so he would soon have the right to evict the poor and elderly tenants in Rienzi Plaza. What would you do if you were Baskin? What obligation does he have to the tenants? To his investors? Is it fair to them if he decides to subsidize the rents of low-income tenants? What about the community? Does it benefit from having elderly members? How will Baskin feel about himself if he puts these elderly tenants out on the street? Or if *The Wall Street Journal* runs a front-page article about his eviction plans? On the other hand, could he argue that it is the government's responsibility to house the poor and elderly? Is there any compromise solution?

## Organization's Responsibility to Its Employees

When James Kilts became CEO of Gillette Co., the consumer products giant had been a mainstay of the Boston community for a hundred years. But the organization was going through hard times: Its stock was trading at less than half its peak price. In four short years, Kilts turned Gillette around—strengthening its brands, cutting jobs, and paying off debt. With its stock up 61 percent, Kilts had added $20 billion in shareholder value.

Then suddenly Kilts sold Gillette to Procter & Gamble Co. (P&G) for $57 billion. So short was Kilts's stay in Boston that he never moved his family from their home in Rye, New York. Shareholders benefited—the company's stock price went up 13 percent in one day. And so did Kilts—his payoff was $153 million, including a $36.5 million sweetener for having made the deal. In addition, P&G agreed to pay him $8 million a year to serve as vice chairman after the merger. When he retires, his pension will be $1.2 million per year. Moreover, two of his top lieutenants were paid a total of $57 million.

Any downside to this deal? Four percent of the Gillette workforce—6,000 employees—were fired. If the payouts to the top three Gillette executives were divided among these 6,000, each unemployed worker would receive $35,000. The loss of this many employees (4,000 of whom live in New England) had a ripple effect throughout the area economy. Although Gillette shareholders certainly benefited in the short run from the sale, their profit would have been even greater without this $210 million payout to the executives. Moreover, about half the increase in Gillette revenues during the time that Kilts was running the show were attributable to currency fluctuations. A cheaper dollar increased revenue overseas. If the dollar had moved in the opposite direction, there might not have been any increase in revenue. Indeed, for the first two years after Kilts joined Gillette, the stock price declined. It wasn't until the dollar turned down that the stock price improved.

Should CEOs be paid so much when many employees will lose their jobs? One study found that CEOs who receive sweeteners negotiate a lower sale price than those who do not.[7] But shareholders certainly profited during his tenure.

## Organization's Responsibility to Its Shareholders

Staples, Inc. is the world's largest office products company. It also strives to be socially responsible. The company has prepared a document entitled "Staples Soul: It's what moves us" that reports on its corporate responsibility efforts. (This report is available at the company website.) For example, 20 percent of its energy consumption in the United States is from renewable sources. The company has reconfigured its fleet of vehicles to save 500,000 gallons of fuel a year. It donates to hundreds of worthy organizations. If you were a shareholder of Staples, would you approve of these efforts?

Milton Friedman, a Nobel Laureate in economics, famously observed, "The one and only social responsibility of business is to increase its profits."[8] He argued that an executive should act

---

[7] Mark Maremont, "No Razor Here: Gillette Chief to Get a Giant Payday," *Wall Street Journal*, Jan. 31, 2005, p. 1.

[8] Milton Friedman, "The Social Responsibility of Business Is to Increase Its Profits," *New York Times Magazine*, Sept. 13, 1970, p. 32.

for the benefit of the owners of the company. His primary responsibility is to them. If an individual wishes to support other responsibilities, such as a charity, a church, a city, or a country, let him do so with his own time and money, not that of the shareholders.

Look at some of the Staples corporate responsibility initiatives listed on its website. Is that how you would choose to spend your money? If you were a Staples shareholder, perhaps you would prefer to earn higher returns on your stock so that you could give money to other projects you consider more compelling. If the air needs to be cleaner or the schools richer, why shouldn't private donors or public institutions be responsible, not one company's shareholders?[9]

Reading deeper into the "Staples Soul" report, you would discover that the total giving to community organizations was $26 million out of $5.2 billion in revenue. Then you might have the opposite feeling—$26 million out of $5 billion? Should the company be *more* generous? How should companies balance their obligation to their shareholders and their world?

## Organization's Responsibility Overseas

An American company's ethical obligations do not end at the border. What ethical duties does an American manager owe to stakeholders in countries where the culture and economic circumstances are very different?

Here is a typical story from Guatemala:

> My father left home a long time ago. My mother supported me and my five brothers and sisters by selling tortillas and corn. Our house was a tin shack on the side of the road. We were crowded with all of us in one room. One day the police came and cleared us all out saying that we couldn't come back unless we paid rent. How could we afford that? I was 12 and my mother said it was time for me to work. Lots of other kids shine shoes or beg, but I heard that the maquila [clothing factory] was willing to hire children if we would work as hard as older people.
>
> I can keep up with the grown-ups. We work from 6:00 in the morning to 6:30 at night, with half an hour break at noon. We have no other breaks the whole rest of the day. If I don't work fast enough, they hit me, not too hard, and threaten to fire me. Sometimes, if there is too much work to do, they'll lock the doors and not let us out until everything is finished. I earn $30 a week and without that money, we would not have enough to eat. My mother hopes all of my brothers and sisters can get jobs in the factory, too. Of course, I'd rather be in school where I could wear a uniform and have friends. Then I could get a job as a clerk at the medical clinic. I would find people's files and tell them how long before the doctor could see them.[10]

This description paints a distasteful picture indeed: children being beaten as they work 12-hour days. Should American companies (and consumers) buy goods that are produced in sweatshop factories? Jeffrey Sachs, a leading economist and adviser to developing nations, says, "My concern is not that there are too many sweatshops but that there are too few."[11] Why would he support sweatshops and child labor?

Historically, poor children have worked to help support their family. In England in 1860, almost 40 percent of 14-year-old boys worked, and that was not just a few hours at Burger Box, but more likely 60 hours a week. That percentage is higher than in Africa or India today. For a child in a desperately poor family, the choice is not work or school, it is work, starvation, or prostitution.

Industrialization has always been the first stepping stone out of dire poverty—it was in England, it is now in the Third World. Eventually, higher productivity leads to higher wages. During the past 50 years, Taiwan and South Korea welcomed sweatshops while India resisted

---

[9] See, for instance, David Henderson, "Misguided Virtue: False Notions of Corporate Social Responsibility," Hobart Paper 142, Institute of Economic Affairs, London, cited in *The Economist,* Nov. 17, 2001, p. 70.

[10] Adapted from the *Boston Globe,* June 15, 1997.

[11] Allen R. Meyerson, "In Principle, a Case for More 'Sweatshops,'" *New York Times,* June 22, 1997, p. E5.

what it perceived to be foreign exploitation. Although all three countries started at the same economic level, Taiwan and South Korea today have much lower levels of infant mortality and much higher levels of education than India.[12]

When governments or customers try to force Third World factories to pay higher wages, the factory owners typically either relocate to lower wage countries or mechanize, thereby reducing the need for workers. In either case, the local economy suffers.

The difference, however, between the twenty-first and the nineteenth centuries is that now there are wealthy countries able to help their poorer neighbors. In the nineteenth century, England was among the richest countries, so it was on its own to solve its economic problems. Is America ethically obligated to assist the people around the world who live in abject poverty? Already, owing to pressure from activists, many companies have introduced better conditions in their factories. Workers are less likely to be beaten. They can go to the bathroom without asking permission. They might even receive rudimentary medical care. Manufacturing processes use fewer dangerous chemicals. Factories are cleaner, with better lighting and more ventilation. But hours are still long and wages low.

Many of these sweatshops produce clothing. As a consumer, how much would be you willing to pay in higher clothing prices to eliminate sweatshops and child labor? As a taxpayer, how much are you willing to pay in taxes to subsidize Third World incomes so that sweatshops and child labor are no longer necessary?

## EXAM *Strategy*

**Question:** Many of America's largest consumer product companies, such as Wal-Mart, Nike, and Land's End, buy fabric produced in China by Fountain Set Holdings Ltd. Chinese government investigators recently discovered that Fountain Set has contaminated a local river by dumping dye waste into it. What responsibility do U.S. companies have to ensure safe environmental practices by overseas suppliers?

**Strategy:** Look at the ethics checklist. Citizens of China are stakeholders of American companies. Although it is legal to buy fabric from a company that is polluting overseas, this is surely information that Nike would not want to be well known. Does the company have values? What does its website say? Do any of us want to live in a world where Chinese children are poisoned so that our running shoes cost less?

**Result:** Do Wal-Mart and Nike have an obligation to source their products more carefully?

---

[12] The data in this and the preceding paragraph are from Nicholas D. Kristof and Sheryl WuDunn, "Two Cheers for Sweatshops," *New York Times Magazine,* Sept. 24, 2000, p. 70.

## CHAPTER CONCLUSION

Even employees who are ethical in their personal lives may find it difficult to uphold their standards at work if those around them behave differently. Managers wonder what they can do to create an ethical environment in their companies. The surest way to infuse ethics throughout an organization is for top executives to behave ethically themselves. Few employees will bother to "do the right thing" unless they observe that their bosses value and support such behavior. To ensure a more ethical world, managers must be an example for others, both within and outside their organizations.

# EXAM REVIEW

**1.** **WHY BOTHER WITH ETHICS?** There are at least five reasons to be concerned about ethics in a business environment:
- Society as a whole benefits from ethical behavior.
- Money does not buy happiness.
- People feel better when they behave ethically.
- Unethical behavior can be very costly.
- Ethical behavior is more likely to pay off.

**2.** **THE ETHICS CHECKLIST**
- What are the facts?
- What are the critical issues?
- Who are the stakeholders?
- What are the alternatives?
- What are the ethical implications of each alternative?
  - Is it legal?
  - How would it look in the light of day?
  - What are the consequences?
  - Does it violate important values?
  - What kind of world would this be if everyone behaved this way?

**EXAM Strategy**

**Question:** Rap artist Ice-T and his band, Body Count, recorded a song called "Cop Killer," in which the singer gleefully anticipates slitting a policeman's throat. (The lyrics to this song are readily available on the Internet.) Recorded music was an important source of profits for the company, which was struggling with a $15 billion debt and a depressed stock price. If Time Warner renounced rap albums, its reputation in the music business—and its future profits—might have suffered.

**Strategy:** Review the ethics checklist. The company was concerned about several important stakeholders—shareholders, consumers, suppliers (rap musicians), and society. What are the alternatives? Would it be possible to work with rap musicians to tone down such hateful lyrics? Find other sources of music? Does this music violate important values? What about the artists' free speech rights? Are the Time Warner executives creating the kind of world in which they would want to raise their children? Do they care about anything other than profitability? (See the "Result" at the end of this section.)

**2. Result:** You decide.

# PRACTICE EXAM

## MATCHING QUESTIONS

Match the following people with their views.
\_\_\_ A. Martin Luther King, Jr.
\_\_\_ B. John Akers

1. Argued that "Ethics and competitiveness are inseparable."
2. Argued that "Third World countries need more sweatshops, not fewer."

___ C. Jeffrey Sachs

___ D. Milton Friedman

3. Argued that "The one and only social responsibility of business is to increase its profits."

4. Argued that "An unjust law is not law at all."

## SHORT ANSWER QUESTIONS

1. Executives were considering the possibility of moving their company to a different state. They wanted to determine if employees would be willing to relocate, but they did not want the employees to know the company was contemplating a move because the final decision had not yet been made. Instead of asking the employees directly, the company hired a firm to carry out a telephone survey. When calling the employees, these "pollsters" pretended to be conducting a public opinion poll and identified themselves as working for the new state's Chamber of Commerce. Has this company behaved in an ethical manner? Would there have been a better way to obtain this information?

2. H. B. Fuller Co. of St. Paul is a leading manufacturer of industrial glues. Its mission statement says the company "will conduct business legally and ethically." It has endowed a university chair in business ethics and donates 5 percent of its profits to charity. But now it is under attack for selling its shoemakers' glue, Resistol, in Central America. Many homeless children in these countries have become addicted to Resistol's fumes. So widespread is the problem that glue-sniffers in Central America are called "resistoleros." Glue manufacturers in Europe have added a foul-smelling oil to their glue that discourages abusers. Fuller fears that the smell may also discourage legitimate users. What should Fuller do?

3. Genentech, Inc., manufactures Protropin, a genetically engineered version of the human growth hormone. This drug's purpose is to enhance the growth of short children. Protropin is an important product for Genentech, accounting for more than one-third of the company's total revenue of $217 million. Although the drug is approved for the treatment of children whose bodies make inadequate quantities of growth hormone, many doctors prescribe it for children with normal amounts of growth hormone who simply happen to be short. There is no firm evidence that the drug actually increases growth for short children with normal growth hormone. Moreover, many people question whether it is appropriate to prescribe such a powerful drug for cosmetic reasons, especially when the drug may not work. Nor is there proof that it is safe over the long term. Is Genentech behaving ethically? Should it discourage doctors from prescribing the drug to normal, short children?

4. Mark is an executive for a multinational office equipment company that would like to enter the potentially vast Chinese market. The official tariffs on office equipment imported into China are so high that these goods are uncompetitive in the local market. Mark discovers, however, that many companies sell their goods to importers offshore. These importers then negotiate "special" tariff rates with Chinese officials. Because these customs officials are under pressure to meet revenue targets, sometimes they are willing to negotiate lower, unofficial rates. What would you do if you were Mark?

5. ROLE REVERSAL Write one or two paragraphs that could be used as an essay question describing an ethical dilemma that you have faced in your own life.

## INTERNET RESEARCH PROBLEM

Find on the Internet an example of a real-life ethical dilemma. How did the person involved solve it? What would you have done if you had been in that situation? Use the ethics checklist in this chapter to guide you.

**You can find further practice problems in the Online Quiz at www.cengage.com/blaw/beatty.**

# COURTS, LITIGATION, AND ALTERNATIVE DISPUTE RESOLUTION

**Tony Caruso** had not returned for dinner, and his wife, Karen, was nervous. She put on some sandals and hurried across the dunes to the ocean shore a half mile away. She soon came upon Tony's dog, Blue, tied to an old picket fence. Tony's shoes and clothing were piled neatly nearby. Karen and friends searched frantically throughout the evening. A little past midnight, Tony's body washed ashore, his lungs filled with water. A local doctor concluded he had accidentally drowned.

Karen and her friends were not the only ones distraught. Tony had been partners with Beth Smiles in an environmental consulting business, Enviro-Vision. They were good friends, and Beth was emotionally devastated. When she was able to focus on business issues, Beth filed an insurance claim with the Coastal Insurance Group. Beth hated to think about Tony's death in financial terms, but she was relieved that the struggling business would receive $2 million on the life insurance policy.

> **A little past midnight, Tony's body washed ashore, his lungs filled with water.**

Several months after filing the claim, Beth received this reply from Coastal: "Under the policy issued to Enviro-Vision, we are liable in the amount of $1 million in the event of Mr. Caruso's death. If his death is accidental, we are liable to pay double indemnity of $2 million. But pursuant to section H(5), death by suicide is not covered. After a thorough investigation, we have concluded that Anthony Caruso's death was an act of suicide. Your claim is denied in its entirety." Beth was furious. She was convinced Tony was incapable of suicide. And her company could not afford the $2 million loss. She decided to consult her lawyer, Chris Pruitt.

## · THREE FUNDAMENTAL AREAS OF LAW ·

This case is a fictionalized version of several real cases based on double indemnity insurance policies. In this chapter we follow Beth's dispute with Coastal from initial interview through appeal, using it to examine three fundamental areas of law: the structure of our court systems, litigation, and alternative dispute resolution.

When Beth Smiles meets with her lawyer, Chris Pruitt brings a second attorney from his firm, Janet Booker, who is an experienced **litigator,** that is, a lawyer who handles court cases. If they file a lawsuit, Janet will be in charge, so Chris wants her there for the first meeting. Janet probes about Tony's home life, the status of the business, his personal finances, everything. Beth becomes upset that Janet doesn't seem sympathetic, but Chris explains that Janet is doing her job: she needs all the information, good and bad.

## LITIGATION VERSUS ALTERNATIVE DISPUTE RESOLUTION

**Litigation**
is the process of resolving disputes in court.

**Alternative dispute resolution**
Resolving disputes out of court, through formal or informal processes.

Janet starts thinking about the two methods of dispute resolution: litigation and alternative dispute resolution. **Litigation** refers to lawsuits, the process of filing claims in court, trying the case, and living with the court's ruling. **Alternative dispute resolution** is any other formal or informal process used to settle disputes without resorting to a trial. It is increasingly popular with corporations and individuals alike because it is generally cheaper and faster than litigation.

## · ALTERNATIVE DISPUTE RESOLUTION ·

Janet Booker knows that even after expert legal help, vast expense, and years of work, litigation may leave clients unsatisfied. If she can use alternative dispute resolution (ADR) to create a mutually satisfactory solution in a few months, for a fraction of the cost, she is glad to do it. In most cases the parties **negotiate,** whether personally or through lawyers. Fortunately, the great majority of disputes are resolved this way. Negotiation often begins as soon as a dispute arises and may last a few days or several years.

# MEDIATION

Mediation is the fastest growing method of dispute resolution in the United States. Here, a neutral person, called a mediator, attempts to coax the two disputing parties toward a voluntary settlement.

A mediator does not render a decision in the dispute but uses a variety of skills to prod the parties toward agreement. Mediators must earn the trust of both parties, listen closely, defuse anger and fear, explore common ground, cajole the parties into different perspectives, and build the will to settle. Good mediators do not need a law degree, but they must have a sense of humor and low blood pressure.

Of all forms of dispute resolution, mediation probably offers the strongest "win-win" potential. Because the goal is voluntary settlement, neither party needs to fear that it will end up the loser. This is in sharp contrast to litigation, where one party is very likely to lose. Removing the fear of defeat often encourages thinking and talking that are more open and realistic than negotiations held in the midst of a lawsuit. Studies show that more than 75 percent of mediated cases do reach a voluntary settlement.

> **Mediation**
> A form of ADR in which a neutral third party coaxes the disputing parties toward a voluntary settlement.

# ARBITRATION

In this form of ADR, the parties agree to bring in a neutral third party, but with a major difference: the arbitrator has the power to impose an award. The arbitrator allows each side equal time to present its case and, after deliberation, issues a binding decision, generally without giving reasons. Unlike mediation, arbitration ensures that there will be a final result, although the parties lose control of the outcome. Arbitration is generally faster and cheaper than litigation.

Parties in arbitration give up many rights that litigants retain, including discovery. *Discovery*, as we see below, allows the two sides in a lawsuit to obtain documentary and other evidence from the opponent before trial. Arbitration permits both sides to keep secret many files that would have to be divulged in a court case, potentially depriving the opposing side of valuable evidence. A party may have a stronger case than it realizes, and the absence of discovery may permanently deny it that knowledge.

Janet Booker proposes to Coastal Insurance that they use ADR to expedite a decision in their dispute. Coastal rejects the offer. Coastal's lawyer, Rich Stewart, insists that suicide is apparent.

It is a long way to go before trial, but Janet has to prepare her case. The first thing she thinks about is where to file the lawsuit.

> **Arbitration**
> A form of ADR in which a neutral third party has the power to impose a binding decision.

## · COURT SYSTEMS ·

The United States has over 50 systems of courts. One nationwide system of *federal* courts serves the entire country. In addition, each *state* has its own court system. The state and federal courts are in different buildings, have different judges, and hear different kinds of cases. Each has special powers and certain limitations.

# STATE COURTS

The typical state court system forms a pyramid, as Exhibit 3.1 shows. You may use the Internet to learn the exact names and powers of the courts in your state. Go to **http://www.state.[name of state].gov**, and click on "agencies," "courts," or a similar link.

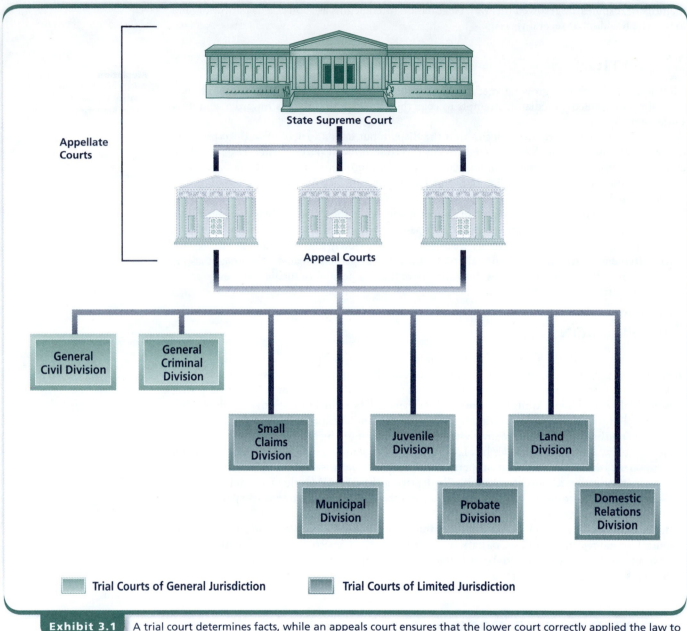

State Supreme Court

**Appellate Courts**

Appeal Courts

**General Civil Division**

**General Criminal Division**

**Small Claims Division**

**Municipal Division**

**Juvenile Division**

**Probate Division**

**Land Division**

**Domestic Relations Division**

Trial Courts of General Jurisdiction          Trial Courts of Limited Jurisdiction

**Exhibit 3.1** A trial court determines facts, while an appeals court ensures that the lower court correctly applied the law to those facts.

## Trial Courts

Almost all cases start in trial courts, the ones endlessly portrayed on television and in film. There is one judge and there will often (but not always) be a jury. This is the only court to hear testimony from witnesses and receive evidence. **Trial courts** determine the facts of a particular dispute and apply to those facts the law given by earlier appellate court decisions.

In the Enviro-Vision dispute, the trial court will decide all important facts that are in dispute. Did Tony Caruso die? Did he drown? Assuming he drowned, was his death an accident or a suicide? Once the jury has decided the facts, it will apply the law to those facts. If Tony Caruso

**Trial courts**
determine the facts and apply to them the law given by appellate courts.

died accidentally, contract law provides that Beth Smiles is entitled to double indemnity benefits. If the jury decides he killed himself, Beth gets nothing.

**Jurisdiction** refers to a court's power to hear a case. A plaintiff may start a lawsuit only in a court that has jurisdiction over that kind of case. Some state trial courts have very limited jurisdiction, while others have the power to hear almost any case. In Exhibit 3.1, notice that some courts have power only to hear cases of small claims, domestic relations, and so forth.

## Appellate Courts

Appellate courts are entirely different from trial courts. Three or more judges hear the case. There are no juries, ever. These courts do not hear witnesses or take new evidence. They hear appeals of cases already tried below. **Appeal courts** generally accept the facts given to them by trial courts and review the trial record to see if the court made errors of law.

An appeal court reviews the trial record to make sure that the lower court correctly applied the law to the facts. If the trial court made an **error of law**, the appeal court may require a new trial. Suppose the jury concludes that Tony Caruso committed suicide but votes to award Enviro-Vision $1 million because it feels sorry for Beth Smiles. That is an error of law: if Tony committed suicide, Beth is entitled to nothing. An appellate court will reverse the decision, declaring Coastal the victor.

The party that loses at the trial court generally is entitled to be heard at the intermediate court of appeals. The party filing the appeal is the **appellant**. The party opposing the appeal (because it won at trial) is the **appellee**. A party that loses at the court of appeals may *ask* the state supreme court to hear an appeal, but the state's highest court may choose not to accept the case.

# FEDERAL COURTS

As discussed in Chapter 1, federal courts are established by the United States Constitution, which limits what kinds of cases can be brought in any federal court. For our purposes, two kinds of civil lawsuits are permitted in federal court: federal question cases and diversity cases.

## Federal Question Cases

A claim based on the United States Constitution, a federal statute, or a federal treaty is called a **federal question case**.[1] Federal courts have jurisdiction over these cases. If the Environmental Protection Agency orders Logging Company not to cut in a particular forest, and Logging Company claims that the agency has wrongly deprived it of its property, that suit is based on a federal statute (a law passed by Congress) and is thus a federal question. Enviro-Vision's potential suit merely concerns an insurance contract. The federal district court has no federal question jurisdiction over the case.

## Diversity Cases

Even if no federal law is at issue, federal courts have jurisdiction when (1) the plaintiff and defendant are citizens of different states and (2) the amount in dispute exceeds $75,000. The theory behind diversity jurisdiction is that courts of one state might be biased against citizens of another state. To ensure fairness, the parties have the option of federal court.

Enviro-Vision is located in Oregon and Coastal Insurance is incorporated in Georgia.[2] They are citizens of different states and the amount in dispute far exceeds $75,000. Janet could file this case in United States District Court based on diversity jurisdiction.

---

[1] 28 U.S.C. §1331 governs federal question jurisdiction and 28 U.S.C. §1332 covers diversity jurisdiction.

[2] For diversity purposes, a corporation is a citizen of the state in which it is incorporated and the state in which it has its principal place of business.

---

**Jurisdiction**
A court's power to hear a case.

**Appellate courts**
generally accept the facts provided by trial courts and review the record for legal errors.

**Error of law**
A wrong decision made in a trial that leads to the reversal of a decision or a new trial.

**Appellant**
The party filing an appeal of a trial verdict.

**Appellee**
The party opposing an appeal.

**Federal question case**
A claim based on the United States Constitution, a federal statute, or a federal treaty.

**Diversity case**
A lawsuit in which the plaintiff and defendant are citizens of different states *and* the amount in dispute exceeds $75,000.

## Trial Courts

United States District Courts are the primary trial courts in the federal system. The nation is divided into about 94 districts, and each has a district court. States with smaller populations have one district, while those with larger populations have several districts. There are also specialized trial courts such as Bankruptcy Court, Tax Court, and others, which are, you will be happy to know, beyond the scope of this book.

## Appellate Courts

**United States Courts of Appeals**    These are the intermediate courts of appeals. As the map below shows, they are divided into "circuits," most of which are geographical areas. For example, an appeal from the Northern District of Illinois would go to the Court of Appeals for the Seventh Circuit. You will find an interactive map of the District and Circuit Courts at **http://www.uscourts.gov**.

**United States Supreme Court**    This is the highest court in the country. There are nine justices on the Court. One justice is the chief justice and the other eight are associate justices. When they decide a case, each justice casts an equal vote. For a face-to-face meeting with Supreme Court justices, past and present, introduce yourself to **http://www.oyez.org**.

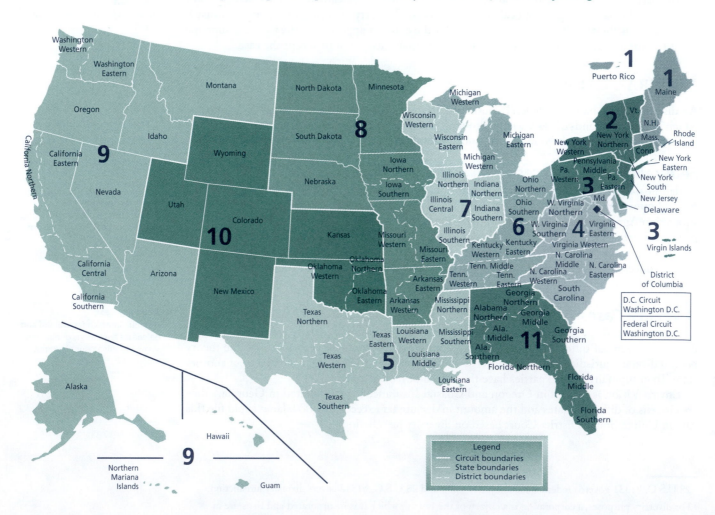

## EXAM *Strategy*

**Question:**  Mark has sued Janelle, based on the state common law of negligence. He is testifying in court, explaining how Janelle backed a rented truck out of her driveway and slammed into his Lamborghini, doing $82,000 in damages. Where is this taking place?

A   State appeals court
B   United States Court of Appeals
C   State trial court
D   Federal District Court
E   Either state trial court or Federal District Court

**Strategy:**  The question asks about trial and appellate courts, and also about state versus federal courts. One issue at a time, please. What are the different functions of trial and appellate courts? *Trial* courts use witnesses, and often juries, to resolve factual disputes. *Appellate* courts never hear witnesses and never have juries. Applying that distinction to these facts tells us whether we are in a trial or appeals court.

   *State* trial courts may hear lawsuits on virtually any issue. *Federal District Courts* may only hear two kinds of cases: federal question (those involving a statute or constitutional provision); or diversity (where the parties are from different states *and* the amount at issue is $75,000 or higher). Apply what we know to the facts here.

**Result:**  We are in a trial court, because Mark is testifying. Could we be in Federal District Court? No. The suit is based on state common law. This is not a diversity case, because the parties live in the same state, and this is not an appeal of a previous trial, so this is not an appeals court.

## · LITIGATION ·

Janet Booker decides to file the Enviro-Vision suit in the Oregon trial court. She thinks that a state court judge may take the issue more seriously than a Federal District Court judge.

## Pleadings

The documents that begin a lawsuit are called the **pleadings**. The most important are the complaint and the answer.

### Complaint

The plaintiff files in court a **complaint**, which is a short, plain statement of the facts she is alleging and the legal claims she is making. The purpose of the complaint is to inform the defendant of the general nature of the claims and the need to come into court and protect his interests.

   Janet Booker files the complaint, as shown below. Because Enviro-Vision is a partnership, she files the suit on behalf of Beth, personally.

**Pleadings**
The documents that begin a lawsuit, consisting of a complaint, the answer, and sometimes a reply.

**Complaint**
The pleading that starts a lawsuit, this is a short statement of the facts alleged by the plaintiff, and his or her legal claims.

STATE OF OREGON
CIRCUIT COURT

Multnomah County                                             Civil Action No. _____

Elizabeth Smiles,
Plaintiff

                                                             JURY TRIAL DEMANDED

v.

Coastal Insurance Company, Inc.,
Defendant

COMPLAINT

Plaintiff Elizabeth Smiles states that:

1.   She is a citizen of Multnomah County, Oregon.
2.   Defendant Coastal Insurance Company, Inc., is incorporated under the laws of Georgia and has as its usual place of business 148 Thrift Street, Savannah, Georgia.
3.   On or about July 5, 2009, plaintiff Smiles ("Smiles"), Defendant Coastal Insurance Co, Inc. ("Coastal") and Anthony Caruso entered into an insurance contract ("the contract"), a copy of which is annexed hereto as Exhibit "A." This contract was signed by all parties or their authorized agents, in Multnomah County, Oregon.
4.   The contract obligates Coastal to pay to Smiles the sum of two million dollars ($2 million) if Anthony Caruso should die accidentally.
5.   On or about September 18, 2009, Anthony Caruso accidentally drowned and died while swimming.
6.   Coastal has refused to pay any sum pursuant to the contract.
7.   Coastal has knowingly, willingly and unreasonably refused to honor its obligations under the contract.

WHEREFORE, plaintiff Elizabeth Smiles demands judgment against defendant Coastal for all monies due under the contract; demands triple damages for Coastal's knowing, willing, and unreasonable refusal to honor its obligations; and demands all costs and attorney's fees, with interest.

ELIZABETH SMILES,
By her attorney,
[Signed]
Janet Booker
Pruitt, Booker & Bother
983 Joy Avenue
Portland, OR
October 18, 2009

---

**Answer**
The defendant's response to the complaint.

## Answer

Coastal has 20 days in which to file an answer. Coastal's **answer** is a brief reply to each of the allegations in the complaint. The answer tells the court and the plaintiff exactly what issues are in dispute. Since Coastal admits that the parties entered into the contract that Beth claims they did, there is no need for her to prove that in court. The court can focus its attention on the issue that Coastal disputes: whether Tony Caruso died accidentally.

**Default judgment**
A decision that the plaintiff in a case wins without going to trial.

   If the defendant fails to answer in time, the plaintiff will ask for a **default judgment**, meaning a decision that the plaintiff wins without a trial.

## Class Actions

Suppose Janet uncovers evidence that Coastal denies 80 percent of all life insurance claims, calling them suicide. She could ask the court to permit a **class action**. If the court granted her request, she would represent the entire group of plaintiffs, including those who are unaware of the lawsuit or even unaware they were harmed. Class actions can give the plaintiffs much greater leverage, since the defendant's potential liability is vastly increased. Because Janet has no such evidence, she decides not to pursue a class action.

## Discovery

**Discovery** is the critical, pre-trial opportunity for both parties to learn the strengths and weaknesses of the opponent's case.

The theory behind civil litigation is that the best outcome is a negotiated settlement and that parties will move toward agreement if they understand the opponent's case. That is likeliest to occur if both sides have an opportunity to examine the evidence their opponent will bring to trial. Further, if a case does go all the way to trial, efficient and fair litigation cannot take place in a courtroom filled, like a piñata, with surprises. On television dramas, witnesses say astonishing things that amaze the courtroom. In real trials the lawyers know in advance the answers to practically all questions asked because discovery has allowed them to see the opponent's documents and question its witnesses. The following are the most important forms of discovery.

**Interrogatories**    These are written questions that the opposing party must answer, in writing, under oath.

**Depositions**    These provide a chance for one party's lawyer to question the other party, or a potential witness, under oath. The person being questioned is the **deponent**. Lawyers for both parties are present.

**Production of Documents and Things**    Each side may ask the other side to produce relevant documents for inspection and copying; to produce physical objects, such as part of a car alleged to be defective; and for permission to enter on land to make an inspection, for example, at the scene of an accident.

**Physical and Mental Examination**    A party may ask the court to order an examination of the other party, if his physical or mental condition is relevant, for example, in a case of medical malpractice.

Janet Booker begins her discovery with interrogatories. Her goal is to learn Coastal's basic position and factual evidence and then follow up with more detailed questioning during depositions. Her interrogatories ask for every fact Coastal relied on in denying the claim. She asks for the names of all witnesses, the identity of all documents, the description of all things or objects that they considered. She requests the names of all corporate officers who played any role in the decision and of any expert witnesses Coastal plans to call.

Coastal has 30 days to answer Janet's interrogatories. Before it responds, Coastal mails to Janet a notice of deposition, stating its intention to depose Beth Smiles. Beth and Janet will go to the office of Coastal's lawyer, and Beth will answer questions under oath. But at the same time Coastal sends this notice, it sends 25 other notices of deposition. It will depose Karen Caruso as soon as Beth's deposition is over. Coastal also plans to depose all seven employees of Enviro-Vision; three neighbors who lived near Tony and Karen's beach house; two policemen who participated in the search; the doctor and two nurses involved in the case; Tony's physician; Jerry Johnson, Tony's tennis partner; Craig Bergson, a college roommate; a couple who had dinner with Tony and Karen a week before his death; and several other people.

**Class action**
A suit filed by a group of plaintiffs with related claims.

**Discovery**
The pre-trial opportunity for both parties to learn the other side's case.

**Deponent**
The person being questioned in a deposition.

Rich, the Coastal lawyer, proceeds to take Beth's deposition. It takes two full days. He asks about Enviro-Vision's past and present. He learns that Tony appeared to have won their biggest contract ever from Rapid City, Oregon, but that he then lost it when he had a fight with Rapid City's mayor. He inquires into Tony's mood, learns that he was depressed, and probes in every direction he can to find evidence of suicidal motivation. Janet and Rich argue frequently over questions and whether Beth should have to answer them. At times Janet is persuaded and permits Beth to answer; other times she instructs Beth not to answer. For example, toward the end of the second day, Rich asks Beth whether she and Tony had been sexually involved. Janet instructs Beth not to answer. This fight necessitates a trip into court. As both lawyers know, **the parties are entitled to discover anything that could reasonably lead to valid evidence.** Rich wants his questions answered and files a motion to compel discovery. The judge will have to decide whether Rich's questions are reasonable.

**Motion**
A formal request to the court.

A **motion** is a formal request to the court. Before, during and after trial, both parties will file many motions. A **motion to compel discovery** is a request to the court for an order requiring the other side to answer discovery. The judge rules that Beth must discuss Tony's romantic life only if Coastal has evidence that he was involved with someone outside his marriage. Because the company lacks any such evidence, the judge denies Coastal's motion.

At the same time, the judge hears one of Beth's **motions for a protective order.** Beth claims that Rich has scheduled too many depositions; the time and expense are a huge burden to a small company. The judge limits Rich to 10 depositions. Rich cancels several depositions, including that of Craig Bergson, Tony's old roommate. As we will see, Craig knows crucial facts about this case, and Rich's decision not to depose him will have major consequences.

**E-Discovery** The biggest change in litigation in the last decade is the explosive rise of electronic discovery (e-discovery). Companies send hundreds, thousands, or even millions of e-mails every day. Many of the e-mails have attachments that are sometimes hundreds of pages long. In addition, businesses large and small have vast amounts of data stored electronically. All this information is potentially subject to discovery.

It is enormously time-consuming and expensive for companies to locate all the relevant material, separate it from irrelevant or confidential matter, and furnish it. A firm may be obligated to furnish *millions* of e-mails to the opposing party. In one recent case, a defendant had to pay 31 lawyers full time for six months just to wade through an ocean of e-documents and figure out which had to be supplied and how to produce it. Not surprisingly, this data eruption has created a new industry: high-tech companies that assist law firms in finding, sorting, and delivering electronic data.

Who is to say what must be supplied? What if an e-mail string contains individual e-mails that are clearly privileged (meaning a party need not divulge them), but others that are not privileged? May a company refuse to furnish the entire string? Many will try. However, some courts have ruled that companies seeking to protect e-mail strings must create a log describing every individual e-mail and allow the court to determine which are privileged.[3]

When the cost of furnishing the data becomes burdensome, who should pay, the party seeking the information or the one supplying it? In a recent $4 million corporate lawsuit, the defendant turned over 3,000 e-mails and 211,000 other documents. But the trial judge noted that many of the e-mail attachments—sometimes 12 to an e-mail—had gone missing, and it required the company to produce them. The defendant protested that finding the attachments would cost an additional $206,000. The judge ordered the company to do it and bear the full cost.

The following case illustrates a common discovery problem: refusal by one side to appear for deposition. Did the defendant cynically believe that long delays would win the day, given that the plaintiff was 78 years old? What can a court do in such a case?

---

[3] *Universal Service Fund Telephone Billing Practices Litigation*, 232 F.R.D. 669 (D. Kan. 2005).

## STINTON V. ROBIN'S WOOD, INC.

45 A.D. 3D 203, 842 NYS2D 477
NEW YORK APP. DIV., 2007

### CASE SUMMARY

**Facts:** Ethel Flanzraich, 78 years old, slipped and fell on the steps of property owned by Robin's Wood. She broke her left leg and left arm. Flanzraich sued, claiming that Robin's Wood caused her fall by negligently painting the stairs. The defendant's employee, Anthony Monforte, had painted the steps. In its answer to the complaint, Robin's Wood denied all the significant allegations.

During a preliminary conference with the trial judge, the parties agreed to hold depositions of both parties on August 4. Flanzraich appeared for deposition, but Robin's Wood did not furnish its employee, Monforte, nor did it offer any other company representative. The court then ordered the deposition of the defendant to take place the following April 2. Again, Robin's Wood produced neither Monforte nor anyone else. On July 16, the court ordered the defendant to produce its representative within 30 days. Once more, no one showed up for deposition.

On August 18—over *one year* after the original deposition date—Flanzraich moved to strike the defendant's answer, meaning that the plaintiff would win by default. The company argued that it had made diligent efforts to locate Monforte and force him to appear. However, all the letters sent to Monforte were addressed care of Robin's Wood. Finally, the company stated that it no longer employed Monforte.

The trial judge granted the motion to strike the answer. That meant that Robin's Wood was liable for Flanzraich's fall. The only remaining issue was damages. The court determined that Robin's Wood owed $22,631 for medical expenses, $150,000 for past pain and suffering, and $300,000 for future pain and suffering. One day later, Flanzraich died of other causes. Robin's Wood appealed.

**Issue:** *Did the trial court abuse its discretion by striking the defendant's answer?*

**Decision:** No, the trial court did not abuse its discretion. Affirmed.

**Reasoning:** Normally, a lawsuit must be decided on the evidence and reasonable conclusions. However, if a defendant fails to respond to discovery requests, and its failure is willful, extreme, and disrespectful of the court, a trial judge may strike the defendant's answer altogether.

Robin's Wood failed to comply with three orders to appear for deposition. The company never produced Monforte while he worked there. It failed to notify the plaintiff when Monforte left, and it made no effort to produce another employee for deposition. The company did everything it could to ensure that Flanzraich would never speak with its worker. Had the company at least produced another representative, Flanzraich could have learned where Monforte had gone, because the record indicates Robin's Wood knew his whereabouts.

These delays were particularly menacing to Flanzraich's case because she was elderly—a fact well known to the company. A trial judge may respond to such offensive conduct with appropriate orders.

## Summary Judgment

When discovery is completed, both sides may consider seeking summary judgment. **Summary judgment** is a ruling by the court that no trial is necessary because some essential facts are not in dispute. The purpose of a trial is to determine the facts of the case, that is, to decide who did what to whom, why, when, and with what consequences. If relevant facts are not in dispute, then there is no need for a trial.

Suppose Joe sues EZBuck Films, claiming that the company's new movie, *Lover Boy*, violates the copyright of a screenplay that he wrote, called *Love Man*. Discovery establishes that the two stories are suspiciously similar. But EZBuck's lawyer also learns that Joe sold the copyright for *Love Man* to HotShot Pix. EZBuck may or may not have violated a copyright, but there is no need for a trial because Joe cannot win even if there is a copyright violation. He does not own the copyright. When EZBuck moves for summary judgment, the court will grant the motion, terminating the case before trial.

In the following case, the defendant won summary judgment, meaning that the case never went to trial. And yet, this was only the beginning of trouble for that defendant, William Jefferson Clinton.

**Summary judgment**
A ruling that no trial is necessary because essential facts are not in dispute.

## JONES V. CLINTON

990 F. SUPP. 657, 1998 U.S. DIST. LEXIS 3902
UNITED STATES DISTRICT COURT FOR THE EASTERN DISTRICT OF ARKANSAS, 1998

### CASE SUMMARY

**Facts:** In 1991, Bill Clinton was governor of Arkansas. Paula Jones worked for a state agency, the Arkansas Industrial Development Commission (AIDC). When Clinton became president, Jones sued him, claiming that he had sexually harassed her. She alleged that, in May 1991, the governor arranged for her to meet him in a hotel room in Little Rock, Arkansas. When they were alone, he put his hand on her leg and slid it toward her pelvis. She escaped from his grasp, exclaimed, "What are you doing?" and said she was "not that kind of girl." She was upset and confused, and sat on a sofa near the door. She claimed that Clinton approached her, "lowered his trousers and underwear, exposed his penis, and told her to kiss it." Jones was horrified, jumped up, and said she had to leave. Clinton responded by saying, "Well, I don't want to make you do anything you don't want to do," and pulled his pants up. He added that if she got in trouble for leaving work, Jones should "have Dave call me immediately and I'll take care of it." He also said, "You are smart. Let's keep this between ourselves." Jones remained at AIDC until February 1993, when she moved to California because of her husband's job transfer.

President Clinton denied all the allegations. He also filed for summary judgment, claiming that Jones had not alleged facts that justified a trial. Jones opposed the motion for summary judgment.

**Issue:** *Was Clinton entitled to summary judgment, or was Jones entitled to a trial?*

**Decision:** Jones failed to make out a claim of sexual harassment. Summary judgment is granted for the President.
**Reasoning:** To establish this type of sexual harassment case, a plaintiff must show that her refusal to submit to unwelcome sexual advances resulted in specific harm to her job.

Jones received every merit increase and cost-of-living allowance for which she was eligible. Her only job transfer involved a minor change in working conditions, with no reduction in pay or benefits. Jones claims that she was obligated to sit in a less private area, often with no work to do, and was the only female employee not to receive flowers on Secretary's Day. However, even if these allegations are true, all are trivial and none is sufficient to create a sexual harassment suit. Jones has demonstrated no specific harm to her job.

In other words, the court acknowledged that there were factual disputes, but concluded that even if Jones proved each of her allegations, she would still lose the case, because her allegations fell short of a legitimate case of sexual harassment. Jones appealed the case. Later the same year, as the appeal was pending and the House of Representatives was considering whether to impeach President Clinton, the parties settled the dispute. Clinton, without acknowledging any of the allegations, agreed to pay Jones $850,000 to drop the suit.

Janet and Rich each consider moving for summary judgment, but both correctly decide that they would lose. There is one major fact in dispute: Did Tony Caruso commit suicide? Only a jury may decide that issue. As long as there is some evidence supporting each side of a key factual dispute, the court may not grant summary judgment.

### EXAM *Strategy*

**Question:** You are a judge. Mel has sued Kevin, claiming that while Kevin was drunk, he negligently drove his car down Mel's street and destroyed rare trees on a lot that Mel owns, next to his house. Mel's complaint stated that three witnesses, at a bar, saw Kevin take at least eight drinks less than an hour before the damage was done. In Kevin's answer, he denied causing the damage and denied being in the bar that night.

Kevin's lawyer has moved for summary judgment. He proves that three weeks before the alleged accident, Mel sold the lot to Tatiana.

Mel's lawyer opposes summary judgment. He produces a security camera tape proving that Kevin was in the bar, drinking beer, 34 minutes before the damage was done. He produces a signed statement from Sandy, a landscape gardener who lives across the street from the scene. Sandy states that she heard a crash, hurried to the windows, and saw Kevin's car weaving away from the damaged trees. She is a landscape gardener and estimates the tree damage at $30,000 to $40,000. How should you rule on the motion?

**Strategy:**  Do not be fooled by red herrings about Kevin's drinking or the value of the trees. Stick to the question: Should you grant summary judgment? Trials are necessary to resolve disputes about essential factual issues. Summary judgment is appropriate when some essential facts are not disputed. Is there an essential fact not in dispute? Find it. Apply the rule. Being a judge is easy!

**Result:**  It makes no difference whether Kevin was drunk or sober, whether he caused the harm, or whether he was at home in bed. Mel did not own the property at the time of the accident. He cannot win. You should grant Kevin's summary judgment motion.

...............................................................................................................................

Well over 90 percent of all lawsuits are settled before trial. But the parties in the Enviro-Vision dispute are unable to compromise, and are headed for trial.

> **Well over 90 percent of all lawsuits are settled before trial.**

## · TRIAL ·

## ADVERSARY SYSTEM

Our system of justice assumes that the best way to bring out the truth is for the two contesting sides to present the strongest case possible to a neutral fact-finder. Each side presents its witnesses and then the opponent has a chance to cross-examine. The **adversary system** presumes that by putting a witness on the stand and letting both lawyers "go at" her, the truth will emerge.

The judge runs the trial. Each lawyer sits at a large table near the front. Beth, looking tense and unhappy, sits with Janet. Rich Stewart sits with a Coastal executive. In the back of the courtroom are benches for the public. Today there are only a few spectators. One is Tony's old roommate, Craig Bergson, who has a special interest in the trial.

**Adversary system**
A system based on the assumption that if two sides present their best case before a neutral party, the truth will be established.

## RIGHT TO JURY TRIAL

Not all cases are tried to a jury. As a general rule, both plaintiff and defendant have a right to demand a jury trial when the lawsuit is for money damages. For example, in a typical contract lawsuit, such as Beth's insurance claim, both plaintiff and defendant have a jury trial right whether they are in state or federal court. Even in such a case, though, the parties may waive the jury right, meaning they agree to try the case to a judge.

If the plaintiff is seeking an equitable remedy, such as an injunction (an order not to do something), there is no jury right for either party. Equitable rights come from the old Court of Chancery in England, where there was never a jury. Even today, only a judge may give an equitable remedy.

Although jury selection for some cases takes many days, in the Enviro-Vision case the first day of the hearing ends with the jury selected. In the hallway outside the court, Rich offers Janet $200,000 to settle. Janet reports the offer to Beth and they agree to reject it. Craig Bergson drives home, emotionally confused. Only three weeks before his death, Tony had accidentally met his old roommate and they had had several drinks. Craig believes that what Tony told him answers the riddle of this case.

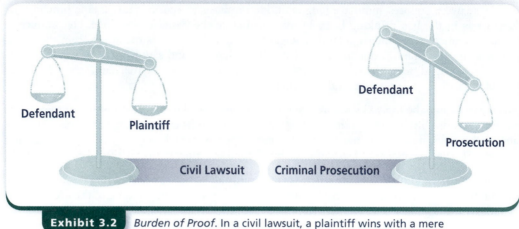

**Exhibit 3.2** *Burden of Proof.* In a civil lawsuit, a plaintiff wins with a mere preponderance of the evidence. But the prosecution must persuade a jury beyond a reasonable doubt in order to win a criminal conviction.

## OPENING STATEMENTS

The next day, each attorney makes an opening statement to the jury, summarizing the proof he or she expects to offer, with the plaintiff going first. Janet focuses on Tony's successful life, his business and strong marriage, and the tragedy of his accidental death.[4]

Rich works hard to establish a friendly rapport with the jury. He expresses regret about the death. Nonetheless, suicide is a clear exclusion from the policy. If insurance companies are forced to pay claims they did not bargain for, everyone's insurance rates will go up.

## BURDEN OF PROOF

**Burden of proof**
The plaintiff must convince the jury that its version of the case is correct.

In civil cases, the plaintiff has the **burden of proof**. That means that the plaintiff must convince the jury that its version of the case is correct; the defendant is not obligated to disprove the allegations.

**Preponderance of the evidence**
The plaintiff's burden to convince a jury that his version of the facts is at least *slightly* more convincing than the defendant's. The standard of proof required for a civil case.

The plaintiff's burden in a civil lawsuit is to prove its case by a **preponderance of the evidence**. The plaintiff must convince the jury that his or her version of the facts is at least *slightly* more likely than the defendant's version. Some courts describe this as a "51–49" persuasion, that is, that plaintiff's proof must "just tip" credibility in its favor. By contrast, in a criminal case, the prosecution must demonstrate **beyond a reasonable doubt** that the defendant is guilty. The burden of proof in a criminal case is much tougher because the likely consequences are, too. See Exhibit 3.2.

**Beyond a reasonable doubt**
The government's burden in a criminal prosecution.

## PLAINTIFF'S CASE

Since the plaintiff has the burden of proof, Janet puts in her case first. She wants to prove two things. First, that Tony died. That is easy, since the death certificate clearly demonstrates it and since Coastal does not seriously contest it. Second, in order to win double indemnity damages, she must show that the death was accidental. She will do this with the testimony of the witnesses

---

[4] Janet Booker has dropped her claim for triple damages against Coastal. To have any hope of such a verdict, she would have to show that Coastal had no legitimate reason at all for denying the claim. Discovery has convinced her that Coastal will demonstrate some rational reasons for what it did.

she calls, one after the other. Her first witness is Beth. When a lawyer asks questions of her own witness, it is **direct examination**. Janet brings out all the evidence she wants the jury to hear: that the business was basically sound, though temporarily troubled, that Tony was a hard worker, why the company took out life insurance policies, and so forth.

Then Rich has a chance to **cross-examine** Beth, which means to ask questions of an opposing witness. He will try to create doubt in the jury's mind. He asks Beth only questions for which he is certain of the answers, based on discovery. Rich gets Beth to admit that the firm was not doing well the year of Tony's death; that Tony had lost the best client the firm ever had; that Beth had reduced salaries; and that Tony had been depressed about business.

Janet uses her other witnesses, Tony's friends, family and co-workers, to fortify the impression that his death was accidental.

**Direct examination**
is when a lawyer asks questions of his or her own witness.

**Cross-examination**
is when a lawyer asks questions of an opposing witness.

## DEFENDANT'S CASE

Rich now puts in his case, exactly as Janet did, except that he happens to have fewer witnesses. He calls the examining doctor, who admits that Tony could have committed suicide by swimming out too far. On cross-examination, Janet gets the doctor to acknowledge that he has no idea whether Tony intentionally drowned. Rich also questions several neighbors as to how depressed Tony had seemed and how unusual it was that Blue was tied up. Some of the witnesses Rich deposed, such as the tennis partner Jerry Johnson, have nothing that will help Coastal's case, so he does not call them.

Craig Bergson, sitting in the back of the courtroom, thinks how different the trial would have been had he been called as a witness. When he and Tony had the fateful drink, Tony had been distraught: business was terrible, he was involved in an extramarital affair that he could not end, and he saw no way out of his problems. He had no one to talk to and had been hugely relieved to speak with Craig. Several times Tony had said, "I just can't go on like this. I don't want to, anymore." Craig thought Tony seemed suicidal and urged him to see a therapist Craig knew. Tony had said that it was good advice, but Craig is unsure whether Tony sought any help.

This evidence would have affected the case. Had Rich Stewart known of the conversation, he would have deposed Craig and the therapist. Coastal's case would have been far stronger, perhaps overwhelming. But Craig's evidence will never be heard. Facts are critical. Rich's decision to depose other witnesses and omit Craig may influence the verdict more than any rule of law.

## CLOSING ARGUMENT

Both lawyers sum up their case to the jury, explaining how they hope the jury will interpret what they have heard. Judge Rowland instructs the jury as to its duty. He tells them that they are to evaluate the case based only on the evidence they heard at trial, relying on their own experience and common sense.

He explains the law and the burden of proof, telling the jury that it is Beth's obligation to prove her case. If Beth has proven that Tony died by means other than suicide but not by accident, she is entitled to $1 million; if she has proven that his death was accidental, she is entitled to $2 million. However, if Coastal has proven suicide, Beth receives nothing. Finally, he states that if they are unable to decide between accidental death and suicide, there is a legal presumption that it was accidental. Rich asks Judge Rowland to rephrase the "legal presumption" part, but the judge declines.

## VERDICT

The jury deliberates informally, with all jurors entitled to voice their opinion. Some deliberations take two hours; some take two weeks. Many states require a unanimous verdict; others require only, for example, a 10–2 vote in civil cases.

This case presents a close call. No one saw Tony die. Yet even though they cannot know with certainty, the jury's decision will probably be the final word on whether he took his own life. After a day and a half of deliberating, the jury notifies the judge that it has reached a verdict. Rich Stewart quickly makes a new offer: $350,000. Beth hesitates but turns it down.

The judge summons the lawyers to court, and Beth goes as well. The judge asks the foreman if the jury has reached a decision. He states that it has: the jury finds that Tony Caruso drowned accidentally, and awards Beth Smiles $2 million.

## • APPEALS •

Two days later, Rich files an appeal to the court of appeal. The same day, he phones Janet and increases his settlement offer to $425,000. Beth is tempted but wants Janet's advice. Janet says the risks of an appeal are that the court will order a new trial, and they would start all over. But to accept this offer is to forfeit over $1.5 million. Beth is unsure what to do. The firm desperately needs cash now. Janet suggests they wait until oral argument, another eight months.

Rich files a brief arguing that there were two basic errors at the trial: first, that the jury's verdict is clearly contrary to the evidence; and second, that the judge gave the wrong instructions to the jury. Janet files a reply brief, opposing Rich on both issues. In her brief, Janet cites many cases that she claims are **precedent**: earlier decisions by the state supreme court on similar or identical issues.

### APPEAL COURT OPTIONS

The court of appeal can **affirm** the trial court, allowing the decision to stand. The court may **modify** the decision, for example, by affirming that the plaintiff wins but decreasing the size of the award. (That is unlikely here; Beth is entitled to $2 million or nothing.) The court might **reverse and remand**, meaning it nullifies the lower court's decision and returns the case to the trial court for a new trial. Or it could simply **reverse**, turning the loser (Coastal) into the winner, with no new trial.

Janet and Beth talk. Beth is very anxious and wants to settle. She does not want to wait four or five months, only to learn that they must start all over. With Beth's approval, Janet phones Rich and offers to settle for $1.2 million. Rich snorts, "Yeah, right." Then he snaps, "$750,000. Take it or leave it. Final offer." After a short conversation with her client, Janet calls back and accepts the offer.

---

**Precedent**
Earlier decisions by a court on similar or identical issues, on which subsequent court decisions can be based.

**Affirm**
To allow a court decision to stand as is.

**Modify**
To let a court decision stand, but with changes.

**Reverse and remand**
To nullify a lower court's decision and return a case to trial.

**Reverse**
To rule that the loser in a previous case actually wins, with no new trial.

---

| LITIGATION | | |
|---|---|---|
| **1. PLEADINGS**<br>Complaint<br>Answer | **2. DISCOVERY**<br>Interrogatories<br>Depositions<br>Production of documents<br>   and things<br>Physical and mental<br>   examinations | **3. PRE-TRIAL MOTIONS**<br>Class action<br>Summary judgment |
| **4. TRIAL**<br>Jury selection<br>Opening statements<br>Plaintiff's case<br>Defendant's case<br>Closing argument | **5. JURY'S ROLE**<br>Judge's instructions<br>Deliberation<br>Verdict | **6. APPEALS**<br>Affirm<br>Modify<br>Reverse<br>Remand |

## CHAPTER CONCLUSION

**No one will ever know for sure whether Tony took his own life.** Craig Bergson's evidence might have tipped the scales in favor of Coastal. But even that is uncertain, since the jury could have found him unpersuasive. After two years, the case ends with a settlement and uncertainty—both typical lawsuit results. The vaguely unsatisfying feeling about it all is only too common and indicates why litigation is best avoided—by reasonable negotiation.

## EXAM REVIEW

1. **ALTERNATIVE DISPUTE RESOLUTION** Alternative dispute resolution (ADR) is any formal or informal process to settle disputes without a trial. Mediation and arbitration are the two most common forms. (p. 28)

2. **COURT SYSTEMS** There are many systems of courts, one federal and one in each state. A federal court will hear a case only if it involves a federal question or diversity jurisdiction. (pp. 29–31)

3. **TRIAL AND APPELLATE COURTS** Trial courts determine facts and apply the law to the facts; appeal courts generally accept the facts found by the trial court and review the trial record for errors of law. (p. 32)

**EXAM Strategy**

**Question:** Jade sued Kim, claiming that Kim promised to hire her as an in-store model for $1,000 per week for eight weeks. Kim denied making the promise, and the jury was persuaded: Kim won. Jade has appealed, and now offers Steve as a witness. Steve will testify to the appeals court that he saw Kim hire Jade as a model, exactly as Jade claimed. Will Jade win on appeal?

**Strategy:** Before you answer, make sure you know the difference between trial and appellate courts. (See the "Result" at the end of this section.)

4. **PLEADINGS** A complaint and an answer are the two most important pleadings, that is, documents that start a lawsuit. (p. 33)

5. **DISCOVERY** Discovery is the critical pretrial opportunity for both parties to learn the strengths and weaknesses of the opponent's case. Important forms of discovery include interrogatories, depositions, production of documents and objects, physical and mental examinations, and requests for admission. (p. 35)

6. **MOTIONS** A motion is a formal request to the court. (p. 36)

7. **SUMMARY JUDGMENT** Summary judgment is a ruling by the court that no trial is necessary because some essential facts are not in dispute. (p. 37)

**8. RIGHT TO A JURY** Generally, both plaintiff and defendant may demand a jury in any lawsuit for money damages. (p. 39)

**9. BURDEN OF PROOF** The plaintiff's burden of proof in a civil lawsuit is preponderance of the evidence, meaning that its version of the facts must be at least slightly more persuasive than the defendant's. In a criminal prosecution, the government must offer proof beyond a reasonable doubt in order to win a conviction. (p. 40)

**EXAM Strategy**

**Question:** In Courtroom 1, Asbury has sued Park, claiming that Park drove his motorcycle negligently and broke Asbury's leg. The jury is deliberating. The jurors have serious doubts about what happened, but they find Asbury's evidence slightly more convincing than Park's. In Courtroom 2, the state is prosecuting Patterson for drug possession. The jury in that case is also deliberating. The jurors have serious doubts about what happened, but they find the government's evidence slightly more convincing than Patterson's. Who will win in each case?

**Strategy:** A different burden of proof applies in the two cases. (See the "Result" at the end of this section.)

**10. VERDICT** The verdict is the jury's decision in a case. (p. 41)

**11. APPELLATE COURT RULINGS** An appeal court has many options. The court may affirm, upholding the lower court's decision; modify, changing the verdict but leaving the same party victorious; reverse, transforming the loser into the winner; and/or remand, sending the case back to the lower court. (p. 42)

**3. Result:** Trial courts use witnesses to help resolve factual disputes. Appellate courts review the record to see if there have been errors of law. Appellate courts never hear witnesses, and they will not hear Steve. Jade will lose her appeal.

**9. Result:** In the civil lawsuit, Asbury must merely convince the jury by a preponderance of the evidence. He has done this, so he will win. In the prosecution, the government must demonstrate proof beyond a reasonable doubt. It has failed to do so, and Patterson will be acquitted.

## PRACTICE EXAM

## MATCHING QUESTIONS

Match the following terms with their definitions.

| | |
|---|---|
| ___ A. Arbitration | 1. A pretrial procedure involving written questions to be signed under oath |
| ___ B. Diversity jurisdiction | 2. A form of ADR in which the parties themselves craft the settlement |
| ___ C. Mediation | 3. A pretrial procedure involving oral questions answered under oath |
| ___ D. Interrogatories | 4. The power of a federal court to hear certain cases between citizens of different states |
| ___ E. Deposition | 5. A form of ADR that leads to a binding decision |

## TRUE/FALSE QUESTIONS

1. T  F  One advantage of arbitration is that it provides the parties with greater opportunities for discovery than litigation does.

2. T  F  In the United States, there are many separate courts, but only one court *system*, organized as a pyramid.

3. T  F  If we are listening to witnesses testify, we must be in a trial court.

4. T  F  About one-half of all lawsuits settle before trial.

5. T  F  In a lawsuit for money damages, both the plaintiff and the defendant are generally entitled to a jury.

## MULTIPLE CHOICE QUESTIONS

6. A federal court has the power to hear
   A. Any case.
   B. Any case between citizens of different states.
   C. Any criminal case.
   D. Appeals of any cases from lower courts.
   E. Any lawsuit based on a federal statute.

7. Before trial begins, a defendant in a civil lawsuit believes that even if the plaintiff proves everything he has alleged, the law requires the defendant to win. The defendant should
   A. Request arbitration.
   B. Request a mandatory verdict.
   C. Move for recusal.
   D. Move for summary judgment.
   E. Demand mediation.

8. In a civil lawsuit
   A. The defendant is presumed innocent until proven guilty.
   B. The defendant is presumed guilty until proven innocent.
   C. The plaintiff must prove her case by a preponderance of the evidence.
   D. The plaintiff must prove her case beyond a reasonable doubt.
   E. The defendant must establish his defenses to the satisfaction of the court.

9. Mack sues Jasmine, claiming that she caused an automobile accident. At trial, Jasmine's lawyer is asking her questions about the accident. This is
   A. An interrogatory.
   B. A deposition.
   C. Direct examination.
   D. Cross-examination.
   E. Opening statement.

10. Jurisdiction refers to
    A. The jury's decision.
    B. The judge's instructions to the jury.
    C. Pretrial questions posed by one attorney to the opposing party.
    D. The power of a court to hear a particular case.
    E. A decision by an appellate court to send the case back to the trial court.

## SHORT-ANSWER QUESTIONS

11. State which court(s) have jurisdiction as to each of these lawsuits:

    (a) Pat wants to sue his next-door neighbor Dorothy, claiming that Dorothy promised to sell him the house next door.

(b) Paula, who lives in New York City, wants to sue Dizzy Movie Theatres, whose principal place of business is Dallas. She claims that while she was in Texas on holiday, she was injured by their negligent maintenance of a stairway. She claims damages of $30,000.

(c) Phil lives in Tennessee. He wants to sue Dick, who lives in Ohio. Phil claims that Dick agreed to sell him 3,000 acres of farmland in Ohio, worth over $2 million.

(d) Pete, incarcerated in a federal prison in Kansas, wants to sue the United States government. He claims that his treatment by prison authorities violates three federal statutes.

12. Students are now suing schools for sexual harassment. The cases raise important issues about the limits of discovery. In a case in Petaluma, California, a girl claimed that she was harassed for years and that the school knew about it and failed to act. According to press reports, she alleges that a boy stood up in class and asked, "I have a question. I want to know if [Jane Doe] has sex with hot dogs." In discovery, the school district sought the parents' therapy records, the girl's diary, and a psychological evaluation of the girl. Should they get those things?

13. ETHICS Trial practice is dramatically different in Britain. The lawyers for the two sides, called solicitors, do not go into court. Courtroom work is done by different lawyers, called barristers. The barristers are not permitted to interview any witnesses before trial. They know the substance of what each witness intends to say but do not rehearse questions and answers, as in the United States. Which approach do you consider more effective? More ethical? What is the purpose of a trial? Of pretrial preparation?

14. Claus Scherer worked for Rockwell International and was paid over $300,000 per year. Rockwell fired Scherer for alleged sexual harassment of several workers, including his secretary, Terry Pendy. Scherer sued in United States District Court, alleging that Rockwell's real motive in firing him was his high salary.

   Rockwell moved for summary judgment, offering deposition transcripts of various employees. Pendy's deposition detailed instances of harassment, including comments about her body, instances of unwelcome touching, and discussions of extramarital affairs. Another deposition, from a Rockwell employee who investigated the allegations, included complaints by other employees as to Scherer's harassment. In his own deposition, which he offered to oppose summary judgment, Scherer testified that he could not recall the incidents alleged by Pendy and others. He denied generally that he had sexually harassed anyone. The district court granted summary judgment for Rockwell. Was its ruling correct?

15. ROLE REVERSAL Write a multiple-choice question that illustrates the unique significance of summary judgment. First, be sure you understand when and why a party is entitled to summary judgment.

# INTERNET RESEARCH PROBLEM

You may be called for jury duty before long. Online, find a summary of a juror's responsibilities. Some people try hard to get out of jury duty. Why is that a problem in a democratic society?

**You can find further practice problems in the Online Quiz at www.cengage.com/blaw/beatty.**

# CONSTITUTIONAL, STATUTORY, ADMINISTRATIVE, AND COMMON LAW

**Gregory Johnson** was angry. On a public street in Dallas, the young man lit an American flag on fire, protesting the nearby political convention. Law officers arrested and convicted him of violating Texas law, but Johnson appealed his case all the way to the United States Supreme Court, claiming that the First Amendment protected this form of demonstration. Did it? Should it? Which has a higher social value, Johnson's urge to protest, or the government's decision to protect the flag? How do we decide the issue? Where do we find the law that will answer this question? In this chapter, we look at four vital sources of law: the United States Constitution, statutes, administrative agencies, and the common law.

> **Which has a higher social value, Johnson's urge to protest, or the government's decision to protect the flag?**

Let us consider a very different—yet related—question. What if a state legislature passes a law prohibiting new construction along a lakefront? This measure will protect the environment and keep beaches open for all of us. In the process, though, it will render some very expensive waterfront property worthless, because the owners will not be able to build. Whose interest is more important, that of the public or that of the property owners?

Does your state have the power to prohibit flag burning? If so, does that mean it could outlaw a campaign poster on your front lawn? Prohibit political protest entirely? Ban waterfront development? How much power have we granted to the government? What rights do the people retain? Those important questions lead to our first law source.

## · CONSTITUTIONAL LAW ·

## GOVERNMENT POWER

The Constitution of the United States is the greatest legal document ever written. No other written constitution has lasted so long, governed so many, or withstood such challenge.

In 1783, 13 American colonies gained surprising independence from Great Britain. Four years later, the colonies sent delegates to craft a new constitution, but the men (no women among them) faced conflicts on a basic issue. How much power should the federal government be given? The Framers, as they have come to be called because they made or "framed" the original document, had to compromise. **The Constitution is a series of compromises about power.**

### Separation of Powers

One method of limiting power was to create a national government divided into three branches, each independent and equal. Each branch would act as a check on the power of the other two, avoiding the despotic rule that had come from London. Article I of the Constitution created a Congress, which was to have legislative power. Article II created the office of president, defining the scope of executive power. Article III established judicial power by creating the Supreme Court and permitting additional federal courts.

Consider how the three separate powers balance one another: Congress was given the power to pass statutes, a major grant of power. But the president was permitted to veto legislation, a nearly equal grant. Congress, in turn, had the right to override the veto, ensuring that the president would not become a dictator. The president was allowed to appoint federal judges and members of his cabinet, but only with a consenting vote from the Senate.

### Federalism

The national government was indeed to have considerable power, but it would still be *limited* power. Article I, section 8, enumerates those issues on which Congress may pass statutes. If an issue is not on the list, Congress has no power to legislate. Thus Congress may create and regulate a post office because postal service is on the list. But Congress may not pass statutes regulating child custody in a divorce: That issue is not on the list. Only the states may legislate child custody issues.

## POWER GRANTED

### Congressional Power

Article I of the Constitution creates the Congress, with its two houses. Representation in the House of Representatives is proportionate with a state's population, but each state elects two senators. Congress may perform any of the functions enumerated in Article I, section 8, such as imposing taxes, spending money, creating copyrights, supporting the military, declaring war, and so forth. None of these rights is more important than the authority to raise and spend money (the "power of the purse"), because every branch of government is dependent upon Congress for its money.

One of the most important items on this list of congressional powers concerns trade.

**Interstate Commerce**   "The Congress shall have power to regulate commerce with foreign nations, and among the several states." This is the **Commerce Clause**: Congress is authorized to regulate trade between states. For example, if Congress passed a law imposing a new tax on all trucks engaged in interstate transportation, the law is valid. Congress can regulate television broadcasts because many of them cross state lines.

States have less power in this area. **A state statute that discriminates against interstate commerce is unconstitutional and void.** Suppose that Ohio, in order to protect its dairy industry, imposes a special tax on milk produced outside the state. That law discriminates against interstate trade and violates the Commerce Clause.

> **The Commerce Clause** gives Congress the power to regulate commerce with foreign nations and among states. A state statute that discriminates against interstate trade is void.

## Executive Power

Article II of the Constitution defines the executive power. Once again, the Constitution gives powers in general terms. **The basic job of the president is to enforce the nation's laws.** Three of his key powers concern appointment, legislation, and foreign policy.

**Appointment**   As we see later in this chapter, administrative agencies play a powerful role in business regulation. The president nominates the heads of most of them. These choices dramatically influence what issues the agencies choose to pursue and how aggressively they do it. For example, a president who believes that it is vital to protect our natural resources may appoint a forceful environmentalist to run the Environmental Protection Agency (EPA), whereas a president who dislikes federal regulations will choose a more passive agency head.

**Legislation**   The president and his advisers propose bills to Congress and lobby hard for their passage. The executive also has veto power.

**Foreign Policy**   The president conducts the nation's foreign affairs, coordinating international efforts, negotiating treaties, and so forth. The president is also the commander in chief of the armed forces, meaning that he heads the military.

## Judicial Power

Article III of the Constitution creates the Supreme Court and permits Congress to establish lower courts within the federal court system. Federal courts have two key functions: adjudication and judicial review.

**Adjudicating Cases**   The federal court system hears criminal and civil cases. All prosecutions of federal crimes begin in United States District Court. That same court has limited jurisdiction to hear civil lawsuits, a subject discussed in Chapter 3, on dispute resolution.

**Judicial Review**   **Judicial review** refers to the power of federal courts to declare a statute or governmental action unconstitutional and void. The courts can examine acts from any branch of federal or state government. If Ohio did pass a tax on milk produced in other states, a federal court would declare the law void, as a violation of the Commerce Clause. Exhibit 4.1 illustrates the balance among Congress, the president, and the Court.

> **Judicial review** refers to the power of federal courts to declare a statute or governmental action unconstitutional and void.

Is judicial review good for the nation? Those who oppose it argue that federal court judges are all appointed, not elected, and that we should not permit judges to nullify a statute passed by elected officials because that diminishes the people's role in their government. Those who favor judicial review insist that there must be one cohesive interpretation of the Constitution and the judicial branch is the logical one to provide it. The following example of judicial review shows how immediate and emotional the issue can be. This is a criminal prosecution for a brutal crime. Cases like this force us to examine two questions about judicial review. What is the proper punishment for such a horrible crime? Just as important, *who should make that decision*—appointed judges, or elected legislators?

# YOU *be the* JUDGE

## KENNEDY v. LOUISIANA
### 128 S.Ct. 2641
### United States Supreme Court, 2008

**Facts:** Patrick Kennedy raped his 8-year-old stepdaughter, referred to as L.H. He then phoned 911 and reported that two neighborhood boys had dragged the girl to a side yard of the property and committed the crime. A forensic expert testified that L.H.'s physical injuries were the most severe he had ever witnessed from a sexual assault. L.H. at first corroborated Kennedy's version of the crime, but in court acknowledged that her stepfather had assaulted her. The jury also heard evidence that the defendant had raped another 8-year-old. Kennedy was convicted of aggravated rape, because the victim was under 12 years of age.

The jury voted to sentence Kennedy to death, which was permitted by the Louisiana statute. The state supreme court affirmed the death sentence, and Kennedy appealed to the United States Supreme Court. He argued that the Louisiana statute was unconstitutional. The Eighth Amendment prohibits cruel and unusual punishment, which includes penalties that are out of proportion to the crime. Kennedy claimed that capital punishment was out of proportion to rape and violated the Eighth Amendment.

Six states had passed laws permitting capital punishment for child rape, though the remaining 44 states had not. Louisiana argued that the statute did not violate the amendment and that the voters must be allowed to express their abhorrence of so evil an act.

**You Be the Judge:  Did the Louisiana statute violate the Constitution by permitting the death penalty in a case of child rape? Is it proper for the Supreme Court to decide this issue?**

**Argument for Kennedy:** The court's interpretation of the Constitution must evolve with society. The Eighth Amendment requires that punishment be proportionate to the crime. A national consensus opposes the death penalty for any crime other than murder. Capital punishment exists in 36 states, but only 6 of those states allow it for child rape. No state has executed a defendant for rape since 1964. As horrifying as child rape is, society merely brutalizes itself when it sinks to the level of capital punishment for a crime other than murder.

There are also policy reasons to prohibit this punishment. Children may be more reluctant to testify against perpetrators if they know that a prosecution could lead to execution. Also, a young child may be an unreliable witness for a case where the stakes are so high. It is the responsibility of this court to nullify such a harmful law.

**Argument for Louisiana:** Child rape is one of the most horrifying of crimes. The defendant damages a young person, destroys her childhood, and terrifies a community. Only the severest of penalties is sufficient.

Six states have recently passed statutes permitting capital punishment in these cases. It is possible that a consensus is developing *in favor* of the death penalty for these brutal assaults. If the court strikes down this law, it will effectively stifle a national debate and destroy any true consensus.

Kennedy argues that capital punishment might be bad policy—but that is a question for voters and legislatures, not for courts. Obviously, the citizens of Louisiana favor this law. If they are offended by the statute, they have the power to replace legislators who support it. The court should leave this issue to the citizens. That is how a democracy is intended to function.

# PROTECTED RIGHTS

The original Constitution was silent about the rights of citizens. This alarmed many, who feared that the new federal government would have unlimited power over their lives. So in 1791, the first 10 amendments, known as the Bill of Rights, were added to the Constitution, guaranteeing many liberties directly to individual citizens.

The amendments to the Constitution protect the people of this nation from the power of state and federal government. The **First Amendment** guarantees rights of free speech, free press, and religion; the **Fourth Amendment** protects against illegal searches; the **Fifth Amendment** ensures due process; the **Sixth Amendment** demands fair treatment for defendants in criminal prosecutions; and the **Fourteenth Amendment** guarantees equal protection of the law. We

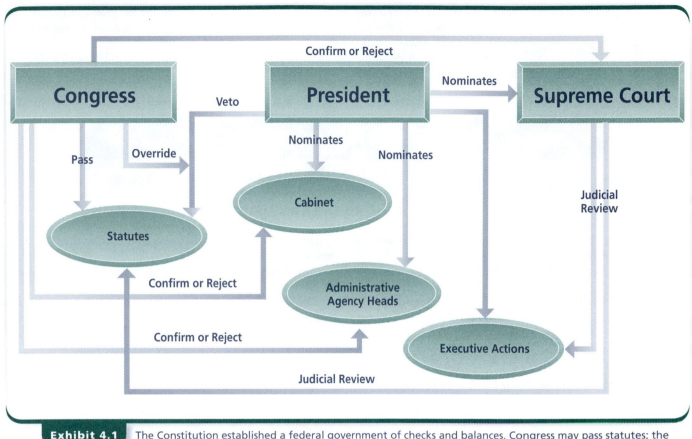

**Exhibit 4.1**   The Constitution established a federal government of checks and balances. Congress may pass statutes; the president may veto them; and Congress may override the veto. The president nominates cabinet officers, administrative heads, and Supreme Court justices, but the Senate must confirm his nominees. Finally, the Supreme Court (and lower federal courts) exercise judicial review over statutes and executive actions. Unlike the other checks and balances, judicial review is not provided for in the Constitution but is a creation of the Court itself in *Marbury v. Madison.*

consider the First, Fifth, and Fourteenth Amendments in this chapter and the Fourth, Fifth, and Sixth Amendments in Chapter 7, on crime.

The "people" who are protected include citizens and, for most purposes, corporations. Corporations are considered persons and receive most of the same protections. The great majority of these rights also extend to citizens of other countries who are in the United States.

**Constitutional rights** generally protect only against governmental acts. The Constitution generally does not protect us from the conduct of private parties, such as corporations or other citizens. Constitutional protections apply to federal, state, and local governments.

### First Amendment: Free Speech

The First Amendment states that "Congress shall make no law . . . abridging the freedom of speech. . . ." In general, we expect our government to let people speak and hear whatever they choose. The Framers believed democracy would work only if the members of the electorate were free to talk, argue, listen, and exchange viewpoints in any way they wanted. If a city government prohibited an antiabortion group from demonstrating, its action would violate the First Amendment. Government officers may not impose their political beliefs on the citizens. The

**Constitutional rights**
generally protect only against *government* acts.

**The First Amendment**
protects freedom of speech.

government may regulate the *time, place,* and *manner* of speech, for example, by prohibiting a midnight rally, or insisting that demonstrators remain within a specified area. But outright prohibitions are unconstitutional.

"Speech" includes symbolic conduct. Does that mean flag burning is permissible? The following case, introduced at the beginning of this chapter, is about that issue.

## TEXAS V. JOHNSON

### 491 U.S. 397, 109 S. Ct. 2533, 1989 U.S. LEXIS 3115
### UNITED STATES SUPREME COURT, 1989

### CASE SUMMARY

**Facts:** Outside the Republican National Convention in Dallas, Gregory Johnson participated in a protest against policies of the Reagan administration. Participants gave speeches and handed out leaflets. Johnson burned an American flag. He was arrested and convicted under a Texas statute that prohibited desecrating the flag, but the Texas Court of Criminal Appeals reversed on the grounds that the conviction violated the First Amendment. Texas appealed to the United States Supreme Court.

**Issue:** *Does the First Amendment protect flag burning?*

**Decision:** Affirmed. The First Amendment protects flag burning.

**Reasoning:** The First Amendment literally applies only to "speech," but this Court has already ruled that the Amendment also protects written words and other conduct that will convey a specific message. For example, earlier decisions protected a student's right to wear a black armband in protest against American military actions. Judged by this standard, flag burning is symbolic speech.

Texas argues that its interest in honoring the flag justifies its prosecution of Johnson, since he knew that his action would be deeply offensive to many citizens. However, if there is a bedrock principle underlying the First Amendment, it is that the government may not prohibit the expression of an idea simply because society finds it offensive.

The best way to preserve the flag's special role in our lives is not to punish those who feel differently, but to persuade them that they are wrong. We do not honor our flag by punishing those who burn it, because in doing so we diminish the freedom that this cherished emblem represents.

# FIFTH AMENDMENT: DUE PROCESS AND THE TAKINGS CLAUSE

Ralph is a first-semester senior at State University, where he majors in finance. With a 3.6 grade point average and outstanding recommendations, he has an excellent chance of admission to an elite business school—until his life suddenly turns upside down. Professor Watson, who teaches Ralph in marketing, notifies the school's dean that the young man plagiarized material that he included in his recent paper. Dean Holmes reads Watson's report and sends Ralph a brief letter: "I find that you have committed plagiarism in violation of school rules. Your grade in Dr. Watson's marketing course is an 'F.' You are hereby suspended from the University for one full academic year."

Ralph is shocked. He is convinced he did nothing wrong, and wants to tell his side of the story, but Dean Holmes refuses to speak with him. What can he do? The first step is to read the Fifth Amendment.

Two related provisions of the Fifth Amendment, called the Due Process Clause and the Takings Clause, prohibit the government from arbitrarily depriving us of our most valuable assets. Together, they state: "No person shall be . . . deprived of life, liberty, or property without due process of law; nor shall private property be taken for public use, without just compensation."

We will discuss the civil law aspects of these clauses, but due process also applies to criminal law. The reference to "life" refers to capital punishment. The criminal law issues of this subject are discussed in Chapter 7.

## Procedural Due Process

The government deprives citizens or corporations of their property in a variety of ways. The Internal Revenue Service may fine a corporation for late payment of taxes. The Customs Service may seize goods at the border. As to liberty, the government may take it by confining someone in a mental institution or by taking a child out of the home because of parental neglect. The purpose of **procedural due process** is to ensure that before the government takes liberty or property, the affected person has a fair chance to oppose the action.[1]

The Due Process Clause protects Ralph because State University is part of the government. Ralph is entitled to due process. Does this mean that he gets a full court trial on the plagiarism charge? No. **The type of hearing the government must offer depends upon the importance of the property or liberty interest.** The more important the interest, the more formal the procedures must be. Regardless of how formal the hearing, one requirement is constant: The fact finder must be neutral.

In a criminal prosecution, the liberty interest is very great. A defendant can lose his freedom or even his life. The government must provide the defendant with a lawyer if he cannot afford one, adequate time to prepare, an unbiased jury, an opportunity to present his case and cross-examine all witnesses, and many other procedural rights.

A student faced with academic sanctions receives less due process but still has rights. State University has failed to provide Ralph with due process. The school has accused the young man of a serious infraction. The school must promptly provide details of the charge, give Ralph all physical evidence, and allow him time to plan his response. The university must then offer Ralph a hearing, before a neutral person or group, who will listen to Ralph (as well as Dr. Watson) and examine any evidence the student offers. Ralph is not, however, entitled to a lawyer or a jury.

## The Takings Clause

Kabrina owns a 10-acre parcel of undeveloped land on Lake Halcyon. She plans to build a 20-bedroom inn of about 35,000 square feet—until the state environmental agency abruptly halts the work. The agency informs Kabrina that, to protect the lake from further harm, it will allow no shoreline development except single-family houses of 2,000 square feet or less. Kabrina is furious. Does the state have the power to wreck Kabrina's plans? To learn the answer, we look to another section of the Fifth Amendment.

**The Takings Clause** prohibits a state from taking private property for public use without just compensation. A town wishing to build a new football field *does* have the right to boot you out of your house. But the town must compensate you. The government takes your land through the power of eminent domain. Officials must notify you of their intentions and give you an opportunity to oppose the project and to challenge the amount the town offers to pay. When the hearings are done, though, the town may write you a check and grind your house into goalposts, whether you like it or not.

If the state actually wanted to take Kabrina's land and turn it into a park, the Takings Clause would force it to pay the fair market value. However, the state is not trying to seize the land—it merely wants to prevent large development.

"My land is worthless," Kabrina replies. "You might just as well kick me off my own property!" **A regulation that denies *all beneficial use* of property is a taking, and requires compensation.** Has the government denied Kabrina all beneficial use? No, it has not. Kabrina retains the right

**Procedural due process** ensures that before the government takes liberty or property, the affected person has a fair chance to oppose the action.

**The Takings Clause** prohibits a state from taking private property for public use without just compensation.

---

[1] In *criminal* cases, procedural due process also protects against the taking of *life*.

to build a private house; she just can't build the inn she wants. The environmental agency has decreased the value of the land, but it owes her nothing. Had the state forbidden *any construction* on her land, it would have been obligated to pay Kabrina.

# FOURTEENTH AMENDMENT: EQUAL PROTECTION CLAUSE

Shannon Faulkner wanted to attend The Citadel, a state-supported military college in South Carolina. She was a fine student who met every admission requirement that The Citadel set except one: She was not a male. The Citadel argued that its long and distinguished history demanded that it remain all male. Faulkner responded that she was a citizen of the state and ought to receive the benefits that others got, including the right to a military education. Could the school exclude her on the basis of gender?

**The Equal Protection Clause** dictates that the government must generally treat people equally.

The Fourteenth Amendment provides that "No State shall . . . deny to any person within its jurisdiction the equal protection of the laws." This is the **Equal Protection Clause**, and it means that, generally speaking, all levels of government must treat people equally. Unfair classifications among people or corporations will not be permitted. **Regulations based on gender, race, or fundamental rights are generally void.** Shannon Faulkner won her case and was admitted to The Citadel. The Court found no justification for discriminating against women. Any regulation based on race or ethnicity is *certain* to be void; one based on gender is *likely* to be void. Similarly, all citizens enjoy the *fundamental right* to travel between states. If Kentucky limited government jobs to those who had lived in the state for two years, it would be discriminating against a fundamental right, and the restriction would be struck down.

## EXAM *Strategy*

**Question:** Megan is a freshman at her local public high school; her older sister, Jenna, attends a nearby private high school. Both girls are angry because their schools prohibit them from joining their respective wrestling teams, where only boys are allowed. The two girls sue based on the United States Constitution. Discuss the relevant law and predict the outcomes.

**Strategy:** One girl goes to private and one to public school. Why does that matter? Now ask what provision of the Constitution is involved, and what legal standard it establishes.

**Result:** The Constitution offers protection from the *government*. A private high school is not part of the government, and Jenna has no constitutional case. Megan's suit is based on the Equal Protection Clause. Regulations based on gender are generally void. The school will probably argue that wrestling with stronger boys will be dangerous for girls. However, courts are increasingly suspicious of any sex discrimination and are unlikely to find the school's argument persuasive.

# · STATUTORY LAW ·

**Statutes** are laws passed by Congress or state legislatures.

Most new law is statutory law. **Statutes** affect each of us every day, in our business, professional, and personal lives. When the system works correctly, this is the one part of the law over which we the people have control. We elect the local legislators who pass state statutes; we vote for the senators and representatives who create federal statutes. If we understand the system, we can affect the largest source of contemporary law. If we live in ignorance of its strengths and pitfalls, we delude ourselves that we participate in a democracy.

As we saw in Chapter 1, there are many systems of government operating in the United States: a national government and 50 state governments. Each level of government has a legislative body. In Washington, D.C., Congress is our national legislature. Congress passes the statutes that govern the nation. In addition, each state has a legislature, which passes statutes for that state only. In this section, we look at how Congress does its work creating statutes. State legislatures operate similarly, but the work of Congress is better documented and obviously of national importance.

## COMMITTEE WORK

Congress is organized into two houses, the House of Representatives and the Senate. Either house may originate a proposed statute, which is called a **bill**. After a bill has been proposed, it is sent to an appropriate committee.[2]

**Bill**
A proposed statute.

If you visit either house of Congress, you will probably find half a dozen legislators on the floor, with one person talking and no one listening. This is because most of the work is done in committees. Both houses are organized into dozens of committees, each with special functions. The House currently has about 27 committees (further divided into about 150 subcommittees), and the Senate has approximately 20 committees (with about 86 subcommittees). For example, the Armed Services committee of each house oversees the huge defense budget and the workings of the armed forces. Labor committees handle legislation concerning organized labor and working conditions. Banking committees develop expertise on financial institutions. Judiciary committees review nominees to the federal courts. There are dozens of other committees, some very powerful, because they control vast amounts of money, and some relatively weak.

When a bill is proposed in either house, it is referred to the committee that specializes in that subject. Why are bills proposed in the first place? For any of several reasons:

- *New Issue, New Worry.* During the early years of this millennium, voters were increasingly irate about abuses in campaign financing, and, after years of hearings, Congress finally passed legislation designed to reduce excessive political donations.

- *Unpopular Judicial Ruling.* If Congress disagrees with a judicial interpretation of a statute, the legislators may pass a new statute to modify or "undo" the court decision. For example, if the Supreme Court misinterprets a statute about musical copyrights, Congress may pass a new law correcting the Court's error.

- *Criminal Law.* When legislators perceive that social changes have led to new criminal acts, they may respond with new statutes. The rise of Internet fraud has led to many new statutes outlawing such things as computer trespass and espionage, fraud in the use of cell phones, identity theft, and so on.

Congressional committees hold hearings to investigate the need for new legislation and consider the alternatives. Suppose a congressperson believes that a growing number of American corporations locate their headquarters offshore to escape taxes. She requests committee hearings on the subject, hoping to discover the extent of the problem, its causes, and possible remedies. After hearings, she proposes a bill she believes will remedy the problem. If the committee votes in favor of the bill, it goes to the full body, meaning either the House of Representatives or the Senate. If the full body approves the bill, it goes to the other house.

The bill must be voted on and approved by both branches of Congress. If both houses pass the bill, the legislation normally must go to a conference committee, made of members from each

---

[2] See the chart of state and federal governments in Chapter 1. A vast amount of information about Congress is available on the Internet. The House of Representatives has a Web page at **http://www.house.gov/**. The Senate's site appears at **http://www.senate.gov**. Each page provides links to current law, pending legislation, votes, committees, and more.

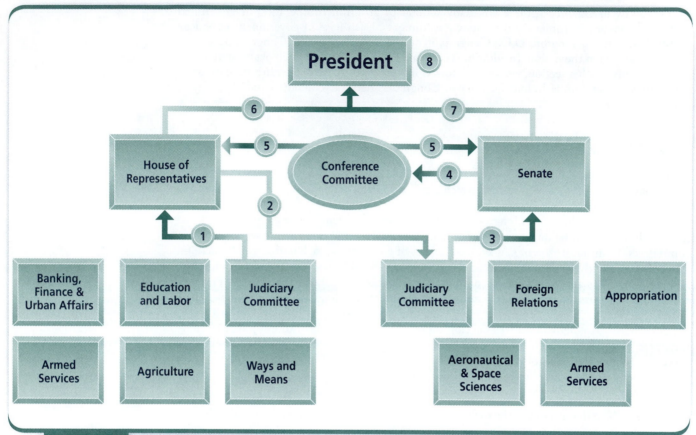

The two houses of Congress are organized into dozens of committees, a few of which are shown here. The path of the 1964 Civil Rights Act (somewhat simplified) was as follows: (1) The House Judiciary Committee approved the bill and sent it to the full House; (2) the full House passed the bill and sent it to the Senate, where it was assigned to the Senate Judiciary Committee; (3) the Senate Judiciary Committee passed an amended version of the bill and sent it to the full Senate; (4) the full Senate passed the bill with additional amendments. Because the Senate version was now different from the bill the House passed, the bill went to a Conference Committee. The Conference Committee (5) reached a compromise and sent the new version of the bill back to both houses. Each house passed the compromise bill (6 and 7) and sent it to the president, who signed it into law (8).

house, to resolve differences between the two versions. Assuming both houses then pass the same version of the bill, the bill goes to the president. If the president signs the bill, it becomes law. If the president opposes the bill, he will veto it, in which case it is not law. When the president vetoes a bill, Congress has one last chance to make it law: an override. Should both houses re-pass the bill, each by a two-thirds margin, it becomes law over the president's veto.

## · COMMON LAW ·

Jason observes a toddler wander onto the railroad tracks and hears a train approaching. He has plenty of time to pull the child from the tracks with no risk to himself, but he chooses to do nothing. The youngster is killed. The child's family sues Jason for his callous behavior, and a court determines that Jason owes—nothing. How can that be?

Jason and the toddler present a classic legal puzzle: What, if anything, must a bystander do when he sees someone in danger? We will examine this issue to see how the common law works.

The **common law** is judge-made law. It is the sum total of all the cases decided by appellate courts. The common law of Pennsylvania consists of all cases decided by appellate courts in that state. The Illinois common law of bystander liability is all the cases on that subject decided by Illinois appellate courts. Two hundred years ago, almost all the law was common law. Today, most new law is statutory. But common law still predominates in tort, contract, and agency law, and it is very important in property, employment, and some other areas.

We focus on appellate courts because they are the only ones to make rulings of law, as discussed in Chapter 3. In a bystander case, it is the job of the state's highest court to say what legal obligations, if any, a bystander has. The trial court, on the other hand, must decide facts: Was this defendant able to see what was happening? Was the plaintiff really in trouble? Could the defendant have assisted without peril to himself?

> **Jason observes a toddler wander onto the railroad tracks and hears a train approaching.**

**Common law**
is made by appellate courts.

## STARE DECISIS

Nothing perks up a course like Latin. ***Stare decisis*** means "let the decision stand." It is the essence of the common law. The phrase indicates that once a court has decided a particular issue, it will generally apply the same rule in future cases. Suppose the highest court of Arizona must decide whether a contract for a new car, signed by a 16-year-old, can be enforced against him. The court will look to see if there is precedent, that is, whether the high court of Arizona has already decided a similar case. The Arizona court looks and finds several earlier cases, all holding that such contracts may not be enforced against a minor. The court will apply that precedent and refuse to enforce the contract in this case. Courts do not always follow precedent but they generally do: *Stare decisis*.

Two words explain why the common law is never as easy as we might like: *predictability* and *flexibility*. The law is trying to accommodate both goals. The need for predictability is apparent: People must know what the law is. If contract law changed daily, an entrepreneur who leased factory space and then started buying machinery would be uncertain if the factory would actually be available when she was ready to move in. Will the landlord slip out of the lease? Will the machinery be ready on time? The need for predictability created the doctrine of *stare decisis*.

Yet there must also be flexibility in the law, some means to respond to new problems and changing social mores. In this new millennium, we cannot be encumbered by ironclad rules established before electricity was discovered. These two ideas may be obvious, but they also conflict: The more flexibility we permit, the less predictability we enjoy. We will watch the conflict play out in the bystander cases.

*Stare decisis*
means "let the decision stand," and describes a court's tendency to follow earlier cases.

## BYSTANDER CASES

This country inherited from England a simple rule about a bystander's obligations: You have no duty to assist someone in peril unless you created the danger. In *Union Pacific Railway Co. v. Cappier*,[3] through no fault of the railroad, a train struck a man, severing an arm and a leg. Railroad employees saw the incident happen but did nothing to assist him. By the time help arrived, the victim had died. In this 1903 case, the court held that the railroad had no duty to help the injured man. The court declared that it was legally irrelevant whether the railroad's conduct was inhumane.

---

[3] 66 Kan. 649, 72 P. 281 (1903).

As harsh as this judgment might seem, it was an accurate statement of the law at that time in both England and the United States: Bystanders need do nothing. With a rule this old and well established, no court was willing to scuttle it. What courts did do was seek openings for small changes.

Eighteen years after the Kansas case of *Cappier,* the court in nearby Iowa found the basis for one exception. Ed Carey was a farm laborer, working for Frank Davis. While in the fields, Carey fainted from sunstroke and remained unconscious. Davis simply hauled him to a nearby wagon and left him in the sun for an additional four hours, causing serious permanent injury. The judges said that was not good enough. Creating a modest exception to the bystander rule, the court ruled that when an employee suffers a serious injury *on the job,* the employer must take reasonable measures to help him. Leaving a stricken worker in the hot sun was not reasonable, and Davis was liable.[4]

And this is how the common law changes: bit by tiny bit. In the 1970s, changes came more quickly.

## TARASOFF V. REGENTS OF THE UNIVERSITY OF CALIFORNIA

17 CAL. 3D 425, 551 P.2D 334, 131 CAL. RPTR. 14
SUPREME COURT OF CALIFORNIA, 1976

### CASE SUMMARY

**Facts:** On October 27, 1969, Prosenjit Poddar killed Tatiana Tarasoff. Tatiana's parents claimed that two months earlier, Poddar had confided his intention to kill Tatiana to Dr. Lawrence Moore, a psychologist employed by the University of California at Berkeley. They sued the university, claiming that Dr. Moore should have warned Tatiana and/or should have arranged for Poddar's confinement.

**Issue:** *Did Dr. Moore have a duty to Tatiana Tarasoff?*

**Decision:** Yes, Dr. Moore had a duty to Tatiana Tarasoff.
**Reasoning:** Under the common law, one person generally owes no duty to control the conduct of another or to warn anyone who is in danger. However, courts make an exception when the defendant has a special relationship to a dangerous person or potential victim. A therapist is someone who has just such a special relationship with a patient.

No one can be expected to do a perfect job. A therapist must only exercise the reasonable degree of skill, knowledge, and care ordinarily possessed by others in the field. In this case, however, there is no dispute about whether Dr. Moore could have foreseen violence. He actually predicted Poddar would kill Tatiana. Once a therapist determines that a patient poses a serious danger of violence, he must make reasonable efforts to protect the victim. The Tarasoffs have stated a legitimate claim against Dr. Moore.

The Tarasoff exception applies in the limited circumstance of a special relationship, such as therapist–patient. Does the decision mean an end to the bystander rule? By no means. Ernesto Parra was a customer at the Jiminez Restaurant when food became lodged in his throat. The employees did not use the Heimlich maneuver or any other method to try to save him. Parra choked to death. Was the restaurant liable? No, said the Illinois Appeals Court. The restaurant had no obligation to do anything.[5] The bystander rule, that hardy oak, is still alive and well.

---

[4] *Carey v. Davis,* 190 Iowa 720, 180 N.W. 889 (1921).

[5] 230 Ill. App. 3d 819, 595 N.E.2d 1186, 1992 Ill. App. LEXIS 935 (1992).

## EXAM *Strategy*

**Question:** When Rachel is walking her dog, Bozo, she watches a skydiver float to earth. He lands in an enormous tree, suspended 45 feet above ground. "Help!" the man shouts. Rachel hurries to the tree and sees the skydiver bleeding profusely. She takes out her cell phone to call 911 for help, but just then Bozo runs away. Rachel darts after the dog, afraid he will jump in a nearby pond and emerge smelling of mud. She forgets about the skydiver and takes Bozo home in a shopping bag. After bleeding for three hours, the skydiver expires.

The victim's family sues Rachel. She defends by saying she feared that Bozo would have an allergic reaction to mud, and that in any case, she could not have climbed 45 feet up a tree to save the man. The family argues that the dog is not allergic to mud, that even if he is, a pet's inconvenience pales compared to human life, and that Rachel could have phoned for emergency help without climbing an inch. Please rule.

**Strategy:** The family's arguments might seem compelling, but are they relevant? Rachel is a bystander, someone who perceives another in danger. What is the rule concerning a bystander's obligation to act? Apply the rule to the facts of this case.

**Result:** A bystander has no duty to assist someone in peril unless she created the danger. Rachel did not create the skydiver's predicament. She had no obligation to do anything. Rachel wins.

## · ADMINISTRATIVE LAW ·

Before beginning this section, please return your seat to its upright position. Stow the tray firmly in the seat back in front of you. Turn off any cell phones, laptops, or other electronic devices. Sound familiar? Administrative agencies affect each of us every day in hundreds of ways. They have become the fourth branch of government. Supporters believe that they provide unique expertise in complex areas; detractors regard them as unelected government run amok.

Many administrative agencies are familiar. The Federal Aviation Administration, which requires all airlines to ensure that your seats are upright before takeoff and landing, is an administrative agency. The Internal Revenue Service haunts us every April 15. The Environmental Protection Agency (EPA) regulates the water quality of the river in your town. The Federal Trade Commission (FCC) oversees the commercials that shout at you from your television set.

Other agencies are less familiar. You may never have heard of the Bureau of Land Management, but if you go into the oil and gas industry, you will learn that this powerful agency has more control over your land than you do. If you develop real estate in Palos Hills, Illinois, you will tremble every time the Appearance Commission of the City of Palos Hills speaks, since you cannot construct a new building without its approval. If your software corporation wants to hire an Argentine expert on databases, you will get to know the complex workings of Immigration and Customs Enforcement: no one lawfully enters this country without its nod of approval.

Administrative agencies use three kinds of power to do the work assigned to them: they make rules, investigate, and adjudicate.

## RULE MAKING

One of the most important functions of an administrative agency is to make rules. In doing this, the agency attempts, prospectively, to establish fair and uniform behavior for all businesses in the affected area. To create a new rule is to promulgate it. Agencies promulgate two types of rules: legislative and interpretive.

### Legislative Rules

These are the most important agency rules, and they are much like statutes. Here, an agency is changing the law by requiring businesses or private citizens to act in a certain way. For example, the FCC promulgated a rule requiring all cable television systems with more than 3,500 subscribers to develop the capacity to carry at least 20 channels and to make some of those channels available to local community stations. This legislative rule has a heavy financial impact on many cable systems. As far as a cable company is concerned, it is more important than most statutes passed by Congress. Legislative rules have the full effect of a statute.

### Interpretive Rules

These rules do not change the law. They are the agency's interpretation of what the law already requires. But they can still affect all of us.

In 1977, Congress passed the Clean Air Act in an attempt to reduce pollution from factories. The act required the EPA to impose emission standards on "stationary sources" of pollution. But what did "stationary source" mean? It was the EPA's job to define that term. Obscure work, to be sure, yet the results could be seen and even smelled, because the EPA's definition would determine the quality of air entering our lungs every time we breathe. Environmentalists wanted the term defined to include every smokestack in a factory so that the EPA could regulate each one. The EPA, however, developed the "bubble concept," ruling that "stationary source" meant an entire factory, but not the individual smokestacks. As a result, polluters could shift emission among smokestacks in a single factory to avoid EPA regulation. Environmentalists howled that this gutted the purpose of the statute, but to no avail. The agency had spoken, merely by interpreting a statute.

### Investigation

Agencies do an infinite variety of work, but they all need broad factual knowledge of the field they govern. Some companies cooperate with an agency, furnishing information and even voluntarily accepting agency recommendations. For example, the United States Product Safety Commission investigates hundreds of consumer products every year and frequently urges companies to recall goods that the agency considers defective. Many firms comply. Other companies, however, jealously guard information, often because corporate officers believe that disclosure would lead to adverse rules. To force disclosure, agencies use subpoenas and searches. A **subpoena** is an order to appear at a particular time and place to provide evidence. A **subpoena** *duces tecum* requires the person to appear and bring specified documents. Businesses and other organizations intensely dislike subpoenas and resent government agents plowing through records and questioning employees. Nonetheless, a subpoena is generally lawful if it is *relevant* to a valid investigation, does not create an *unreasonable burden* on the company, and does not seek *privileged material*, such as documents exchanged between an executive and the company's lawyer.

**Subpoena**
An order to appear at a particular time and place. A **subpoena** *duces tecum* requires the person to produce certain documents or things.

## ADJUDICATION

To **adjudicate** a case is to hold a hearing about an issue and then decide it. Agencies adjudicate countless cases. The FCC adjudicates which applicant for a new television license is best qualified. The Occupational Safety and Health Administration (OSHA) holds adversarial hearings to determine whether a manufacturing plant is dangerous.

Most adjudications begin with a hearing before an **administrative law judge** (ALJ). There is no jury. An ALJ is an employee of the agency but is expected to be impartial in her rulings. All parties are represented by counsel. The rules of evidence are informal, and an ALJ may receive any testimony or documents that will help resolve the dispute.

After all evidence is taken, the ALJ makes a decision. The losing party has a right to appeal to an appellate board within the agency. The appellate board has the power to make a *de novo* decision, meaning it may ignore the ALJ's decision. A party unhappy with that decision may appeal to federal court.

**Adjudicate**
To hold a formal hearing about an issue and then decide it.

**Administrative law judge**
An agency employee who acts as an impartial decision maker.

## CHAPTER CONCLUSION

**The legal battle over power never stops.** When may a state outlaw waterfront development? Prohibit symbolic speech? Other issues are just as thorny, such as when a bystander is liable to assist someone in peril, or whether a government agency may subpoena corporate documents. Some of the questions will be answered by that extraordinary document, the Constitution, while others require statutory, common law, or administrative responses. There are no easy answers to any of the questions because there has never been a democracy so large, so diverse, or so powerful.

## EXAM REVIEW

1.  **CONSTITUTION**  The Constitution is a series of compromises about power. (p. 48)

.................................................................................................

2.  **CONSTITUTIONAL POWERS**  Article I of the Constitution creates the Congress and grants all legislative power to it. Article II establishes the office of president and defines executive powers. Article III creates the Supreme Court and permits lower federal courts; the article also outlines the powers of the federal judiciary. (p. 48)

.................................................................................................

3.  **COMMERCE CLAUSE**  Under the Commerce Clause, Congress may regulate interstate trade. A state law that interferes with interstate commerce is void. (p. 49)

**EXAM Strategy**

**Question:**  Maine exempted many charitable institutions from real estate taxes but denied this benefit to a charity that primarily benefited out-of-state residents. Camp Newfound was a Christian Science organization, and 95 percent of its summer campers came from other states. Camp Newfound sued Maine. Discuss.

**Strategy:**  The state was treating organizations differently depending on the states their campers come from. This raised Commerce Clause issues. What does that clause state? (See the "Result" at the end of this section.)

4.  **PRESIDENTIAL POWERS**  The president's key powers include making agency appointments, proposing legislation, conducting foreign policy, and acting as commander in chief of the armed forces. (p. 49)

.................................................................................................

5.  **FEDERAL COURTS**  The federal courts adjudicate cases and also exercise judicial review, which is the right to declare a statute or governmental action unconstitutional and void. (p. 49)

.................................................................................................

6.  **FIRST AMENDMENT**  The First Amendment protects most freedom of speech, although the government may regulate the time, place, and manner of speech. (p. 50)

.................................................................................................

7.  **PROCEDURAL DUE PROCESS**  Procedural due process is required whenever the government attempts to take liberty or property. (p. 53)

.................................................................................................

**8.** **TAKINGS CLAUSE** The Takings Clause prohibits a state from taking private property for public use without just compensation. (p. 53)

**9.** **EQUAL PROTECTION CLAUSE** The Equal Protection Clause generally requires the government to treat people equally. (p. 54)

**10.** **LEGISLATION** Bills originate in congressional committees and go from there to the full House of Representatives or Senate. If both houses pass the bill, the legislation normally must go to a conference committee to resolve differences between the two versions. If the president signs the bill, it becomes a statute; if he vetoes it, Congress can pass it over his veto with a two-thirds majority in each house. (p. 55)

**11.** ***STARE DECISIS*** *Stare decisis* means "let the decision stand," and it indicates that once a court has decided a particular issue, it will generally apply the same rule in future cases. (p. 56)

**12.** **COMMON LAW** The common law evolves in awkward fits and starts because courts attempt to achieve two contradictory purposes: predictability and flexibility. (p. 56)

**13.** **BYSTANDER RULE** The common-law bystander rule holds that, generally, no one has a duty to assist someone in peril unless the bystander himself created the danger. Courts have carved some exceptions during the last 100 years, but the basic rule still stands. (p. 56)

**14.** **ADMINISTRATIVE AGENCIES** Congress creates federal administrative agencies to supervise many industries. Agencies promulgate rules and investigate and adjudicate cases. (p. 59)

**EXAM Strategy**

**Question:** Hiller Systems, Inc. was performing a safety inspection on board the M/V *Cape Diamond,* an oceangoing vessel, when an accident occurred involving the fire extinguishing equipment. Two men were killed. The Occupational Safety and Health Administration (OSHA), a federal agency attempted to investigate, but Hiller refused to permit any of its employees to speak to OSHA investigators. What could OSHA do to pursue the investigation? What limits would there be on OSHA's work?

**Strategy:** Agencies makes rules, investigate, and adjudicate. Which is involved here? (Investigation.) During an investigation, what power has an agency to force a company to produce data? What are the limits on that power? (See the "Result" at the end of this section.)

**3. Result:** The Commerce Clause holds that a state statute that discriminates against interstate commerce is almost always invalid. Maine was subsidizing charities that served in-state residents and penalizing those that attracted campers from elsewhere. The tax rule violated the Commerce Clause and was void.

**14. Result:** OSHA can issue a subpoena *duces tecum,* demanding that those on board the ship, and their supervisors, appear for questioning and bring with them all relevant documents. OSHA may ask for anything that is (1) relevant to the investigation, (2) not unduly burdensome, and (3) not privileged. Conversations between one of the ship inspectors and his supervisor is clearly relevant; a discussion between the supervisor and the company's lawyer is privileged due to attorney-client privilege.

# PRACTICE EXAM

## MATCHING QUESTIONS

Match the following terms with their definitions:

___ A. Statute

___ B. Equal Protection Clause

___ C. Judicial review

___ D. Takings Clause

___ E. *Stare decisis*

___ F. Promulgate

1. The power of federal courts to examine the constitutionality of statutes and acts of government.

2. The part of the Constitution that requires compensation in eminent domain cases.

3. The rule that requires courts to decide cases based on precedent.

4. The act of an administrative agency creating a new rule.

5. A law passed by a legislative body.

6. Generally prohibits regulations based on gender, race, or fundamental rights.

## TRUE/FALSE QUESTIONS

Circle true or false:

1. T  F  The government may not prohibit a political rally, but it may restrict when and where the demonstrators meet.

2. T  F  The Due Process Clause requires that any citizen is entitled to a jury trial before any right or property interest is taken.

3. T  F  The government has the right to take a homeowner's property for a public purpose.

4. T  F  A subpoena is an order punishing a defendant who has violated a court ruling.

5. T  F  A bystander who sees someone in peril must come to that person's assistance, but only if he can do so without endangering himself or others.

6. T  F  Administrative agencies play an advisory role in the life of many industries but do not have the legal authority to enforce their opinions.

## MULTIPLE-CHOICE QUESTIONS

7. Colorado passes a hotel tax of 8 percent for Colorado residents and 15 percent for out-of-state visitors. The new law

   A. Is valid, based on the Supremacy Clause

   B. Is void, based on the Supremacy Clause

   C. Is valid, based on the Commerce Clause

   D. Is void, based on the Commerce Clause

   E. Is void, based on the Takings Clause

8. Suppose a state legislature approves an education plan for the next year that budgets $35 million for boys' athletics and $25 million for girls' athletics. Legislators explain the difference by saying, "In our experience, boys simply care more about sports than girls do." The new plan is

   A. Valid

   B. Void

   C. Permissible, based on the legislators' statutory research

   D. Permissible, but probably unwise

   E. Subject to the Takings Clause

9. Congress has passed a new bill, but the president does not like the law. What could happen next?

   A. The president must sign the bill whether he likes it or not.

   B. The president may veto the bill, in which case it is dead.

   C. The president may veto the bill, but Congress may attempt to override the veto.

   D. The president may ask the citizens to vote directly on the proposed law.

   E. The president may discharge the Congress and order new elections.

10. Which of these is an example of judicial review?

    A. A trial court finds a criminal defendant guilty.

    B. An appeals court reverses a lower court's ruling.

    C. An appeals court affirms a lower court's ruling.

    D. A federal court declares a statute unconstitutional.

    E. A Congressional committee interviews a potential Supreme Court justice.

11. Martine, a psychiatrist, is convinced that Lance, her patient, intends to kill his own father.

    A. Martine may not contact the father, because she is obligated to protect patient–therapist confidentiality.

    B. Martine *may* contact the father, but she is *not obligated* to take any steps at all.

    C. Martine must warn the father.

    D. Martine may seek judicial review of the case.

    E. Martine may warn Lance not to do anything, but she herself may not become involved.

12. What is an example of a subpoena?

    A. A court order to a company to stop polluting the air.

    B. A court order requiring a deponent to answer questions.

    C. A federal agency demands various internal documents from a corporation.

    D. The president orders troops called up in the national defense.

    E. The president orders Congress to pass a bill on an expedited schedule.

## SHORT-ANSWER QUESTIONS

13. In the early 1970s, President Richard Nixon became embroiled in the Watergate dispute. He was accused of covering up a criminal break-in at the national headquarters of the Democratic Party. Nixon denied any wrongdoing. A United States District Court judge ordered the president to produce tapes of conversations held in his office. Nixon knew that complying with the order would produce damaging evidence, probably destroying his presidency. He refused, claiming executive privilege. The case went to the Supreme Court. Nixon strongly implied that even if the Supreme Court ordered him to produce the tapes, he would refuse. What major constitutional issue did this raise?

14. Gilleo opposed American participation in the war in the Persian Gulf. She displayed a large sign on her front lawn that read, "Say No to War in the Persian Gulf, Call Congress Now." The city of Ladue prohibited signs on front lawns, and Gilleo sued. The city claimed that it was regulating "time, place, and manner." Explain that statement, and decide who should win.

15. ETHICS: Suppose you were on a state supreme court and faced with a restaurant choking case. Should you require restaurant employees to know and employ the Heimlich maneuver to assist a choking victim? If they do a bad job, they could cause additional injury. Should you permit them to do nothing at all? Is there a compromise position? What social policies are most important?

16. ROLE REVERSAL: Write an exam question that involves any two of these important Fifth Amendment protections: procedural due process, the Takings Clause, and the Equal Protection Clause.

# INTERNET RESEARCH PROBLEM

Research some pending legislation in Congress. Go to **http://www.senate.gov**, and click on "bills." Choose some key words that interest you, and see what your government is doing. Read the summary of the bill, if one is provided, or go to the text of the bill and scan the introduction. What do the sponsors of this bill hope to accomplish? Do you agree or disagree with their goals?

**You can find further practice problems in the Online Quiz at www.cengage.com/blaw/beatty.**

## CHAPTER 5

# INTENTIONAL TORTS AND BUSINESS TORTS

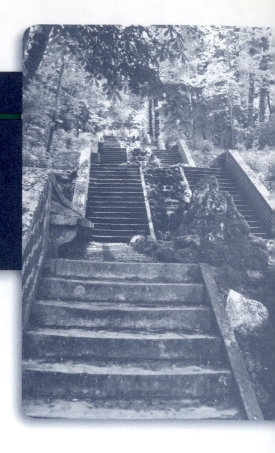

In a small Louisiana town, Don Mashburn ran a restaurant called Maison de Mashburn. *The New Orleans States-Item* newspaper reviewed his eatery, and here is what the article said:

> "'Tain't Creole, 'tain't Cajun, 'tain't French, 'tain't country American,'tain't good. I don't know how much real talent in cooking is hidden under the mélange of hideous sauces which make this food and the menu a travesty of pretentious amateurism but I find it all quite depressing. Put a yellow flour sauce on top of the duck, flame it for drama, and serve it with some horrible multi-flavored rice in hollowed-out fruit and what have you got? A well-cooked duck with an ugly sauce that tastes too sweet and thick and makes you want to scrape off the glop to eat the plain duck. [The stuffed eggplant was prepared by emptying] a shaker full (more or less) of paprika on top of it. [One sauce created] trout à la green plague [while another should have been called] yellow death on duck."

'Tain't Creole, 'tain't Cajun, 'tain't French, 'tain't country American,'tain't good.

Mashburn sued, claiming that the newspaper had committed libel, damaging his reputation and hurting his business.[1] Trout à la green plague will be the first course on our menu of tort law. Mashburn learned, as you will, why filing such a lawsuit is easier than winning it.

This odd word "tort" is borrowed from the French, meaning "wrong." And that is what it means in law: A tort is a wrong. More precisely, a **tort** is a violation of a duty imposed by the *civil* law. When a person breaks one of those duties and injures another, it is a tort. The injury could be to a person or her property. Libel is one example of a tort where, for example, a newspaper columnist falsely accuses someone of being an alcoholic. A surgeon who removes the wrong kidney from a patient commits a different kind of tort, called negligence. A business executive who deliberately steals a client away from a competitor, interfering with a valid contract, commits a tort called interference with a contract. A con artist who tricks money out of you with a phony offer to sell you a boat commits fraud, yet another tort.

> **Tort**
> A violation of a duty imposed by the civil law.

Because tort law is so broad, it takes a while to understand its boundaries. To start with, we must distinguish torts from criminal law.

It is a crime to steal a car, to embezzle money from a bank, to sell cocaine. As discussed in Chapter 1, society considers such behavior so threatening that the government itself will prosecute the wrongdoer, whether or not the car owner or bank president wants the case to go forward. A district attorney, who is paid by the government, will bring the case to court, seeking to send the defendant to prison and/or to fine him. If there is a fine, the money goes to the state, not to the victim.

In a tort case, it is up to the injured party, the plaintiff, to seek compensation. She must hire her own lawyer, who will file a lawsuit. Her lawyer must convince the court that the defendant breached some legal duty and ought to pay money damages to the plaintiff. The plaintiff has no power to send the defendant to jail. Bear in mind that a defendant's action might be both a crime *and* a tort. The con artist who tricks money out of you with a fake offer to sell you a boat has committed the tort of fraud. You may file a civil suit against him and will collect money damages if you can prove your case. The con artist has also committed the crime of fraud. The state will prosecute, seeking to imprison and fine him.

## EXAM *Strategy*

**Question:** Keith is driving while intoxicated. He swerves into the wrong lane and causes an accident, seriously injuring Marta. Who is more likely to file a tort lawsuit in this case, Marta or the state? Who is more likely to prosecute Keith for drunk driving? Could there be a lawsuit and a prosecution at the same time? In which case is Keith more likely to be found *guilty*, a civil suit or a criminal prosecution?

**Strategy:** Only one of these parties can prosecute a criminal case. And in only one kind of case can a defendant be found guilty.

**Result:** Only the government prosecutes criminal cases. Marta may urgently request a prosecution, but the District Attorney will make the final decision. And only in a criminal case can a defendant be found guilty. However, Marta is free to sue Keith for the injuries he has caused, even if he is simultaneously prosecuted. She can recover money damages for her injuries, whether or not Keith is found guilty in the criminal case.

---

[1] *Mashburn v. Collins*, 355 So.2d 879 (La. 1977).

Tort law is divided into categories. In this chapter, we consider **intentional torts**, that is, harm caused by a deliberate action. The newspaper columnist who wrongly accuses someone of being a drunk has committed the intentional tort of libel. The con artist who tricks money from you has committed the intentional tort of fraud. In the next chapter, we examine **negligence and strict liability,** which are injuries caused by neglect and oversight rather than by deliberate conduct.

## · INTENTIONAL TORTS ·

## DEFAMATION

The First Amendment guarantees the right to free speech, a vital freedom that enables us to protect other rights. But that freedom is not absolute. Courts have long recognized that we cannot permit irresponsible speech to harm another's reputation. Free speech should not include the right to falsely accuse your neighbor of selling drugs. That sounds sensible enough, yet once we say that free speech and personal reputation both deserve protection, we have guaranteed perpetual conflict.

The law of defamation concerns false statements that harm someone's reputation. Defamatory statements can be written or spoken. Written defamation is **libel**. Suppose a newspaper accuses a local retail store of programming its cash registers to overcharge customers, when the store has never done so. That is libel. Oral defamation is **slander**. If Professor Wilson, in class, refers to Sally Student as a drug dealer, and Sally has never sold anything stronger than Arm & Hammer, he has slandered her. (Defamatory comments made on television and radio are considered libel because the vast audiences mean that the damage is similar to that done by newspapers.)

There are four elements to a defamation case. An **element** is a fact that a plaintiff must prove to win a lawsuit. The plaintiff in any kind of lawsuit must prove all the elements to prevail. The elements in a defamation case are:

- *Defamatory statement.* This is a statement likely to harm another person's reputation. When Professor Wisdom accuses Sally of dealing drugs, that will clearly harm her reputation.
- *Falseness.* The statement must be false to be defamatory. If Sally Student actually sold marijuana to a classmate, then Professor Wisdom has a defense to slander.
- *Communicated.* The statement must be communicated to at least one person other than the plaintiff. If Wisdom speaks only to Sally and accuses her of dealing drugs, there is no slander. But there is if he shouts the accusation in a crowded hall.
- *Injury.* In slander cases, the plaintiff generally must show some injury. Sally's injury would be a damaged reputation in the school, embarrassment, and humiliation. But in libel cases, the law is willing to assume injury. Because libel is written, and more permanent than slander, courts award damages even without proof of injury.

## OPINION

Remember that the plaintiff must demonstrate a "false" statement. Opinions, though, cannot be proven true or false. For that reason, **opinion is generally a valid defense in a defamation suit.**

Mr. Mashburn, who opened the chapter suing over his restaurant review, lost his case. The court held that a reasonable reader would have understood the statements to be opinion only. "A shaker full of paprika" and "yellow death on duck" were not to be taken literally but were merely the author's expression of his personal dislike. What about a crude description of a college official, appearing in the school's newspaper? You be the judge.

# YOU *be the* JUDGE

## YEAGLE v. COLLEGIATE TIMES
255 Va. 293, 497 S.E.2d 136, 1998 Va. LEXIS 32
Virginia Supreme Court, 1998

**Facts:** Sharon Yeagle was assistant to the vice-president of student affairs at the Virginia Polytechnic Institute and State University. The state had an academic honors program called the Governor's Fellows Program, and one of Yeagle's duties was to help students apply. The school newspaper, the *Collegiate Times,* published an article describing the university's success at placing students in the Fellows Program. The article included a block quotation in larger print, attributed to Yeagle. Underneath Yeagle's name was the phrase "Director of Butt Licking."

Yeagle sued the *Collegiate Times,* alleging that the vulgar phrase defamed her. The trial court dismissed the case, ruling that no reasonable person would take the words literally and that the phrase conveyed no factual information. Yeagle appealed to the Virginia Supreme Court.

**You Be the Judge: Was the phrase defamatory, or was it deliberate exaggeration that no reasonable person would take literally?**

**Argument for Yeagle:** The disgusting phrase that the *Collegiate Times* used to describe Ms. Yeagle is defamatory for several reasons. The conduct described by the words happens to be a crime in Virginia, a violation of the state sodomy statute. Thus the paper is accusing her of criminal offenses that she has never committed. That is defamation, and in itself entitles Ms. Yeagle to damages.

If, however, defendants argue that the phrase must be interpreted figuratively, then the newspaper has accused Ms. Yeagle of currying favor, or directing others to do so, in a uniquely degrading fashion. The *Collegiate Times* is informing its readers that she performs her job in a sleazy, unprofessional manner evidently because she cannot succeed by merit. The paper is suggesting that she is devoid of integrity and capable of achieving goals only by devious, deviant methods.

**Argument for Collegiate Times:** Statements are defamatory only if a reasonable reader would understand them as asserting facts that can be proven true or false. There is no such statement in this case, and no defamation. No reasonable reader, after finishing an article about the Fellows Program, would believe that Ms. Yeagle was actually the director as described, or even that there is such a job.

The paper chose to inject humor into its coverage of a mundane issue, for the entertainment of its readers. The great majority of the paper's readers appreciate lively language that is at times irreverent. For anyone who is quick to take offense, the proper recourse is not to file suit, but to put down the paper.

# PUBLIC PERSONALITIES

The rules of the game change for those who play in the open. Public officials and public figures receive less protection from defamation. An example of a public official is a police chief. A public figure is a movie star, for example, or a multimillionaire playboy constantly in the news. In the landmark case *New York Times Co. v. Sullivan,* the Supreme Court ruled that the free exchange of information is vital in a democracy and is protected by the First Amendment to the Constitution. If the information wounds public people, that may just be tough luck.

The rule from the *New York Times v. Sullivan* case is that a public official or public figure can win a defamation case only by proving actual malice by the defendant. **Actual malice** means that the defendant knew the statement was false or acted with reckless disregard of the truth. If the plaintiff merely shows that the defendant newspaper printed incorrect statements, even very damaging ones, that will not suffice to win the suit. In the *New York Times v. Sullivan* case, the police chief of Birmingham, Alabama claimed that the *Times* falsely accused him of racial violence in his job. He lost because he could not prove that the *Times* had acted with actual malice. If he had shown that the *Times* knew the accusation was false and published it anyway, he would have won.

**Actual malice**
means that the defendant in a defamation suit knew his or her statement was false or acted with reckless disregard of the truth.

## False Imprisonment

**False imprisonment**
The intentional restraint of another person without reasonable cause or consent.

**False imprisonment** is the intentional restraint of another person without reasonable cause and without consent. False imprisonment cases most commonly arise in retail stores, which sometimes detain employees or customers for suspected theft. Most states now have statutes governing the detention of suspected shoplifters. **Generally, a store may detain a customer or worker for alleged shoplifting provided there is a reasonable basis for the suspicion and the detention is done reasonably.** To detain a customer in the manager's office for 20 minutes and question him about where he got an item is lawful. To chain that customer to a display counter for three hours and humiliate him in front of other customers is unreasonable and false imprisonment.

## Battery and Assault

**Battery**
Intentional, offensive touching.

These torts are related but not identical. **Battery** is an intentional touching of another person in a way that is unwanted or offensive. There need be no intention to hurt the plaintiff. If the defendant intended to do the physical act, and a reasonable plaintiff would be offended by it, battery has occurred.

Suppose an irate parent throws a chair at a referee during his daughter's basketball game, breaking the man's jaw. It is irrelevant that the father did not intend to injure the referee. But a parent who cheerfully slaps the winning coach on the back has not committed battery because a reasonable coach would not be offended.

**Assault**
An action that causes another person to fear an imminent battery.

**Assault** occurs when a defendant performs some action that makes a plaintiff fear an imminent battery. It is assault even if the battery never occurs. Suppose Ms. Wilson shouts "Think fast!" at her husband and hurls a toaster at him. He turns and sees it flying at him. His fear of being struck is enough to win a case of assault, even if the toaster misses. If the toaster happens to strike him, Ms. Wilson has also committed battery.

### EXAM *Strategy*

**Question:** Patrick owns a fast food restaurant that is repeatedly painted with graffiti. He is convinced that 15-year-old Juan, a frequent customer, is the culprit. The next time Juan comes to the restaurant, Patrick locks the men's room door while Juan is inside. Patrick calls the police, but because of a misunderstanding, the police are very slow to arrive. Juan shouts for help, banging on the door, but Patrick does not release him for two hours. Juan sues for assault, battery, and false imprisonment. A psychiatrist testifies that Juan has suffered serious psychological harm. Will Juan win?

**Strategy:** The question focuses on the distinction between three intentional torts. Battery: an offensive touching. Assault: causing an imminent fear of battery. False imprisonment: a store may detain someone if it does so reasonably.

**Result:** Locking Juan up for two hours, based on an unproven suspicion, was clearly unreasonable. Patrick has committed false imprisonment and Juan will win. However, Patrick did not touch Juan, or create a reasonable fear of contact, so there has been no battery or assault.

## Fraud

**Fraud**
is injuring someone by deliberate deception.

**Fraud** is injuring another person by deliberate deception. It is fraud to sell real estate knowing that there is a large toxic waste deposit underground, of which the buyer is ignorant. Fraud is a tort, but it typically occurs during the negotiation or performance of a contract, and it is discussed in detail in Unit 2, on contracts.

## Intentional Infliction of Emotional Distress

A credit officer was struggling in vain to locate Sheehan, who owed money on his car. The officer finally phoned Sheehan's mother, falsely identified herself as a hospital employee, and said she needed to find Sheehan because his children had been in a serious auto accident. The horrified mother provided Sheehan's whereabouts, which enabled the company to seize his car. But Sheehan himself spent seven hours frantically trying to locate his supposedly injured children, who in fact were fine. He was not injured physically, but he sued for his emotional distress—and won. The **intentional infliction of emotional distress** results from extreme and outrageous conduct that causes serious emotional harm. The credit company was liable for the intentional infliction of emotional distress.[2] The following case arose in a setting that guarantees controversy—an abortion clinic.

> **Intentional infliction of emotional distress**
> Extreme and outrageous conduct that causes serious emotional harm.

## JANE DOE AND NANCY ROE v. LYNN MILLS

212 MICH. APP. 73, 536 N.W.2D 824, 1995 MICH. APP. LEXIS 313
MICHIGAN COURT OF APPEALS, 1995

### CASE SUMMARY

**Facts:** Late one night, an antiabortion protestor named Robert Thomas climbed into a Dumpster located behind the Women's Advisory Center, an abortion clinic. He found documents indicating that the plaintiffs were soon to have abortions at the clinic. Thomas gave the information to Lynn Mills. The next day, Mills and Sister Lois Mitoraj created signs, using the women's names, indicating that they were about to undergo abortions, and urging them not to "kill their babies."

Doe and Roe (not their real names) sued, claiming intentional infliction of emotional distress (as well as breach of privacy, discussed later in this chapter). The trial court dismissed the lawsuit, ruling that the defendants' conduct was not extreme and outrageous. The plaintiffs appealed.

**Issue:** *Have the plaintiffs made a valid claim of intentional infliction of emotional distress?*

**Decision:** The plaintiffs have made a valid claim of intentional infliction of emotional distress.

**Reasoning:** A defendant is liable for the intentional infliction of emotional distress only when his conduct is outrageous in character, extreme in degree, and utterly intolerable in a civilized community. A good test is whether the average member of the community would respond to the defendant's conduct by exclaiming, "Outrageous!"

These defendants have a constitutional right to protest against abortions, but they have no such right to publicize private matters. Their behavior here might well cause the average person to say, "Outrageous!" The plaintiffs are entitled to a trial, so that a jury can decide whether the defendants have inflicted emotional distress.

## · DAMAGES ·

### COMPENSATORY DAMAGES

Mitchel Bien, a deaf mute, enters the George Grubbs Nissan dealership, where folks sell cars aggressively. Very aggressively. Maturelli, a salesman, and Bien communicate by writing messages back and forth. Maturelli takes Bien's own car keys, and the two then test drive a 300ZX. Bien says he does not want the car, but Maturelli escorts him back inside and fills out a sales sheet. Bien repeatedly asks for his keys, but Maturelli only laughs, pressuring him to buy the new car. Minutes pass. Hours pass. Bien becomes frantic, writing a dozen notes, begging to leave, threatening to call the police. Maturelli mocks Bien and his physical disabilities. Finally, after four hours, the customer escapes.

> Bien becomes frantic, writing a dozen notes, begging to leave, threatening to call the police.

---

[2] *Ford Motor Credit Co. v. Sheehan,* 373 So. 2d 956, 1979 Fla. App. LEXIS 15416 (Fla. Dist. Ct. App. 1979).

Bien sues for the intentional infliction of emotional distress. Two former salesmen from Grubbs testify that they have witnessed customers cry, yell, and curse as a result of the aggressive tactics. Doctors state that the incident has traumatized Bien, dramatically reducing his confidence and self-esteem and preventing his return to work even three years later.

The jury awards Bien damages. But how does a jury calculate the money? For that matter, why should a jury even try? Money can never erase pain or undo a permanent injury. The answer is simple: Money, however inexact and ineffective, is the only thing a court has to give. A successful plaintiff generally receives **compensatory damages**, meaning an amount of money that the court believes will restore him to the position he was in before the defendant's conduct caused an injury. Here is how damages are figured.

**Compensatory damages** are intended to restore the plaintiff to the position he was in before the defendant's conduct caused injury.

First, a plaintiff receives money for medical expenses that he has proven by producing bills from doctors, hospitals, physical therapists, and psychotherapists. If a doctor testifies that he needs future treatment, Bien will offer evidence of how much that will cost. The **single recovery principle** requires a court to settle the matter once and for all, by awarding a lump sum for past and future expenses.

**Single recovery principle** requires a court to settle a legal case once and for all, by awarding a lump sum for past and future expenses.

Second, the defendants are liable for lost wages, past and future. The court takes the number of days or months that Bien has missed (and will miss) work and multiplies that times his salary.

Third, a plaintiff is paid for pain and suffering. Bien testifies about how traumatic the four hours were and how the experience has affected his life. He may state that he now fears shopping, suffers nightmares, and seldom socializes. To bolster the case, a plaintiff uses expert testimony, such as the psychiatrists who testified for Bien. In this case, the jury awarded Bien $573,815, calculated as in the following table.[3]

| | |
|---|---:|
| Past medical | $ 70.00 |
| Future medical | 6,000.00 |
| Past rehabilitation | 3,205.00 |
| Past lost earning capacity | 112,910.00 |
| Future lost earning capacity | 34,650.00 |
| Past physical symptoms and discomfort | 50,000.00 |
| Future physical symptoms and discomfort | 50,000.00 |
| Past emotional injury and mental anguish | 101,980.00 |
| Future emotional injury and mental anguish | 200,000.00 |
| Past loss of society and reduced ability to socially interact with family, former fiancee, and friends, and hearing (i.e., nondeaf) people in general | 10,000.00 |
| Future loss of society and reduced ability to socially interact with family, former fiancee, and friends, and hearing people | 5,000.00 |
| TOTAL | $573,815.00 |

# Punitive Damages

Richard Boeken began smoking Marlboro cigarettes at the age of 10. Decades later, as he was dying of lung cancer, he sued Philip Morris, the company that manufactured the cigarettes. While

---

[3] The compensatory damages are described in *George Grubbs Enterprises v. Bien,* 881 S.W.2d 843, 1994 Tex. App. LEXIS 1870 (Tex. Ct. App. 1994). In addition to the compensatory damages described, the jury awarded $5 million in punitive damages. The Texas Supreme Court reversed the award of punitive damages, but not the compensatory. Id., 900 S.W.2d 337, 1995 Tex. LEXIS 91 (Tex. 1995). The high court did not dispute the appropriateness of punitive damages, but reversed because the trial court failed to instruct the jury properly as to how it should determine the assets actually under the defendants' control, an issue essential to punitive damages but not compensatory damages.

the lawsuit was pending, Boeken died. When the jury heard all the evidence, it was clearly angry about the tobacco company's behavior. The jurors awarded Boeken's widow $5.5 million in compensatory damages. As we will see in a moment, they also awarded a larger sum in punitive damages—much, much larger.

Punitive damages are not designed to compensate the plaintiff for harm, because compensatory damages will have done that. **Punitive damages** are intended to punish the defendant for conduct that is extreme and outrageous. Courts award these damages in relatively few cases. When an award of punitive damages is made, it is generally in a case of intentional tort, although they also occur in negligence suits. The idea behind punitive damages is that certain behavior is so unacceptable that society must make an example of it. A large award of money should deter the defendant from repeating the mistake and others from ever making it.

Although a jury has wide discretion in awarding punitive damages, the U.S. Supreme Court has ruled that a verdict must be reasonable. In awarding punitive damages, a court must consider three "guideposts":

- The reprehensibility of the defendant's conduct.
- The ratio between the harm suffered and the award. Generally, the punitive award should not be more than nine times the compensatory award.
- The difference between the punitive award and any civil penalties used in similar cases.

Despite the guidelines, dramatic cases may still lead to large awards, as Richard Boeken's lawsuit illustrates.

**Punitive damages**
punish the defendant for conduct that is extreme and outrageous.

## Boeken v. Philip Morris, Incorporated

127 Cal. App. 4th 1640, 26 CalRptr. 3d 638
California Court of Appeals, 2005

### CASE SUMMARY

**Facts:** Richard Boeken began smoking Marlboro cigarettes in the 1950s. Countless advertisements, targeted at boys aged 10 to 18, convinced him and his friends that the "Marlboro man" was powerful, healthy, and macho. Eventually Richard changed to Marlboro Lights cigarettes, but continued smoking into the 1990s, when he was diagnosed with lung cancer. He filed suit against Philip Morris, the cigarette manufacturer, for fraud and other torts. He died of cancer before the case was concluded.

The jury found Philip Morris liable for fraudulently concealing that cigarettes were addictive and carcinogenic. It awarded Boeken $5.5 million in compensatory damages, and also assessed punitive damages—of $3 *billion.* The trial judge reduced the punitive award to $100 million. Philip Morris appealed.

**Issue:** *Was the punitive damage award excessive?*

**Decision:** The appellate court reduced the punitive damages award to $50 million.

**Reasoning:** Philip Morris manufactured a product that it knew caused addiction, disease, and death. The company added chemicals to make Marlboros more addictive and easier to draw into the lungs. It targeted adolescent males and lured them to the product with misleading advertisements.

Philip Morris knew that there was no reason to believe Marlboro Lights or Ultralights were any safer than its Reds, yet the company was still marketing "light" cigarettes at the time of trial. And Philip Morris was still adding urea to Marlboro tobacco, causing more nicotine to reach the smoker's lungs. One expert testified that of the people who die every year in this country from smoking-related disease, 200,000 are attributable to Philip Morris products.

Punitive damages would not deter wrongdoers if they could easily absorb the award. Philip Morris earned a profit of nearly $15 million per day. The company's conduct and profits justified a punitive to compensatory damages ratio of at least 9 to 1. A reduced punitive damages award of $50 million was fair.

### *Tort Reform and the* Exxon Valdez

Some people believe that jury awards are excessive and need statutory reform, while others argue that the evidence demonstrates punitive awards are rare and modest in size. About half of the states have passed limits. The laws vary, but many work this way. A jury is permitted to award whatever it considers fair for economic damages, meaning lost wages and medical expenses. However, noneconomic damages (pain and suffering), together with any punitive award, may not exceed a prescribed limit, such as three times the economic damages, or sometimes a flat cap, such as $250,000 total. These restrictions can drastically lower the total verdict.

In the famous *Exxon Valdez* case, the U.S. Supreme Court placed a severe limit on a certain type of punitive award. The ship's captain had been drunk, and when the *Exxon Valdez* ran aground, it caused massive, permanent environmental damage. The jury awarded $5 billion in punitive damages, which the Supreme Court reduced to $507 million, equivalent to the compensatory damages awarded. However, it is unclear how influential the decision will be. The case arose in the isolated area of maritime law. Courts may decide not to apply the *Exxon Valdez* reasoning in other cases.

## · BUSINESS TORTS ·

## TORTIOUS INTERFERENCE WITH A CONTRACT

Competition is the essence of business. Successful corporations compete aggressively, and the law permits and expects them to. But there are times when healthy competition becomes illegal interference. This is called **tortious interference with a contract**. To win such a case, a plaintiff must establish four elements:

**Tortious interference with a contract**
occurs when a defendant deliberately harms a contractual relationship between two other parties.

• There was a contract between the plaintiff and a third party.

• The defendant knew of the contract.

• The defendant improperly induced the third party to breach the contract or made performance of the contract impossible; and

• There was injury to the plaintiff.

Because businesses routinely compete for customers, employees, and market share, it is not always easy to identify tortious interference. There is nothing wrong with two companies bidding against each other to buy a parcel of land, and nothing wrong with one corporation doing everything possible to convince the seller to ignore all competitors. But once a company has signed a contract to buy the land, it is improper to induce the seller to break the deal. The most commonly disputed issues in these cases concern elements 1 and 3: Was there a contract between the plaintiff and another party? Did the defendant improperly induce a party to breach it? Defendants will try to show that the plaintiff had no contract.

## INTRUSION

**Intrusion**
into someone's private life is a tort if a reasonable person would find it offensive

**Intrusion** into someone's private life is a tort if a reasonable person would find it offensive. Peeping through someone's windows or wiretapping his telephone are obvious examples of intrusion. In a famous case involving a "paparazzo" photographer and Jacqueline Kennedy Onassis, the court found that the photographer had invaded her privacy by making a career out of photographing her. He had bribed doormen to gain access to hotels and restaurants she visited, had jumped out of bushes to photograph her young children, and had driven powerboats dangerously close to her.

The court ordered him to stop.[4] Nine years later, the paparazzo was found in contempt of court for again taking photographs too close to Ms. Onassis. He agreed to stop once and for all—in exchange for a suspended contempt sentence.

# COMMERCIAL EXPLOITATION

**Commercial exploitation** prohibits the unauthorized use of another person's likeness or voice for commercial purposes. For example, it would be illegal to run a magazine ad showing actress Keira Knightley holding a can of soda, without her permission. The ad would imply that she endorses the product. Someone's identity is her own, and it cannot be exploited unless she permits it. Ford Motor Company hired a singer to imitate Bette Midler's version of a popular song. The imitation was so good that most listeners were fooled into believing that Ms. Midler was endorsing the product. That, ruled a court, violated her right to commercial exploitation.

> **Commercial exploitation** prohibits the unauthorized use of another person's likeness or voice for business purposes.

---

[4] *Galella v. Onassis,* 487 F. 2d 986, 1973 U.S.App.LEXIS 7901 (2d Cir. 1973).

## CHAPTER CONCLUSION

This chapter has been a potpourri of sin, a bubbling cauldron of conduct best avoided. Although tortious acts and their consequences are diverse, two generalities apply. First, the boundaries of intentional torts are imprecise, the outcome of a particular case depending to a considerable extent upon the fact finder who analyzes it. Second, the thoughtful executive and the careful citizen, aware of the shifting standards and potentially vast liability, will strive to ensure that his or her conduct never provides that fact finder an opportunity to give judgment.

## EXAM REVIEW

1.  **TORT**  A tort is a violation of a duty imposed by the civil law. (p. 67)

..................................................................................................

2.  **DEFAMATION**  Defamation involves a defamatory statement that is false, uttered to a third person, and causes an injury. (p. 68)

**EXAM Strategy**

**Question:**  Benzaquin had a radio talk show. On the program, he complained about an incident in which state trooper Fleming had stopped his car, apparently for lack of a proper license plate and safety sticker. Benzaquin explained that the license plate had been stolen and the sticker fallen onto the dashboard, but Fleming refused to let him drive away. Benzaquin and two young grandsons had to find other transportation. On the show, Benzaquin angrily recounted the incident, then described Fleming and troopers generally: "arrogants wearing trooper's uniforms like tights"; "little monkey, you wind him up and he does his thing"; "we're not paying them to be dictators and Nazis"; "this man is an absolute barbarian, a lunkhead, a meathead." Fleming sued Benzaquin for defamation. Comment.

**Strategy:**  Review the elements of defamation. Can these statements be proven true or false? If not, what is the result? Look at the defenses. Does one apply? (See the "Result" at the end of this section.)

**3.** **FALSE IMPRISONMENT** False imprisonment is the intentional restraint of another person without reasonable cause and without consent. (p. 70)

**4.** **BATTERY AND ASSAULT** Battery is an intentional touching of another person in a way that is unwanted or offensive. Assault involves an act that makes the plaintiff fear an imminent battery. (p. 70)

**EXAM Strategy**

**Question:** Caudle worked at Betts Lincoln-Mercury dealer. During an office party, many of the employees, including president Betts, were playing with an electric auto condenser, which gave a slight shock when touched. Some employees played catch with it. Betts shocked Caudle on the back of his neck, and chased him around. The shock later caused Caudle to suffer headaches, to pass out, numbness, and eventually to require nerve surgery. He sued Betts for battery. Betts defended by saying that it was all horseplay and that he had intended no harm. Please rule.

**Strategy:** Betts argues that he intended no harm. Is intent to harm an element of Caudle's case? (See the "Result" at the end of this section.)

**5.** **INTENTIONAL INFLICTION OF EMOTIONAL DISTRESS** The intentional infliction of emotional distress involves extreme and outrageous conduct that causes serious emotional harm. (p. 71)

**6.** **COMPENSATORY DAMAGES** Compensatory damages are the normal remedy in a tort case. In unusual cases, the court may award punitive damages, not to compensate the plaintiff but to punish the defendant. (p. 72)

**7.** **TORTIOUS INTERFERENCE WITH A CONTRACT** Tortious interference with a contract involves the defendant unfairly harming an existing contract. (p. 74)

**8.** **COMMERCIAL EXPLOITATION** protects the exclusive right to use one's own name, likeness, or voice. (p. 75)

**2. Result:** The court ruled in favor of Benzaquin, because a reasonable person would understand the words to be opinion and ridicule. They are not statements of fact because most of them could not be proven true or false. A statement like "dictators and Nazis" is not taken literally by anyone.[5]

**4. Result:** The court held that it was irrelevant that Betts had shown no malice toward Caudle nor intended to hurt him. Betts intended the *physical contact* with Caudle, and even though he could not foresee everything that would happen, he is liable for all consequences of his intended physical action.

---

[5] *Fleming v. Benzaquin*, 390 Mass. 175, 454 N.E.2d 95 (1983).

# PRACTICE EXAM

## MATCHING QUESTIONS

Match the following terms with their definitions:

___ A. Interference with a contract

___ B. Fraud

___ C. Defamation

___ D. False imprisonment

___ E. Punitive damages

___ F. Intentional infliction of emotional distress

___ G. Commercial exploitation

1. Money awarded to punish the wrongdoer
2. Intentionally restraining another person without reasonable cause
3. Intentional deception, frequently used to obtain a contract with another party
4. Deliberately stealing a client who has a contract with another
5. Violation of the exclusive right to use one's own name, likeness, or voice
6. Using a false statement to damage someone's reputation
7. An act so extreme that an average person would say, "Outrageous!"

## TRUE/FALSE QUESTIONS

Circle true or false:

1. T  F  A store manager who believes a customer has stolen something may question him but not restrain him.

2. T  F  Becky punches Kelly in the nose. Becky has committed the tort of assault.

3. T  F  A defendant cannot be liable for defamation if the statement, no matter how harmful, is true.

4. T  F  In most cases, a winning plaintiff receives compensatory and punitive damages.

5. T  F  A beer company that wishes to include a celebrity's picture in its magazine ads must first obtain the celebrity's permission.

## MULTIPLE-CHOICE QUESTIONS

6. A valid defense in a defamation suit is

   A. Falseness
   B. Honest error
   C. Improbability
   D. Opinion
   E. Third-party reliance

7. Joe Student, irate that on an exam he received a B− rather than a B, stands up in class and throws his laptop at the professor. The professor sees it coming and ducks just in time; the laptop smashes against the chalkboard. Joe has committed

   A. Assault
   B. Battery
   C. Negligence
   D. Slander
   E. No tort, because the laptop missed the professor

8. Marsha, a supervisor, furiously berates Ted in front of 14 other employees, calling him "a loser, an incompetent, a failure as an employee and as a person." She hands around copies of Ted's work and for twenty minutes mocks his efforts. If Ted sues Marsha, his best claim will be

   A. Assault
   B. Battery
   C. Intentional infliction of emotional distress
   D. Negligence
   E. Interference with a contract

9. Rodney is a star player on the Los Angeles Lakers basketball team. He has two years remaining on his four-year contract. The Wildcats, a new team in the league, try to lure Rodney away from the Lakers by offering him more money, and Rodney agrees to leave Los Angeles. The Lakers sue. The Lakers will

A. Win a case of defamation

D. Win a case of negligence

B. Win a case of commercial exploitation

E. Lose

C. Win a case of intentional interference with a contract

10. Hank and Antonio, drinking in a bar, get into an argument that turns nasty. Hank punches Antonio several times, knocking him down and breaking his nose and collarbone. Which statement is true?

A. Antonio could sue Hank, who might be found guilty in his suit.

D. The state could prosecute Hank, but only with Antonio's permission.

B. Antonio and the state could start separate criminal cases against Hank.

E. If the state prosecutes Hank, he will be found liable or not liable, depending on the evidence.

C. Antonio could sue Hank, and the state could prosecute Hank.

## SHORT-ANSWER QUESTIONS

11. Caldwell was shopping in a K-Mart store, carrying a large purse. A security guard observed her look at various small items such as stain, hinges, and antenna wire. On occasion she bent down out of sight of the guard. The guard thought he saw Caldwell put something in her purse. Caldwell removed her glasses from her purse and returned them a few times. After she left, the guard approached her in the parking lot and said that he believed she had store merchandise in her pocketbook, but was unable to say what he thought was put there. Caldwell opened the purse, and the guard testified that he saw no K-Mart merchandise in it. The guard then told Caldwell to return to the store with him. They walked around the store for approximately 15 minutes, while the guard said six or seven times that he saw her put something in her purse. Caldwell left the store after another store employee indicated she could go. Caldwell sued. What kind of suit did she file, and what should the outcome be?

12. Tata Consultancy of Bombay, India, is an international computer consulting firm. It spends considerable time and effort recruiting the best personnel from India's leading technical schools. Tata employees sign an initial three-year employment commitment, often work overseas, and agree to work for a specified additional time when they return to India. Desai worked for Tata, but then he quit and formed a competing company, which he called Syntel. His new

company contacted Tata employees by phone, offering more money to come work for Syntel, bonuses, and assistance in obtaining permanent resident visas in the United States. At least sixteen former Tata employees left their work without completing their contractual obligations and went to work for Syntel. Tata sued. What did it claim, and what should be the result?

13. Johnny Carson was for many years the star of a well-known television show, *The Tonight Show*. For about twenty years, he was introduced nightly on the show with the phrase, "Here's Johnny!" A large segment of the television-watching public associated the phrase with Carson. A Michigan corporation was in the business of renting and selling portable toilets. The company chose the name "Here's Johnny Portable Toilets," and coupled the company name with the marketing phrase, "The World's Foremost Comedian." Carson sued. What claim is he making? Who should win, and why?

14. ETHICS: Fifteen-year-old Terri Stubblefield was riding in the backseat of a Ford Mustang II when the car was hit from behind. The Mustang was engulfed in a ball of fire, and Terri was severely burned. She died. Terri's family sued Ford, alleging that the car was badly designed—and that Ford knew it. At trial, Terri's family introduced evidence that Ford knew the fuel tank was dangerous and that it could have taken measures to make the tank safe. There was evidence that

Ford consciously decided not to remedy the fuel tanks in order to save money. The jury awarded $8 million in punitive damages to the family. Ford appealed. Should the punitive damages be affirmed? What are the obligations of a corporation when it knows that one of its products may be dangerous? Should we require a manufacturer to improve the safety of its cars if doing so will make them too expensive for many drivers? What would you do if you were a mid-level executive and saw evidence that your company was endangering the lives of consumers to save money? What would you do if you were on a jury and saw such evidence?

15. ROLE REVERSAL: Write a multiple-choice question about defamation in which one, and only one, element is missing from the plaintiff's case. Choose a set of answers that forces the student to isolate the missing element.

## INTERNET RESEARCH PROBLEM

Using the Internet, find a recent case in which a court awarded punitive damages for the intentional tort of assault, battery, intentional infliction of emotional distress, or false imprisonment. What facts led to the punitive damages award? Make your own award of punitive damages, and then compare your judgment with the court's.

You can find further practice problems in the Online Quiz at **www.cengage.com/blaw/beatty.**

# NEGLIGENCE AND STRICT LIABILITY

**Party time!** A fraternity at the University of Arizona welcomed new members, and the alcohol flowed freely. Several hundred people danced and shrieked and drank, and no one checked for proof of age. A common occurrence—but one that ended tragically. A minor student drove away, intoxicated, and slammed into another car. The other driver was gravely injured. The drunken student was obviously liable, but his insurance did not cover the huge medical bills. The injured man also sued the fraternity. Should the organization be legally responsible? The issue is one of negligence law. In this contentious area, courts continually face one question: When someone is injured, how far should responsibility extend?

> **Several hundred people danced and shrieked and drank, and no one checked for proof of age.**

# ▪ NEGLIGENCE ▪

We might call negligence the "unintentional" tort because it concerns harm that arises by accident. A person, or perhaps an organization, does some act, not expecting to hurt anyone, yet someone is harmed. Should a court impose liability? The fraternity members who gave the party never wanted—or thought—that an innocent man would suffer terrible damage. But he did. Is it in society's interest to hold the fraternity responsible?

**Palsgraf**   Before we can answer this question, we need some guidance. Things go wrong all the time, and people are hurt in large ways and small. Society needs a method of analyzing negligence cases consistently and fairly. One of America's greatest judges, Benjamin Cardozo, offered his thoughts more than 75 years ago. In a case called *Palsgraf v. Long Island Railroad,* he made a decision that still dominates negligence thinking today.

Helen Palsgraf was waiting on a railroad platform. As a train began to leave the station, a man carrying a package ran to catch it. He jumped aboard but looked unsteady, so a guard on the car reached out to help him as another guard, on the platform, pushed from behind. The man dropped the package, which struck the tracks and exploded—it was packed with fireworks. The shock knocked over some heavy scales at the far end of the platform, and one of them struck Palsgraf. She sued the railroad.

Judge Cardozo ruled that the guard's conduct might have been a wrong as to the passenger, but it was not a wrong as to Ms. Palsgraf, standing far away. The guard could not anticipate that anything he did might injure her. A defendant can be liable for negligence only if he had a duty *to the injured plaintiff.* Because the guard could not foresee injuring Ms. Palsgraf, he had no duty to her. Her negligence case failed. "Proof of negligence in the air, so to speak, will not do," declared the judge.

**To win a negligence case, the plaintiff must prove *all five* of these elements:**

- *Duty of due care.* The defendant had a duty of due care *to this plaintiff.* This is Judge Cardozo's point in the *Palsgraf* case.

- *Breach.* The defendant breached her duty.

- *Factual cause.* The defendant's conduct actually caused the injury.

- *Foreseeable harm.* It was foreseeable that conduct like the defendant's might cause this type of harm.

- *Injury.* The plaintiff has actually been hurt.

## DUTY OF DUE CARE

The first issue may be the most difficult in all of tort law: Did the defendant have a duty of due care to the injured person? Judges draw an imaginary line around the defendant and say that she owes a duty to the people within this circle, but not to those outside it. The test is generally "foreseeability." If a defendant can foresee injury to a particular person, she has a **duty** to him. If she cannot foresee the harm, there is usually no duty.

Some cases are easy. Suppose Glorious University operates a cafeteria. Does the school have a duty of due care to its diners? Absolutely. Management can foresee that a grimy kitchen will cause serious illness, so the university has a duty to each of its patrons. On the other hand, assume the school bookstore sells a road map of Greece to a student. During spring break, the student drives recklessly along a narrow country lane in Greece, injuring a farmer. The university could never have foreseen harm to a Greek farmer merely from selling a map, so it had no duty to the man.

Let us apply these principles to the fraternity case.

**Duty**
If a defendant can foresee injury to a particular person, she has a duty to him.

## HERNANDEZ V. ARIZONA BOARD OF REGENTS

177 ARIZ. 244, 866 P.2D 1330, 1994 ARIZ. LEXIS 6
ARIZONA SUPREME COURT, 1994

### CASE SUMMARY

**Facts:** At the University of Arizona, the Epsilon Epsilon chapter of Delta Tau Delta fraternity gave a welcoming party for new members. The fraternity's officers knew that the majority of its members were under the legal drinking age but permitted everyone to consume alcohol. John Rayner, who was under 21 years of age, left the party. He drove negligently and caused a collision with an auto driven by Ruben Hernandez. At the time of the accident, Rayner's blood alcohol level was 0.15, exceeding the legal limit. The crash left Hernandez blind, severely brain damaged, and quadriplegic.

Hernandez sued Rayner, who settled the case based on the amount of his insurance coverage. The victim also sued the fraternity, its officers and national organization, all the fraternity members who contributed money to buy the alcohol, the university, and others. The trial court granted summary judgment for all defendants and the court of appeals affirmed. Hernandez appealed to the Arizona Supreme Court.

**Issue:** *Did the fraternity and the other defendants have a duty of due care to Hernandez?*

**Decision:** Yes, the defendants did have a duty of due care to Hernandez. Reversed and remanded.

**Reasoning:** Historically, Arizona and most states have considered that *consuming* alcohol led to liability, but not *furnishing* it. However, the common law also has had a longstanding rule that a defendant could be liable for supplying some object to a person who is likely to endanger others. Giving a car to an intoxicated youth is an example of such behavior. The youth might easily use the object (the car) to injure other people.

There is no difference between giving a car to an intoxicated youth and giving alcohol to a young person with a car. Both acts involve minors who, because of their age and inexperience, are likely to endanger third parties. Furthermore, furnishing alcohol to a minor violates several state statutes. The defendants did have a duty of due care to Hernandez and to the public in general.

## LANDOWNER'S DUTY

The common law applies special rules to a landowner for injuries occurring on her property. In most states, the owner's duty depends on why the injured person came onto the property.

**Trespasser**
A person on someone else's property without consent.

- *Lowest Liability: Trespasser.* A **trespasser** is anyone on the property without consent. A landowner is liable to a trespasser only for intentionally injuring him or for some other gross misconduct. The landowner has no liability to a trespasser for mere negligence. Jake is not liable if a vagrant wanders onto his land and is burned by defective electrical wires.

**Licensee**
A person on property for her own purposes, but with the owner's permission.

- *Higher Liability: Licensee.* A **licensee** is anyone on the land for her own purposes but with the owner's permission. A social guest is a typical licensee. A licensee is entitled to a warning of hidden dangers that the owner knows about. If Juliet invites Romeo for a late supper on the balcony and fails to mention that the wooden railing is rotted, she is liable when her hero plunges to the courtyard.

**Invitee**
A person on property because it is a public place.

- *Highest Liability: Invitee.* An **invitee** is someone on the property as of right because it is a public place or a business open to the public. The owner has a duty of reasonable care to an invitee. Perry is an invitee when he goes to the town beach. If riptides have existed for years and the town fails to post a warning, it is liable if Perry drowns. Perry is also an invitee when he shops at Daphne's Boutique. Daphne is liable if she ignores spilled coffee that causes Perry to slip.

# CRIME AND TORT: LANDOWNER'S LIABILITY

Law shows us trends in social issues. Regrettably, a major concern of tort law today is how to respond to injury caused by criminals. If a criminal assaults and robs a pedestrian in a shopping mall, that act is a crime and may be prosecuted by the state. But prosecution leaves the victim uncompensated. The assault is also an intentional tort (discussed in Chapter 5), and the victim could file a civil lawsuit against the criminal. But most violent criminals have no assets. Given this economic frustration and the flexibility of the common law, it is inevitable that victims of violence look elsewhere for compensation, as they did in the following tragic case.

## WIENER v. SOUTHCOAST CHILDCARE CENTERS, INC.

32 CA.4TH 1138, 88 P.3D. 517, 12 CAL. RPTR.3D. 615
SUPREME COURT OF CALIFORNIA, 2004

### CASE SUMMARY

**Facts:** Southcoast operated a child-care facility on a property on a busy street corner that it leased from First Baptist Church. A 4-foot-high, chain-link fence enclosed the playground located adjacent to the sidewalk and street. Steven Abrams intentionally drove his large Cadillac through the fence, onto the playground, and into a group of children, causing horrific carnage. He killed two children and injured many others. Abrams was convicted of first-degree murder.

The parents of the killed and injured youngsters sued Southcoast and the church, alleging the defendants knew that the fence was inadequate to protect the children. The trial judge granted summary judgment for the defendants, ruling that Southcoast and the others owed no duty to prevent such harm. The appellate court reversed, and Southcoast appealed to the state's highest panel.

**Issue:** *Did Southcoast have a duty to the plaintiffs to prevent this kind of harm?*

**Holding:** No, Southcoast had no duty to the plaintiffs.
**Reasoning:** The parents allege that Southcoast and the church knew the chain-link fence was inadequate to protect their children. There had in fact been a few earlier accidents. According to one neighbor, when a mail-truck driver fell out of his truck, the vehicle took off, bounced over the curb, and drove through the fence before striking a tree inside the yard. No one was injured. Neighbors testified that other traffic incidents occurred near the premises involving vehicles that hit the curb.

The parents argue that it makes no difference whether the driver who killed the children acted negligently or with criminal intent. The risk of harm from an unsafe fence was the same, and the two defendants owed a duty to make the fence stronger.

In fact, the law treats third-party criminal acts differently from ordinary negligence. A court must find heightened foreseeability before holding a defendant liable for the criminal acts of third parties. It is difficult or impossible to predict when a criminal might strike. And if a criminal decides on a particular goal or victim, it is very hard to remove his every means for achieving that goal.

Abrams's brutal criminal act was unforeseeable. Southcoast had never been the target of violence before. The attack was outrageous and bizarre. It was impossible for anyone to anticipate a perpetrator committing premeditated murder against the children. Southcoast and the church owed no duty to the children.

The case is reversed, and summary judgment is granted for the defendants.

---

## EXAM *Strategy*

**Question:** Compare the *Wiener* decision with a case from Chapter 1: *Kuehn v Pub Zone*, on page 8. Both are negligence cases in which the harm is caused by criminal conduct. However, the two cases have opposite outcomes. Why is that?

**Strategy:** What standard did the *Pub Zone* court use to decide that the bar owner was liable? Who won? Apply the same standard to the *Wiener* case. Who should win?

**Result:** The *Pub Zone* court declared that a property owner was not an insurer against criminal acts but would be liable if the violent conduct was *foreseeable*, based on experience. Kerkoulas knew from earlier incidents that gang members wearing insignia presented a danger to patrons, and she was liable when violence erupted. In the *Wiener* case, the court used the same standard but found there was no history of violence at the day care center. Harm to the children was unforeseeable. The law was the same in both cases, but different facts led to contrasting results.

..................................................................................................................................

# BREACH OF DUTY

**Breach of duty**
A defendant breaches his duty of due care by failing to behave the way a reasonable person would under similar circumstances.

The second element of a plaintiff's negligence case is **breach of duty**. Courts apply the *reasonable person* standard: **A defendant breaches his duty of due care by failing to behave the way a reasonable person would under similar circumstances.** Reasonable "person" means someone of the defendant's occupation. A taxi driver must drive as a reasonable taxi driver would. An architect who designs a skyscraper's safety features must bring to the task far greater knowledge than the average person possesses.

Two medical cases illustrate the reasonable person standard. A doctor prescribes a powerful drug without asking his 21-year-old patient about other medicines she is currently taking. The patient suffers a serious drug reaction from the combined medications. The physician is liable for the harm. A reasonable doctor always checks current medicines before prescribing new ones.

On the other hand, assume that an 84-year-old patient dies on the operating table in an emergency room. While the surgeon was repairing heart damage, the man had a fatal stroke. If the physician followed normal medical procedures, and acted with reasonable speed, he is not liable. A doctor must do a reasonable professional job, but cannot guarantee a happy outcome.

# FACTUAL CAUSE AND FORESEEABLE HARM

A plaintiff must also show that the defendant's breach of duty *caused* the plaintiff's harm. Courts look at two issues to settle causation: Was the defendant's behavior the *factual cause* of the harm? Was *this type of harm foreseeable?*[1]

## Factual Cause

**Factual cause**
The defendant's breach led to the ultimate harm.

Nothing mysterious here. If the defendant's breach physically led to the ultimate harm, it is the **factual cause**. Suppose that Dom's Brake Shop tells Customer his brakes are now working fine, even though Dom knows that is false. Customer drives out of the shop, cannot stop at a red light, and hits Bicyclist crossing at the intersection. Dom is liable to Bicyclist. Dom's unreasonable behavior was the *factual cause* of the harm. Think of it as a row of dominoes. The first domino (Dom's behavior) knocked over the next one (failing brakes), which toppled the last one (the cyclist's injury).

Suppose, alternatively, that just as Customer is exiting the repair shop, Bicyclist hits a pothole and tumbles off her cycle, avoiding Customer's auto. Bicyclist's injuries stem from her fall, not from the auto. Customer's brakes still fail, and Dom has breached his duty to Customer, but Dom is not liable to Bicyclist. She would have been hurt anyway. No factual causation.

## Foreseeable Type of Harm

**Foreseeable type of harm**
Refers to injury that a reasonable person could anticipate.

For the defendant to be liable, the *type of harm* must have been reasonably **foreseeable**. In the case above, Dom could easily foresee that bad brakes would cause an automobile accident. He need not have foreseen exactly what happened. He did not know there would be a cyclist nearby.

---

[1] Courts often refer to these two elements, grouped together, as *proximate cause* or *legal cause*. However, as many judges have acknowledged, those terms have created legal confusion, so we use *factual cause* and *foreseeable type of harm,* the issues on which most decisions ultimately focus.

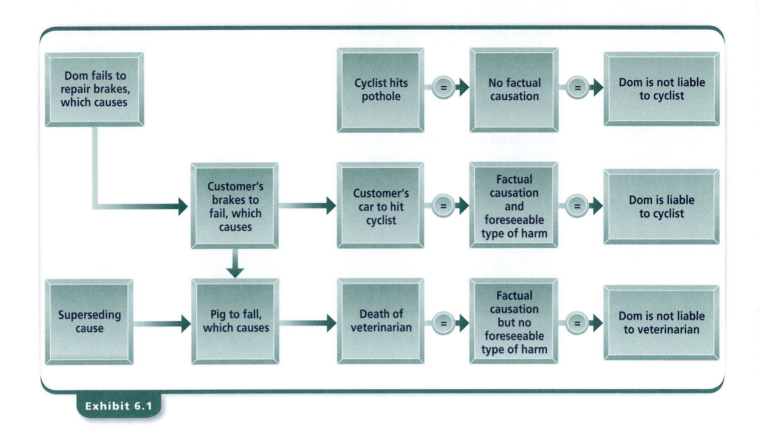

**Exhibit 6.1**

What he could foresee was this general type of harm involving defective brakes. Because the accident that occurred was of the type he could foresee, he is liable.

By contrast, assume the collision of car and bicycle produces a loud crash. Two blocks away, a pet pig, asleep on the window ledge of a 12th-story apartment, is startled by the noise, awakens with a start, and plunges to the sidewalk, killing a veterinarian who was making a house call. If the vet's family sues Dom, should it win? Dom's negligence was the factual cause: It led to the collision, which startled the pig, which flattened the vet. Most courts would rule, though, that Dom is not liable. The *type of harm* is too bizarre. Dom could not reasonably foresee such an extraordinary chain of events, and it would be unfair to make him pay for it. See Exhibit 6.1.

## EXAM *Strategy*

**Question:** Jenny asked a neighbor, Tom, to water her flowers while she was on vacation. For three days, Tom did this without incident, but on the fourth day, when he touched the outside faucet, he received a violent electric shock that shot him through the air, melted his sneakers and glasses, set his clothes on fire, and seriously scalded him. Tom sued, claiming that Jenny had caused the damage when she negligently repaired a second-floor toilet. Water from the steady leak had flooded through the walls, soaking wires and eventually causing the faucet to become electrified. You are Jenny's lawyer. Use one (and only one) element of negligence law to move for summary judgment.

**Strategy:** The four elements of negligence we have examined thus far are duty to this plaintiff, breach, factual cause, and foreseeable type of injury. Which element seems to be most helpful to Jenny's defense? Why?

**Result:** Jenny is entitled to summary judgment because this was not a foreseeable type of injury. Even if she did a bad job of fixing the toilet, she could not possibly have anticipated that her poor workmanship could cause *electrical* injuries—and violent ones, at that—to anybody.[2]

..................................................................................................................

## Res Ipsa Loquitur

*Res ipsa loquitur*
means "the thing speaks for itself"
and refers to cases where the
facts *imply* that the defendant's
negligence caused the harm.

Normally, a plaintiff must prove factual cause and foreseeable type of harm to establish negligence. But in a few cases, a court may be willing to infer that the defendant caused the harm, under the doctrine of **res ipsa loquitur** ("the thing speaks for itself"). Suppose a pedestrian is walking along a sidewalk when an air conditioning unit falls on his head from a third-story window. The defendant, who owns the third-story apartment, denies any wrongdoing, and it may be difficult or impossible for the plaintiff to prove why the air conditioner fell. In such cases, many courts will apply *res ipsa loquitur* and declare that the facts imply that the defendant's negligence caused the accident. If a court uses this doctrine, then the defendant must come forward with evidence establishing that it did not cause the harm.

Because *res ipsa loquitur* dramatically shifts the burden of proof from plaintiff to defendant, it applies only when (1) the defendant had exclusive control of the thing that caused the harm; (2) the harm normally would not have occurred without negligence; and (3) the plaintiff had no role in causing the harm. In the air conditioner example, most states would apply the doctrine and force the defendant to prove she did nothing wrong.

## INJURY

**Injury**
must be genuine, not speculative.

Finally, a plaintiff must prove that he has been injured. In some cases, **injury** is obvious. For example, Ruben Hernandez suffered grievous harm when struck by a drunk driver. But in other cases, injury is unclear. **The plaintiff must persuade the court that he has suffered a harm that is genuine, not one that is merely speculative.**

Angelina and her family have been given a defective hotel room, and they are repacking to move to a better one. Angelina feels under the bed and picks up what she believes to be a candy wrapper. She feels a "gush" as she retrieves the item, which turns out to be a wet condom. She screams, washes her hands, and rushes to an emergency room, terrified she has been exposed to AIDS. Because of technical problems at the hospital, the condom is never tested. Angelina's hand happens to have a burn on one finger and bloody cuticles. However, over a 12-month period, she tests negative for HIV four times.

Angelina sues the hotel, claiming fear that she will die of AIDS. Outcome? In most states, she will lose. A plaintiff may win a suit based on fear of a future disease or condition, but only if her anxiety is reasonable. She must show a substantial probability that her present injury will develop into a future ailment. If the medical evidence indicates that will not happen, the plaintiff loses. In Angelina's case, it is more than 99 percent likely that she will never develop HIV. She would have won if she had tested positive. She would also have prevailed if the condom had tested positive *and* evidence indicated that touching it could transmit the disease. Fortunately, neither of those things was true; unfortunately, she loses her lawsuit.

The following case prompts a different issue: may a plaintiff recover damages for emotional injury when a *relative* is harmed?

---

[2] Based on *Hebert v. Enos*, 60 Mass. App. Ct. 817, 806 N.E.2d 452 (Massachusetts Court of Appeals, 2004).

## RA V. SUPERIOR COURT

154 CAL. APP. 4TH 142, 64 CA. RPTR. 3D 539
CALIFORNIA COURT OF APPEALS, 2007

### CASE SUMMARY

**Facts:** Michelle Ra and her husband, Phil, were shopping in an Armani Exchange in Old Town, Pasadena. Michelle was looking at merchandise in the women's section while Phil examined men's sweaters, about 10 or 15 feet away. Michelle was not facing her husband when she heard a loud bang. A large, overhead store sign had fallen, striking Phil and seriously injuring him. Michelle turned, saw her husband bent over in pain, and hurried to him. Ten days later, Michelle suffered a miscarriage, which she attributed to the accident.

The Ras sued Armani for negligence in permitting the sign to fall, and also for the emotional distress suffered by Michelle. This case concerns only Michelle's claim. The trial court granted summary judgment to the store, declaring that Michelle had not made out a valid claim of bystander recovery because she had not seen the accident occur. She appealed.

**Issue:** *May a bystander recover for emotional distress caused by an accident that she did not see?*

**Decision:** A bystander may not recover for emotional distress caused by an accident unless she witnessed it. Summary judgment affirmed.

**Reasoning:** Michelle testified that when she heard the crash, "I was not sure if he was involved, but I knew the sound came from the direction—the part of the store he was in."

To recover for negligent infliction of emotional distress as a bystander, a plaintiff must prove she (1) is closely related to the injury victim; (2) is present at the scene of the event and is aware it is injuring the victim; and (3) as a result suffers serious emotional distress. Someone who hears an accident but does not then know it is causing injury to a relative does not have a viable bystander claim for emotional distress, even if she learns the truth moments later.

It is the trauma caused by *witnessing* the injury to a close relative that gives rise to a lawsuit. Michelle did not witness the accident and cannot prevail.

## DAMAGES

The plaintiff's damages in a negligence case are generally **compensatory damages,** meaning an amount of money that the court believes will restore him to the position he was in before the defendant's conduct caused an injury. In unusual cases, a court may award **punitive damages,** that is, money intended not to compensate the plaintiff but to punish the defendant. We discussed both forms of damages in Chapter 5.

## · DEFENSES ·

## ASSUMPTION OF THE RISK

Quick, duck! Close call—that baseball nearly knocked your ear off. If it had, the home team would owe you . . . nothing. Here at the ballpark, there is always a slight chance of injury, and you are expected to realize it. Wherever there is an obvious hazard, a special rule applies. **Assumption of the risk**: A person who voluntarily enters a situation that has an obvious danger cannot complain if she is injured. If you are not willing to tolerate the risk of being hurt by a batted ball, stay home and watch the game on television. And while you are here—pay attention, will you?

Suppose that Good Guys, a restaurant, holds an ice-fishing contest on a frozen lake to raise money for accident victims. Margie grabs a can full of worms and strolls to the middle of the lake to try her luck, but slips on the ice and suffers a concussion. When she returns to consciousness, Margie should not bother filing suit—she assumed the risk.

**Assumption of the risk**
A person who voluntarily enters a situation of obvious danger cannot complain if she is injured.

# CONTRIBUTORY AND COMPARATIVE NEGLIGENCE

Sixteen-year-old Michelle Wightman was out driving at night, with her friend Karrie Wieber in the passenger seat. They came to a railroad crossing, where the mechanical arm had descended and warning bells were sounding, in fact, had been sounding for a long time. A Conrail train, SEEL-7, had suffered mechanical problems and was stopped 200 feet from the crossing, where it had stalled for roughly an hour. Michelle and Karrie saw several cars ahead of them go around the barrier and cross the tracks. Michelle had to decide whether she would do the same.

Long before Michelle made her decision, the train's engineer had seen the heavy Saturday night traffic crossing the tracks and realized the danger. A second train had passed the crossing at 70 miles per hour, without incident. SEEL-7's conductor and brakeman also understood the peril, but rather than posting a flagman, who could have stopped traffic when a train approached, they walked to the far end of their train to repair the mechanical problem. A police officer had come upon the scene, told his dispatcher to notify Conrail of the danger, and left.

Michelle decided to cross the tracks. She slowly followed the cars ahead of her. TV-9, a freight train traveling at 60 miles per hour, struck the car broadside, killing both girls instantly.

Michelle's mother sued Conrail for negligence. The company claimed that it was Michelle's foolish risk that led to her death. Who wins when both parties are partly responsible? It depends on whether the state uses a legal theory called contributory negligence. Under **contributory negligence**, if the plaintiff is even *slightly* negligent she recovers nothing. If Michelle's death occurred in a contributory negligence state, and the jury considered her even minimally responsible, her estate would receive no money.

> ...the mechanical arm had descended and warning bells were sounding, in fact, had been sounding for a long time.

**Contributory negligence**
A plaintiff who is even *slightly* negligent recovers nothing.

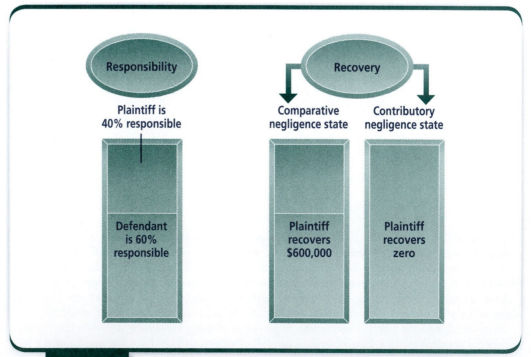

**Exhibit 6.2**   Defendant's negligence injures plaintiff, who suffers $1 million in damages.

Critics attacked this rule as unreasonable. A plaintiff who was 1 percent negligent could not recover from a defendant who was 99 percent responsible under those terms. So most states threw out the contributory negligence rule, replacing it with comparative negligence. In a **comparative negligence** state, a plaintiff may generally recover even if she is partially responsible. The jury will be asked to assess the relative negligence of the two parties.

Michelle died in Ohio, which is a comparative negligence state. The jury concluded that reasonable compensatory damages were $1 million. It also concluded that Conrail was 60 percent responsible for the tragedy and Michelle 40 percent. See Exhibit 6.2. The girl's mother received $600,000 in compensatory damages.[3]

> **Comparative negligence**
> A plaintiff may generally recover even if she is partially responsible.

# · STRICT LIABILITY ·

Some activities are so naturally dangerous that the law places an especially high burden on anyone who engages in them. A corporation that produces toxic waste can foresee dire consequences from its business that a stationery store cannot. This higher burden is **strict liability**. There are two main areas of business that incur strict liability: ultrahazardous activity and defective products. We discuss **defective products** in Chapter 20, on product liability.

> **Strict liability**
> A high level of liability assumed by people or corporations who engage in activities that are very dangerous.
>
> **Defective products**
> generally lead to strict liability. See Chapter 20.

## Ultrahazardous Activity

Ultrahazardous activities include using harmful chemicals, operating explosives, keeping wild animals, bringing dangerous substances onto property, and a few similar activities where the danger to the general public is especially great. **A defendant engaging in an ultrahazardous activity is virtually always liable for any harm that results.** Plaintiffs do not have to prove duty or breach or foreseeable harm. Recall the deliberately bizarre case we posed earlier of the pig falling from a window ledge and killing a veterinarian. Dom, the mechanic whose negligence caused the car crash, could not be liable for the veterinarian's death because the plunging pig was not foreseeable. But if the pig had been jolted off the window ledge by Sam's Blasting Company doing perfectly lawful blasting for a new building down the street, Sam would be liable. Even if Sam had taken extraordinary care, he would lose. The "reasonable person" rule is irrelevant in a strict liability case.

> **Ultrahazardous activities**
> A defendant engaging in such acts is virtually always liable for resulting harm.

---

[3] *Wightman v. Consolidated Rail Corporation*, 86 Ohio St. 3d 431, 715 N.E.2d 546 (Ohio, 1999).

## YOU *be the* JUDGE

**NEW JERSEY DEPARTMENT OF ENVIRONMENTAL PROTECTION v. ALDEN LEEDS, INC.**
153 N.J. 272; 708 A.2d 1161; 1998 N.J. LEXIS 212; 46 ERC(BNA) 1447
Supreme Court of New Jersey, 1998

**Facts:** The Alden Leeds company packages, stores, and ships swimming pool chemicals. The firm does most of its work at its facility in Kearns, New Jersey. At any given time, about 21 different hazardous chemicals are present.

The day before Easter, a fire of unknown origin broke out in "Building One" of the company's site, releasing chlorine gas and other potentially dangerous by-products into the air. There were no guards or other personnel on duty. The fire caused $9 million in damage to company property. Because of the danger, the Department of Environmental Protection (DEP) closed the New Jersey Turnpike along with half a dozen other major highways, halted all commuter rail and train service in the area, and urged residents to stay indoors with windows closed. An unspecified number of residents went to local hospitals with respiratory problems.

Based on New Jersey's air pollution laws, the DEP fined Alden Leeds for releasing the toxic chemicals. The appellate court reversed, declaring that there was no evidence the company had caused the fire or the harm. The case reached the state's high court.

*continued*

**You Be the Judge:** **Is the company responsible for the harm?**

**Argument for Alden Leeds:** Alden Leeds did nothing wrong. Why should the company pay a fine? The firm was licensed to use these chemicals and did so in a safe manner. There is no evidence the company caused the fire. Sometimes accidents just happen. Do not penalize a responsible business simply to make somebody pay. The state should go after careless firms that knowingly injure the public. Leave good companies alone so they can get on with business and provide jobs.

**Argument for the Department of Environmental Protection:** This accident made innocent people sick and caused massive difficulties for tens of thousands. It makes no difference why the accident happened. That is the whole point of strict liability. When a company chooses to participate in an ultrahazardous activity, it accepts full liability for anything that goes wrong, regardless of the cause. If you want the profits, you accept the responsibility. Alden Leeds must pay.

## CHAPTER CONCLUSION

Negligence issues necessarily remain in flux, based on changing social values and concerns. A working knowledge of these issues and pitfalls can help everyone—business executive and ordinary citizen alike.

## EXAM REVIEW

1. **ELEMENTS OF NEGLIGENCE** The five elements of negligence are duty of due care, breach, factual causation, foreseeable type of harm, and injury. (p. 81)

2. **DUTY** If the defendant could foresee that misconduct would injure a particular person, he probably has a duty to her. (p. 81)

3. **LANDOWNER'S LIABILITY** In most states, a landowner's duty of due care is lowest to trespassers; higher to a licensee (anyone on the land for her own purposes but with the owner's permission); and highest of all to an invitee (someone on the property as of right). (p. 82)

4. **BREACH** A defendant breaches his duty of due care by failing to behave the way a reasonable person would under similar circumstances. (p. 84)

5. **FACTUAL CAUSE** If an event physically led to the ultimate harm, it is the factual cause. (p. 84)

6. **FORESEEABLE TYPE OF HARM** For the defendant to be liable, the type of harm must have been reasonably foreseeable. (p. 84)

7. **INJURY** The plaintiff must persuade the court that he has suffered a harm that is genuine, not speculative. (p. 86)

8. **CONTRIBUTORY AND COMPARATIVE NEGLIGENCE** In a contributory negligence state, a plaintiff who is even slightly responsible for his own injury recovers nothing; in a comparative negligence state, the jury may apportion liability between plaintiff and defendant. (p. 88)

EXAM Strategy

**Question:** There is a collision between cars driven by Candy and Zeke. The evidence is that Candy is about 25 percent responsible, for failing to stop quickly enough, and Zeke about 75 percent responsible, for making a dangerous turn. Candy is most likely to win:

   (a) A lawsuit for battery

   (b) A lawsuit for negligence, in a comparative negligence state

   (c) A lawsuit for negligence, in a contributory negligence state

   (d) A lawsuit for strict liability

   (e) A lawsuit for assault

**Strategy:** Battery and assault are intentional torts, which are irrelevant in a typical car accident. Are such collisions strict liability cases? No; therefore, the answer must be either (b) or (c). Apply the distinction between comparative and contributory negligence to the evidence here. (See the "Result" at the end of this section.)

9. **STRICT LIABILITY** A defendant is strictly liable for harm caused by an ultrahazardous activity or a defective product. Ultrahazardous activities include using harmful chemicals, blasting, and keeping wild animals. Strict liability means that if the defendant's conduct led to the harm, the defendant is liable, even if she exercises extraordinary care. (p. 89)

EXAM Strategy

**Question:** Marko owned a cat and allowed it to roam freely outside. In the three years he had owned the pet, the animal had never bitten anyone. The cat entered Romi's garage. When Romi attempted to move it outside, the cat bit her. Romi underwent four surgeries, was fitted with a plastic finger joint, and spent more than $39,000 in medical bills. She sued Marko, claiming both strict liability and ordinary negligence. Assume that state law allows a domestic cat to roam freely. Evaluate both of Romi's claims.

**Strategy:** Negligence requires proof that the defendant breached a duty to the plaintiff by behaving unreasonably and that the resulting harm was foreseeable. Was it? When would harm by a domestic cat be foreseeable? A defendant can be strictly liable for keeping a wild animal. Apply that rule as well. (See the "Result" at the end of this section.)

**8. Result:** In a contributory negligence state, a plaintiff who is even 1 percent responsible for the harm loses. Candy was 25 percent responsible. She can win *only* in a comparative negligence state.

**9. Result:** If Marko's cat had bitten or attacked people in the past, this harm was foreseeable and Marko is liable. If the cat had never done so, and state law allows domestic animals to roam, Romi probably loses her suit for negligence. Her strict liability case definitely fails: a house cat is not a wild animal.

# PRACTICE EXAM

## MATCHING QUESTIONS

Match the following terms with their definitions:

\_\_\_ A. Breach

\_\_\_ B. Strict liability

\_\_\_ C. Compensatory damages

\_\_\_ D. Invitee

\_\_\_ E. Negligence

1. Money awarded to an injured plaintiff

2. Someone who has a legal right to enter upon land

3. A defendant's failure to perform a legal duty

4. A tort caused accidentally

5. Legal responsibility that comes from performing ultrahazardous acts

## TRUE/FALSE QUESTIONS

Circle true or false:

1. T   F   There are five elements in a negligence case, and a plaintiff wins who proves at least three of them.

2. T   F   Max, a 19-year-old sophomore, gets drunk at a fraternity party and then causes a serious car accident. Max can be found liable and so can the fraternity.

3. T   F   Some states are comparative negligence states but the majority are contributory negligence states.

4. T   F   A landowner might be liable if a dinner guest fell on a broken porch step but not liable if a trespasser fell on the same place.

5. T   F   A defendant can be liable for negligence even if he never intended to cause harm.

6. T   F   When Ms. Palsgraf sued the railroad, the court found that the railroad should have foreseen what might go wrong.

## MULTIPLE-CHOICE QUESTIONS

7. In which case is a plaintiff most likely to sue based on strict liability?

A. Defamation

B. Injury caused on the job

C. Injury caused by a tiger that escapes from a zoo

D. Injury caused partially by plaintiff and partially by defendant

E. Injury caused by defendant's careless driving

8. Martha signs up for a dinner cruise on a large commercial yacht. While the customers are eating dinner, the yacht bangs into another boat. Martha is thrown to the deck, breaking her wrist. She sues. At trial, which of these issues is likely to be the most important?

A. Whether the yacht company had permission to take Martha on the cruise

B. Whether the yacht company improperly restrained Martha

C. Whether Martha feared an imminent injury

D. Whether the yacht's captain did a reasonable job of driving the yacht

E. Whether Martha has filed similar suits in the past

9. Dolly, an architect, lives in Pennsylvania, which is a comparative negligence state. While she is inspecting a construction site for a large building she designed, she is injured when a worker drops a hammer from two stories up. Dolly was not wearing a safety helmet at the time. Dolly sues the construction company. The jury concludes that Dolly has

suffered $100,000 in damages. The jury also believes that Dolly was 30 percent liable for the accident, and the construction company was 70 percent liable. Outcome?

A. Dolly wins nothing.

B. Dolly wins $30,000.

C. Dolly wins $50,000.

D. Dolly wins $70,000.

E. Dolly wins $100,000.

10. A taxi driver, hurrying to pick up a customer at the airport, races through a 20 mph hospital zone at 45 mph and strikes May, who is crossing the street in a pedestrian crosswalk. May sues the driver and the taxi company. What kind of suit is this?

A. Contract

B. Remedy

C. Negligence

D. Assault

E. Battery

## SHORT-ANSWER QUESTIONS

11. At approximately 7:50 p.m., bells at the train station rang and red lights flashed, signaling an express train's approach. David Harris walked onto the tracks, ignoring a yellow line painted on the platform instructing people to stand back. Two men shouted to Harris, warning him to get off the tracks. The train's engineer saw him too late to stop the train, which was traveling at approximately 99 mph. The train struck and killed Harris as it passed through the station. Harris's widow sued the railroad, arguing that the railroad's negligence caused her husband's death. Evaluate the widow's argument.

12. A new truck, manufactured by General Motors Corp. (GMC), stalled in rush hour traffic on a busy interstate highway because of a defective alternator, which caused a complete failure of the truck's electrical system. The driver stood nearby and waved traffic around his stalled truck. A panel truck approached the GMC truck. Immediately behind the panel truck, Davis was driving a Volkswagen fastback. Because of the panel truck, Davis was unable to see the stalled GMC truck. The panel truck swerved out of the way of the GMC truck, and Davis drove straight into it. The accident killed him. Davis's widow sued GMC. GMC moved for summary judgment, alleging (1) no duty to Davis; (2) no factual causation; and (3) no foreseeable harm. Comment on the three defenses that GMC has raised.

13. A prison inmate bit a hospital employee. The employee sued the state for negligence and lack of supervision, claiming a fear of AIDS. The plaintiff had tested negative for the AIDS virus three times, and there was no proof that the inmate had the virus. Comment on the probable outcome.

14. ETHICS: Koby, age 16, works after school at Fast-Food from 4 p.m. until 11 p.m. On Friday night, the restaurant manager sees that Koby is exhausted, but insists that he remain until 4:30 a.m., cleaning up, then demands that he work Saturday morning from 8 a.m. until 4 p.m. On Saturday afternoon, as Koby drives home, he falls asleep at the wheel and causes a fatal car accident. Should FastFood be liable? What important values are involved in this issue? How does the Golden Rule apply?

15. ROLE REVERSAL: Create a short-answer question that focuses on either factual cause, foreseeable type of harm, or *res ipsa loquitur*.

## INTERNET RESEARCH PROBLEM

Everyone knows that drunk driving is bad, but many people still do it. Online, find something that you did not know about drunk driving. What role should the law play in this problem, and what role should parents, students, and schools play?

**You can find further practice problems in the Online Quiz at www.cengage.com/blaw/beatty.**

# CRIMINAL LAW AND PROCEDURE

**A major crime has occurred during the 90 minutes Stacey was at her desk, but she will never report it to the police.**

**Crime can** take us by surprise. Stacey tucks her nine-year-old daughter, Beth, into bed. Promising her husband, Mark, that she will be home by 11 p.m., she jumps into her car and heads back to Be Patient, Inc. She puts a compact disk in the player of her $85,000 sedan and tries to relax. Be Patient is a health care organization that owns five geriatric hospitals. Most of its patients use Medicare, and Stacey supervises all billing to their largest client, the federal government.

She parks in a well-lighted spot on the street and walks to her building, failing to notice two men, collars turned up, watching from a parked truck. Once in her office, she goes straight to her computer and works on billing issues. Tonight's work goes more quickly than she expected, thanks to new software she helped develop. At 10:30 p.m., she emerges from the building with a quick step and a light heart, walks to her car—and finds it missing.

A major crime has occurred during the 90 minutes Stacey was at her desk, but she will never report it to the police. It is a crime that costs Americans countless dollars each year, yet Stacey will not even mention it to friends or family. Stacey is the criminal.

When we think of crime, we imagine the drug dealers and bank robbers endlessly portrayed on television. We do not picture corporate executives sitting at polished desks. "Street crimes" are indeed serious threats to our security and happiness. But when measured only in dollars, street crime takes second place to white-collar crime, which costs society tens of billions of dollars annually.

The hypothetical about Stacey is based on many real cases and is used to illustrate that crime does not always dress the way we expect. Her car was never stolen; it was simply towed. Two parking bureau employees, watching from their truck, saw Stacey park illegally and did their job. It is Stacey who committed a crime—Medicare fraud. Stacey has learned the simple but useful lesson that company profits rise when she charges the government for work that Be Patient has never done. For months she billed the government for imaginary patients. Then she hired a computer hacker to worm into the Medicare computer system and plant a "Trojan horse," a program that seemed useful to Medicare employees but actually contained a series of codes opening the computer to Stacey. Stacey simply entered the Medicare system and altered the calculations for payments owed to Be Patient. Every month, the government paid Be Patient about $10 million for imaginary work. Stacey's scheme was quick and profitable—and a distressingly common crime.

## · CRIME, SOCIETY, AND LAW ·

### CIVIL LAW/CRIMINAL LAW

Conduct is criminal when society outlaws it. When a state legislature or Congress concludes that certain behavior threatens the population generally, it passes a statute forbidding that behavior, in other words, declaring it criminal. Medicare fraud, which Stacey committed, is a crime because Congress has outlawed it.

#### Prosecution

Suppose the police arrest Roger and accuse him of breaking into a video store and stealing 25 video cameras, videos, and other equipment. The owner of the video store is the one harmed, but it is the government that prosecutes crimes. The local prosecutor will decide whether or not to charge Roger and bring him to trial.

#### Jury Right

The facts of the case will be decided by a judge or jury. A criminal defendant has a right to a trial by jury for any charge that could result in a sentence of six months or longer. The defendant may demand a jury trial or may waive that right, in which case the judge will be the fact finder.

#### Punishment

In a civil lawsuit, the plaintiff seeks a verdict that the defendant is liable for harm caused to her. But in a criminal case, the government asks the court to find the defendant guilty of the crime. If the judge or jury finds the defendant guilty, the court will punish him with a fine, and/or a prison sentence. The fine is paid to the government, not to the injured person (although the court will sometimes order restitution, meaning that the defendant must reimburse the victim for harm suffered). It is generally the judge who imposes the sentence. If the jury is not persuaded of the defendant's guilt, it will acquit him, that is, find him not guilty.

## Felony/Misdemeanor

**Felony**
A serious crime, for which a defendant can be sentenced to spend one year or more in prison.

**Misdemeanor**
A less serious crime, often punishable by a year or less in jail.

A **felony** is a serious crime, for which a defendant can be sentenced to spend one year or more in prison. Murder, robbery, rape, drug dealing, wire fraud, and embezzlement are felonies. A **misdemeanor** is a less serious crime, often punishable by a year or less in a county jail. Driving without a license and simple possession of one marijuana cigarette are considered misdemeanors in most states.

# THE PROSECUTION'S CASE

In all criminal cases, the prosecution faces several basic issues.

## Conduct Outlawed

Virtually all crimes are created by statute. The prosecution must demonstrate to the court that the defendant's alleged conduct is indeed outlawed by a statute. Returning to Roger, the alleged video thief, the state charges that he stole video cameras from a store, a crime clearly defined by statute as burglary.

## Burden of Proof

**Beyond a reasonable doubt**
The prosecution's burden of proof in a criminal case; the case against the defendant must be proved to such an extent that no reasonable person would doubt it.

In a civil case, the plaintiff must prove her case by a preponderance of the evidence. But in a criminal case, the government must prove its case **beyond a reasonable doubt**. This is because the potential harm to a criminal defendant is far greater. The stigma of a criminal conviction will stay with him, making it more difficult to obtain work and housing.

## Actus Reus

**Actus reus**
Meaning, "the guilty act," this term refers to an act prohibited by law.

***Actus reus*** means the "guilty act." The prosecution must prove that the defendant voluntarily committed a prohibited act. Suppose Mary Jo files an insurance claim for a stolen car, knowing that her car was not stolen. That is insurance fraud. Filing the claim is the *actus reus:* Mary Jo voluntarily filled out the insurance claim and mailed it. At a bar, Mary Jo describes the claim to her friend, Chi Ling, who laughs and replies, "That's great. It'll serve the company right." Has Chi Ling committed a crime? No. She may be cynical, but Chi Ling has committed no *actus reus*.

## Mens Rea

**Mens rea**
Meaning "guilty state of mind," this term refers to what the defendant was thinking or intended when she committed the crime in question.

**General intent**
means that the defendant intended to do the prohibited physical act.

**Specific intent**
means that the defendant intended to do something beyond the mere prohibited physical act.

The prosecution must also show ***mens rea***, a "guilty state of mind," on the defendant's part. This is harder to prove than *actus reus*—it requires convincing evidence about something that is essentially psychological. Precisely what "state of mind" the prosecution must prove varies, depending on the crime. Most crimes require a showing of **general intent**, meaning that the defendant intended to do the prohibited physical action (the *actus reus*). Suppose Miller, a customer in a bar, picks up a bottle and smashes it over the head of Bud. In a trial for criminal assault, the *mens rea* would simply be the intention to hit Bud. The prosecution need not show that Miller intended serious harm, only that he intended the blow.

Some crimes require **specific intent**. The prosecution must prove that the defendant willfully intended to do something beyond the physical act. For example, burglary requires proof that the defendant entered a building at night and intended to commit a felony inside, such as stealing property.

# DEFENSES

A criminal defendant will frequently dispute the facts that link her to the crime. For example, she might claim mistaken identity (that she merely resembles the real criminal) or offer an alibi (that she can prove she was elsewhere when the crime was committed). In addition, a defendant may offer legal defenses. One of the most controversial is the insanity defense.

## *Insanity*

In most states, a defendant who can prove that he was insane at the time of the criminal act will be declared not guilty. This reflects the moral basis of our criminal law. Insane people, though capable of great harm, historically have not been considered responsible for their acts. A defendant found to be insane will generally be committed to a mental institution. If and when that hospital determines that he is no longer a danger to society, he will, in theory, be released.

States use different rules to gauge sanity. The most common test is the **M'Naghten Rule**. The defendant must show (1) that he suffered a serious, identifiable mental disease and that because of it (2) he did not understand the nature of his act or did not know that it was wrong. Suppose Jerry, a homeless man, stabs Phil. At trial, a psychiatrist testifies that Jerry suffers from chronic schizophrenia, that he does not know where he is or what he is doing, and that when he stabbed Phil, he believed he was sponging down his pet giraffe. If the jury believes the psychiatrist, it may find Jerry not guilty by reason of insanity.

What if the alleged mental defect is a result of the defendant's own behavior? You be the judge.

**M'Naghten Rule**
A test to gauge sanity that evaluates whether a criminal suffered a serious, identifiable mental disease that kept him from understanding the nature of his act or know that it was wrong.

---

# YOU *be the* JUDGE

### BIEBER v. PEOPLE
856 P.2d 811, 1993 Colo. LEXIS 630
Supreme Court of Colorado, 1993

**Facts:** Donald Bieber walked up to a truck in which William Ellis was sitting and shot Ellis, whom he did not know, in the back of his head. He threw Ellis's body from the truck and drove away. Shortly before and after the killing, Bieber encountered various people in different places. He sang "God Bless America" and the "Marine Hymn" to them and told them he was a prisoner of war and was being followed by communists. He told people he had killed a Communist on "War Memorial Highway." The police arrested him.

Bieber had a long history of drug abuse. Several years before the homicide, Bieber voluntarily sought treatment for mental impairment, entering a hospital and saying he thought he was going to hurt someone. He was later released into a long-term drug program.

Bieber was charged with first-degree murder. He pleaded not guilty by reason of insanity. An expert witness testified that he was insane, suffering from "amphetamine delusional disorder" (ADD), a recognized psychiatric illness resulting from long-term use of amphetamines and characterized by delusions. At trial, Bieber's attorney argued that he was not intoxicated at the time of the crime but that he was insane due to ADD. The trial court refused to instruct that Bieber could be legally insane due to ADD, and the jury found Bieber guilty of first-degree murder. He appealed.

**You Be the Judge: May a jury find that a defendant with ADD is legally insane?**

**Argument for Bieber:** It is morally and legally proper to distinguish between people who commit a crime out of viciousness and those who suffer serious mental illness. Mr. Bieber suffered from a serious psychotic illness recognized by the American Psychiatric Association. There was overwhelming evidence that he was out of control and did not know what he was doing at the time of the homicide. The fact that ADD is brought about by years of amphetamine use should make no difference in an insanity case. This man's reason was destroyed by a serious illness. He should not be treated the same as a cold-blooded killer.

**Argument for the State:** Your honors, there is no qualitative difference between a person who drinks or takes drugs knowing that he or she will be momentarily "mentally defective" as an immediate result and one who drinks or takes drugs knowing that he or she may be "mentally defective" as an eventual,

*continued*

long-term result. In both cases, the person is aware of the possible consequences of his or her actions.

As a matter of public policy, we must not excuse a defendant's actions, which endanger others, based upon a mental disturbance or illness that he or she actively and voluntarily contracted. If anything, the moral blameworthiness would seem to be even greater with respect to the long-term effects of many, repeated instances of voluntary intoxication occurring over an extended period of time. We ask that you affirm.

# · CRIMES THAT HARM BUSINESS ·

## LARCENY

It is holiday season at the mall, the period of greatest profits—and the most crime. At the Foot Forum, a teenager limps in wearing ragged sneakers and sneaks out wearing Super Rags, valued at $195. Down the aisle at a home furnishing store, a man is so taken by a $375 power saw that he takes it.

**Larceny**
is the trespassory taking of personal property with intent to steal.

**Larceny** is the trespassory taking of personal property with the intent to steal it. "Trespassory taking" means that someone else originally had the property. The Super Rags are personal property (not real estate), they were in the possession of the Foot Forum, and the teenager deliberately left without paying, intending never to return the goods. That is larceny. By contrast, suppose Fast Eddie leaves Bloomingdale's in New York, descends to the subway system, and jumps over a turnstile without paying. Larceny? No. He has "taken" a service—the train ride—but not personal property.

## COMPUTER CRIME

Shalon Dragon and his friend Durham were stopped by police in Jersey City, N.J., for driving erratically. The back seat was crammed with packages from Macy's department store. Durham first told the officer that he had bought the items in New Jersey and then changed his story, saying he had purchased them in Pennsylvania. A check revealed that both men had outstanding warrants, and each was arrested. A search of the car uncovered the following items: several fictitious New York state non-driver identification cards in the names of various individuals but containing either Dragon or Durham's picture; records titled "Mount Sinai Medical Center" listing names that matched those on the identification cards, as well as additional identifying information, such as addresses, dates of birth, and social security numbers; receipts from Macy's department stores located in New Jersey, New York, and Pennsylvania; 19 boxes of Timberland boots; five Macy's shopping bags containing new merchandise; and one shopping bag containing cellular phones.

What is going on here? Identity theft, that's what. The ascent of the Internet inevitably brings with it new forms of crime. In a moment, we will see the payoff Dragon received for his efforts. First, let us look at various federal statutes that apply to computer crimes.

- The **Computer Fraud and Abuse Act** prohibits using a computer to commit theft, espionage, trespass, fraud, and damage to another computer. An angry employee who hacks into his company's central computer system and damages the billing system has violated this law.

- The **Access Device Fraud Act** outlaws the fraudulent use of cards, codes, account numbers, and other devices to obtain money, goods, or services. For example, it is a violation of this act to reprogram a cellular telephone so that calls are charged to an improper account.

- The **Wire and Electronic Communications Interception Act** makes it a crime to intercept most wire, oral, and electronic communications. (This law does not prohibit recording your own conversations.) We warned you not to tape your roommate's conversations!

- The **Identity Theft and Assumption Deterrence Act** bars the use of false identification to commit fraud or other crime. This is the crime with which Dragon and Durham were charged. The Federal Trade Commission receives hundreds of thousands of complaints of identity theft every year: guard identifying data carefully.

How does identify theft work? Dragon and friend will explain—as they did in court.

## UNITED STATES V. DRAGON

### 471 F.3d 501
### THIRD CIRCUIT COURT OF APPEALS, 2006

### CASE SUMMARY

**Facts:** After his arrest, described above, Shalon Dragon was convicted of identity theft and sentenced to 44 months in prison. He appealed, claiming his punishment was too harsh.

**Issue:** *Did Dragon's identity theft warrant this sentence?*

**Decision:** Yes, the punishment fit the crime. Affirmed.

**Reasoning:** Durham obtained the personal information of 45 hospital patients from a contact he had at Mount Sinai Medical Center. Dragon and Durham then obtained false identification cards from photo stores in New York City, reflecting the patients' names and identifying information. They used the false identification to charge merchandise and gift cards to the real account-holder at Macy's stores in New Jersey, New York, and Pennsylvania.

After hearing from Dragon's counsel, Dragon himself, and the government, the District Court imposed a sentence of 44 months. The District Court commented on the complexity of the fraud scheme and the harm caused to victims of identity theft. The District Court twice acknowledged Dragon's request for leniency. It first stated, "Mr. Dragon, you're right you're a young man, but you're a young man that's found a pretty nifty way to get extra cash with very little danger to yourself." In imposing a higher sentence, the District Court emphasized Dragon's long history of fraudulent criminal conduct and the fact that Dragon had been given "a second chance" by various courts "over and over again." In light of his failure to take advantage of this past leniency, the District Court found it necessary to sentence Dragon "to a serious term of imprisonment."

Affirmed.

# FRAUD

Robert Dorsey owned Bob's Chrysler in Highland, Illinois. He ordered cars from the manufacturer, the First National Bank of Highland paid Chrysler, and Dorsey—supposedly—repaid the loans as he sold autos. Dorsey, though, began to suffer financial problems, and the bank suspected he was selling cars without repaying his loans. A state investigator notified Dorsey that he planned to review all dealership records. One week later, a fire engulfed the dealership. An arson investigator discovered that an electric iron, connected to a timer, had been placed on a pile of financial papers doused with accelerant.

The saddest part of this true story is that it is only too common. Some experts suggest that 1 percent of corporate revenues are wasted on fraud alone. Dorsey was convicted and imprisoned for committing two crimes that cost business billions of dollars annually—fraud and arson.[1]

> An electric iron, connected to a timer, had been placed on a pile of financial papers doused with accelerant.

---

[1] *United States v. Dorsey*, 27 F.3d 285 (7th Cir. 1994).

**Fraud**
is the deception of another person for the purpose of obtaining money or property.

**Bank fraud**
Using deceit to obtain money, assets, securities, or other property under the control of any financial institution.

**Wire fraud** and **mail fraud**
involve the use of mail, telegram, telephone, radio or television to obtain property by deceit.

**Medicare fraud**
Using false statements, bribes, or kickbacks to obtain Medicare payments from the federal or state government.

**Fraud** refers to various crimes, all of which have a common element: the deception of another person for the purpose of obtaining money or property from him. Robert Dorsey's precise violation was bank fraud, a federal crime. It is **bank fraud** to use deceit to obtain money, assets, securities, or other property under the control of any financial institution.

**Wire fraud** and **mail fraud** are additional federal crimes, involving the use of interstate mail, telegram, telephone, radio, or television to obtain property by deceit. For example, if Marsha makes an interstate phone call to sell land that she does not own, that is wire fraud.

Finally, Stacey, the hospital executive described in the chapter's introduction, committed a fourth type of fraud. **Medicare fraud** includes using false statements, bribes, or kickbacks to obtain Medicare payments from the federal or state government.

## EXAM *Strategy*

**Question:** Eric mails glossy brochures to 25,000 people, offering to sell them a one-month time-share in a stylish apartment in Las Vegas. The brochure depicts an imposing building, an opulent apartment, and spectacular pools. To reserve a space, customers need only send in a $2,000 deposit. Three hundred people respond, sending in the money. In fact, there is no such building. Eric, planning to flee with the cash, is arrested and prosecuted. His sentence could be as long as 20 years. (1) With what crime is he charged? (2) Is this a felony or misdemeanor prosecution? (3) Does Eric have a right to a jury trial? (4) Describe the burden of proof, *actus reus*, and *mens rea* in this case.

**Strategy:** (1) Eric is deceiving people, and that should tell you the *type* of crime. (2, 3) The potential 20-year sentence determines whether Eric's crime is a misdemeanor or felony and whether or not he is entitled to a jury trial. (4) We know that the government has the burden of proof in a criminal prosecutions—but *how much* evidence must it offer? Finally, distinguish *actus reus* from *mens rea*.

**Result:** Eric is charged with mail fraud. The potential penalty here is 20 years, so the crime is a felony. Eric has a right to a jury, as does any defendant whose sentence could be six months or longer. The prosecution must prove its case beyond a reasonable doubt, a much higher burden than that in a civil case. The *actus reus* in this case is mailing 25,000 brochures about a nonexistent building. The *mens rea* is Eric's guilty knowledge that the brochure is intended to swindle people.

## Arson

**Arson**
is the malicious use of fire or explosives to damage real estate or personal property.

Robert Dorsey, the Chrysler dealer, committed a second serious crime. **Arson** is the malicious use of fire or explosives to damage or destroy any real estate or personal property. It is both a federal and a state crime. Dorsey used arson to conceal his bank fraud. Most arsonists hope to collect on insurance policies. Every year thousands of buildings burn, particularly in economically depressed neighborhoods, as owners try to make a quick kill or extricate themselves from financial difficulties. We involuntarily subsidize their immorality by paying higher insurance premiums.

## EMBEZZLEMENT

**Embezzlement**
is the fraudulent conversion of property already in the defendant's possession.

This crime also involves illegally obtaining property, but with one big difference: The culprit begins with legal possession. **Embezzlement** is the fraudulent conversion of property already in the defendant's possession. A bank teller is expected to handle thousands of bills every day. But when she decides to tidy her cash drawer by putting all the wrinkled hundred-dollar bills in her pocket, she has embezzled.

# · CRIMES COMMITTED BY BUSINESS ·

A corporation can be found guilty of a crime based on the conduct of any of its agents, who include anyone undertaking work on behalf of the corporation. An agent can be a corporate officer, an accountant hired to audit a statement, a sales clerk, or almost any other person performing a job at the company's request.

If an agent commits a criminal act within the scope of his employment and with the intent to benefit the corporation, the company is liable. This means that the agent himself must first be guilty. The normal requirements of *actus reus* and *mens rea* apply. If the agent is guilty, the corporation is, too. The most common punishment for a corporation is a fine. This makes sense in that the purpose of a business is to earn a profit, and a fine, if large enough, hurts. Critics believe that the criminal law has gone too far. It is unfair, they argue, to impose *criminal* liability on a corporation, and thus penalize the shareholders, unless high-ranking officers were directly involved in the illegal conduct. The following case concerns a corporation's responsibility for a death caused by its employee.

## COMMONWEALTH v. ANGELO TODESCA CORP.

446 Mass. 128, 842 N.E. 2d 930
Supreme Judicial Court of Massachusetts, 2006

### CASE SUMMARY

**Facts:** Brian Gauthier, an experienced truck driver, worked for Todesca, a paving company. After about a year driving a particular 10-wheel tri-axle dump truck, Gauthier noticed that the backup alarm had stopped working. When he reported this, the company mechanic realized that the old alarm needed replacement. The mechanic had none in stock, so the company instructed Gauthier to drive the truck without the alarm.

About a month later, Gauthier and other Todesca drivers were delivering asphalt to the work site on a highway at the entrance to a shopping mall. A police officer directed the construction vehicles and the routine mall traffic. A different driver asked the officer to "watch our backs" as the trucks backed through the intersection. All the other trucks were equipped with backup alarms. When it was Gauthier's turn to back up, he struck the police officer, killing him.

The state charged the Todesca Corporation with motor vehicle homicide, and the jury found the company guilty. The trial judge imposed a fine—of $2,500. The court of appeals reversed the conviction, and the prosecution appealed to the state's highest court.

**Issue:** *Could the company be found guilty of motor vehicle homicide?*

**Decision:** Yes, the company was guilty of motor vehicle homicide.

**Reasoning:** The defendant maintains that a corporation never can be criminally liable for motor vehicle homicide because a corporation cannot "operate" a vehicle. We disagree. A corporation can act only through its agents. By the defendant's reasoning, a corporation never could be liable for any crime. A corporation can no more serve alcohol to minors, or bribe government officials, than operate a vehicle negligently. Only human agents are capable of these actions. Nevertheless, we consistently have held that a corporation may be criminally liable for such acts when performed by corporate employees, acting within the scope of their employment and on behalf of the corporation.

Gauthier's truck was not equipped with a functioning backup alarm, and he knew the alarm was missing. The defendant had a written safety policy mandating that all its trucks be equipped with such alarms. An employee's violation of his employer's rules, intended to protect the safety of third persons, is evidence of the employee's negligence, for which the employer may be held liable.

Gauthier never informed the victim that his truck did not have an alarm. The jury could have inferred that the victim, a veteran police officer, knew that the defendant routinely equipped its trucks with backup alarms. The victim expected to hear a backup alarm and would have, almost right in his ear—had the truck been properly maintained.

Affirmed.

# COMPLIANCE PROGRAMS

The **federal sentencing guidelines** are the detailed rules that judges must follow when sentencing defendants convicted of crimes in federal court. The guidelines instruct judges to determine whether, at the time of the crime, the corporation had in place a serious compliance program, that is, a plan to prevent and detect criminal conduct at all levels of the company. A company that can point to a detailed, functioning compliance program may benefit from a dramatic reduction in the fine or other punishment meted out. Indeed, a tough compliance program may even convince federal investigators to curtail an investigation and to limit any prosecution to those directly involved, rather than attempting to get a conviction against high-ranking officers or the company itself.

# RICO

The **Racketeer Influenced and Corrupt Organizations Act (RICO)** is one of the most powerful and controversial statutes ever written. Congress passed the law primarily to prevent gangsters from taking money they earned illegally and investing it in legitimate businesses. But RICO has expanded far beyond the original intentions of Congress and is now used more often against ordinary businesses than against organized criminals.

The government may prosecute both individuals and organizations for violating RICO. For example, the government may prosecute a mobster, claiming that he has run a heroin ring for years. It may also prosecute an accounting firm, claiming that it lied about corporate assets in a stock sale to make the shares appear more valuable than they really were. If the government proves its case, the defendant can be hit with large fines and a prison sentence of up to 20 years.

What is a violation of this law? **RICO prohibits using two or more racketeering acts to accomplish any of these goals:** (1) investing in or acquiring legitimate businesses with criminal money; (2) maintaining or acquiring businesses through criminal activity; or (3) operating businesses through criminal activity.

What does that mean in English? It is a two-step process to prove that a person or an organization has violated RICO:

- The prosecutor must show that the defendant committed two or more racketeering acts, which are any of a long list of specified crimes: embezzlement, arson, mail fraud, wire fraud, and so forth. If a stockbroker told two customers that Bronx Gold Mines was a promising stock, when she knew that it was worthless, that would be two racketeering acts.

- The prosecutor must show that the defendant used these racketeering acts to accomplish one of the three purposes listed above. If the stockbroker gave fraudulent advice and used the commissions to buy advertising for her firm, that would violate RICO.

# MONEY LAUNDERING

**Money laundering** consists of taking the proceeds of certain criminal acts and either (1) using the money to promote crime, or (2) attempting to conceal the source of the money.

Money laundering is an important part of major criminal enterprises. Successful criminals earn enormous sums, and they strive to filter their profits back into the flow of commerce so that their crimes go undetected. Laundering is an essential part of the corrosive traffic in drugs. Profits, all in cash, mount so swiftly that the most difficult step for a successful dealer can be to use the money without attracting the government's attention. However, as the following case illustrates, it is not only drug dealers who seek to launder their wrongfully obtained cash. But, really . . . a minister?

# United States v. Kennard

472 F.3d 851
11th Circuit Court of Appeals, 2006

## CASE SUMMARY

**Facts:** The Rev. Abraham Kennard bilked hundreds of churches and other nonprofits out of millions of dollars. He set up the Network International Investment Corporation and then approached churches and other nonprofit organizations that needed funds for capital improvements. Kennard made a simple offer: for every $3,000 in membership fees that an organization paid into the Network, they would receive $500,000 in grants. He told investors that the grants were possible because he had lined up famous investors who would provide tens of millions of dollars in financing. The Network would also be profiting from its own Christian resorts from around the country. Victims believed Kennard: More than 1,600 churches and other nonprofits around the nation paid in over $8.7 million.

Kennard deposited the money in an escrow account of his attorney, Scott Cunningham, and from there, he transferred the money to various locations, including the bank account of Promotional Time International, Inc., which was controlled by Abraham's brother, Laboyce Kennard.

Needless to say, the "investors" never received their money. Abraham was prosecuted and found guilty of various crimes. This case concerns Laboyce Kennard, who was convicted of money laundering. He appealed, arguing there was insufficient proof that he knowingly laundered money.

**Issue:** *Was there sufficient evidence that Laboyce knowingly laundered money?*

**Decision:** Yes, there was sufficient evidence that Laboyce knowingly laundered money. Affirmed.

**Reasoning:** This case demonstrates two important truths: "The love of money is the root of all evil," and "There's a sucker born every minute."

To convict Laboyce on the money laundering conspiracy charge, the government had to prove that some agreement existed to launder the proceeds of Abraham's church fraud, and that Laboyce knowingly and voluntarily participated in that agreement. Conspiracy may be proven by circumstantial evidence.

Laboyce made most of the account withdrawals, generally in cash. He went with Abraham to a Network meeting in Charlotte, N.C., at which Abraham gave Network members fake, oversized disbursement checks instead of the grant money they had been promised. Two months later, Laboyce videotaped Abraham conducting a sham groundbreaking ceremony for one of the Christian resorts Abraham had promised that Network would build, the plan being to show the video to members in an attempt to forestall their complaints. Laboyce later "worked security" for Abraham at a July Network meeting in Orlando where those in attendance reacted angrily to Abraham's announcement that their grants would again be delayed. And in October, Laboyce attended a meeting at which Abraham informed him that an FBI investigation of Network had led to the seizure of Cunningham's escrow account. All of this evidence is enough for a jury to find beyond a reasonable doubt that Laboyce knowingly participated in the conspiracy to launder the proceeds of the fraud.

## EXAM *Strategy*

**Question:** Explain the difference between embezzlement and money laundering. Give an example of each.

**Strategy:** Both crimes involve money illegally obtained, but they are very different. As to embezzlement, how did the criminal obtain the funds? In a laundering case, to what use is the criminal trying to put the cash?

**Result:** Embezzlement refers to fraudulently taking money that is already in the defendant's possession. For example, if a financial advisor, *lawfully entrusted* with his client's funds for investing, uses some of the cash to buy himself a luxurious yacht, he has embezzled the client's money. Money laundering consists of taking *illegally obtained* money and either using the funds to promote additional crimes or attempting to *conceal* the source of the cash. In the preceding case, the defendant laundered money when he took "investment" funds and transferred them, first to the lawyer's account, and then to various other banks, trying to disguise their origin.

·············································································································

## · THE CRIMINAL PROCESS ·

How does the government investigate and prosecute criminal cases? The steps vary from case to case, but the summary in Exhibit 7.1 highlights the important steps.

### *Informant*

Yasmin is a secretary to Stacey, the Be Patient executive who opened this chapter. She speaks to Moe, an FBI agent. She reports that Stacey routinely charges the government for patients who do not exist. Moe prepares an affidavit for Yasmin to sign, detailing everything she told him. An **affidavit** is simply a written statement signed under oath.

**Affidavit**
A written statement signed under oath.

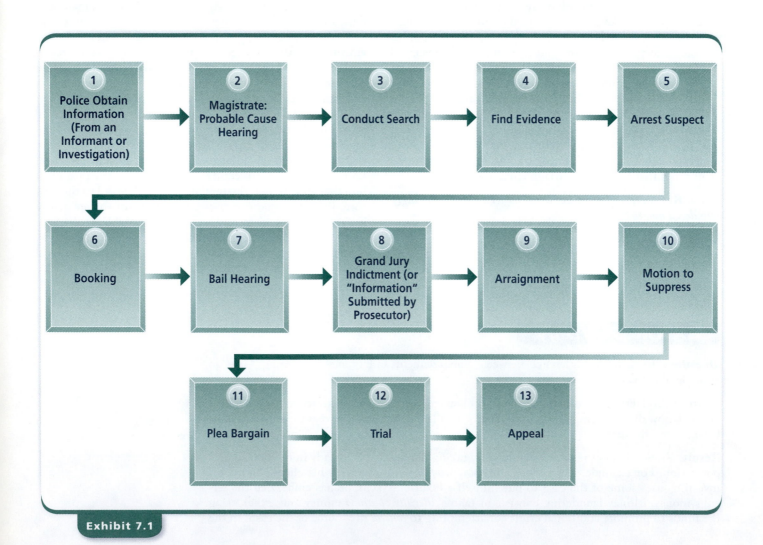

**Exhibit 7.1**

# WARRANT

Moe takes Yasmin's affidavit to a United States magistrate, an employee of the federal courts who is similar to a judge. Moe asks the magistrate to issue search warrants for Be Patient's patient records. A **search warrant** is written permission from a neutral official, such as the magistrate, to conduct a search. A warrant must specify with reasonable certainty the place to be searched and the items to be seized.

**Search warrant**
Written permission to conduct a search, given by a neutral official.

## Probable Cause

The magistrate will issue a warrant only if there is probable cause. **Probable cause** means that, based on all of the information presented, it is likely that evidence of crime will be found in the place to be searched. The magistrate will look at Yasmin's affidavit to determine (1) whether the informant (Yasmin) is reliable, and (2) whether she has a sound basis for the information. In this case, both are true, and the magistrate issues the warrant.

# SEARCH AND SEIZURE

Armed with the warrants, Moe and other agents arrive at Be Patient hospitals, show the warrants, and take away the appropriate records. The search may not exceed what is described in the warrant. The agents cart the records back to headquarters and enter the data into a computer. The computer compares the records of actual patients with the bills submitted to the government and indicates that 10 percent of all bills are for fictional patients. Moe summarizes the new data on additional affidavits and presents the affidavits to the magistrate, who issues arrest warrants.

## Fourth Amendment

The **Fourth Amendment** prohibits the government from making illegal searches and seizures. This amendment protects individuals, corporations, partnerships, and other organizations. In general, the police must obtain a warrant before conducting a search. If the police search without one, they have probably violated the Fourth Amendment.

**The Fourth Amendment**
prohibits the government from making illegal searches and seizures.

## Exclusionary Rule

Under the **exclusionary rule**, evidence obtained illegally may not be used at trial against the victim of the search. Suppose when Yasmin called the FBI, Moe simply drove straight to one of Be Patient's hospitals and grabbed patient records. Moe lacked a warrant, the search was illegal, and the evidence would be excluded from trial.

**Exclusionary rule**
holds that evidence obtained illegally may not be used at trial against the victim of the search.

# ARREST

Moe arrives at Be Patient and informs Stacey that she is under arrest. He informs her of her right to remain silent. He drives Stacey to FBI headquarters, where she is booked; that is, her name, photograph, and fingerprints are entered in a log. She is entitled to a prompt bail hearing. A judge or magistrate will set an amount of bail that she must pay in order to go free pending the trial. The purpose of bail is to ensure that Stacey will appear for all future court hearings.

## Self-Incrimination

The **Fifth Amendment** bars the government from forcing any person to testify against himself. In other words, the police may not use mental or physical coercion to force a confession out of someone. Society does not want a government that engages in torture. Such abuse might occasionally catch a criminal, but it would grievously injure innocent people and make all citizens fearful of the government that is supposed to represent and protect them. Before the police obtain a confession, the defendant must be told that he has the right to remain silent; that anything he says can be used against him at trial; that he has the right to a lawyer; and that if he cannot afford a lawyer, the court will appoint one for him.

**The Fifth Amendment**
prohibits self-incrimination.

# INDICTMENT

**Indictment**
The government's formal charge that the defendant has committed a crime and must stand trial.

Moe turns all of his evidence over to Larry, the local prosecutor for the United States. Larry presents the evidence to a grand jury. It is the grand jury's job to determine whether there is probable cause that this defendant committed the crime with which she is charged. The grand jury votes to indict Stacey. An **indictment** is the government's formal charge that the defendant has committed a crime and must stand trial. The grand jury is persuaded that there is probable cause that Stacey billed for 1,550 nonexistent patients, charging the government for $290 million worth of services that were never performed. The grand jury indicts her for (1) Medicare fraud, (2) mail fraud, (3) computer crimes, and (4) RICO violations. It also indicts Be Patient, Inc., and other employees.

# ARRAIGNMENT

Stacey is ordered back to court. A clerk reads her the formal charges of the indictment. The judge asks whether Stacey has a lawyer, and of course she does. If she did not, the judge would urge her to get one quickly. If a defendant cannot afford a lawyer, the court will appoint one to represent her free of charge. The judge now asks the lawyer how Stacey pleads to the charges. Her lawyer answers that she pleads not guilty to all charges.

## Plea Bargaining

**Plea bargain**
An agreement between prosecution and defense that the defendant will plead guilty to a reduced charge in exchange for a reduced sentence.

Sometime before trial, the two attorneys will meet to consider a plea bargain. A **plea bargain** is an agreement between prosecution and defense that the defendant will plead guilty to a reduced charge, and the prosecution will recommend to the judge a relatively lenient sentence. Based on the RICO violations alone, Stacey faces a possible 20-year prison sentence, along with a large fine and a devastating forfeiture order. The government makes this offer: Stacey will plead guilty to 100 counts of mail fraud; Be Patient will repay all $290 million and an additional $150 million in fines; the government will drop the RICO and computer crime charges and recommend to the judge that Stacey be fined only $1 million and sentenced to three years in prison. In the federal court system, about 75 percent of all prosecutions end in a plea bargain. In state court systems, the number is often higher.

Stacey agrees to the government's offer. The judge accepts the plea, and Stacey is fined and sentenced accordingly. A judge need not accept the bargain but usually does.

# TRIAL AND APPEAL

When there is no plea bargain, the case must go to trial. The mechanics of a criminal trial are similar to those for a civil trial, described in Chapter 3, on dispute resolution. It is the prosecution's job to convince the jury beyond a reasonable doubt that the defendant committed every element of the crime charged.

## The Revised Patriot Act

In response to the devastating attacks of September 11, 2001, Congress passed a sweeping antiterrorist law known as the Patriot Act. The statute was designed to give law enforcement officials greater power to investigate and prevent potential terrorist assaults, but it was controversial from the start. In a particularly troublesome section, the law permitted the FBI to issue a **national security letter** (NSL) to communications firms such as Internet service providers and telephone companies. An NSL typically demanded that the recipient furnish to the government its customer records and that the recipient never divulge to anyone what it has done. NSLs could be used to obtain access to subscriber billing records, phone, financial, credit and other information—even records of books taken from libraries. A federal court declared this provision an unconstitutional violation of rights under the Fourth Amendment (illegal searches) and the First Amendment (free speech).

Congress revised and reauthorized the Patriot Act, but a year later, the same court found the new NSL provisions unconstitutional. Evidence indicated that between 2003 and 2005, the FBI had issued over 143,000 NSLs. The trial judge declared that the NSLs permitted the government to learn the identity of Internet users engaged in anonymous speech in online discussions, obtain a list of all e-mails the person had sent, and then gather information on all recipients. The court declared: "The Constitution was designed so that the dangers of any given moment would never suffice as justification for discarding fundamental individual liberties or circumscribing the judiciary's unique role under our governmental system in protecting those liberties and upholding the rule of law."[2]

---

[2] *Doe v. Gonzalez*, 500 Fed. Supp. 2d 379 (SDNY, 2007).

## CHAPTER CONCLUSION

**Business crime appears in unexpected places, with surprising suspects.** Classic fraud and embezzlement schemes are often foiled with commonsense preventive measures. Federal sentencing guidelines make it eminently worthwhile for corporations to establish aggressive compliance programs. Sophisticated computer and money laundering crimes can be thwarted only with determination and the cooperation of citizens and police agencies.

## EXAM REVIEW

**1.** **PROSECUTION'S CASE** In all prosecutions, the government must establish that the defendant's conduct was outlawed, that the defendant committed the *actus reus*, and that he had the necessary *mens rea*. The government must prove its case beyond a reasonable doubt. (p. 96)

**Question:** Arnie owns a two-family house in a poor section of the city. A fire breaks out, destroying the building and causing $150,000 damage to an adjacent store. The state charges Arnie with arson. Simultaneously, Vickie, the store owner, sues Arnie for the damage to her property. Both cases are tried to juries, and the two juries hear identical evidence of Arnie's actions. But the criminal jury acquits Arnie, while the civil jury awards Vickie $150,000. How did that happen?

**Strategy:** The opposite outcomes are probably due to the different burdens of proof in a civil and criminal case. Make sure that you know that distinction. (See the "Result" at the end of this section.)

**2.** **DEFENSE CASE** In addition to factual defenses, such as mistaken identity or alibi, a defendant may offer various legal defenses, such as insanity. (p. 97)

**3.   LARCENY**  Larceny is the trespassory taking of personal property with the intent to steal. (p. 98)

........................................................................................................

**4.   FRAUD**  Fraud refers to a variety of crimes, all of which involve the deception of another person for the purpose of obtaining money or property. (p. 100)

........................................................................................................

**5.   ARSON**  Arson is the malicious use of fire or explosives to damage or destroy real estate or personal property. (p. 100)

........................................................................................................

**6.   EMBEZZLEMENT**  Embezzlement is the fraudulent conversion of property already in the defendant's possession. (p. 100)

........................................................................................................

**7.   COMPUTER CRIMES**  Computer crime statutes prohibit computer trespass and fraud; wrongful use of cards, codes, and identification; and most intercepting or taping of conversations. (p. 98)

........................................................................................................

**8.   CORPORATE LIABILITY**  If a company's agent commits a criminal act within the scope of her employment and with the intent to benefit the corporation, the company is liable. (p. 101)

........................................................................................................

**9.   RICO**  RICO prohibits using two or more racketeering acts to invest in legitimate business or carry on certain other criminal acts. RICO permits civil lawsuits as well as criminal prosecutions. (p. 102)

**EXAM Strategy**

**Question:** Cheryl is a bank teller. She figures out a way to steal $99.99 per day in cash without getting caught. She takes the money daily for 8 months and invests it in a catering business she is starting with Floyd, another teller. When Floyd learns what she is doing, he tries it, but is caught in his first attempt. He and Cheryl are both prosecuted.

   (a)  Both are guilty only of larceny.
   (b)  Both are guilty of larceny and violating RICO.
   (c)  Both are guilty of embezzlement; Cheryl is also guilty of violating RICO.
   (d)  Both are guilty of embezzlement and violating RICO.
   (e)  Both are guilty of larceny and violating RICO.

**Strategy:** You need to know the difference between larceny and embezzlement. What is it? Once you have that figured out, focus on RICO. The government must prove two things. First, that the defendant committed crimes more than once—how many times? Second, that the defendant used the criminal proceeds for a specific purpose—what? (See the "Result" at the end of this section.)

**10.   MONEY LAUNDERING**  Money laundering consists of taking the proceeds of certain criminal acts and either (1) using the money to promote crime, or (2) attempting to conceal the source of the money. (p. 102)

........................................................................................................

**1. Result:** The plaintiff offered enough proof in the civil case to convince a jury *by a preponderance of the evidence* that Arnie had damaged her store. However, that same evidence, offered in a criminal prosecution, was not enough to persuade the jury *beyond a reasonable doubt* that Arnie had lit the fire.

**9. Result:** Cheryl and Floyd both committed embezzlement, which refers to fraudulently taking money that was properly in their possession. Floyd did it once, but a RICO conviction requires two or more racketeering acts—Floyd has not violated RICO. Cheryl embezzled dozens of times and invested the money in a legitimate business. She is guilty of embezzlement and RICO.

## PRACTICE EXAM

## MATCHING QUESTIONS

Match the following terms with their definitions:

___ A. Larceny

___ B. RICO

___ C. Felony

___ D. *Mens rea*

___ E. M'Naghten Rule

___ F. Embezzlement

1. A statute designed to prevent the use of criminal proceeds in legitimate businesses
2. Fraudulently keeping property already in the defendant's possession
3. A test used to gauge a defendant's sanity
4. The most serious type of crime, usually punishable by a year or more in prison
5. The trespassory taking of personal property
6. A guilty state of mind

## TRUE/FALSE QUESTIONS

Circle true or false:

1. T  F    Both the government and the victim are entitled to prosecute a crime.

2. T  F    A misdemeanor is a less serious crime, punishable by less than a year in jail.

3. T  F    In all criminal cases, the prosecution must prove *actus reus*.

4. T  F    Corporate officers can be convicted of crimes; corporations themselves cannot be.

5. T  F    An affidavit is the government's formal charge of criminal wrongdoing.

## MULTIPLE-CHOICE QUESTIONS

6. The insanity defense

A. Is available in less than five states nationwide

B. Means that if the jury finds that a defendant was insane at the time of the crime, the defendant goes free

C. Means that if the jury finds that a defendant was insane at the time of the crime, the defendant is locked in prison for the same time period as if he had been found guilty

D. Means that if the jury finds that a defendant was insane at the time of the crime, the defendant will be locked in a mental hospital until he is no longer a danger to society

E. Used to be the law in all states, but has now been outlawed by court rulings

7. Probable cause means

A. Substantial evidence that the person signing the affidavit has legitimate reasons for requesting the warrant

B. Substantial similarity between the items sought and the items found

C. Substantial likelihood that a crime has taken place or is about to take place

D. Trustworthy evidence that the victim of the search is known to have criminal tendencies

E. That based on all of the information presented, it is likely that evidence of crime will be found in the place mentioned

8. Police believe that Jay is dealing drugs from his apartment. They search his apartment without a warrant and find 3 kilos of cocaine. The cocaine

A. Will be excluded from Jay's trial

B. Is valid evidence provided the police reasonably believed Jay was a drug dealer

C. Is valid evidence provided the police had spoken to neighbors before searching

D. Was improperly obtained but may be used in Jay's trial

E. May not be used in Jay's trial but may be used during his sentencing

9. A prosecutor concerned that he may lack sufficient evidence to obtain a conviction may agree to

A. An affidavit

B. A warrant

C. An appeal

D. An indictment

E. A plea bargain

10. Professor asks Janice, his teaching assistant, to please drive the professor's car to the repair shop. Janice gets in and drives, not to the garage, but 1,400 miles farther west, to Las Vegas. Janice has committed

A. Fraud

B. Embezzlement

C. Larceny

D. RICO violation

E. Access Device Fraud

## SHORT-ANSWER QUESTIONS

11. ETHICS: What is the rationale for treating an insane defendant differently from others? Do you find the theory persuasive? Why or why not?

12. Northwest Telco Corp. (Telco) provides long-distance telephone service. Customers dial a general access number, then enter a six-digit access code and then the phone number they want to call. A computer places the call and charges the account. On January 10, 1990, Cal Edwards, a Telco engineer, noticed that Telco's general access number was being dialed exactly every 40 seconds. After each dialing, a different six-digit number was entered, followed by a particular long-distance number. This continued from 10 p.m. to 6 a.m. Why was Edwards concerned?

13. ROLE REVERSAL: Write a short-answer question that focuses on the elements of a RICO violation.

## INTERNET RESEARCH PROBLEM

Search for a Web site devoted to Internet crime. Find a current crime that might victimize you. What steps should you take to avoid harm?

**You can find further practice problems in the Online Quiz at www.cengage.com/blaw/beatty.**

# INTERNATIONAL LAW

**The day** after Anfernee graduates from business school, he opens a shop specializing in sports caps and funky hats. Sales are brisk, but Anfernee is making little profit because his American-made caps are expensive. Then an Asian company offers to sell him identical merchandise for 45 percent less than the American suppliers charge. Anfernee is elated, but he quickly begins to wonder. Why is the new price so low? Are the foreign workers paid a living wage? Could the Asian company be using child labor? The sales representative requests a $50,000 cash "commission" to smooth the export process in his country. That sounds suspicious. The questions multiply without end. Will the contract be written in English or a foreign language? Must Anfernee pay in dollars or some other currency? The foreign company wants a letter of credit. What does that mean?

Anfernee should put this lesson under his cap: The world is now one vast economy, and negotiations quickly cross borders. Transnational business grows

> **The world is now one vast economy, and negotiations quickly cross borders.**

with breathtaking speed. The United States now exports more than $800 billion worth of goods each year, and an additional $330 billion worth of services. Leading exports include industrial machinery, computers, aircraft and other transportation equipment, electronic equipment, and chemicals.

Here are the nations that trade the most goods with the United States as of 2007:[1]

| Rank | Country | Exports (in billions of U.S. dollars) | Imports (in billions of U.S. dollars) | Total, All Trade (in billions of U.S. dollars) | Percent of Total Trade |
|---|---|---|---|---|---|
| | Total, All Countries | 1,061.4 | 1,791.8 | 2,853.3 | 100.0 |
| | Total, Top 15 Countries | 750.4 | 1,325.2 | 2,075.6 | 72.7 |
| 1 | Canada | 229.1 | 288.7 | 517.8 | 18.1 |
| 2 | China | 58.3 | 295.8 | 354.2 | 12.4 |
| 3 | Mexico | 126.3 | 194.1 | 320.4 | 11.2 |
| 4 | Japan | 57.4 | 133.6 | 191.0 | 6.7 |
| 5 | Germany | 45.5 | 86.3 | 131.8 | 4.6 |
| 6 | United Kingdom | 46.4 | 52.5 | 98.9 | 3.5 |
| 7 | South Korea | 31.6 | 44.1 | 75.7 | 2.7 |
| 8 | France | 25.2 | 38.5 | 63.7 | 2.2 |
| 9 | Taiwan | 23.6 | 35.2 | 58.7 | 2.1 |
| 10 | Netherlands | 29.8 | 16.8 | 46.6 | 1.6 |
| 11 | Brazil | 22.0 | 23.6 | 45.6 | 1.6 |
| 12 | Venezuela | 9.5 | 35.5 | 45.0 | 1.6 |
| 13 | Italy | 12.9 | 32.1 | 44.9 | 1.6 |
| 14 | Singapore | 23.9 | 17.0 | 40.9 | 1.4 |
| 15 | Saudi Arabia | 9.0 | 31.5 | 40.5 | 1.4 |

**Multinational enterprises (MNEs)**
Companies that do business in several countries simultaneously.

Who are the people who do all this trading? Anfernee's modest sports cap concern is at one end of the spectrum. At the other are **multinational enterprises (MNEs)**, that is, companies doing business in several countries simultaneously.

[1] United States Census Bureau. Data is year-to-date through November, 2007.

## ▪ MNEs AND POWER ▪

An MNE can take various forms. It may be an Italian corporation with a wholly owned American subsidiary that manufactures electrical components in Alabama and sells them in Brazil. Or it could be a Japanese company that licenses a software company in India to manufacture computer programs for sale throughout Europe. One thing is constant: the power of these huge enterprises. Each of the top 10 MNEs earns annual revenue greater than the gross domestic product of two-thirds of the world's nations. More than 200 MNEs have annual sales exceeding $1 billion and more cash available at any one time than the majority of countries do. Money means power. This corporate might can be used to create jobs, train workers, and build lifesaving medical equipment. Such power can also be used to corrupt government officials, rip up the environment, and exploit already impoverished workers. International law is vital.

## ▪ TRADE REGULATION ▪

Nations regulate international trade in many ways. In this section we look at export and import controls that affect trade out of and into the United States. **Exporting** is shipping goods or services out of a country. The United States, with its huge farms, is the world's largest exporter of agricultural products. **Importing** is shipping goods and services into a country. The United States suffers trade deficits every year because the value of its imports exceeds that of its exports, as the following table demonstrates.

**Export**
To ship goods or services out of a country.

**Import**
To ship goods or services into a country.

| U.S. INTERNATIONAL TRADE IN GOODS AND SERVICES (IN MILLIONS OF DOLLARS) | | | | | | | | |
|---|---|---|---|---|---|---|---|---|
| | Balance | | | Exports | | | Imports | | |
| Year | Total | Goods | Services | Total | Goods | Services | Total | Goods | Services |
| 1980 | −19,407 | −25,500 | 6,093 | 271,834 | 224,250 | 47,584 | 291,241 | 249,750 | 41,491 |
| 1990 | −80,864 | −111,037 | 30,173 | 535,233 | 387,401 | 147,832 | 616,097 | 498,438 | 117,659 |
| 2000 | −378,344 | −452,414 | 74,070 | 1,070,980 | 771,994 | 298,986 | 1,449,324 | 1,224,408 | 224,916 |
| 2006 | −758,522 | −838,271 | 79,749 | 1,445,703 | 1,023,109 | 422,594 | 2,204,225 | 1,861,380 | 342,845 |

*Source:* United States Census Bureau

## EXPORT CONTROLS

You and a friend open an electronics business, intending to purchase goods in this country for sale abroad. A representative of Interlex stops in to see you. Interlex is an Asian electronics company, and the firm wants you to obtain for it a certain kind of infrared dome. The representative explains that this electronic miracle helps helicopters identify nearby aircraft. You find a Pennsylvania company that manufactures the domes, and you realize that you can buy and sell them to Interlex for a handsome profit. Any reason not to? As a matter of fact, there is.

All nations limit what may be exported. In the United States, several statutes do this, including the **Arms Export Control Act** (AECA). This statute permits the president to create a list of controlled goods, all related to military weaponry. No one may export any listed item without a license.

**Arms Export Control Act**
Prohibits the export of specific weapons.

The AECA prohibits exports of the infrared domes. The equipment is used in the guidance system of one of the most sophisticated weapons in the American defense arsenal. Foreign governments have attempted to obtain the equipment through official channels, but the American government has placed the domes on the list of restricted military items. When a U.S. citizen did send such goods to a foreign country, he was convicted and imprisoned.

# IMPORT CONTROLS

## *Tariffs*

**Tariff**
A tax imposed on goods when they enter a country. Also called *duty.*

Tariffs are the most widespread method of limiting what may be imported into a nation. A **tariff** is a tax imposed on goods when they enter a country. Tariffs are also called *duties.* Nations use tariffs primarily to protect their domestic industries. Because the company importing the goods must pay this duty, the importer's costs increase, making the merchandise more expensive for consumers. This renders domestic products more attractive. High tariffs unquestionably help local industry, but they proportionately harm local buyers. Consumers benefit from zero tariffs, because the unfettered competition drives down prices.

Tariffs change frequently and vary widely from one country to another. For manufactured goods, the United States imposes an average tariff of less than 4 percent, about the same as that of the European Union. However, major trading partners around the world set tariffs of 10 to 30 percent for identical items, with those duties generally being highest in developing countries. Foodstuffs show even greater diversity. For agricultural products, average tariffs are about 25 percent in North America, 30 percent in the European Union, 39 percent in South America, 75 percent in sub-Saharan Africa, and 113 percent in South Asia. You can export potatoes to Israel duty-free, but the same produce sent to Norway will cost you a tariff of 476 percent. Rice is welcome in Iceland, but not in Japan, where the duty is 648 percent. Tariffs count.[2]

**Classification**
The Customs Service decision about the precise nature of imported goods.

**Classification** The U.S. Customs Service imposes tariffs at the point of entry into the United States. A customs official inspects the merchandise as it arrives and **classifies** it, in other words, decides precisely what the goods are. This decision is critical because the tariff will vary depending on the classification. The goods in the following case were not designed to hold money—but that is what the case was really about.

## AVENUES IN LEATHER, INC. V. U.S.

423 F.3D 1326, COURT OF APPEALS FOR THE FEDERAL CIRCUIT, 2005

### CASE SUMMARY

**Facts:** Avenues in Leather (Avenues) imported Presentation Calcu-Folios. What are they, you ask? It took two courts to supply the answer.

Calcu-Folios are 13 inches tall, 11 inches wide, and 1.5 inches deep. They are made of paperboard covered with plastic. A padded handle is fitted to the spine. The goods are zippered on three sides and contain an interior sleeve, several small pockets, a solar-powered calculator, and a three-ring binder.

The Customs Service (Customs) classified the merchandise under tariff Heading 4202, which covers "Trunks, suitcases, vanity cases, attaché cases, briefcases, school satchels, and similar containers." Avenues argued the Calcu-Folios should be classified under Heading 4820, which applies to "Binders, folders, file covers, memorandum pads, letter pads, and similar articles."

That distinction might sound pretty dull (in fact, it *is* pretty dull), but of course the real difference is profit and loss.

---

[2] World Bank; Economic Research Service, United States Department of Agriculture.

Heading 4820 carries a tariff of about 3 percent, while Heading 4202 imposes a 20 percent rate. Avenues filed suit and the Court of International Trade agreed with the company, awarding the lower duty. Customs appealed.

**Issue:** *Should the Calcu-Folio be classified as a briefcase or a binder?*

**Decision:** The Calcu-Folio was a binder, and should have received the lower tariff rate.

**Reasoning:** The Calcu-Folio's designer testified that the article was designed as an aid for taking and organizing notes. Customs submitted dictionary definitions of "briefcase" to argue that the merchandise was classifiable as a briefcase or similar container. It also introduced evidence that the items had been marketed as business travel goods, useful for carrying non-paper personal objects.

While the Calcu-Folios may be used to organize and protect small, flat items, they have an internal capacity of only 1 inch. They cannot carry newspapers, books, and other objects normally carried in briefcases.

The Court of International Trade correctly concluded that the Calcu-Folios are neither classifiable as a form of briefcase, nor as a "similar container," under Heading 4202. Affirmed.

**Valuation**   After classifying the imported goods, customs officials impose the appropriate duty *ad valorem,* meaning "according to the value of the goods." In other words, the Customs Service must determine the value of the merchandise before it can tax a percentage of that value. This step can be equally contentious, since goods will have different prices at each stage of manufacturing and delivery. The question is supposed to be settled by the transaction value of the goods, meaning the price actually paid for the merchandise when sold for export to the United States (plus shipping and other minor costs). But there is often room for debate, so importers use customs agents to help negotiate the most favorable valuation.

> **Valuation**
> The Customs Service's determination of the tariff, based on the value of the goods.

## Dumping

**Dumping**   means selling merchandise at one price in the domestic market and at a cheaper, unfair price in an international market. Suppose a Singapore company, CelMaker, makes cellular telephones for $20 per unit and sells them in the United States for $12 each, vastly undercutting domestic American competitors. CelMaker may be willing to suffer short-term losses in order to drive out competitors for the American market. Once it has gained control of that market, it will raise its prices, more than compensating for its initial losses. And CelMaker may get help from its home government. Suppose the Singapore government prohibits foreign cellular phones from entering Singapore. CelMaker may sell its phones for $75 at home, earning such high profits that it can afford the temporary losses in America.

> **Dumping**
> Selling merchandise at one price in the domestic market and at a cheaper, unfair price in the international market.

In the United States, the Commerce Department investigates suspected dumping. If the Department concludes that the foreign company is selling items at **less than fair value,** and that this harms an American industry, it will impose a **dumping duty** sufficiently high to put the foreign goods back on fair footing with domestic products.

### EXAM *Strategy*

**Question:**  California producers of sea salt protest to the American government that they cannot compete with the same product imported from China. How do the California producers want the United States government to respond? May the U.S. government legally oblige?

**Strategy:**  Domestic producers who cannot compete with foreign competition typically ask their government to impose higher tariffs on the imported goods. However, the whole point of GATT and the WTO is to avoid trade wars. There are two instances in which the United States government is free to levy increased duties on the Chinese goods. What are they?

**Result:**  When a company *dumps* goods, it sells them overseas at an artificially low price, generally to destroy competition and gain a foothold. That is illegal, and the domestic (United States) government may impose dumping duties to protect local producers. Subsidized goods—those supported by foreign company's government—are also illegal. If the United States government can demonstrate illegal subsidies, it imposes countervailing duties designed to give all producers an equal chance.

## Quotas

**Quota**
A limit on the quantity of a particular good that may enter a nation.

A **quota** is a limit on the quantity of a particular good that may enter a nation. For example, the United States, like most importing nations, has agreements with many developing nations, placing a quota on imported textiles. In some cases, textile imports from a particular country may grow by only a small percentage each year. Without such a limit, textile imports from the developing world would increase explosively because costs are so much lower there. As part of the GATT treaty (discussed below), the wealthier nations pledged to increase textile imports from the developing countries.

Money and politics are a volatile mix, as demonstrated by all recorded history from 3000 B.C. to the present. As long as nations have existed, they have engaged in disputes about quotas and tariffs. And that is why more than 100 countries negotiated and signed the GATT treaty.

## General Agreement on Tariffs and Trade (GATT)

**GATT**
The General Agreement on Tariffs and Trade is a massive international treaty designed to eliminate trade barriers and bolster international commerce.

What is GATT—the greatest boon to American commerce in a century, or the worst assault on the American economy in 200 years? It depends on whom you ask. Let's start where everyone agrees.

**GATT** is the General Agreement on Tariffs and Trade. This massive international treaty has been negotiated on and off since the 1940s to eliminate trade barriers and bolster commerce. GATT has already had considerable effect. In 1947, the worldwide average tariff on industrial goods was about 40 percent. Now it is about 4 percent (although agricultural duties still average over 40 percent). The world's economies have exploded over that half century. Proponents of GATT applaud the agreement. Opponents scoff that both lower duties and higher trade would have arrived without GATT.

**Signatory**
A nation that signs a treaty.

**Ratification**
The vote by a nation's legislature to honor an international agreement.

In 1994, the United States and 125 other countries signed the treaty. A **signatory** is a nation that signs a treaty. However, a signatory is not bound by the agreement until it is **ratified**, that is, until the nation's legislature votes to honor it. In the United States, Congress voted to ratify GATT. If the latest round of cuts is fully implemented, average duties in all signatories should drop to about 3.7 percent. Further, nearly half of all trade in industrial goods will be duty free, at least in developed countries. That must be good—or is it?

## Trade

Leading supporters of GATT suggest that its lower tariffs vastly increase world trade. The United States should be one of the biggest beneficiaries because for decades this country has imposed lower duties than most other nations. American companies will for once compete on equal footing.

But opponents claim that the United States will be facing nations with unlimited pools of exploited labor. These countries will dominate labor-intensive merchandise such as textiles, eliminating millions of American jobs.

## World Trade Organization and the Environment

**The World Trade Organization** is a group created by GATT to resolve trade disputes.

GATT created the **World Trade Organization (WTO)** to resolve trade disputes. The WTO is empowered to hear arguments from any signatory nation about tariff violations or nontariff barriers. This international "court" may order compliance from any nation violating GATT and may penalize countries by imposing trade sanctions.

Here is how the WTO decides a trade dispute. Suppose that the United States believes that Brazil is unfairly restricting trade. The United States asks the WTO's Dispute Settlement Body

(DSB) to form a panel, which consists of three nations uninvolved in the dispute. After the panel hears testimony and arguments from both countries, it releases its report. The DSB generally approves the report, unless either nation appeals. If there is an appeal, the WTO Appellate Body hears the dispute and generally makes the final decision, subject to approval by the entire WTO. No single nation has the power to block final decisions. If a country refuses to comply with the WTO's ruling, affected nations may retaliate by imposing punitive tariffs.

**ETHICS**  Child labor is an even more wrenching issue. The practice exists to some degree in all countries and is common throughout the developing world. The International Labor Organization, an affiliate of the United Nations, estimates that 120 million children between the ages of 5 and 14 work full time, and 130 million more labor part time. As the world generally becomes more prosperous, this ugly problem has actually increased. Children in developing countries typically work in agriculture and domestic work, but many toil in mines and others in factories, making rugs, glass, clothing, and other goods.

The rug industry highlights this tragedy. Tens of millions of children, some as young as four, toil in rug workrooms, seven days a week, 12 hours a day. Many, shackled to the looms they operate, are essentially slaves, working for pennies a day or, in some cases, for no money at all. As we confront such brutal conditions, we must bear in mind that child labor is truly universal. The United Farm Workers union estimates that 800,000 underage children help their migrant parents harvest U.S. crops—work that few Americans are willing to do. ◆

## WTO Summary

The WTO continues to grow, adding China (and a quarter of the world's population) early in this millennium. The WTO has resolved many trade disputes that otherwise might have caused bitter tariff wars. The United States has been the most active user of the dispute settlement process, bringing almost one quarter of all cases to the WTO. The United States has prevailed in the majority of its cases, though not all. For example, as a result of WTO consultations, Japan changed its law to grant full copyright protection to sound recordings, a case worth about $500 million annually to the American recording industry.

In a case that did not settle, India was ordered to eliminate import bans on 2,700 types of goods, including consumer products, textiles, agricultural products, petrochemicals, and other commodities. On the other hand, Japan prevailed in another case brought by the United States, when a WTO panel determined, contrary to assertions made on behalf of Eastman Kodak, that Japan did not discriminate against imported film.

# REGIONAL AGREEMENTS

Many regional agreements also regulate international trade. We will briefly describe the two that most closely affect the United States.

## The European Union

The **European Union (EU)** used to be known as the Common Market. The original six members—Belgium, France, Luxembourg, the Netherlands, West Germany, and Italy—have been joined by 21 additional countries. See the map on this page.

The EU is one of the world's most powerful associations, with a prosperous population of nearly half a billion people. Its sophisticated legal system sets Union-wide standards for tariffs, dumping, subsidies, antitrust, transportation, and many other issues. The first goals of the EU were to eliminate trade barriers between member nations; establish common tariffs with respect to external countries; permit the free movement of citizens across its borders; and coordinate its agricultural and fishing policies for the collective

**European Union**
An association of 27 European countries joined together for the purpose of facilitating trade, free movement between nations, and setting economic and foreign policy.

**The EU (European Union) Countries)**

good. The EU has largely achieved these goals. Most but not all of the EU countries have adopted a common currency, the euro. During the next decade, the Union will focus on further economic integration and effective coordination of foreign policy.

### NAFTA

**North American Free Trade Agreement**
An commercial association among Mexico, Canada and the United States designed to eliminate almost all trade barriers among the three nations.

In 1993, the United States, Canada, and Mexico signed the **North American Free Trade Agreement (NAFTA)**. The principal goal was to eliminate almost all trade barriers, tariff and nontariff, among the three nations. Like GATT, this trilateral (three-nation) compact has been controversial, and there will probably never be agreement on NAFTA's value because the treaty has enriched some while impoverishing others. Unquestionably, trade among the three nations has increased enormously. Mexico now sells more to the United States than do Germany and the United Kingdom combined.

Opponents of the treaty argue that NAFTA costs the United States jobs and lowers the living standards of American workers by forcing them to compete with low-paid labor. For example, Swingline Staplers closed a factory in Queens, New York after 75 years of operation and moved to Mexico. Instead of paying its American workers $11.58 per hour, Swingline paid Mexican workers 50 cents an hour to do the same work. Proponents contend that although some jobs are lost, many others are gained, especially in fields with a future, such as high technology. They claim that as new jobs invigorate the Mexican economy, consumers there will be able to afford American goods for the first time, providing an enormous new market.

## · INTERNATIONAL SALES AGREEMENTS ·

> **You must focus on two principal issues: the sales contract and letters of credit.**

Cowboy boots are hot in France. Big Heel, Inc., your small company in Tucson, Arizona, makes superb boots with exquisite detailing, and you realize that France could be a bonanza.

Le Pied D'Or, a new, fast-growing French chain of shoe stores, is interested in buying 10,000 pairs of your boots, at about $300 per pair. You must focus on two principal issues: the sales contract and letters of credit. You are wise enough to know that you must have a written contract—$3 million is a lot of money for Big Heel.

This is a contract for the sale of goods. Goods are things that can be moved, such as boots, airplanes, pencils, and computers. A sale of goods is governed by different law than the sale of real estate (e.g., a house) or services (e.g., accounting).

## WHAT LAW GOVERNS THE SALE OF GOODS?

Potentially, three conflicting laws could govern your boot contract: Arizona law, French law, and an international treaty. Each is different, and it is therefore essential to negotiate which law will control.

Because this contract is for the sale of goods, your local law is the **Arizona Uniform Commercial Code (UCC).** The UCC is discussed throughout Units 2 and 3, on contracts and commercial transactions. It is a statute that has taken the common law principles of contract and modified them to meet the needs of contemporary business. Article 2 of the UCC governs the sale of goods. American business lawyers are familiar with the UCC and will generally prefer that it govern. French law is based on **Roman law** and the **Napoleonic Code** and is obviously different. French lawyers and business executives are naturally partial to it. How to compromise? Perhaps by using a neutral law.

**The United Nations Convention on Contracts for the International Sale of Goods (CISG)** is the result of 50 years of work by various international groups, all seeking to create a uniform, international law on this important subject. Finally, in 1980, a United Nations conference adopted the CISG, though it became the law in individual nations only if and when they adopted it. The United States and most of its principal trading partners have adopted this important treaty.

**The CISG applies automatically to any contract for the sale of goods between two parties from different countries, each of which is a signatory.** France and the United States have both signed. Thus the CISG automatically applies to the Big Heel–Pied D'Or deal unless the parties specifically opt out. If the parties want to be governed by other law, they must state very clearly that they exclude the CISG and elect, for example, the UCC.

> **The United Nations Convention on Contracts for the International Sale of Goods**
> A uniform, international law on trade that has been adopted by the United States and most of its principal trading partners.

## CHOICE OF FORUM

The parties must decide not only what law governs, but where disagreements will be resolved. The French and American legal systems are dramatically different. In a French civil lawsuit, generally neither side is entitled to depose the other or to obtain interrogatories or even documents, in sharp contrast to the American system where such discovery methods dominate litigation. American lawyers, accustomed to discovery to prepare a case and advance settlement talks, are unnerved by the French system. Similarly, French lawyers are dismayed at the idea of spending two years taking depositions, exchanging paper, and arguing motions, all at great expense. At trial, the contrasts grow. In a French civil trial, there is generally no right to a jury. The rules of evidence are more flexible (and unpredictable), neither side employs its own expert witnesses, and the parties themselves never appear as witnesses.

## FINAL CHOICES

The parties must select a language for the contract and a currency for payment. Language counts, because legal terms seldom translate literally. Currency is vital, because the exchange rate may alter between the signing and payment.

The parties agree that the contract price will be paid in U.S. dollars. Pied D'Or is unfamiliar with the UCC and absolutely refuses to make a deal unless either French law or the CISG governs. Your lawyer recommends accepting the CISG, provided that the contract is written in English and that any disputes will be resolved in Arizona courts. Pied D'Or reluctantly agrees. You have a deal!

## LETTER OF CREDIT

Because Pied D'Or is new and fast growing, you are not sure it will be able to foot the bill. Your lawyer recommends that payment be made by letter of credit. Here is how the letter will work.

Big Heel demands that the contract include a provision requiring payment by **confirmed irrevocable letter of credit**. Le Pied D'Or agrees. The French company now contacts its bank, La Banque Bouffon, and instructs Bouffon to issue a letter of credit to Big Heel. The letter of credit is a promise by the bank itself to pay Big Heel, if Big Heel presents certain documents. Banque Bouffon, of course, expects to be repaid by Pied D'Or. The bank is in a good position to assess Pied D'Or's creditworthiness, since it is local and can do any investigating it wants before issuing the credit. It may also insist that Pied D'Or give Bouffon a mortgage on property, or that Pied D'Or deposit money in a separate Bouffon account.

But at Big Heel, you are still not entirely satisfied about getting paid because you don't know anything about Bouffon. That is why you have required a *confirmed* letter of credit. Bouffon will forward its letter of credit to Big Heel's own bank, the Bandito Trust Company of Tucson. Bandito examines the letter and then confirms the letter. This is *Bandito's own guarantee* that it will pay Big Heel. Bandito will do this only if it knows, through international banking contacts,

> **Confirmed irrevocable letter of credit**
> A promise made by the seller's bank to pay for the goods, and then guaranteed by the buyer's bank.

that Bouffon is a sound bank. The risk has now been spread to two banks, and at Big Heel you are confident of payment.

Why do banks do this? For a fee. When will Bandito pay Big Heel? As soon as Big Heel presents documents indicating that the boots have been placed on board a ship bound for France.

The following case shows why sellers often demand a letter of credit.

## CENTRIFUGAL CASTING MACHINE CO., INC. v. AMERICAN BANK & TRUST CO.

966 F.2D 1348, 1992 U.S. APP. LEXIS 13089
UNITED STATES COURT OF APPEALS FOR THE TENTH CIRCUIT, 1992

### CASE SUMMARY

**Facts:** Centrifugal Casting Machine Co. (CCM) entered into a contract with the State Machinery Trading Co. (SMTC), an agency of the Iraqi government. CCM agreed to manufacture cast iron pipe plant equipment for a total price of $27 million. The contract specified payment of the full amount by confirmed irrevocable letter of credit. The Central Bank of Iraq then issued the letter, on behalf of SMTC (the "account party") to be paid to CCM (the "beneficiary"). The Banca Nazionale del Lavorov (BNL) confirmed the letter.

Following Iraq's invasion of Kuwait on August 2, 1990, President George H. W. Bush issued two executive orders blocking the transfer of property in the United States in which Iraq held any interest. In other words, no one could use, buy, or sell any Iraqi property or cash. When CCM attempted to draw upon the letter of credit, the United States government intervened. The government claimed that like all Iraqi money in the United States, this money was frozen by the executive order. The United States District Court rejected the government's claim, and the government appealed.

**Issue:**  *Is CCM entitled to be paid pursuant to the letter of credit?*

**Decision:** CCM is entitled to payment. Affirmed.

**Reasoning:** United States claims that it is freezing Iraqi assets to punish international aggression. That is a legitimate foreign policy argument. However, no court has the power to rewrite basic principles of international trade.

A letter of credit has unique value for two reasons. First, the bank that issues the letter is substituting its credit for that of the buyer. Because the bank is promising to pay with its own funds, the seller is confident of receiving its money.

Second, the bank's obligation to pay on the letter of credit is entirely separate from the underlying bargain between buyer and seller. The bank must pay, even if the seller has breached the contract or the buyer has gone bankrupt. The money in this case came from the bank that issued the letter; the government may not seize it. Any other ruling would undermine all letters of credit.

## EXAM *Strategy*

**Question:**  In an international contract for the sale of goods, Seller is to be paid by a confirmed irrevocable letter of credit. Buyer claims that the goods are defective and threatens to sue. If the parties are going to end up in court anyway, why bother with a letter of credit?

**Strategy:**  A confirmed letter of credit is unique because the seller is assured of payment as soon as it presents a proper bill of lading to the appropriate local bank—regardless of the quality of the goods. Seller would much rather defend this lawsuit against Buyer than sue for its money in foreign courts.

**Result:**  There *may* be a lawsuit, but Seller is not worried. It is Buyer who must sue, probably in Seller's home country. Buyer now risks substantial time and cash for an uncertain outcome. When the parties discuss a settlement, as surely they will, Seller is holding a big advantage—the cash.

## Extraterritoriality

The United States has many statutes designed to protect employees, such as those that prohibit discrimination on the basis of race, religion, gender, and so on. Do these laws apply overseas? This is an issue of **extraterritoriality**—the power of one nation to impose its laws in other countries.[3] Many American companies do business through international **subsidiaries**—foreign companies which they control. The subsidiary may be incorporated in a nation that denies workers the protection they would receive in the United States. What happens when an employee of a foreign subsidiary argues that his rights under an *American* statute have been violated? You make the call.

**Extraterritoriality**
The power of one nation to impose its laws in other countries.

**Subsidiary**
A company controlled by a foreign company.

[3] Extraterritoriality can also refer to exemption from local laws. For example, ambassadors are generally exempt from the law of the nation in which they serve.

## YOU *be the* JUDGE

### CARNERO v. BOSTON SCIENTIFIC CORPORATION
433 F.3d 1
First Circuit Court of Appeals, 2006

**Facts:** Boston Scientific (BSC) was an American company that manufactured medical equipment. The company had its headquarters in Massachusetts but did business around the world through foreign subsidiaries. One of the company's subsidiaries was Boston Scientific Argentina (BSA), and it was there that Ruben Carnero began working. His employment contract stated that he would work at BSA's headquarters in Buenos Aires and be paid in pesos. Argentine law was to govern the contract. Four years later, Carnero took an assignment to work as a country manager for a different BSC subsidiary, Boston Scientific Do Brasil (BSB). Carnero frequently traveled to Massachusetts to meet with company executives, but did most of his work in South America.

About a year later, BSB fired Carnero, and BSA soon did the same. Carnero claimed that the companies terminated him in retaliation for his reporting to BSC executives that the Argentine and Brazilian subsidiaries inflated sales figures and engaged in other accounting fraud. Carnero filed suit in Massachusetts, alleging that his firing violated an American statute, the Sarbanes-Oxley Act of 2002 (SOX).

Congress passed that law in response to the massive fraud cases involving Enron, Arthur Andersen, and other companies. The law was passed primarily to protect investors, but it included a "whistleblower" provision. That section was designed to guard employees who informed superiors or investigating officials of fraud within the company. The law allows injured employees reinstatement and back pay.

BSC argued that SOX did not apply overseas and the District Court agreed, dismissing the case. Carnero appealed.

**Issue:** Does SOX protect a whistleblower employed overseas by a subsidiary of an American company?

**Argument for Carnero:** Congress passed SOX because the American people were appalled by the massive fraud in major corporations, and the resulting harm to employees, investors, the community, and the economy. The whistleblower protection is designed to encourage honest employees to come forward and report wrongdoing—an act that no employee wants to do, and one which has historically led to termination. Mr. Carnero knew his report would be poorly received but believed he had an ethical obligation to protect his company. For that effort he was fired, and now Boston Scientific attempts to avoid liability using the technicality of corporate hierarchy.

Yes, Mr. Carnero was employed by BSB and BSA. But both of those companies are owned and operated by Boston Scientific. It is the larger company, with headquarters in the United States, which calls the shots. That is why executives in Massachusetts frequently asked Mr. Carnero to report to them—and why he brought them his unhappy news.

A whistleblower deserves gratitude and a pay raise. Mr. Carnero may well have saved his employer from massive losses and public disgrace. Would Boston Scientific like to wind up as Enron did—the company in bankruptcy court, its executives in prison? If Boston Scientific is too petty to acknowledge Mr. Carnero's contribution, the company should at least honor the purpose and intent of SOX by protecting his job.

*continued*

**Argument for Boston Scientific:** First, we do not know whether there have been any accounting irregularities or not. Second, the fact that Mr. Carnero is employed by companies incorporated in Argentina and Brazil is more than a technicality. He is asking an American court to go into two foreign countries—sovereign nations with good ties to the United States—and investigate accounting and employment practices of companies incorporated and operating there. The very idea is offensive. No nation can afford to treat its allies and trading partners with such contempt.

If the United States can impose its whistleblowing law in foreign countries, may those nations impose their rules and values here? Suppose that a country forbids women to do certain work. May companies in those nations direct American subsidiaries to reject all female job applicants? Neither the citizens nor courts of this country would tolerate such interference for a moment.

Mr. Carnero's idea is also impractical. How would an American court determine why he was fired? Must the trial judge here subpoena Brazilian witnesses and demand documentary evidence from that country?

Finally, the SOX law does not apply overseas because Congress never said it did. The legislators—well aware that American corporations operate subsidiaries abroad—made no mention of those companies when they passed this statute.

# · FOREIGN CORRUPT PRACTICES ACT ·

Foreign investment is another major source of international commerce. Assume that Fonlink is an American communications corporation that wants to invest in the growing overseas market. As a Fonlink executive, you travel to a small, new republic that was formerly part of the Soviet Union. You meet a trade official who tells you that Fonlink is the perfect company to install a new, nationwide telephone/digital system for his young country. You are delighted with his enthusiasm. Over lunch, the official tells you that he can obtain an exclusive contract for Fonlink to do the work, but you will have to pay him a commission of $750,000. Such a deal would be worth millions of dollars for Fonlink, and a commission of $750,000 is economically sensible. Should you pay it?

**Foreign Corrupt Practices Act**
prohibits an American businessperson from giving anything of value to a foreign official to influence an official decision.

The **Foreign Corrupt Practices Act (FCPA)** makes it illegal for an American businessperson to give "anything of value" to any foreign official in order to influence an official decision. The classic example of an FCPA violation is bribing a foreign official to obtain a government contract. You must find out exactly why the minister needs so much money, what he plans to do with it, and how he will obtain the contract.

You ask these questions, and the trade official responds, "I am a close personal friend of the minister of the interior. In my country, you must know people to make things happen. The minister respects my judgment, and some of my fee will find its way to him. Do not trouble yourself with details."

Bad advice. A prison sentence is not a detail. The FCPA permits fines of $100,000 for individuals and $1 million for corporations, as well as prison sentences of up to five years. If you pay money that "finds its way to the minister," you have violated the act.

It is sad but true that in many countries bribery is routine and widely accepted. When Congress investigated foreign bribes to see how common they were, more than 300 U.S. companies admitted paying hundreds of millions of dollars in bribes to foreign officials. Legislators concluded that such massive payments distorted competition among American companies for foreign contracts, interfered with the free market system, and undermined confidence everywhere in our way of doing business. The statutory response was simple: Foreign bribery is illegal, plain and simple. The FCPA has two principal requirements:

- *Bribes.* The statute makes it illegal for U.S. companies and citizens to bribe foreign officials to influence a governmental decision. The statute prohibits giving anything of value and also bars using third parties as a conduit for such payments.

- *Record Keeping.* All publicly traded companies—whether they engage in international trade or not—must keep detailed records that prevent hiding or disguising bribes. These records must be available for U.S. government officials to inspect.

Transparency International, a nonprofit agency based in Germany, publishes a "Corruption Perception Index," gauging how much dishonesty businesspeople and scholars encounter in different nations. In 2004, the agency listed 145 nations on its index. The highest-ranking countries (perceived *least* corrupt) were Finland, New Zealand, Denmark, Iceland, Singapore, Sweden, Switzerland, Norway, Australia, and the United Kingdom. The agency listed the United States as the 17th least corrupt. The countries ranking lowest (perceived *most* corrupt) were Côte d'Ivoire, Georgia, Indonesia, Tajikstan, Turkmenistan, Azerbaijan, Paraguay, Chad, Myanmar, Nigeria, Bangladesh, and Haiti. The full index is available from Transparency International at **http://www.transparency.org.**

## CHAPTER CONCLUSION

**Overseas investment, like sales abroad, offers potentially great rewards but significant pitfalls.** A working knowledge of international law is essential to any entrepreneur or executive seriously considering foreign commerce. As the WTO lowers barriers, international trade will increase, and your awareness of these principles will grow still more valuable.

## EXAM REVIEW

1. **AECA** The Arms Export Control Act (AECA) restricts exports from the United States that would harm national security or foreign policy. (p. 113)

..................................................................................................................

2. **TARIFF** A tariff is a tax imposed on goods when they enter a country. Tariffs are also known as duties. The U.S. Customs Service classifies goods when they enter the United States and imposes appropriate tariffs. (p. 114)

**Question:** Sports Graphics, Inc. imports "Chill" brand coolers from Taiwan. Chill coolers have an outer shell of vinyl, with handles and pockets, and an inner layer of insulation. In a recent lawsuit, the issue was whether "Chill" coolers were "luggage" or "articles used for preparing, serving, or storing food or beverages," as Sports Graphics claimed. Who was the other party to the dispute, why did the two sides care about this, and what arguments did they make?

**Strategy:** The Customs Service (the other party) classifies goods and then imposes an appropriate *ad valorem* tax. What is at stake, of course, is money. (See the "Result" at the end of this section.)

3. **DUMPING** Most countries, including the United States, impose duties for goods that have been dumped (sold at an unfairly low price in the international market). (p. 115)

..................................................................................................................

4. **GATT** The General Agreement on Tariffs and Trade (GATT) is lowering the average duties worldwide. Proponents see it as a boon to trade; opponents see it as a threat to workers and the environment. (p. 116)

.................................................................................................................................

5. **WTO** GATT created the World Trade Organization (WTO), which resolves disputes between signatories to the treaty. (p. 116)

.................................................................................................................................

6. **CISG** A sales agreement between an American company and a foreign company may be governed by the UCC, by the law of the foreign country, or by the United Nations Convention on Contracts for the International Sale of Goods (CISG). The CISG differs from the UCC in several important respects. (p. 119)

.................................................................................................................................

7. **LETTERS OF CREDIT** A confirmed, irrevocable letter of credit is an important means of facilitating international sales contracts, because the seller is assured of payment by a local bank as long as it delivers the specified goods. (p. 119)

**EXAM Strategy**

**Question:** Flyby Knight (FK) contracts to sell 12 helicopters to Air Nigeria, for $8 million each. Payment is to be made by letter of credit, issued by the Bank of Nigeria, confirmed by Citibank in New York, and due when the confirming bank receives a bill of lading indicating that all helicopters are on board ship, ready for sailing to Nigeria. FK loads the aircraft on board ship, and the next day delivers the bill of lading to Citibank. The same day, Air Nigeria informs FK that its inspectors onboard ship have discovered serious flaws in the rotator blades and the fuel lines. Air Nigeria states it will neither accept nor pay for the helicopters. Is FK entitled to its $96 million?

   (a) FK is entitled to no money.

   (b) FK is entitled to no money *provided* Air Nigeria can prove the helicopters are defective.

   (c) Air Nigeria is obligated to pay FK the full price.

   (d) Bank of Nigeria is obligated to pay FK the full price.

   (e) Citibank is obligated to pay FK the full price.

**Strategy:** Payment is to be made by confirmed letter of credit. Ask yourself what that means. In such a case, the confirming bank is obligated to pay the seller when the bank receives a bill of lading indicating that conforming goods have been delivered. What about the fact that the goods seem defective? That is irrelevant. It is precisely to avoid long-distance arguments over such problems that sellers insist on these letters. (See the "Result" at the end of this section.)

8. **FCPA** The Foreign Corrupt Practices Act (FCPA) makes it illegal for an American business person to bribe foreign officials. (p. 122)

.................................................................................................................................

**2. Result:** Customs evidently claimed that the goods were luggage, which carries a much higher tariff than food storage articles. Customs argued that the handles and portability made the articles luggage. But Sports Graphics prevailed, convincing the court that the primary purpose of the containers was the storage of food. The lawsuit reduced the company's tariff from 20 percent to 3.4 percent.

**7. Result:** When Citibank receives the bill of lading, indicating delivery of the helicopters, it is obligated to pay. The correct answer is E.

# PRACTICE EXAM

## MATCHING QUESTIONS

Match the following terms with their definitions:

___ A. Signatory        1. A trade agreement between Mexico, the United States, and Canada

___ B. NAFTA            2. Selling goods at a cheaper, unfair price internationally

___ C. Tariff           3. An international convention that governs the sale of goods

___ D. CISG             4. A nation that signs a treaty

___ E. Dumping          5. A duty imposed on imports

## TRUE/FALSE QUESTIONS

Circle true or false:

1. T   F   A problem for many international merchants is that tariffs have been rising for the last decade.

2. T   F   The United States imports more goods and services (combined) than it exports.

3. T   F   "Valuation" is the process by which the Customs Services decides the nature of goods being imported into the United States.

4. T   F   The United States helped negotiate GATT but ironically has refused to sign the agreement.

5. T   F   Decisions of the WTO are nonbinding recommendations.

## MULTIPLE-CHOICE QUESTIONS

6. With which country does the United States trade more than any other?

   A. Mexico                      D. United Kingdom

   B. Germany                     E. Canada

   C. China

7. The Commerce Department alleges that Interlex, a foreign company, is selling Palm Pilots in the United States for less than the cost of production. The department is charging Interlex with

   A. A NAFTA violation           D. An AECA violation

   B. Dumping                     E. A CISG violation

   C. An FCPA infraction

8. "Choice of forum" refers to

   A. The exporting venue         D. The method of payment in an international contract

   B. The importing venue

   C. The country where legal disputes will be settled        E. An inter-banking agreement designed to ensure payment for goods

9. The WTO rules that the nation of Lugubria must lower tariffs on software from the United States from 45 percent to 8 percent, but Lugubria refuses to comply. What can the United States do?

    A. Nothing, because the WTO's ruling is only a recommendation

    B. Appeal to the United Nations

    C. Appeal to the World Court

    D. Impose retaliatory tariffs

    E. File suit in federal court in the U.S.

10. Your Chicago company negotiates an agreement with a British company for the sale of goods. The contract does not specify the law that governs the agreement. If there is a dispute, what law *will* govern?

    A. The UCC

    B. The CISG

    C. British law

    D. Illinois law

    E. EU law

## SHORT-ANSWER QUESTIONS

11. Jean-François, a French wine exporter, sues Bob Joe, a Texas importer, claiming that Bob Joe owes him $2 million for wine. Jean-François takes the witness stand to describe how the contract was created. Where is the trial taking place?

12. Blondek and Tull were two employees of an American company called Eagle Bus. They hoped that the Saskatchewan provincial government would award Eagle a contract for buses. To bolster their chances, they went to Saskatchewan and paid $50,000 to two government employees. Back in the United States, they were arrested and charged with a crime. Suppose they argue that even if they did something illegal, it occurred in Canada, and that Canada is the only nation that can prosecute them. Comment on the defense.

13. ETHICS: Hector works in Zoey's importing firm. Zoey overhears Hector on the phone say, "OK, 30,000 ski parkas at $80 per parka. You've got yourself a deal. Thanks a lot." When Hector hangs up, Zoey is furious, yelling, "I told you not to make a deal on those Italian ski parkas without my permission! I think I can get a better price elsewhere." "Relax, Zoey," replies Hector. "I wanted to lock them in, to be sure we had some in case your deal fell through. It's just an oral contract, so we can always back out if we need to." Is that ethical? How far can a company go to protect its interests? Does it matter that another business might make serious financial plans based on the discussion? Apart from the ethics, is Hector's idea smart?

14. Continental Illinois National Bank issued an irrevocable letter of credit on behalf of Bill's Coal Company for $805,000, with the Allied Fidelity Insurance Co. as beneficiary. Bill's Coal Co. then went bankrupt, and subsequently Allied presented to Continental documents that were complete and conformed to the letter of credit. Continental refused to pay. Because Bill's Coal was bankrupt, there was no way Continental would collect once it had paid on the letter. Allied filed suit. Who should win?

15. ROLE REVERSAL: Draft an essay or short-answer question that focuses on how a confirmed, irrevocable letter of credit works.

## INTERNET RESEARCH PROBLEM

Read about the worldwide problem of sweatshops. Is this a serious problem? If so, what role should the law play in its resolution? What can one student do about it?

**You can find further practice problems in the Online Quiz at www.cengage.com/blaw/beatty.**

# 2

# Contracts

# CHAPTER
# 9

# INTRODUCTION TO CONTRACTS

**Have a seat.** Great to see you. Here, grab a menu. Yes, you're right: the tables at this café are jammed together. In fact, *that's why I chose* the spot. Listen to the conversations around us. Oh, go on, don't worry—eavesdropping is acceptable for academic purposes. To our right, a famous director is chatting with Katrina, the glamorous actress. He is trying to sign her up for a new film, *Body Work,* but she seems hesitant.

> **Katrina hesitates; Bob nods encouragingly, then sticks out his hand and . . . Katrina shakes! It's a wrap—I guess.**

KATRINA (doubtful): I'm intrigued with the character, Bob, and I'd love to work with you. I *am* concerned about the nude scenes. The one on the toboggan run was okay. But that scene in the poultry factory—very explicit. I don't work fully nude.

BOB: We'll solve it—what am I, a sleaze? This is fine art; don't give it another thought. We're talking $2.5 million, Katrina. $600,000 up front, the rest deferred, the usual percentages.

KATRINA: As you know, my fee is $3 million. I should talk with my agent. I'd need something in writing about the nudity, the percentages, all of it.

BOB: I have to settle this fast. Julia is seriously considering the role.

KATRINA (worried): *Julia!* Are you kidding? Bob, I said I'm interested.

Oh my, look at that. Katrina hesitates; Bob nods encouragingly, then sticks out his hand and . . . Katrina shakes! It's a wrap—I guess. Now bend your ear toward the table on our left. The man wants to quit his job and accept a position with a competing company, but the woman, his boss, is insisting he stay.

EMILY: I taught you everything you know about computer encryption, Jake, and you're not taking that sophisticated training to my number one competitor.

JAKE: Emily, their offer is just too good to turn down. I deserve a chance to expand my horizons. Come on, be human!

EMILY (waving a document): Look here, my friend. Page four of your employment contract: "I agree that if I leave the company for any reason, I will not work for a competing firm anywhere in the United States for a period of three years." And here is your lovely, rounded signature. You work for me, Jake, or you go flip burgers.

Gee, that Emily is tough. I guess poor Jake is stuck in his present job. We need something cheerier. Listen to the two women behind you. While I was waiting, they have been bargaining over a vacation condo.

LI-LI: I don't think I can go lower than 485.

MARIA: Well . . . $450,000. I guess.

LI-LI: Maria, it has the best ocean view in the whole complex. And you would be on the top floor!

MARIA: 460.

Li-Li: 475. My final offer. Do you happen to have the time?

Maria: The time? What's the hurry? Oh . . . okay, 475. Shake, partner.

Li-Li: It's a deal. That's great. I'm so happy for you. You're going to love it. Do we need to put this in writing?

Maria: Are you kidding? How long have we known each other, since we were six?

Li-Li: Five and a half! You're right, why spend the money on lawyers and boring documents? Let's spend it on champagne. Waiter!

The café is a hotbed of contract negotiations—but then, so is our society. These three conversations demonstrate why it is important to understand contract law. Bob and Katrina think they have an agreement, but in fact *they do not,* because the parties have not achieved a meeting of the minds. Jake, if he reads the next chapter, will be delighted to learn that *he is free to change jobs:* a court will not enforce Emily's noncompetition agreement. Finally, Li-Li should skip the champagne and instead scratch a simple contract onto a napkin. Without Maria's signature, Li-Li *cannot enforce her friend's promise* to pay.

## · THE PURPOSE OF A CONTRACT ·

Parties enter into contracts attempting to control their future. **Contracts exist to make business matters more predictable.** Most contracts work out precisely as the parties intended because the parties fulfill their obligations. Most—but not all. We will study contracts that have gone wrong. We look at these errant deals to learn how to avoid the problems they manifest.

### Judicial Activism versus Judicial Restraint

In most contract cases, judges do their best simply to enforce whatever terms the parties agreed to. Even if the contract results in serious harm to one party, a court will generally enforce it. This is **judicial restraint.** On the other hand, some courts practice **judicial activism.** In contract law, this means that a court will ignore certain provisions of a contract, or an entire agreement, if the judge believes that enforcing the deal would be unjust. A court may even be willing to create a contract where none existed if it appears necessary to avoid injustice. Judicial activism makes the law **more flexible but less predictable.**

# ISSUES (AND ANSWERS)

The three contract negotiations described earlier illustrate several basic principles, and we will consider each. A contract has four elements:

1. **Agreement.** One party must make a valid offer, and the other party must accept it. (Bob failed to make a clear offer to Katrina.)
2. **Consideration.** There has to be bargaining that leads to an exchange between the parties.
3. **Legality.** The contract must be for a lawful purpose. (Emily's noncompetition agreement is probably illegal.)
4. **Capacity.** The parties must be adults of sound mind.

Contract cases often raise several other important issues, which we examine throughout the next three chapters:

- **Consent.** Neither party may trick or force the other into the agreement.
- **Written Contracts.** Some contracts must be in writing to be enforceable. (Neither Li-Li nor Maria may enforce the condo contract unless there is a signed agreement.)
- **Third-Party Interests.** Some contracts affect people other than the parties themselves.
- **Performance and Discharge.** If a party fully accomplishes what the contract requires, his duties are discharged.
- **Remedies.** A court will award money or other relief to a party injured by a breach of contract.

# CONTRACTS DEFINED

A **contract** is a promise that the law will enforce. As we look more closely at the elements of contract law, we will encounter some intricate issues, but remember that we are usually interested in answering three basic questions of common sense, all relating to promises:

- Is it certain that the defendant promised to do something?
- If she did promise, is it fair to make her honor her word?
- If she did not promise, are there unusual reasons to hold her liable anyway?

**Contract**
A promise that the law will enforce.

# · TYPES OF CONTRACTS ·

## BILATERAL AND UNILATERAL CONTRACTS

In a **bilateral contract**, both parties make a promise. Suppose a producer says to Gloria, "I'll pay you $2 million to star in my new romantic comedy, *A Promise for a Promise*, which we are shooting three months from now in Santa Fe." Gloria says, "It's a deal." That is a bilateral contract. Each party has made a promise to do something. The producer is now bound to pay Gloria $2 million, and Gloria is obligated to show up on time and act in the movie. The vast majority of contracts are bilateral contracts.

In a **unilateral contract**, one party makes a promise that the other party can accept only by *doing* something. These contracts are less common. Suppose the movie producer says to Leo, "I'll give you a hundred bucks if you mow my lawn this weekend." Leo is not promising to do it. If he mows the lawn, he has accepted the offer and is entitled to his hundred dollars. If he spends the weekend at the beach, neither he nor the producer owes anything.

**Bilateral contract**
A contract where both parties make a promise.

**Unilateral contract**
A contract where one party makes a promise that the other party can accept only by doing something.

# EXPRESS AND IMPLIED CONTRACTS

In an **express contract**, the two parties explicitly state all important terms of their agreement. *The great majority* of binding agreements are express contracts. The contract between the producer and Gloria is an express contract, because the parties explicitly state what Gloria will do, where and when she will do it, and how much she will be paid. Some express contracts are oral, as that one was, and some are written.

In an **implied contract**, the words and conduct of the parties indicate that they intended an agreement. Suppose every Friday, for two months, the producer asks Leo to mow his lawn, and loyal Leo does so each weekend. Then for three more weekends, Leo simply shows up without the producer asking, and the producer continues to pay for the work done. But on the twelfth weekend, when Leo rings the doorbell to collect, the producer suddenly says, "I never asked you to mow it. Scram." The producer is correct that there was no express contract, because the parties had not spoken for several weeks. But a court will probably rule that the conduct of the parties has *implied* a contract. Not only did Leo mow the lawn every weekend, but the producer even paid on three weekends when they had not spoken. It was reasonable for Leo to assume that he had a weekly deal to mow and be paid. Naturally, there is no implied contract thereafter.

Today, the hottest disputes about implied contracts often arise in the employment setting. Many employees have "at-will" agreements. This means that the employees are free to quit at any time and the company has the right to fire them at any time, for virtually any reason. Courts routinely enforce at-will contracts. But often a company provides its workers with personnel manuals that guarantee certain rights. The legal issue is whether the handbook implies a contract guaranteeing the specified rights.

## DEMASSE v. ITT CORPORATION

194 ARIZ. 500, 984 P.2D 1138, SUPREME COURT OF ARIZONA, 1999

### CASE SUMMARY

**Facts:** Roger Demasse and five others were employees-at-will at ITT Corporation, where they started working at various times between 1960 and 1979. Each was paid an hourly wage.

ITT issued an employee handbook, which it revised four times over two decades.

The first four editions of the handbook stated that within each job classification, any layoffs would be made in reverse order of seniority. The fifth handbook made two important changes. First, the document stated that "nothing contained herein shall be construed as a guarantee of continued employment. ITT does not guarantee continued employment to employees and retains the right to terminate or lay off employees."

Second, the handbook stated that "ITT reserves the right to amend, modify, or cancel this handbook, as well as any or all of the various policies [or rules] outlined in it." Four years later, ITT notified its hourly employees that layoff guidelines for hourly employees would be based not on seniority but on ability and performance. About 10 days later, the six employees were laid off, though less senior employees kept their jobs. The six employees sued. ITT argued that because the workers were employees

at-will, the company had the right to lay them off at any time, for any reason. The case reached the Arizona Supreme Court.

**Issue:** *Did ITT have the right unilaterally to change the layoff policy?*

**Decision:** ITT did not have the right unilaterally to change the layoff policy, because a valid implied contract prevented the company from doing so.

**Reasoning:** An employer has the right to lay off an at-will employee for virtually any reason. That means that the employer also has the right unilaterally to change the layoff policy. However, when the words or conduct of the parties establish an implied contract, the employee is no longer at-will.

In deciding whether there is an implied contract concerning job security, the key issue is whether a reasonable person would conclude that the parties intended to limit the employer's right to terminate the employee. A company makes a contract offer when it puts in the handbook a statement about job security that a reasonable employee would consider a commitment. The worker can then accept that offer by beginning or continuing employment. At that point, the parties have created a binding implied contract. Here, the first handbook declared that lay-offs would be based on seniority. The employees accepted that offer by working, and from that time on, an implied contract governed the employment relationship. ITT had no right unilaterally to change the layoff policy.

**ETHICS** Other than the workers and the company, who are the stakeholders? What *alternatives* were available to Demasse? What are the most important *values* involved in this dispute? If there are conflicting values, which are most important? ◆

## EXECUTORY AND EXECUTED CONTRACTS

A contract is **executory** when one or more parties have not fulfilled their obligations. Recall Gloria, who agrees to act in the producer's film beginning in three months. The moment Gloria and the producer strike their bargain, they have an executory bilateral express contract. A contract is **executed** when all parties have fulfilled their obligations. When Gloria finishes acting in the movie and the producer pays her final fee, their contract will be fully executed.

**Executory contract**
A binding agreement in which one or more of the parties has not fulfilled its obligations.

**Executed contract**
An agreement in which all parties have fulfilled their obligations.

## VALID, UNENFORCEABLE, VOIDABLE, AND VOID AGREEMENTS

A **valid contract** is one that satisfies all the law's requirements. A court will therefore enforce it. The contract between Gloria and the producer is a valid contract, and if the producer fails to pay Gloria, she will win a lawsuit to collect the unpaid fee.

An **unenforceable agreement** occurs when the parties intend to form a valid bargain but a court declares that some rule of law prevents enforcing it. Suppose Gloria and the producer orally agree that she will star in his movie, which he will start filming in 18 months. The statute of frauds requires that this contract be in writing, because it cannot be completed within one year. If the producer signs up another actress two months later, Gloria has no claim against him.

A **voidable contract** occurs when the law permits one party to terminate the agreement. This happens, for example, when the other party has committed fraud or misrepresentation. Suppose that Klene Corp. induces Smart to purchase 1,000 acres of Klene land by telling Smart that there is no underground toxic waste, even though Klene knows that just under the topsoil lies an ocean of bubbling purple sludge. Klene is committing fraud. Smart may void the contract—that is, terminate it and owe nothing.

A **void agreement** is one that neither party can enforce, usually because the purpose of the deal is illegal or because one of the parties had no legal authority to make a contract.

**Valid contract**
A contract that satisfies all the law's requirements.

**Unenforceable agreement**
A contract where the parties intend to form a valid bargain but a court declares that some rule of law prevents enforcing it.

**Voidable contract**
An agreement that, because of some defect, may be terminated by one party, such as a minor, but not by both parties.

**Void agreement**
An agreement that neither party may legally enforce, usually because the purpose of the bargain was illegal or because one of the parties lacked capacity to make it.

## ▪ REMEDIES CREATED BY JUDICIAL ACTIVISM ▪

Now we turn away from true contracts and consider two remedies created by judicial activism: promissory estoppel and quasi-contract. Each of these remedies has grown in importance over the last 100 years. In each case, a sympathetic plaintiff can demonstrate an injury. But the crux of the matter is this: there is no contract. The plaintiff must hope for more "creative" relief. The two remedies can be confusingly similar. The best way to distinguish them is this:

- In **promissory estoppel** cases, the defendant made a promise that the plaintiff relied on.
- In **quasi-contract** cases, the defendant did not make any promise, but did receive a benefit from the plaintiff.

# Promissory Estoppel

A fierce fire swept through Dana and Derek Andreason's house in Utah, seriously damaging it. The good news was that agents for Aetna Casualty promptly visited the Andreasons and helped them through the crisis. The agents reassured the couple that all the damage was covered by their insurance, instructed them on which things to throw out and replace, and helped them choose materials for repairing other items. The bad news was that the agents were wrong: the Andreasons' policy had expired six weeks before the fire. When Derek Andreason presented a bill for $41,957 worth of meticulously itemized work that he had done under the agents' supervision, Aetna refused to pay.

The Andreasons sued—but not for breach of contract, because the insurance agreement had expired. They sued Aetna under the legal theory of promissory estoppel: **Even when there is no contract, a plaintiff may use promissory estoppel to enforce the defendant's promise if he can show that:**

**Promissory estoppel**
A doctrine in which a court may enforce a promise made by the defendant even when there is no contract, if the defendant knew that the plaintiff was likely to rely on the promise, the plaintiff did in fact rely, and enforcement of it is the only way to avoid injustice.

- The defendant made a promise knowing that the plaintiff would likely rely on it;
- The plaintiff did rely on the promise; and
- The only way to avoid injustice is to enforce the promise.

> **Is enforcing the promise the only way to avoid injustice?**

Aetna made a promise to the Andreasons, namely, its assurance that all the damage was covered by insurance. The company knew that the Andreasons would rely on that promise, which they did by ripping up a floor that might have been salvaged, throwing out some furniture, and buying materials to repair the house. Is enforcing the promise the only way to avoid injustice? Yes, ruled the Utah Court of Appeals.[1] The Andreasons' conduct was reasonable, based on what the Aetna agent said. Under promissory estoppel, the Andreasons received virtually the same amount they would have obtained had the insurance contract been valid.

# Quasi-Contract

Don Easterwood leased more than 5,000 acres of farmland in Jackson County, Texas, from PIC Realty for one year. The next year he obtained a second one-year lease. During each year, Easterwood farmed the land, harvested the crops, and prepared the land for the following year's planting. Toward the end of the second lease, after Easterwood had harvested his crop, he and PIC began discussing the terms of another lease. As they negotiated, Easterwood prepared the land for the following year, cutting, plowing, and disking the soil. But the negotiations for a new lease failed, and Easterwood moved off the land. He sued PIC Realty for the value of his work preparing the soil.

Easterwood had neither an express nor an implied contract for the value of his work. How could he make any legal claim? By relying on the legal theory of a quasi-contract: **Even when there is no contract, a court may use quasi-contract to compensate a plaintiff who can show that:**

**Quasi-contract**
A legal fiction in which, to avoid injustice, the court awards damages as if a contract had existed, although one did not.

- The plaintiff gave some benefit to the defendant;
- The plaintiff reasonably expected to be paid for the benefit and the defendant knew this; and
- The defendant would be unjustly enriched if he did not pay.

**Quantum meruit**
"As much as he deserves." The damages awarded in a quasi-contract case.

If a court finds all these elements present, it will generally award the value of the goods or services that the plaintiff has conferred. The damages awarded are called **quantum meruit**, meaning that the plaintiff gets "as much as he deserved." The court is awarding money that it believes the plaintiff *morally ought to have*, even though there was no valid contract entitling her to it. This is judicial activism. The purpose is justice; the term is contradictory.

---

[1] *Andreason v. Aetna Casualty & Surety Co.*, 848 P.2d 171, 1993 Utah App. LEXIS 26 (Utah App. 1993).

Don Easterwood testified that in Jackson County, it was common for a tenant farmer to prepare the soil for the following year but then move. In those cases, he claimed, the landowner compensated the farmer for the work done. Other witnesses agreed. The court ruled that indeed there was no contract but that all elements of quasi-contract had been satisfied. Easterwood gave a benefit to PIC because the land was ready for planting. Easterwood reasonably assumed he would be paid, and PIC Realty knew it. Finally, said the court, it would be unjust to let PIC benefit without paying anything. The court ordered PIC to pay the fair market value of Easterwood's labors.

Almost all courts would agree with the result in the Easterwood case. But, once again, if a court "invents" a contract where none existed, it may have opened the door to an infinite variety of claims. When is the enrichment "unjust"? When would a defendant "reasonably know that the plaintiff expects compensation"? In the following case, the defendant knew nothing at all about what doctors did for him—how could he?

## NOVAK V. CREDIT BUREAU COLLECTION SERVICE

877 N.E. 2D 1253, IND. APP., 2007.

### CASE SUMMARY

**Facts:** David Novak was unconscious. He suffered a brain aneurysm, a weakness in the brain's blood vessels that can be life-threatening. An ambulance took him to Saint Regional Medical Center, where doctors operated successfully. He remained in the hospital for two months and was discharged, able to go about life's normal activities.

Novak did not pay the Medical Center's bill. The hospital assigned its claim to a credit bureau, meaning that the credit bureau acquired the right to sue Novak for the full debt. Which it promptly did.

The trial court found that because Novak had been unconscious, he could not give consent to the treatment. The medical services had been necessary to avoid serious injury or death. When Novak recovered, he remained in the hospital and participated in his own recovery, without objecting to the services he received. Based on all of that, the trial court gave judgment to the credit bureau on a theory of quasi-contract. Novak appealed.

**Issue:** *Was the credit bureau entitled to damages based on quasi-contract?*

**Decision:** Yes, the bureau was entitled to damages based on quasi-contract.

**Reasoning:** Novak argues that the credit bureau is entitled to nothing because he never expressly or impliedly requested medical services. However, the real issue in a case of quasi-contract is whether the plaintiff supplied a benefit under circumstances in which compensation is essential to avoid unjust enrichment.

A plaintiff who has supplied services to the defendant, although acting without the defendant's consent, is entitled to restitution if he expected to charge for his work, the services were necessary to prevent serious bodily harm, and it was impossible for the defendant to give consent.

The hospital saved Novak's life, and its doctors assumed they would be paid. Novak could not give consent because he was unconscious. Novak would be unjustly enriched if he received these vital services for free.

Affirmed.

## • SOURCES OF CONTRACT LAW •

## COMMON LAW

Express and implied contracts, promissory estoppel, and quasi-contract were all crafted, over centuries, by appellate courts deciding one contract lawsuit at a time. In this country, the basic principles are similar from one state to another, but there have been significant differences concerning most important contract doctrines. In part because of these differences, the twentieth century saw the rise of two major new sources of contract law: the **Uniform Commercial Code** and the **Restatement of Contracts.**

# UNIFORM COMMERCIAL CODE

Business methods changed quickly during the first half of the last century. Executives used new forms of communication, such as telephone and wire, to make deals. Transportation speeded up. Corporations routinely conducted business across state borders and around the world. Executives, lawyers, and judges wanted a body of law for commercial transactions that reflected modern business methods and provided uniformity throughout the United States. That desire gave birth to the Uniform Commercial Code (UCC), created in 1952. The drafters intended the UCC to facilitate the easy formation and enforcement of contracts in a fast-paced world. The Code governs many aspects of commerce, including the sale and leasing of goods, negotiable instruments, bank deposits, letters of credit, investment securities, secured transactions, and other commercial matters. Every state has adopted at least part of the UCC to govern commercial transactions within that state. For our purposes in studying contract, the most important part of the Code is Article 2. The entire UCC is available online at **http://www.law.cornell.edu**.

**Goods**
are things that are movable, other than money and investment securities.

**UCC Article 2 governs the sale of goods. "Goods"** means anything movable, except for money, securities, and certain legal rights. Goods include pencils, commercial aircraft, books, and Christmas trees. Goods do not include land or a house, because neither is movable, nor do they include a stock certificate. A contract for the sale of 10,000 sneakers is governed by the UCC; a contract for the sale of a condominium in Los Angeles is governed by the California common law and its statute of frauds. Thus, when analyzing any contract problem as a student or business executive, you must note whether the agreement concerns the sale of goods.

---

**EXAM** *Strategy*

**Question:** Leila agrees to pay Kendrick $35,000 to repair windmills. Confident of this cash, Kendrick contracts to buy Derrick's used Porsche for $33,000. Then Leila informs Kendrick she does not need his help and will not pay him. Kendrick tells Derrick that he no longer wants the Porsche. Derrick sues Kendrick, and Kendrick files suit against Leila. What law or laws govern these lawsuits?

**Strategy:** Always be conscious of whether a contract is for services or the sale of goods. Different laws govern. To make that distinction, you must understand the term "goods." If you are clear about that, the question is easily answered.

**Result:** *Goods* means anything movable, and a Porsche surely qualifies. The UCC will control Derrick's suit. Repairing windmills is a service. Kendrick's lawsuit is governed by the common law of contracts.

---

# RESTATEMENT (SECOND) OF CONTRACTS

In 1932, the American Law Institute (ALI), a group of lawyers, scholars, and judges, drafted the Restatement of Contracts, attempting to codify what its members regarded as the best rulings of contract law. In 1979, the ALI issued a new version, the Restatement (Second) of Contracts. Like its predecessor, the Restatement (Second) is not the law anywhere, and in this respect it differs from the common law and the UCC. However, judges often refer to the Restatement (Second) when they decide cases, so we too will seek its counsel from time to time.

## · AGREEMENT ·

## MEETING OF THE MINDS

**Two parties can form a contract only if they have had a meeting of the minds.** This requires that they (1) understood each other and (2) intended to reach an agreement. Recall the café conversation between Katrina and Bob, concerning the new film. Was there a meeting of the minds? Judges make an objective assessment of each party's intent. A court will not try to get inside Katrina's head and decide what she was thinking as she shook hands. It will look at the handshake objectively, deciding how a reasonable person would interpret the words and conduct. Katrina may honestly have meant to conclude a deal for $3 million with no nude scenes, while Bob might in good faith have believed he was committing himself to $2.5 million and absolute control of the script. Neither belief will control the outcome. A reasonable person observing their discussion would not have known what terms they agreed to, and hence there is no agreement.

## OFFER

Bargaining begins with an offer. An offer is a serious matter because it permits the other party to create a contract by accepting. An **offer** is an act or a statement that proposes definite terms and permits the other party to create a contract by accepting those terms.

The person who makes an offer is the **offeror**. The person to whom he makes that offer is the **offeree**. The terms are annoying but inescapable because, like handcuffs, all courts use them. In most contract negotiations, two parties bargain back and forth, maybe for minutes, perhaps for months. Each may make several offers, revoke some proposals, suggest counteroffers, and so forth. For our purposes, the offeror remains the one who made the first offer.

Two questions determine whether a statement is an offer:

- Did the offeror intend to make a bargain?
- Are the terms of the offer definite?

**Offer**
In contract law, an act or statement that proposes definite terms and permits the other party to create a contract by accepting those terms.

**Offeror**
The party in contract negotiations who makes the first offer.

**Offeree**
The party in contract negotiations who receives the first offer.

### Invitations to Bargain

**An invitation to bargain is not an offer.** Suppose Martha telephones Joe and leaves a message on his answering machine, asking if Joe would consider selling his vacation condo on Lake Michigan. Joe faxes a signed letter to Martha saying, "There is no way I could sell the condo for less than $150,000." Martha promptly sends Joe a cashier's check for that amount. Does she own the condo? No. Joe's fax is not an offer. It is merely an invitation to bargain. Joe is indicating that he would be happy to receive an offer from Martha. He is not promising to sell the condo for $150,000 or for any amount.

## PROBLEMS WITH DEFINITENESS

It is not enough that the offeror intends to enter into an agreement. **The terms of the offer must be definite.** If they are vague, then even if the offeree "accepts" the deal, a court does not have enough information to enforce it and there is no contract.

You want a friend to work in your store for the holiday season. This is a definite offer: "I offer you a job as a salesclerk in the store from November 1 through December 29, 40 hours per week at $10 per hour." But suppose, by contrast, you say: "I offer you a job as a salesclerk in the store from November 1 through December 29, 40 hours per week. We will work out a fair wage once we see how busy things get." Your friend replies, "That's fine with me." This offer is indefinite. What is a fair wage? $6 per hour? $15 per hour? How will the determination be made? There is no binding agreement.

The following case presents a problem with definiteness, concerning a famous television show. You want to know what happened? Go to the place. See the guy. No, not the guy in hospitality. Our friend in waste management. Don't say nothing. Then get out.

# BAER V. CHASE

392 F.3D 609, THIRD CIRCUIT COURT OF APPEALS, 2004

## CASE SUMMARY

**Facts:** David Chase was a television writer-producer with many credits, including a detective series called *The Rockford Files*. He became interested in a new program, set in New Jersey, about a "mob boss in therapy," a concept he eventually developed into *The Sopranos*. Robert Baer was a prosecutor in New Jersey who wanted to write for television. He submitted a *Rockford Files* script to Chase, who agreed to meet with Baer.

When they met, Baer pitched a different idea, concerning "a film or television series about the New Jersey Mafia." He did not realize Chase was already working on such an idea. Later that year, Chase visited New Jersey. Baer arranged meetings for Chase with local detectives and prosecutors, who provided the producer with information, material, and personal stories about their experiences with organized crime. Detective Thomas Koczur drove Chase and Baer to various New Jersey locations, and introduced Chase to Tony Spirito. Spirito shared stories about loan sharking, power struggles between family members connected with the mob, and two colorful individuals known as Big Pussy and Little Pussy, both of whom later became characters on the show.

Back in Los Angeles, Chase wrote and sent to Baer a draft of the first *Sopranos* teleplay. Baer called Chase and commented on the script. The two spoke at least four times that year, and Baer sent Chase a letter about the script.

When *The Sopranos* became a hit television show, Baer sued Chase. He alleged that on three separate occasions, Chase had agreed that if the program succeeded, Chase would "take care of" Baer, and would "remunerate Baer in a manner commensurate to the true value of his services." This happened twice on the phone, Baer claimed, and once during Chase's visit to New Jersey. The understanding was that if the show failed, Chase would owe nothing. Chase never paid Baer anything.

The district court dismissed the case, holding that the alleged promises were too vague to be enforced. Baer appealed.

**Issue:** *Was Chase's promise definite enough to be enforced?*

**Decision:** No, the promise was too indefinite to be enforced.

**Reasoning:** To create a binding agreement, the offer and acceptance must be definite enough that a court can tell what the parties were obligated to do. The parties need to agree on all of the essential terms; if they do not, there is no enforceable contract.

One of the essential terms is price. The agreement must either specify the compensation to be paid or describe a method by which the parties can calculate it. The duration of the contract is also basic: how long do the mutual obligations last?

There is no evidence that the parties agreed on how much Chase would pay Baer, or when or for what period. The parties never defined what they meant by the "true value" of Baer's services, or how they would determine it. The two never discussed the meaning of "success" as applied to *The Sopranos*. They never agreed on how "profits" were to be calculated. The parties never discussed when the alleged agreement would begin or end.

Baer argues that the courts should make an exception to the principle of definiteness when the agreement concerns an "idea submission." The problem with his contention is that there is not the slightest support for it in the law. There is no precedent whatsoever for ignoring the definiteness requirement, in this type of contract or any other.

Affirmed.

---

**ETHICS** Was it fair for Chase to use Baer's services without compensation? Did Baer really *expect* to get paid, or was he simply hoping that his work would land him a job? Has either party violated the *Golden Rule?* What are the most important *values* involved? ◆

# TERMINATION OF OFFERS

As we have seen, the great power that an offeree has is to form a contract by accepting an offer. But this power is lost when the offer is terminated, which can happen in several ways:

## Revocation

In general, the offeror may revoke the offer any time before it has been accepted. Revocation is effective as soon as the offeree receives it.

## Rejection

If an offeree rejects an offer, the rejection immediately terminates the offer. Suppose a major accounting firm telephones you and offers a job, starting at $80,000. You respond, "Nah. I'm gonna work on my surfing for a year or two." The next day you come to your senses and write the firm, accepting its offer. No contract. Your rejection terminated the offer and ended your power to accept.

## Counteroffer

Frederick faxes Kim, offering to sell a 50 percent interest in the Fab Hotel in New York for only $135 million. Kim faxes back, offering to pay $115 million. Moments later, Kim's business partner convinces her that Frederick's offer was a bargain, and she faxes an acceptance of his $135 million offer. Does Kim have a binding deal? No. A counteroffer is a rejection. The parties have no contract at any price.

## Expiration

When an offer specifies a time limit for acceptance, that period is binding. If the offer specifies no time limit, the offeree has a reasonable period in which to accept.

## Destruction of the Subject Matter

A used car dealer offers to sell you a rare 1938 Bugatti for $75,000 if you bring cash the next day. You arrive, suitcase stuffed with century notes, just in time to see the dealer fall out of a blimp, dropping 3,000 feet through the air and crushing the Bugatti. The dealer's offer terminated.

# ACCEPTANCE

As we have seen, when there is a valid offer outstanding, the offeree can create a contract by accepting. **The offeree must say or do something to accept.** Silence, though golden, is not acceptance. Marge telephones Vick and leaves a message on his answering machine: "I'll pay $75 for your law textbook from last semester. I'm desperate to get a copy, so I will assume you agree unless I hear from you by 6:00 tonight." Marge hears nothing by the deadline and assumes she has a deal. She is mistaken. Vick neither said nor did anything to indicate that he accepted.

**When the offer is for a bilateral contract, the offeree generally must accept by making a promise.** An employer calls you and says, "If you're able to start work two weeks from today, we can pay you $5,000 per month. Can you do it?" That is an offer for a bilateral contract. You must accept by promising to start in two weeks.

**When the offer is for a unilateral contract, the offeree must accept by performing.** A newspaper telephones you: "If you write us a 5,000-word article on iguanas that can play bridge, and get it to us by Friday at noon, we'll pay you $750." The newspaper does not want a promise, it wants the article. If—and only if—your work is ready on time, you get paid.

# MIRROR IMAGE RULE

If only he had known! A splendid university, an excellent position as department chair—gone. And all because of the mirror image rule. The Ohio State University wrote to Philip Foster offering him an appointment as a professor and chair of the art history department. His position was to begin July 1, and he had until June 2 to accept the job. On June 2, Foster telephoned the Dean and left a message accepting the position, **effective July 15.** Later, Foster thought better of it and wrote the university, accepting the school's starting date of July 1. Too late! Professor Foster never did occupy that chair at Ohio State. The court held that since his acceptance varied the starting date, it was a counteroffer. And a counteroffer, as we know, is a rejection.[2]

**Mirror image rule**
A contract doctrine that requires acceptance to be on exactly the same terms as the offer.

The common law **mirror image rule** requires that acceptance be on precisely the same terms as the offer. If the acceptance contains terms that add to or contradict the offer, even in minor ways, courts generally consider it a counteroffer. The rule worked reasonably well in the nineteenth century, when parties would write an original contract and exchange it, penciling in any changes. But now that businesses use standardized forms to purchase most goods and services, the rule creates enormous difficulties. Sellers use forms they have prepared, with all conditions stated to their advantage, and buyers employ their own forms, with terms they prefer. The forms are exchanged in the mail (or electronically), with neither side clearly agreeing to the other party's terms.

The problem is known as the "battle of forms." Once again, the UCC has entered the fray, attempting to provide flexibility and common sense for those contracts involving the sale of goods. But for contracts governed by the common law, such as Professor Foster's, the mirror image rule is still the law.

## UCC AND THE BATTLE OF FORMS

UCC §2-207 dramatically modifies the mirror image rule for the sale of goods. Under this provision, an acceptance that adds additional or different terms **will often create a contract.** The rule is intricate, but may be summarized this way:

> For the sale of goods, the most important factor is whether the parties believe they have a binding agreement. If their conduct indicates that they have a deal, they probably do.
>
> If the offeree *adds new* terms to the offer, acceptance by the offeror generally creates a binding agreement.
>
> If the offeree *changes* the terms of the offer, a court will probably rely on general principles of the UCC to create a fair contract.
>
> If a party wants a contract on its terms only, with no changes, it must clearly indicate that.

Suppose Wholesaler writes to Manufacturer, offering to buy "10,000 wheelbarrows at $50 per unit. Payable on delivery, 30 days from today's date." Manufacturer writes back, "We accept your offer of 10,000 wheelbarrows at $50 per unit, payable on delivery. Interest at normal trade rates for unpaid balances." Manufacturer clearly intends to form a contract. The company has added a new term, but there is still a valid agreement.

### EXAM *Strategy*

**Question:** Elaine faxes an offer to Raoul. Raoul writes, "I accept. Please note, I will charge 2 percent interest per month for any unpaid money." He signs the document and faxes it back to Elaine. Do the two have a binding contract?

**Strategy:** Slow down, this is trickier than it seems. Raoul has added a term to Elaine's offer. In a contract for services, acceptance must mirror the offer, but not so in an agreement for the sale of goods.

**Result:** If this is an agreement for services, there is no contract. However, if this agreement is for goods, the additional term *may* become part of an enforceable contract.

---

[2] *Foster v. Ohio State University*, 41 Ohio App. 3d 86, 534 N.E.2d 1220, 1987 Ohio App. LEXIS 10761 (Ohio Ct. App. 1987).

**Question:** Assume that Elaine's offer concerns goods. Is there an agreement?

**Strategy:** Under UCC 2-207, an additional term will generally become part of a binding agreement for goods, unless . . . ?

**Result:** The parties have probably created a binding contract unless Elaine indicated in her offer that she would accept her terms only, with no changes.

.................................................................................

## ▪ CONSIDERATION ▪

We have all made promises that we soon regretted. Mercifully, the law does not hold us accountable for everything we say. Yet some promises must be enforced. Which ones? The doctrine of consideration exists for one purpose: to distinguish promises that are binding from those that are not.

Consideration is a required element of any contract. **Consideration** means that there must be bargaining that leads to an exchange between the parties. (See Exhibit 9.1.) *Bargaining* indicates that each side is obligating itself in some way to *induce the other side to agree*. Generally, a court will enforce one party's promise only if the other party did something or promised something in exchange.

If one party makes a promise without some kind of bargaining, there is generally no contract. Carol Kelsoe had worked at International Wood Products for many years. One day, her supervisor surprised her by promising her 5 percent of the company's stock. Unfortunately, he never gave her those shares. Heartbroken, Kelsoe sued—and lost.[3] Kelsoe had given nothing in exchange for her supervisor's words. There was no consideration on her part, and she could not enforce his promise.

**Consideration**
Bargaining that leads to an exchange between the parties.

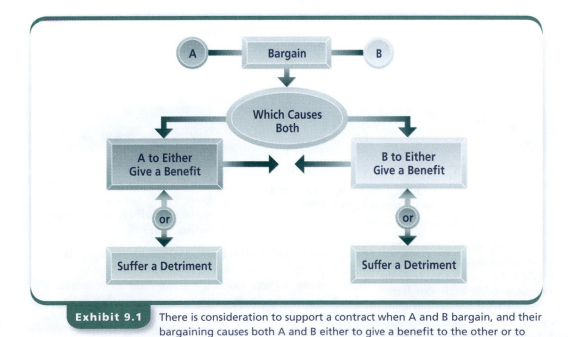

**Exhibit 9.1** There is consideration to support a contract when A and B bargain, and their bargaining causes both A and B either to give a benefit to the other or to suffer a detriment.

--------

[3] *Kelsoe v. International Wood Products, Inc.,* 588 So. 2d 877, 1991 Ala. LEXIS 1014 (Supreme Court of Alabama, 1991).

If Kelsoe had assured him that she would remain at International Wood for three extra years (or three extra days) in exchange for the stock, that would have been consideration, and she would have collected her shares.

**The thing bargained for can be another promise or action.** Usually one party bargains for another promise. Jennifer says to Ben, "I'm supposed to fly to Chicago in a week, to give a speech. Will you do it for me? I'll give you $15,000." "Sure," Ben responds, "I'll do that for $15,000." The very next day Jennifer changes her mind. Too late. Ben's *promise* to go to Chicago was consideration. The parties have a deal that either one can enforce.

**The thing bargained for can be action, rather than a promise.** Manny tells Sandra, "I need someone to hook up my cable TV by tonight at 8:00. If you get it done, I'll give you $200." Manny seeks action, not a promise. If Sandra connects the television on time, her work is consideration and the parties have a binding deal.

**The thing bargained for can be a promise to do something or a promise to refrain from doing something.** Megan promises to deliver 1,000 canoes in two months if Casey agrees to pay $300 per canoe. Megan's promise to act is consideration. The most famous of all consideration lawsuits involved a promise to refrain. The case began in 1869, when a well-meaning uncle made a promise to his nephew. Ever since the nephew responded, generations of American law students have dutifully inhaled the facts and sworn by its wisdom; now you, too, may drink it in.

## ILLUSORY PROMISE

Annabel calls Jim and says, "I'll sell you my bicycle for 325 bucks. Interested?" Jim says, "I'll look at it tonight in the bike rack. If I like what I see, I'll pay you three and a quarter in the morning." At sunrise, Jim shows up with the $325 but Annabel refuses to sell. Can Jim enforce their deal? No. He said he would buy the bicycle *if he liked it,* keeping for himself the power to get out of the agreement for any reason at all. He is not committing himself to do anything, and the law considers his promise illusory, that is, not really a promise at all. **An illusory promise is not consideration.** Because he has given no consideration, there is no contract and *neither party* can enforce the deal. Was the promise in the following case illusory? You decide.

---

### YOU *be the* JUDGE

#### CULBERTSON v. BRODSKY
788 S.W.2d 156, 1990 Tex. App. LEXIS 1008
Texas Court of Appeals, 1990

**Facts:** Sam Culbertson had some Texas real estate to sell. He and Frederick Brodsky signed an option contract. Brodsky was to deliver a check for $5,000, representing "earnest money," to a bank. The bank would hold the check in escrow for 60 days. During that period, the bank would not cash it. Brodsky could inspect the property and perform engineering studies to determine whether the real estate could be used for his purposes. If he decided that the land was of no use to him, he could terminate the agreement and demand return of his earnest money. Ultimately, Brodsky decided that he did want to buy the land, but Culbertson refused to sell, claiming that Brodsky gave no consideration to support their contract. The trial court gave judgment for Brodsky, ordering Culbertson to convey the land. Culbertson appealed.

**You Be the Judge:** Did Brodsky give valid consideration that makes Culbertson's promise enforceable?

**Argument for Culbertson:** Your honors, Mr. Brodsky made a very sly promise, since it was in fact no promise at all. Brodsky insisted on keeping the right to terminate this phony agreement at any time, for any reason. Mr. Culbertson was expected to leave the property off the market for 60 valuable days while Brodsky took his own sweet time to inspect the land, perform engineering tests, make feasibility calculations, reconsider his position, and ultimately decide whether he had any interest in the property. If he decided for any reason that he no longer wanted the land, Brodsky could simply walk away from the deal. Please note that he didn't even lose

*continued*

the use of the $5,000. The bank was not permitted to cash the check until Brodsky made up his mind. No money ever left Brodsky's account—indeed, no money even had to be in his account, unless and until he decided to exercise his option.

A true option contract provides something for each party. The landowner is obligated to hold the property open for the buyer, but the buyer pays a fee for this privilege. Here, Brodsky was obligated to pay nothing and do nothing. He made no promise at all, and we urge that no contract resulted.

**Argument for Brodsky:** Your honors, it is rather disingenuous of Mr. Culbertson to pose as an injured party here. He is, in fact, a sophisticated property owner. He voluntarily entered into a contract with Mr. Brodsky for one reason: it was in his own interest. He concluded that the best way to

"land" Mr. Brodsky was first to "hook" him with an option contract. He wanted Mr. Brodsky to show serious interest, and demanded earnest money. He got it. He insisted that Mr. Brodsky's check be held in escrow. He got it. Culbertson hoped that by getting this degree of commitment, Mr. Brodsky would perform the necessary tests on the land and conclude that he wanted to buy it. And that is *precisely what happened*. Mr. Brodsky, in total good faith, performed his tests, decided the land was what he had wanted, and exercised the option that Culbertson had sold him. But Culbertson decided to back out of the deal—presumably to sell elsewhere.

Now Culbertson comes into court and relies on a technical rule of contract law to try to weasel out of a good faith deal. The law of consideration was never intended to permit such chicanery.

## CHAPTER CONCLUSION

**Contracts govern countless areas of our lives, from intimate family issues to multibillion dollar corporate deals.** Understanding contract principles is essential for a successful business or a professional career and is invaluable in private life. Courts no longer rubber-stamp any agreement that two parties have made. If we know the issues that courts scrutinize, the agreement we draft is likelier to be enforced. We thus achieve greater control over our affairs—the very purpose of a contract.

## EXAM REVIEW

1. **CONTRACTS** A contract is a promise that the law will enforce. Contracts are intended to make business matters more predictable. (p. 131)

........................................................................................

2. **COMMON LAW AND UCC** The common law governs contracts for services, employment, and real estate. The Uniform Commercial Code (UCC), Article 2, governs contracts for the sale of goods. (p. 135)

........................................................................................

3. **EXPRESS AND IMPLIED CONTRACTS** In an express contract, the two parties explicitly state all important terms of their agreement. In an implied contract, the words and conduct of the parties indicate that they intended an agreement. (p. 132)

........................................................................................

4. **PROMISSORY ESTOPPEL** A claim of promissory estoppel requires that the defendant made a promise knowing that the plaintiff would likely rely, the plaintiff did rely, and it would be wrong to deny recovery. (p. 134)

........................................................................................

5. **QUASI-CONTRACT** A claim of quasi-contract requires that the defendant received a benefit, knowing that the plaintiff would expect compensation, and it would be unjust not to grant it. (p. 134)

........................................................................................

**EXAM Strategy**

**Question:** The Hoffmans owned and operated a successful small bakery and grocery store. They spoke with Lukowitz, an agent of Red Owl Stores, who told them that for $18,000, Red Owl would build a store and fully stock it for them. The Hoffmans sold their bakery and grocery store and purchased a lot on which Red Owl was to build the store. Lukowitz then told Hoffman that the price had gone up to $26,000. The Hoffmans borrowed the extra money from relatives, but then Lukowitz informed them that the cost would be $34,000. Negotiations broke off and the Hoffmans sued. The court determined that there was no contract because too many details had not been worked out—the size of the store, its design, and the cost of constructing it. Can the Hoffmans recover any money?

**Strategy:** Because there is no contract, the Hoffmans must rely on either promissory estoppel or quasi-contract. Promissory estoppel focuses on the defendant's promise and the plaintiff's reliance. Those suing in quasi-contract must show that the defendant received a benefit for which it should reasonably expect to pay. Does either fit here? (See the "Result" at the end of this section.)

**6.    MEETING OF THE MINDS** The parties can form a contract only if they have a meeting of the minds. (p. 137)

**EXAM Strategy**

**Question:** Norv owned a Ford dealership and wanted to expand by obtaining a BMW outlet. He spoke with Jackson and other BMW executives on several occasions. Norv now claims that those discussions resulted in an oral contract that requires BMW to grant him a franchise, but the company disagrees. Norv's strongest evidence of a contract is the fact that Jackson gave him forms on which to order BMWs. Jackson answered that it was his standard practice to give such forms to prospective dealers, so that if the franchise were approved, car orders could be processed quickly. Norv states that he was "shocked" when BMW refused to go through with the deal. Is there a contract?

**Strategy:** A court makes an *objective* assessment of what the parties did and said to determine whether they had a meeting of the minds and intended to form a contract. Norv's "shock" is irrelevant. Do the order forms indicate a meeting of the minds? Was there additional evidence that the parties had reached an agreement? (See the "Result" at the end of this section.)

**7.    OFFER** An offer is an act or a statement that proposes definite terms and permits the other party to create a contract by accepting. The terms of the offer must be definite. (p. 137)

**8.    ACCEPTANCE** The offeree must say or do something to accept. The common law mirror image rule requires acceptance on precisely the same terms as the offer. (p. 139)

**9.    CONSIDERATION** A promise is normally binding only if it is supported by consideration, which requires a bargaining and exchange between the parties. (p. 141)

**5. Result:** Red Owl received no benefit from the Hoffmans' sale of their store or purchase of the lot. However, Red Owl did make a promise, and expected the Hoffmans to rely on it, which they did. The Hoffmans won their claim of promissory estoppel.

**6. Result:** The order forms are neither an offer nor an acceptance. Norv has offered no evidence that the parties agreed on price, date of performance, or any other key terms. There is no contract. Norv allowed eagerness and optimism to replace common sense.

# PRACTICE EXAM

## MATCHING QUESTIONS

Match the following terms with their definitions:

___ A. Implied contract

___ B. Mirror image rule

___ C. Consideration

___ D. Liquidated debt

___ E. Bilateral contract

1. A debt in which the amount is undisputed.

2. An agreement based on one promise in exchange for another.

3. Bargaining that leads to an exchange between the parties.

4. An agreement based on the words and actions of the parties.

5. A common law principle requiring the acceptance to be on exactly the terms of the offer.

## TRUE/FALSE QUESTIONS

Circle true or false:

1. T  F  To be enforceable, all contracts must be in writing.

2. T  F  Abdul hires Sean to work in his store, and agrees to pay him $9 per hour. This agreement is governed by the UCC.

3. T  F  If an offer demands a reply within a stated period, the absence of a reply indicates acceptance.

4. T  F  Without a meeting of the minds there cannot be a contract.

5. T  F  As long as one party gives consideration, there is a binding contract.

## MULTIPLE-CHOICE QUESTIONS

6. Mark, a newspaper editor, walks into the newsroom and announces to a group of five reporters: "I'll pay a $2,000 bonus to the first reporter who finds definitive evidence that Senator Blue smoked marijuana at the celebrity party last Friday." Anna, the first reporter to produce the evidence, claims her bonus based on

   A. Unilateral contract.

   B. Promissory estoppel.

   C. Quasi-contract.

   D. Implied contract.

   E. Express contract.

7. Raul has finished the computer installation he promised to perform for Tanya, and she has paid him in full. This is

   A. An express contract.

   B. An implied contract.

   C. An executed contract.

   D. A bilateral contract.

   E. No contract.

8. Alejandro sees an ad in the newspaper, with a beautiful sweater pictured: "Versace sweaters, normally $600, today only: $300." He phones the store and says that he wants two sweaters, a black one and a gray one. When he arrives at the store, the sweaters are sold out. He sues, based on a contract. Alejandro will

   A. Win, because the store never revoked its offer.

   B. Win, because he accepted within a reasonable time.

   C. Win, because there was a meeting of the minds.

   D. Lose, because he needed to accept in person.

   E. Lose, because the store never made an offer.

9. On Monday night, Louise is talking on her cell phone with Bill. "I'm desperate for a manager in my store," says Louise. "I'll pay you $45,000 per year, if you can start tomorrow morning. What do you say?"

"It's a deal," says Bill. "I can start tomorrow at 8 a.m. I'll take $45,000 and I also want 10 percent of any profits you make above last year's." Just then Bill loses his cell phone signal. The next morning he shows up at the store, but Louise refuses to hire him. Bill sues. Bill will

A. Win, because there was a valid offer and acceptance.

B. Win, based on promissory estoppel.

C. Lose, because he rejected the offer.

D. Lose, because the agreement was not put in writing.

E. Lose, because Louise revoked the offer.

10. At Lorenza's 90th birthday party, she gives a speech to the 25 guests, praising her maid, Anna. "Anna has worked faithfully for me for 55 years. In appreciation, next week I am going to give Anna $100,000." Anna is ecstatic, but next week, Lorenza changes her mind. Is Anna entitled to the money?

A. Yes, provided the witnesses agree she made the promise.

B. Yes, provided Lorenza *intended* to make the gift.

C. Yes, because there is adequate consideration: Anna's work and Lorenza's promise.

D. Yes, provided Lorenza actually has the money.

E. No.

## SHORT-ANSWER QUESTIONS

11. Interactive Data Corp. hired Daniel Foley as an assistant product manager at a starting salary of $18,500. Over the next six years Interactive steadily promoted Foley until he became Los Angeles branch manager at a salary of $56,116. Interactive's officers repeatedly told Foley that he would have his job as long as his performance was adequate. In addition, Interactive distributed an employee handbook that specified "termination guidelines," including a mandatory seven-step, pretermination procedure. Two years later Foley learned that his recently hired supervisor, Robert Kuhne, was under investigation by the FBI for embezzlement at his previous job. Foley reported this to Interactive officers. Shortly thereafter, Interactive fired Foley. He sued, claiming that Interactive could only fire him for good cause, after the seven-step procedure. What kind of a claim is he making? Should he succeed?

12. ETHICS: John Stevens owned a dilapidated apartment that he rented to James and Cora Chesney for a low rent. The Chesneys began to remodel and rehabilitate the unit. Over a four-year period, they installed two new bathrooms, carpeted the floors, installed new septic and heating systems, and rewired, replumbed, and painted. Stevens periodically stopped by and saw the work in progress. The Chesneys transformed the unit into a respectable apartment. Three years after their work was done, Stevens served the Chesneys with an eviction notice. The Chesneys counterclaimed, seeking the value of the work they had done. Are they entitled to it? Comment on the law and the ethics.

13. Arnold owned a Pontiac dealership and wanted to expand by obtaining a Buick outlet. He spoke with Patricia Roberts and other Buick executives on several occasions. He now claims that those discussions resulted in an oral contract that requires Buick to grant him a franchise, but the company disagrees. His strongest evidence of a contract is the fact that Roberts gave him forms on which to order Buicks. Roberts answered that it was her standard practice to give such forms to prospective dealers, so that if the franchise were approved, car orders could be processed quickly. Is there a contract?

14. Tindall operated a general contracting business in Montana. He and Konitz entered into negotiations for Konitz to buy the business. The parties realized that Konitz could succeed with the business only if Tindall gave support and assistance for a year or so after the purchase, especially by helping with the process of bidding for jobs and obtaining bonds to guarantee performance. Konitz bought the business and Tindall helped with the bidding and bonding. Two years later, Tindall presented Konitz with a contract for his services up to that point. Konitz did not want

to sign but Tindall insisted. Konitz signed the agreement, which said: "Whereas Tindall sold his contracting business to Konitz and thereafter assisted Konitz in bidding and bonding without which Konitz would have been unable to operate, NOW THEREFORE

Konitz agrees to pay Tindall $138,629." Konitz later refused to pay. Comment.

15. ROLE REVERSAL: Write a multiple-choice question focusing on UCC 2-207.

## INTERNET RESEARCH PROBLEM

Online, find a current case concerning "quasi-contract." What are the details of the dispute? Who won and why?

**You can find further practice problems in the Online quiz at www.cengage.com/blaw/beatty.**

# LEGALITY, CONSENT, AND WRITING

**Soheil Sadri,** a California resident, did some serious gambling at Caesar's Tahoe casino in Nevada. And lost. To keep gambling, he wrote checks to Caesar's and then signed two memoranda pledging to repay money advanced. After two days, with his losses totaling more than $22,000, he went home. Back in California, Sadri stopped payment on the checks and refused to pay any of the money he owed Caesar's. The casino sued and recovered . . . nothing. Sadri relied on an important legal principle to defeat the suit: **A contract that is illegal is void and unenforceable.** We will examine a variety of contracts that may be void.

Gambling is one of America's fastest growing businesses, but a controversial one. Because our citizens—and our states—are divided over the ethics of wagering, conflicts such as the dispute between Sadri and Caesar's are inevitable. The basic rule, however, is clear: **A gambling contract is illegal unless it is specifically authorized by state statute.** In California, as in many states, gambling on credit is not allowed. In other words, it is illegal to lend money to help someone wager. However, in Nevada, gambling on credit is legal and debt memoranda such as Sadri's are enforceable contracts. Caesar's sued Sadri in California (where he lived). The court admitted that California's attitude toward gambling had changed and that bingo, poker clubs, and lotteries were common. Nonetheless, the court denied that the new tolerance extended to wagering on credit, stating: "The judiciary cannot protect pathological gamblers from themselves, but we can refuse to participate in their financial ruin."[1]

Caesar's lost, and Sadri kept his money. However, do not become too excited at the prospect of risk-free wagering. Casinos responded to cases like *Sadri* by changing their practices. Most now extend credit only to a gambler who agrees that disputes about repayment will be settled in *Nevada* courts. Because such contracts are legal in that state, the casino is able to obtain a judgment against a defaulting debtor and—yes—enforce that judgment in the gambler's home state. In *your* home state.

Despite these more restrictive casino practices, Sadri's dispute is a useful starting place from which to examine contract legality because it illustrates two important themes. First, morality is a significant part of contract legality. In refusing to enforce an obligation that Sadri undeniably had made, the California court relied on the human and social consequences of gambling and on the ethics of judicial enforcement of gambling debts. Second, "void" really means just that: **a court will not assist either party to an illegal agreement,** even if its refusal leaves one party obviously shortchanged.

---

[1] *Metropolitan Creditors Service of Sacramento v. Sadri*, 15 Cal. App. 4th 1821, 1993 Cal App. LEXIS 559, 19 Cal. Rptr. 2d 646 (Cal. Ct. App. 1993).

## · LEGALITY ·

## RESTRAINT OF TRADE

Free trade is the basis of the American economy, and any bargain that restricts it is suspect. Most restraint of free trade is barred by antitrust law. But it is the common law that still regulates one restriction on trade: agreements to refrain from competition. Some of these agreements are legal, some are void. They are *very* common. Many readers of this book will find such a clause in their own employment contracts.

**To be valid, an agreement not to compete must be ancillary to a legitimate bargain.** "Ancillary" means that the noncompetition agreement must be part of a larger agreement. Suppose Cliff sells his gasoline station to Mina and the two agree that Cliff will not open a competing gas station within five miles any time during the next two years. Cliff's agreement not to compete is ancillary to the sale of his service station. His noncompetition promise is enforceable. But suppose that Cliff and Mina already had the only two gas stations within 35 miles. They agree between themselves not to hire each other's workers. Their agreement might be profitable to them, because each could now keep wages artificially low. But their deal is ancillary to no legitimate bargain, and it is therefore void.

The two most common settings for legitimate noncompetition agreements are the *sale of a business* and an *employment relationship*.

## SALE OF A BUSINESS

Kory has operated a real estate office, Hearth Attack, in a small city for 35 years, building an excellent reputation and many ties with the community. She offers to sell you the business and its goodwill for $300,000. But you need assurance that Kory will not take your money and promptly open a competing office across the street. With her reputation and connections, she would ruin your chances of success. You insist on a noncompete clause in the sale contract. In this clause, Kory promises that for one year she will not open a new real estate office or go to work for a competing company within a 10-mile radius of Hearth Attack. Suppose, six months after selling you the business, Kory goes to work for a competing realtor, two blocks away. You seek an injunction (a court order) to prevent her from working. Who wins?

**When a noncompete agreement is ancillary to the sale of a business, it is enforceable if reasonable in time, geographic area, and scope of activity.** In other words, a court will not enforce a noncompete agreement that lasts an unreasonably long time, covers an unfairly large area, or prohibits the seller of the business from doing a type of work that she never had done before. Measured by this test, Kory is almost certainly bound by her agreement. One year is a reasonable time to allow you to get your new business started. A 10-mile radius is probably about the area that Hearth Attack covers, and realty is obviously a fair business from which to prohibit Kory. A court will grant the injunction, barring Kory from her new job.

If, on the other hand, the noncompetition agreement had prevented Kory from working anywhere within 200 miles of Hearth Attack, and she started working 50 miles away, a court would refuse to enforce the contract.

## EMPLOYMENT

When you sign an employment contract, the document may well contain a noncompete clause. Employers have legitimate worries that employees might go to a competitor and take with them trade secrets or other proprietary information. Some employers, though, attempt to place harsh restrictions on their employees, perhaps demanding a blanket agreement that the employee will never go to work for a competitor. Once again, courts look at the reasonableness of restrictions placed on an employee's future work. Because the agreement now involves the very livelihood of the worker, a court scrutinizes the agreement more closely.

**A noncompete clause in an employment contract is generally reasonable—and enforceable—only to the extent necessary to protect (1) trade secrets, (2) confidential information, or (3) customer lists developed over an extended period.** In general, other restrictions on future employment are unenforceable.[2] Suppose that Gina, an engineer, goes to work for Fission Chips, a silicon chip manufacturer that specializes in defense work. She signs a noncompete agreement promising never to work for a competitor. Over a period of three years, Gina learns some of Fission's proprietary methods of etching information onto the chips. She acquires a great deal of new expertise about chips generally. And she periodically deals with Fission Chips' customers, all of whom are well-known software and hardware manufacturers.

Gina accepts an offer from WriteSmall, a competitor. Fission Chips races into court, seeking an injunction to block Gina from working for WriteSmall. This injunction threatens Gina's career. If she cannot work for a competitor, or use her general engineering skills, what will she do? And for exactly that reason, no court will grant such a broad order. The court will allow Gina to work for competitors, including WriteSmall. It will order her not to use or reveal any trade secrets belonging to Fission. She will, however, be permitted to use the general expertise she has acquired, and she may contact former customers because anyone could get their names from the yellow pages.

Was the noncompete in the following case styled fairly, or was the employee clipped?

## KING v. HEAD START FAMILY HAIR SALONS, INC.

886 So.2d 769, Supreme Court of Alabama, 2004

### CASE SUMMARY

**Facts:** Kathy King was a single mother supporting a college-age daughter. For 25 years, she had worked as a hair stylist. For the most recent 16 years, she had worked at Head Start, which provided haircuts, coloring, and styling for men and women. King was primarily a stylist, though she had also managed one of the Head Start facilities.

King quit Head Start and began working as manager of a Sports Clips shop, located in the same mall as the store she just left. Sports Clip offered only haircuts and primarily served men and boys. Head Start filed suit, claiming that King was violating the noncompetition agreement that she had signed. The agreement prohibited King from working at a competing business within a two-mile radius of any Head Start facility for 12 months after leaving the company. The trial court issued an injunction enforcing the noncompete. King appealed.

**Issue:** *Was the noncompetition agreement valid?*

**Decision:** The agreement was only partly valid.

**Reasoning:** Head Start does business in 30 locations throughout Jefferson and Shelby counties. Virtually every hair-care facility in those counties is located within 2 miles of a Head Start business and is thus covered by the noncompetition agreement. The contract is essentially a blanket restriction, entirely barring King from this business.

King must work to support herself and her daughter. She is 40 years old and has worked in the hair-care industry for 25 years. She cannot be expected at this stage in life to learn new job skills. Enforcing the noncompetition agreement would work a grave hardship on her. The contract cannot be permitted to impoverish King and her daughter.

On the other hand, Head Start is entitled to some of the protection it sought in this agreement. The company has a valid concern that if King is permitted to work anywhere she wants, she could take away many customers from Head Start. The trial court should fashion a more reasonable geographic restriction, one that will permit King to ply her trade while ensuring that Head Start does not unfairly lose customers. For example, the lower court could prohibit King from working within two miles of the Head Start facility where she previously worked, or some variation on that idea.

Reversed and remanded.

---

[2] If the agreement restricts the employee from *starting a new business,* a court may apply the more lenient standard used for the sale of a business; the noncompete clause will be enforced if reasonable in time, geography, and scope of activity.

The following chart summarizes the factors that courts look at in noncompete agreements.

## THE LEGALITY OF NONCOMPETE CLAUSES

| Type of Noncompete Agreement | When Enforceable | |
|---|---|---|
| Not ancillary to a sale of business or employment | Never | |
| Ancillary to a sale of business | If reasonable in time, geography, and scope of activity | |
| Ancillary to employment | Contract is more likely to be enforced when it:<br>• Involves trade secrets or confidential information: These are almost always protected<br>• Includes customer lists developed over an extended period and carefully protected<br>• Encompasses limited time and geographical scope<br>• Is vital to protect the employer's business | Contract is less likely to be enforced when it:<br>• Involves an employee who already had the skills when he arrived, or merely developed general skills on the job<br>• Includes customer lists that can be derived from public sources<br>• Encompasses excessive time or geographical scope<br>• Is unduly harsh on the employee or contrary to public interest |

# EXCULPATORY CLAUSES

You decide to capitalize on your expert ability as a skier and open a ski school in Colorado, "Pike's Pique." But you realize that skiing sometimes causes injuries, so you require anyone signing up for lessons to sign this form:

> I agree to hold Pike's Pique and its employees entirely harmless in the event that I am injured in any way or for any reason or cause, including but not limited to any acts, whether negligent or otherwise, of Pike's Pique or any employee or agent thereof.

The day your school opens, Sara Beth, an instructor, deliberately pushes Toby over a cliff because Toby criticizes her color combinations. Eddie, a beginning student, "blows out" his knee attempting an advanced racing turn. And Maureen, another student, reaches the bottom of a steep run and slams into a snowmobile that Sara Beth parked there. Maureen, Eddie, and Toby's families all sue Pike's Pique. You defend based on the form you had them sign. Does it save the day?

**Exculpatory clause**
A contract provision that attempts to release one party from liability in the event the other party is injured.

The form on which you are relying is an **exculpatory clause**, that is, one that attempts to release you from liability in the event of injury to another party. Exculpatory clauses are common. Ski schools use them, and so do parking lots, landlords, warehouses, and daycare centers. All manner of businesses hope to avoid large tort judgments by requiring their customers to give up any right to recover. Is such a clause valid? Sometimes. Courts often—but not always—ignore exculpatory clauses, finding that one party was forcing the other party to give up legal rights that no one should be forced to surrender.

**An exculpatory clause is generally unenforceable when it attempts to exclude an intentional tort or gross negligence.** When Sara Beth pushes Toby over a cliff, that is the intentional tort of battery. A court will not enforce the exculpatory clause. Sara Beth is clearly liable.[3] As to the snowmobile at the bottom of the run, if a court determines that was gross negligence (carelessness far greater than ordinary negligence), then the exculpatory clause will again be ignored. If, however, it was ordinary negligence, then we must continue the analysis.

**An exculpatory clause is generally unenforceable when the affected activity is in the public interest, such as medical care, public transportation, or some essential service.** What about Eddie's suit against Pike's Pique? Eddie claims that he should never have been allowed to attempt an advanced maneuver. His suit is for ordinary negligence, and the exculpatory clause probably does bar him from recovery. Skiing is a recreational activity. No one is obligated to do it, and there is no strong public interest in ensuring that we have access to ski slopes.

**An exculpatory clause is generally unenforceable when the parties have greatly unequal bargaining power.** When Maureen flies to Colorado, suppose that the airline requires her to sign a form contract with an exculpatory clause. Because the airline almost certainly has much greater bargaining power, it can afford to offer a "take it or leave it" contract. But because the bargaining power is so unequal, the clause is probably unenforceable.

**An exculpatory clause is generally unenforceable unless the clause is clearly written and readily visible.** Thus, if Pike's Pique gave all ski students an eight-page contract, and the exculpatory clause was at the bottom of page seven in small print, the average customer would never notice it. The clause would be void.

## EXAM *Strategy*

**Question:** Shauna flew a World War II fighter aircraft as a member of an exhibition flight team. While the team was performing in a delta formation, another plane collided with Shauna's aircraft, causing her to crash-land, leaving her permanently disabled. Shauna sued the other pilot and the team. The defendants moved to dismiss, based on an exculpatory clause that Shauna had signed. The clause was one paragraph long and stated that Shauna knew team flying was inherently dangerous and could result in injury or death. She agreed not to hold the team or any members liable in case of an accident. Shauna argued that the clause should not be enforced against her if she could prove the other pilot was negligent. Please rule.

**Strategy:** The issue is whether the exculpatory clause is valid. Courts are likely to declare such clauses void if they concern vital activities like medical care, exclude an intentional tort or gross negligence, or arise from unequal bargaining power.

**Result:** This is a clear, short clause, between parties with equal bargaining power, and does not exclude an intentional tort or gross negligence. The activity is unimportant to the public welfare. The clause is valid. Even if the other pilot was negligent, Shauna will lose, meaning the court should dismiss her lawsuit.

## · UNCONSCIONABLE CONTRACTS ·

Gail Waters was young, naive, and insecure. A serious injury when she was 12 years old left her with an annuity, that is, a guaranteed annual payment for many years. When Gail was 21, she became involved with Thomas Beauchemin, an ex-convict, who introduced her to drugs. Beauchemin suggested that Gail sell her annuity to some friends of his, and she agreed.

---

[3] Note that Pike's Pique is probably not liable under agency law principles that preclude an employer's liability for an employee's intentional tort.

Beauchemin arranged for a lawyer to draw up a contract, and Gail signed it. She received one $50,000 payment for her annuity, which at that time had a cash value of $189,000 and was worth, over its remaining 25 years, $694,000. Gail later decided this was not an excellent bargain. Was the contract enforceable? That depends on the law of unconscionability.

**An unconscionable contract is one that a court refuses to enforce because of fundamental unfairness.** Historically, a contract was considered unconscionable if it was "such as no man in his senses and not under delusion would make on the one hand, and as no honest and fair man would accept on the other."[4] The two factors that most often lead a court to find unconscionability are (1) **oppression**, meaning that one party used its superior power to force a contract on the weaker party, and (2) **surprise**, meaning that the weaker party did not fully understand the consequences of its agreement.

Gail Waters won her case. The Massachusetts high court ruled:

> Beauchemin introduced the plaintiff to drugs, exhausted her credit card accounts, unduly influenced her, suggested that the plaintiff sell her annuity contract, initiated the contract negotiations, was the agent of the defendants, and benefited from the contract between the plaintiff and the defendants. The defendants were represented by legal counsel; the plaintiff was not. The cash value of the annuity policy at the time the contract was executed was approximately four times greater than the price to be paid by the defendants. For payment of not more than $50,000 the defendants were to receive an asset that could be immediately exchanged for $189,000, or they could elect to hold it for its guaranteed term and receive $694,000.
>
> The disparity of interests in this contract is so gross that the court cannot resist the inference that it was improperly obtained and is unconscionable.[5]

## · CAPACITY AND CONSENT ·

For Kevin Green, it was love at first sight. She was sleek, as quick as a cat, and a beautiful deep blue. He paid $4,600 cash for the used Camaro. The car soon blew a gasket, and Kevin demanded his money back. But the Camaro came with no guarantee, and Star Chevrolet, the dealer, refused. Kevin repaired the car himself. Next, some unpleasantness on the highway left the car a worthless wreck. Kevin received the full value of the car from his insurance company. Then he sued the dealer, seeking a refund of his purchase price. The dealer pointed out that it was not responsible for the accident, and that the car had no warranty of any kind. Yet the court awarded Kevin the full value of his car. How can this be?

The automobile dealer ignored *legal capacity*. Kevin Green was only 16 years old when he bought the car, and a minor, said the court, has the right to cancel any agreement he made, for any reason. Capacity concerns the legal ability of a party to enter a contract. Someone may lack capacity because of his young age or mental infirmity. Consent refers to whether a contracting party truly understood what he was getting into and whether he made the agreement voluntarily. Consent issues arise most often in cases of fraud and mistake.

### CAPACITY

**Capacity** is the legal ability to enter into a contract. An adult of sound mind has the legal capacity to contract. Generally, any deal she enters into will be enforced if all elements we have

---

**Unconscionable contract**
A contract that is shockingly one-sided and fundamentally unfair.

**Oppression**
One party uses superior power to force a contract on another party.

**Surprise**
A party does not fully understand the consequences of its agreement to a contract.

**Capacity**
The legal ability to enter into a contract.

---

[4] *Hume v. United States*, 132 U.S. 406, 411, 10 S. Ct. 134, 1889 U.S. LEXIS 1888 (1889), quoting *Earl of Chesterfield v. Janssen*, 38 Eng. Rep. 82, 100 (Ch. 1750).

[5] *Waters v. Min Ltd.*, 412 Mass. 64, 587 N.E.2d 231, 1992 Mass. LEXIS 66 (1992).

seen—agreement, consideration, and so forth—are present. But two groups of people usually lack legal capacity: minors and those with a mental impairment.

## Minors

A minor is someone under the age of 18. Because a minor lacks legal capacity, she normally can create only a voidable contract. **A voidable contract may be canceled by the party who lacks capacity.** Notice that *only the party lacking capacity* may cancel the agreement. So a minor who enters into a contract generally may choose between enforcing the agreement or negating it. The other party, however, has no such right.

## Disaffirmance

A minor who wishes to escape from a contract generally may **disaffirm** it; that is, he may notify the other party that he refuses to be bound by the agreement. Because Kevin was 16 when he signed, the deal was voidable. When the Camaro blew a gasket and the lad informed Star Chevrolet that he wanted his money back, he was disaffirming the contract, which he could do for any reason at all. Kevin was entitled to his money back. If Star Chevrolet had understood the law of capacity, it would have towed the Camaro away and returned the young man's $4,600. At least the dealership would have had a repairable automobile.

**Disaffirm**
To give notice of refusal to be bound by an agreement.

## Restitution

**A minor who disaffirms a contract must return the consideration he has received, to the extent he is able.** Restoring the other party to its original position is called **restitution**. The consideration that Kevin Green received in the contract was, of course, the Camaro. If Star Chevrolet had delivered a check for $4,600, Kevin would have been obligated to return the car.

What happens if the minor is not able to return the consideration because he no longer has it or it has been destroyed? Most states hold that the minor is still entitled to his money back. Kevin Green got his money and Star Chevrolet received a fine lesson.

**Restitution**
Restoring an injured party to its original position.

## Mentally Impaired Persons

**A person suffers from a mental impairment if by reason of mental illness or defect he is unable to understand the nature and consequences of the transaction.**[6] The mental impairment can be insanity that has been formally declared by a court or mental illness that has never been ruled on but is now evident. The impairment may also be due to some other mental illness, such as schizophrenia, or to mental retardation, brain injury, senility, or any other cause that renders the person unable to understand the nature and consequences of the contract.

**A party suffering a mental impairment generally creates only a voidable contract.** The impaired person has the right to disaffirm the contract just as a minor does. But again, the contract is voidable, not void. The mentally impaired party generally has the right to full performance if she wishes. Similar rules apply in cases of drug or alcohol **intoxication.** When one party is so intoxicated that he cannot understand the nature and consequences of the transaction, the contract is voidable.

# REALITY OF CONSENT

Smiley offers to sell you his house for $300,000, and you agree in writing to buy. After you move in, you discover that the house is sinking into the earth at the rate of six inches per week. In 12 months, your only access to the house will be through the chimney. You sue, asking to **rescind**, which means to cancel the agreement. You argue that when you signed the contract, you did not truly consent because you lacked essential information. In this section, we look at issues of misrepresentation, fraud, and mistake.

**Rescind**
To cancel a contract.

---

[6] Restatement (Second) of Contracts §15.

## Misrepresentation and Fraud

**Misrepresentation**
A statement that is factually wrong.

**Misrepresentation** occurs when a party to a contract says something that is factually wrong. "This house has no termites," says a homeowner to a prospective buyer. If the house is swarming with the nasty pests, the statement is a misrepresentation. The misrepresentation might be innocent or fraudulent. If the owner believes the statement to be true and has a good reason for that belief, he has made an **innocent misrepresentation.** If the owner knows that it is false, the statement is **fraudulent misrepresentation.** To explain these concepts, we will assume that two people are discussing a possible deal. One is the "maker"—that is, the person who makes the statement that is later disputed. The other is the "injured person," the one who eventually claims to have been injured by the statement. In order to rescind the contract, the injured person must show that the maker's statement was either fraudulent or a material misrepresentation. She does not have to show both. Innocent misrepresentation and fraud each make a contract voidable. **To rescind a contract based on misrepresentation or fraud, a party must show three things: (1) There was a false statement of fact; (2) the statement was fraudulent or material; and (3) the injured person justifiably relied on the statement.**

### Element One: False Statement of Fact

The injured party must show a false statement of fact. Notice that this does not mean the statement was a lie. If a homeowner says that the famous architect Stanford White designed his house, but Bozo Loco actually did the work, it is a false statement. The owner might have a good reason for the error. Perhaps a local history book identifies the house as a Stanford White. Or the owner's words might be an intentional lie. In either case, it is a false statement of fact.

An **opinion,** though, is not a statement of fact. A realtor says, "I think land values around here will be going up 20 or 30 percent for the foreseeable future." That statement is pretty enticing to a buyer, but it is not a false statement of fact. The maker is clearly stating her own opinion, and the buyer who relies on it does so at his peril. A close relative of opinion is something called puffery. A statement is **puffery** when a reasonable person would realize that it is a sales pitch, representing the exaggerated opinion of the seller. Puffery is not a statement of fact and is never a basis for rescission.

**Fraud**
Intending to induce the other party to contract, knowing the words are false or uncertain that they are true.

### Element Two: Fraud or Materiality

This is the heart of the case. The injured party must demonstrate that the statement was fraudulent or material:

- The statement was fraudulent if the maker intended to induce the other party to contract, either knowing that her words were false or uncertain that they were true.

**Material**
The maker expected the other party to rely on her words.

- The statement was **material** if the maker expected the other party to rely on her words in reaching an agreement.

So the injured party can win by showing either of two very different things. **Fraud** indicates a bad faith statement, whereas material misrepresentation signifies that the words were inaccurate—and effective.

Consider the examples in the following chart.

### Element Three: Justifiable Reliance

The injured party must also show that she actually did rely on the false statement and that her reliance was reasonable. Suppose the seller of a gas station lies through his teeth about the structural soundness of the building. The buyer believes what he hears but does not much care, because he plans to demolish the building and construct a daycare center. There was fraud but no reliance, and the buyer may not rescind.

### Plaintiff's Remedy for Misrepresentation or Fraud

Both innocent and fraudulent misrepresentation permit the injured party to rescind the contract. In other words, the injured party who proves all three elements will get her money back. She will, of course, have to make restitution to the other party. If she bought land and now wants to rescind, she must return the property to the seller.

| Statement: In each case, the words are false | Owner's Belief | Legal Result | Explanation |
|---|---|---|---|
| 1. "The heating system is perfect." | Owner knows this is false. | Fraud. | Owner knew the statement was false and intended to induce the buyer to enter into a contract. |
| 2. "The house is built on solid bedrock." | Owner has no idea what is under the surface. | Fraud. | Owner was not certain the statement was true and intended to induce the buyer to enter into a contract. |
| 3. "The roof is only six years old." | Owner believes the statement is accurate, because when he bought the house six years ago, he was told the roof was new. | Material misrepresentation. | Owner acted in good faith, but the statement is material because owner expects the buyer to rely on it. |
| 4. "The pool is 30 feet long." | Owner believes the statement is accurate because he measured the pool himself, though in fact it is only 29 feet. | Not a material misrepresentation. | Although this is a misrepresentation, it is not material, because a reasonable buyer would not make a decision based on a one-foot error in the pool length. |

But the injured party is not forced to rescind the deal if it makes financial sense to go forward with it. After signing a contract to buy a new house, Nancy learns that the building has a terrible heating system. A new one will cost $12,000. If the seller told her the system was "like new," Nancy may rescind the deal. But it may be economically harmful for her to do so. She might have sold her old house, hired a mover, taken a new job, and so forth. She has the option of fully performing the contract and moving into the new house. What are her other remedies? That will depend on whether the misstatement ("the system is like new") was fraudulent or simply a material misrepresentation.

If the maker's statement is fraudulent, the injured party generally has a choice of rescinding the contract or suing for damages. If the seller's mistake was fraudulent, Nancy will generally be allowed to carry out the contract and sue for damages. She could move into the new house and sue for the difference between what she got and what was promised, which is probably about $12,000, the cost of replacing the heating system. But if the seller's mistake was innocent, and Nancy can prove only material misrepresentation, she has no remedy other than rescission. If she goes forward with the contract, she must accept the house as she finds it.

**Special Problem: Silence**    We know that a party negotiating a contract may not misrepresent a material fact. But what about silence? Suppose the seller knows the roof is in dreadful condition (since she sleeps under an umbrella), but the buyer never asks. Must the seller disclose what she knows?

This is perhaps the hottest topic today in the law of misrepresentation. A seller who knows something that the buyer does not know is often required to divulge it. The Restatement (Second) of Contracts offers guidance.

**Nondisclosure of a fact amounts to misrepresentation when:**

- Disclosure is necessary to correct a previous assertion. During the course of negotiations, one party's perception of the facts may change. When an earlier statement later appears inaccurate, the change generally must be reported.

- Disclosure would correct a basic mistaken assumption that the other party is relying on. When one party knows that the other is negotiating with a mistaken assumption about an important fact, the party who knows of the error must correct it. Most courts require a property seller to disclose hidden defects. The judge in the following case states the rule somewhat differently, but the reasoning and outcome are the same.

# FIMBEL V. DECLARK

695 N.E.2D 125, INDIANA COURT OF APPEALS, 1998

## CASE SUMMARY

**Facts:** Ronald and Patricia Fimbel bought two lakefront lots on Lake Latonka in Indiana, intending to build a summer cottage. However, they discovered that the soil was not suitable for a septic system. They would have to hire an engineer at a substantial expense to determine if it was even possible to construct an alternative system. They decided to sell the land.

The Fimbels met with several interested buyers, including Thomas and Joan DeClark. The Fimbels said nothing about the septic problems. The DeClarks bought the property and, one week later, learned that the property was unbuildable. They sued, and the trial court granted them rescission. The Fimbels appealed.

**Issue:** *Did the Fimbels have a duty to disclose the septic problems?*

**Decision:** Yes, the Fimbels had a duty to disclose. Affirmed.

**Reasoning:** If a buyer questions the condition or quality of property, a seller is obligated to disclose what he knows. When asked if he had ever planned to construct a house on the lots, Fimbel replied that he had considered doing so but decided instead to build on land he owned in Minnesota, near a friend's residence. DeClark mentioned that he did in fact want to erect a house on the property. That conversation obligated Fimbel to inform DeClark about the septic problem.

Fimbel argues that he never misrepresented the soil's condition. Although that is technically accurate, Fimbel's statement as to why he preferred to build in Minnesota was only partially correct, at best. He concealed what he knew about the land he was selling. Creating a false impression by partially disclosing facts is misrepresentation. The Fimbels' silence, together with their misrepresentation, makes them liable for fraud.

**ETHICS** There are various disclosure rules that a state could adopt:

- *Caveat emptor*—let the buyer beware.
- Seller has a duty to disclose only if asked.
- Seller has a duty to disclose regardless of whether asked.
- Seller's only duty is to notify buyer of important considerations that buyer may wish to investigate (soil condition, building laws, problems with neighboring property, etc.).

Which rule do you prefer, and why? As you answer this question, apply these concepts from the Chapter 2 ethics checklist: What are the alternatives? What outcome does the Golden Rule require? ◆

## *Mistake*

Most contract principles come from appellate courts, but in the area of "legal mistake" a cow wrote much of the law. The cow was Rose 2d of Aberlone, a gentle animal that lived in Michigan in 1886. Rose's owner, Hiram Walker & Sons, had bought her for $850. After a few years, the company concluded that Rose could have no calves. As a barren cow she was worth much less, so Walker contracted to sell her to T. C. Sherwood for $80. But when Sherwood came to collect Rose, the parties realized she was pregnant. Walker refused to part with the happy mother, and Sherwood sued. Walker defended, claiming that both parties had made a mistake and that the contract was voidable.

**Bilateral Mistake**  A **bilateral mistake** occurs when both parties negotiate based on the same factual error. Sherwood and Walker both thought Rose was barren, both negotiated accordingly, and both were wrong. The Michigan Supreme Court gave judgment for Walker, the seller, permitting him to rescind the contract because the parties were both wrong about the essence of what they were bargaining for.

   **If the parties contract based on an important factual error, the contract is voidable by the injured party.** Sherwood and Walker were both wrong about Rose's reproductive ability, and the error was basic enough to cause a tenfold difference in price. Walker, the injured party, was entitled to rescind the contract. Note that the error must be *factual*. Suppose Walker sold Rose thinking that the price of beef was going to drop, when in fact the price rose 60 percent in five months. He made a mistake, but it was simply a business prediction that proved wrong. Walker would have no right to rescind.

> **Bilateral mistake**
> occurs when both parties negotiate based on the same factual error.

**Conscious Uncertainty**  No rescission is permitted where one of the parties knows he is taking on a risk—that is, he realizes there is uncertainty about the quality of the thing being exchanged. Rufus offers 10 acres of mountainous land to Priscilla. "I can't promise you anything about this land," he says, "but they've found gold on every adjoining parcel." Priscilla, panting with gold lust, buys the land, digs long and hard and discovers—mud. She may not rescind the contract. She understood her risk, and there was no mutual mistake.

**Unilateral Mistake**  Sometimes only one party enters a contract under a mistaken assumption, a situation called **unilateral mistake**. In these cases, it is more difficult for the injured party to rescind a contract. To rescind for unilateral mistake, a party must demonstrate that she entered the contract because of a basic factual error and that either (1) enforcing the contract would be unconscionable or (2) the nonmistaken party knew of the error.

> **Unilateral mistake**
> occurs when only one party negotiates based on a factual error.

## EXAM *Strategy*

**Question:** Joe buys an Otterhound named Barky from Purity Dog Shop. He pays $2,500 for the puppy, the high cost due to the certificate Purity gives him, indicating that the puppy's parents were both AKC champions (elite dogs). Two months later, Joe sells the hound to Emily for $2,800. Joe and Emily both believe that Barky is descended from champions. Then a state investigation reveals that Purity has been cheating and its certificates are fakes. Barky is a mixed-breed dog, worth about $100. Emily sues Joe. Who wins?

**Strategy:** Both parties are mistaken about the kind of dog Joe is selling, so this is an instance of bilateral mistake. What is the rule in such cases?

**Result:** If the two sides agree based on an important factual error, the contract is voidable by the injured party. A mutt is entirely different from a dog that might become a champion. The parties erred about the essence of their deal. Joe's good faith does not save him, and Emily is entitled to rescind.

# · CONTRACTS IN WRITING ·

> **Perry moved out of their dorm room into a suite at the Ritz and refused to give Oliver one red cent.**

Oliver and Perry were college roommates, two sophomores with contrasting personalities. They were sitting in the cafeteria with some friends, Oliver chatting away, Perry slumped on a plastic bench. Oliver suggested that they buy a lottery ticket, as the prize for that week's drawing was $3 million. Perry muttered, "Nah. You never win if you buy just one ticket." Oliver bubbled up, "OK, we'll buy a ticket every week. We'll keep buying them from now until we graduate. Come on, it'll be fun. This month, I'll buy the tickets. Next month, you will, and so on." Other students urged Perry to do it and, finally, grudgingly, he agreed. The two friends carefully reviewed their deal. Each party was providing consideration, namely, the responsibility for purchasing tickets during his month. The amount of each purchase was clearly defined at one dollar. They would start that week and continue until graduation day, two and a half years down the road. Finally, they would share equally any money won. As three witnesses looked on, they shook hands on the bargain. That month, Oliver bought a ticket every week, randomly choosing numbers, and won nothing. The next month, Perry bought a ticket with equally random numbers—and won $52 million. Perry moved out of their dorm room into a suite at the Ritz and refused to give Oliver one red cent. Oliver sued, seeking $26 million and the return of an Eric Clapton CD that he had loaned to Perry.

If the former friends had read this chapter, they would never have slid into such a mess. In the last chapter, we covered the basics of contract law, and now we put the icing on the cake. We will examine which contracts must be in writing, when third parties have rights or obligations under an agreement, what problems arise in the performance of contracts, and the remedies available when a deal goes awry. Oliver and Perry's case involves the statute of frauds, which tells us which contracts must be written.

## WRITTEN CONTRACTS

The rule we examine in this chapter is not exactly news. Parliament passed the original statute of frauds in 1677. The purpose was to prevent lying (fraud) in civil lawsuits. The statute required that in several types of cases, a contract would be enforced only if it was in writing. Almost all states in our own country later passed their own statutes making the same requirements. It is important to remember, as we examine the rules and exceptions, that Parliament and the state legislatures all had a commendable, straightforward purpose in passing their respective statutes of fraud: *to provide a court with the best possible evidence of whether the parties intended to make a contract.*

**Statute of frauds**
Requires certain contracts to be in writing.

The **statute of frauds**: A plaintiff may not enforce any of the following agreements, unless the agreement, or some memorandum of it, is in writing and signed by the defendant. The agreements that must be in writing are those:

- For any interest in **land**;
- That **cannot be performed within one year**;
- To pay the **debt of another**;
- Made by an **executor of an estate**;
- Made in **consideration of marriage**; and
- For the **sale of goods worth $500 or more**.

### *Unenforceable (Sorry, Oliver)*

In other words, when two parties make an agreement covered by any one of these six topics, it must be in writing to be enforceable. Oliver and Perry made a definite agreement to purchase lottery tickets during alternate months and share the proceeds of any winning ticket. But their agreement was to last two and one-half years. As the second item on the list indicates, a contract must be in writing if it cannot be performed within one year. The good news is that Oliver gets back his Eric Clapton CD. The bad news is that he gets none of the lottery money. Even though three witnesses saw the deal made, it is unlikely to be enforced in any state. Perry the pessimist will probably walk away with all $52 million.[7]

# CONTRACTS THAT MUST BE IN WRITING

## Agreements for an Interest in Land

A contract for the sale of any interest in land must be in writing to be enforceable. Notice the phrase "interest in land." This means any legal right regarding land. A house on a lot is an interest in land. A mortgage, an easement, and a leased apartment are all interests in land. As a general rule, leases must therefore be in writing, although many states have created an exception for short-term leases of a year or less.

### Exception: Full Performance by the Seller

If the seller completely performs her side of a contract for an interest in land, a court is likely to enforce the agreement even if it was oral. Adam orally agrees to sell his condominium to Maggie for $150,000. Adam delivers the deed to Maggie and expects his money a week later, but Maggie fails to pay. Most courts will allow Adam to enforce the oral contract and collect the full purchase price from Maggie.

### Exception: Part Performance by the Buyer

The buyer of land may be able to enforce an oral contract if she paid part of the purchase price and either entered upon the land or made improvements to it. Suppose that Eloise sues Grover to enforce an alleged oral contract to sell a lot in Happydale. She claims they struck a bargain in January. Grover defends based on the statute of frauds, saying that even if the two did reach an oral agreement, it is unenforceable. Eloise proves that she paid 10 percent of the purchase price and that in February she began excavating on the lot to build a house, and that Grover knew of the work. Eloise has established part performance and will be allowed to enforce her contract.

In the following case, the defendant seems to have acknowledged *in court* that she agreed to sell her property. Does that satisfy the statute of frauds?

## BAKER v. DAVES

83 Ark. App. 145, 119 S.W.3d 53, Court of Appeals of Arkansas, 2003

### CASE SUMMARY

**Facts:** Tommy and Eleanor Daves had a daughter, Lisa Baker. The Daves gave Lisa a deed to a 2-acre property with a house on it, keeping for themselves a *life interest* in the parcel. In other words, the Daves each had a half interest in the land for the rest of their lives; they could live in the house and use the land any way they wished. When they died, the property would go to their daughter.

Tommy and Eleanor divorced and settled their affairs amicably. In court, with Lisa watching from the second row, their lawyers informed the court of an agreement that all three

---

[7] Perry might also raise *illegality* as a defense, claiming that a contract for gambling is illegal. That defense is likely to fail. Courts appear to distinguish between the simple purchase of a legal lottery ticket, which friends often share, and the more traditional—and socially dangerous—gambling contracts involving horse racing or casino betting. See, for example, *Pando v. Fernandez*, 118 A.D.2d 474, 499 N.Y.S.2d 950, 1986 N.Y. App. Div. LEXIS 54345 (N.Y. App. Div. 1986), finding no illegality in an agreement to purchase a lottery ticket, even where the purchaser was a minor! Because an illegality defense would probably fail Perry, it is all the more unfortunate that Oliver did not jot down their agreement in writing.

parties had allegedly made to sell the 2-acre property. Lisa would be reimbursed for taxes and insurance she had paid during the two years she owned the property, and the Daveses would split the rest of the money.

After the agreement was announced, Lisa put the property on the market, but then withdrew it and refused to sell. Tommy Daves sued his daughter. Lisa defended based on the statute of frauds, saying she had never agreed in court to the deal, and never signed any contract to sell. The trial court acknowledged that Lisa had signed nothing but found that the courtroom statements proved the parties had formed a binding contract. The judge ordered Lisa to sell the house, and she appealed.

**Issue:** *Was Lisa obligated to sell the house?*

**Decision:** No, Lisa was not obligated to sell the house.

**Reasoning:** In the trial court, the lawyers for Tommy and Eleanor Daves summarized what they considered to be an agreement to sell the property:

**Attorney for Eleanor Daves:** The parties have a joint life estate in 2.2 acres of property and a house on Vimy Ridge Road in Alexander, Arkansas. The parties have agreed to sell the house and 2.2 acres and split the proceeds. They have agreed that Mr. Daves will contact a real estate agency.

**Attorney for Tommy Daves:** They have a life estate. It was placed in her daughter's name and the daughter is the title owner. She is going to cooperate in listing the property for sale. They are actually selling the property, not just the life estate.

**Attorney for Eleanor Daves:** The daughter has agreed to sell her interest in the property as well as the life estate of the two parties.

Tommy Daves argues that because Lisa was in court while the statements were made, she implicitly agreed to them and is bound by the oral contract that was formed. Lisa argues that she made no such agreement.

Lisa Baker was not a party to the divorce proceedings. She was not represented by counsel during the trial. The trial court never asked whether she had heard the purported agreement or whether she agreed to it. In the absence of clear evidence that Lisa orally agreed in court to sell the property, the statute of frauds must control this case. There is no written evidence of a contract, and Lisa is not bound by any alleged oral agreement.

Reversed and remanded.

**Reasoning of the Dissent:** Lisa admitted she was present in the hallway with her mother at the time of the divorce hearing when the agreement was being discussed. She acknowledged that she was in the courtroom when the agreement was being read into the record, although she claimed she could not hear what the lawyers were saying. Lisa also admitted that she listed the property for sale pursuant to the agreement. Her conduct unequivocally demonstrates her assent to the agreement.

## Agreements That Cannot Be Performed Within One Year

Contracts that cannot be performed within one year are unenforceable unless they are in writing. This one-year period begins on the date the parties make the agreement. The critical phrase here is "*cannot* be performed within one year." If a contract could be completed within one year, it need not be in writing. Betty gets a job at Burger Brain, throwing fries in oil. Her boss tells her she can have Fridays off for as long as she works there. That oral contract is enforceable, whether Betty stays one week or 57 years. It could have been performed within one year if, say, Betty quit the job after six months. Therefore it does not need to be in writing.[8]

If the agreement will necessarily take longer than one year to finish, it must be in writing to be enforceable. If Betty is hired for three years as manager of Burger Brain, the agreement is unenforceable unless put in writing. She cannot perform three years of work in one year.

---

[8] This is the majority rule. In most states, if a company hires an employee "for life," the contract need not be in writing because the employee could die within one year. "Contracts of uncertain duration are simply excluded [from the statute of frauds]; the provision covers only those contracts whose performance cannot possibly be completed within a year." Restatement (Second) of Contracts §130, Comment a, at 328 (1981). However, a few states disagree. The Illinois Supreme Court ruled that a contract for lifetime employment is enforceable only if written. *McInerney v. Charter Golf, Inc.*, 176 Ill. 2d 482, 680 N.E.2d 1347, 1997 Ill. LEXIS 56 (Ill. 1997).

| Type of Agreement | Enforceability |
| --- | --- |
| *Cannot* be performed within one year.<br>*Example:* An offer of employment for three years. | Must be in writing to be enforceable. |
| *Might* be performed within one year, although could take many years to perform.<br>*Example:* "As long as you work here at Burger Brain you may have Fridays off." | Enforceable whether it is oral or written, because the employee might quit working a month later. |

The following case starts with a notorious diet pill and ends with a paralegal suing her boss. Which argument carries greater weight?

## YOU *be the* JUDGE

### SAWYER v. MILLS

2007 WL 1113038
Kentucky Court of Appeals, 2007

**Facts:** Barbara Sawyer, a paralegal, worked for attorney Melbourne Mills, assisting him in a class action lawsuit against the makers of a popular diet drug called Fen-Phen. Mills promised Sawyer a large bonus "when the ship comes in," but never specified how much he would pay her. Mills successfully settled the Fen-Phen case for millions of dollars and later met with Sawyer and her husband to discuss her bonus. The Sawyers secretly recorded the conversation.

The Sawyers asked Mills for a $1 million bonus, to be paid as a lump sum. Mills refused. However, the parties kept talking and Mills eventually agreed to pay Sawyer $1 million, plus $65,000 for a luxury automobile. Payments were to be made in monthly installments of $10,000, for 10 years. Mills also agreed to sign a document confirming his promise. Sawyer's lawyer drafted the writing but Mills never signed it. He did pay nine monthly installments, along with an extra payment of $100,000.

At trial, jurors heard the tape recording, which confirmed the oral agreement. The jury concluded that the parties had reached a binding agreement, and awarded Sawyer $900,000. However, the court granted a judgment notwithstanding the verdict for Mills. He ruled that the agreement was barred by the statute of frauds. Sawyer appealed.

**You Be the Judge: Does the statute of frauds prevent enforcement of Mills's promise?**

**Argument for Sawyer:** The statute of frauds exists to make sure that a plaintiff does not come into court and allege an oral promise that never existed. The fear of fraudulent claims is legitimate but obviously does not apply in this case. We *know* that Mills agreed to pay $1 million because we can *hear* him make the promise. We know the exact terms of the agreement, we know it was a reasonable arrangement based on years of work and a massive settlement. We even hear Mills agree to sign a document confirming his promise.

The statute of frauds was designed to prevent fraud—not encourage it. Mills's tiresome, technical arguments did not fool the jurors. After hearing—literally—the evidence, the jury knew there had been a deal and awarded Sawyer her fair share. Let's stop playing legal games, start doing justice, and restore the verdict.

**Argument for Mills:** This is a simple case. The plaintiffs allege an oral contract for 10 years' worth of installment payments. In other words, *if* there was an agreement, it was for 10 years' duration. Sawyer's own lawyer drafted a contract—never signed—for compensation lasting a full decade. Under the statute of frauds, an agreement that cannot be performed within one year is unenforceable unless written and signed. End of case.

If our legislature wanted to encourage secret tape recordings and deception, it could have included an exception to the statute of frauds, giving tricky plaintiffs a reward for bad-faith negotiating. However, the legislators wisely have made no such exception. The alleged oral contract is worthless.

### Promise to Pay the Debt of Another

When one person agrees to pay the debt of another as a favor to that debtor, it is called a collateral promise, and it must be in writing to be enforceable. A student applies for a $10,000 loan to help pay for college, and her father agrees to repay the bank if the student defaults. The bank will insist that the father's promise be in writing because his oral promise alone is unenforceable.

### Promise Made by an Executor of an Estate

An executor is the person who is in charge of an estate after someone dies. The executor's job is to pay debts of the deceased, obtain money owed to him, and disburse the assets according to the will. In most cases, the executor will use only the estate's assets to pay those debts, but occasionally she might offer her own money. An executor's promise to use her own funds to pay a debt of the deceased must be in writing to be enforceable.

## PROMISE MADE IN CONSIDERATION OF MARRIAGE

Barney is a multimillionaire with the integrity of a gangster and the charm of a tax collector. He proposes to Li-Tsing, who promptly rejects him. Barney then pleads that if Li-Tsing will be his bride, he will give her an island he owns off the coast of California. Li-Tsing begins to see his good qualities and accepts. After they are married, Barney refuses to deliver the deed. Li-Tsing will get nothing from a court either, because a promise made in consideration of marriage must be in writing to be enforceable.

## WHAT THE WRITING MUST CONTAIN

Each of the five types of contract described earlier must be in writing in order to be enforceable. What must the writing contain? It may be a carefully typed contract, using precise legal terminology, or an informal memorandum scrawled on the back of a paper napkin at a business lunch. The writing may consist of more than one document, written at different times, with each document making a piece of the puzzle. However, there are some general requirements. The contract or memorandum:

- Must be signed by the defendant, and
- Must state with reasonable certainty the name of each party, the subject matter of the agreement, and all the essential terms and promises.[9]

### Signature

A statute of frauds typically states that the writing must be "signed by the party to be charged therewith," in other words, the defendant. Judges define "signature" very broadly. Using a pen to write one's name, though sufficient, is not required. A secretary who stamps an executive's signature on a letter fulfills this requirement. Any other mark or logo placed on a document to indicate acceptance, even an "X," will likely satisfy the statute of frauds. Electronic commerce creates new methods of signing—and new controversies, discussed later in this chapter.

### Reasonable Certainty

Suppose Garfield and Hayes are having lunch, discussing the sale of Garfield's vacation condominium. They agree on a price and want to make some notation of the agreement even before their lawyers work out a detailed purchase and sales agreement. A perfectly adequate memorandum

---

[9] Restatement (Second) of Contracts §131.

might say, "Garfield agrees to sell Hayes his condominium at 234 Baron Boulevard, apartment 18, for $350,000 cash, payable on June 18, 2004, and Hayes promises to pay the sum on that day." They should make two copies of their agreement and sign both.

## Sale of Goods

The UCC requires a writing for the sale of goods worth $500 or more. This is the sixth and final contract that must be written, although the Code's requirements are easier to meet than those of the common law. In some cases, the Code dispenses altogether with the writing requirement. To read the UCC online, go to **http://www.law.cornell.edu** and click on "Contracts and Codes," then "Uniform Commercial Code." The basic statute of frauds rule is Section 2-201(1). Important exceptions are found at Section 2-201(2) and (3).

The basic UCC rule: A contract for the sale of goods worth $500 or more is not enforceable unless there is some writing, signed by the defendant, indicating that the parties reached an agreement. The key difference between the common-law rule and the UCC rule is that the Code does not require all the terms of the agreement to be in writing. The Code demands only an indication that the parties reached an agreement. The two things that are essential are the signature of the defendant and the quantity of goods being sold. The quantity of goods is required because this is the one term for which there will be no objective evidence. Suppose a short memorandum between textile dealers indicates that Seller will sell to Buyer "grade AA 100% cotton, white athletic socks." If the writing does not state the price, the parties can testify at court about what the market price was at the time of the deal. But how many socks were to be delivered? One hundred pairs or 100,000? The quantity must be written. (A basic sale of goods contract appears at **http://www.lectlaw.com/**. Click on "Legal Forms," then "General Business Forms.")

**Electronic Contracts and Signatures**   E-commerce has grown at a dazzling rate, and U.S. enterprises buy and sell tens of billions of dollars worth of goods and services over the Internet. What happens to the writing requirement, though, when there is no paper? The present statute of frauds requires some sort of "signing" to ensure that the defendant committed to the deal. Today, an "electronic signature" could mean a name typed (or automatically included) at the bottom of an e-mail message, a retinal or vocal scan, or a name signed by electronic pen on a writing tablet, among others.

Are electronic signatures valid? Yes. State legislatures and Congress are struggling to craft a cohesive law, and the job is incomplete, but here are the rules so far:

- **The Uniform Electronic Transaction Act (UETA).** This law was drafted by the National Conference of Commissioners on Uniform State Laws, who also draft the UCC. As this book goes to press, UETA is the law in 48 states and territories. **UETA declares that a contract or signature may not be denied enforceability simply because it is in electronic form.** In other words, the normal rules of contract law apply, but one party may not avoid such a deal merely because it originated in cyberspace.

- **The Electronic Signatures in Global and National Commerce Act (E-Sign).** This federal statute, which applies in any state that has not adopted UETA, also declares that contracts will not be denied enforcement simply because they are in electronic form, or signed electronically.

With cyberlaw in its early stages, how can an executive take advantage of the Internet's commercial opportunities while protecting his company against losses unique to the field?

First, acknowledge the risks, which include lost or intercepted communications, fraudulently altered documents, and difficulties authenticating the source of an offer or acceptance. Second, be cautious about "electronic signatures." Assume that any commitments you make electronically can be enforced against you. Paradoxically, if the contract is important, do not assume that the other party's promises, if made electronically, are enforceable. Get a hard copy, signed in ink.

# CHAPTER CONCLUSION

**It is not enough to bargain effectively and obtain a contract that gives you exactly what you want.** Bargaining a contract with a noncompete or exculpatory clause that is too one-sided may lead a court to ignore it. Both parties must be adults of sound mind and must give genuine consent. Misrepresentation and mistakes indicate that at least one party did not truly consent. Some contracts must be in writing to be enforceable, and the writing must be clear and unambiguous.

# EXAM REVIEW

**1.** **ILLEGAL CONTRACTS** Illegal contracts are void and unenforceable. Claims of illegality often arise concerning noncompete clauses, exculpatory clauses, and unconscionable clauses. (p. 149)

**EXAM Strategy**

**Question:** The purchaser of a business insisted on putting this clause in the sales contract: The seller would not compete, for five years, "anywhere in the United States, the continent of North America, or anywhere else on earth." What danger does that contract represent *to the purchaser?*

**Strategy:** This is a noncompete clause based on the sale of a business. Such clauses are valid if reasonable. Is this clause reasonable? If it is unreasonable, what might a court do? (See the "Result" at the end of this section.)

**2.** **MINORITY AND MENTAL IMPAIRMENT** Minors and mentally impaired persons generally may disaffirm contracts. (p. 155)

**3.** **FRAUD AND MISREPRESENTATION** Fraud and material misrepresentation are grounds for disaffirming a contract. The injured party must prove a false statement of fact, fraud or materiality, and justifiable reliance. (p. 156)

**4.** **MISTAKE** In a bilateral mistake, either party may rescind the contract. In a case of unilateral mistake, the injured party may rescind only in limited circumstances. (p. 159)

**5.** **WRITING REQUIRED** Contracts that must be in writing to be enforceable concern:

- The sale of any interest in land;
- Agreements that cannot be performed within one year;
- Promises to pay the debt of another;
- Promises made by an executor of an estate;
- Promises made in consideration of marriage; and
- The sale of goods worth $500 or more. (p. 160)

**Question:** Donald Waide had a contracting business. He bought most of his supplies from Paul Bingham's supply center. Waide fell behind on his bills, and Bingham told Waide that he would extend no more credit to him. That same day, Donald's father, Elmer Waide, came to Bingham's store and said to Bingham that he would "stand good" for any sales to Donald made on credit. Based on Elmer's statement, Bingham again gave Donald credit, and Donald ran up $10,000 in goods before Bingham sued Donald and Elmer. What defense did Elmer make and what was the outcome?

**Strategy:** This was an oral agreement, so the issue is whether the promise had to be in writing to be enforceable. Review the list of six contracts that must be in writing. Is this agreement there? (See the "Result" at the end of this section.)

6. **WRITING CONTENTS** The writing must be signed by the defendant and must state the name of all parties, the subject matter of the agreement, and all essential terms and promises. (p. 164)

**1. Result:** "Anywhere else on earth"? This is almost certainly unreasonable. It is hard to imagine a purchaser who would legitimately need such wide-ranging protection. In some states, a court might rewrite the clause, limiting the effect to the seller's state or some other reasonable area. However, in other states, a court finding a clause unreasonable will declare it void in its entirety—enabling the seller to open a competing business next door.

**5. Result:** Elmer made a promise to pay the debt of another. He did so as a favor to his son. This is a collateral promise. Elmer never signed any such promise, and the agreement cannot be enforced against him.

## PRACTICE EXAM

### MATCHING QUESTIONS

___ A. Fraud

___ B. Restitution

___ C. Part performance

___ D. Exculpatory clause

___ E. Unconscionable

1. A contract clause intended to relieve one party from potential tort liability

2. A contract provision that no one would sign who understood it

3. The intention to deceive the other party

4. Restoring the other party to its original position

5. Entry onto land, or improvements made to it, by a buyer who has no written contract

### TRUE/FALSE QUESTIONS

1. T  F  A contract may not be rescinded based on puffery.

2. T  F  An agreement for the sale of a house does not need to be in writing if the deal will be completed within one year.

3. T  F  Noncompete clauses are suspect because they tend to restrain free trade.

4. T  F  A seller of property must generally disclose latent defects that he knows about.

5. T    F    A court is unlikely to enforce an exculpatory clause included in a contract for surgery.

6. T    F    An agreement for the sale of 600 plastic cups, worth $0.50 each, must be in writing to be enforceable.

## MULTIPLE-CHOICE QUESTIONS

7. In which case is a court most likely to enforce an exculpatory clause?
   A. Dentistry
   B. Hang gliding
   C. Parking lot
   D. Public transportation
   E. Accounting

8. Sarah, age 17, uses $850 of her hard-earned, summer-job money to pay cash for a diamond pendant for the senior prom. She has a wonderful time at the dance but decides the pendant was an extravagance, returns it, and demands a refund. The store has a "no refund" policy that is clearly stated on a sign on the wall. There was no defect in the pendant. The store refuses the refund. When Sarah sues, she will
   A. Win $850
   B. Win $425
   C. Win, but only if she did not notice the "no refund" policy
   D. Win, but only if she did not think the "no refund" policy applied to her
   E. Lose

9. Tobias is selling a surrealist painting. He tells Maud that the picture is by the famous French artist Magritte, although in fact Tobias has no idea whether that is true or not. Tobias's statement is
   A. Bilateral mistake
   B. Unilateral mistake
   C. Fraud
   D. Misrepresentation
   E. Legal, as long as he acted in good faith

10. Louise e-mails Sonya, "I will sell you my house at 129 Brittle Blvd. for $88,000, payable in one month. Best, Louise." Sonya e-mails back, "Louise, I accept the offer to buy your house at that price. Sonya." Neither party prints a copy of the two e-mails.
    A. The parties have a binding contract for the sale of Louise's house.
    B. Louise is bound by the agreement but Sonya is not.
    C. Sonya is bound by the agreement but Louise is not.
    D. Neither party is bound because the agreement was never put in writing.
    E. Neither party is bound because the agreement was never signed.

11. You drive up to a fancy restaurant and hand your car keys to the valet. You have created
    A. An exculpatory clause
    B. A noncompete clause
    C. A bailment
    D. An illusory contract
    E. An adhesion contract

12. In February, Chuck orally agrees to sell his hunting cabin, with 15 acres, to Kyle for $35,000, with the deal to be completed in July, when Kyle will have the money. In March, while Chuck is vacationing on his land, he permits Kyle to enter the land and dig the foundation for a new cottage. In July, Kyle arrives with the money but Chuck refuses to sell. Kyle sues.
    A. Chuck wins because the contract was never put in writing.
    B. Chuck wins because the contract terms were unclear.
    C. Kyle wins because a contract for vacation property does not need to be written.
    D. Kyle wins because Chuck allowed him to dig the foundation.
    E. Kyle wins because Chuck has committed fraud.

## SHORT-ANSWER QUESTIONS

13. Brockwell left his boat to be repaired at Lake Gaston Sales. The boat contained electronic equipment and other personal items. Brockwell signed a form stating that Lake Gaston had no responsibility for any loss to any property in or on the boat. Brockwell's electronic equipment was stolen and other personal items were damaged, and he sued. Is the exculpatory clause enforceable?

14. Guyan Machinery, a West Virginia manufacturing corporation, hired Albert Voorhees as a salesman and required him to sign a contract stating that if he left Guyan, he would not work for a competing corporation anywhere within 250 miles of West Virginia for a two-year period. Later, Voorhees left Guyan and began working at Polydeck Corp., another West Virginia manufacturer. The only product Polydeck made was urethane screens, which comprised half of 1 percent of Guyan's business. Is Guyan entitled to enforce its noncompete clause?

15. ETHICS: Richard and Michelle Kommit traveled to New Jersey to have fun in the casinos. While in Atlantic City, they used their MasterCard to withdraw cash from an ATM conveniently located in the "pit," which is the gambling area of a casino. They ran up debts of $5,500 on the credit card and did not pay. The Connecticut National Bank sued for the money. What argument should the Kommits make? Which party, if any, has the moral high ground here? Should a casino offer ATM services in the gambling pit? If a credit card company allows customers to withdraw cash in a casino, is it encouraging them to lose money? Do the Kommits have any ethical right to use the ATM, attempt to win money by gambling, and then seek to avoid liability?

16. The McAllisters had several serious problems with their house, including leaks in the ceiling, a buckling wall, and dampness throughout. They repaired the buckling wall by installing I-beams to support it. They never resolved the leaks and the dampness. When they decided to sell the house, they said nothing to prospective buyers about the problems. They stated that the I-beams had been added for reinforcement. The Silvas bought the house for $60,000. Soon afterward, they began to have problems with leaks, mildew, and dampness. Are the Silvas entitled to any money damages? Why or why not?

17. Lonnie Hippen moved to Long Island, Kansas, to work at an insurance company owned by Griffiths. After he moved there, Griffiths offered to sell Hippen a house he owned and Hippen agreed in writing to buy it. He did buy the house and moved in, but two years later, Hippen left the insurance company. He then claimed that at the time of the sale, Griffiths had orally promised to buy back his house at the selling price if Hippen should happen to leave the company. Griffiths defended based on the statute of frauds. Hippen argued that the statute of frauds did not apply because the repurchase of the house was essentially part of his employment with Griffiths. Comment.

18. ROLE REVERSAL: Write one multiple-choice question with two noncompete clauses, one of which is valid and the other void.

You can find further practice problems in the Online Quiz at **www.cengage.com/blaw/beatty.**

## CHAPTER 1

# CONCLUSION TO CONTRACTS

> **Christopher then claimed ownership of Howdy Doody and refused to give him to the museum.**

**During television's** formative days, Howdy Doody was one of the medium's biggest stars. His acting was wooden—as were his head and body— but for 13 years, Howdy and an assorted group of puppets starred in one of the most popular children's programs of all time. Rufus Rose maintained and repaired the puppets. When Howdy took his last double-jointed bow (to a chorus of toddler wails), NBC permitted Rose to keep the various puppets temporarily. Six years later, NBC became concerned that Rose was inadequately maintaining them. The network wanted Howdy and friends moved to a safe, public location. Rose claimed the puppets were in good shape and wanted payment for the maintenance he had provided. The two parties agreed in writing that Rose would give Howdy and the other stars of the show (including Dilly Dally and Flub-A-Dub) to a puppet museum at the Detroit Institute of Arts (DIA). NBC agreed to pay the puppeteer for his work. The company permitted Rose to keep some of the minor puppets from the program, provided they were not used for commercial purposes.

When Rose died, his son Christopher took possession of the famous puppet. At about that time, a copy of Howdy sold at auction for $113,000. Christopher then claimed ownership of Howdy Doody and refused to give him to the museum. The DIA wanted its famous puppet, but the museum had never been a party to the agreement between NBC and Rose. Did the DIA have any rights to Howdy? The museum filed suit, making a third party claim.

The basic pattern in third party law is quite simple. Two parties make a contract, and their rights and obligations are subject to the rules that we have already studied: offer and acceptance, consideration, legality, and so forth. However, sometimes their contract affects a third party, one who had no role in forming the agreement itself. The two contracting parties may intend to benefit a third person. Those are cases of third party beneficiary. In other cases, one of the contracting parties may actually transfer his rights or responsibilities to a third party, raising issues of assignment or delegation. We consider the issues one at a time. Then we examine issues of contract performance and remedies.

## · THIRD PARTY BENEFICIARY ·

The two parties who make a contract always intend to benefit themselves. Oftentimes their bargain will also benefit someone else. A **third party beneficiary** is someone who was not a party to the contract but stands to benefit from it. Many contracts create third party beneficiaries. In the chapter's introduction, NBC and Rufus Rose contracted to give Howdy Doody to the Detroit Institute of Arts. The museum stood to benefit from this agreement.

As another example, suppose a city contracts to purchase from Seller 20 acres of an abandoned industrial site in a rundown neighborhood to be used for a new domed stadium. The owner of a pizza parlor on the edge of Seller's land might benefit enormously. A once marginal operation could become a gold mine of cheese and pepperoni.

When the two contracting parties fulfill their obligations and the third party receives her benefit, there is no dispute to analyze. If Christopher Rose had walked Howdy Doody into the puppet museum, and if the city completed the stadium, there would be no unhappy third parties. Problems arise when one of the parties fails to perform the contract as expected. The issue is this: *May the third party beneficiary enforce the contract?* The museum had no contract with the Rose family. Is the museum entitled to the puppet? The pizza parlor owner was not a party to the contract for the sale of the stadium land. If the city breaks its agreement to buy the property, should the owner recover profits for unsold sausage and green pepper?

**Third party beneficiary**
Someone who is not a party to a contract but stands to benefit from it.

The outcome in cases like these depends upon the intentions of the two contracting parties. If they intended to benefit the third party, she will probably be permitted to enforce their contract. If they did not intend to benefit her, she probably has no power to enforce the agreement. The Restatement uses a bit more detail to analyze these cases. We must first understand the terms "promisor" and "promisee." The **promisor** is the one who makes the promise that the third party beneficiary is seeking to enforce. Parts of the contract may not interest her, so the Restatement looks only at the relevant promise, not at the entire contract. The **promisee** is the other party to the contract.

According to the **Restatement (Second) of Contracts §302: A beneficiary of a promise is an intended beneficiary and may enforce a contract if the parties *intended* her to benefit *and if either* (a) enforcing the promise will satisfy a duty of the promisee to the beneficiary, or (b) the promisee intended to make a gift to the beneficiary.**

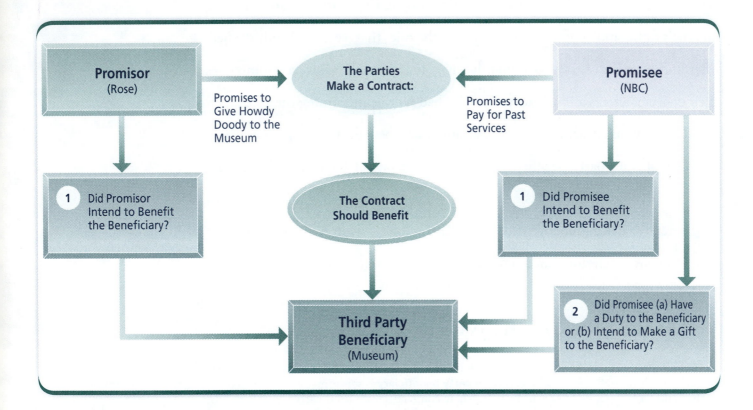

Any beneficiary who is not an intended beneficiary is an **incidental beneficiary** and may not enforce the contract. In other words, a third party beneficiary must show two things in order to enforce a contract that two other people created. First, she must show that the two contracting parties were aware of her situation and knew that she would receive something of value from their deal. Second, she must show that the promisee wanted to benefit her for one of two reasons: either to satisfy some duty owed or to make her a gift.

If the promisee is fulfilling some duty, the third party beneficiary is called a creditor beneficiary. Most often, the "duty" that a promisee will be fulfilling is a debt already owed to the beneficiary. If the promisee is making a gift, the third party is a donee beneficiary.[1] As long as the

---

[1] **Donee** comes from the word **donate,** meaning to give.

third party is either a creditor or a donee beneficiary, she may enforce the contract. If she is only an incidental beneficiary, she may not.

We will apply this rule to the dispute over Howdy Doody. Like most contracts, the deal between NBC and Rufus Rose had two promises: Rose's agreement to give the puppet to the museum, and NBC's promise to pay for the work done on Howdy. The promise that interests us is the one concerning Howdy's destination in Detroit. Rose was the promisor and NBC was the promisee.

Did the two parties intend to benefit the museum? Yes, they did. NBC wanted Howdy to be displayed to the general public, and in a noncommercial venue. Rose, who wanted payment for work already done, was happy to go along with the network's wishes. Did NBC owe a duty to the museum? No. Did the network intend to make a gift to the museum? Yes. The museum wins! The Detroit Institute of Arts was an intended third party beneficiary and is entitled to Howdy Doody.[2]

By contrast, the pizza parlor owner will surely lose. A stadium is a multimillion dollar investment, and it is most unlikely that the city and the seller of the land were even aware of the owner's existence, let alone that they intended to benefit him. He probably cannot prove either the first element or the second element, and certainly not both.

In the following case, a dazzling diamond loses its luster. Who is entitled to sue?

## SCHAUER V. MANDARIN GEMS OF CALIFORNIA, INC.

2005 WL 5730 COURT OF APPEAL OF CALIFORNIA, 2005

### CASE SUMMARY

**Facts:** Sarah Schauer and her fiancé, Darin Erstad, went shopping for an engagement ring, first at Tiffany and Cartier, then at Mandarin Gems, where they were captivated by a 3.01 carat diamond with a clarity grading of S11. Erstad bought the ring the same day for $43,121. Later, Mandarin supplied Erstad with a written appraisal, again rating the ring as an S11, and valuing it at $45,500. Paul Lam, a certified gemologist, signed the appraisal.

Diamonds may last forever but this marriage was short-lived. The divorce decree gave each party the right to keep whatever personal property they currently held, meaning that Schauer could keep the ring. She had the ring appraised by the Gem Trade Laboratory, which gave it a poorer clarity rating, and a value of $20,000.

Schauer sued Mandarin for misrepresentation and breach of contract, but the jeweler defended by saying that it had never contracted with her, and that she was not a third party beneficiary of the company's agreement with Erstad. The trial court dismissed Schauer's suit, and she appealed.

**Issue:** *Does Schauer have any right to sue for breach of contract?*

**Decision:** Yes, she is entitled to sue.

**Reasoning:** A true third party beneficiary may enforce a contract made by others, unless they rescinded the agreement. Persons who expect to incidentally or remotely benefit from a bargain may not enforce it.

A plaintiff claiming status as a third party beneficiary must demonstrate that the promisor understood that the promisee intended to benefit the third party. It is not necessary that both parties intended to benefit the third party.

Schauer alleged that she and Erstad went shopping for an engagement ring. They were together when they looked at the ring, and they explained to the jeweler that Erstad was buying the diamond to give to Schauer as an engagement ring. The jeweler *must* have understood that Erstad was entering into a sales contract intending to benefit Schauer.

Schauer has alleged facts that, if found to be true, establish her as a third party beneficiary. She is entitled to proceed with her contract claim against Mandarin Gems.

Reversed and remanded.

---

[2] *The Detroit Institute of Arts Founders Society v. Rose*, 127 F. Supp.2d 117 (D.Conn. 2001).

# · ASSIGNMENT AND DELEGATION ·

**Assignment of rights**
A contracting party transfers his rights under a contract to someone else.

**Delegation of duties**
A contracting party transfers her duties pursuant to a contract to someone else.

**Assignor**
The person making an assignment.

**Assignee**
The person receiving an assignment.

**Obligor**
The person obligated to do something under a contract.

**Obligee**
The person who has an obligation coming to her.

A contracting party may transfer his rights under the contract, which is called an **assignment of rights**. Or a contracting party may transfer her duties pursuant to the contract, which is a **delegation of duties**. Frequently, a party will do both simultaneously.

For our purposes, the Restatement serves as a good summary of common-law provisions. The UCC rules are generally similar. Our first example is a sale of goods case, governed by the UCC, but the outcome would be the same under the Restatement.

Lydia needs 500 bottles of champagne. Bruno agrees to sell them to her for $10,000, payable 30 days after delivery. He transports the wine to her. Bruno happens to owe Doug $8,000 from a previous deal, so he says to Doug, "I don't have the money, but I'll give you my claim to Lydia's $10,000." Doug agrees. Bruno then *assigns* to Doug *his rights* to Lydia's money, and in exchange Doug gives up his claim for $8,000. Bruno is the **assignor**, the one making an assignment, and Doug is the **assignee**, the one receiving an assignment.

Why would Bruno offer $10,000 when he owed Doug only $8,000? Because all he has is a *claim* to Lydia's money. Cash in hand is often more valuable. Doug, however, is willing to assume some risk for a potential $2,000 gain.

Bruno notifies Lydia of the assignment. Lydia, who owes the money, is called the **obligor**—that is, the one obligated to do something. At the end of 30 days, Doug arrives at Lydia's doorstep, asks for his money, and gets it, because Lydia is obligated to him.

Lydia bought the champagne because she knew she could sell it at a profit. She promptly agrees to sell and deliver the 500 bottles to Coretta, at a mountaintop wilderness camp. Lydia has no four-wheel drive cars, so she finds Keith, who is willing to deliver the bottles for $1,000. Lydia *delegates her duty* to Keith to deliver the bottles to Coretta. Keith is now obligated to deliver the bottles to Coretta, the **obligee**—that is, the one who has the obligation coming to her. Lydia also remains obligated to Coretta, the obligee, to ensure that the bottles are delivered.

Assignment and delegation can each create problems. We will examine the most common ones.

## Assignment

### *What Rights Are Assignable?*
**Any contractual right may be assigned unless assignment**

(a) would substantially change the obligor's rights or duties under the contract, or

(b) is forbidden by law or public policy, or

(c) is validly precluded by the contract itself.[3]

**Substantial Change**  Assignment is prohibited if it would substantially change the obligor's situation. For example, Bruno may assign to Doug the payment from Lydia because it makes no difference to Lydia whether she writes a check to one or the other. But suppose Erica, who lives on a quarter-acre lot in Hardscrabble, hires Keith to mow her lawn once per week for the summer, for a total fee of $700. Erica pays up front before she leaves for the summer. May she assign her right to weekly lawn care to Lloyd, who enjoys a three-acre estate in Halcyon, 60 miles distant? No. The extra travel and far larger yard would dramatically change Keith's obligations.

**Public Policy**  Some assignments are prohibited by public policy. For example, someone who has suffered a personal injury in an automobile accident may not assign her claim to a third person.

**Contract Prohibition**  Finally, one of the contracting parties may try to prohibit assignment in the agreement itself. Most landlords include in the written lease a clause prohibiting the

---

[3] Restatement (Second) of Contracts §317(2). And note that UCC §2-210(2) is, for our purposes, nearly identical.

tenant from assigning the tenancy without the landlord's written permission. Such clauses are generally, but not always, enforced by a court.

### How Rights Are Assigned

An assignment may be written or oral, and no particular formalities are required. However, when someone wants to assign rights governed by the statute of frauds, she must do it in writing. Suppose City contracts with Seller to buy Seller's land for a domed stadium and then brings in Investor to complete the project. If City wants to assign to Investor its rights to the land, it must do so in writing.

### Rights of the Parties After Assignment

**Once the assignment is made and the obligor notified, the assignee may enforce her contractual rights against the obligor.** If Lydia fails to pay Doug for the champagne she gets from Bruno, Doug may sue to enforce the agreement. The law will treat Doug as though he had entered into the contract with Lydia.

But the reverse is also true. **The obligor may generally raise all defenses against the assignee that she could have raised against the assignor.** Suppose Lydia opens the first bottle of champagne—silently. "Where's the pop?" she wonders. All 500 bottles have gone flat. Bruno has failed to perform his part of the contract, and Lydia may use Bruno's nonperformance as a defense against Doug. If the champagne was indeed worthless, Lydia owes Doug nothing.

## DELEGATION OF DUTIES

Garret has always dreamed of racing stock cars. He borrows $250,000 from his sister, Maybelle, in order to buy a car and begin racing. He signs a promissory note in that amount, guaranteeing that he will repay Maybelle the full amount, plus interest, on a monthly basis over 10 years. Regrettably, during his first race, on a Saturday night, Garret discovers that he has a speed phobia. He finally finishes the race at noon on Sunday and quits the business. Garret transfers the car and equipment to Brady, who agrees in writing to pay all money owed to Maybelle. For a few months Brady sends a check, but he is killed while watching bumper cars at a local carnival. Maybelle sues Garret, who defends based on the transfer to Brady. Will his defense work?

Most duties are delegable. But delegation does not by itself relieve the delegator of his own liability to perform the contract.

Garret was the **delegator** and Brady was the **delegatee**. Garret has legally delegated to Brady his duty to repay Maybelle. However, Garret remains personally obligated. When Maybelle sues, she will win. Garret, like many debtors, would have preferred to wash his hands of his debt, but the law is not so obliging.

Garret's delegation to Brady was typical in that it included an assignment at the same time. If he had merely transferred ownership, that would have been only an assignment. If he had convinced Brady to pay off the loan without getting the car, that would have been merely a delegation. He did both at once.

**Delegator**
A person who gives his obligation under a contract to someone else.

**Delegatee**
A person who receives an obligation under a contract from someone else.

### What Duties Are Delegable

The rules concerning what duties may be delegated mirror those about the assignment of rights.

> **An obligor may delegate his duties unless**

1. delegation would violate public policy, or

2. the contract prohibits delegation, or

3. the obligee has a substantial interest in personal performance by the obligor.[4]

**Public Policy**   Delegation may violate public policy, for example, in a public works contract. If City hires Builder to construct a subway system, state law may prohibit Builder from delegating

---

[4] Restatement (Second) of Contracts §318. And see UCC §2-210, establishing similar limits.

his duties to Subcontractor. A public agency should not have to work with parties that it never agreed to hire.

**Contract Prohibition**    The parties may forbid almost any delegation, and the courts will enforce the agreement. Hammer, a contractor, is building a house and hires Spot as his painter, including in his contract a clause prohibiting delegation. Just before the house is ready for painting, Spot gets a better job elsewhere and wants to delegate his duties to Brush. Hammer may refuse the delegation even if Brush is equally qualified.

**Substantial Interest in Personal Performance**    Suppose Hammer had omitted the "nondelegation" clause from his contract with Spot. Could Hammer still refuse the delegation on the grounds that he has a substantial interest in having Spot do the work? No. Most duties are delegable. There is nothing so special about painting a house that one particular painter is required to do it. But some kinds of work do require personal performance, and obligors may not delegate these tasks. The services of lawyers, doctors, dentists, artists, and performers are considered too personal to be delegated. There is no single test that will perfectly define this group, but generally when the work will test *the character, skill, discretion, and good faith* of the obligor, she *may not* delegate her job.

## · PERFORMANCE AND DISCHARGE ·

A party is discharged when she has no more duties under a contract. Most contracts are discharged by full performance. In other words, the parties generally do what they promise. Sally agrees to sell Arthur 300 tulip-shaped wine glasses for his new restaurant. Right on schedule, Sally delivers the correct glasses and Arthur pays in full. Contract, full performance, discharge, end of case.

Sometimes the parties discharge a contract by agreement. For example, the parties may agree to **rescind** their contract, meaning that they terminate it by mutual agreement. At times, a court may discharge a party who has not performed. When things have gone amiss, a judge must interpret the contract and issues of public policy to determine who in fairness should suffer the loss. We will analyze the most common issues of performance and discharge.

**Rescind**
To terminate a contract by mutual agreement.

## PERFORMANCE

Caitlin has an architect draw up plans for a monumental new house, and Daniel agrees to build it by September 1. Caitlin promises to pay $900,000 on that date. The house is ready on time but Caitlin has some complaints. The living room ceiling was supposed to be 18 feet high but it is only 17 feet; the pool was to be azure yet it is aquamarine; the maid's room was not supposed to be wired for cable television but it is. Caitlin refuses to pay anything for the house. Is she justified? Of course not; it would be absurd to give her a magnificent house for free when it has only tiny defects. And that is how a court would decide the case. But in this easy answer lurks a danger. How much leeway will a court permit? Suppose the living room is only 14 feet high, or 12 feet, or 5 feet? What if Daniel finishes the house a month late? Six months late? Three years late? At some point, a court will conclude that Daniel has so thoroughly botched the job that he deserves little or no money. Where is that point? That is a question that businesses—and judges—face every day.

### Strict Performance and Substantial Performance

**Strict Performance**    Courts dislike strict performance because it enables one party to benefit without paying and sends the other one home empty-handed. **A party is generally not required to render strict performance unless the contract expressly demands it and such a demand is reasonable.** Caitlin's contract never suggested that Daniel would forfeit all payment if there were minor problems. Even if Caitlin had insisted on such a clause, a court would be unlikely to enforce it, because the requirement is unreasonable.

In some cases, strict performance does make sense. Marshall agrees to deliver 500 sweaters to Leo's store, and Leo promises to pay $20,000 cash on delivery. If Leo has only $19,000 cash and a promissory note for $1,000, he has failed to perform, and Marshall need not give him the sweaters. Leo's payment represents 95 percent of what he promised, but there is a big difference between cash and a promissory note.

**Substantial Performance**    Daniel, the house builder, won his case against Caitlin because he fulfilled most of his obligations, even though he did an imperfect job. Courts often rely on the substantial performance doctrine, especially in cases involving services as opposed to those concerning the sale of goods or land. **In a contract for services, a party that substantially performs its obligations will receive the full contract price, minus the value of any defects.** Daniel receives $900,000, the contract price, minus the value of a ceiling that is one foot too low, a pool the wrong color, and so forth. It will be for the trial court to decide how much those defects are worth. If the court decides the low ceiling is a $10,000 damage, the pool color worth $5,000, and the cable television worth $500, then Daniel receives $884,500.

On the other hand, a party that fails to perform substantially receives nothing on the contract itself and will only recover the value of the work if any. If the foundation cracks in Caitlin's house and the walls collapse, Daniel will not receive his $900,000. In such a case, he collects only the market value of the work he has done, which is probably zero.

*When* is performance substantial? There is no perfect test, but courts look at these issues:

- How much benefit has the promisee received?
- If it is a construction contract, can the owner use the thing for its intended purpose?
- Can the promisee be compensated with money damages for any defects?
- Did the promisor act in good faith?

## EXAM *Strategy*

**Question:** Jade owns a drag strip. She hires Trevor to resurface it for $180,000, paying $90,000 down. When the project is completed, Jade refuses to pay the balance and sues Trevor for her down payment. He counterclaims for the $90,000 still due. At trial, Trevor proves that all of the required materials were applied by trained workers in an expert fashion, the dimensions were perfect, and his profit margin very modest. The head of the national drag racing association testifies that his group considers the strip unsafe. He noticed puddles in both asphalt lanes, found the concrete starting pads unsafe, and believed the racing surface needed to be ground off and reapplied. His organization refuses to sanction races at the track until repairs are made. Who wins the suit?

**Strategy:** When one party has performed imperfectly, we have an issue of substantial performance. To decide whether Trevor is entitled to his money, we apply four factors: (1) How much benefit did Jade receive? (2) Can she use the racing strip for its intended purpose? (3) Can Jade be compensated for defects? (4) Did Trevor act in good faith?

**Result:** Jade has received no benefit whatsoever. She cannot use her drag strip for drag racing. Compensation will not help Jade—she needs a new strip. Trevor's work must be ripped up and replaced. Trevor may have acted in good faith, but he failed to deliver what Jade bargained for. Jade wins all of the money she paid. (As we will see later in this chapter, she may win additional sums for her lost profits.)

## GOOD FAITH

The parties to a contract must carry out their obligations in good faith. The Restatement (Second) of Contracts §205 states: **"Every contract imposes upon each party a duty of good faith and fair dealing in its performance and its enforcement."** The UCC establishes a similar requirement for all contracts governed by the Code.[5] How far must one side go to meet its good faith burden? The Restatement emphasizes that the parties must remain faithful to the "agreed common purpose and justified expectations of the other party."

In the following case, one party to a contract played its cards very close to its chest. Too close?

## BRUNSWICK HILLS RACQUET CLUB INC. v. ROUTE 18 SHOPPING CENTER ASSOCIATES

182 N.J. 210, 864 A.2d 387, SUPREME COURT OF NEW JERSEY, 2005

### CASE SUMMARY

**Facts:** Brunswick Hills Racquet Club (Brunswick) owned a tennis club on property that it leased from Route 18 Shopping Center Associates (Route 18). The lease ran for 25 years, and Brunswick had spent about $1 million in capital improvements. The lease expired March 30, 2002. Brunswick had the option of either buying the property or purchasing a 99-year lease, both on very favorable terms. To exercise its option, Brunswick had to notify Route 18 no later than September 30, 2001, and had to pay the option price of $150,000. If Brunswick failed to exercise its options, the existing lease automatically renewed as of September 30, for 25 more years, but at more than triple the current rent.

In February 2000—19 months before the option deadline—Brunswick's lawyer, Gabriel Spector, wrote to Rosen Associates, the company that managed Route 18, stating that Brunswick intended to exercise the option for a 99-year lease. He requested that the lease be sent well in advance so that he could review it. He did not make the required payment of $150,000.

In March, Rosen replied that it had forwarded Spector's letter to its attorney, who would be in touch. In April, Spector again wrote, asking for a reply from Rosen or its lawyer.

Over the next six months, Spector continually asked for a copy of the lease, or information, but neither Route 18's lawyer nor anyone else provided any data. In January 2001, Spector renewed his requests for a copy of the lease. Route 18's lawyer never replied. Sadly, in May 2001, after a long illness, Spector died. In August 2001, Spector's law partner, Arnold Levin, wrote to Rosen, again stating Brunswick's intention to buy the 99-year lease, and requesting a copy of all relevant information. He received no reply, and the September deadline passed.

In February 2002, Route 18's lawyer dropped the hammer, notifying Levin that Brunswick could not exercise its option to lease, because it had failed to pay the $150,000 by September 30, 2001.

Brunswick sued, claiming that Route 18 had breached its duty of good faith and fair dealing. The trial court found that Route 18 had no duty to notify Brunswick of impending deadlines, and gave summary judgment for Route 18. The appellate court affirmed, and Brunswick appealed to the state supreme court.

**Issue:** *Did Route 18 breach its duty of good faith and fair dealing?*

**Holding:** Yes, Route 18 breached its duty of good faith and fair dealing.

**Reasoning:** Courts generally should not tinker with precisely drafted agreements entered into by experienced business people. Nonetheless, every party to a contract is bound by a duty of good faith and fair dealing in its performance. Good faith is conduct that conforms to community standards of decency and reasonableness. Neither party may do anything that will prevent the other from receiving the contract benefits.

Route 18 and its agents acted in bad faith. Nineteen months before the deadline, Brunswick Hills notified the landlord that it intended to exercise its option to purchase a 99-year lease. Brunswick Hills mistakenly believed that its payment was not due until closing. During that year and a half, Route 18 engaged in a pattern of evasion, sidestepping every request by Brunswick Hills to move forward on closing the lease. After Spector's death, Route 18's lawyer continued to play possum, despite the obvious risk to Brunswick Hills. Route 18 acknowledged that it did not want the lease payment, because the long-term lease was not in its financial interest.

Neither a landlord nor its attorney is required to act as his brother's keeper. However, there are ethical norms that apply even in the harsh world of commercial transactions. All parties must behave in good faith and deal fairly with the other side. Brunswick Hills' repeated letters and calls to close the lease placed an obligation on Route 18 to respond in a timely, honest manner. The company failed to do that, and Brunswick Hills is entitled to exercise the 99-year lease.

---

[5] UCC §1-203.

# BREACH

**When one party *materially* breaches a contract, the other party is discharged.** A material breach is one that substantially harms the innocent party. The discharged party has no obligation to perform and may sue for damages. Edwin promises that on July 1 he will deliver 20 tuxedos, tailored to fit male chimpanzees, to Bubba's circus for $300 per suit. After weeks of delay, Edwin concedes he hasn't a cummerbund to his name. This is a material breach and Bubba is discharged. Notice that a trivial breach, such as a one-day delay in delivering the tuxedos, would not have discharged Bubba.

## Statute of Limitations

A party injured by a breach of contract should act promptly. **A statute of limitations begins to run at the time of injury and will limit the time within which the injured party may file suit.** Statutes of limitation vary widely. In some states, for example, an injured party must sue on oral contracts within three years, on a sale of goods contract within four years, and on some written contracts within five years. Failure to file suit within the time-limits discharges the breaching party.

**Statute of limitations**
limits the time within which an injured party may file suit.

# IMPOSSIBILITY

"Your honor, my client wanted to honor the contract. He just couldn't. Honest." Does the argument work? It depends. A court will discharge an agreement if performing a contract was truly impossible but not if honoring the deal merely imposed a financial burden. **True impossibility means that something has happened making it utterly impossible to do what the promisor said he would do.** Francoise owns a vineyard that produces Beaujolais Nouveau wine. She agrees to ship 1,000 cases *of her wine* to Tyrone, a New York importer, as soon as this year's vintage is ready. Tyrone will pay $50 per case. But a fungus wipes out her entire vineyard. Francoise is discharged. It is theoretically impossible for Francoise to deliver wine from her vineyard, and she owes Tyrone nothing.

True impossibility is generally limited to these three causes:

- *Destruction of the Subject Matter.* This happened with Francoise's vineyard.
- *Death of the Promisor in a Personal Services Contract.* When the promisor agrees personally to render a service that cannot be transferred to someone else, her death discharges the contract.
- *Illegality.* If the purpose of a contract becomes illegal, that change discharges the contract.

It is rare for contract performance to be truly impossible but common for it to become a financial burden to one party. Suppose Bradshaw Steel in Pittsburgh agrees to deliver 1,000 tons of steel beams to Rice Construction in Saudi Arabia at a given price, but a week later, the cost of raw ore increases 30 percent. A contract once lucrative to the manufacturer is suddenly a major liability. Does that change discharge Bradshaw? Absolutely not. Rice signed the deal *precisely to protect itself against price increases.* The whole purpose of contracts is to enable the parties to control their futures.

# · REMEDIES ·

A remedy is the method a court uses to compensate an injured party. The most common remedy, used in the great majority of lawsuits, is money damages.

The first step that a court takes in choosing a remedy is to decide what interest it is trying to protect. An **interest** is a legal right in something. Someone can have an interest in property, for example, by owning it, or renting it to a tenant, or lending money so someone else may buy it.

**Interest**
A legal right in something.

He can have an interest in a *contract* if the agreement gives him some benefit. There are four principal contract interests that a court may seek to protect:

- *Expectation Interest.* This refers to what the injured party reasonably thought she would get from the contract.
- *Reliance Interest.* The injured party may be unable to demonstrate expectation damages but may still prove that he expended money in reliance on the agreement.
- *Restitution Interest.* An injured party may only be able to demonstrate that she has conferred a benefit on the other party. Here, the objective is to restore to the injured party the benefit she has provided.
- *Equitable Interest.* In some cases, something more than money is needed, such as an order to transfer property to the injured party (specific performance) or an order forcing one party to stop doing something (an injunction).

We will look at all four interests. The first two, expectation and reliance, create what are known as *legal* remedies, because they developed in English courts of *law*. The other interests lead to what are termed *equitable* remedies. Historically, when law courts were unable to help a plaintiff, the injured party would sometimes appeal to the Chancellor in London, who had more flexible authority. The Chancellor's powers became known as equitable remedies, a term still used today.

## EXPECTATION INTEREST

This is the most common remedy. **The expectation interest is designed to put the injured party in the position she would have been in had both sides fully performed their obligations.** A court tries to give the injured party the money she would have made from the contract. If accurately computed, this should take into account all the gains she reasonably expected and all the expenses and losses she would have incurred. The injured party should not end up better off than she would have been under the agreement, nor should she suffer serious loss.

William Colby was a former director of the CIA. He wanted to write a book about his 15 years in Vietnam. He paid James McCarger $5,000 for help in writing an early draft and promised McCarger another $5,000 if the book was published. Then he hired Alexander Burnham to co-write the book. Colby's agent secured a contract with Contemporary Books, which included a $100,000 advance. But Burnham was hopelessly late with the manuscript, and Colby missed his publication date. Colby fired Burnham and finished the book without him. Contemporary published *Lost Victory* several years late, and the book flopped, earning no significant revenue. Because the book was so late, Contemporary paid Colby a total of only $17,000. Colby sued Burnham for his lost expectation interest. The court awarded him $23,000, calculated as follows:

| | | | |
|---|---|---|---|
| | $ | 100,000 | advance, the only money Colby was promised |
| | − | 10,000 | agent's fee |
| | = | 90,000 | fee for the two authors, combined |
| divided by 2 | = | 45,000 | Colby's fee |
| | − | 5,000 | owed to McCarger under the earlier agreement |
| | = | 40,000 | Colby's expectation interest |
| | − | 17,000 | fee Colby received from Contemporary |
| | = | 23,000 | Colby's expectation damages—that is, the amount he would have received had Burnham finished on time[6] |

---

[6] *Colby v. Burnham*, 31 Conn. App. 707, 627 A.2d 457, 1993 Conn. App LEXIS 299 (Conn. App. Ct. 1993).

The *Colby* case presented an easy calculation of damages. Other contracts are complex. Courts typically divide the expectation damages into three parts: (1) compensatory (or "direct") damages, which represent harm that flowed directly from the contract's breach; (2) consequential (or "special") damages, which represent harm caused by the injured party's unique situation; and (3) incidental damages, which are minor costs such as storing or returning defective goods, advertising for alternative goods, and so forth. The first two—compensatory and consequential—are the important ones.

## Compensatory Damages

**Compensatory damages** are the most common monetary awards for the expectation interest. Courts also refer to these as "direct damages." **Compensatory damages** are those that flow directly from the contract. In other words, these are the damages that inevitably result from the breach. Suppose Ace Productions hires Reina to star in its new movie, *Inside Straight*. Ace promises Reina $3 million, providing she shows up June 1 and works until the film is finished. But in late May, Joker Entertainment offers Reina $6 million to star in its new feature, and on June 1 Reina informs Ace that she will not appear. Reina has breached her contract, and Ace should recover compensatory damages.

What are the damages that flow directly from the contract? Ace obviously has to replace Reina. If Ace hires Kween as its star and pays her a fee of $4 million, Ace is entitled to the difference between what it expected to pay ($3 million) and what the breach forced it to pay ($4 million), or $1 million in compensatory damages. Suppose the rest of the cast and crew are idle for two weeks because of the delay in hiring a substitute, and the lost time costs the producers an extra $2.5 million. Reina is also liable for those expenses. Both the new actress and the delay are inevitable.

**Reasonable Certainty**   The injured party must prove the breach of contract caused damages that can be quantified with reasonable certainty. What if *Inside Straight*, now starring Kween, bombs at the box office? Ace proves that each of Reina's last three movies grossed over $60 million, but *Inside Straight* grossed only $28 million. Is Reina liable for the lost profits? No. Ace cannot prove that it was Reina's absence that caused the film to fare poorly. The script may have been mediocre, or Kween's co-stars dull, or the publicity efforts inadequate. Mere "speculative damages" are worth nothing.

## Consequential Damages

In addition to compensatory damages, the injured party may seek consequential damages or, as they are also known, "special damages." These do not flow directly from the contract. **Consequential damages** are those resulting from the unique circumstances of *this injured plaintiff*. The rule comes from a famous 1854 case, *Hadley v Baxendale*.

The Hadleys operated a flour mill, but a shaft broke and their business ground to a halt. The family hired Baxendale to cart the damaged part to a foundry, where a new one could be manufactured. Baxendale promised to make the delivery in one day, but he was late transporting the shaft, and as a result the Hadleys' mill was shut for five extra days. They sued for their lost profit—and lost. The court declared: **The injured party may recover consequential damages only if the breaching party should have foreseen them when the two sides formed the contract.** Baxendale had no way of knowing that this was the Hadleys' only shaft, or that his delay in transport would cost them substantial profit. The Hadleys would have won had they *told* Baxendale this was their only shaft. They failed to do that, and they failed to win their profits.

Let us return briefly to *Inside Straight*. Suppose that, long before shooting began, Ace had sold the film's soundtrack rights to Spinem Sound for $2 million. Spinem believed it would make a profit only if Reina appeared in the film, so it demanded the right to discharge the agreement if Reina dropped out. When Reina quit, Spinem terminated the contract. Now, when Ace sues Reina, it will also seek $2 million in consequential damages for the lost music revenue. If Reina knew about Ace's contract with Spinem when she signed to do the film, she is liable for $2 million. If she never realized she was an essential part of the music contract, she owes nothing for

---

**Compensatory damages** are those that flow directly from the contract.

**Consequential damages** Damages that result from the unique circumstances of the plaintiff. Also known as *special damages*.

the lost profits. In the following case, the plaintiffs lost not only profits—but their entire business. Can they recover for harm that is so extensive? You decide.

## YOU *be the* JUDGE

### BI-ECONOMY MARKET, INC. v. HARLEYSVILLE INS. CO. OF NEW YORK

2008 WL 423451
New York Court of Appeals, 2008

**Facts:** Bi-Economy Market was a family-owned meat market in Rochester, NY. The company was insured by Harleysville Insurance. The "Deluxe Business Owner's" policy provided replacement cost for damage to buildings and inventory. Coverage also included "business interruption insurance" for one year, meaning the loss of pretax profit plus normal operating expenses, including payroll.

The company suffered a disastrous fire, which destroyed its building and all inventory. Bi-Economy immediately filed a claim with Harleysville, but the insurer responded slowly. Harleysville eventually offered a settlement of $163,000. A year later, an arbitrator awarded the Market $407,000. During that year, Harleysville paid for seven months of lost income but declined to pay more. The company never recovered or reopened.

Bi-Economy sued, claiming that Harleysville's slow, inadequate payments destroyed the company. The company also sought consequential damages for the permanent destruction of its business. Harleysville claimed that it was responsible only for damages specified in the contract: the building, inventory, and lost income. The trial court granted summary judgment for Harleysville. The appellate court affirmed, claiming that when they entered into the contract, the parties did not contemplate damages for termination of the business. Bi-Economy appealed to the state's highest court.

**You Be the Judge:** Is Bi-Economy entitled to consequential damages for the destruction of its business?

**Argument for Bi-Economy:** Bi-Economy is a small, family business. We paid for business interruption insurance for an obvious reason: in the event of a disaster, we lacked the resources to keep going while buildings were constructed and inventory purchased. We knew that in such a calamity, we would need prompt reimbursement—compensation covering the immediate damage and our on-going lost income. Why else would we pay the premiums?

At the time we entered into the contract, Harleysville could easily foresee that if it responded slowly, with insufficient payments, we could not survive. They knew that is what we wanted to avoid—and it is just what happened. The insurer's bad faith offer of a low figure, and its payment of only seven months' lost income, ruined a fine family business. When the insurance company agreed to business interruption coverage, it was declaring that it would act fast and fairly to sustain a small firm in crisis. The insurer should now pay for the full harm it has wrought.

**Argument for Harleysville:** We contracted to insure the Market for three losses: its building, inventory, and lost income. After the fire, we performed a reasonable, careful evaluation and made an offer we considered fair. An arbitrator later awarded Bi-Economy additional money, which we paid. However, it is absurd to suggest that in addition to that, we are liable for an open-ended commitment for permanent destruction of the business.

Consequential damages are appropriate in cases where a plaintiff suffers a loss that was not covered in the contract. In this case, though, the parties bargained over exactly what Harleysville would pay in the event of a major fire. If the insurer has underpaid for lost income, let the court award a fair sum. However, the parties never contemplated an additional, enormous payment for cessation of the business. There is almost no limit as to what that obligation could be. If Bi-Economy was concerned that a fire might put the company permanently out of business, it should have said so at the time of negotiating for insurance. The premium would have been dramatically higher.

Neither Bi-Economy nor Harleysville ever imagined such an open-ended insurance obligation, and the insurer should not pay an extra cent.

## Incidental Damages

**Incidental damages**
are the relatively minor costs that the injured party suffers when responding to the breach.

**Incidental damages** are the relatively minor costs that the injured party suffers when responding to the breach. When Reina, the actress, breaches the film contract, the producers may have to leave the set and fly back to Los Angeles to hire a new actress. The cost of travel, renting a room for auditions, and other related expenses are incidental damages.

## RELIANCE INTEREST

George plans to manufacture and sell silk scarves during the holiday season. In the summer, he contracts with Cecily, the owner of a shopping mall, to rent a high-visibility stall for $100 per day. George then buys hundreds of yards of costly silk and gets to work cutting and sewing. Then in September, Cecily refuses to honor the contract. George sues and easily proves Cecily breached a valid contract. But what is his remedy?

George cannot establish an expectation interest in his scarf business. He hoped to sell each scarf for a $40 gross profit and wanted to make $2,000 per day. But how much would he actually have earned? Enough to retire on—or enough to buy a salami sandwich for lunch? A court cannot give him an expectation interest, so George will ask for *reliance damages*. **The reliance interest is designed to put the injured party in the position he would have been in had the parties never entered into a contract.** This remedy focuses on the time and money the injured party spent performing his part of the agreement.

Assuming he is unable to sell the scarves to a retail store (which is probable because retailers will have made purchases long ago), George should be able to recover the cost of the silk fabric he bought and perhaps something for the hours of labor he spent cutting and sewing. However, reliance damages can be difficult to win because *they are harder to quantify*. Judges dislike vague calculations. How much was George's time worth in making the scarves? How good was his work? How likely were the scarves to sell? If George has a track record in the industry, he will be able to show a market price for his services. Without such a record, his reliance claim becomes a tough battle.

> **How much would he actually have earned? Enough to retire on—or enough to buy a salami sandwich for lunch?**

## RESTITUTION INTEREST

Jim and Bonnie Hyler bought an expensive recreational vehicle (RV) from Autorama. The salesman promised the Hylers that a manufacturer's warranty covered the entire vehicle for a year. The Hylers had a succession of major problems with their RV, including windows that wouldn't shut, a door that fell off, a loose windshield, and defective walls. Then they learned that the manufacturer had gone bankrupt. In fact, the Autorama salesman knew of the bankruptcy when he made the sales pitch.

The Hylers returned the RV to Autorama and demanded their money back. They wanted restitution.

The restitution interest is designed to return to the injured party a benefit that he has conferred on the other party, which it would be unjust to leave with that person. Restitution is a common remedy in contracts involving fraud, misrepresentation, mistake, and duress. In these cases, restitution often goes hand-in-hand with **rescission**, which means to "undo" a contract and put the parties where they were before they made the agreement. The court declared that Autorama had misrepresented the manufacturer's warranty by omitting the small fact that the manufacturer itself no longer existed. Autorama was forced to return to the Hylers the full purchase price plus the value of the automobile they had traded. The dealer, of course, was allowed to keep the defective RV and stare out the ill-fitting windows.[7]

**Rescission**
The undoing of a contract, which puts both parties in the positions they were in when they made the agreement.

## OTHER EQUITABLE INTERESTS

In addition to restitution, the other two equitable powers that concern us are specific performance and injunction.

### Specific Performance

Leona Claussen owned Iowa farmland. She sold some of it to her sister-in-law, Evelyn Claussen, and, along with the land, granted Evelyn an option to buy additional property at $800 per acre.

---

[7] *Hyler v. Garner*, 548 N.W.2d 864, 1996 Iowa Sup. LEXIS 322 (Iowa, 1966).

Evelyn could exercise her option any time during Leona's lifetime or within six months of Leona's death. When Leona died, Evelyn informed the estate's executor that she was exercising her option. But other relatives wanted the property, and the executor refused to sell. Evelyn sued and asked for *specific performance*. She did not want an award of damages; she wanted the land itself. The remedy of **specific performance** forces the two parties to perform their contract.

**A court will award specific performance, ordering the parties to perform the contract, only in cases involving the sale of land or some other asset that is unique.** Courts use this equitable remedy when money damages would be inadequate to compensate the injured party. If the subject is unique and irreplaceable, money damages will not put the injured party in the same position she would have been in had the agreement been kept. So a court will order the seller to convey the rare object and the buyer to pay for it.

Historically, every parcel of land has been regarded as unique, and therefore specific performance is always available in real estate contracts. Evelyn Claussen won specific performance. The Iowa Supreme Court ordered Leona's estate to convey the land to Evelyn for $800 per acre.[8] Generally speaking, either the seller or the buyer may be granted specific performance.

Other unique items, for which a court will order specific performance, include such things as rare works of art, secret formulas, patents, and shares in a closely held corporation. By contrast, a contract for a new Jeep Grand Cherokee is not enforceable by specific performance. An injured buyer can use money damages to purchase a virtually identical auto.

> **Specific performance** compels parties to perform the contract they agreed to when the contract concerns the sale of land or some other unique asset.

### EXAM *Strategy*

**Question:** The Monroes, a retired couple who live in Illinois, want to move to Arizona to escape the northern winter. In May, the Monroes contract in writing to sell their house to the Temples for $450,000. Closing is to take place June 30. The Temples pay a deposit of $90,000. However, in early June, the Monroes travel through Arizona and discover it is too hot for them. They promptly notify the Temples they are no longer willing to sell and return the $90,000, with interest. The Temples sue, seeking the house. In response, the Monroes offer evidence that the value of the house has dropped from about $450,000 to about $400,000. They claim that the Temples have suffered no loss. Who will win?

**Strategy:** Most contract lawsuits are for money damages, but not this one. The Temples want the house. Because they want the house itself, and not money damages, the drop in value is irrelevant. What legal remedy are the Temples seeking? They are suing for specific performance. When will a court grant specific performance? Should it do so here?

**Result:** In cases involving the sale of land or some other unique asset, a court will grant specific performance, ordering the parties to perform the agreement. All houses are regarded as unique. The court will force the Monroes to sell their house, provided the Temples have sufficient money to pay for it.

### Injunction

You move into your new suburban house on two acres of land, and the fresh air is exhilarating. But the wind shifts to the west, and you find yourself thinking of farm animals, especially pigs. Your next-door neighbor just started an organic bacon ranch, and the first 15 porkers have checked in. You check out the town's zoning code, discover that it is illegal to raise livestock in the neighborhood, and sue. Money damages will not suffice, because you want the bouquet to disappear. You seek the equitable remedy of injunction. An **injunction** is a court order that requires someone to do something or refrain from doing something.

> **Injunction** A court order to do something or to refrain from doing something.

---

[8] *In re Estate of Claussen*, 482 N.W.2d 381, 1992 Iowa Sup. LEXIS 52 (Iowa 1992).

The court will order your neighbor immediately to cease and desist raising any pigs or other farm animals on his land. "Cease" means to stop, and "desist" means to refrain from doing it in the future. The injunction will not get you any money, but it will move the pigs out of town, and that was your goal.

In the increasingly litigious world of professional sports, injunctions are commonplace. In the following basketball case, the trial court issued a preliminary injunction—that is, an order issued early in a lawsuit prohibiting a party from doing something during the course of the lawsuit. The court attempts to protect the interests of the plaintiff immediately. If, after trial, it appears that the plaintiff has been injured and is entitled to an injunction, the trial court will make its order a permanent injunction. If it appears that the preliminary injunction should never have been issued, the court will terminate the order.

## MILICIC V. BASKETBALL MARKETING COMPANY, INC.

2004 PA.A SUPER. 333, 857 A.2D 689, SUPERIOR COURT OF PENNSYLVANIA, 2004

### CASE SUMMARY

**Facts:** The Basketball Marketing Company (BMC) markets, distributes, and sells basketball apparel and related products. BMC signed a long-term endorsement contract with a 16-year-old Serbian player, Darko Milicic, who was virtually unknown in the United States. Two years later, Milicic became the second pick in the National Basketball Association (NBA)'s draft, making him an immensely marketable young man.

Four days after his 18th birthday, Milicic made a buyout offer to BMC, seeking release from his contract so that he could arrange a more lucrative one elsewhere. BMC refused to release him. A week later, Milicic notified BMC in writing that he was disaffirming the contract and returned all money and goods he had received from the company. BMC again refused to release Milicic.

Believing that Milicic was negotiating an endorsement deal with either Reebok or Adidas, BMC sent both companies letters informing them it had an enforceable endorsement deal with Milicic that was valid for several more years. Because of BMC's letter, Adidas ceased negotiating with Milicic just short of signing a contract. Milicic sued BMC, seeking a preliminary injunction that would prohibit BMC from sending such letters to competitors. The trial court granted the preliminary injunction and BMC appealed.

**Issue:** *Is Milicic entitled to a preliminary injunction?*

**Decision:** Yes, Milicic is entitled to a preliminary injunction.

**Reasoning:** Like any plaintiff seeking a preliminary injunction, Milicic must prove four elements.

First, Milicic had a strong likelihood of success on the merits. Under Pennsylvania law, a minor may void a contract by disaffirming it within a reasonable time of turning 18 years old. Milicic sent BMC a letter only 11 days after his 18th birthday, unequivocally stating that he disavowed the agreement made when he was a minor. In all likelihood, Milicic will succeed in nullifying the contract with BMC.

Second, injunctive relief was necessary to prevent immediate and irreparable harm for which money damages would not adequately compensate Milicic. Top NBA picks negotiate and secure endorsements quickly to take advantage of the excitement and publicity generated by the draft. BMC blocked Milicic's efforts to conclude an agreement with Adidas. Continued obstruction would cause Milicic irreparable harm.

Third, denying the injunction would cause greater injury than granting it. BMC violates important public policy by refusing to acknowledge a minor's power to disaffirm. The law presumes that a minor lacks the maturity to negotiate such an important agreement. When a company wants to conclude a contract with a minor, it is well-established practice to ask that a court appoint a guardian for the minor. It is astonishing that BMC, a company whose business is based entirely on contract law, failed to protect Milicic's interest—and its own—by requesting a guardian.

Finally, a preliminary injunction will restore the parties to the status quo that existed when Milicic turned 18, by preventing BMC from further interfering with Milicic's negotiations. The lower court properly granted injunctive relief. Affirmed.

## *Mitigation of Damages*

Note one limitation on *all* contract remedies: **A party injured by a breach of contract may not recover for damages that he could have avoided with reasonable efforts.** In other words, when one party perceives that the other has breached or will breach the contract, the injured party must try to prevent unnecessary loss. A party is expected to **mitigate** his damages—that is, to keep damages as low as he reasonably can.

## CHAPTER CONCLUSION

A moment's caution! Often that is the only thing needed to avoid years of litigation. Yes, the broad powers of a court may enable it to compensate an injured party, but problems of proof and the uncertainty of remedies demonstrate that the best solution is a carefully drafted contract and socially responsible behavior.

## EXAM REVIEW

1.  **THIRD PARTY BENEFICIARY** A third party beneficiary is an intended beneficiary and may enforce a contract only if the parties intended her to benefit from the agreement and (1) enforcing the promise will satisfy a debt of the promisee to the beneficiary or (2) the promisee intended to make a gift to the beneficiary. (p. 171)

    .................................................................................................................

2.  **ASSIGNMENT AND DELEGATION** An assignment transfers the assignor's contract rights to the assignee. A delegation transfers the delegator's duties to the delegatee. (p. 173)

    .................................................................................................................

3.  **RIGHT TO ASSIGN** A party generally may assign contract rights unless doing so would substantially change the obligor's rights or duties; is forbidden by law; or is validly precluded by the contract. (p. 174)

    .................................................................................................................

4.  **RIGHT TO DELEGATE** Duties are delegable unless delegation would violate public policy; the contract prohibits delegation; or the obligee has a substantial interest in personal performance by the obligor. (p. 175)

    .................................................................................................................

5.  **DISCHARGE** Unless the obligee agrees otherwise, delegation does not discharge the delegator's duty to perform. (p. 176)

    .................................................................................................................

6.  **SUBSTANTIAL PERFORMANCE** Strict performance, which requires one party to fulfill its duties perfectly, is unusual. In construction and service contracts, substantial performance is generally sufficient to entitle the promisor to the contract price, minus the cost of defects. (p. 177)

    .................................................................................................................

7.  **GOOD FAITH** Good faith performance is required in all contracts. (p. 177)

    .................................................................................................................

8.  **IMPOSSIBILITY** True impossibility means that some event has made it impossible to perform an agreement. (p. 179)

    .................................................................................................................

EXAM *Strategy*

**Question:** Omega Concrete had a gravel pit and factory. Access was difficult, so Omega contracted with Union Pacific Railroad (UP) for the right to use a private road that crossed UP property and tracks. The contract stated that use of the road was solely for Omega employees and that Omega would be responsible for closing a gate that UP planned to build where the private road joined a public highway. In fact, UP never constructed the gate; Omega had no authority to construct the gate. Mathew Rogers, an Omega employee, was killed by a train while using the private road. Rogers's family sued Omega, claiming that Omega failed to keep the gate closed as the contract required. Is Omega liable?

**Strategy:** Impossibility means that the promisor cannot do what he promised to do. Is this such a case? (See the "Result" at the end of this section.)

9. **REMEDIES** A remedy is the method a court uses to compensate an injured party. (p. 179)

10. **EXPECTATION INTEREST** The expectation interest puts the injured party in the position she would have been in had both sides fully performed. It has three components: compensatory, consequential, and incidental damages. (p. 180)

EXAM *Strategy*

**Question:** Mr. and Ms. Beard contracted for Builder to construct a house on property he owned and sell it to the Beards for $785,000. The house was to be completed by a certain date, and Builder knew that the Beards were selling their own home in reliance on the completion date. Builder was late with construction, forcing the Beards to spend $32,000 in rent. Ultimately, Builder never finished the house, and the Beards moved elsewhere. They sued. At trial, expert testimony indicated the market value of the house as promised would have been $885,000. How much money are the Beards entitled to, and why?

**Strategy:** Normally, in cases of property, an injured plaintiff may use specific performance to obtain the land or house. However, there *is* no house, so there will be no specific performance. The Beards will seek their expectation interest. Under the contract, what did they reasonably expect? They anticipated a finished house, on a particular date, worth $885,000. They did not expect to pay rent while waiting. Calculate their losses. (See the "Result" at the end of this section.)

11. **RELIANCE INTEREST** The reliance interest puts the injured party in the position he would have been in had the parties never entered into a contract. (p. 183)

12. **RESTITUTION INTEREST** The restitution interest returns to the injured party a benefit that she has conferred on the other party, which it would be unjust to leave with that person. (p. 183)

13. **SPECIFIC PERFORMANCE** Specific performance, ordered only in cases of a unique asset, requires both parties to perform the contract. (p. 184)

14. **INJUNCTION** An injunction is a court order that requires someone to do something or refrain from doing something. (p. 184)

**8. Result:** There was no gate, and Omega had no right to build one. This is a case of true impossibility. Omega was not liable.

**10. Result:** The Beards' compensatory damages represent the difference between the market value of the house and the contract price. They expected a house worth $100,000 more than their contract price, and they are entitled to that sum. They also suffered consequential damages. The Builder knew they needed the house as of the contract date, and he could foresee that his breach would force them to pay rent. He is liable for a total of $132,000.

## PRACTICE EXAM

## MATCHING QUESTIONS

___ A. Material      1. A type of breach that substantially harms the innocent party

___ B. Intended beneficiary      2. When a party has no more obligations under a contract

___ C. Discharged      3. Damages that can be recovered only if the breaching party should have foreseen them

___ D. Consequential      4. A third party who should be able to enforce a contract between two others

## TRUE/FALSE QUESTIONS

**1.** T   F    Contract dates and deadlines are strictly enforceable unless the parties agree otherwise.

**2.** T   F    Where one party has clearly breached, the injured party must mitigate damages.

**3.** T   F    Courts award the expectation interest more often than any other remedy.

**4.** T   F    A party who delegates duties remains liable for contract performance.

## MULTIPLE-CHOICE QUESTIONS

**7.** Bob, a mechanic, claims that Cathy owes him $1,500 on a repair job. Bob wants to assign his claim to Hardknuckle Bank. The likeliest reason that Bob wants to do this is

     A. Cathy also owes Hardknuckle Bank money.

     B. Hardknuckle Bank owes Bob money on a consumer claim.

     C. Hardknuckle Bank owes Bob money on a repair job.

     D. Bob owes Hardknuckle Bank money.

     E. Bob and Cathy are close friends.

**8.** The agreement between Bob and Cathy says nothing about assignment. May Bob assign his claim to Hardknuckle?

     A. Bob may assign his claim but only with Cathy's agreement.

     B. Bob may assign his claim, but only if Cathy and Hardknuckle agree.

     C. Bob may assign his claim without Cathy's agreement.

     D. Bob may assign his claim but Cathy may nullify the assignment.

     E. Bob may not assign his claim because it violates public policy.

9. Jody is obligated under a contract to deliver 100,000 plastic bottles to a spring water company. Jody's supplier has just gone bankrupt; any other suppliers will charge her more than she expected to pay. This is

   A. Consequential damages

   B. Impossibility

   C. Expectation interest

   D. Substantial performance

   E. Legally irrelevant

10. An example of true impossibility is

    A. Strict performance

    B. Failure of condition

    C. Illegality

    D. Material breach

    E. Consequential interest

11. Museum schedules a major fundraising dinner, devoted to a famous Botticelli picture, for September 15. Museum then hires Sue Ellen to restore the picture, her work to be done no later than September 14. Sue Ellen is late with the restoration, forcing the Museum to cancel the dinner and lose at least $500,000 in donations. Sue Ellen delivers the picture, in excellent condition, two weeks late. Museum sues.

    A. Museum will win.

    B. Museum will win if, when the parties made the deal, Sue Ellen knew the importance of the date.

    C. Museum will win provided that it was Sue Ellen's fault she was late.

    D. Museum will win provided that it was *not* Sue Ellen's fault she was late.

    E. Museum will lose.

12. Tara is building an artificial beach at her lakefront resort. She agrees in writing to buy 1,000 tons of sand from Frank for $20 per ton, with delivery on June 1, at her resort. Frank fails to deliver any sand, and Tara is forced to go elsewhere. She buys 1,000 tons from Maureen at $25 per ton, and then is forced to pay Walter $5,000 to haul the sand to her resort. Tara sues Frank. Tara will recover

    A. Nothing

    B. $5,000

    C. $10,000

    D. $15,000

    E. $30,000

## SHORT-ANSWER QUESTIONS

1. Nationwide Discount Furniture hired Rampart Security to install an alarm in its warehouse. A fire would set off an alarm in Rampart's office, and the security company was then supposed to notify Nationwide immediately. A fire did break out, but Rampart allegedly failed to notify Nationwide, causing the fire to spread next door and damage a building owned by Gasket Materials Corp. Gasket sued Rampart for breach of contract, and Rampart moved for summary judgment. Comment.

2. Evans built a house for Sandra Dyer, but the house had some problems. The garage ceiling was too low. Load-bearing beams in the "great room" cracked and appeared to be steadily weakening. The patio did not drain properly. Pipes froze. Evans wanted the money promised for the job, but Dyer refused to pay. Comment.

3. Racicky was in the process of buying 320 acres of ranch land. While that sale was being negotiated, Racicky signed a contract to sell the land to Simon. Simon paid $144,000, the full price of the land. But Racicky then went bankrupt, before he could complete the purchase of the land, let alone its sale. Which of these remedies should Simon seek: expectation, restitution, or specific performance?

4. ETHICS: The National Football League (NFL) owns the copyright to the broadcasts of its games. It licenses local television stations to telecast certain games and maintains a "blackout rule," which prohibits stations from broadcasting home games that are not sold out 72 hours before the game starts. Certain home games of the Cleveland team were not sold out, and the NFL blocked local broadcast. But

several bars in the Cleveland area were able to pick up the game's signal by using special antennas. The NFL wanted the bars to stop showing the games. What did it do? Was it unethical of the bars to broadcast the games that they were able to pick up? Apart from the NFL's legal rights, do you think it had the moral right to stop the bars from broadcasting the games?

5. ROLE REVERSAL: Write a short-answer question that highlights the difference between an assignment and a delegation.

## INTERNET RESEARCH PROBLEM

You represent a group of neighborhood residents in a large city who are protesting construction of a skyscraper that will violate building height limitations. Draft a complaint, requesting an appropriate injunction. Online, find a sample complaint seeking an injunction.

**You can find further practice problems in the Online Quiz at www.cengage.com/blaw/beatty.**

# SALES AND
# PRODUCT LIABILITY

*He Sued,* She Sued. Harold and Maude made a great couple because both were compulsive entrepreneurs. One evening they sat on their penthouse roof deck, overlooking the twinkling Chicago skyline. Harold sipped a decaf coffee while negotiating, over the phone, with a real estate developer in San Antonio. Maude puffed a cigar as she bargained on a different line with a toy manufacturer in Cleveland. They hung up at the same time. "I did it!" shrieked Maude, "I made an incredible deal for the robots—five bucks each!" "No, *I* did it!" triumphed Harold, "I sold the 50 acres in Texas for $300,000 more than it's worth." They dashed indoors.

Maude quickly scrawled a handwritten memo, which read, "Confirming our deal—100,000 Psychopath Robots—you deliver Chicago— end of summer." She didn't mention a price, or an exact delivery date, or when payment would be made. She signed her memo and faxed it to the toy manufacturer. Harold took more time. He typed a thorough contract, describing

> "Confirming our deal—100,000 Psychopath Robots—you deliver Chicago—end of summer."

precisely the land he was selling, the $2.3 million price, how and when each payment would be made, and what the deed conveyed. He signed the contract and faxed it, along with a plot plan showing the surveyed land. Then the happy couple grabbed a bottle of champagne, returned to the deck—and placed a side bet on whose contract would prove more profitable. The loser would have to cook and serve dinner for six months.

Neither Harold nor Maude ever heard again from the other parties. The toy manufacturer sold the robots to another retailer at a higher price. Maude was forced to buy comparable toys elsewhere for $9 each. She sued. And the Texas property buyer changed his mind, deciding to develop a Club Med in Greenland and refusing to pay Harold for his land. He sued. Only one of the two plaintiffs succeeded. Which one?

## · SALES ·

The adventures of Harold and Maude illustrate the Uniform Commercial Code (UCC) in action. The Code is the single most important source of law for people engaged in commerce and controls the vast majority of contracts made every day in every state. The Code is old in origin, contemporary in usage, admirable in purpose, and flawed in application. "Yeah, yeah, that's fascinating," snaps Harold, "but who wins the bet?" Relax, Harold, we'll tell you in a minute.

## DEVELOPMENT OF THE UCC

Throughout the first half of the twentieth century, commercial transactions changed dramatically in this country, as advances in transportation and communication revolutionized negotiation and trade. The nation needed a modernized business law to give nationwide uniformity and predictability in a new and faster world. In 1942, two groups of scholars, the American Law Institute (ALI) and the National Conference of Commissioners on Uniform State Laws (NCCUSL), began the effort to draft a modern, national law of commerce. The scholars debated and formulated for nearly a decade. Finally, in 1952, the lawyers published their work-the Uniform Commercial Code. The entire Code is available online at **http://www.law.cornell.edu** by clicking on "Constitutions and Codes," then "Uniform Commercial Code."

The ALI and the NCCUSL have revised the Code several times since then, with important changes coming as recently as 2003. Remember, though, that the UCC is the creation of scholars. No section of the Code has any legal effect until a state legislature adopts it. In fact, all 50 states and the District of Columbia have adopted the UCC, but not all have used identical versions.

This book discusses and applies provisions of the Code that have been widely adopted. The commissioners completely rewrote Article 9, on secured transactions, at the turn of the millennium, and this text reflects those changes because every state has adopted them. The commissioners have also revised Article 1, which provides definitions and general guidance, and Article 2, on sales. However, as this book goes to press, very few states have adopted revised Article 1, and none have adopted revised Article 2. We focus on existing law, not the proposed changes to Articles 1 and 2.

This chapter is designed to:

- illustrate key elements of the Code *that have changed the common law rules* of contracts, and
- survey the leading doctrines of product liability.

| | |
|---|---|
| Article 1: General Provisions | The purpose of the Code, general guidance in applying it, and definitions. |
| Article 2: Sale of Goods | The sale of *goods,* such as a new car, 20,000 pairs of gloves, or 101 dalmatians. This is one of the two most important articles in the UCC. |
| Article 2A: Leases | A temporary exchange of goods for money, such as renting a car. |
| Article 3: Negotiable Instruments | The use of checks, promissory notes, and other negotiable instruments. |
| Article 4: Bank Deposits and Collections | The rights and obligations of banks and their customers. |
| Article 4A: Funds Transfers | An instruction, given by a bank customer, to credit a sum of money to another's account. |
| Article 5: Letters of Credit | The use of credit, extended by two or more banks, to facilitate a contract between two parties who do not know each other and require guarantees by banks they trust. |
| Article 6: Bulk Transfers | The sale of a major part of a company's inventory or equipment. |
| Article 7: Warehouse Receipts, Bills of Lading, and Other Documents of Title | Documents proving ownership of goods that are being transported or stored. |
| Article 8: Investment Securities | Rights and liabilities concerning shares of stock or other ownership of an enterprise. |
| Article 9: Secured Transaction | A sale of goods in which the seller keeps a financial stake in the goods he has sold, such as a car dealer who may repossess the car if the buyer fails to make payments. This is one of the two most important articles in the Code. |

## Harold and Maude, Revisited

Harold and Maude each negotiated what they believed was an enforceable agreement, and both filed suit: Harold for the sale of his land, Maude for the purchase of toy robots. Only one prevailed. The difference in outcome demonstrates why everyone in business needs a working knowledge of the Code. As we revisit the happy couple, Harold is clearing the dinner dishes. Maude sits back in her chair, lights a cigar, and compliments her husband on the apple tart.

Harold's contract was for the sale of land and was governed by the common law of contracts, which requires any agreement for the sale of land to be in writing and *signed by the defendant,* in this case the buyer in Texas. Harold signed it, but the buyer never did, so Harold's meticulously detailed document was worth less than a five-cent cigar.

Maude's quickly scribbled memorandum, concerning robot toys, was for the sale of goods and was governed by Article 2 of the UCC. The Code requires less detail and formality in a writing. Because Maude and the seller were both merchants, the document she scribbled could be enforced *even against the defendant,* who had never signed anything. The fact that Maude left out the price and other significant terms was not fatal to a contract under the UCC, though under the common law such omissions would have made the bargain unenforceable.

## Scope of Article 2

Because the UCC changes the common law, it is essential to know whether the Code applies in a given case. Negotiations may lead to an enforceable agreement when the UCC applies, even though the same bargaining would create no contract under the common law.

**Goods**
are things that are movable, other than money and investment securities.

**UCC §2-102: Article 2 applies to the sale of goods.**[1] **Goods are things that are movable, other than money and investment securities.** Hats are goods, and so are railroad cars, lumber, books, and bottles of wine. Land is not a good, nor is a house. Article 2 regulates sales, which means that one party transfers title to the other in exchange for money. If you sell your motorcycle to a friend, that is a sale of goods.[2]

## Merchants

The UCC evolved to provide merchants with rules that would meet their unique business needs. However, while the UCC offers a contract law that is more flexible than the common law, it also requires a higher level of responsibility from the merchants it serves. Those who make a living by crafting agreements are expected to understand the legal consequences of their words and deeds. Thus, many sections of the Code offer two rules: one for "merchants" and one for everybody else.

**Merchant**
Someone who routinely deals in the particular goods involved.

**UCC §2-104: A merchant is someone who routinely deals in the particular goods involved, or who appears to have special knowledge or skill in those goods, or who uses agents with special knowledge or skill in those goods.** A used car dealer is a "merchant" when it comes to selling autos, because he routinely deals in them. He is not a merchant when he goes to a furniture store and purchases a new sofa.

**The UCC frequently holds a merchant to a higher standard of conduct than a non-merchant.** For example, a merchant may be held to an oral contract if she received written confirmation of it, even though the merchant herself never signed the confirmation. That same confirmation memo, arriving at the house of a non-merchant, would not create a binding deal.

## CONTRACT FORMATION

The common law expected the parties to form a contract in a fairly predictable and traditional way: the offeror made a clear offer that included all important terms, and the offeree agreed to all terms. Nothing was left open. The drafters of the UCC recognized that businesspeople frequently do not think or work that way and that the law should reflect business reality.

---

[1] Officially, Article 2 tells us that it applies to *transactions* in goods, which is a slightly broader category than sale of goods. But most sections of Article 2, and most court decisions, focus exclusively on sales, and so shall we.

[2] Because leasing is so important, the drafters of the Code added Article 2A to cover the subject. Article 2A is similar to Article 2, but there are important differences, and anyone engaging in a significant amount of commercial leasing must become familiar with Article 2A. For our purposes, leasing law is a variation on the theme of Article 2, and we will concentrate on the principal melody of sales.

## Formation Basics: Section 2-204

UCC §2-204 provides three important rules that enable parties to make a contract quickly and informally:

1. *Any Manner That Shows Agreement.* The parties may make a contract in any manner sufficient to show that they reached an agreement. They may show the agreement with words, writings, or even their conduct. Lisa negotiates with Ed to buy 300 barbecue grills. The parties agree on a price, but other business prevents them from finishing the deal. Then six months later Lisa writes, "Remember our deal for 300 grills? I still want to do it if you do." Ed does not respond, but a week later a truck shows up at Lisa's store with the 300 grills, and Lisa accepts them. The combination of their original discussion, Lisa's subsequent letter, Ed's delivery, and her acceptance all adds up to show that they reached an agreement. The court will enforce their deal, and Lisa must pay the agreed-upon price.

2. *Moment of Making Is Not Critical.* The UCC will enforce a deal even though it is difficult, in common-law terms, to say exactly when it was formed. Was Lisa's deal formed when they orally agreed? When he delivered? She accepted? The Code's answer: it does not matter. The contract is enforceable.

3. *One or More Terms May Be Left Open.* The common law insisted that the parties clearly agree on all important terms. The Code changes that. **Under the UCC, a court may enforce a bargain even though one or more terms were left open.** Lisa's letter never said when she required delivery of the barbecue grills or when she would pay. Under the UCC, the omission is not fatal. As long as there is some certain basis for giving damages to the injured party, the court will do just that. If Lisa refused to pay, a court would rule that the parties assumed she would pay within a commercially reasonable time, such as 30 days.

In the following case, we can almost see the roller coasters, smell the cotton candy—and hear the carnival owners arguing.

## JANNUSCH V. NAFFZIGER

2008 WL 540877, ILLINOIS COURT OF APPEALS, 2008

### CASE SUMMARY

**Facts:** Gene and Martha Jannusch owned Festival Foods, which served snacks at events throughout Illinois and Indiana. The business included a truck, servicing trailer, refrigerators, roasters, chairs, and tables.

Lindsey and Louann Naffziger orally agreed to buy Festival Foods for $150,000, the deal including all the assets and the opportunity to work at events secured by the Jannuschs. The Naffzigers paid $10,000 immediately, with the balance due when they received their bank loan. They took possession the next day and operated Festival Foods for the remainder of the season.

In a pretrial deposition, Louann Naffziger acknowledged orally agreeing to buy the business for $150,000. (Her admission under oath made the lack of a written contract irrelevant.) However, she could not recall making the agreement on any particular date. Gene Jannusch suggested the parties sign something, but the Naffzigers replied that they were "in no position to sign anything" because they had received no loan

money from the bank and lacked a lawyer. Lindsey admitted taking possession of Festival Foods, receiving the income from the business, purchasing inventory, replacing equipment, and paying taxes and employees.

Two days after the business season ended, they returned Festival Foods to the Jannuschs, stating that the income was lower than expected. The Jannuschs sued. The trial court ruled that there had been no meeting of the minds and hence no contract. The Jannuschs appealed.

**Issue:** *Did the parties form a contract?*

**Decision:** Yes, the parties formed a contract.

**Reasoning:** The Naffzigers argue that nothing was said in the contract about a price for good will, a covenant not to compete, the value of individual assets, release from earlier liens, or the consequences should their loan be denied.

Under the UCC, a contract may be enforced even though some contract terms are missing or left to be agreed upon. However, if the essential terms are so uncertain that a court cannot decide whether the agreement has been broken, there is no contract.

The essential terms were agreed upon. The purchase price was $150,000, and the parties specified all assets to be transferred. No essential terms remained to be agreed upon. The only action remaining was the performance of the contract, and the Naffzigers took possession and used all items as their own.

Louann Naffziger could not recall making the oral agreement on any particular date, but parties may form a binding agreement even though the moment of its making is undetermined. Returning the goods at the end of the season was not a rejection of the Jannusches' offer to sell; it was a breach of contract.

The parties agreed to a sale of Festival Foods for $150,000, and the Naffzigers violated the agreement. Reversed and remanded.

---

Based on the UCC, the Jannusches won a case they would have lost under the common law. Next we look at changes the Code has made in the centuries-old requirement of a writing.

## Statute of Frauds

**UCC §2-201 requires a writing for any sale of goods worth $500 or more.** However, under the UCC, the writing need not completely summarize the agreement. The Code only requires a writing *sufficient to indicate* that the parties made a contract. In other words, the writing need not be a contract. A simple memo is enough, or a letter or informal note, mentioning that the two sides reached an agreement.

**In general, the writing must be signed by the defendant**—that is, whichever party is claiming there was no deal. Dick signs and sends to Shirley a letter saying, "This is to acknowledge your agreement to buy all 650 books in my rare book collection for $188,000." Shirley signs nothing. A day later, Louis offers Dick $250,000. Is Dick free to sell? No. He signed the memo, it indicates a contract, and Shirley can enforce it against him.

Now reverse the problem. Suppose that after Shirley receives Dick's letter, she decides against rare books in favor of original scripts from the *South Park* television show. Dick sues. Shirley wins because she signed nothing.

**Enforceable Only to Quantity Stated**   Because the writing only has to indicate that the parties agreed, it need not state every term of their deal. But one term is essential: quantity. **The Code will enforce the contract only up to the quantity of goods stated in the writing.** This is logical, since a court can surmise other terms, such as price, based on market conditions. Buyer agrees to purchase pencils from Seller. The market value of the pencils is easy to determine, but a court would have no way of knowing whether Buyer meant to purchase 1,000 pencils or 100,000; the quantity must be stated.

**Merchant Exception**   This is a major change from the common law. **When two merchants make an oral contract, and one sends a confirming memo to the other within a reasonable time, and the memo is sufficiently definite that it could be enforced against the sender herself, then the memo is also valid against the merchant who receives it, unless he objects within 10 days.** Laura, a tire wholesaler, signs and sends a memo to Scott, a retailer, saying, "Confm yr order today—500 tires cat #886—cat price." Scott realizes he can get the tires cheaper elsewhere and ignores the memo. Big mistake. Both parties are merchants, and Laura's memo is sufficient to bind her. So it also satisfies the statute of frauds against Scott, unless he objects within 10 days.

## EXAM *Strategy*

**Question:** Marko, a sporting goods retailer, speaks on the phone with Wholesaler about buying 500 footballs. After the conversation, Marko writes this message by hand: "Confirming our discussion—you will deliver to us 'Pro Bowl' model footballs—$45 per unit—arrival our store no later than July 20 this year." Marko signs and faxes the note to Wholesaler. Wholesaler reads the fax but then gets an order from Lana for the same model football at $51 per unit. Wholesaler never responds to Marko's fax and sells his entire supply to Lana. Two weeks later, Marko is forced to pay more from another seller and sues Wholesaler. Marko argues that under merchant exception, his fax was sufficient to satisfy the statute of frauds. Is he right?

**Strategy:** These two parties are merchants, and the merchant exception applies. Under this exception, a memo that could be enforced against the sender himself may bind the merchant who receives it. Could this memo be enforced against Marko? Make sure that you know what terms must be included to make a writing binding.

**Result:** The writing must indicate that the two parties reached an agreement. Marko's memo does so because he says he is confirming their discussion. Even if some terms are omitted, the writing may still suffice. However, the memo will be enforced only to the quantity of goods stated. Marko stated no quantity—a fatal error. His writing fails to satisfy the statute of frauds, and he loses the suit.

..................................................................................................................

## Added Terms: Section 2-207

Under the common law's mirror image rule, when one party makes an offer, the offeree must accept those exact terms. If the offeree adds or alters any terms, the acceptance is ineffective, and the offeree's response becomes a counteroffer. In one of its most significant modifications of contract law, the UCC changes that outcome. **Under §2-207, an acceptance that adds or alters terms will often create a contract.** The Code has made this change in response to the *battles of the form.* Every day, corporations buy and sell millions of dollars of goods using preprinted forms. The vast majority of all contracts involve such documents. Typically, the buyer places an order by using a preprinted form, and the seller acknowledges with its own preprinted acceptance form. Because each form contains language favorable to the party sending it, the two documents rarely agree. The Code's drafters concluded that the law must cope with real practices.

**Intention** The parties must still *intend* to create a contract. Section 2-207 is full of exceptions, but there is no change in this basic requirement of contract law. If the differing forms indicate that the parties never reached agreement, there is no contract.

**Additional or Different Terms** An offeree may include a new term in his acceptance and still create a binding deal. Suppose Breeder writes to Pet Shop, offering to sell 100 guinea pigs at $2 each. Pet Shop faxes a memo saying, "We agree to buy 100 g.p. We receive normal industry credit for any unhealthy pig." Pet Shop has added a new term, concerning unhealthy pigs, but the parties have created a binding contract because the writings show they intended an agreement. Now the court must decide what the terms of the contract are because there is some discrepancy. The first step is to decide whether the new language is an *additional term* or a *different term.*

**Additional terms** are those that raise issues not covered in the offer. The "unhealthy pig" issue is an additional term because the offer said nothing about it. **When both parties are *merchants*, additional terms generally become part of the bargain.**[3] Both Pet Shop and Breeder are merchants, and the additional term about credit for unhealthy animals does become part of their agreement.

**Additional terms**
raise issues not covered in the offer.

**Different terms** *contradict* those in the offer. Suppose Brilliant Corp. orders 1,500 cell phones from Makem Co., for use by Brilliant's sales force. Brilliant places the order by using a preprinted

**Different terms**
contradict those in the offer.

_____

[3] There are three circumstances in which additional terms do *not* become part of the agreement: when the original offer *insisted on its own terms;* when the additional term *materially alters* the offer—that is, makes a dramatic change in the proposal; and when the offeror *promptly objects* to the new terms.

form stating that the product is fully warranted for normal use and that seller is liable for compensatory *and consequential* damages. This means, for example, that Makem could be liable for lost profits if a salesperson's phone fails during a lucrative sales pitch. Makem responds with its own memo stating that in the event of defective phones, Makem is liable only to repair or replace and *is not liable for consequential damages, lost profits, or any other damages.*

Makem's acceptance has included a different term because its language contradicts the offer. **Different terms cancel each other out. The Code then supplies its own terms, called gap-fillers,** which cover prices, delivery dates and places, warranties, and other subjects. The Code's gap-filler about warranties does permit recovery of compensatory and consequential damages. Therefore, Makem would be liable for lost profits.

**Gap fillers**
UCC rules for supplying missing terms.

# PERFORMANCE AND REMEDIES

The Code's practical, flexible approach also shapes its rules about contract performance and remedy. Once again, our goal in this chapter is to highlight doctrines that demonstrate a *change or an evolution in common-law principles.*

## Buyer's Remedies

**Conforming goods**
satisfy the contract terms.

A seller is expected to deliver what the buyer ordered. **Conforming goods** satisfy the contract terms. Nonconforming goods do not.[4] Frame Shop orders from Wholesaler a large quantity of walnut wood, due on March 15, to be used for picture frames. If Wholesaler delivers, on March 8, high-quality *cherry* wood, it has shipped nonconforming goods.

A buyer has the right to **inspect the goods** before paying or accepting[5] and may **reject nonconforming goods** by notifying the seller within a reasonable time.[6] Frame Shop may lawfully open Wholesaler's shipping crates before paying and is entitled to refuse the cherry wood. However, when the buyer rejects nonconforming goods, **the seller has the right to cure,** by delivering conforming goods before the contract deadline.[7] If Wholesaler delivers walnut wood by March 15, Frame Shop must pay in full. The Code even permits the seller to cure *after* the delivery date if doing so is reasonable. Notice the UCC's eminently pragmatic goal: to make contracts work.

**Cover**
To reasonably obtain substitute goods because another party has not honored a contract.

**Cover**   If the seller breaches, the buyer may *cover* by reasonably obtaining substitute goods; it may then obtain the difference between the contract price and its cover price, plus incidental and consequential damages, minus expenses saved.[8] Retailer orders 10,000 pairs of ballet shoes from Shoemaker, at $55 per pair, to be delivered August 1. When no shoes dance through the door, Shoemaker explains that its workers in Europe are on strike and no delivery date can be guaranteed. Retailer purchases comparable shoes elsewhere for $70 and files suit. Retailer will win $150,000, representing the increased cost of $15 per pair.

**Consequential damages**
Damages resulting from the unique circumstances of the injured party.

**Incidental and Consequential Damages**   **An injured buyer is generally entitled to incidental and consequential damages.** Incidental damages cover such costs as advertising for replacements, sending buyers to obtain new goods, and shipping the replacement goods. Consequential damages are those resulting from the unique circumstances of *this injured party.* They can be much more extensive and may include lost profits. **A buyer expecting to resell goods may obtain the loss of profit caused by the seller's failure to deliver.** In the ballet shoes case, suppose

---

[4] UCC §2-106(2).

[5] UCC §2-513.

[6] UCC §§2-601, 602.

[7] UCC §2-508.

[8] UCC §2-712.

Retailer has contracts to resell the goods to ballet companies at an average profit of $10 per pair. Retailer is also entitled to those lost profits.

### Seller's Remedies

Of course, a seller has rights, too. Sometimes a buyer breaches before the seller has delivered the goods, for example, by failing to make a payment due under the contract. If that happens, **the seller may refuse to deliver the goods.**[9]

If a buyer unjustly refuses to accept or pay for goods, the injured seller may resell them. **If the resale is commercially reasonable, the seller may recover the difference between the resale price and contract price, plus incidental damages, minus expenses saved.**[10] Incidental damages are expenses the seller incurs in holding the goods and reselling them, costs such as storage, shipping, and advertising for resale. The seller must deduct expenses saved by the breach. For example, if the contract required the seller to ship heavy machinery from Detroit to San Diego, and the buyer's breach enables the seller to market its goods profitably in Detroit, the seller must deduct from its claimed losses the transportation costs that it saved.

Finally, the seller may simply sue **for the contract price** if the buyer has accepted the goods *or if* the goods are conforming and resale is impossible.[11] If the goods were manufactured to the buyer's unique specifications, there might be no other market for them, and the seller should receive the contract price.

## • WARRANTIES AND PRODUCT LIABILITY •

> **He waves angrily at the absurdity, takes a ferocious bite from his burger—and with a loud CRACK breaks a tooth.**

You are sitting in a fast-food restaurant in Washington, D.C. Your friend Harley, who works for a member of Congress, is eating with one hand and gesturing with the other. "We want product liability reform and we want it now," he proclaims, stabbing the air with his free hand. "It's absurd, these multimillion dollar verdicts, just because something has a *slight defect*." He waves angrily at the absurdity, takes a ferocious bite from his burger—and with a loud CRACK breaks a tooth. Harley howls in pain and throws down the bun, revealing a large piece of bone in the meat. As he tips back in misery, his defectively manufactured chair collapses, and Harley slams into the tile, knocking himself unconscious. Hours later, when he revives in the hospital, he refuses to speak to you until he talks with his lawyer. They will discuss **product liability**, which refers to goods that have caused an injury. The harm may be physical, as it was in Harley's case. Or it can be purely economic, as when a corporation buys a computer so defective it must be replaced, costing the buyer lost time and profits. The injured party may have a choice of possible remedies, including:

**Product liability**
refers to goods that have caused an injury.

- *Warranty,* which is an assurance provided in a sales contract;
- *Negligence,* which refers to unreasonable conduct by the defendant; and
- *Strict liability,* which prohibits defective products whether the defendant acted reasonably or not.

We discuss each of these remedies in this chapter. What all product liability cases have in common is that a person or business has been hurt by goods. We begin with warranties.

---

[9] UCC §2-705.

[10] UCC §2-706.

[11] UCC §2-709.

# EXPRESS WARRANTIES

**Warranty**
A guarantee that goods will meet certain standards.

**A warranty is a contractual assurance that goods will meet certain standards.** It is normally a manufacturer or a seller who gives a warranty, and a buyer who relies on it. A warranty might be explicit and written: "The manufacturer warrants that the lightbulbs in this package will provide 100 watts of power for 2,000 hours." Or a warranty could be oral: "Don't worry, this machine can harvest any size of wheat crop ever planted in the state."

**Express warranty**
A guarantee, created by the words or actions of the seller, that goods will meet certain standards.

**An express warranty is one that the seller creates with his words or actions.**[12] Whenever a seller *clearly indicates* to a buyer that the goods being sold will meet certain standards, she has created an express warranty. For example, if the salesclerk for a paint store tells a professional house painter that "this exterior paint will not fade for three years, even in direct sunlight," that is an express warranty and the store is bound by it. The store is also bound by express warranty if the clerk gives the painter a brochure making the same promise or a sample that indicates the same thing.

**Disclaimer**
A statement that a particular warranty does not apply.

The seller may **disclaim** a warranty. A **disclaimer** is a statement that a particular warranty *does not* apply. The seller may disclaim an oral express warranty by including in the sales contract a statement such as "sold as is," or "any oral promises are disclaimed." Written express warranties generally *cannot* be disclaimed.

In the following case, a ventilation company wrote a letter hoping to clear the air (and sell the product). Was the letter an express warranty? You decide.

---

[12] UCC §2-313.

---

# YOU *be the* JUDGE

## KELLER v. INLAND METALS ALL WEATHER CONDITIONING, INC.
### 139 Idaho 233, 76 P.3d 977
### Supreme Court of Idaho, 2003

**Facts:** When Brian and Clarice Keller installed an indoor swimming pool in the athletic club they owned, customers began to complain that the air near the pool was hot, humid, and foul-smelling. The Kellers sought help from two contractors. Inland Metal submitted a bid to install a 7½-ton dehumidifier for about $30,000, and another company offered to install a 10-ton machine for about $40,000.

The Kellers were worried that the 7½-ton dehumidifier might be too small, so Inland's president visited the club, accompanied by a representative of the machine's manufacturer. The men assured the Kellers that the 7½-ton dehumidifier would work. Inland's president followed up with a letter to the Kellers, which said:

As in any indoor pool, the air needs to be treated with outdoor fresh air, dehumidified, air conditioned in the summer, and heated in the winter. This ducted system will rid you of the sweating walls and eliminate those offensive odors, and overall "bad air." This is not an uncommon problem, and all commercial pool owners face the same thing until they install one of these systems.

Once you complete this installation, your air problems should be over, and your customers should be satisfied and happy.

The Kellers bought the system from Inland, but the dehumidifier did not improve the problem. The Kellers sued, and the trial court found that Inland had breached an express warranty. Inland appealed.

**You Be the Judge:  Did Inland make an express warranty?**

**Argument for Inland:**  Inland never made an express warranty. The company never said, "We guarantee that this unit will resolve all of the problems described." In its letter, the company described what it expected the dehumidifier to do and mentioned that customers "should be satisfied and happy" with the improved air. That is a far cry from promising to return the cost of the machine in the event that anyone claimed the machine was imperfect. Customers complain about many things, some legitimate, some not. Inland cannot prevent finicky clients from finding fault with a good dehumidifier. If Inland had intended its product to be guaranteed against any and all complaints, it would have said so—and charged much more.

*continued*

**Argument for the Kellers:** When Inland representatives visited the health club, they assured the Kellers that the dehumidifier would do the job. An express warranty can be created orally, and that is exactly what Inland did. That is all the Kellers need to win, but they have more. Inland's follow-up letter repeated the reassurance: "This ducted system will rid you of the sweating walls and eliminate those offensive odors." That is a clear affirmation that the machine will meet certain standards—in other words, it is an express warranty. Inland made an oral and a written warranty and must be bound by its words.

# IMPLIED WARRANTIES

Emily sells Sam a new jukebox for his restaurant, but the machine is so defective it never plays a note. When Sam demands a refund, Emily scoffs that she never made any promises. She is correct that she made no express warranties but is liable nonetheless. Many sales are covered by implied warranties.

    **Implied warranties are those created by the Code itself, not by any act or statement of the seller.**

## Implied Warranty of Merchantability

This is the most important warranty in the Code. **Unless excluded or modified, a warranty that the goods shall be merchantable is implied in a contract for their sale if the seller is a merchant with respect to goods of that kind.** *Merchantable* means that the goods are fit for the ordinary purposes for which they are used.[13] This rule contains several important principles:

- *Unless excluded or modified* means that the seller does have a chance to escape this warranty. A seller may disclaim this warranty provided he actually mentions the word "merchantability." A seller also has the option to disclaim *all* warranties, by stating that the goods are sold "as is" or "with all faults."

- *Merchantability* requires that goods be fit for their normal purposes. A ladder, to be merchantable, must be able to rest securely against a building and support someone who is climbing it. The ladder need not be serviceable as a boat ramp.

- *Implied* means that the law itself imposes this liability on the seller.

- *A merchant with respect to goods of that kind* means that the seller is someone who routinely deals in these goods or holds himself out as having special knowledge about these goods.

    Dacor Corp. manufactured and sold scuba diving equipment. Dacor ordered air hoses from Sierra Precision, specifying the exact size and couplings so that the hose would fit safely into Dacor's oxygen units. Within a year, customers returned a dozen Dacor units, complaining that the hose connections had cracked and were unusable. Dacor recalled 16,000 units and refit them at a cost of $136,000. Dacor sued Sierra and won its full costs. Sierra was a merchant with respect to scuba hoses because it routinely manufactured and sold them. The defects were life-threatening to scuba divers, and the hoses could not be used for normal purposes.[14]

    The scuba equipment was not merchantable because a properly made scuba hose should never crack under normal use. What if the product being sold is food, and the food contains something that is harmful—yet quite normal?

**Implied warranty**
Guarantees created by the Uniform Commercial Code and imposed on the seller of goods.

**Implied warranty of merchantability**
Goods must be of at least average, passable quality in the trade.

---

[13] UCC §2-314(1).

[14] *Dacor Corp. v. Sierra Precision*, 1993 U.S. Dist. LEXIS 8009 (N.D. Ill. 1993).

## GOODMAN V. WENCO FOODS, INC.

333 N.C. 1, 423 S.E.2D 444, 1992 N.C. LEXIS 671
SUPREME COURT OF NORTH CAROLINA, 1992

### CASE SUMMARY

**Facts:** Fred Goodman and a friend stopped for lunch at a Wendy's restaurant in Hillsborough, North Carolina. Goodman had eaten about half of his double hamburger when he bit down and felt immediate pain in his lower jaw. He took from his mouth a triangular piece of cow bone, about one-sixteenth to one-quarter inch thick and one-half inch long, along with several pieces of his teeth. Goodman's pain was intense and his dental repairs took months.

The restaurant purchased all of its meat from Greensboro Meat Supply Company (GMSC). Wendy's required its meat to be chopped and "free from bone or cartilage in excess of 1/8 inch in any dimension." GMSC beef was inspected continuously by state regulators and was certified by the United States Department of Agriculture (USDA). The USDA considered any bone fragment less than three-quarters of an inch long to be "insignificant."

Goodman sued, claiming a breach of the implied warranty of merchantability. The trial court dismissed the claim, ruling that the bone was natural to the food and that the hamburger was therefore fit for its ordinary purpose. The appeals court reversed this, holding that a hamburger could be unfit even if the bone occurred naturally. Wendy's appealed to the state's highest court.

**Issue:** *Was the hamburger unfit for its ordinary purpose because it contained a harmful but natural bone?*

**Decision:** Affirmed. Even if the harmful bone occurred naturally, the hamburger could be unfit for its ordinary purpose.

**Reasoning:** When an object in food harms a consumer, the injured person may recover even if the substance occurred naturally, provided that a reasonable consumer would not expect to encounter it. A triangular, one-half-inch bone shaving may be inherent to a cut of beef, but whether a reasonable consumer would anticipate it is normally a question for the jury.

Wendy's hamburgers need not be perfect, but they must be fit for their intended purpose. It is difficult to imagine how a consumer could guard against bone particles, short of removing the hamburger from its bun, breaking it apart, and inspecting its small components.

Wendy's argues that, since its meat complied with federal and state standards, the hamburgers were merchantable as a matter of law. However, while compliance with legal standards is evidence for the juries to consider, it does not ensure merchantability. A jury could still conclude that a bone this size in hamburger meat was reasonably unforeseeable and that an injured consumer was entitled to compensation.

---

**Implied warranty of fitness for a particular purpose**

If the seller knows that the buyer plans to use the goods for a particular purpose, the seller generally is held to warrant that the goods are in fact fit for that purpose. Also known as *warranty of fitness.*

## Implied Warranty of Fitness for a Particular Purpose

The other warranty that the law imposes on sellers is the implied warranty of fitness for a particular purpose. This cumbersome name is often shortened to the *warranty of fitness.* **Where the seller at the time of contracting knows about a particular purpose for which the buyer wants the goods, and knows that the buyer is relying on the seller's skill or judgment, there is (unless excluded or modified) an implied warranty that the goods shall be fit for such purpose.**[15]

Notice that the seller must know about some special use the buyer intends and realize that the buyer is relying on the seller's judgment. Suppose a lumber sales clerk knows that a buyer is relying on his advice to choose the best wood for a house being built in a swamp. The Code implies a warranty that the wood sold will withstand those special conditions.

Once again, a seller may disclaim this warranty if she clearly states "as is" or "sold with all faults," or some similar language.

## Consumer Sales

The Code often provides stronger protection for consumers than for businesses. Many states prohibit a seller from disclaiming implied warranties in the sale of consumer goods. In these

---

[15] UCC §2-315.

states, if a home furnishings store sells a bunk bed to a consumer and the top bunk tips out the window on the first night, the seller is liable. If the sales contract clearly stated "no warranties of merchantability or fitness," the court would reject the clause and find that the seller breached the implied warranty of merchantability.

# NEGLIGENCE

A buyer of goods may have remedies other than warranty claims. One is negligence. Here we focus on how this law applies to the sale of goods. Negligence is notably different from contract law. In a contract case, the two parties have reached an agreement, and the terms of their bargain will usually determine how to settle any dispute. If the parties agreed that the seller disclaimed all warranties, then the buyer may be out of luck. But in a negligence case, there has been no bargaining between the parties, who may never have met. A consumer injured by an exploding cola bottle is unlikely to have bargained for her beverage with the CEO of the cola company. Instead, the law *imposes* a standard of conduct on everyone in society, corporation and individual alike. The two key elements of this standard, for present purposes, are *duty* and *breach*. A plaintiff injured by goods she bought must show that the defendant, usually a manufacturer or seller of a product, had a duty to her and breached that duty. A defendant has a duty of due care to anyone who could foreseeably be injured by its misconduct. Generally, it is the duty to act as *a reasonable person* would in like circumstances; a defendant who acts unreasonably has breached his duty.

   In negligence cases concerning the sale of goods, plaintiffs most often raise one or more of these claims:

- *Negligent Design.* The buyer claims that the product injured her because the manufacturer designed it poorly. Negligence law requires a manufacturer to design a product free of *unreasonable* risks. The product does not have to be absolutely safe. An automobile that guaranteed a driver's safety could be made but would be prohibitively expensive. Reasonable safety features must be built in if they can be included at a tolerable cost.
- *Negligent Manufacture.* The buyer claims that the design was adequate but that failure to inspect or some other sloppy conduct caused a dangerous product to leave the plant.
- *Failure to Warn.* A manufacturer is liable for failing to warn the purchaser or users about the dangers of normal use and also foreseeable misuse. However, there is no duty to warn about obvious dangers, a point evidently lost on some manufacturers. A Batman costume unnecessarily included this statement: "For play only: Mask and chest plate are not protective; cape does not enable user to fly."

# STRICT LIABILITY

The other tort claim that an injured person can bring against the manufacturer or seller of a product is strict liability. Like negligence, strict liability is a burden created by the law rather than by the parties. And, as with all torts, strict liability concerns claims of physical harm. But there is a key distinction between negligence and strict liability: in a negligence case, the injured buyer must demonstrate that the seller's conduct was unreasonable. Not so in strict liability.

   **In strict liability, the injured person need not prove that the defendant's conduct was unreasonable.** The injured person must show only that the defendant manufactured or sold a product that was defective and that the defect caused harm. Almost all states permit such lawsuits, and most adopted the summary of strict liability provided by the Restatement (Second) of Torts §402A. Because §402A is the most frequently cited section in all of tort law, we quote it in full:

1. One who sells any product in a defective condition unreasonably dangerous to the user or consumer or to his property is subject to liability for physical harm thereby caused to the ultimate user or consumer, or to his property, if

   a. the seller is engaged in the business of selling such a product, and

    **b.** it is expected to and does reach the user or consumer without substantial change in the condition in which it is sold.

**2.** The rule stated in Subsection (1) applies although

    **a.** the seller has exercised all possible care in the preparation and sale of his product, and

    **b.** the user or consumer has not bought the product from or entered into any contractual relation with the seller.

These are the key terms in subsection (1):

- *Defective condition unreasonably dangerous to the user.* The defendant is liable only if the product is defective when it leaves his hands. There must be something wrong with the goods. If they are reasonably safe and the buyer's mishandling of the goods causes the harm, there is no strict liability. If you attempt to open a soda bottle by knocking the cap against a counter, and the glass shatters and cuts you, the manufacturer owes nothing.

  The article sold must be *more dangerous* than the ordinary consumer would expect. A carving knife can produce a lethal wound, but everyone knows that, and a sharp knife is not unreasonably dangerous. On the other hand, prescription drugs may harm in ways that neither a layperson nor a doctor would anticipate. The manufacturer *must provide adequate warnings* of any dangers that are not apparent.

- *In the business of selling.* The seller is liable only if she normally sells this kind of product. Suppose your roommate makes you a peanut butter sandwich and, while eating it, you cut your mouth on a sliver of glass that was in the jar. The peanut butter manufacturer faces strict liability, as does the grocery store where your roommate bought the goods. But your roommate is not strictly liable because he does not serve sandwiches as a business.

- *Reaches the user without substantial change.* Obviously, if your roommate put the glass in the peanut butter thinking it was funny, neither the manufacturer nor the store is liable.

And here are the important phrases in subsection (2):

- *Has exercised all possible care.* This is the heart of strict liability, which makes it a potent claim for consumers. *It is no defense that the seller used reasonable care.*

  If the product is dangerously defective and injures the user, the seller is liable even if it took every precaution to design and manufacture the product safely. Suppose the peanut butter jar did in fact contain a glass sliver when it left the factory. The manufacturer proves that it uses extraordinary care in keeping foreign particles out of the jars and thoroughly inspects each container before it is shipped. The evidence is irrelevant. The manufacturer has shown that it was not negligent in packaging the food, but reasonable care is irrelevant in strict liability.

- *No contractual relation.* This means that the injured party need not have bought the goods directly from the party responsible for the defect. Suppose the manufacturer that made the peanut butter sold it to a distributor, which sold it to a wholesaler, which sold it to a grocery store, which sold it to your roommate. You may sue the manufacturer, distributor, wholesaler, and store, even though you never contracted with any of them.

**Restatement (Third) and Contemporary Trends**    We saw that under traditional negligence law, a company could be found liable based on design, manufacture, or failure to warn. The same three activities can give rise to a claim of strict liability. It will normally be easier for a plaintiff to win a claim of strict liability, because she does not need to demonstrate that the manufacturer's conduct was unreasonable.

    If the steering wheel on a brand new car falls off, and the driver is injured, that is a clear case of defective manufacturing, and the company will be strictly liable. Those are the easy cases. As courts have applied §402A, defective design cases have been more contentious. Suppose a vaccine that prevents serious childhood illnesses inevitably causes brain damage in a very small number of children, because of the nature of the drug. Is the manufacturer liable? What if a racing sailboat, designed only for speed, is dangerously unstable in the hands of a less experienced sailor? Is the boat's maker responsible for fatalities? Suppose an automobile made of lightweight metal uses less fuel but exposes its occupants to more serious injuries in an accident. How is a court to decide whether the design was defective? Often, these design cases also involve issues of warnings: Did drug designer diligently detail dangers to doctors? Should sailboat seller sell speedy sailboat solely to seasoned sailors?

Over the years, most courts have adopted one of two tests for design and warning cases. The first is consumer expectation. Here, a court finds the manufacturer liable for defective design if the product is less safe than a reasonable consumer would expect. If a smoke detector has a 3 percent failure rate, and the average consumer has no way of anticipating that danger, effective cautions must be included, though the design may be defective anyway. Many states have moved away from that test and now use a *risk-utility test.* Here, a court must weigh the benefits for society against the dangers that the product poses. Principal factors in the risk-utility test include:

- The *value* of the product;
- The *gravity* of the danger (how bad will the harm be);
- The *likelihood* that such danger will occur (the odds);
- The mechanical feasibility of a *safer alternative design;* and
- The *adverse consequences* of an alternative design (greater cost, different risks created).

Because of the conflicting court decisions, the American Law Institute drafted the Restatement (Third) of Torts: Product Liability, in an attempt to harmonize judicial opinions about product liability generally and design defects in particular. The new Restatement treats manufacturing cases differently from those involving design defects and failure to warn.

- In manufacturing cases, a product is defective whenever it departs from its intended design, regardless of how much care was taken. This is the traditional standard.
- In design and warnings cases, a product is defective only when the *foreseeable* risks of harm could have been reduced by using a reasonable alternative design or warning. So-called strict liability in these cases is beginning to resemble plain old negligence. If courts adopt this new approach, it will become more difficult for plaintiffs to win a design or warning case because they will need to prove that the manufacturer should have foreseen the danger and could have done something about it.

There is no strong trend in how judges examine these cases: courts tend to pick and choose the analytic tools they use. Most still regard §402A as the basic law for all strict liability lawsuits. In design cases, many courts use the risk-utility test, quite a few still examine consumer expectation, and some permit both analyses. Most states consider the availability of alternative designs to be important, and some consider it essential. And finally, as the following case indicates, some courts employ elements of the Restatement (Third)—with plenty of disagreement.

## UNIROYAL GOODRICH TIRE COMPANY V. MARTINEZ

977 S.W.2D 328, TEXAS SUPREME COURT, 1998

### CASE SUMMARY

**Facts:** When Roberto Martinez, a mechanic, attempted to mount a 16-inch tire on a 16.5-inch rim (wheel), the tire exploded, causing him serious, permanent injuries. He sued Goodrich, the tire manufacturer; the Budd Company, which made the rim; and Ford Motor Company, which designed it. Budd and Ford settled out of court, and the case proceeded against Goodrich.

The tire had a conspicuous label, advising users never to mount a 16-inch tire on a 16.5-inch rim, warning of the danger of severe injury or death, and including a picture of a worker thrown into the air by an explosion. The label also urged the user never to lean or reach over the assembly while working. Martinez ignored the warnings.

Martinez admitted that the warnings were adequate but claimed that Goodrich was strictly liable for failing to use a safer "bead" design. The bead, a rubber-encased steel wire, encircles the tire and holds it to the rim. Martinez's expert testified that an alternate design, used by other tire manufacturers, would have prevented his injury. The trial court gave judgment for Martinez in the amount of $10,308,792.45, the Court of Appeals affirmed, and Goodrich appealed to the state's highest court.

**Issue:** *When warnings are adequate, is a manufacturer still obligated to use a safer alternative design?*

**Decision:** The manufacturer was obligated to use a safer design. Affirmed.

**Reasoning:** The Restatement (Second) declared that a product was not defectively designed if it included adequate warnings. However, the Restatement (Third) has rejected this view. Under the new Restatement, the key question remains whether a safer alternative existed. To decide the issue, a court should look at a broad range of factors: the probability and magnitude of potential harm, instructions and warnings included, consumer expectations, cost of alternative design, and product longevity.

Goodrich urges this court to follow the old rule, from the Restatement (Second). We decline. People often ignore warnings. A redesigned tire would have prevented this accident. The company's competitors incorporated the safer bead design almost a decade before this accident occurred, and Goodrich itself followed suit a year after Martinez was hurt. A Goodrich expert acknowledged that if one of his loved ones were inflating a tire, he would prefer the tire to have a single-bead design.

**Dissent's Reasoning:** Goodrich put a prominent, pictographic warning on the tire. Martinez saw it and ignored it. Thousands of these tires were sold, but only one other person ever claimed this type of injury. When the probability of harm is so low, and the warnings adequate, the company has done all that should be required.

---

## EXAM *Strategy*

**Question:** Warm, Inc. sells large, portable space heaters for industrial use. Warm sells Little Factory a unit and installs it. The sales contract states, "This heating unit is sold as is. There are no warranties, express or implied." On the third night the unit is used, it causes a fire and burns down the factory. Little sues Warm. At trial, the evidence indicates that a defect in the unit caused the fire, but also that this was unprecedented at Warm. The company employed more than the usual number of quality inspectors, and its safety record was the best in the entire industry. Discuss the effect of the sales contract and Warm's safety record. Predict who will win.

**Strategy:** The question raises three separate issues: warranty (the disclaimer), negligence (the safety record), and strict liability (the defect). What language most effectively disclaims warranties? What must a plaintiff prove to win a negligence case? To prove a strict liability case?

**Result:** A company may disclaim all warranties by stating the product is sold "as is," especially when selling to a corporate buyer. Warm's disclaimer is effective. The company's safety record is so good that there seems to be no case for negligence. However, Little Factory still wins its lawsuit. The product was unreasonably dangerous to the user. Warm was in the business of selling such heaters and installed the heater itself. In a strict liability case, Warm's safety efforts will not save it.

## CHAPTER CONCLUSION

**The development of the UCC was an enormous and ambitious undertaking.** Its goal was to facilitate the free flow of commerce across this large nation. By any measure, the UCC has been a success. Remember, though: the terms of the UCC are precise. Failure to comply with these exacting provisions can close opportunities, and open courtroom doors.

## EXAM REVIEW

1. **THE UCC** The Code is designed to modernize commercial law and make it uniform throughout the country. Article 2 applies to the sale of goods. (p. 192)

2. **MERCHANTS** A merchant is someone who routinely deals in the particular goods involved, or who appears to have special knowledge or skill in those goods, or who uses agents with special knowledge or skill. (p. 194)

3. **CONTRACT FORMATION** UCC §2-204 permits the parties to form a contract in any manner that shows agreement. (p. 194)

4. **WRITING REQUIREMENT** For the sale of goods worth $500 or more, UCC §2-201 requires some writing that indicates an agreement. (p. 196)

**EXAM Strategy**

**Question:** To satisfy the UCC statute of frauds regarding the sale of goods, which of the following must generally be in writing?

   (a) Designation of the parties as buyer and seller

   (b) Delivery terms

   (c) Quantity of the goods

   (d) Warranties to be made

**Strategy:** O.K., this may be overkill. But the question illustrates two basic points of UCC law: First, the Code allows a great deal of flexibility in the formation of contracts. Second, there is one term for which no flexibility is allowed. Make sure you know which it is. (See the "Result" at the end of this section.)

5. **MERCHANT EXCEPTION** A merchant who receives a signed memo confirming an oral contract may become liable if he fails to object within 10 days. (p. 196)

6. **UCC §2-207** UCC §2-207 governs an acceptance that does not "mirror" the offer. *Additional* terms usually become part of the contract. *Different* terms contradict the offer, and are generally replaced by the Code's own gap-filler terms. (p. 197)

**EXAM Strategy**

**Question:** Cookie Co. offered to sell Distrib Markets 20,000 pounds of cookies at $1 per pound, subject to certain specified terms for delivery. Distrib replied in writing as follows: "We accept your offer for 20,000 pounds of cookies at $1 per pound, weighing scale to have valid city certificate." Under the UCC:

    (a) A contract was formed between the parties.

    (b) A contract will be formed only if Cookie agrees to the weighing scale requirement.

    (c) No contract was formed because Distrib included the weighing scale requirement in its reply.

    (d) No contract was formed because Distrib's reply was a counteroffer.

**Strategy:** Distrib's reply included a new term. That means it is governed by UCC §2-207. Is the new term an additional term or a different term? An additional term goes beyond what the offeror stated. Additional terms become a part of the contract except in three specified instances. A different term contradicts one made by the offeror. Different terms generally cancel each other out. (See the "Result" at the end of this section.)

**7.** **REMEDIES** An injured seller may resell the goods and obtain the difference between the contract and resale prices. An injured buyer may buy substitute goods and obtain the difference between the contract and cover prices. (p. 198)

**8.** **PRODUCT LIABILITY** Product liability may arise in various ways:
- A party may create an express warranty with words or actions. The Code may *imply* a warranty of merchantability or fitness for a particular purpose.
- A seller will be liable if her conduct is not that of a reasonable person.
- A seller may be strictly liable for a defective product that reaches the user without substantial change. (p. 199)

**4. Result:** (C). The contract will be enforced only to the extent of the quantity stated.

**6. Result:** The "valid city certificate" phrase raises a new issue; it does not contradict anything in Cookie's offer. That means it is an additional term, and becomes part of the deal unless Cookie insisted on its own terms, the additional term materially alters the offer, or Cookie promptly rejects it. Cookie did not insist on its terms, this is a minor addition, and Cookie never rejected it. The new term is part of a valid contract and the answer is "a."

# PRACTICE EXAM

## MATCHING QUESTIONS

___ A. Additional terms

___ B. Strict liability

___ C. Merchantability

___ D. Different terms

1. An implied warranty that goods are fit for their ordinary purpose
2. Generally become part of a contract between merchants
3. The reasonableness of defendant's conduct is irrelevant
4. Generally cancel each other out

## TRUE/FALSE QUESTIONS

1. T   F   In a contract for the sale of goods, the offer may include any terms the offeror wishes; the offeree must accept on exactly those terms or reject the deal.

2. T   F   Seller can be bound by written warranties but not by oral statements.

3. T   F   Under strict liability, an injured consumer could potentially recover damages from the product's manufacturer and the retailer who sold the goods.

4. T   F   A contract for the sale of $300 worth of decorative stone must be in writing to be enforceable.

## MULTIPLE-CHOICE QUESTIONS

5. Marion orally agrees to sell Ashley her condominium in Philadelphia for $700,000. The parties have known each other for 20 years and do not bother to put anything in writing. Based on the agreement, Marion hires a moving company to pack up all her goods and move them to a storage warehouse. Ashley shows up with a cashier's check, and Marion says, "You're going to love it here." But at the last minute, Marion declines to take the check and refuses to sell. Ashley sues and wins

   A. Nothing

   B. The condominium

   C. $700,000

   D. The difference between $700,000 and the condominium's market value

   E. Damages for fraud

6. Seller's sales contract states that "The model 8J flagpole will withstand winds up to 150 mph, for a minimum of 35 years." The same contract includes this: "This contract makes no warranties, and any implied warranties are hereby disclaimed." School buys the flagpole, which blows down six months later in a 105-mph wind.

   A. Seller is not liable because it never made any express warranties.

   B. Seller is not liable because it disclaimed any warranties.

   C. Seller is liable because the disclaimer was invalid.

   D. Seller is liable because implied warranties may not be disclaimed.

7. Manufacturer sells a brand-new, solar-powered refrigerator. Because the technology is new, Manufacturer sells the product "as is." Plaintiff later sues Manufacturer for breach of warranty and wins. Plaintiff is probably

   A. A distributor with no understanding of legal terminology

   B. A retailer who had previously relied on manufacturer

   C. A retailer who had never done business before with manufacturer

   D. A retailer who failed to notice the "as is" label

   E. A consumer

8. CPA QUESTION: To establish a cause of action based on strict liability in tort for personal injuries resulting from using a defective product, one of the elements the plaintiff must prove is that the seller (defendant)

   A. Failed to exercise due care

   B. Was in privity of contract with the plaintiff

   C. Defectively designed the product

   D. Was engaged in the business of selling the product

## SHORT-ANSWER QUESTIONS

9. Nina owns a used car lot. She signs and sends a fax to Seth, a used car wholesaler who has a huge lot of cars in the same city. The fax says, "Confirming our agrmt—I pick any 15 cars fr yr lot—30% below blue book." Seth reads the fax, laughs, and throws it away. Two weeks later, Nina arrives and demands to purchase 15 of Seth's cars. Is he obligated to sell?

10. **YOU BE THE JUDGE: WRITING PROBLEM** United Technologies advertised a used Beechcraft Baron airplane for sale in an aviation journal. Attorney Thompson Comerford spoke with a United agent who described the plane as "excellently maintained" and said it had been operated "under §135 flight regulations," meaning the plane had been subject to airworthiness inspections every 100 hours. Comerford arrived at a Dallas airport to pick up the plane, where he paid $80,000 for it. He signed a sales agreement stating that the plane was sold "as is" and that there were "no representations or warranties, express or implied, including the condition of the aircraft, its merchantability or its fitness for any particular purpose." Comerford attempted to fly the plane home but immediately experienced problems with its brakes, steering, ability to climb, and performance while cruising. (Otherwise it was fine.) He sued, claiming breach of express and implied warranties. Did United Technologies breach express or implied warranties? **Argument for Comerford:** United described the airplane as "excellently maintained," knowing that Mr. Comerford would rely. The company should not be allowed to say one thing and put the opposite in writing. **Argument for United Technologies:** Comerford is a lawyer, and we assume he can read. The contract clearly stated that the plane was sold as is. There were no warranties.

11. **ETHICS:** Texaco, Inc., and other oil companies sold mineral spirits in bulk to distributors, which then resold to retailers. Mineral spirits are used for cleaning and are harmful or fatal if swallowed. Texaco allegedly knew that the retailers, such as hardware stores, frequently packaged the mineral spirits (illegally) in used half-gallon milk containers and sold them to consumers, often with no warnings on the packages. David Hunnings, age 21 months, found a milk container in his home, swallowed the mineral spirits, and died. The Hunningses sued Texaco in negligence. The trial court dismissed the complaint, and the Hunningses appealed. What is the legal standard in a negligence case? Have the plaintiffs made out a valid case of negligence? Assume that Texaco knew about the repackaging and the grave risk but continued to sell in bulk because doing so was profitable. (If the plaintiffs cannot prove those facts, they will lose even if they do get to a jury.) Would that make you angry? Should the case go to a jury? Or did the fault still lie with the retailer and/or the parents?

12. Lewis River Golf, Inc., grew and sold sod. It bought seed from defendant, O. M. Scott & Sons, under an express warranty. But the sod grown from the Scott seeds developed weeds, a breach of Scott's warranty. Several of Lewis River's customers sued, unhappy with the weeds in their grass. Lewis River lost most of its customers, cut back its production from 275 acres to 45 acres, and destroyed all remaining sod grown from Scott's seeds. Eventually, Lewis River sold its business at a large loss. A jury awarded Lewis River $1,026,800, largely for lost profits. Scott appealed, claiming that a plaintiff may not recover for lost profits. Comment.

13. **ROLE REVERSAL:** Write a multiple-choice question that contrasts the common-law rules of contract formation with those of UCC §2-204.

# INTERNET RESEARCH PROBLEM

Online, find out which cars are safer than average. Which are less safe? How important is auto safety to you? Are you willing to pay more for a safe car? Who should be the final judge of auto safety: auto companies, insurance companies, juries, government regulators, or consumers?

**You can find further practice problems in the Online Quiz at www.cengage.com/blaw/beatty.**

# NEGOTIABLE INSTRUMENTS

**As a freshman** in college, Bemis was having lots of new experiences: For the first time in his life, he was living away from home and also had his own bank account and checkbook. He was discovering that being on his own offered new freedom, but it also imposed new responsibilities.

Bemis bought a combination refrigerator and microwave from a fellow selling them out on the sidewalk in front of the dorm. Since Bemis could not afford the entire $300 purchase price, he put down $100 in cash and signed a promissory note for the balance. When the microwave burst into flames, Bemis was relieved to think that at least he was only out $100. That was until Samantha showed up at his door demanding payment on the note. It turns out that the seller had sold the note to Samantha and Bemis was liable to her for the full amount.

During fraternity rush week, Bemis pledged Freaks House. Late one night, the pledge captain threatened Bemis that if he did not write a substantial check

> **The pledge captain threatened Bemis that if he did not write a substantial check to the fraternity, he would be held down in a bathtub filled with ice water until his eyes popped.**

to the fraternity, he would be held down in a bathtub filled with ice water until his eyes popped. Bemis wrote the check. The next morning he went to the bank where he discovered, to his relief, that the check was not valid for two reasons: he was a minor, and he had signed the check under duress. Bemis is now a member of Geeks House.

Because Bemis's college distributed free iPods to all freshmen, he sold his old MP3 player to Vanessa. When she handed him the check, he glanced at it and saw "$50." What he failed to notice was that the *words* on the check said "five dollars." When Bemis took the check to the bank, he discovered that it was worth only five dollars because, when words and numbers disagree, it is the words that win.

## · COMMERCIAL PAPER ·

The law of commercial paper is important to anyone who writes checks or borrows money. Historically speaking, however, commercial paper is a relatively new development. In early human history, people lived on whatever they could hunt, grow, or make for themselves. Imagine what your life would be like if you had to subsist only on what you could make yourself. Over time, people improved their standard of living by bartering for goods and services they could not make themselves. But traders needed a method for keeping account of who owed how much to whom. That was the role of currency. Many items have been used for currency over the years, including silver, gold, copper, and cowrie shells. These currencies have two disadvantages—they are easy to steal and difficult to carry.

Paper currency weighs less than gold or silver, but it is even easier to steal. As a result, money had to be kept in a safe place, and banks developed to meet that need. However, money in a vault is not very useful unless it can be readily spent. Society needed a system for transferring paper funds easily. Commercial paper is that system. Electronic alternatives may ultimately dominate the marketplace, but for now paper is still king.

## · TYPES OF NEGOTIABLE INSTRUMENTS ·

There are two kinds of commercial paper: negotiable and non-negotiable instruments. Article 3 of the Uniform Commercial Code (UCC) covers only negotiable instruments; non-negotiable instruments are governed by ordinary contract law. There are also two categories of negotiable instruments: notes and drafts.

A **note** (also called a **promissory note**) is your promise that you will pay money. A promissory note is used in virtually every loan transaction, whether the borrower is buying a multimillion

**Promissory note**
The maker of the instrument promises to pay a specific amount of money.

dollar company or a TV set. For example, when you borrow money from Aunt Leila to buy a car, you will sign a note promising to repay the money. You are the **maker** because you are the one who has made the promise. Aunt Leila is the **payee** because she expects to be paid.

**Maker**
The issuer of a promissory note.

**Payee**
Someone who is owed money under the terms of an instrument.

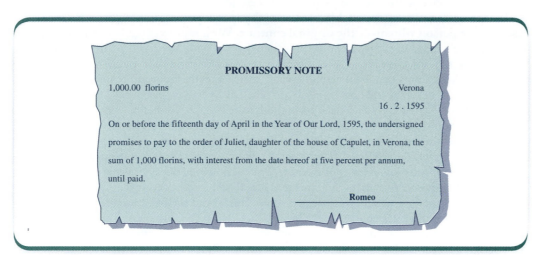

PROMISSORY NOTE

1,000.00 florins                                                  Verona

                                                      16 . 2 . 1595

On or before the fifteenth day of April in the Year of Our Lord, 1595, the undersigned

promises to pay to the order of Juliet, daughter of the house of Capulet, in Verona, the

sum of 1,000 florins, with interest from the date hereof at five percent per annum,

until paid.

                                                      Romeo

In this note, Romeo is the maker and Juliet is the payee.

A **draft** is an order directing someone else to pay money for you. A **check** is the most common form of a draft—it is an order telling a bank to pay money. In a draft, three people are involved: the **drawer** orders the **drawee** to pay money to the payee. Now before you slam the book shut in despair, let us sort out the players. Suppose that Maria Sharapova wins the River Oaks Club Open. River Oaks writes her a check for $500,000. This check is simply an order by River Oaks (the drawer) to its bank (the drawee) to pay money to Sharapova (the payee). The terms make sense if you remember that, when you take money out of your account, you *draw* it out. Therefore, when you write a check, you are the draw*er* and the bank is the draw*ee*. The person to whom you make out the check is being paid, so she is called the pay*ee*.

The following table illustrates the difference between notes and drafts. Even courts sometimes confuse the terms *drawer* (the person who signs a check) and *maker* (someone who signs a promissory note). **Issuer** is an all-purpose term that means both maker and drawer.

**Draft**
The drawer of this instrument orders someone else to pay money.

**Check**
An instrument in which the drawer orders the drawee bank to pay money to the payee.

**Drawer**
The person who issues a draft.

**Drawee**
The person who pays a draft. In the case of a check, the bank is the drawee.

**Issuer**
The maker of a promissory note or the drawer of a draft.

|       | Who Pays                             | Who Plays                                              |
|-------|--------------------------------------|-------------------------------------------------------|
| Note  | You make a promise that you will pay.| Two people are involved: maker and payee.             |
| Draft | You order someone else to pay.       | Three people are involved: drawer, drawee, and payee. |

## THE FUNDAMENTAL "RULE" OF COMMERCIAL PAPER

The possessor of a piece of commercial paper has an unconditional right to be paid, as long as (1) the paper is *negotiable*; (2) it has been *negotiated* to the possessor; (3) the possessor is a *holder in due course*; and (4) the issuer cannot claim a valid defense.

# Negotiability

To work as a substitute for money, commercial paper must be freely transferable in the market-place, just as money is. In other words, it must be *negotiable*.

**The possessor of *non*-negotiable commercial paper has the same rights—no more, no less—as the person who made the original contract.** With non-negotiable commercial paper, the transferee's rights are *conditional* because they depend upon the rights of the original party to the contract. If, for some reason, the original party loses his right to be paid, so does the transferee. The value of non-negotiable commercial paper is greatly reduced because the transferee cannot be absolutely sure what his rights are or whether he will be paid at all.

Suppose that Krystal buys a used car from the Trustie Car Lot for her business, Krystal Rocks. She cannot afford to pay the full $15,000 right now, but she is willing to sign a note promising to pay later. As long as Trustie keeps the note, Krystal's obligation to pay is contingent upon the validity of the underlying contract. If, for example, the car is defective, then Krystal might not be liable to Trustie for the full amount of the note. Trustie, however, does not want to keep the note. He needs the cash *now* so that he can buy more cars to sell to other customers. Reggie's Finance Co. is happy to buy Krystal's promissory note from Trustie, but the price Reggie is willing to pay depends upon whether her note is negotiable.

If Krystal's promissory note is non-negotiable, Reggie gets exactly the same rights that Trustie had. As the saying goes, he steps into Trustie's shoes. Suppose that Trustie tampered with the odometer and, as a result, Krystal's car is worth only $12,000. If, under contract law, she owes Trustie only $12,000, then that is all she has to pay Reggie, even though the note *says* $15,000.

**The possessor of *negotiable* commercial paper has *more* rights than the person who made the original contract.** With negotiable commercial paper, the transferee's rights are *unconditional.* He is entitled to be paid the full amount of the note, regardless of the relationship between the original parties. If Krystal's promissory note is a negotiable instrument, she must pay the full amount to whoever has possession of it, no matter what complaints she might have against Trustie.

Exhibit 13.1 illustrates the difference between negotiable and non-negotiable commercial paper.

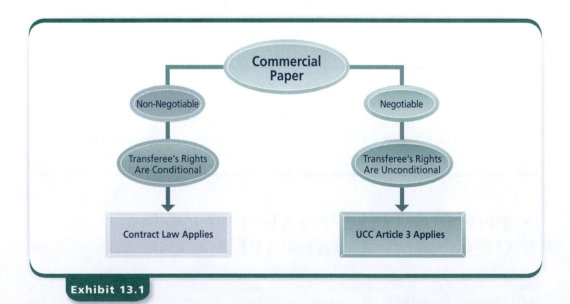

**Exhibit 13.1**

Because negotiable instruments are more valuable than non-negotiable ones, it is important for buyers and sellers to be able to tell, easily and accurately, if an instrument is indeed negotiable. To be negotiable:

1. **The instrument must be in *writing*.**

2. **The instrument must be *signed* by the maker or drawer.**

3. **The instrument must contain an *unconditional promise* or *order to pay*.** If Krystal's promissory note says, "I will pay $15,000 as long as the car is still in working order," it is not negotiable because it is making a conditional promise. The instrument must also contain a promise or order to pay. It is not enough simply to say, "Krystal owes Trustie $15,000." She has to indicate that she owes the money and also that she intends to pay it. "Krystal promises to pay Trustie $15,000" would work.

4. **The instrument must state a *definite amount* of money which is clear "within its four corners."** "I promise to pay Trustie one-third of my profits this year" would not work, because the amount is unclear. If Krystal's note says, "I promise to pay $15,000 worth of diamonds," it is not negotiable because it does not state a definite amount of *money*.

5. **The instrument must be payable on *demand* or at a *definite time*.** A demand instrument is one that must be paid whenever the holder requests payment. If an instrument is undated, it is treated as a demand instrument and is negotiable. An instrument can be negotiable even if it will not be paid until some time in the future, provided that the payment date can be determined when the document is made. A graduate of a well-known prep school wrote a generous check to his alma mater, but for payment date he put, "The day the headmaster is fired." This check is not negotiable because it is payable neither on demand nor at a definite time.

6. **The instrument must be payable to *order* or to *bearer*. Order paper** must include the words "Pay to the order of" someone. By including the word "order," the maker is indicating that the instrument is not limited to only one person. "Pay to the order of Trustie Car Lot" means that the money will be paid to Trustie *or to anyone Trustie designates*. If the note is made out "To bearer," it is **bearer paper** and can be redeemed by *any* holder in due course.

The rules for checks are different from other negotiable instruments. If properly filled out, checks are negotiable. And sometimes they are negotiable even if not filled out correctly. Most checks are preprinted with the words "Pay to the order of," but sometimes people inadvertently cross out "order of." Even so, the check is still negotiable. Checks are frequently received by consumers who, sadly, have not completed a course on business law. The drafters of the UCC did not think it fair to penalize them when the drawer of the check was the one who made the mistake.

**Order paper**
An instrument that includes the words "pay to the order of" or their equivalent.

**Bearer paper**
An instrument payable "to bearer."

## EXAM *Strategy*

**Question:** Sam had a checking account at Piggy Bank. Piggy sent him special checks that he could use to draw down a line of credit. When Sam used these checks, Piggy did not take money out of his account; instead the bank treated the checks as loans and charged him interest. Piggy then sold these used checks to Wolfe. Were the checks negotiable instruments?

**Strategy:** When faced with a question about negotiability, begin by looking at the list of six requirements. In this case, there is no reason to doubt that the checks are in writing, signed by the issuer, and with an unconditional promise to pay to order at a definite time. But do the checks state a definite amount of money? Can the holder "look at the four corners of the check" and determine how much Sam owes?

**Result:** Sam was supposed to pay Piggy the face amount of the check plus interest. Wolfe does not know the amount of the interest unless he reads the loan agreement. Therefore, the checks are not negotiable.

## Interpretation of Ambiguities

Perhaps you have noticed that people sometimes make mistakes. Although the UCC establishes simple and precise rules for creating negotiable instruments, people do not always follow these rules to the letter. It might be tempting simply to invalidate defective documents (after all, money is at stake here). But instead, the UCC favors negotiability and has rules to resolve uncertainty and supply missing terms.

Notice anything odd about the check pictured here? Is it for $1,500 or $15,000? When the terms in a negotiable instrument contradict each other, three rules apply:

- Words take precedence over numbers.
- Handwritten terms prevail over typed and printed terms.
- Typed terms win over printed terms.

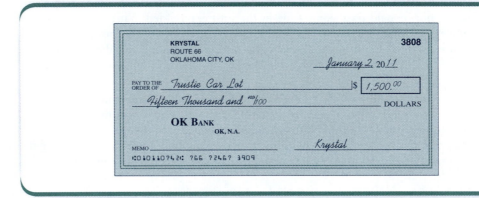

According to these rules, Krystal's check is for $15,000 because, in a conflict between words and numbers, words win.

In the following case, the amount of the check was not completely clear. Was it a negotiable instrument?

# YOU *be the* JUDGE

### BLASCO v. MONEY SERVICES CENTER

2006 Bankr. LEXIS 2899
United States Bankruptcy Court for the Northern District of Alabama, 2006

**Facts:** Christina Blasco ran out of money. She went to the Money Services Center (MSC) and borrowed $500. To repay the loan, she gave MSC a check for $587.50, which it promised not to cash for two weeks. This kind of transaction is called a "payday loan" because it is made to someone who needs money to tide them over until the next paycheck.

(Note that in this case, Blasco was paying 17.5 percent interest for a two-week loan, which is an annual compounded interest rate of 6,500 percent. This is the dark side of payday loans—interest rates are often exorbitant.)

Before MSC could cash the check, Blasco filed for bankruptcy protection. Although MSC knew about Blasco's filing,

*continued*

it deposited the check. It is illegal for creditors to collect debts after a bankruptcy filing, except that creditors are entitled to payment on negotiable instruments.

Ordinarily checks are negotiable instruments, but only if they are for a definite amount. This check had a wrinkle: the numerical amount of the check was $587.50 but the amount in words was written as "five eighty-seven and 50/100 dollars." Did the words mean "five hundred eighty-seven" or "five thousand eighty-seven" or perhaps "five million eighty-seven"? Was the check negotiable despite this ambiguity?

**You Be the Judge:** **Was this check a negotiable instrument? Was it for a definite amount?**

**Argument for Blasco:** For a check to be negotiable, two rules apply:

1. The check must state a definite amount of money, which is clear within its four corners.

2. If there is a contradiction between the words and numbers, words take precedence over numbers.

Words prevail over numbers, which means that the check is for "five eighty-seven and 50/100 dollars." This amount is not definite. A holder cannot be sure of the precise amount of the check. Therefore the check is not a negotiable instrument, and MSC had no right to submit it for payment.

**Argument for MSC:** Blasco is right about the two rules. However, she is wrong in their interpretation. If there is a contradiction between the words and numbers, words take precedence over numbers. In this case, there was no contradiction. The words were ambiguous, but they did not contradict the numbers. If the words had said "five thousand eighty-seven," that would have been a contradiction. Instead, the numbers simply clarified the words. Even someone who was a stranger to this transaction could safely figure out the amount of the check. Therefore, it is negotiable and MSC is not liable.

## NEGOTIATION

**Negotiation** means that an instrument has been transferred to the holder by someone *other than the issuer*. If the issuer has transferred the instrument to the holder, then it has not been negotiated and the issuer can refuse to pay the holder if there was some flaw in the underlying contract. Thus, if Jake gives Madison a promissory note for $2,000 in payment for a new computer, but the computer crashes and burns the first week, Jake has the right to refuse to pay the note. Jake was the issuer and the note was not negotiated. But if, before the computer self-destructs, Madison indorses and transfers the note to Kayla, then Jake is liable to Kayla for the full amount of the note, regardless of his claims against Madison.

**To be negotiated, order paper must first be** *indorsed* **and then** *delivered* **to the transferee. Bearer paper must simply be** *delivered* **to the transferee; no indorsement is required.**[1]

An **indorsement** is the signature of the payee. Tess writes a rent check for $475 to her landlord, Larnell. If Larnell signs the back of the check and delivers it to Patty, he has met the two requirements for negotiating order paper: indorsement and delivery. If Larnell delivers the check to Patty but forgets to sign it, the check has not been indorsed and therefore cannot be negotiated—it has no value to Patty.

> **If the computer crashes and burns the first week, Jake has the right to refuse to pay the note.**

**Negotiation**
means that an instrument has been transferred to the holder by someone other than the issuer.

**Indorsement**
The signature of the payee.

**EXAM** *Strategy*

**Question:** Antoine makes a check out to cash and delivers it to Barley. He writes on the back, "Pay to the order of Charlotte." She signs her name. Is this check bearer paper or order paper? Has it been negotiated?

---

[1] §3-201. The UCC spells the word "indorsed." Outside the UCC, the word is more commonly spelled "endorsed."

**Strategy:** Whenever a negotiable instrument is transferred, it is important to ask if the instrument has been properly negotiated. To be negotiated, order paper must be indorsed and delivered; bearer paper need only be delivered, but in both cases by someone other than the issuer.

**Result:** This check changes back and forth between order and bearer paper, depending on what the indorsement says. When Antoine makes out a check to cash, it is bearer paper. When he gives it to Barley, it is not negotiated because he is the issuer. When Barley writes on the back "Pay to the order of Charlotte," it becomes order paper. When he gives it to Charlotte, it is properly negotiated because he is not the issuer and he has both indorsed the check and transferred it to her. When she signs it, the check becomes bearer paper. And so on it could go forever.[2]

## HOLDER IN DUE COURSE

**A holder in due course has an automatic right to receive payment for a negotiable instrument (unless the issuer can claim a valid defense).** If the possessor of an instrument is not a holder in due course, then his right to payment depends upon the relationship between the issuer and payee. He inherits whatever claims and defenses arise out of that contract. Clearly, then, holder in due course status dramatically increases the value of an instrument because it enhances the probability of being paid.

### Requirements for Being a Holder in Due Course

Under §3-302 of the UCC, **a holder in due course** is a *holder* who has given *value* for the instrument, in *good faith, without notice* of outstanding claims or other defects.

**Holder**    For order paper, a **holder** is anyone in possession of the instrument if it is payable to or indorsed to her. For bearer paper, a holder is anyone in possession. Tristesse gives Felix a check payable to him. Because Felix owes his mother money, he indorses the check and delivers it to her. This is a valid negotiation because Felix has both indorsed the check (which is order paper) and delivered it. Therefore, Felix's mother is a holder.

**Value**    A holder in due course must give value for an instrument. **Value** means that the holder has *already* done something in exchange for the instrument. Felix's mother has already loaned him money, so she has given value.

**Good Faith**    There are two tests to determine if a holder acquired an instrument in good faith. The holder must meet *both* these tests:

- **Subjective Test.** Did the holder *believe* the transaction was honest in fact?
- **Objective Test.** Did the transaction *appear* to be commercially reasonable?

Felix persuades his elderly neighbor, Faith, that he has invented a fabulous beauty cream guaranteed to remove wrinkles. She gives him a $10,000 promissory note, payable in 90 days, in return for exclusive sales rights in Pittsburgh. Felix sells the note to his old friend Griffin for $2,000. Felix never delivers the sales samples to Faith. When Griffin presents the note to Faith, she refuses to pay on the grounds that Griffin is not a holder in due course. She contends that he did not buy the note in good faith.

Griffin fails both tests. Any friend of Felix knows he is not trustworthy, especially when presenting a promissory note signed by an elderly neighbor. Griffin did not believe the transaction was honest in fact. Also, $10,000 notes are not usually discounted to $2,000; $9,000 would be more normal. This transaction is not commercially reasonable, and Griffin should have realized immediately that Felix was up to no good.

---

**Holder in due course**
Someone who has given value for an instrument, in good faith, without notice of outstanding claims or other defenses.

**Holder**
For order paper, anyone in possession of the instrument if it is payable to or indorsed to her. For bearer paper, anyone in possession.

**Value**
The holder has *already* done something in exchange for the instrument.

---

[2] Even when all the space on the back of the check is filled, the holder can attach a separate paper for indorsements, called an **allonge.**

**Notice of Outstanding Claims or Other Defects**   In certain circumstances, a holder is on notice that an instrument has an outstanding claim or other defect:

1.  **The instrument is overdue.** An instrument is overdue the day after its due date. At that point, the recipient ought to wonder why no one has bothered to collect the money owed. A check is overdue 90 days after its date. Any other demand instrument is overdue (1) the day after a request for payment is made or (2) a reasonable time after the instrument was issued.

2.  **The instrument is dishonored.** To dishonor an instrument is to refuse to pay it. For example, once a check has been stamped "Insufficient Funds" by the bank, it has been dishonored, and no one who obtains it afterward can be a holder in due course.

3.  **The instrument is altered, forged, or incomplete.** Anyone who knows that an instrument has been altered or forged cannot be a holder in due course. Suppose Joe wrote a check to Tony for $200. While showing the check to Liza, Tony cackles to himself and says, "Can you believe what that goof did? Look, he left the line blank after the words 'two hundred.'" Taking his pen out with a flourish, Tony changes the zeroes to nines and adds the words "ninety-nine." He then indorses the check over to Liza, who is definitely not a holder in due course.

4.  **The holder has notice of certain claims or disputes.** No one can qualify as a holder in due course if she is on notice that (1) someone else has a claim to the instrument or (2) there is a dispute between the original parties to the instrument. Matt hires Sheila to put aluminum siding on his house. In payment, he gives her a $15,000 promissory note with the due date left blank. They agree that the note will not be due until 60 days after completion of the work. Despite the agreement, Sheila fills in the date immediately and sells the note to Rupert at American Finance Corp., who has bought many similar notes from Sheila. Rupert knows that the note is not supposed to be due until after the work is finished. Usually, before he buys a note from her, he demands a signed document from the home owner certifying that the work is complete. Also, he lives near Matt and can see that Matt's house is only half finished. Rupert is not a holder in due course because he has reason to suspect there is a dispute between Sheila and Matt.

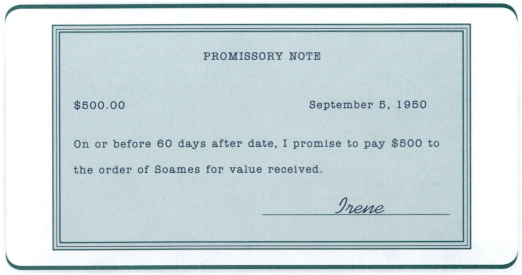

The holder of this note should realize that there may be a problem.

## Defenses against a Holder in Due Course

Negotiable instruments are meant to be a close substitute for money, and, as a general rule, holders expect to be paid. **However, the issuer of a negotiable instrument is not required to pay if:**

1.  His signature on the instrument was forged.

2.  After signing the instrument, his debts were discharged in bankruptcy.

3. He was a minor at the time he signed the instrument.

4. The amount of the instrument was altered after he signed it. (Although, if he left the instrument blank, he is liable for any amounts later filled in.)

5. He signed the instrument under duress, while mentally incapacitated, or as part of an illegal transaction.

6. He was tricked into signing the instrument without knowing what it was and without any reasonable way to find out.

## CONSUMER EXCEPTION

In the eighteenth and nineteenth centuries, negotiable instruments often circulated through several hands. The business community treated them as money. The concept of holder in due course was essential because the instruments had little use if they could not be transferred for value. In the modern banking system, however, instruments are much less likely to circulate. Currently, the most common use for negotiable instruments is in consumer transactions. A consumer pays for a refrigerator by giving the store a promissory note. The store promptly sells the note to a finance company. Even if the refrigerator is defective, under Article 3 the consumer must pay full value on the note because the finance company is a holder in due course.

Some commentators have argued that the concept of holder in due course no longer serves a useful purpose and that it should be eliminated once and for all (and with it Article 3 of the UCC). No state has yet taken such a dramatic step. Instead, some states require promissory notes given by a consumer to carry the words "consumer paper." Notes with this legend are non-negotiable.

**Consumer credit contract**
A contract in which a consumer borrows money from a lender to purchase goods and services from a seller who is affiliated with the lender.

Meanwhile, the Federal Trade Commission (FTC) has special rules for consumer credit contracts. A **consumer credit contract** is one in which a consumer borrows money from a lender to purchase goods and services from a seller who is affiliated with the lender. If Sears loans money to Gerald to buy a high-definition TV at Sears, that is a consumer credit contract. It is not a consumer credit contract if Gerald borrows money from his cousin Vinnie to buy the TV from Sears. The FTC requires all promissory notes in consumer credit contracts to contain the following language:

NOTICE
ANY HOLDER OF THIS CONSUMER CREDIT CONTRACT IS SUBJECT TO ALL CLAIMS AND DEFENSES WHICH THE DEBTOR COULD ASSERT AGAINST THE SELLER OF GOODS OR SERVICES OBTAINED WITH THE PROCEEDS HEREOF.

Under §3-106(d) of the UCC, no one can be a holder in due course of an instrument with this language. If the language is omitted from a consumer note, it is possible to be a holder in due course, but the seller is subject to a fine.

In the following case, the plaintiff borrowed money from Sterling to pay Mayflower. The FTC rule applied because the two companies were "affiliated."

## SCOTT v. MAYFLOWER HOME IMPROVEMENT CORP.

363 N.J. Super. 145; 831 A.2d 564; 2001 N.J. Super. LEXIS 524
Superior Court of New Jersey, 2001

### CASE SUMMARY

**Facts:** Mary Johnson signed a contract with Mayflower Home Improvement Corporation for repair work on her home. The contract specified a fee of $25,900. Later, Mayflower arranged for Johnson to pay for this work by borrowing money from

Sterling Resources. In the note she signed with Sterling, the price was unconscionably high—$50,108.60—and so was the interest rate—17.98 percent.

Johnson alleges that Mayflower was running a scam. It hired unlicensed salespeople who targeted minority neighborhoods. The contracts prepared by the salespeople specified the work in general terms but omitted the name, make, quality, and model of the products and materials to be used. The contracts did not specify the interest rate or the total cost. The contractor's work was done in a shoddy or incomplete manner often using poor-quality materials.

Sterling routinely loaned money to Mayflower customers. The interest rates on these loans were between 15 percent and 19 percent. Sterling then sold the loans to banks and other financial institutions (the Lender).

When Johnson failed to make the payments due on the note, the Lender sued her. It moved for summary judgment against Johnson on the grounds that, as a holder in due course, it was entitled to enforce the note regardless of her claims against Mayflower or Sterling. She responded that, under the FTC consumer exception rule, the Lender was not a holder in due course. Therefore, the Lender was subject to whatever defenses she had against Sterling or Mayflower.

**Issue:** *Was the Lender a holder in due course?*

**Decision:** No, the Lender was not a holder in due course.

**Reasoning:** Before the FTC adopted its Holder Rule, unethical merchants used the Holder in Due Course doctrine to victimize thousands of innocent consumers. They sold shoddy furniture, defective aluminum siding, and cars that were lemons. The defrauded consumer paid with a note that the merchants immediately sold. Even after discovering the fraud, the consumer still had to pay the note when a holder in due course presented it. But, under the FTC Holder Rule, the holder of a consumer note must step into the shoes of the seller. If the seller has no right to be paid, then neither does any subsequent holder. A lender who is offered a consumer note with the FTC Holder notice should either refuse to buy it or should purchase insurance against any losses if the note turns out to be unenforceable.

In this case, the FTC Holder notice was conspicuously printed on Mary Johnson's note. As a result, all holders knew that the FTC Holder Rule applied.

## CHAPTER CONCLUSION

**Commercial paper provides essential grease to the wheels of commerce.** We could scarcely imagine our lives without it. It is worth remembering, however, that the terms of the UCC are precise and that failure to comply with these exacting provisions can lead to unfortunate consequences. In some ways, the UCC is like a marine drill instructor: rigid, but predictable if you follow the rules.

## EXAM REVIEW

1. **NEGOTIABILITY** The possessor of non-negotiable commercial paper has the same rights—no more, no less—as the person who made the original contract. The possessor of negotiable commercial paper has more rights than the person who made the original contract. (p. 214)

2. **THE FUNDAMENTAL RULE OF COMMERCIAL PAPER** The possessor of a piece of commercial paper has an unconditional right to be paid, as long as:
   - The paper is negotiable;
   - It has been negotiated to the possessor;
   - The possessor is a holder in due course; and
   - The issuer cannot claim a valid defense. (p. 213)

**3.** **REQUIREMENTS FOR NEGOTIABILITY** To be negotiable, an instrument must:
- Be in writing;
- Be signed by the maker or drawer;
- Contain an unconditional promise or order to pay;
- State a definite amount of money which is clear "within its four corners";
- Be payable on demand or at a definite time; and
- Be payable to order or to bearer. (p. 215)

**4.** **AMBIGUITY** When the terms in a negotiable instrument contradict each other, three rules apply:
- Words take precedence over numbers.
- Handwritten terms prevail over typed and printed terms.
- Typed terms win over printed terms. (p. 216)

**5.** **NEGOTIATION** To be negotiated, order paper must first be indorsed and then delivered to the transferee. Bearer paper must simply be delivered to the transferee; no indorsement is required. (p. 217)

**6.** **HOLDER IN DUE COURSE** A holder in due course is a holder who has given value for the instrument, in good faith, without notice of outstanding claims or other defects. (p. 218)

**EXAM Strategy**

**Question:** After Irene Nusor fell behind on her mortgage payments, she answered an advertisement from Best Financial Consultants offering attractive refinancing opportunities. During a meeting at a McDonald's restaurant, a Best representative told her that the company would arrange for a complete refinancing of her home, pay off two of her creditors, and give her an additional $5,000 in spending money. Nusor would only have to pay Best $4,000. Nusor signed a blank promissory note that was filled in later by Best representatives for $14,986.61. Best did not fulfill its promises to Nusor, but within two weeks, it sold the note to Robin Parkhill for just under $14,000. Nusor refused to pay the note, alleging that Parkhill was not a holder in due course. Is Nusor liable to Parkhill?

**Strategy:** Whenever a question asks if someone is a holder in due course, begin by reviewing the requirements for being a holder in due course. Is this person a *holder* who has given *value* for the instrument, in *good faith, without notice* of outstanding claims or other defects? (See the "Result" at the end of this section.)

**7.** **DEFENSES** The issuer of a negotiable instrument is not required to pay if:
- His signature was forged.
- After signing the instrument, his debts were discharged in bankruptcy.
- He was a minor at the time he signed the instrument.
- The amount of the instrument was altered after he signed it.
- He signed the instrument under duress, while mentally incapacitated, or as part of an illegal transaction.
- He was tricked into signing the instrument without knowing what it was and without any reasonable way to find out. (p. 219)

8.  **CONSUMER EXCEPTION** The Federal Trade Commission requires all promissory notes in consumer credit contracts to contain language preventing any subsequent holder from being a holder in due course. (p. 220)

**Question:** Gina and Douglas Felde purchased a Chrysler car with a 70,000-mile warranty. They signed a loan contract with the dealer to pay for the car in monthly installments. The dealer sold the contract to the Chrysler Credit Corp. Soon, the car developed a tendency to accelerate abruptly and without warning. Two Chrysler dealers were unable to correct the problem. The Feldes filed suit against Chrysler Credit Corp., but the company refused to rescind the loan contract. The company argued that, as a holder in due course on the note, it was entitled to be paid regardless of any defects in the car. How would you decide this case if you were the judge?

**Strategy:** Whenever consumers are involved, consider the possibility that there is a consumer credit contract. The plaintiffs in this case are consumers who have borrowed money from a lender to purchase goods from a seller who is affiliated with the lender (both seller and lender are owned by Chrysler). Thus the contract is a consumer credit contract. (See the "Result" at the end of this section.)

**6. Result:** In this case, Parkhill is a holder who has given value. Did she act in good faith? We don't know if she actually *believed* the transaction was honest, but the court held that the transaction did not *appear* to be commercially reasonable because Parkhill's profit was so high. Thus, Parkhill was not a holder in due course and Nusor was not liable to her.

**8. Result:** Chrysler Credit was not a holder in due course. Therefore, it is subject to any defenses the Feldes might have against the dealer, including that the car was defective.

# PRACTICE EXAM

## MATCHING QUESTIONS

Match the following terms with their definitions:

___ A. Note
___ B. Check
___ C. Draft
___ D. Order paper
___ E. Bearer paper

1. An instrument that is not made out to any specific person
2. An order to someone else to pay money
3. An instrument with the words "pay to the order of"
4. A promise to pay money
5. An order to a bank to pay money

## TRUE/FALSE QUESTIONS

Circle true or false:

1. T  F  The possessor of a piece of commercial paper always has an unconditional right to be paid.

2. T  F  Three parties are involved in a draft.

3. T  F  To be negotiable, bearer paper must be indorsed and delivered to the transferee.

4. T  F  Negotiation means that an instrument has been transferred to the holder by the issuer.

5. T  F  A promissory note may be valid even if it does not have a specific due date.

## MULTIPLE-CHOICE QUESTIONS

**6.** CPA QUESTION: In order to negotiate bearer paper, one must:

A. Indorse the paper

B. Indorse and deliver the paper with consideration

C. Deliver the paper

D. Deliver and indorse the paper

**7.** The possessor of a piece of order paper does not have an unconditional right to be paid if:

A. The paper is negotiable.

B. The possessor is the payee.

C. The paper has been indorsed to the possessor.

D. The possessor is a holder in due course.

E. The issuer changed his mind after signing the instrument.

**8.** An instrument is negotiable unless:

A. It is in writing.

B. It is signed only by the drawee.

C. It contains an order to pay.

D. It is payable on demand.

E. It is payable only to bearer.

**9.** Chloe buys a motorcycle on eBay from Junior. In payment she gives him a promissory note for $7,000. He immediately negotiates the note to Terry. After the motorcycle arrives, Chloe discovers that it is not as advertised. One week later, she notifies Junior. She still has to pay Terry because:

A. On eBay, the rule is "buyer beware."

B. Terry's rights are not affected by Junior's misdeeds.

C. Terry indorsed the note.

D. Chloe is the drawee.

E. Chloe waited too long to complain.

**10.** Donna gives a promissory note to C. J. Which of the following errors would make the note invalid?

A. The instrument was written on a dirty sock.

B. The instrument promised to pay 15,000 euros.

C. The note stated that Donna owed C. J. "$1,500: One thousand and five dollars."

D. Donna signed the note without reading it.

E. The due date was specified as "three months after Donna graduates from college."

## SHORT-ANSWER QUESTIONS

**11.** Shelby wrote the check shown below to Dana. When is it payable and for how much?

**12.** In the prior question, who are the drawer, drawee, and payee of this check?

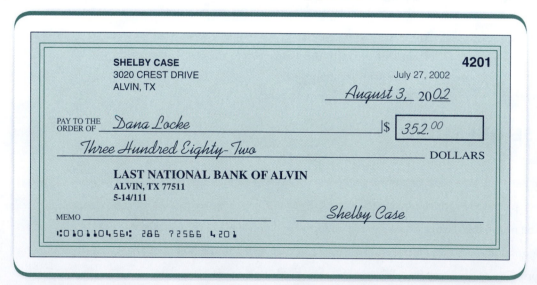

13. Giggle, Inc. writes a check to Computer Co. to pay for a truckload of hard drives. The next day, Giggle discovers that all the boxes on the truck are filled with bricks. The company asks its bank to stop payment on the check. In the meantime, Computer has indorsed the check to Cosmo to pay him for the food he provided for Computer's annual holiday party . Does Giggle have to pay Cosmo?

14. Catherine Wagner suffered serious physical injuries in an automobile accident and became acutely depressed as a result. One morning, she received a check for $17,400 in settlement of her claims arising out of the accident. She indorsed the check and placed it on the kitchen table. She then called Robert Scherer, her long-time roommate, to tell him the check had arrived. That afternoon, she jumped from the roof of her apartment building, killing herself. The police found the check and a note from her, stating that she was giving it to Scherer. Had Wagner negotiated the check to Scherer?

15. ROLE REVERSAL: Write a multiple-choice question that raises the issue of an instrument's negotiability.

# INTERNET RESEARCH PROBLEM

Go to http://www.legaldocs.com (or an equivalent site) and fill in the blanks of a promissory note. Who is the maker and who is the payee of your note? Did you create a demand note?

You can find further practice problems in the Online Quiz at www.cengage.com/blaw/beatty.

# Secured Transactions

### Dear Help-for-All:

Somebody must be crazy. When I got out of school, I paid $18,000 for a used Lexus. I made every payment for over two years. I shelled out over 9,000 bucks for that car.

Then I got laid off through no fault of my own. I missed a few payments, and the bank repossessed the car. They auctioned off the Lexus. Now the bank's lawyer phones and says I'm still liable for over $5,000. They take my car away, they sell it—and still I owe money?

Signed,

Still Sane, I Hope

> **They take my car away, they sell it—and still I owe money?**

Dear Still Sane,

I am sympathetic, but unfortunately the bank is entitled to its money. When you bought the car, you signed two documents: a note, in which you promised to pay the full balance owed, and a security agreement, which said that if you stopped making payments, the bank could repossess the vehicle and sell it.

There are two problems. First, even after two years of writing checks, you might still have owed about $10,000 (because of interest). Second, cars depreciate quickly. Your $18,000 vehicle probably had a market value of about $8,000 30 months later. The security agreement allowed the bank to sell the Lexus at auction, where prices are still lower. Your car evidently fetched about $5,000. That leaves a deficiency of $5,000—for which you are legally responsible, regardless of who is driving the car.

Sorry,

Help-for-Almost-All

## · SECURED TRANSACTIONS ·

We can sympathize with "Still Sane," but the bank is entitled to its money. The buyer and the bank had entered into a secured transaction, meaning that one party gave credit to another, insisting on full repayment and the right to seize certain property if the debt went unpaid. It is essential to understand the basics of this law, because we live and work in a world economy based solidly—or shakily—on credit.

Article 9 of the Uniform Commercial Code (UCC) governs secured transactions in personal property. Article 9 employs terms not used elsewhere, so we must lead off with some definitions:

- **Fixtures** are goods that have become attached to real estate. For example, heating ducts are goods when a company manufactures them, but they become fixtures when installed in a house.
- **Security interest** means an interest in personal property or fixtures that secures the performance of some obligation. If an automobile dealer sells you a new car on credit and retains a security interest, it means she is keeping legal rights in your car, including the right to drive it away if you fall behind in your payments.
- **Secured party** is the person or company that holds the security interest. The automobile dealer who sells you a car on credit is the secured party.
- **Collateral** is the property subject to a security interest. When a dealer sells you a new car and keeps a security interest, the vehicle is the collateral.
- **Debtor** For our purposes, debtor refers to a person who has some original ownership interest in the collateral. If Alice borrows money from a bank and uses her Mercedes as collateral, she is the debtor because she owns the car.
- **Security agreement** is the contract in which the debtor gives a security interest to the secured party. This agreement protects the secured party's rights in the collateral.
- **Perfection** is a series of steps the secured party must take to protect its rights in the collateral against people other than the debtor.
- **Financing statement** is a record intended to notify the general public that the secured party has a security interest in the collateral.

**Fixtures**
Goods that have become attached to real estate.

**Security interest**
An interest in personal property or fixtures that secures the performance of an obligation.

**Secured party**
A person or company that holds a security interest.

**Collateral**
Property that is subject to a security interest.

**Debtor**
A person who has original ownership interest in the collateral.

**Security agreement**
A contract in which the debtor gives a security interest to the secured party.

**Perfection**
A series of steps the secured party must take to protect its rights in the collateral against people other than the debtor.

**Financing statement**
A document that the secured party files to give the general public notice that it has a secured interest in the collateral.

**Record**
Information written on paper or stored in an electronic or other medium.

**Authenticate**
To sign a document or to use any symbol or encryption method that identifies the person and clearly indicates she is adopting the record as her own.

- **Record** refers to information written on paper or stored in an electronic or other medium.
- **Authenticate** means to sign a document or to use any symbol or encryption method that identifies the person and clearly indicates she is adopting the record as her own. You authenticate a security agreement when you sign the papers at an auto dealership. A company may authenticate by using the Internet to transmit an electronic signature.

Here is an example using the terms just discussed. A medical equipment company manufactures a CT scanner and sells it to a clinic for $2 million, taking $500,000 cash and the clinic's promise to pay the rest over five years. The clinic simultaneously authenticates a security agreement, giving the manufacturer a security interest in the CT scanner. The manufacturer then electronically files a financing statement in an appropriate state agency. This perfects the manufacturer's rights, meaning that its security interest in the CT scanner is now valid against all the world. Exhibit 14.1 illustrates this transaction.

If the clinic goes bankrupt and many creditors try to seize its assets, the manufacturer has first claim to the CT scanner. The clinic's bankruptcy is of great importance. When a debtor has money to pay all of its debts, there are no concerns about security interests. A creditor insists on a security interest to protect itself in the event the debtor cannot pay all of its debts.

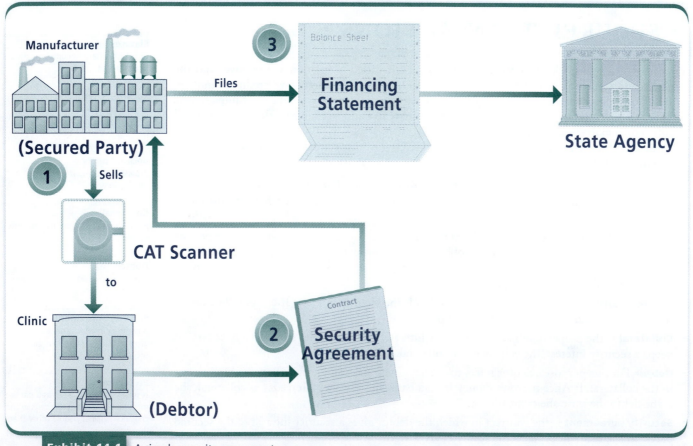

**Exhibit 14.1**   A simple security agreement:
(1) The manufacturer sells a CT scan machine to a clinic, taking $500,000 and the clinic's promise to pay the balance over five years.
(2) The clinic simultaneously authenticates a security agreement.
(3) The manufacturer perfects by electronically filing a financing statement.

# REVISED ARTICLE 9

The American Law Institute and the National Conference of Commissioners on Uniform State Laws rewrote Article 9 early in this millennium, and the revisions are now the law in all states. All citations in this chapter are to the revised Article 9. The Uniform Commercial Code is available online at **http://www.law.cornell.edu/ucc/ucc.table.html**.

Article 9 applies to any transaction intended to create a security interest in personal property or fixtures. The personal property that may be used as collateral includes:

- Goods, which are things that are movable.
- Inventory, meaning goods held by someone for sale or lease, such as all the beds and chairs in a furniture store.
- Instruments, such as drafts, checks, certificates of deposit, and notes.
- Investment property, which refers primarily to securities and related rights.
- Other property, including documents of title, accounts, general intangibles (copyrights, patents, goodwill, and so forth), and chattel paper (for example, a sales document indicating that a retailer has a security interest in goods sold to a consumer). Slightly different rules apply to some of these forms of property, but the details are less important than the general principles on which we shall focus.

Article 9 applies any time the parties intended to create a security interest in any of the items listed above.

## ᐧ ATTACHMENT OF A SECURITY INTEREST ᐧ

**Attachment** is a vital step in a secured transaction. This means that the secured party has taken three steps to create an enforceable security interest:

**Attachment**
A three-step process that creates an enforceable security interest.

- The two parties made a security agreement and either the debtor has authenticated a security agreement describing the collateral, or the secured party has obtained possession.
- The secured party has given value to obtain the security agreement; and
- The debtor has rights in the collateral.[1]

## AGREEMENT

Without an agreement, there can be no security interest. Generally, the agreement must be either written on paper and signed by the debtor, or electronically recorded and authenticated by the debtor. The agreement must reasonably identify the collateral. For example, a security agreement may properly describe the collateral as "all equipment in the store at 123 Periwinkle Street."

A security agreement at a minimum might:

- State that Happy Homes, Inc. and Martha agree that Martha is buying an Arctic Co. refrigerator, and identify the exact unit by its serial number.
- Give the price, the down payment, the monthly payments, and interest rate.

---

[1] UCC §9-203.

- State that because Happy Homes is selling Martha the refrigerator on credit, it has a security interest in the refrigerator; and
- Provide that if Martha defaults (fails to make payments when due), Happy Homes is entitled to repossess the refrigerator.

## POSSESSION

In certain cases, the security agreement need not be in writing if the parties have an oral agreement and the secured party has possession. For some kinds of collateral, for example stock certificates, it is safer for the secured party actually to take the item than to rely upon a security agreement.

### EXAM *Strategy*

**Question:** Hector needs money to keep his business afloat. He asks his uncle for a $1 million loan. The uncle agrees, but he insists that his nephew grant him a security interest in Hector's splendid gold clarinet, worth over $2 million. Hector agrees. The uncle prepares a handwritten document summarizing the agreement and asks his nephew to sign it. Hector hands the clarinet to his uncle and receives his money, but he forgets to sign the document. Has a security agreement attached?

**Strategy:** Attachment occurs if the parties made a security agreement and there was authentication or possession; the secured party has given value; and the debtor had rights in the collateral.

**Result:** Hector agreed to give his uncle a security interest in the instrument. He never authenticated (signed) the agreement, but the uncle did take possession of the clarinet. The uncle gave Hector $1 million, and Hector owned the instrument. Yes, the security interest attached.

## VALUE

For the security interest to attach, the secured party must give value. Usually, the value will be apparent. If a bank loans $400 million to an airline, that money is the value, and the bank may therefore obtain a security interest in the planes that the airline is buying.

## DEBTOR RIGHTS IN THE COLLATERAL

The debtor can only grant a security interest in goods if he has some legal right to those goods himself. Typically, the debtor owns the goods. But a debtor may also give a security interest if he is leasing the goods or even if he is a bailee, meaning that he is lawfully holding them for someone else.

### Result

Once the security interest has attached to the collateral, the secured party is protected against the debtor. If the debtor fails to pay, the secured party may repossess the collateral, meaning take it away.

## ATTACHMENT TO FUTURE PROPERTY

**After-acquired property**
Items that the debtor obtains after the parties have made their security agreement.

**After-acquired property** refers to items that the debtor obtains after the parties have made their security agreement. The parties may agree that the security interest attaches to after-acquired property. Basil is starting a catering business but owns only a beat-up car. He borrows $55,000 from the Pesto Bank, which takes a security interest in the car. But Pesto also insists on an after-acquired clause. When Basil purchases a commercial stove, cooking equipment, and freezer, Pesto's security interest attaches to each item as Basil acquires it.

A security agreement automatically applies to proceeds—whatever a debtor obtains who sells the collateral or otherwise disposes of it. The secured party obtains a security interest in the proceeds of the collateral, unless the security agreement states otherwise.[2]

## • PERFECTION •

### NOTHING LESS THAN PERFECTION

Once the security interest has attached to the collateral, the secured party is protected against the debtor. Pesto Bank loaned money to Basil and has a security interest in all of his property. If Basil defaults on his loan, Pesto may insist he deliver the goods to the bank. If he fails to do that, the bank can seize the collateral. But Pesto's security interest is valid only against Basil; if a third person claims some interest in the goods, the bank may never get them. For example, Basil might have taken out another loan, from his friend Olive, and used the same property as collateral. Olive knew nothing about the bank's original loan. To protect itself against Olive, and all other parties, the bank must perfect its interest.

There are several kinds of perfection, including:

- Perfection by filing.
- Perfection by possession.
- Perfection of consumer goods.

In some cases the secured party will have a choice of which method to use; in other cases only one method works.

### PERFECTION BY FILING

The most common way to perfect is by filing a financing statement with the appropriate state agency. A financing statement gives the names of all parties, describes the collateral, and outlines the security interest, enabling any interested person to learn about it. Suppose the Pesto Bank obtains a security interest in Basil's catering equipment and then perfects by filing with the secretary of state in the state capital. When Basil asks his friend Olive for a loan, she will check the records to see if anyone has a security interest in the catering equipment. Olive's search uncovers Basil's previous security agreement, and she realizes it would be unwise to make the loan. If Basil were to default, the collateral would go straight to Pesto Bank, leaving Olive empty-handed. See Exhibit 14.2.

Article 9 prescribes one form, to be used nationwide for financing statements. The financing form is available online at many websites. Remember that the filing may be done on paper or electronically.

The most common problems that arise in filing cases are (1) whether the financing statement contained enough information to put other people on notice of the security interest; and (2) whether the secured party filed the papers in the right place.

---

[2] UCC §9-204 and §9-203.

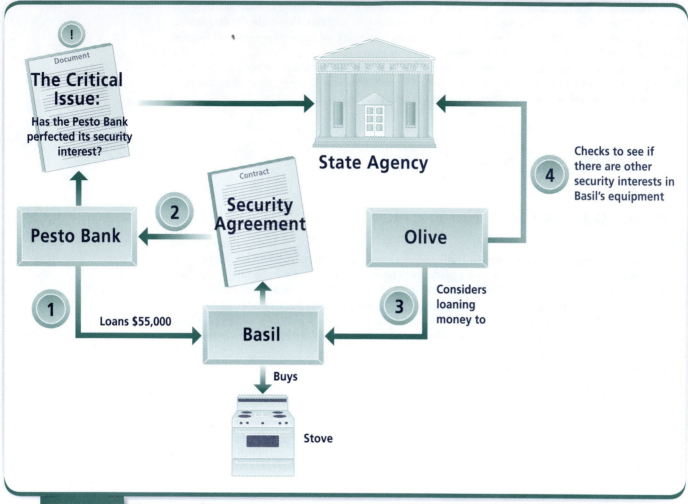

**State Agency**

**The Critical Issue:**

**Document**

Has the Pesto Bank perfected its security interest?

**Pesto Bank**

**2**

**Contract**

**Security Agreement**

**Olive**

**4** Checks to see if there are other security interests in Basil's equipment

**1**

**Loans $55,000**

**Basil**

**3** Considers loaning money to

**Buys**

**Stove**

**Exhibit 14.2** The Pesto Bank:
(1) Loans money to Basil and
(2) Takes a security interest in his equipment.
Later, when Olive:
(3) Considers loaning Basil money, she will
(4) Check to see if any other creditors already have a security interest in his goods.

## Contents of the Financing Statement

**A financing statement is sufficient if it provides the name of the debtor, the name of the secured party, and an indication of the collateral.**[3]

The name of the debtor is critical because that is what an interested person will use to search among the millions of other financing statements on file. Faulty descriptions of the debtor's name have led to thousands of disputes and untold years of litigation, as subsequent creditors have failed to locate any record of an earlier claim on the debtor's property. In response, the Code is now very precise about what name must be used. If the debtor is a "registered organization," such as a corporation, limited partnership, or limited liability company, the official, registered name of the company is the only one acceptable. If the debtor is a person, or an unregistered organization (such as a club), then the *correct* name is required. Trade names are not sufficient. Because

[3] UCC §9-502(a).

misnamed debtors have created so much conflict, the Code now offers a straightforward test: A financing statement is effective if a computer search run under the debtor's correct name produces it. That is true even if the financing statement used the *incorrect* name. If the search does not reveal the document, then the financing statement is ineffective as a matter of law. The burden is on the secured party to file accurately, not on the searcher to seek out erroneous filings.[4]

The collateral must be described reasonably so that another party contemplating a loan to the debtor will understand which property is already secured. A financing statement could properly state that it applies to "all inventory in the debtor's Houston warehouse." If the debtor has given a security interest in everything he owns, then it is sufficient to state simply that the financing statement covers "all assets" or "all personal property."

The filing must be done by the debtor's last name. But which name is the last? Conflicting cultural traditions create ambiguity, as the following case indicates. Did the court get it right?

## CORONA FRUITS & VEGGIES, INC. V. FROZSUN FOODS, INC.

143 Cal. App. 4th 319, 48 Cal. Rptr. 3d 868
California Court of Appeals, 2006.

### CASE SUMMARY

**Facts:** Corona Fruits & Veggies (Corona) leased farmland to a strawberry farmer named Armando Munoz Juarez. He signed the lease, "Armando Munoz." Corona advanced money for payroll and farm production expenses. The company filed a UCC-1 financing statement, claiming a security interest in the strawberry crop. The financing statement listed the debtor's name as "Armando Munoz." Six months later, Armando Munoz Juarez contracted with Frozsun Foods, Inc., to sell processed strawberries. Frozsun advanced money and filed a financing statement listing the debtor's name as "Armando Juarez."

By the next year, our good farmer owed Corona $230,000 and Frozsun $19,600. When the farmer was unable to make payments on Corona's loan, the company repossessed the farmland and harvested the strawberry crop. Both Corona and Frozsun claimed the proceeds of the crop. The trial court awarded the money to Frozsun, finding that Corona had filed its financing statement under the wrong last name, and therefore had failed to perfect its security interest in the strawberry crop. Corona appealed.

**Issue:** *Did Corona correctly file its financing statement?*

**Decision:** No, Corona did not correctly file. Affirmed.

**Reasoning:** Because UCC-1 financing statements are indexed by last name, it is essential that a creditor use the correct surname. This debtor's true last name was "Juarez," not "Munoz." Corona's own business records, receipts, and checks all refer to him as "Juarez," as do his green card and photo ID.

The record indicates that Frozsun's agent conducted a "Juarez" debtor name search and did not discover appellants' UCC-1 financing statement. The secured party, not the debtor or uninvolved third parties, has the duty of ensuring proper filing and indexing of the notice.

Corona contends that since the debtor is from Mexico, we should follow the traditions of that country, where the surname is formed by listing the father's name, then the mother's. But the strawberries were planted in California, not Mexico. This is where the debt arose and the UCC-1 was filed. The state cannot organize a filing system that will accommodate naming practices in all foreign countries.

Corona failed to file properly, and its security interest never perfected.

## Place and Duration of Filing

Article 9 specifies where a secured party must file. These provisions may vary from state to state, so it is essential to check local law: A misfiled record accomplishes nothing. Generally speaking, a party must file in a central filing office located in the state where an individual debtor lives or where an organization has its executive office.[5]

---

[4] UCC §9-506(c).

[5] UCC §9-307.

Once a financing statement has been filed, it is effective for five years (except for a manufactured home, where it lasts 30 years). After five years the statement will expire and leave the secured party unprotected, unless she files a continuation statement within six months prior to expiration. The continuation statement is valid for an additional five years, and a secured party may file one periodically, forever.

## PERFECTION BY POSSESSION

For most types of collateral, in addition to filing, a secured party generally may perfect by possession. So if the collateral is a diamond brooch or 1,000 shares of stock, a bank may perfect its security interest by holding the items until the loan is paid off. **However, possession imposes one important duty: A secured party must use reasonable care in the custody and preservation of collateral in her possession.**[6] Reliable Bank holds 1,000 shares of stock as collateral for a loan it made to Grady. Grady instructs the bank to sell the shares and use the proceeds to pay off his debt in full. If Reliable neglects to sell the stock for five days, and the share price drops by 40 percent during that period, the bank will suffer the loss, not Grady.

## PERFECTION OF CONSUMER GOODS

**The Code gives special treatment to security interests in most consumer goods.** Merchants cannot file a financing statement for every bed, television, and stereo for which a consumer owes money. To understand the UCC's treatment of these transactions, we need to know two terms. The first is consumer goods, which are those used primarily for personal, family, or household purposes. The second term is purchase money security interest.

**Purchase money security interest (PMSI)**

An interest taken by the person who sells the collateral or advances money so the debtor can buy it.

A **purchase money security interest (PMSI)** is one taken by the person who sells the collateral or by the person who advances money so the debtor can buy the collateral.[7] Assume the Gobroke Home Center sells Marion a $5,000 stereo system. The sales document requires a payment of $500 down and $50 per month for the next three centuries, and gives Gobroke a security interest in the system. Because the security interest was "taken by the seller," the document is a PMSI. It would also be a PMSI if a bank had loaned Marion the money to buy the system and the document gave the bank a security interest. See Exhibit 14.3.

But aren't all security interests PMSIs? No, many are not. Suppose a bank loans a retail company $800,000 and takes a security interest in the store's present inventory. That is not a PMSI, since the store did not use the money to purchase the collateral.

What must Gobroke Home Center do to perfect its security interest? Nothing. **A PMSI in consumer goods perfects automatically, without filing.**[8] Marion's new stereo is clearly consumer goods, because she will use it only in her home. Gobroke's security interest is a PMSI, so the interest has perfected automatically.

The Code provisions about perfecting generally do not apply to motor vehicles, trailers, mobile homes, boats, or farm tractors. These types of secured interests are governed by state law, which frequently require a security interest to be noted directly on the vehicle's certificate of title.

---

[6] UCC §9-207.

[7] UCC §9-103.

[8] UCC §9-309(1).

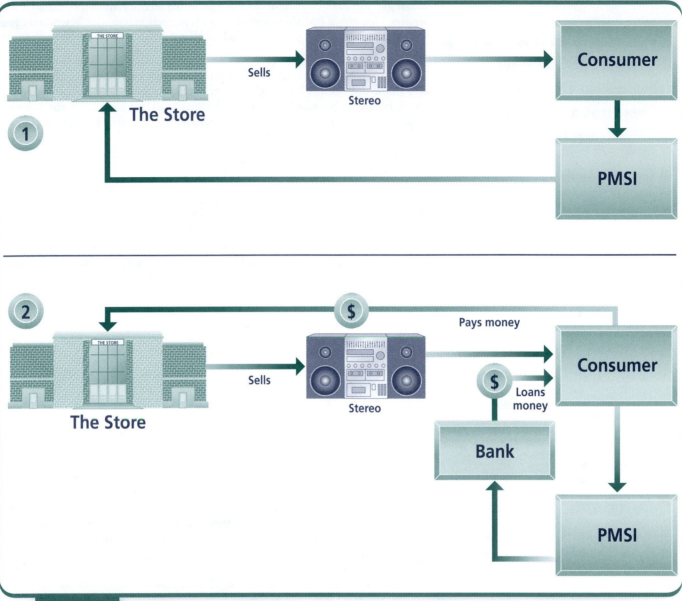

**Exhibit 14.3** A purchase money security interest can arise in either of two ways. In the first example, a store sells a stereo to a consumer on credit; the consumer in turn signs a PMSI, giving the store a security interest in the stereo. In the second example, the consumer buys the stereo with money loaned from a bank; the consumer signs a PMSI giving the *bank* a security interest in the stereo.

## EXAM *Strategy*

**Question:** Winona owns a tropical fish store. To buy a spectacular new tank, she borrows $25,000 from her sister, Pauline, and signs an agreement giving Pauline a security interest in the tank. Pauline never files the security agreement. Winona's business goes belly up, and both Pauline and other creditors angle to repossess the tank. Does Pauline have a perfected interest in the tank?

> ## Winona does not sleep with the fish—we hope—so the fish tank was not a consumer purchase.

**Strategy:** Generally, a creditor obtains a perfected security interest by filing or possession. However, a PMSI in consumer goods perfects automatically, without filing. Was Pauline's security agreement a PMSI? Was the fish tank a consumer good?

**Result:** A PMSI is one taken by the person who sells the collateral or advances money for its purchase. Pauline advanced the money for Winona to buy the tank, so Pauline does have a PSMI. Consumer goods are those used primarily for personal, family, or household purposes. Winona does not sleep with the fish—we hope—so this was not a consumer purchase. Pauline failed to perfect and is unprotected against other creditors.

## · PROTECTION OF BUYERS ·

Generally, once a security interest is perfected, it remains effective regardless of whether the collateral is sold, exchanged, or transferred in some other way. Bubba's Bus Co. needs money to meet its payroll, so it borrows $150,000 from Francine's Finance Co., which takes a security interest in Bubba's 180 buses and perfects its interest. Bubba, still short of cash, sells 30 of his buses to Antelope Transit. But even that money is not enough to keep Bubba solvent: He defaults on his loan to Francine and goes into bankruptcy. Francine pounces on Bubba's buses. May she repossess the 30 that Antelope now operates? Yes. The security interest continued in the buses even after Antelope purchased them, and Francine can whisk them away.

There are some exceptions to this rule. The Code gives a few buyers special protection.

### Buyers in Ordinary Course of Business

**Buyer in ordinary course of business (BIOC)**
Someone who buys goods in good faith from a seller who routinely deals in such goods.

A **buyer in ordinary course of business (BIOC)** is someone who buys goods in good faith from a seller who routinely deals in such goods. For example, Plato's Garden Supply purchases 500 hemlocks from Socrates' Farm, a grower. Plato is a BIOC: He is buying in good faith and Socrates routinely deals in hemlocks. This is an important status, because a BIOC is generally not affected by security interests in the goods. However, if Plato realized that the sale violated another party's rights in the goods, there would be no good faith. If Plato knew that Socrates was bankrupt and had agreed with a creditor not to sell any of his inventory, Plato would not achieve BIOC status.

A buyer in ordinary course of business takes the goods free of a security interest created by his seller, even though the security interest is perfected.[9] Suppose that, a month before Plato made his purchase, Socrates borrowed $200,000 from the Athenian Bank. Athenian took a security interest in all of Socrates' trees and perfected by filing. Then Plato purchased his 500 hemlocks. If Socrates defaults on the loan, Athenian will have no right to repossess the 500 trees that are now at the Garden Supply. Plato took them free and clear. (Of course, Athenian can still attempt to repossess other trees from Socrates.) The BIOC exception is designed to encourage ordinary commerce. A buyer making routine purchases should not be forced to perform a financing check before buying.

But the rule creates its own problems. A creditor may extend a large sum of money to a merchant based on collateral, such as inventory, only to discover that by the time the merchant

---

[9] UCC §9-320(a). In fact, the buyer takes free of the security interest *even if the buyer knew of it.* Yet a BIOC, by definition, must be acting in good faith. Is this a contradiction? No. Plato might know that a third party has a security interest in Socrates' crops yet not realize that his purchase violates the third party's rights. Generally, for example, a security interest will permit a retailer to sell consumer goods, the presumption being that part of the proceeds will go to the secured party. A BIOC cannot be expected to determine what a retailer plans to do with the money he is paid.

defaults, the collateral has been sold. Because the BIOC exception undercuts the basic protection given to a secured party, the courts interpret it narrowly. BIOC status is available only if the seller created the security interest. Oftentimes, a buyer will purchase goods that have a security interest created by someone other than the seller. If that happens, the buyer is not a BIOC. However, should that rule be strictly enforced even when the results are harsh? You make the call.

## YOU *be the* JUDGE

### CONSECO FINANCE SERVICING CORP. v. LEE
2004 WL 1243417
Court of Appeals of Texas, 2004

**Facts:** Lila Williams purchased a new Roadtrek 200 motor home from New World R.V. Inc. She paid about $14,000 down and financed $63,000, giving a security interest to New World. The RV company assigned its security interest to Conseco Finance, which perfected. Two years later, Williams returned the vehicle to New World (the record does not indicate why), and New World sold the RV to Robert and Ann Lee for $42,800. A year later, Williams defaulted on her payments to Conseco.

The Lees sued Conseco, claiming to be BIOCs and asking for a court declaration that they had sole title to the Roadtrek. Conseco counterclaimed, seeking title based on its perfected security interest. The trial court ruled that the Lees were BIOCs, with full rights to the vehicle. Conseco appealed.

**You Be the Judge:  Were the Lees BIOCs?**

**Conseco's Argument:**  Under UCC §9-319, a buyer in ordinary course takes free of a security interest *created by the buyer's*  *seller.* The buyers were the Lees. The seller was New World. New World did not create the security interest—Lila Williams did. There is no security interest created by New World. The security interest held by Conseco was created by someone else (Williams) and is not affected by the Lees' status as BIOCs. The law is clear and Conseco is entitled to the Roadtrek.

**The Lees' Argument:**  Conseco weaves a clever argument, but let's remove the mumbo-jumbo and look at what they are saying. Two honest buyers, acting in perfect good faith, can walk into an RV dealership, spend $42,000 for a used vehicle, and end up with—nothing. Conseco claims it is entitled to an RV that the Lees paid for because someone that the Lees have never dealt with, never even heard of, gave *to this RV seller* a security interest which the seller, years earlier, passed on to a finance company. Conseco's argument defies common sense and the goals of Article 9.

## · PRIORITIES AMONG CREDITORS ·

What happens when two creditors have a security interest in the same collateral? The party who has **priority** in the collateral gets it. Typically, the debtor lacks assets to pay everyone, so all creditors struggle to be the first in line. After the first creditor has repossessed the collateral, sold it, and taken enough of the proceeds to pay off his debt, there may be nothing left for anyone else. (There may not even be enough to pay the first creditor all that he is due, in which case that creditor will sue for the deficiency.) Who gets priority? There are three principal rules.[10]

The first rule is easy: A party with a perfected security interest takes priority over a party with an unperfected interest. This is the whole point of perfecting: to ensure that your security interest gets priority over everyone else's. On August 15, Meredith's Market, an antique store, borrows $100,000 from the Happy Bank, which takes a security interest in all of Meredith's inventory.

---

[10] UCC §9-322(a)(2), UCC §9-322(a)(3), and UCC §9-322(a)(1).

Happy Bank does not perfect. On September 15, Meredith uses the same collateral to borrow $50,000 from the Suspicion Bank, which files a financing statement the same day. On October 15, as if on cue, Meredith files for bankruptcy and stops paying both creditors. Suspicion wins because it holds a perfected interest, whereas the Happy Bank holds merely an unperfected interest.

The second rule: If neither secured party has perfected, the first interest to attach gets priority. Suppose that Suspicion Bank and Happy Bank had both failed to perfect. In that case, Happy Bank would have the first claim to Meredith's inventory, since Happy's interest attached first.

And the third rule follows logically: Between perfected security interests, the first to file or perfect wins. Diminishing Perspective, a railroad, borrows $75 million from the First Bank, which takes a security interest in Diminishing's rolling stock (railroad cars) and immediately perfects by filing. Two months later, Diminishing borrows $100 million from Second Bank, which takes a security interest in the same collateral and also files. When Diminishing arrives, on schedule, in bankruptcy court, both banks will race to seize the rolling stock. First Bank gets the railcars because it perfected first.

| March 1 | April 2 | May 3 | The Winner: |
|---------|---------|-------|-------------|
| First Bank lends money and perfects its security interest by filing a financing statement. | Second Bank lends money and perfects its security interest by filing a financing statement. | Diminishing goes bankrupt, and both banks attempt to take the rolling stock. | First Bank, because it perfected first. |

# · DEFAULT AND TERMINATION ·

We have reached the end of the line. Either the debtor has defaulted, or it has performed its obligations and may terminate the security agreement.

## DEFAULT

The parties define "default" in their security agreement. Generally, a debtor defaults when he fails to make payments due or enters bankruptcy proceedings. The parties can agree that other acts will constitute default, such as the debtor's failure to maintain insurance on the collateral. When a debtor defaults, the secured party has two principal options: (1) It may take possession of the collateral; or (2) it may file suit against the debtor for the money owed. The secured party does not have to choose between these two remedies; it may try one after the other, or both simultaneously.

### Taking Possession of the Collateral
When the debtor defaults, the secured party may take possession of the collateral.[11] The secured party may act on its own, without any court order, and simply take the collateral, provided this can be done without a breach of the peace. Otherwise, the secured party must file suit against the debtor and request that the court order the debtor to deliver the collateral.

---

[11] UCC §9-609.

### Disposition of the Collateral

Once the secured party has obtained possession of the collateral, it has two choices. The secured party may (1) dispose of the collateral; or (2) retain the collateral as full satisfaction of the debt. Notice that until the secured party disposes of the collateral, the debtor has the right to redeem it, that is, to pay the full value of the debt and retrieve her property.

A secured party may sell, lease, or otherwise dispose of the collateral in any commercially reasonable manner.[12] Typically, the secured party will sell the collateral in either a private or a public sale. First, however, the debtor must receive reasonable notice of the time and place of the sale, so that she may bid on the collateral.

When the secured party has sold the collateral, it applies the proceeds of the sale: first, to its expenses in repossessing and selling the collateral, and second, to the debt. Sometimes the sale leaves a deficiency, that is, insufficient funds to pay off the debt. The debtor remains liable for the deficiency, and the creditor will sue for it. On the other hand, the sale of the collateral may yield a surplus, that is, a sum greater than the debt. The secured party must pay the surplus to the debtor.

## · TERMINATION ·

Finally, we need to look at what happens when a debtor does not default, but pays the full debt. (You are forgiven if you lost track of the fact that things sometimes work out smoothly.) Once that happens, the secured party must complete a termination statement, a document indicating that it no longer claims a security interest in the collateral.[13]

---

[12] UCC §9-610.
[13] UCC §9-513.

## CHAPTER CONCLUSION

Borrowed money is the lubricant that keeps a modern economy motoring smoothly. Without it, many consumers would never own a car or stereo, and many businesses would be unable to grow. But unless these debts are repaid, the economy will falter. Secured transactions are one method for ensuring that creditors are paid.

## EXAM REVIEW

1.  **ARTICLE 9** Article 9 applies to any transaction intended to create a security interest in personal property or fixtures. (p. 229)

    ................................................................................................................

2.  **ATTACHMENT** Attachment means that (1) the two parties made a security agreement and either the debtor has authenticated a security agreement describing the collateral or the secured party has obtained possession; and (2) the secured party gave value in order to get the security agreement; and (3) the debtor has rights in the collateral. (p. 229)

    ................................................................................................................

3.  **PERFECTION** Attachment protects against the debtor. Perfection of a security interest protects the secured party against parties other than the debtor. (p. 231)

    ................................................................................................................

**4.** **FILING** Filing is the most common way to perfect. For many forms of collateral, the secured party may also perfect by obtaining either possession or control. (p. 233)

**5.** **PMSI** A purchase money security interest (PMSI) is one taken by the person who sells the collateral or advances money so the debtor can buy the collateral. A PMSI in consumer goods perfects automatically. (p. 234)

**EXAM Strategy**

**Question:** John and Clara Lockovich bought a 22-foot Chaparrel Villian II boat from Greene County Yacht Club for $32,500. They paid $6,000 cash and borrowed the rest of the purchase price from Gallatin National Bank, which took a security interest in the boat. Gallatin filed a financing statement in Greene County, Pennsylvania, where the bank was located. But Pennsylvania law requires financing statements to be filed in the county of the debtor's residence, and the Lockoviches lived in Allegheny County. The Lockoviches soon washed up in bankruptcy court. Other creditors demanded that the boat be sold, claiming that Gallatin's security interest had been filed in the wrong place. Who wins? (Please be advised: this is a trick question.)

**Strategy:** Gallatin National Bank obtained a special kind of security interest in the boat. Identify that type of interest. What special rights does this give to the bank? (See the "Result" at the end of this section.)

**6.** **BIOC** A buyer in ordinary course of business (BIOC) takes the goods free of a security interest created by his seller even though the security interest is perfected. (p. 236)

**7.** **PRIORITY** Priority among secured parties is generally as follows:

(a) A party with a perfected security interest takes priority over a party with an unperfected interest.

(b) If neither secured party has perfected, the first interest to attach gets priority.

(c) Between perfected security interests, the first to file or perfect wins. (p. 237)

**EXAM Strategy**

**Question:** Barwell, Inc., sold McMann Golf Ball Co. a "preformer," a machine that makes golf balls, for $55,000. Barwell delivered the machine on February 20. McMann paid $3,000 down, the remainder to be paid over several years, and signed an agreement giving Barwell a security interest in the preformer. Barwell did not perfect its interest. On March 1, McMann borrowed $350,000 from First of America Bank, giving the bank a security interest in McMann's present and after-acquired property. First of America perfected by filing on March 2. McMann, of course, became insolvent, and both Barwell and the bank attempted to repossess the preformer. Who gets it?

**Strategy:** Two parties have a valid security interest in this machine. When that happens, there is a three-step process to determine which party gets priority. Apply them. (See the "Result" at the end of this section.)

**8.** **DEFAULT** When the debtor defaults, the secured party may take possession of the collateral and then sell, lease, or otherwise dispose of the collateral in any commercially reasonable way, or it may ignore the collateral and sue the debtor for the full debt. (p. 238)

**5. Result:** Gallatin advanced the money that the Lockoviches used to buy the boat, meaning the bank obtained a PMSI. A PMSI in consumer goods perfects automatically, without filing. The boat was a consumer good. Gallatin's security interest perfected without any filing at all, and so the bank wins.

**7. Result:** This question is resolved by the first of those three steps. A party with a perfected security interest takes priority over a party with an unperfected interest. The bank wins because its perfected security interest takes priority over Barwell's unperfected interest.

## PRACTICE EXAM

### MATCHING QUESTIONS

Match the following terms with their definitions:

___ A. Attachment

___ B. BIOC

___ C. Perfection

___ D. PMSI

___ E. Priority

1. Someone who buys goods in good faith from a seller who deals in such goods
2. Steps necessary to make a security interest valid against the whole world
3. A security interest taken by the person who sells the collateral or advances money so the debtor can buy it
4. The order in which creditors will be permitted to seize the property of a bankrupt debtor
5. Steps necessary to make a security interest valid against the debtor, but not against third parties

### TRUE/FALSE QUESTIONS

Circle true or false:

1. T   F   A party with a perfected security interest takes priority over a party with an unperfected interest.

2. T   F   A buyer in ordinary course of business takes goods free of an unperfected security interest, but does not take them free of a perfected security interest.

3. T   F   When a debtor defaults, a secured party may seize the collateral and hold it, using reasonable care, but may not sell or lease it.

4. T   F   A party may take a security interest in tangible things, such as goods, but not in intangible things, such as bank accounts.

5. T   F   Without an agreement of the parties there can be no security interest.

### MULTIPLE-CHOICE QUESTIONS

Note to the student: The following cases and problems were decided under the former Article 9. In each instance, the outcome would be the same under the revised laws.

6. CPA QUESTION: Under the UCC Secured Transactions Article, perfection of a security interest by a creditor provides added protection against other parties in the event the debtor does not pay its debts. Which of the following parties is not affected by perfection of a security interest?

A. Other prospective creditors of the debtor

B. The trustee in a bankruptcy case

C. A buyer in the ordinary course of business

D. A subsequent personal injury judgment creditor

7. CPA QUESTION: Mars, Inc., manufactures and sells VCRs on credit directly to wholesalers, retailers, and consumers. Mars can perfect its security interest in the VCRs it sells without having to file a financing statement or take possession of the VCRs if the sale is made to which of the following:

    A. Retailers

    B. Wholesalers that sell to distributors for resale

    C. Consumers

    D. Wholesalers that sell to buyers in ordinary course of business

8. Bank has loaned unsecured money to Retailer, which still owes $700,000. Bank becomes nervous that Retailer is on the verge of bankruptcy, and sends a "notice of security interest" to Retailer, claiming a security interest in all inventory and real estate of Retailer. Retailer does not respond. Bank files its notice in the state's central filing office. When Retailer goes bankrupt, Bank

    A. Has a perfected security interest in the inventory but not the real estate

    B. Has a perfected security interest in the real estate but not the inventory

    C. Has a perfected security interest in both the real estate and the inventory

    D. Has no security interest in either the real estate or the inventory

    E. Has an unperfected security interest in both the real estate and the inventory

9. Which case does *not* represent a purchase money security interest?

    A. Auto dealer sells consumer a car on credit.

    B. Wholesaler sells retailer 5,000 pounds of candy on credit.

    C. Bank lends money to Retailer, using Retailer's existing inventory as collateral.

    D. Bank lends money to auto dealer to purchase 150 new cars, which are the collateral.

    E. Consumer applies to credit agency for loan with which to buy a yacht.

10. Millie lends Arthur, her next-door neighbor, $25,000. He gives her his diamond ring as collateral for the loan. Which statement is true?

    A. Millie has no valid security interest in the ring because the parties did not enter into a security agreement.

    B. Millie has no valid security interest in the ring because she has not filed appropriate papers.

    C. Millie has an attached, unperfected security interest in the ring.

    D. Millie has an attached, unperfected security interest in the ring but can perfect her interest by filing.

    E. Millie has an attached, perfected security interest in the ring.

# SHORT-ANSWER QUESTIONS

11. The Copper King Inn, Inc., had money problems. It borrowed $62,500 from two of its officers, Noonan and Patterson, but that did not suffice to keep the inn going. So Noonan, on behalf of Copper King, arranged for the inn to borrow $100,000 from Northwest Capital, an investment company that worked closely with Noonan in other ventures. Copper King signed an agreement giving Patterson, Noonan, and Northwest a security interest in the inn's furniture and equipment. But the financing statement that the parties filed made no mention of Northwest. Copper King went bankrupt. Northwest attempted to seize assets, but other creditors objected. Is Northwest entitled to Copper King's furniture and equipment?

12. Sears sold a lawn tractor to Cosmo Fiscante for $1,481. Fiscante paid with his personal credit card. Sears kept a valid security interest in the lawnmower but did not perfect. Fiscante had the machine delivered to his business, Trackers Raceway Park, the only place he ever used the machine. When Fiscante was unable to meet his obligations, various creditors attempted to seize the lawnmower. Sears argued that because it had a purchase money security interest (PMSI) in the lawnmower, its interest had perfected automatically. Is Sears correct?

13. ETHICS: The Dannemans bought a Kodak copier worth over $40,000. Kodak arranged financing by

GECC and assigned its rights to that company. Although the Dannemans thought they had purchased the copier on credit, the papers described the deal as a lease. The Dannemans had constant problems with the machine and stopped making payments. GECC repossessed the machine and, without notifying the Dannemans, sold it back to Kodak for $12,500, leaving a deficiency of $39,927. GECC sued the Dannemans for that amount. The Dannemans argued that the deal was not a lease but a sale on credit.

Why does it matter whether the parties had a sale or a lease? Is GECC entitled to its money? Finally, comment on the ethics. Why did the Dannemans not understand the papers they had signed? Who is responsible for that? Are you satisfied with the ethical conduct of the Dannemans? Kodak? GECC?

14. ROLE REVERSAL: Write a multiple-choice question with a conflict between a secured party and a buyer in ordinary course of business.

# INTERNET RESEARCH PROBLEM

Draft a security agreement in which your friend gives you a security interest in her $20,000 home entertainment system, in exchange for a loan of $12,000. Because the collateral is something that she uses daily, what special concerns do you have? How will you protect yourself? Next, find a UCC-1 financing form online. Print the form, then complete it. In what office of your state should you file in order to perfect?

**You can find further practice problems in the Online Quiz at www.cengage.com/blaw/beatty.**

# BANKRUPTCY

**George Bryan Brummell,** known as Beau Brummell, was a celebrity in nineteenth-century England. Known for his impeccable sense of style, he was the leading arbiter of taste and fashion for more than 20 years. This role was demanding—he routinely spent five hours a day simply getting dressed. After bathing in eau de cologne and water, he would spend an hour with his hairdresser and another two hours tying his cravat (a fancy necktie). Although he had inherited modest wealth, his extravagant lifestyle brought him to ruin. He fled to France to escape his creditors, taking his lavish tastes with him. After 14 years in France, he was thrown in debtors' prison.

> **Despite being in bankruptcy, Basinger continued to spend $43,000 per month, including $6,000 for clothes.**

For actor Kim Basinger, a modern celebrity, bankruptcy had a different outcome. After signing a contract to appear in *Boxing Helena,* a movie about a doctor who cut off his lover's arms and legs, she changed her mind and refused to show up for filming. A jury found that she had breached her contract and ordered her to pay $8.1 million. She filed for bankruptcy protection, claiming $5 million in assets and $11 million in liabilities.

Despite being in bankruptcy, Basinger continued to spend $43,000 per month, including $6,000 for clothes, $4,000 for entertainment, and $7,000 for pet care and other personal expenses. She also reported owning $192,000 of jewelry. In the meantime, her creditors received nothing.[1]

## • OVERVIEW OF BANKRUPTCY •

The U.S. Bankruptcy Code (Code) has three primary goals:

- To preserve as much of the debtor's property as possible.
- To divide the debtor's assets fairly between the debtor and creditors.
- To divide the debtor's assets fairly among creditors.

The following options are available under the Bankruptcy Code:

| Number | Topic | Description |
|---|---|---|
| Chapter 7 | Liquidation | The bankrupt's assets are sold to pay creditors. If the debtor owns a business, it terminates. The creditors have no right to the debtor's future earnings. |
| Chapter 9 | Municipal bankruptcies | This chapter is not covered in this book. |
| Chapter 11 | Reorganization | This chapter is designed for businesses and wealthy individuals. Businesses continue in operation, and creditors receive a portion of both current assets and future earnings. |
| Chapter 12 | Family farmers | This chapter is not covered in this book. |
| Chapter 13 | Consumer reorganizations | Chapter 13 offers reorganization for the typical consumer. Creditors usually receive a portion of the individual's current assets and future earnings. |

All of the Code's chapters have one of two objectives—rehabilitation or liquidation. Chapters 11 and 13, for example, focus on rehabilitation. These chapters hold creditors at bay while the debtor develops a payment plan. In return for retaining some of their assets, debtors typically

---

[1] A California appeals court overturned the judgment against Basinger and ordered a new trial. On the eve of retrial, Basinger settled for $3.8 million.

promise to pay creditors a portion of their future earnings. However, when debtors are unable to develop a feasible plan for rehabilitation under Chapter 11 or 13, Chapter 7 provides for liquidation (also known as a **straight bankruptcy**). Most of the debtor's assets are distributed to creditors, but the debtor has no obligation to share future earnings.

Debtors are sometimes eligible to file under more than one chapter. No choice is irrevocable because both debtors and creditors have the right to ask the court to convert a case from one chapter to another at any time during the proceedings.

**Straight bankruptcy**
Also known as liquidation, this form of bankruptcy mandates that the bankrupt's assets be sold to pay creditors but the bankrupt has no obligation to share future earnings.

## ▪ CHAPTER 7 LIQUIDATION ▪

All bankruptcy cases proceed in a roughly similar pattern, regardless of chapter. We use Chapter 7 as a template to illustrate common features of all bankruptcy cases. Later on, the discussions of the other chapters will indicate how they differ from Chapter 7.

### FILING A PETITION

**Any individual, partnership, corporation, or other business organization that lives, conducts business, or owns property in the United States can file under the Code.** (Chapter 13, however, is available only to individuals.) The traditional term for someone who could not pay his debts was "**bankrupt**," but the Code uses the term "**debtor**" instead. We use both terms interchangeably.

A case begins with the filing of a bankruptcy petition in federal district court. Debtors may go willingly into the bankruptcy process by filing a **voluntary petition,** or they may be dragged into court by creditors who file an **involuntary petition.**

**Bankrupt**
Another term for debtor.

**Debtor**
Someone who cannot pay his debts and files for protection under the Bankruptcy Code.

### VOLUNTARY PETITION

Any debtor (corporation or individual) has the right to file for bankruptcy. It is not necessary that the debtor's liabilities exceed assets. Debtors sometimes file a bankruptcy petition because cash flow is so tight they cannot pay their debts, even though they are not technically insolvent. However, *individuals* must meet two requirements before filing:

- Within 180 days before the filing, an individual debtor must undergo credit counseling with an approved agency.
- Individual debtors may file under Chapter 7 if they earn less than the median income in their state *or* they cannot afford to pay back at least $6,575 over five years.[2] Generally, all other debtors must file under Chapters 11 or 13. (These Chapters require the bankrupt to repay some debt.)

The voluntary petition must include the following documents:

| Document | Description |
| --- | --- |
| Petition | Begins the case. Easy to fill out, it requires checking a few boxes and typing in name, address, and Social Security number. |
| List of Creditors | The names and addresses of all creditors. |

[2] In some circumstances, debtors with income higher than $6,575 may still be eligible to file under Chapter 7, but the formula is highly complex and more than most readers want to know. The formula is available at 11 USC §707(b)(2)(A).

| Schedule of Assets and Liabilities | A list of the debtor's assets and debts. |
| --- | --- |
| Claim of Exemptions | A list of all assets that the debtor is entitled to keep. |
| Schedule of Income and Expenditures | The debtor's job, income, and expenses. |
| Statement of Financial Affairs | A summary of the debtor's financial history and current financial condition. In particular, the debtor must list any recent payments to creditors and any other property held by someone else for the debtor. |

## INVOLUNTARY PETITION

Creditors may force a debtor into bankruptcy by filing an involuntary petition. The creditors' goals are to preserve as much of the debtor's assets as possible and to ensure that all creditors receive a fair share. Naturally, the Code sets strict limits—debtors cannot be forced into bankruptcy every time they miss a credit card payment. **An involuntary petition must meet all of the following requirements:**

- The debtor must owe at least $13,475 in unsecured claims to the creditors who file.
- If the debtor has at least 12 creditors, three or more must sign the petition. If the debtor has fewer than 12 creditors, any one of them can file a petition.
- The creditors must allege either that a custodian for the debtor's property has been appointed in the prior 120 days or that the debtor has generally not been paying debts that are due.

What does "a custodian for the debtor's property" mean? *State* laws sometimes permit the appointment of a custodian to protect a debtor's assets. The Code allows creditors to pull a case out from under state law and into federal bankruptcy court by filing an involuntary petition.

Once a voluntary petition is filed or an involuntary petition approved, the bankruptcy court issues an **order for relief**. This order is an official acknowledgment that the debtor is under the jurisdiction of the court, and it is, in a sense, the start of the bankruptcy process. An involuntary debtor must now make all the filings that accompany a voluntary petition.

**Order for relief**
An official acknowledgment that a debtor is under the jurisdiction of the bankruptcy court.

## TRUSTEE

**The trustee is responsible for gathering the bankrupt's assets and dividing them among creditors.** Creditors have the right to elect the trustee, but often they do not bother. In this case, the **U.S. Trustee** makes the selection. The U.S. Attorney General appoints a U.S. Trustee for each region of the country to administer the bankruptcy law.

**U.S. Trustee**
Oversees the administration of bankruptcy law in a region.

## CREDITORS

**After the order for relief, the U.S. Trustee calls a meeting of creditors.** At the meeting the bankrupt must answer (under oath) any question the creditors pose about his financial situation. If the creditors want to elect a trustee, they do so at this meeting.

**After the meeting of creditors, unsecured creditors must submit a proof of claim.** The proof of claim is a simple form stating the name of the creditor and the amount of the claim. Secured creditors do not file proofs of claim.

**Proof of claim**
A form stating the name of an unsecured creditor and the amount of the claim against the debtor.

# AUTOMATIC STAY

A fox chased by hounds has no time to make rational long-term decisions. What that fox needs is a safe burrow. Similarly, it is difficult for debtors to make sound financial decisions when hounded night and day by creditors shouting, "Pay me! Pay me!" The Code is designed to give debtors enough breathing space to sort out their affairs sensibly. An **automatic stay** is a safe burrow for the bankrupt. It goes into effect as soon as the petition is filed. An automatic stay prohibits creditors from collecting debts that the bankrupt incurred before the petition was filed. Creditors may not sue a bankrupt to obtain payment nor may they take other steps, outside of court, to pressure the debtor for payment. The following case illustrates how persistent creditors can be.

**Automatic stay**
Prohibits creditors from collecting debts that the bankrupt incurred before the petition was filed.

## JACKSON V. HOLIDAY FURNITURE

309 B.R. 33, 2004 BANKR. LEXIS 548
UNITED STATES BANKRUPTCY COURT FOR THE WESTERN DISTRICT OF MISSOURI, 2004

### CASE SUMMARY

**Facts:** In April, Cora and Frank Jackson purchased a recliner chair on credit from Dan Holiday Furniture. They made payments until November. That month, they filed for protection under the Bankruptcy Code. Dan Holiday received a notice of the bankruptcy. This notice stated that the store must stop all efforts to collect on the Jacksons' debt.

Despite this notice, a Dan Holiday collector telephoned the Jacksons' house 10 times between November 15 and December 1 and left a card in their door threatening repossession of the chair. On December 1, Frank—without Cora's knowledge—went to Dan Holiday to pay the $230.00 owed for November and December. He told the store owner about the bankruptcy filing, but allegedly added that he and his wife wanted to continue making payments directly to Dan Holiday.

In early January, employees at Dan Holiday learned that Frank had died the month before. Nevertheless, after Cora failed to make the payment for the month of January, a collector telephoned her house 26 times between January 14 and February 19. The store owner's sister left the following message on Cora's answering machine:

Hello. This is Judy over at Dan Holiday Furniture. And this is the last time I am going to call you. If you do not call me I will be at your house. And I expect you to call me today. If there is a problem I need to speak to you about it. You need to call me. We need to get this thing going. You are a January and February payment behind. And if you think you are going to get away with it, you've got another thing coming.

When Cora returned home on February 18, she found seven bright yellow slips of paper in her door jamb stating that a Dan Holiday truck had stopped by to repossess her furniture. The cards read:

> "OUR TRUCK was here to **REPOSSESS** Your furniture [sic]. 241-6933 Dan Holiday Furn. & Appl. Co."

The threat to send a truck was merely a ruse designed to frighten Cora. In truth, Dan Holiday did not really want the recliner back. The owner just wanted to talk directly with Cora about making payments.

Also on February 18, Dan Holiday sent Cora a letter stating that she had 24 hours to bring her account current or else **"Repossession** Will Be Made and **Legal Action Will Be Taken."** That same day, Cora's bankruptcy attorney contacted Dan Holiday. Thereafter all collection activity ceased.

**Issues:** *Did Dan Holiday violate the automatic stay provisions of the Bankruptcy Code? What is the penalty for a violation?*

**Decision:** Dan Holiday was in violation of the Bankruptcy Code. The court awarded the Jacksons their actual damages, attorneys' fees, court costs, and punitive damages.

**Reasoning:** Anyone injured by a creditor who violates the automatic stay provisions is entitled to recover both actual damages (including court costs and attorneys' fees) as well as punitive damages where appropriate. In this case, the court awards actual damages of $230.00, because that is how much Dan Holiday coerced from Frank Jackson on December 1. The Court also awards the Jacksons their attorneys' fees and court costs in the amount of $1,142.42.

In addition, the Jacksons are entitled to punitive damages because Dan Holiday intentionally and flagrantly violated the automatic stay provision. Dan Holiday's conduct was remarkably bad—employees called the Jackson household no less than 26 times in January and February.

It is not clear how much the punitive damages should be because there was no evidence presented at trial about how much Dan Holiday can afford. The court is only aware that Dan Holiday is a family-owned business that has been in existence for 52 years. It seems likely that it is a relatively small business. Therefore, the Court is assessing a penalty of $100.00

for each illegal contact with the Jacksons after December 1, when it was crystal clear that Dan Holiday knew about the Jacksons' bankruptcy filing. Under this calculation, punitive damages total $2,800.00. The Court believes that this penalty will be enough to sting the pocketbook of Dan Holiday and impress upon the company, its owners, and its employees the importance of complying with the provisions of the Bankruptcy Code.

# BANKRUPTCY ESTATE

The filing of the bankruptcy petition creates a new legal entity separate from the debtor—the **bankruptcy estate**. All of the bankrupt's assets pass to the estate, except exempt property and new property that the debtor acquires after the petition is filed.

**Bankruptcy estate**
The new legal entity created when a debtor files a bankruptcy petition. All of the debtor's existing assets pass into the estate.

## Exempt Property

**The Code permits *individual* debtors (but not organizations) to keep some property for themselves.** This exempt property saves the debtor from destitution during the bankruptcy process and provides the foundation for a new life once the process is over.

In this one area of bankruptcy law, the Code defers to state law. Although the Code lists various types of exempt property, it permits states to opt out of the federal system and define a different set of exemptions. However, debtors can take advantage of state exemptions only if they have lived in that state for two years prior to the bankruptcy.

Under the *federal* Code, a debtor is allowed to exempt only $20,200 of the value of her home. Most *states* exempt items such as the debtor's home, household goods, cars, work tools, disability and pension benefits, alimony, and health aids. Indeed, some states set no limit on the value of exempt property. Both Florida and Texas, for example, permit debtors to keep homes of unlimited value and a certain amount of land. But the federal statute limits this state exemption to $136,875 for any house that was acquired during the 40 months before the bankruptcy.

## Voidable Preferences

A major goal of the bankruptcy system is to divide the debtor's assets fairly among creditors. It would not be fair if debtors were permitted to pay off some of their creditors immediately before filing a bankruptcy petition. Such a payment is called a **preference** because it gives unfair preferential treatment to a creditor. **The trustee can void any transfer to a creditor that took place in the 90-day period before the filing of a petition.**

**Preference**
When a debtor unfairly pays creditors immediately before filing a bankruptcy petition.

## Fraudulent Transfers

Suppose that a debtor sees bankruptcy inexorably approaching across the horizon like a tornado. He knows that, once the storm hits and he files a petition, everything he owns except a few items of exempt property will become part of the bankruptcy estate. Before that happens, he may be tempted to give some of his property to friends or family to shelter it from the tornado. If he succumbs to temptation, however, he is committing a fraudulent transfer. **A transfer is fraudulent if it is made within the year before a petition is filed and its purpose is to hinder, delay, or defraud creditors.** The trustee can void any fraudulent transfer. The debtor has committed a crime and may be prosecuted.

**Question:** Lawrence Williams and his wife, Diana, enjoyed a luxurious lifestyle while his investment bank flourished. But when the bank failed, Lawrence was faced with debts of $6 million. On the eve of the bankruptcy filing, Diana suddenly announced that she wanted a divorce. In what had to be the most amicable breakup ever, Lawrence willingly transferred all of his assets to her. The unhappy couple went on to obtain their divorce in only two months, a speed that the bankruptcy court referred to as "astonishing." Was this transfer a voidable preference or a fraudulent transfer? What difference does it make?

**Strategy:** Begin by looking at the differences between these two types of wrongful transfers. Fraudulent transfers sound similar to voidable preferences, but there is an important distinction: voidable preferences pay legitimate debts, while fraudulent transfers protect the debtor's assets from legitimate creditors. A voidable transfer is a civil offense; a fraudulent transfer is a crime.

**Result:** The court found that Williams had committed a fraudulent transfer because he was attempting to protect his assets from creditors.[3]

## Payment of Claims

Imagine a crowded delicatessen on Saturday evening. People are pushing and shoving because they know there is not enough food for everyone; some customers will go home hungry. The delicatessen could simply serve whoever pushes to the front of the line, or it could establish a number system to ensure that the most deserving customers are served first. The Code has, in essence, adopted a number system to prevent a free-for-all fight over the bankrupt's assets. Indeed, one of the Code's primary goals is to ensure that creditors are paid in the proper order, not according to who pushes to the front of the line.

All claims are placed in one of three classes: (1) secured claims, (2) priority claims, and (3) unsecured claims. **The trustee pays the bankruptcy estate to the various classes of claims in order of rank.** A higher class is paid in full before the next class receives any payment at all. The debtor is entitled to any funds remaining after all claims have been paid. The payment order is shown in Exhibit 15.1.

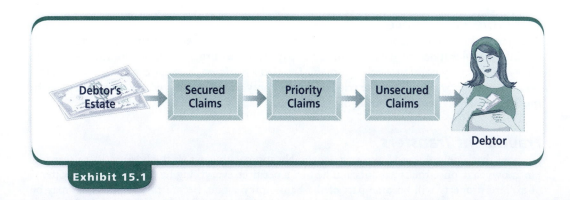

**Exhibit 15.1**

---

[3] *In re Williams*, 159 B.R. 648, 1993 Bankr. LEXIS 1482 (Bankr. D.R.I. 1993), remanded, 190 B.R. 728, 1996 U.S. Dist. LEXIS 539.

### Secured Claims

Creditors whose loans are secured by specific collateral are paid first. Secured claims are fundamentally different from all other claims because they are paid not out of the general funds of the estate, but by selling a specific asset.

### Priority Claims

Each category of priority claims is paid in order, with the first group receiving full payment before the next group receives anything. Priority claims include:

- Alimony and child support.
- Administrative expenses (such as fees to the trustee, lawyers, and accountants).
- Back wages to the debtor's employees for work performed during the 180 days prior to the date of the petition.
- Income and property taxes.

### Unsecured Claims

Last, and frequently very much least, unsecured creditors have now reached the delicatessen counter. They can only hope that some food remains (and that they will be paid).

## DISCHARGE

Filing a bankruptcy petition is embarrassing and time consuming. It can affect the debtor's credit rating for years, making the simplest car loan a challenge. To encourage debtors to file for bankruptcy despite the pain involved, the Code offers a powerful incentive: the **fresh start**. Once a bankruptcy estate has been distributed to creditors, they cannot make a claim against the debtor for money owed before the filing, *whether or not they actually received any payment*. These prepetition debts are **discharged**. All is forgiven, if not forgotten.

**Discharge** is an essential part of bankruptcy law. Without it, debtors would have little incentive to take part. To avoid abuses, however, the Code limits both the type of debts that can be discharged and the circumstances under which discharge can take place. In addition, a debtor must complete a course on financial management before receiving a discharge.

**Fresh start**
After the termination of a bankruptcy case, creditors cannot make a claim against the debtor for money owed before the initial bankruptcy petition was filed.

**Discharge**
The debtor no longer has an obligation to pay a debt.

### Debts That Cannot Be Discharged

The following debts are among those that can never be discharged. The debtor remains liable in full until they are paid:

- Recent income and property taxes.
- Money obtained by fraud.
- Cash advances on a credit card totaling more than $825 that an individual debtor takes out within 70 days before the order of relief.
- Debts omitted from the Schedule of Assets and Liabilities.
- Money owed for alimony, maintenance, or child support.
- Debts stemming from intentional and malicious injury.
- Debts that result from a violation of securities laws.
- Student loans made or guaranteed by the government for which repayment would cause undue hardship to the debtor.

**EXAM** *Strategy*

**Question:** James Hartley, the owner of an auto parts store, told an employee, Rickey D. Jones, to clean and paint some tires in the basement. Highly flammable gasoline fumes accumulated in the poorly ventilated space. Hartley threw a firecracker into the basement, as a joke, intending only to startle Jones. Sparks from the firecracker caused an explosion and fire that severely burned Jones. He filed a personal injury suit against Hartley for $1 million. Is this debt dischargeable under Chapter 7?

**Strategy:** Review the list of debts that cannot be discharged. You will see that injuries caused by a stupid accident are dischargeable, not those caused intentionally or maliciously.

**Result:** Hartley's behavior was foolish, but his debt to Jones was dischargeable because the injury was not intentional or malicious.

........................................................................................................................................

## Circumstances That Prevent Debts from Being Discharged

The Code also prohibits the discharge of debts under the following circumstances:

- *Business organizations.* Under Chapter 7 (but not the other chapters), only the debts of individuals can be discharged, not those of business organizations. Once its assets have been distributed, an organization must cease operation. If the company resumes business again, it becomes responsible for all its prefiling debts.

- *Revocation.* A court can revoke a discharge within one year if it discovers the debtor engaged in fraud or concealment.

- *Dishonesty or bad-faith behavior.* The court may deny discharge altogether if the debtor has made fraudulent transfers, hidden assets, or otherwise acted in bad faith.

- *Repeated filings for bankruptcy.* A debtor who has received a discharge under Chapter 7 or 11 cannot receive another discharge under Chapter 7 for at least eight years after the prior filing.

**ETHICS**    Banks and credit card companies lobbied Congress hard to insert the prohibition against repeat bankruptcy filings. They argued that irresponsible consumers run up debt and then blithely walk away. You might think that, if this were true, lenders would avoid customers with a history of bankruptcy. New research indicates, though, that lenders actually *target* those consumers, repeatedly sending them offers to borrow money. The reason is simple: These consumers are much more likely to take cash advances, which carry very high interest rates. And this is one audience that *must* repay its loans for the simple reason that these borrowers cannot declare bankruptcy again.[4] Is this strategy ethical? ◆

## Reaffirmation

**Reaffirm**
To promise to pay a debt even after it is discharged.

Sometimes debtors are willing to **reaffirm** a debt, meaning they promise to pay even after discharge. They may want to reaffirm a secured debt to avoid losing the collateral. For example, a debtor who has taken out a loan secured by a car may reaffirm that debt so that the finance company will agree not to repossess it. Sometimes debtors reaffirm because they feel guilty, or they want to maintain a good relationship with the creditor. They may have borrowed from a family member or an important supplier.

Because discharge is a fundamental pillar of the bankruptcy process, courts look closely at each reaffirmation to ensure that the creditor has not unfairly pressured the bankrupt. To be valid, either the court must determine that the reaffirmation is in the debtor's best interest and does

---

[4] See Porter, Katherine M., "Bankrupt Profits: The Credit Industry's Business Model for Postbankruptcy Lending." U Iowa Legal Studies Research Paper No. 07-26 Available at SSRN: http://ssrn.com/abstract=1004276.

not impose undue hardship, or the attorney representing the debtor must file an affidavit in court stating that the debtor's consent was informed and voluntary and the agreement does not create a hardship.

Money has never been known to simplify family relationships. In the following case, the debtors' finances were complicated by the fact that they had borrowed from her mother and were living with his parents. The court stepped in to protect the (adult) children from reaffirming a debt.

## In Re: John & Julie Hoffman

358 B.R. 839; 2006 Bankr. LEXIS 3841
United States Bankruptcy Court for the Western District of Virginia, 2006

### CASE SUMMARY

**Facts:** The Hoffmans filed for relief under Chapter 7. Among their debts was a loan for $11,500.00, secured by their 1999 Dodge Caravan. The car was worth less than half the amount of the loan. There was no economic sense to paying back twice the value of the car, so ordinarily, they would have defaulted on the loan. The problem was that Mrs. Hoffman's mother was a co-signer. If they defaulted, she would have to pay. To protect her, the Hoffmans signed a reaffirmation agreement promising to repay the car loan at the rate of $96 a week for four years. To further darken an already unhappy picture, the Hoffmans' monthly income of $4,799.12 was $35.87 less than their expenses. Because they had lost their house, they were living with his parents and paying $600 a month in rent.

The Hoffmans' lawyer refused to approve the reaffirmation agreement because it had a negative monthly budget. They asked the Court for approval.

**Issue:** *Will the court approve a reaffirmation agreement that shows a negative monthly budget?*

**Decision:** The court did not approve the reaffirmation agreement.

**Reasoning:** For the court to approve a reaffirmation agreement, there must be some evidence that the debtors are able to make the required payments. The Hoffmans' income is $36 a month less than their expenses and their financial position is likely to get even worse because Mrs. Hoffman has accepted a job that pays $2,000 a month less than she is earning now.

Although the Court appreciates the Hoffmans' desire to protect her mother, the court must base its decision on their economic best interest. They can always make voluntary payments on the car, but the court will not approve an agreement that requires them to do so.

## · CHAPTER 11 REORGANIZATION ·

For a business, the goal of a Chapter 7 bankruptcy is euthanasia—putting it out of its misery by shutting it down and distributing its assets to creditors. Chapter 11 has a much more complicated and ambitious goal—resuscitating a business so that it can ultimately emerge as a viable economic concern.

Both individuals and businesses can use Chapter 11. Businesses usually prefer Chapter 11 over Chapter 7 because Chapter 11 does not require them to dissolve at the end as Chapter 7 does. The threat of death creates a powerful incentive to try rehabilitation under Chapter 11. Individuals, however, tend to prefer Chapter 13 because it is specifically designed for them.

A Chapter 11 proceeding follows many of the same steps as Chapter 7: a petition (either voluntary or involuntary), an order for relief, a meeting of creditors, proofs of claim, and an automatic stay. There are, however, some significant differences.

## DEBTOR IN POSSESSION

Chapter 11 does not require a trustee. The bankrupt is called the **debtor in possession** and, in essence, serves as trustee. The debtor in possession has two jobs: to operate the business and to develop a plan of reorganization. A trustee is chosen only if the debtor is incompetent or uncooperative. In that case, the creditors can elect the trustee, but if they do not choose to do so, the U.S. Trustee appoints one.

## CREDITORS' COMMITTEE

In a Chapter 11 case, the creditors' committee plays a particularly important role because typically there is no neutral trustee to watch over the committee's interests. The committee has the right to help develop the plan of reorganization. The U.S. Trustee typically appoints the seven largest *un*secured creditors to the committee, although the court has the right to require the appointment of some small business creditors as well.

## PLAN OF REORGANIZATION

Once the bankruptcy petition is filed, an automatic stay goes into effect to provide the debtor with temporary relief from creditors. The next stage is to develop a plan of reorganization that provides for the payment of debts and the continuation of the business. For the first 120 days after the order for relief, the debtor has the exclusive right to propose a plan. If the shareholders and creditors accept it, then the bankruptcy case terminates. If the creditors or shareholders reject the debtor's plan, they may file their own version.

## CONFIRMATION OF THE PLAN

All the creditors and shareholders have the right to vote on the plan of reorganization. In preparation for the vote, each creditor and shareholder is assigned to a class. Chapter 11 classifies claims in the same way as Chapter 7: (1) secured claims, (2) priority claims, and (3) unsecured claims.

　　**The bankruptcy court will approve a plan if a majority of *each* class votes in favor of it.** Even if some classes vote against the plan, the court can still confirm it under what is called a **cramdown** (as in, "the plan is crammed down the creditors' throats"). If the court rejects the plan of reorganization, the creditors must develop a new one.

## DISCHARGE

A confirmed plan of reorganization is binding on the debtor and creditors. **The debtor now owns the assets in the bankrupt estate, free of all obligations except those listed in the plan.** Under a typical plan of reorganization, the debtor gives some current assets to creditors and also promises to pay them a portion of future earnings. In contrast, the Chapter 7 debtor typically relinquishes all assets (except exempt property) to creditors but then has no obligation to turn over future income. Exhibit 15.2 illustrates the steps in a Chapter 11 bankruptcy.

## SMALL-BUSINESS BANKRUPTCY

Out of concern that the lengthy procedure in Chapter 11 was harming the creditors of small businesses, Congress decided to speed up the bankruptcy process for businesses with less than $2 million in debt. After the order of relief, the bankrupt has the exclusive right to file a plan for 180 days. The court must confirm or reject the plan within 45 days after its filing. If these

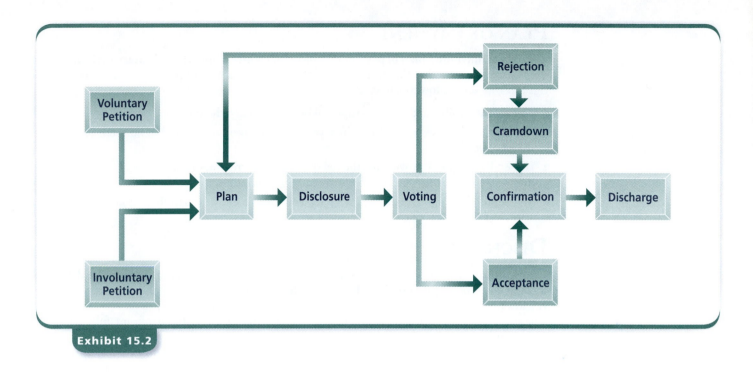

Exhibit 15.2

deadlines are not met, the case can be converted to Chapter 7 or dismissed. The impact of this amendment is uncertain, but some commentators fear that it may well cause more small companies to go out of business.

## · CHAPTER 13 CONSUMER REORGANIZATIONS ·

**The purpose of Chapter 13 is to rehabilitate an individual debtor.** It is not available at all to businesses or to individuals with more than $336,900 in unsecured debts or $1,010,650 in secured debts. Under Chapter 13, the bankrupt consumer typically keeps most of her assets in exchange for a promise to repay some of her debts using future income. Therefore, to be eligible, the debtor must have a regular source of income. Individuals usually choose this chapter because it is easier and cheaper than Chapters 7 and 11.

A bankruptcy under Chapter 13 generally follows the same course as Chapter 11: the debtor files a petition, creditors submit proofs of claim, the court imposes an automatic stay, the debtor files a plan, and the court confirms the plan. But there are some differences.

### BEGINNING A CHAPTER 13 CASE

**To initiate a Chapter 13 case, the debtor must file a voluntary petition.** Creditors cannot use an involuntary petition to force a debtor into Chapter 13. In all Chapter 13 cases, the U.S. Trustee appoints a trustee to supervise the debtor. The trustee also serves as a central clearinghouse for the debtor's payments to creditors. The debtor pays the trustee who, in turn, transmits these funds to creditors. For this service the trustee is allowed to keep 10 percent of the payments.

# PLAN OF PAYMENT

**The debtor must file a plan of payment within 15 days after filing the voluntary petition.** Only the bankruptcy court has the authority to confirm or reject a plan of payment. Creditors have no right to vote on it. However, to confirm a plan, the court must ensure that:

- The plan is feasible and the bankrupt will be able to make the promised payments;
- The plan does not extend beyond three years without good reason and in no event lasts longer than five years;
- If the plan does not provide for the debtor to pay off creditors in full, then all of the debtor's disposable income for the next five years must go to creditors; and
- The debtor is acting in good faith, making a reasonable effort to pay obligations.

# DISCHARGE

Once confirmed, a plan is binding on all creditors, whether they like it or not. **The debtor is washed clean of all prepetition debts except those provided for in the plan.** But if the debtor violates the plan, all of the debts are revived, and the creditors have a right to recover them under Chapter 7. The debts become permanently discharged only when the bankrupt fully complies with the plan.

If the debtor's circumstances change, the debtor, the trustee, or unsecured creditors can ask the court to modify the plan. Most such requests come from debtors whose income has declined. However, if the debtor's income rises, the creditors or the trustee can ask that payments increase, too.

## CHAPTER CONCLUSION

**Bankruptcy law is the safety net that catches those who are not able to meet their financial obligations.** Bankruptcy laws cannot create assets where there are none, but they can ensure that the debtor's assets, however limited, are fairly divided between the debtor and creditors. Any bankruptcy system that accomplishes this goal must be deemed a success.

## EXAM REVIEW

The following chart sets out the important elements of each bankruptcy chapter.

|  | Chapter 7 | Chapter 11 | Chapter 13 |
| --- | --- | --- | --- |
| Objective | Liquidation | Reorganization | Consumer reorganization |
| Who May Use It | Individual or organization | Individual or organization | Individual |
| Type of Petition | Voluntary or involuntary | Voluntary or involuntary | Only voluntary |
| Administration of Bankruptcy Estate | Trustee | Debtor in possession (trustee selected only if debtor is unable to serve) | Trustee |

| Selection of Trustee | Creditors have right to elect trustee; otherwise, U.S. Trustee makes appointment | Usually no trustee | Appointed by U.S. Trustee |
|---|---|---|---|
| Participation in Formulation of Plan | No plan is filed | Both creditors and debtor can propose plans | Only debtor can propose a plan |
| Creditor Approval of Plan | Creditors do not vote | Creditors vote on plan, but court may approve plan without the creditors' support | Creditors do not vote on plan |
| Impact on Debtor's Post-Petition Income | Not affected; debtor keeps all future earnings | Must contribute toward payment of pre-petition debts | Must contribute toward payment of pre-petition debts |

# PRACTICE EXAM

## MATCHING QUESTIONS

Match the following terms with the correct description:

___ A. Fresh start

___ B. Fraudulent transfer

___ C. Exempt property

___ D. Reaffirmation

___ E. Voidable preference

1. Property individual debtors can keep for themselves
2. Debtors are not liable for money owed before the filing
3. Debtor's promise to pay a debt after discharge
4. Payment to a creditor immediately before filing
5. Payment made within the year before a petition is filed with the goal of hindering creditors

## TRUE/FALSE QUESTIONS

Circle true or false:

1. T   F   One of the primary goals of the Code is to punish the debtor.

2. T   F   Each of the Code's chapters has one of two objectives—rehabilitation or liquidation.

3. T   F   A creditor is not permitted to force a debtor into bankruptcy.

4. T   F   The bankruptcy court issues an order for relief to give the debtor a chance to file a petition.

5. T   F   The Code permits *individual* debtors (but not organizations) to keep some property for themselves.

## MULTIPLE CHOICE QUESTIONS

6. CPA QUESTION: Decal Corp. incurred substantial operating losses for the past three years. Unable to meet its current obligations, Decal filed a petition of reorganization under Chapter 11 of the federal Bankruptcy Code. Which of the following statements is correct?

   A. A creditors' committee, if appointed, will consist of unsecured creditors.

   B. The court must appoint a trustee to manage Decal's affairs.

   C. Decal may continue in business only with the approval of a trustee.

   D. The creditors' committee must select a trustee to manage Decal's affairs.

EXAM *Strategy*

7. **CPA QUESTION:** A voluntary petition filed under the liquidation provisions of Chapter 7 of the federal Bankruptcy Code:

    (a) Is not available to a corporation unless it has previously filed a petition under the reorganization provisions of Chapter 11 of the Code

    (b) Automatically stays collection actions against the debtor except by secured creditors

    (c) Will be dismissed unless the debtor has 12 or more unsecured creditors whose claims total at least $5,000

    (d) Does not require the debtor to show that the debtor's liabilities exceed the fair market value of assets

    **Strategy:** One strategy for multiple choice questions is to look down the list quickly to see if you recognize right off the bat that the answers are clearly right or wrong. A is clearly wrong. You may remember that the automatic stay applies to all creditors, so B is wrong. Instead of trying to remember the amount of debt that the unsecured creditors must have, look at the fourth answer. You might remember having read almost that exact sentence in the chapter. (See the "Result" at the end of this section.)

8. CPA QUESTION: Unger owes a total of $50,000 to eight unsecured creditors and one fully secured creditor. Quincy is one of the unsecured creditors and is owed $6,000. Quincy has filed a petition against Unger under the liquidation provisions of Chapter 7 of the federal Bankruptcy Code. Unger has been unable to pay debts as they become due. Unger's liabilities exceed Unger's assets. Unger has filed papers opposing the bankruptcy petition. Which of the following statements regarding Quincy's petition is correct?

    A. It will be dismissed because the secured creditor failed to join in the filing of the petition.

    B. It will be dismissed because three unsecured creditors must join in the filing of the petition.

    C. It will be granted because Unger's liabilities exceed Unger's assets.

    D. It will be granted because Unger is unable to pay Unger's debts as they become due.

9. Why did Kim Basinger (see the chapter introduction) file under Chapter 11 rather than Chapter 13?

    A. Basinger's debts were too low to meet the requirements of Chapter 13.

    B. Basinger had committed fraud.

    C. Basinger had acted in bad faith.

    D. All individuals must file under Chapter 11.

    E. Basinger's debts exceeded the limits permitted by Chapter 13.

10. A debtor is not required to file the following document with his voluntary petition:

    A. Budget statement for the following three years.

    B. Statement of financial affairs.

    C. List of creditors.

    D. Claim of exemptions.

    E. Schedule of income and expenditures.

## SHORT-ANSWER QUESTIONS

11. ETHICS: On November 5, The Fred Hawes Organization, Inc., a small subcontractor, opened an account with Basic Distribution Corp., a supplier of construction materials.

Hawes promised to pay its bills within 30 days of purchase. Although Hawes purchased a substantial quantity of goods on credit from Basic, it made few payments on the accounts until the following March when it paid Basic over $21,000. On May 14, Hawes filed a voluntary petition under Chapter 7. Does the bankruptcy trustee have a right to recover this payment? Is it fair to Hawes's other creditors if Basic is allowed to keep the $21,000 payment?

**EXAM Strategy**

12. **Question:** Mark Milbank built custom furniture in Port Chester, New York. His business was unsuccessful, and he repeatedly borrowed money from his wife and her father. He promised that the loans would enable him to spend more time with his family. Instead, he spent more time in bed with his next-door neighbor. After the divorce, his ex-wife and her father demanded repayment of the loans. Milbank filed for protection under Chapter 13. What could his ex-wife and her father do to help their chances of being repaid?

    **Strategy:** First, ask yourself what kind of creditor they are: secured or unsecured. Then think about what creditors can do to get special treatment. (See the "Result" at the end of this section.)

13. Lydia D'Ettore received a degree in computer programming at DeVry Institute of Technology, with a grade point average of 2.51. To finance her education, she borrowed $20,516.52 from a federal student loan program. After graduation she could not find a job in her field, so she went to work as a clerk at a salary of $12,500. D'Ettore and her daughter lived with her parents free of charge. After setting aside $50 a month in savings and paying bills that included $233 for a new car (a Suzuki Samurai) and $50 for jewelry from Zales, her disposable income was $125 per month. D'Ettore asked the bankruptcy court to discharge the debts she owed for her DeVry education. Should the court do so?

14. After filing for bankruptcy, Yvonne Brown sought permission of the court to reaffirm a $6,000 debt to her credit union. The debt was unsecured and she was under no obligation to pay it. The credit union had published the following notice in its newsletter:

    If you are thinking about filing bankruptcy THINK about the long-term implications. This action, filing bankruptcy, closes the door on TOMORROW. Having no credit means no ability to purchase cars, houses, credit cards. Look into the future—no loans for the education of your children.

    Should the court approve Brown's reaffirmation?

15. Robert Britton was an office manager at the Academy of Cosmetic Surgery Medical Group. Mary Price made an appointment for a consultation about a lipectomy (removal of abdominal fat). Britton wore a name tag that identified him as a doctor, and was addressed as "doctor" by the nurse. Britton and the nurse then examined Price. Britton touched the area of her stomach where there was excess fat and showed her where the incision would be made. A doctor who worked for the Academy actually performed the surgical procedure on Price at the Academy's offices, with Britton present. After the procedure, Price went to a hospital suffering from severe pain. The hospital staff found that a tube had been left in her body at the site of the incision. The jury awarded her $275,000 in damages in a fraud suit against Britton. He subsequently filed a Chapter 7 bankruptcy petition. Is this judgment dischargeable in bankruptcy court?

16. ROLE REVERSAL: Write a multiple-choice question that highlights the difference between Chapters 7 and 11.

**7. Result:** D is the correct answer.

**12. Result:** The father and ex-wife were unsecured creditors who, as a class, come last on the priority list. The court granted their request not to discharge their loans on the grounds that Milbank had acted in bad faith.

## INTERNET RESEARCH PROBLEM

Look on the Web for your state's rules on exempt property. Compared with other jurisdictions, is your state generous or stingy with exemptions? What do you think is a fair exemption?

**You can find further practice problems in the Online Quiz at www.cengage.com/blaw/beatty.**

# AGENCY AND EMPLOYMENT LAW

**Folding shirts** all day long can get pretty boring. What is a guy to do if not bond with the other store clerks? So it was that Justin Kiser and Germania became friends while working at a Ralph Lauren Polo store in San Francisco. She left her job but not her taste for Ralph Lauren clothing. Luckily, Justin was a loyal friend, if not a loyal employee. He let her buy clothing using merchandise credits made out to fake people. He also let her use his employee discount. Not surprisingly, both of these activities were against store policies.

> **Kiser responded that he was such a low-level employee, he had no duty to the company. Call it the "Sales Clerks Don't Count" defense.**

Polo sued Kiser, alleging that he had violated his duty of loyalty. He responded that he was such a low-level employee, he had no duty to the company. Call it the "Sales Clerks Don't Count" defense. What obligation *do* workers have to their employers? Do the same rules apply to clerks and CEOs? Read on in this chapter to find out what happened to Justin Kiser in the case of *Otsuka v. Polo Ralph Lauren Corporation.*

Thus far, this book has primarily dealt with issues of individual responsibility: What happens if *you* knock someone down or *you* sign an agreement? Agency law, on the other hand, is concerned with your responsibility for the actions of others. What happens if your agent assaults someone or enters into an agreement? Agency law presents a significant trade-off: Once you hire other people, you can accomplish a great deal more, but your risk of legal liability increases immensely.

# · CREATING AN AGENCY RELATIONSHIP ·

Principals have substantial liability for the actions of their agents.[1] Therefore, disputes about whether an agency relationship exists are not mere legal quibbles but important issues with potentially profound financial consequences. According to the Restatement of Agency:

> Agency is the fiduciary relationship that arises when one person (a principal) manifests assent to another person (an agent) that the agent shall act on the principal's behalf and subject to the principal's control, and the agent manifests assent or otherwise consents so to act.[2]

To create an agency relationship, there must be:

- A **principal** and
- An **agent**
- Who mutually **consent** that the agent will act on behalf of the principal and
- Be subject to the principal's **control**
- Thereby creating a **fiduciary** relationship.

## CONSENT

To establish consent, the principal must ask the agent to do something, and the agent must agree. In the most straightforward example, you ask a neighbor to walk your dog and she agrees. Matters were more complicated, however, when Steven James met some friends one evening at a restaurant. During the two hours he was there, he drank four to six beers. (It is probably a bad sign that he cannot remember how many.) From then on, one misfortune piled upon another. After leaving the restaurant at about 7:00 p.m., James sped down a highway and crashed into a car that had stalled on the roadway, thereby killing the driver. James told the police at the scene that he had not seen the parked car (another bad sign). In a misguided attempt to help his client, James's lawyer took him to the local hospital for a blood test. Unfortunately, the test confirmed that James had indeed been drunk at the time of the accident.

The attorney knew that if this evidence was admitted at trial, his client would soon be receiving free room and board from the Massachusetts Department of Corrections. So the lawyer argued that the blood test was protected by the client-attorney privilege because the hospital had been his agent and therefore a member of the defense team. The court disagreed, however, holding that the hospital employees were not agents for the lawyer because they had not consented to act in that role. James was convicted of murder in the first degree by reason of extreme atrocity or cruelty.[3]

**Principal**
In an agency relationship, the person for whom an agent is acting.

**Agent**
In an agency relationship, the person who is acting on behalf of a principal.

---

[1] The word "principal" is always used when referring to a person. "Principle," on the other hand, refers to a fundamental idea.

[2] Section 1.01 of the Restatement (Third) of Agency (2006), prepared by the American Law Institute.

[3] *Commonwealth v. James*, 427 Mass. 312, 693 N.E.2d 148, 1998 Mass. LEXIS 175.

## CONTROL

Principals are liable for the acts of their agents because they exercise control over the agents. If principals direct their agents to commit an act, it seems fair to hold the principal liable when that act causes harm. How would you apply that rule to the following situation: William Stanford was an employee of the Agency for International Development. While on his way home to Pakistan to spend the holidays with his family, his plane was hijacked and taken to Iran, where he was killed. Stanford had originally purchased a ticket on Northwest Airlines but had traded it in for a seat on Kuwait Airways (KA). The airlines had an agreement permitting passengers to exchange tickets from one to another. Stanford's widow sued Northwest on the theory that KA was Northwest's agent. The court found, however, that no agency relationship existed because Northwest had no *control* over KA.[4] Northwest did not tell KA how to fly planes or handle terrorists; therefore it should not be liable when KA made fatal errors.

## FIDUCIARY RELATIONSHIP

A fiduciary relationship is a special relationship, with high standards. The beneficiary places special confidence in the fiduciary who, in turn, is obligated to act in good faith and candor, putting his own needs second. The purpose of a fiduciary relationship is for one person to benefit another. **Agents have a fiduciary duty to their principals.** Suppose, for example, that you hire a real estate agent to help you find a house. She shows you a great house, but does not reveal to you the brutal murder that took place there because she is afraid that you would not buy it and she would not receive a commission. She has violated her fiduciary duty to put your interests first.

## ▪ DUTIES OF AGENTS TO PRINCIPALS ▪

## DUTY OF LOYALTY

An agent has a fiduciary duty to act loyally for the principal's benefit in all matters connected with the agency relationship.[5] Remember Justin Kiser from the beginning of the chapter. Did he violate his duty of loyalty?

## OTSUKA V. POLO RALPH LAUREN CORPORATION

2007 U.S. DIST. LEXIS 86523
UNITED STATES DISTRICT COURT FOR THE NORTHERN DISTRICT OF CALIFORNIA, 2007

### CASE SUMMARY

**Facts:** The facts were set out in the opening scenario. Kiser filed a motion to dismiss on the grounds that he was such a low-level employee he did not owe a duty of loyalty to Polo.

**Issue:** *Do all employees owe a duty of loyalty to their employer?*

**Decision:** Yes, all employees owe a duty of loyalty.

**Reasoning:** The cases cited by Polo to support its claim involved higher level employees than Kiser, who was simply a clerk in a Polo store. No matter, the Restatement (Third) of Agency clearly states that all employees are agents and owe a duty of loyalty to their employers. All employees must put their employer's interests first.

---

[4] *Stanford v. Kuwait Airways Corp.*, 648 F. Supp. 1158, 1986 U.S. Dist. LEXIS 18880 (S.D.N.Y. 1986).

[5] Restatement (Third) of Agency §8.01.

## Outside Benefits

**An agent may not receive profits unless the principal knows and approves.** Suppose that Hope is an employee of the agency Big Egos and Talents, Inc. (BEAT). She has been representing Will Smith in his latest movie negotiations.[6] Smith often drives her to meetings in his new Maybach. He is so thrilled that she has arranged for him to star in the new movie *Little Men* that he buys her a Maybach. Can Hope keep this generous gift? Only with BEAT's permission. She must tell BEAT about the Maybach; the company may then take the vehicle itself or allow her to keep it.

## Confidential Information

The ability to keep secrets is important in any relationship, but especially a fiduciary relationship. **Agents can neither disclose nor use for their own benefit any confidential information they acquire during their agency.** For example, after the Beatles fired an employee, he passed on to a competitor confidential information about the royalties on a George Harrison song. The court held that the agent's obligation to keep information confidential continued even after the agency relationship ended.[7]

## Competition with the Principal

**Agents are not allowed to compete with their principal in any matter within the scope of the agency business.** Michael Jackson bought the copyright to many of the Beatles' songs. If, before he made that purchase, one of his employees had bought the songs instead, that employee would have violated her duty to Jackson. Once the agency relationship ends, however, so does the rule against competition. After the employee's job with Jackson ended, she could bid against him for the Beatles' songs.

## Conflict of Interest between Two Principals

**Unless otherwise agreed, an agent may not act for two principals whose interests conflict.** Suppose Travis represents both director Steven Spielberg and actress Angelina Jolie. Spielberg is casting the title role in his new movie, *Nancy Drew: Girl Detective,* a role that Jolie covets. Travis cannot represent these two clients when they are negotiating with each other, unless they both know about the conflict and agree to ignore it.

## Secretly Dealing with the Principal

**If a principal hires an agent to arrange a transaction, the agent may not become a party to the transaction without the principal's permission.** Suppose that actor Matt Damon hired Trang to read scripts for him. Unbeknownst to Damon, Trang had written her own script. She may not sell it to him without revealing that she wrote it herself. Damon may be perfectly happy to buy Trang's script, but he has the right, as her principal, to know that she is the person selling it.

## Appropriate Behavior

**An agent may not engage in inappropriate behavior that reflects badly on the principal.** This rule applies even to *off-duty* conduct. For example, British Airways fired flight attendants for their off-duty behavior in a hotel bar. One of the attendants raised her shirt so that her female colleague could caress her breasts while kissing her on the mouth. She then lowered her trousers, revealing her underwear. Another crew member took off his shirt and poured wine down his trousers.

---

[6] Do not be confused by the fact that Hope works as an agent for movie stars. As an employee of BEAT, her duty is to the company. She is an agent of BEAT, and BEAT works for the celebrities.

[7] *Abkco Music, Inc. v. Harrisongs Music, Ltd.,* 722 F.2d 988, 1983 U.S. App. LEXIS 15562.

# OTHER DUTIES OF AN AGENT

Before Taylor left for a five-week trip to England, he hired Claudia to rent his vacation house. Claudia never got around to listing his house on the regional rental list used by all the area brokers, but when the Fords contacted her looking for rental housing, she did show them Taylor's place. They offered to rent it for $750 per month.

Claudia called Taylor in England to tell him. He responded that he would not accept less than $850 a month, which Claudia thought the Fords would be willing to pay. He told Claudia to call back if there was any problem. The Fords decided that they would go no higher than $800 a month. Instead of calling Taylor in England, Claudia left a message on his home answering machine. When the Fords pressed her for an answer, she said she could not get in touch with Taylor. Not until Taylor returned home did he learn that the Fords had rented another house. Did Claudia violate any of the duties that agents owe to their principals?

## Duty to Obey Instructions

**An agent must obey her principal's instructions unless the principal directs her to behave illegally or unethically.** Taylor instructed Claudia to call him if the Fords rejected the offer. When Claudia failed to do so, she violated this duty.

## Duty of Care

**An agent has a duty to act with reasonable care.** In other words, an agent must act as a reasonable person would, under the circumstances. A reasonable person would not have left a message on Taylor's home answering machine when she knew he was in Europe.

## Duty to Provide Information

**An agent has a duty to provide the principal with all information in her possession that she has reason to believe the principal wants to know.** She also has a duty to provide accurate information. Claudia knew that the Fords had counteroffered for $800 a month. She had a duty to pass this information on to Taylor.

## EXAM *Strategy*

**Question:** Jonah tells his friend Boris that he would like to go parasailing. Boris is very enthusiastic and suggests they try an outfit called "Wind Beneath Your Wings," because he has heard good things about them. Boris makes a reservation, puts the $600 bill on his credit card, and picks Jonah up to drive him to the Wings location. What a friend! The day does not turn out as Jonah had hoped. While up in the air over the Pacific Ocean, his sail springs a leak, he goes plummeting into the sea and breaks both legs. While recuperating in the hospital, he learns that Wings is unlicensed. He also sees an ad for Wings offering parasailing for only $350. And Boris is listed in the ad as one of the company's instructors. Is Boris an agent for Jonah? Has he violated his fiduciary responsibility?

**Strategy:** There are two issues to consider in answering this question: (1) Was there an agency relationship? This requires consent, control, and a fiduciary relationship. (2) Has the agent fulfilled his duties?

**Result:** There is an agency relationship: Boris had agreed to help Jonah; it was Jonah who set the goal for the relationship (parasailing); the purpose of this relationship is for one person to benefit another. Boris has violated his duty to exercise due care. He should not have taken Johan to an unlicensed company. He has also violated his duty to provide information: he should have told Jonah the true cost for the lessons and also revealed that he was a principal of the company. And he violated his duty of loyalty when he worked for two principals whose interests were in conflict.

## PRINCIPAL'S REMEDIES WHEN THE AGENT BREACHES A DUTY

A principal has three potential remedies when an agent breaches her duty:

- The principal can recover from the agent any **damages** the breach has caused. Thus, if Taylor can rent his house for only $600 a month instead of the $800 the Fords offered, Claudia would be liable for $2,400—$200 a month for one year.

- If an agent breaches the duty of loyalty, he must turn over to the principal any **profits** he has earned as a result of his wrongdoing.

- If the agent has violated her duty of loyalty, the principal may **rescind** the transaction. When Trang sold a script to her principal, Matt Damon, without telling him that she was the author, she violated her duty of loyalty. Damon could rescind the contract to buy the script.

## · DUTIES OF PRINCIPALS TO AGENTS ·

**The principal must (1) reimburse the agent for reasonable expenses and (2) cooperate with the agent in performing agency tasks.** The respective duties of agents and principals can be summarized as follows:

| Duties of Agents to Principals | Duty of Principals to Agents |
| --- | --- |
| Duty of loyalty | Duty to reimburse |
| Duty to obey instructions | Duty to cooperate |
| Duty of care | |
| Duty to provide information | |
| Duty to reimburse the agent | |

## · TERMINATING AN AGENCY RELATIONSHIP ·

Either the agent or the principal can terminate the agency relationship at any time. Here are their options:

- *Term Agreement.* The principal and agent can agree in advance how long their relationship will last. Alexandra hires Nicholas to help her purchase exquisite enameled Easter eggs made for the Russian czars by Fabergé. If they agree that the relationship will last five years, they have a term agreement.

- *Achieving a Purpose.* The principal and agent can agree that the agency relationship will terminate when the principal's goals have been achieved. Alexandra and Nicholas might agree that their relationship will end when Alexandra has purchased 10 eggs.

- *Mutual Agreement.* No matter what the principal and agent agree at the start, they can always change their minds later on, as long as the change is mutual. If Nicholas and Alexandra

> **Hiring an agent is not like buying a book. You might not care which copy of the book you buy, but you do care which agent you hire.**

originally agree to a five-year term, but after only three years Nicholas decides he wants to go back to business school and Alexandra runs out of money, they can decide together to terminate the agency.

- *Agency at Will.* If they make no agreement in advance about the term of the agreement, either principal or agent can terminate at any time.

- *Wrongful Termination.* An agency relationship is a personal relationship. Hiring an agent is not like buying a book. You might not care which copy of the book you buy, but you do care which agent you hire. If an agency relationship is not working out, the courts will not force the agent and principal to stay together. **Either party always has the *power* to walk out. They may not, however, have the *right*.** If one party's departure from the agency relationship violates the agreement and causes harm to the other party, the wrongful party must pay damages. He will nonetheless be permitted to leave. If Nicholas has agreed to work for Alexandra for five years but he wants to leave after three, he can leave, provided he pays Alexandra the cost of hiring and training a replacement.

The agency agreement also terminates if either the principal or the agent becomes unable to perform his required duties. For example, if either the principal or the agent dies, the agency agreement automatically terminates. Agreement also terminates if the activity becomes illegal. Andrew and Zach hired Lucia to perform their marriage ceremony in California, but then the voters changed the law to make gay marriage illegal. The agency agreement automatically ended.

## · LIABILITY ·

Although an agent can greatly increase his principal's ability to accomplish her goals, an agency relationship also dramatically increases the risk of the principal's legal liability to third parties.

## Principal's Liability for Contracts

A principal is liable on contracts entered into on her behalf by her agent, if the agent is authorized. She may even be liable if the agent is not authorized but appeared to be so. There are three types of authority: express, implied, and apparent.

**Express authority**
Either by words or conduct, the principal grants an agent permission to act.

**Implied authority**
The agent has authority to perform acts that are reasonably necessary to accomplish an authorized transaction, even if the principal does not specify them.

**Express Authority**   The principal grants **express authority** by words or conduct that, reasonably interpreted, cause the agent to believe the principal desires her to act on the principal's account.[8] In other words, the principal asks the agent to do something and the agent does it. Craig calls his stockbroker, Alice, and asks her to buy 100 shares of Banshee Corp. for his account. She has *express authority* to carry out this transaction.

**Implied Authority**   **Unless otherwise agreed, authority to conduct a transaction includes authority to do acts that are reasonably necessary to accomplish it.**[9] David has recently inherited a house from his grandmother. He hires Nell to auction off the house and its contents. She hires an auctioneer, advertises the event, rents a tent, and generally does everything necessary to conduct a successful auction. After withholding her expenses, she sends the tidy balance to David. Totally outraged, he calls her on the phone, "How dare you hire an auctioneer and rent a tent? I never gave you permission! I *refuse* to pay these expenses!"

David is wrong. A principal almost never gives an agent absolutely complete instructions. Unless some authority is implied, David would have had to say, "Open the car door, get in, put the

---

[8] Restatement (Third) of Agency §2.01.

[9] Restatement (Third) of Agency §2.02.

key in the ignition, drive to the store, buy stickers, mark an auction number on each sticker . . ." and so forth. To solve this problem, the law assumes that the agent has authority to do anything that is reasonably necessary to accomplish her task.

**Apparent Authority**  **A principal can be liable for the acts of an agent who is not, in fact, acting with authority if the principal's conduct causes a third party reasonably to believe that the agent is authorized.** Because the principal has done something to make an innocent third party *believe* the agent is authorized, the principal is every bit as liable to the third party as if the agent did have authority.

For example, two stockbrokers sell fraudulent stock out of their offices at a legitimate brokerage house, using firm e-mail accounts and making presentations to investors in the firm conference rooms. Although the two brokers do not have *actual* or *implied* authority to sell the stock, their employer is nonetheless liable on the grounds that the brokers *appeared* to have authority. Of course, the company has the right to recover from the two brokers if it can compel them to pay.

> **Apparent authority**
> A principal does something to make an innocent third party believe that an agent is acting with the principal's authority, even though the agent is not authorized.

# Agent's Liability for Contracts

The agent's liability on a contract depends upon how much the third party knows about the principal. Disclosure is the agent's best protection against liability.

## Fully Disclosed Principal

**An agent is not liable for any contracts she makes on behalf of a *fully* disclosed principal.** A principal is fully disclosed if the third party knows of his *existence* and his *identity*. Augusta acts as agent for Parker when he buys Tracey's prize-winning show horse. Tracey does not know Parker, but she figures any friend of Augusta's must be OK. She figures wrong—Parker is a charming deadbeat. He injures Tracey's horse, fails to pay the full contract price, and promptly disappears. Tracey angrily demands that Augusta make good on Parker's debt. Unfortunately for Tracey, Parker was a fully disclosed principal—Tracey knew of his *existence* and his *identity*. Augusta is not liable because Tracey knew who the principal was and could have investigated him. Tracey's only recourse is against the principal, Parker (wherever he may be).

## Unidentified Principal

**In the case of an unidentified principal, the third party can recover from either the agent or the principal.** (An unidentified principal is also sometimes called a partially disclosed principal.[10]) A principal is unidentified if the third party knew of his *existence* but not his *identity*. Suppose Augusta had simply said, "I have a friend who is interested in buying your champion." Parker is an unidentified principal because Tracey knows only that he exists, not who he is. She cannot investigate him because she does not know his name. Tracey relies solely on what she is able to learn from the agent, Augusta. Both Augusta and Parker are liable to Tracey. (They are **jointly and severally liable**, which means that Tracey can recover from either or both of them. She cannot, however, recover more than the total that she is owed: if her damages are $100,000, she can recover that amount from either Augusta or Parker, or partial amounts from both, but in no event more than $100,000.)

> **Jointly and severally liable**
> All members of a group are liable. They can be sued as a group, or any one of them can be sued individually for the full amount owing.

## Undisclosed Principal

**In the case of an *undisclosed* principal, the third party can recover from either the agent or the principal.** A principal is undisclosed if the third party did not know of his existence. Suppose that Augusta simply asks to buy the horse herself, without mentioning that she is purchasing it for Parker. In this case Parker is an undisclosed principal because Tracey does not know that Augusta is acting for someone else. Both Parker and Augusta are jointly and severally liable. As Exhibit 16.1 illustrates, the principal is always liable, but the agent is not unless the principal's identity is a mystery.

---

[10] In the past, courts used the term "partially disclosed principal" instead of "unidentified principal." However, the Restatement (Third) of Agency now uses "unidentified principal," so we do, too. (See §1.04.)

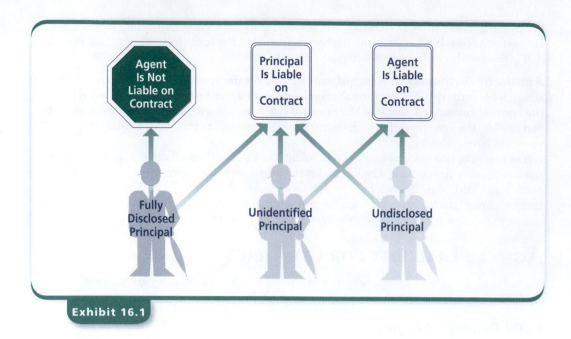

Exhibit 16.1

It is easy to understand why the principal and agent are liable on these contracts, but what about the third party? Is it fair for her to be bound on a contract if she does not even know the identity of the principal? The courts have found these contracts valid for reasons of commercial necessity. For instance, the United Nations headquarters in New York City is located on land purchased secretly. If sellers had known the identity of the purchaser (a wealthy real estate developer), the price of the land would have skyrocketed.

## PRINCIPAL'S LIABILITY FOR TORTS

**An employer is liable for a tort committed by his employee acting within the scope of employment or acting with apparent authority.**[11] This principle of liability is called ***respondeat superior***, which is a Latin phrase that means "let the master answer." Under the theory of *respondeat superior,* the employer (i.e., the principal) is liable for misbehavior by the employee (that is, the agent) whether or not the employer was at fault. Indeed, the employer is liable even if he forbade or tried to prevent the employee from misbehaving. This sounds like a harsh rule. The logic is that, because the principal controls the agent, he should be able to *prevent* misbehavior. If he cannot prevent it, at least he can *insure* against the risks. Furthermore, the principal may have deeper pockets than the agent or the injured third party and thus be better able to *afford* the cost of the agent's misbehavior.

### Employee
There are two kinds of agents: (1) *employees* and (2) *independent contractors.* **A principal *may be* liable for the torts of an employee but generally is *not* liable for the torts of an independent contractor.**[12]

> **Respondeat superior**
> The principle that an employer is liable for a tort committed by an employee acting within the scope of employment or acting with apparent authority.

---

[11] Restatement (Third) Agency §7.07.

[12] In discussions of a principal's liability for an agent, the principal was traditionally referred to as a "master" and the agent as a "servant." The Restatement (Third) of Agency, substitutes the terms "employer" and "employee" and so do we because these terms are more often used in the modern world.

**Employee or Independent Contractor?**   The more control the principal has over an agent, the more likely that the agent will be considered an employee. Therefore, when determining if agents are employees or independent contractors, courts consider whether:

- The principal controls details of the work.
- The principal supplies the tools and place of work.
- The agents work full-time for the principal.
- The agents are paid by time, not by the job.
- The work is part of the regular business of the principal.
- The principal and agents believe they have an employer-employee relationship.
- The principal is in business.

**Negligent Hiring**   As a general rule, principals are not liable for the torts of an independent contractor. There is, however, one exception to this rule: **The principal is liable for the torts of an independent contractor *if* the principal has been negligent in hiring or supervising her.** Thus an employment agency would be liable if it failed to run a background check on a nanny with a criminal record who then harmed a child in her care.

Exhibit 16.2 illustrates the difference in liability between an employee and an independent contractor.

## Scope of Employment

**Principals are only liable for torts that an employee commits within the *scope of employment*.** If an employee leaves a pool of water on the floor of a store and a customer slips and falls, the employer is liable. But if the same employee leaves water on his own kitchen floor and a friend falls, the employer is not liable because the employee is not acting within the scope of employment. An employee is acting within the scope of employment if the act:

- Is one that employees are generally responsible for
- Takes place during hours that the employee is generally employed

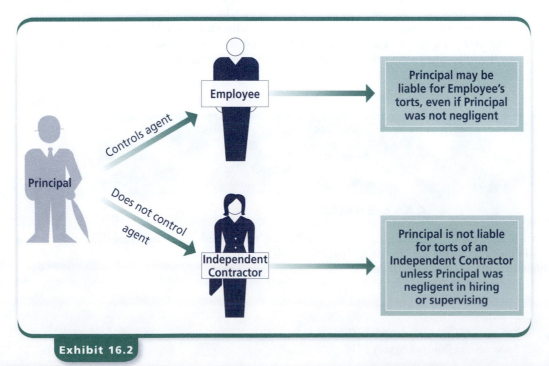

Employee — Principal may be liable for Employee's torts, even if Principal was not negligent

Principal — Controls agent / Does not control agent

Independent Contractor — Principal is not liable for torts of an Independent Contractor unless Principal was negligent in hiring or supervising

**Exhibit 16.2**

- Is part of the principal's business
- Is similar to the one the principal authorized
- Is one for which the principal supplied the tools; and
- Is not seriously criminal

**Authorization**   **An act is within the scope of employment, even if expressly forbidden, if it is of the same general nature as that authorized or if it is incidental to the conduct authorized.**[13] Although Jane has often told Hank not to speed when driving the delivery van, Hank ignores her instructions and plows into Bernadette. Hank was authorized to drive the van but not to speed. However, his speeding was of the same general nature as the authorized act, so Jane is liable to Bernadette.

**Abandonment**   **The principal is liable for the actions of the employee that occur while the employee is at work, but not for actions that occur after the employee has *abandoned* the principal's business.** The employer is liable if the employee is simply on a *detour* from company business, but the employer is not liable if the employee is off on a *frolic of his own.* Suppose that Hank, the delivery van driver, speeds during his afternoon commute home. An employee is generally not acting within the scope of his employment when he commutes to and from work, so his principal, Jane, is not liable. On the other hand, if Hank stops at the Burger Box drive-in window en route to making a delivery, Jane is liable when he crashes into Anna on the way out of the parking lot because this time he is simply making a detour.

### Negligent and Intentional Torts

**The principal is liable if the employee commits a negligent tort that causes physical harm to a person or property.** When Hank crashes into Anna, he is committing a negligent tort, and Jane is liable if all the other requirements for *respondeat superior* are met.

**A principal is *not* liable for the *intentional* torts of the employee unless the employee intended to serve some purpose of the employer.**[14] During an NBA basketball game, Kobe pushes Shaq into some chairs under the basket to prevent him from scoring a breakaway lay-up. Kobe's team is liable for his actions because he was motivated, at least in part, by a desire to help his team. But if Kobe hits Shaq in the parking lot after the playoffs are over, Kobe's team is not liable because he is no longer motivated by a desire to help the team. His motivation now is personal revenge or frustration.

In the following case a priest did wrong. Was the Church liable?

## Doe v. Liberatore

478 F. Supp. 2d 742; 2007 U.S. Dist. LEXIS 19067
United States District Court for the Middle District of Pennsylvania, 2007

### CASE SUMMARY

**Facts:** A number of priests wrote to James Timlin, the Bishop of Scranton, warning him that Father Albert Liberatore was engaging in a sexual relationship with one of his male students.

Bishop Timlin transferred Liberatore from the school to a parish church.

---

[13] Restatement (Third) of Agency §7.07.

[14] Restatement (Third) of Agency §7.07.

Fourteen year-old John Doe was a member of Liberatore's parish. Liberatore befriended Doe, taking him on outings and giving him expensive gifts. Doe routinely slept in Liberatore's bed. A number of priests told Bishop Timlin that they feared Liberatore was sexually abusing Doe. One witness reported that she had seen Doe put his hand down Liberatore's pants. Eventually, Doe himself told a priest that he was being sexually abused. The priest instructed Doe to forgive Liberatore and not to tell other people because it would ruin Doe's life and the lives of others.

Only after Liberatore pleaded guilty to multiple counts of sexual abuse did the Church dismiss him from the priesthood. Doe filed suit against the Church and Bishop Timlin, alleging that they were liable for the torts committed by Liberatore. The defendants filed a motion to dismiss.

**Issues:** *Was Liberatore acting within the scope of his employment? Were the defendants liable for his criminal acts?*

**Decision:** The priest's sexual misconduct was not within the scope of his employment. Nevertheless, the defendants could be liable on the grounds of negligent supervision.

**Reasoning:** Liberatore's sexual abuse of a child was not within the scope of his employment as a priest. In no way did it serve the purposes of the Church or Bishop Timlin. Therefore, the Court granted summary judgment for the defendants on this issue.

However, an employer owes a duty to exercise reasonable care in hiring and supervising employees. The defendants are not negligent for hiring the priest because at that point there was no evidence he would sexually abuse children, but a jury could certainly conclude that both the Church and the Bishop had been negligent in supervising Liberatore.

## Nonphysical Harm

*Nonphysical* torts are those that that harm only reputation, feelings, or wallet. **Nonphysical torts are treated like a contract claim, and the principal is liable if the employee acted with apparent authority.**[15] For example, suppose that Dwayne buys a house insurance policy from Andy, who is an agent of the Balls of Fire Insurance Company. Andy throws away Dwayne's policy and pockets his premiums. When Dwayne's house burns down, Balls of Fire is liable because Andy was acting with apparent authority.

### EXAM *Strategy*

**Question:** Daisy was the founder of an Internet start-up company. Mac was her driver. One day, after he had dropped her at a board meeting, he went to the car wash. There, he told an attractive woman that he worked for a money management firm. She gave him money to invest. On the way out of the car wash, he was so excited that he hit another customer's expensive car. Who is liable for Mac's misdeeds?

**Strategy:** In determining a principal's liability, begin by figuring out whether the agent has committed a physical or nonphysical tort. Remember that the principal is liable for physical torts within the scope of employment, but for nonphysical torts, she is liable only if the employee acted with apparent authority.

**Result:** In this case, Daisy is liable for the damage to the car because that was a physical tort within the scope of employment. But she is not liable for the investment money because Mac did not have apparent authority from her to take those funds.

## AGENT'S LIABILITY FOR TORTS

The focus of this section has been on the *principal's* liability for the agent's torts. But it is important to remember that **agents are always liable for their own torts.** Agents who commit torts are

---

[15] Restatement (Third) Agency §7.08.

personally responsible whether or not their principal is also liable. Even if the tort was committed to benefit the principal, the agent is still liable.

This rule makes obvious sense. If the agent were not liable, he would have little incentive to be careful. Imagine Hank driving his delivery van for Jane. If he were not personally liable for his own torts, he might think, "If I drive fast enough, I can make it through that light even though it just turned red. And if I don't, what the heck, it'll be Jane's problem, not mine." Agents, as a rule, may have fewer assets than their principal, but it is important that their personal assets be at risk in the event of their negligent behavior.

If the agent and principal are *both* liable, which does the injured third party sue? The principal and the agent are *jointly and severally liable,* which means, as we have seen, that the injured third party can sue either one or both, as she chooses. If she recovers from the principal, he can sue the agent.

## CHAPTER CONCLUSION

**Agency is an area of the law that affects us all because each of us has been and will continue to be both an agent and a principal many times in our lives.**

## EXAM REVIEW

1. **CREATING AN AGENCY RELATIONSHIP** A principal and an agent mutually consent that the agent will act on behalf of the principal and be subject to the principal's control, thereby creating a fiduciary relationship. (p. 263)

2. **AN AGENT'S DUTIES TO THE PRINCIPAL** An agent owes these duties to the principal: duty of loyalty, duty to obey instructions, duty of care, and duty to provide information. (pp. 264–266)

**EXAM Strategy**

**Question:** David and Fiona Rookard purchased tickets for a trip through Mexico from a Mexicoach office in San Diego. Mexicoach told them that the trip would be safe. It did not tell them, however, that their tickets had disclaimers written in Spanish warning that, under Mexican law, a bus company is not liable for any harm that befalls its passengers. The Rookards did not read Spanish. They were injured in a bus accident caused by gross negligence on the part of the driver. Did Mexicoach violate its duty to the Rookards?

**Strategy:** An agent has four duties. Which of these might Mexicoach have violated? (See the "Result" at the end of this section.)

3. **THE PRINCIPAL'S REMEDIES IN THE EVENT OF A BREACH** The principal has three potential remedies when the agent breaches her duty: recovery of damages the breach has caused, recovery of any profits earned by the agent from the breach, and rescission of any transaction with the agent. (p. 267)

**4.**  **THE PRINCIPAL'S DUTIES TO THE AGENT** The principal has two duties to the agent: to reimburse legitimate expenses and to cooperate with the agent. (p. 267)

**5.**  **POWER AND RIGHT TO TERMINATE** Both the agent and the principal have the power to terminate an agency relationship, but they may not have the right. If the termination violates the agency agreement and causes harm to the other party, the wrongful party must pay damages. (p. 267)

**6.**  **AUTOMATIC TERMINATION** An agency relationship automatically terminates if the principal or agent can no longer perform the required duties or if the activity becomes illegal. (p. 268)

**7.**  **A PRINCIPAL'S LIABILITY FOR CONTRACTS** A principal is bound by the contracts of the agent if the agent has express, implied, or apparent authority. (p. 268)

**8.**  **EXPRESS AUTHORITY** The principal grants express authority by words or conduct that, reasonably interpreted, cause the agent to believe that the principal desires her to act on the principal's account. (p. 268)

**9.**  **IMPLIED AUTHORITY** Implied authority includes authority to do acts that are incidental to a transaction, usually accompany it, or are reasonably necessary to accomplish it. (p. 268)

**10.**  **APPARENT AUTHORITY** A principal can be liable for the acts of an agent who is not, in fact, acting with authority if the principal's conduct causes a third party reasonably to believe that the agent is authorized. (p. 269)

**EXAM Strategy**

**Question:** Dr. James Leonard wrote Dr. Edward Jacobson offering him a position at a hospital. In the letter, Leonard stated that this appointment would have to be approved by the promotion committee. Jacobson believed that the promotion committee acted only as a "rubber stamp" and its approval was certain. Jacobson accepted the offer, sold his house, and quit his old job. Two weeks later, the promotion committee voted against Jacobson and the offer was rescinded. Did Leonard have apparent authority?

**Strategy:** In cases of apparent authority, begin by asking what the principal did to make the third party believe that the agent was authorized. Did the hospital do anything? (See the "Result" at the end of this section.)

**11.**  **AN AGENT'S LIABILITY FOR A CONTRACT** In the case of a fully disclosed principal, the principal is liable for any contract the agent makes on her behalf, but the agent is not liable. In the case of a unidentified or undisclosed principal, both the agent and the principal are liable on the contract. (p. 269)

**12.**  **A PRINCIPAL'S LIABILITY FOR TORTS** An employer is liable for a tort committed by its employee acting within the scope of employment or acting with apparent authority. (p. 270)

**13.** **INDEPENDENT CONTRACTOR** The principal is liable for the torts of an independent contractor if the principal has been negligent in hiring or supervising her. (p. 271)

................................................................................................

**14.** **INTENTIONAL TORTS** A principal is not liable for the intentional torts of the employee unless the employee intended to serve some purpose of the employer. (p. 272)

................................................................................................

**15.** **AGENT'S LIABILITY FOR TORTS** Agents are always liable for their own torts. (p. 273)

................................................................................................

**2. Result:** From this set of facts, there is no reason to believe that Mexicoach was disloyal or disobeyed instructions. But it seems doubtful that it was careful when hiring the bus company. And it certainly violated its duty to provide information when it failed to translate the disclaimer on the Rookards' tickets.

**10. Result:** No. Indeed, Leonard had told Jacobson that he did not have authority. If Jacobson chose to believe otherwise, that was his problem.

## PRACTICE EXAM

## MATCHING QUESTIONS

Match the following terms with their definitions:

___ A. Term agreement

___ B. Apparent authority

___ C. Agency at will

___ D. A duty of an agent

___ E. Implied authority

1. When two parties make no agreement in advance about the duration of their agreement

2. When an agent has authority to do acts that are necessary to accomplish an assignment

3. When two parties agree in advance on the duration of their agreement

4. When behavior by a principal convinces a third party that the agent is authorized, even though she is not

5. Duty of loyalty

## TRUE/FALSE QUESTIONS

Circle true or false:

**1.** T   F   A principal is always liable on a contract, whether he is fully disclosed, unidentified, or undisclosed.

**2.** T   F   When a contract goes wrong, a third party can always recover damages from the agent, whether the principal is fully disclosed, unidentified, or undisclosed.

**3.** T   F   An agent may receive profits from an agency relationship even if the principal does not know, as long as the principal is not harmed.

**4.** T   F   An agent may never act for two principals whose interests conflict.

**5.** T   F   An agent has a duty to provide the principal with all information in her possession that she has reason to believe the principal wants to know, even if he does not specifically ask for it.

# MULTIPLE-CHOICE QUESTIONS

6. CPA QUESTION: A principal will not be liable to a third party for a tort committed by an agent:
   A. Unless the principal instructed the agent to commit the tort
   B. Unless the tort was committed within the scope of the agency relationship
   C. If the agency agreement limits the principal's liability for the agent's tort
   D. If the tort is also regarded as a criminal act

7. Dorris works in Morris's pet shop. She would *not* be liable for the following activity:
   A. When a salesperson offers to sell the shop a rare parrot, Dorris buys it for her own account instead.
   B. Dorris got drunk and did obscene parrot imitations in the window of the pet shop.
   C. Morris has been trying to acquire a broad-headed snake for years, but they are an endangered species and therefore cannot be sold. Dorris hates snakes, so she refuses to buy a broad-headed snake when it is offered for sale to the shop.
   D. Dorris tells Morris that there are only 10 gerbils in the shop when really there are 20.
   E. The rhesus monkey needed to take his medication every morning. Dorris forgot one day and the monkey died.

8. Someone painting the outside of a building you own crashed through a window, injuring a visiting executive. Which of the following questions would your lawyer *not* need to ask to determine if the painter was your employee?
   A. Did the painter work full-time for you?
   B. Had you checked the painter's references?
   C. Was the painter paid by the hour or the job?
   D. Were you in the painting business?
   E. Did the painter consider herself your employee?

9. Which of the following duties does an agent *not* owe to her principal?
   A. Duty of loyalty
   B. Duty to obey instructions
   C. Duty to reimburse
   D. Duty of care
   E. Duty to provide information

10. Which of the following activities committed by an agent is *not* likely to create liability for the principal?
    A. A car accident while driving to work
    B. Accidentally spilling a glass of water in the company cafeteria, causing another employee to fall
    C. Beating up a visitor because he was rude to the company receptionist
    D. A truck accident while driving drunk in the middle of the workday
    E. Accidentally catching the building on fire while taking a smoking break

# SHORT-ANSWER QUESTIONS

11. Roy Watson sold vacuum cleaners door-to-door as an independent contractor for T & F. Before hiring Watson, the president of T & F checked with two of his former employers but could not remember if he called Watson's two references. Watson had an extensive criminal record. T & F granted Watson sales territory that included Neptune City, New Jersey. This city required that all "peddlers" such as Watson be licensed. Applicants for this license were fingerprinted. T & F never insisted that Watson apply for such a license. Watson attacked Miriam Bennett after selling a vacuum cleaner to her at her home in Neptune City. Is T & F liable to Bennett?

12. ETHICS: Radio TV Reports (RTV) was in the business of recording, transcribing, and monitoring radio and video programming for its clients. The Department of Defense (DOD) in Washington, D.C. was one of RTV's major clients. Paul Ingersoll worked for RTV until August 31. In July, the DOD solicited bids for a new contract for the following year. During this same month, Ingersoll formed his own media

monitoring business, Transmedia. RTV and Transmedia were the only two bidders on the DOD contract, which was awarded to Transmedia. Did Ingersoll violate his fiduciary duty to RTV? Aside from his legal obligations, did Ingersoll behave ethically? How does his behavior look in the light of day? Was it right?

13. Sara Kearns went to an auction at Christie's to bid on a tapestry for her employer, Nardin Fine Arts Gallery. The good news is that she purchased a Dufy tapestry for $77,000. The bad news is that it was not the one her employer had told her to buy. In the excitement of the auction, she forgot her instructions. Nardin refused to pay, and Christie's filed suit. Is Nardin liable for the unauthorized act of its agent?

14. Jack and Rita Powers purchased 312 head of cattle at an auction conducted by Coffeyville Livestock Sales Co. They did not know who owned the cattle they bought. The Powers, in turn, sold 159 of this lot to Leonard Hoefling. He sued the Powers, alleging the cattle were diseased and dying in large numbers, and recovered $38,360. Are the Powers entitled to reimbursement from Coffeyville?

15. This is a tale of marital woe. At the urging of her husband, Phyllis Thropp placed $40,000 in a brokerage account with her husband's friend Richard Gregory, a broker at Bache Halsey. Mrs. Thropp opened the account in her name alone and did not authorize Gregory to discuss the account with Mr. Thropp, nor did she authorize Mr. Thropp to act for her. Undeterred by this technicality, Mr. Thropp forged his wife's name to a power of attorney that authorized him to make decisions for her. He gave this document to Gregory. In the course of the next year, Mr. Thropp ordered Gregory to sell his wife's securities and issue checks to her. After forging her name to the checks, he cashed them and used the money to pay his gambling debts. Gregory did not process the power of attorney form according to standard Bache procedures. When the Thropps saw Gregory socially, Mrs. Thropp frequently asked him how her account was doing. Gregory somehow neglected to mention that it was not doing very well at all. He never told her about the numerous sales. Can this marriage be saved? No, the Thropps were divorced. Did Richard Gregory violate his fiduciary duty to Mrs. Thropp?

16. ROLE REVERSAL: Write a multiple choice question that deals with the liability of employers for the acts of their employees.

# INTERNET RESEARCH PROBLEM

Can you find any examples on the Internet of business dealings in which agents made purchases for an undisclosed principal? Were these business arrangements ethical? What risks did the agents face?

**You can find further practice problems in the Online Quiz at www.cengage.com/blaw/beatty.**

# EMPLOYMENT LAW

**"On the** killing beds you were apt to be covered with blood, and it would freeze solid; if you leaned against a pillar, you would freeze to that, and if you put your hand upon the blade of your knife, you would run a chance of leaving your skin on it. The men would tie up their feet in newspapers and old sacks, and these would be soaked in blood and frozen, and then soaked again, and so on, until by nighttime a man would be walking on great lumps the size of the feet of an elephant. Now and then, when the bosses were not looking, you would see them plunging their feet and ankles into the steaming hot carcass of the steer. . . . The cruelest thing of all was that nearly all of them—all of those who used knives—were unable to wear gloves, and their arms would be white with frost and their hands would grow numb, and then of course there would be accidents."[1]

> . . . you would see them plunging their feet and ankles into the steaming hot carcass of the steer.

---

[1] From Upton Sinclair, *The Jungle* (New York: Bantam Books, 1981), p. 80, a 1906 novel about the meat-packing industry.

## · INTRODUCTION ·

For most of history, the concept of career planning was unknown. By and large, people were born into their jobs. Whatever their parents had been—landowner, soldier, farmer, servant, merchant, or beggar—they became, too. Few people expected that their lives would be better than their parents'. The primary English law of employment reflected this simpler time. Unless the employee had a contract that said otherwise, he was hired for a year at a time. This rule was designed to prevent injustice in a farming society. If an employee worked through harvest time, the landowner could not fire him in the winter. Likewise, a worker could not stay the winter and then leave for greener pastures in the spring.

In the eighteenth and nineteenth centuries, the Industrial Revolution profoundly altered the employment relationship. Many workers left the farms and villages for large factories in the city. Bosses no longer knew their workers personally, so they felt little responsibility toward them. Since employees could quit their factory jobs whenever they wanted, it was thought to be only fair for employers to have the same freedom to fire a worker. Unless workers had an explicit employment contract, they were employees at will. **An *employee at will* could be fired for a good reason, a bad reason, or no reason at all.** For nearly a century, this was the basic common law rule of employment.[2]

However evenhanded this rule may have sounded in theory, in practice it could lead to harsh results. The lives of factory workers were grim. It was not as if they could simply pack up and leave; conditions were no better elsewhere. Courts and legislatures began to recognize that individual workers were generally unable to negotiate fair contracts with powerful employers. Since the beginning of the twentieth century, employment law has changed dramatically. Now, the employment relationship is more strictly regulated by statutes and by the common law. **No longer can a boss discharge an employee for any reason whatsoever.**

Note that many of the statutes discussed in this chapter were passed by Congress and therefore apply nationally. The common law, however, comes from state courts and only applies locally. We will look at a sampling of cases that illustrates national trends, even though the law may not be the same in every state.

This chapter covers three topics in employment law: (1) employment security; (2) safety and privacy in the workplace; and (3) financial protection. Another important topic, employment discrimination, is covered in Chapter 18.

## · EMPLOYMENT SECURITY ·

### National Labor Relations Act

Without unions to represent employee interests, employers could simply fire any troublemaking workers who complained about conditions in factories or mines. By joining together, workers could bargain with their employers on more equal terms. Naturally, the owners fought against the unions, firing organizers and even hiring goons to beat them up. Distressed by anti-union violence, Congress passed the National Labor Relations Act in 1935. Known as the NLRA or the Wagner Act, this statute:

- Prohibits employers from penalizing workers who engage in union activity (for example, joining or forming a union); and
- Requires employers to "bargain in good faith" with unions.

---

[2] You remember that common law rules are those created by the courts.

# FAMILY AND MEDICAL LEAVE ACT

When Randy Seale's wife went into premature labor with triplets, he stayed home from his job as a truck driver with Associated Milk Producers, Inc. However, the milk of human kindness did not flow in this company's veins: It promptly fired the expectant father. Since Seale was an employee at will, the company's action would have been perfectly legal without the Family and Medical Leave Act (FMLA).

The FMLA guarantees both men and women up to 12 weeks of unpaid leave each year for childbirth, adoption, or medical emergencies for themselves or a family member. An employee who takes a leave must be allowed to return to the same or an equivalent job with the same pay and benefits. The FMLA applies only to companies with at least 50 workers and to employees who have been with the company full time for at least a year—this is about 60 percent of all employees. The milk company ultimately agreed to pay Seale $10,000 for its violation of the FMLA.

# COBRA

Many companies provide health insurance for their employees. The problem with this system used to be that losing your job meant losing your health insurance on the spot. Then the U.S. Congress passed the Consolidated Omnibus Budget Reconciliation Act (COBRA). This statute provides that former employees must be allowed to continue their health insurance for 18 months after leaving their job. The catch is that employees must pay for it themselves, up to 102 percent of the cost. (The extra 2 percent covers administrative expenses.)

COBRA applies to any company with 20 or more workers. Both employees and their families are covered. So, for example, if the child of a worker graduates from college and is no longer eligible under her parent's health insurance plan, she can elect to continue her coverage by paying for it herself.

# COMMON LAW PROTECTIONS

The common law employment at will doctrine was created by the courts. Because that rule has sometimes led to absurdly unfair results, the courts have now created a major exception to the rule—**wrongful discharge.**

## *Wrongful Discharge: Violating Public Policy*

Olga Monge was a schoolteacher in her native Costa Rica. After moving to New Hampshire, she attended college in the evenings to earn a U.S. teaching degree. At night, she worked at the Beebe Rubber Co. During the day, she cared for her husband and three children. When she applied for a better job at her plant, the foreman offered to promote her if she would be "nice" and go out on a date with him. When she refused, he assigned her to a lower-wage job, took away her overtime, made her clean the washrooms, and ridiculed her. Finally, she collapsed at work and he fired her.

At that time an employee at will could be fired for any reason. But the New Hampshire Supreme Court decided to change the rule. It held that Monge's firing was a **wrongful discharge.** Under the doctrine of *wrongful discharge,* an employer cannot fire a worker for a reason that violates public policy.

**Although the public policy rule varies from state to state, in essence, it prohibits an employer from firing a worker for a reason that violates basic social rights, duties, or responsibilities.** Here are some examples of the public policy doctrine.

### Refusing to Violate the Law
Larry Downs went to Duke Hospital for surgery on his cleft palate. When he came out of the operating room, the doctor instructed a nurse, Marie Sides, to give Downs enough anesthetic to immobilize him. Sides refused because she thought

**Wrongful discharge**
An employer may not fire a worker for a reason that violates basic social rights, duties or responsibilities.

the anesthetic was wrong for this patient. The doctor angrily administered the anesthetic himself. Shortly thereafter, Downs stopped breathing. Before the doctors could resuscitate him, he suffered permanent brain damage. When Downs's family sued the hospital, Sides was called to testify. A number of Duke doctors told her that she would be "in trouble" if she testified. She did testify and, after three months of harassment, was fired. When she sued Duke University, the court held that the university could not fire an employee for telling the truth in court.

**As a general rule, employees may not be discharged for refusing to break the law.** For example, courts have protected employees who refused to participate in an illegal price-fixing scheme, fake pollution control records required by state law, pollute waters in violation of federal law, or assist a supervisor in stealing from customers.

**ETHICS**   Does an employer ever have the right to require workers to participate in an illegal scheme? Suppose that state pollution control regulations would force a company out of business. When the life of the company is at stake, does the boss have a right to expect a worker to cooperate by fudging records? What guidance does the Chapter 2 Ethics Checklist offer? Is this behavior legal? How would it look in the light of day? ◆

**Exercising a Legal Right**   Dorothy Frampton injured her arm while working at the Central Indiana Gas Co. Her employer (and its insurance company) paid her medical expenses and her salary during the four months she was out of work. When she discovered that she also qualified for benefits under the state's workers' compensation plan, she filed a claim and received payment. One month later, the company fired her. When she sued, the court held the company liable on the theory that if employers can penalize employees for filing workmen's compensation claims, then employees will not file and the whole purpose of the statute will be undermined. **As a general rule, an employer may not fire a worker for exercising a legal right.**

**Performing a Legal Duty**   **Courts have consistently held that an employee may not be fired for serving on a jury.** Jury duty is an important civic obligation that employers are not permitted to undermine.

In the following case, employees objected when their company supplied defective human tissue for transplantation into live patients. Should their behavior be protected as a matter of public policy?

## KOZLOSKI V. AMERICAN TISSUE SERVICES FOUNDATION

2006 U.S. Dist. LEXIS 95435
UNITED STATES DISTRICT COURT FOR THE DISTRICT OF MINNESOTA, 2006

### CASE SUMMARY

**Facts:** American Tissue Services Foundation (ATSF) was in the business of supplying human tissue from cadavers for transplantation into live patients. Mike Slack, an employee of ATSF, revealed to his boss that he had falsified a donor medical record and changed the donor's blood type on the form. This falsification was not only dangerous to recipients of the tissue, it violated Food and Drug Agency (FDA) regulations. Slack was fired and the infractions were reported to the FDA, as required by law.

It turned out, however, that Slack was the foster child of the company's chairman. And, in this case, (foster) blood was thicker

than water. The chairman not only hired Slack at another company as, believe it or not, a quality assurance specialist, but he fired Slack's boss and the two men who had reported the problem to the FDA. The men filed suit against ATSF for wrongful discharge but the company filed a motion to dismiss on the grounds that the public policy doctrine in Minnesota applied only to employees who had refused to violate the law.

**Issues:** *Does the public policy doctrine in Minnesota apply only to employees who refuse to violate the law? Do the plaintiffs have the right to proceed with their lawsuit?*

**Decision:** The wrongful discharge doctrine also applies to situations in which an employee is fired for a reason that clearly violates public policy. The defendants may proceed with their lawsuit.

**Reasoning:** These plaintiffs were fired because they reported to their employer and the FDA their concerns that human tissue was wrongly labeled. This wrongdoing not only created grave risks for the recipients but also violated federal law. ATSF alleges that, under Minnesota law, employees can bring a wrongful discharge claim only if they were fired for refusing to violate the law. This reading of the law is incorrect. Wrongful discharge also applies when the termination is for a reason that *clearly* violates public policy. This termination meets that standard. The safe use of human tissue in live patients is *clearly* a matter of public safety and, therefore, public policy.

## Contract Law

Traditionally, many employers (and employees) thought that only a formal, signed document qualified as an employment contract. Increasingly, however, courts have been willing to enforce an employer's more casual promises, whether written or oral.

**Truth in Hiring**   When the Tanana Valley Medical–Surgical Group, Inc. hired James Eales as a physician's assistant, it promised him that as long as he did his job, he could stay there until retirement age. Six years later the company fired him without cause. The Alaska Supreme Court held **oral promises made during the hiring process are enforceable.**

**Employee Handbooks**   The employee handbook at Blue Cross & Blue Shield stated that employees could be fired only for just cause and then only after warnings, notice, a hearing, and other procedures. Charles Toussaint was fired without warning five years after he joined the company. The court held that **an employee handbook creates a contract.**

## Tort Law

Workers have successfully sued their employers under the following tort theories.

**Defamation**   **Employers may be liable for defamation when they give false and unfavorable references about a former employee**. In his job as a bartender at the Capitol Grille restaurant, Christopher Kane often flirted with customers. After he was fired from his job, his ex-boss claimed that Kane had been "fired from every job he ever had for sexual misconduct." In fact, Kane had never been fired before. He recovered $300,000 in damages for this defamation.

**More than half of the states, however, recognize a** *qualified privilege* **for employers who give references about former employees.** A **qualified privilege** means that employers are liable only for false statements that they know to be false or that are primarily motivated by ill will. After Becky Chambers left her job at American Trans Air, Inc., she discovered that her former boss was telling anyone who called for a reference that Chambers "does not work good with other people," is a "troublemaker," and "would not be a good person to rehire." However, Chambers was unable to prove that her boss had been primarily motivated by ill will. Neither Trans Air nor the boss was held liable for these statements because they were protected by the qualified privilege.

Even if the employer wins, a trial is expensive and takes a lot of time. Therefore, many companies tell their managers that, when asked for a reference, they should only reveal the person's salary and dates of employment and not offer an opinion on job performance.

On the flip side, do employers have any obligation to warn about risky workers? **Generally, courts have held that employers do not have a legal obligation to disclose information about former employees.** For example, while Jeffrey St. Clair worked at the St. Joseph Nursing Home, he was disciplined 24 times for actions ranging from extreme violence to drug and alcohol use. When he applied for a job with Maintenance Management Corp., St. Joseph refused to give any information other than St. Clair's dates of employment. After

**Qualified privilege**
Employers are liable only for false statements that they know to be false or that are primarily motivated by ill will.

he savagely murdered a security guard at his new job, the guard's family sued, but the court dismissed the case.

**In some recent cases, however, courts have held that, when a former worker is potentially dangerous, employers do have an obligation to disclose this information.** For example, officials from two junior high schools gave Robert Gadams glowing letters of recommendation without mentioning that he had been fired for inappropriate sexual conduct with students. While an assistant principal at a new school, he molested a 13-year-old. Her parents sued the former employers. The court held that the writer of a letter of recommendation has "a duty not to misrepresent the facts in describing the qualifications and character of a former employee, if making these misrepresentations would present a substantial, foreseeable risk of physical injury to the third persons." As a result of cases such as this, it makes sense to disclose past violent behavior.

> **ETHICS** What if someone calls you to check references on a former employee who had a drinking problem? The job is driving a van for junior high school sports teams. What is the manager's ethical obligation in this situation? Many managers say that, in the case of a serious problem such as alcoholism, sexual harassment, or drug use, they will find a way to communicate that an employee is unsuitable. What if the ex-employee says she is reformed? Are people entitled to a second chance? Is it right to risk a defamation suit against your company to protect others from harm? What solutions does the Ethics Checklist in Chapter 2 suggest? Would it be just to reveal private information about a former employee? Is the process fair if you provide information that the job applicant has no opportunity to rebut because it is kept secret? ◆

**Intentional Infliction of Emotional Distress** **Employers who permit cruel treatment of their workers face liability under the tort of intentional infliction of emotional distress.** For example, the employer was held liable in the following cases:

- When a 57-year-old social work manager at Yale–New Haven Hospital was fired, she was forced to place her personal belongings in a plastic bag and was escorted out the door by security guards in full view of gaping coworkers. A supervisor told her that she would be arrested for trespassing if she returned. A jury awarded her $105,000.

- An employee swore at a coworker and threatened her with a knife because she rejected his sexual advances. Her superiors fired her for complaining about the incident.

# WHISTLEBLOWING

FMC Corp. sold 9,000 Bradley Fighting Vehicles to the U.S. Army at a price of $1.5 million each. Designed to carry soldiers around battlefields in Eastern Europe, this vehicle was supposed to "swim" across water. But Henry Boisvert, an FMC supervisor, charged that when a test Bradley entered a pond, it immediately filled with water. FMC workers had no time to weld gaps properly, so they filled them in with putty instead. FMC fired Boisvert for raising these quality issues, but the jury sided with him, finding FMC liable for $171.6 million.

No one likes to be accused of wrongdoing even if (or, perhaps, especially if) the accusations are true. **This is exactly what whistleblowers do: They are employees who disclose illegal behavior on the part of their employer.** Not surprisingly, many companies, when faced with such an accusation by an employee, prefer to shoot the messenger.

Whistleblowers are protected in the following situations:

- *The False Claims Act.* Henry Boisvert recovered under the federal False Claims Act, a statute that permits anyone to bring suit against someone who defrauds the government. The Act also prohibits employers from firing workers who file suit under the statute.

- *Employees of Public Companies.* The Sarbanes-Oxley Act of 2002 protects employees of public companies who provide evidence of fraud to investigators. A successful plaintiff must be rehired and given back pay.

- *Common Law.* Most state courts do not permit employers to fire workers who report illegal activity. For example, a Connecticut court held a company liable when it fired a quality control director who reported to his boss that some products had failed quality tests.

### EXAM *Strategy*

**Question:** When Shiloh interviewed for a sales job at a medical supply company, the interviewer promised that she could work exclusively selling medical devices and would not have to be involved in the sale of drugs. Once she began work (as an employee at will), Shiloh discovered that the sales force was organized around regions, not products, so she had to sell both devices and drugs. When she complained to her boss over lunch in the employee lunchroom, he said in a loud voice, "You are a big girl now, it's time you learned that you don't always get what you want." That afternoon, she was fired. Does she have a valid claim against the company?

**Strategy:** First: We know that Shiloh is an employee at will. Is she protected by a *statute*? So far, we have learned about two statutes: the FMLA and COBRA. Neither applies here.

Second: Does the *common law* apply? Shiloh has had two interactions with the company—being hired and being fired. What protections does the common law provide during the hiring process? The employer's promises are enforceable. Here, the company is liable because the interviewer clearly made a promise that the company did not keep. What about the way in which Shiloh was fired? Is it intentional infliction of emotional distress? Was this treatment cruel? Probably not cruel enough to constitute intentional infliction of emotional distress.

**Result:** The company is liable to Shiloh for making false promises to her during the hiring process but not for the manner in which she was fired.

## • SAFETY AND PRIVACY IN THE WORKPLACE •

## WORKPLACE SAFETY

**Congress passed the Occupational Safety and Health Act (OSHA) to ensure safe working conditions.** Under OSHA:

- Employers are under a general obligation to keep their workplace free from hazards that could cause serious harm to employees.

- Employers must comply with specific health and safety standards. For example, health care personnel who work with blood are not permitted to eat or drink in areas where the blood is kept and must not put their mouths on any instruments used to store blood.

- Employers must keep records of all workplace injuries and accidents.

- The Occupational Safety and Health Administration (also known as OSHA) may inspect workplaces to ensure that they are safe. OSHA may assess fines for violations and order employers to correct unsafe conditions.

OSHA has done a lot to make the American workplace safer. In 1900, roughly 35,000 workers died and 350,000 were injured at work. One hundred years later, the workforce had grown five times larger but the number of annual deaths had fallen to 5,100.

# EMPLOYEE PRIVACY

Upon opening the country's first moving assembly line in the early 1900s, Henry Ford issued a booklet, "Helpful Hints and Advice to Employees," that warned against drinking, gambling, borrowing money, taking in boarders, and practicing poor hygiene. Ford also created a department of 100 investigators for door-to-door checks on his employees' drinking habits, sexual practices, and housekeeping skills. It sounds pretty outrageous, but in modern times employees have been fired or disciplined for such extracurricular activities as playing dangerous sports, dating coworkers, or even having high cholesterol. What protection do workers have against intrusive employers?

**Employees are entitled under the common law to a reasonable expectation of privacy.** This protection means that an employer could not, for instance, search an employee's home even if looking for items that the employee might have stolen from the company. What other privacy protections do workers have?

### Off-Duty Conduct

> **Can a boss fire a worker for smoking at home?**

A worker's off-duty conduct may affect her employer. For instance, a smoker may miss many days of work or have higher healthcare costs. Does a boss have the right to control employees outside of the workplace? Can a boss, say, fire a worker for smoking at home? (Someone who smokes over the weekend would still have nicotine in his blood on Monday.) Some states have passed laws that protect the right of employees to engage in any *lawful* activity when off-duty, including smoking, drinking socially, having high cholesterol, being overweight, or engaging in dangerous hobbies—bungee jumping or roller blading, for instance. In the absence of such a statute, however, an employer does have the right to fire an employee for off-duty conduct.

### Alcohol and Drug Testing

Government employees can be tested for drug and alcohol use only if they show signs of use or if they are in a job where this type of abuse endangers the public. Most states permit *private* employers to administer alcohol and drug tests, and a substantial number do.

### Lie Detector Tests

Under the Employee Polygraph Protection Act of 1988, employers may not require, or even suggest, that an employee or job candidate submit to a lie detector test, except as part of an "ongoing investigation" into crimes that have occurred.

### Electronic Monitoring of the Workplace

Technological advances in communications have raised a host of new privacy issues. The **Electronic Communications Privacy Act of 1986 (ECPA) permits employers to monitor workers' telephone calls and e-mail messages if (1) the employee consents; (2) the monitoring occurs in the ordinary course of business; or (3) in the case of e-mail, the employer provides the e-mail system.** However, bosses may not disclose any private information revealed by the monitoring.

In the following case, two employees used company e-mail to trash-talk. Could they be fired for their indiscretion?

# YOU *be the* JUDGE

### MICHAEL A. SMYTH v. THE PILLSBURY CO.

914 F. Supp. 97, 1996 U.S. Dist. LEXIS 776
United States District Court for the Eastern
District of Pennsylvania, 1996

**Facts:** The Pillsbury Co. repeatedly assured its employees that all company e-mail was confidential. The company promised not to intercept e-mail or use it against employees. One evening at home, Michael Smyth and his supervisor engaged in a series of e-mail exchanges that threatened to "kill the backstabbing bastards" (that is, company sales managers) and referred to the planned holiday party as the "Jim Jones Koolaid affair." The company found out about these e-mails and fired both men. Smyth sued, alleging that the company had violated his right to privacy.

**You Be the Judge:** Should employee e-mail be private if the company promises that it is?

**Argument for Smyth:** Pillsbury violated Smyth's privacy rights because:

- It intruded into Smyth's life in a manner that any reasonable person would find offensive.

- Smyth had a reasonable expectation of privacy. The company had told him repeatedly that it would not read his e-mail.

**Argument for Pillsbury:** The company had no choice but to fire Smyth after he made death threats against other employees. What if the company had done nothing and he had carried out those threats? Furthermore, Smyth could not have a reasonable expectation of privacy with an e-mail system that the company established and maintained for the use of its employees.

## EXAM *Strategy*

**Question:** To ensure that its employees did not use illegal drugs in or outside the workplace, Rain Co. required all employees to take a lie detector test. Moreover, managers began to screen the company e-mail system for drug references. Jagger was fired for refusing to take the polygraph test. Jonathan was sacked when a search of his e-mail revealed that he had used marijuana during the prior weekend. Has the company acted legally?

**Strategy:** First: As employees at will, are Jagger and Jonathan protected by a statute? The Employee Polygraph Protection Act permits employers to require a lie detector test as part of an ongoing investigation into crimes that have occurred. Here, Rain has no reason to believe that a crime occurred, so it cannot require a polygraph test. Second: What about Jonathan's marijuana use? The ECPA permits Rain to monitor e-mail messages on its own system. But can the company fire Jonathan for illegal off-duty conduct? Some statutes protect employees for *legal* behavior outside the workplace, but no state protects employees for behavior that violates the law.

**Result:** The company is liable to Jagger for requiring him to take the lie detector test, but not to Jonathan for monitoring his e-mail or firing him for illegal drug use.

## • FINANCIAL PROTECTION •

Congress and the states have enacted laws that provide employees with a measure of financial security. All of the laws in this section were created by statute, not by the courts.

### FAIR LABOR STANDARDS ACT

The Fair Labor Standards Act (FLSA) regulates wages and limits child labor. The wage provisions do not apply to managerial, administrative, or professional staff, which means that accounting, consulting, and law firms (among others) are free to require as many hours a week as their employees can humanly perform without having to pay overtime or the minimum wage.

The FLSA:

- Does not limit the number of hours a week that an employee can work but it does specify that **workers must be paid time and a half for any hours over 40 in one week.**

- **Prohibits "oppressive child labor,"** which means that children under 14 may work only in agriculture and entertainment. Fourteen- and 15-year-olds are permitted to work limited hours after school in nonhazardous jobs. Sixteen- and 17-year-olds may work unlimited hours in nonhazardous jobs.

- **Sets the federal minimum wage.** As of July 2009, the federal minimum wage is $7.25 per hour, although some states have established a higher minimum.

## WORKERS' COMPENSATION

**Workers' compensation statutes provide payment to employees for injuries incurred at work.** In return, employees are not permitted to sue their employers for negligence. The amounts allowed (for medical expenses and lost wages) under workers' comp statutes are often less than a worker might recover in court, but the injured employee trades the certainty of some recovery for the higher risk of rolling the dice at trial.

## SOCIAL SECURITY

The federal Social Security system began in 1935, during the depths of the Great Depression, to provide a basic safety net for the elderly, ill, and unemployed. **The Social Security system pays benefits to workers who are retired, disabled, or temporarily unemployed and to the spouses and children of disabled or deceased workers.** It also provides medical insurance to the retired and disabled. The Social Security program is financed through a tax on wages that is paid by employers, employees, and the self-employed.

Although the Social Security system has done much to reduce poverty among the elderly, many worry that it cannot survive in its current form. When workers pay taxes, the proceeds do not go into a savings account for their retirement, but instead are used to pay benefits to current retirees. In 1940, there were 40 workers for each retiree; currently, there are 3.3. By 2030, when the last Baby Boomers retire, there will be only two workers to support each retiree—a prohibitive burden. No wonder Baby Boomers are often cautioned not to count on Social Security when making their retirement plans.

The Federal Unemployment Tax Act (FUTA) is the part of the Social Security system that provides support to the unemployed. FUTA establishes some national standards, but states are free to set their own benefit levels and payment schedules. While receiving payments, a worker must make a good-faith effort to look for other employment. A worker who quits voluntarily or is fired for just cause is not entitled to benefits.

## CHAPTER CONCLUSION

Although managers sometimes feel overwhelmed by the long list of laws that protect workers, the United States guarantees its workers fewer rights than virtually any other industrialized nation. For instance, Japan, Great Britain, France, Germany, and Canada all require employers to show just cause before terminating workers. Although American employers are no longer insulated from minimum standards of fairness, reasonable behavior, and compliance with important policies, they still have great freedom to manage their employees.

# EXAM REVIEW

1.  **TRADITIONAL COMMON LAW RULE** Traditionally, an employee at will could be fired for a good reason, a bad reason, or no reason at all. This right is now modified by common law and by statute. (p. 280)

2.  **NATIONAL LABOR RELATIONS ACT** The National Labor Relations Act prohibits employers from penalizing workers for union activity. (p. 280)

3.  **FAMILY AND MEDICAL LEAVE ACT** The Family and Medical Leave Act guarantees workers up to 12 weeks of unpaid leave each year for childbirth, adoption, or medical emergencies for themselves or a family member. (p. 281)

4.  **COBRA** This statute provides that former employees must be allowed to continue their health insurance for 18 months after leaving their job, although they must pay for it themselves. (p. 281)

5.  **WRONGFUL DISCHARGE** Under the doctrine of wrongful discharge, an employer cannot fire a worker for a reason that violates public policy. (p. 281)

6.  **PUBLIC POLICY** The public policy rule varies from state to state but, in essence, it prohibits an employer from firing a worker for a reason that violates basic social rights, duties, or responsibilities. (p. 281)

7.  **TRUTH IN HIRING** Promises made during the hiring process are enforceable. (p. 283)

**EXAM Strategy**

**Question:** When Phil McConkey interviewed for a job as an insurance agent with Alexander & Alexander, the company did not tell him that it was engaged in secret negotiations to merge with Aon. When the merger went through soon thereafter, Aon fired McConkey. Was Alexander liable for not telling McConkey about the possible merger?

**Strategy:** Was McConkey protected by a statute? No. Did the company make any promises to him during the hiring process? (See the "Result" at the end of this section.)

8.  **HANDBOOKS** An employee handbook creates a contract. (p. 283)

9.  **DEFAMATION** Employers may be liable for defamation if they give false and unfavorable references. More than half of the states, however, recognize a qualified privilege for employers who give references about former employees. (p. 283)

**EXAM Strategy**

**Question:** Jack was a top salesperson but a real pain in the neck. He argued with everyone, especially his boss, Ross. Finally, Ross had had enough and abruptly fired Jack. But he was worried that if Jack went to work for a competitor, he might take business away. So Ross told everyone who called for a reference that Jack was a difficult human being. Is Ross liable for these statements?

**Strategy:** Ross would be liable for making untrue statements. (See the "Result" at the end of this section.)

10. **INTENTIONAL INFLICTION OF EMOTIONAL DISTRESS** Employers are liable if they treat their workers cruelly. (p. 284)

11. **WHISTLEBLOWERS** Whistleblowers receive some protection under both federal and state laws. (p. 284)

12. **OSHA** The goal of the Occupational Safety and Health Act is to ensure safe conditions in the workplace. (p. 285)

13. **EMPLOYEE PRIVACY** An employer may not violate a worker's reasonable expectation of privacy. However, unless a state has passed a statute to the contrary, employers may monitor many types of off-duty conduct (even legal activities such as smoking). (p. 286)

14. **THE ECPA** The Electronic Communications Privacy Act of 1986 permits employers to monitor workers' telephone calls and e-mail messages if (1) the employee consents, (2) the monitoring occurs in the ordinary course of business, or (3) in the case of e-mail, the employer provides the e-mail system. (p. 286)

15. **THE FLSA** The Fair Labor Standards Act regulates minimum and overtime wages. It also limits child labor. (p. 287)

16. **WORKERS' COMPENSATION** Workers' compensation statutes ensure that employees receive payment for injuries incurred at work. (p. 288)

17. **SOCIAL SECURITY** The Social Security system pays benefits to workers who are retired, disabled, or temporarily unemployed and to the spouses and children of disabled or deceased workers. (p. 288)

**7. Result:** The court held that when Alexander hired him, it was making an implied promise that he would not be fired immediately. The company was liable for not having revealed the merger negotiations.

**9. Result:** These statements were true, so Ross would not be liable. Before making the statements, though, he should ask himself if he wanted the burden of having to prove them true in court.

# PRACTICE EXAM

## MATCHING QUESTIONS

Match the following terms with their definitions:

| | |
|---|---|
| ___ A. Employee at will | 1. A federal statute that ensures safe working conditions |
| ___ B. Public policy rule | 2. When an employee is fired for a bad reason |
| ___ C. FLSA | 3. An employee who discloses illegal behavior on the part of his employer |
| ___ D. Wrongful discharge | 4. An employee without an explicit employment contract |
| ___ E. OSHA | 5. A federal statute that regulates wages and limits child labor |
| ___ F. Whistleblower | 6. An employer may not fire a worker for a reason that violates basic social rights, duties or responsibilities |

## TRUE/FALSE QUESTIONS

Circle true or false:

1. T  F  An employee may be fired for a good reason, a bad reason, or no reason at all.

2. T  F  An employee may be fired if she disobeys a direct order from her boss not to join a labor union.

3. T  F  Promises made by the employer during the hiring process are not enforceable.

4. T  F  In some states, an employer is not liable for false statements they make about former employees unless they know these statements are false or are primarily motivated by ill will.

5. T  F  The federal government has the right to inspect workplaces to ensure that they are safe.

6. T  F  Any employer has the right to insist that employees submit to a lie detector test.

7. T  F  Federal law limits the number of hours every employee can work.

8. T  F  Children under 16 may not hold paid jobs.

9. T  F  Only workers, not their spouses or children, are entitled to benefits under the Social Security system.

## MULTIPLE-CHOICE QUESTIONS

10. Mike is an employee at will. "You're fired!" says Regina, his boss. "Why?" asks Mike. "Never mind why," Regina replies. "I can fire you for any reason at all. Scram!" Can Regina fire Mike for any reason at all?
    A. Yes.
    B. Regina must have a good reason to fire Mike if he has worked at the firm for more than one year.
    C. Regina may fire Mike if he is out for more than three weeks while serving on a jury.
    D. Regina may not fire Mike for logging onto pornographic Web sites at work.
    E. Regina may not fire Mike for testifying in court that Regina was violating federal pollution laws.

11. Under the FMLA:
    A. Both men and women are entitled to leave from their jobs for childbirth, adoption, or medical emergencies.
    B. An employee is entitled to 12 weeks of paid leave.

C. An employee is entitled to leave to care for any member of his household, including pets.

D. An employee who takes a leave is entitled to return to the exact job she left.

E. All employees in the country are covered.

12. Which of the following statements is true under the public policy doctrine?

A. An employee can be fired for any reason.

B. An employee can be fired for threatening a coworker.

C. An employee can be fired for filing a workers' compensation claim.

D. An employee can be fired for violating company policy even if he does so to save someone's life.

E. An employee can be fired for refusing to lie under oath on the witness stand.

13. A whistleblower

A. Is always protected by the law.

B. Is never protected by the law.

C. Is always protected when filing suit under the False Claims Act.

D. Is always protected if she is an employee of the federal government.

E. Is always protected if she works for a private company.

14. Jack was furious when Hermione left the company in the middle of a very busy sales period. He promised that he would get even with her. Another employer called to check Hermione's references. Which of the following statements should Jack make, if his goal is to limit his company's potential liability?

A. Hermione was generally a good worker, but she was often late arriving at the office. (This is true.)

B. Hermione tried to run over a coworker with her car. (This is true.)

C. Hermione wore inappropriate clothing. (This is not true.)

D. Hermione doesn't know her debits from her credits. (This is not true.)

E. Hermione worked for this company for a year and a half. Her title was Chief Knowledge Officer. (This is true.)

15. CPA QUESTION: An unemployed CPA generally would receive unemployment compensation benefits if the CPA:

A. Was fired as a result of the employer's business reversals.

B. Refused to accept a job as an accountant while receiving extended benefits.

C. Was fired for embezzling from a client.

D. Left work voluntarily without good cause.

## SHORT-ANSWER QUESTIONS

16. When Theodore Staats went to his company's "Council of Honor Convention," he was accompanied by a woman who was not his wife, although he told everyone she was. The company fired him. Has Staats's employer violated public policy?

17. ETHICS: When Walton Weiner interviewed for a job with McGraw-Hill, Inc., he was assured that the company would not terminate an employee without "just cause." McGraw-Hill's handbook said, "[The] company will resort to dismissal for just and sufficient cause only, and only after all practical steps toward rehabilitation or salvage of the employee have been taken and failed. However, if the welfare of the company indicates that dismissal is necessary, then that decision is arrived at and is carried out forthrightly." After eight years, Weiner was fired suddenly for "lack of application." Does Weiner have a valid claim against McGraw-Hill? Apart from the legal issue, did McGraw-Hill do the right thing? Was the process fair? Did the company's behavior violate important values?

18. Debra Agis worked in a Ground Round restaurant. The manager, Roger Dionne, informed the waitresses that "there was some stealing going on." Until he found out who was doing it, he intended to fire all

the waitresses in alphabetical order, starting with the letter "A." Dionne then fired Agis. Does she have a valid claim against her employer?

19. Reginald Delaney managed a Taco Time restaurant in Portland, Oregon. Some of his customers told Mr. Ledbetter, the district manager, that they would not be eating there so often because there were too many black employees. Ledbetter told Delaney to fire Ms. White, who was black. Delaney did as he was told. Ledbetter's report on the incident said: "My notes show that Delaney told me that White asked him to sleep with her and that when he would not that she started causing dissension within the crew. She asked him to come over to her house and that he declined." Delaney refused to sign the report because it was untrue, so Ledbetter fired him. What claim might Delaney make against his former employer?

20. Nationwide Insurance Co. circulated a memorandum asking all employees to lobby in favor of a bill that had been introduced in the Pennsylvania House of Representatives. By limiting the damages that an injured motorist could recover from a person who caused an accident, this bill would have saved Nationwide significant money. Not only did John Novosel refuse to lobby, but he privately criticized the bill for harming consumers. Nationwide was definitely not on his side—it fired him. Novosel filed suit, alleging that his discharge had violated public policy by infringing his right to free speech. Did Nationwide violate public policy by firing Novosel?

21. ROLE REVERSAL: Prepare a short-answer question in which an employee alleges that his discharge violated public policy, but you think a court would not agree.

## INTERNET RESEARCH PROBLEM

Go to the Web site of a newspaper in your area or a national newspaper such as *The Wall Street Journal, USA Today,* or *The New York Times.* Find an article that deals with an employment law issue and write a short summary of the issue and the outcome.

**You can find further practice problems in the Online Quiz at www.cengage.com/blaw/beatty.**

# EMPLOYMENT DISCRIMINATION

**Imagine that** you are on the hiring committee of a top San Francisco law firm. Sitting at your desk sorting through résumés, you come across one from a candidate who grew up on an isolated ranch in Arizona. Raised in a house without electricity or running water, he had worked alongside the ranch hands his entire childhood. At the age of 16, he had left home for Stanford University and from there he had gone on to Stanford Law School, where he finished third in his class. "Hm," you think to yourself, "sounds like a real American success story. A great combination of hard work and intelligence." But without hesitation you toss the résumé into the wastebasket. No way you would consider hiring him.

> **You think, "Hm, sounds like a real American success story." But you toss the résumé into the wastebasket.**

This is a true story. Indeed, there was a candidate with these credentials who was unable to find a job in any San Francisco law firm. The only jobs on offer were as a secretary, because this candidate was a woman—Sandra Day O'Connor, who went on to become the first woman Supreme Court Justice and one of the most influential lawyers of her era. But when she graduated from law school, that is the way the world was. In the last four decades, Congress has enacted important legislation to prevent discrimination in the workplace.

## · EQUAL PAY ACT OF 1963 ·

**Under the Equal Pay Act, an employee may not be paid at a lesser rate than employees of the opposite sex for equal work.** "Equal work" means tasks that require equal skill, effort, and responsibility under similar working conditions. If the employee proves that she is not being paid equally, the employer will be found liable unless the pay difference is based on merit, productivity, seniority, or some factor other than sex. A "factor other than sex" includes prior wages, training, profitability, performance in an interview, and value to the company. For example, female agents sued Allstate Insurance Co. because its salary for new agents was based, in part, on prior salary. The women argued that this system was unfair because it perpetuated the historic wage differences between men and women. The court, however, held for Allstate.

## · TITLE VII ·

Prior to 1964, it was legal to treat men and women, whites and people of color, differently in the workplace. Women, for example, could be paid less than men for the same job and could be fired if they got married or pregnant. Newspapers had different pages for men's and women's job ads. **Under Title VII of the Civil Rights Act of 1964, it is illegal for employers to discriminate on the basis of race, color, religion, sex, or national origin.** More specifically, Title VII prohibits (1) discrimination in the workplace; (2) sexual harassment; and (3) discrimination because of pregnancy. It also permits employers to develop affirmative action plans.

Discrimination under Title VII means firing, refusing to hire, failing to promote, or otherwise reducing a person's employment opportunities because of race, color, religion, sex, or national origin. This protection applies to every stage of the employment process from job ads to postemployment references and includes placement, wages, benefits, and working conditions.

### PROOF OF DISCRIMINATION

Plaintiffs in Title VII cases can prove discrimination two different ways: disparate treatment and disparate impact.

#### Disparate Treatment

**To prove a disparate treatment case, the plaintiff must show that she was *treated* differently because of her sex, race, color, religion, or national origin.** The required steps in a disparate treatment case are:

**Step 1.** The plaintiff presents evidence that the defendant has discriminated against her because of a protected trait. This is called a ***prima facie case.*** The plaintiff is not required to prove discrimination; she need only create a *presumption* that discrimination occurred.

Suppose that Louisa applies for a job coaching a boys' high school ice hockey team. She was an All-American hockey star in college. Although Louisa is obviously qualified for the job, Harry, the school principal, rejects her and continues to interview other people.

This is not proof of discrimination, because Harry may have a perfectly good, nondiscriminatory explanation. However, his behavior *could have been* motivated by discrimination.

**Step 2.** The defendant must present evidence that its decision was based on *legitimate, nondiscriminatory* reasons. Harry might say, for example, that he wanted someone with prior coaching experience. Although Louisa is clearly a great player, she has never coached before.

**Step 3.** To win, the plaintiff must now prove that the employer discriminated. She may do so by showing that the reasons offered were simply a *pretext*. Louisa might show that Harry had recently hired a male to coach the tennis team who had no prior coaching experience. Or Harry's assistant might testify that Harry said, "No way I'm going to put a woman on the ice with those guys." If she can present evidence such as this, Louisa wins.

In the following case, was the bartender treated differently because of her sex?

## YOU *be the* JUDGE

### JESPERSEN v. HARRAH'S
444 F.3d 1104, 2006 U.S. App. LEXIS 9307
United States Court of Appeals for the Ninth Circuit, 2006

**Facts:** Darlene Jespersen was a bartender at the sports bar in Harrah's Casino in Reno, Nevada. She was an outstanding employee, frequently praised by both her supervisors and customers.

When Jespersen first went to work for Harrah's, female bartenders were encouraged, but not required, to wear makeup. Jespersen tried for a short period of time, but it made her feel sick, degraded, exposed, and violated. Moreover, wearing makeup interfered with her ability to deal with unruly, intoxicated guests because it "took away [her] credibility as an individual and as a person."

After Jespersen had been at Harrah's for almost 20 years, the casino implemented a program that required bartenders to be "well groomed, appealing to the eye." More explicitly, for men:

- Hair must not extend below top of shirt collar. Ponytails are prohibited.
- Hands and fingernails must be clean and nails neatly trimmed at all times.
- No colored polish is permitted.
- Eye and facial makeup is not permitted.
- Shoes will be solid black leather or leather type with rubber (nonskid) soles.

The rules for women were:

- Hair must be teased, curled, or styled. Hair must be worn down at all times, no exceptions.
- Nail polish can be clear, white, pink, or red color only. No exotic nail art or length.
- Shoes will be solid black leather or leather type with rubber (nonskid) soles.

- Makeup (foundation/concealer and/or face powder, as well as blush and mascara) must be worn and applied neatly in complimentary colors, and lip color must be worn at all times.

An expert was brought in to show the employees (both male and female) how to dress. The workers were then photographed and told that they must look like the photographs every day at work.

When Jespersen refused to wear makeup, Harrah's fired her. She sued under Title VII. The district court granted Harrah's motion for summary judgment. Jespersen appealed.

**You Be the Judge: Did Harrah's requirement that women wear makeup violate Title VII?**

**Argument for Jespersen:** Jespersen refused to wear makeup to work because the cost—in time, money, and personal dignity—was too high.

Employers are free to adopt different appearance standards for each sex, but these standards may not impose a greater burden on one sex than the other. Men were not required to wear makeup; women were. That difference meant a savings for men of hundreds of dollars and hours of time. Harrah's did not have the right to fire Jespersen for violating a rule that applies only to women, with no equivalent for men.

**Argument for Harrah's:** Employers are permitted to impose different appearance rules on women than on men as long as the overall burden on employees is the same. For example, it is not discriminatory to require men to wear their hair short. On balance, Harrah's rules did not impose a heavier burden on women than on men.

**EXAM** *Strategy*

**Question:** Although Kim was an able accountant, she offended a lot of her male colleagues because she was unattractive and had a loud, masculine voice. She was also aggressive about demanding raises. Kim was denied promotion. Has the firm violated Title VII?

**Strategy:** Was Kim being treated differently because of her sex?

**Result:** The firm had to have the same expectations for men as it did for women. If it only promoted attractive men with soft voices, then it had the right not to promote Kim, either. But if the standards were different for men and women, then the firm was in violation.

## Disparate Impact

**Disparate impact applies if the employer has a rule that, *on its face*, is not discriminatory, but *in practice* excludes too many people in a protected group.** The steps in a disparate impact case are:

**Step 1.** The plaintiff must present a *prima facie* case. The plaintiff is not required to prove discrimination; he need only show a disparate impact—that the employment practice in question excludes a disproportionate number of people in a protected group (women and minorities, for instance).

Suppose that Harry will hire only teachers who are at least 5 feet 10 inches tall and weigh 170 pounds. He says he is afraid that students will literally push around anyone smaller. When Chou Ping, an Asian male, applies for a job, he cannot meet Harry's physical requirements. Chou Ping must show that Harry's rule, *in fact*, eliminates more women or minorities than white males. He might offer evidence that 50 percent of all white males can meet Harry's standard, but only 20 percent of white women and Asian males qualify.

**Step 2.** The defendant must offer some evidence that the employment practice was a *job-related business necessity*. Harry might produce evidence that teachers are regularly expected to wrestle students into their classroom seats. Further, he might cite studies showing his standards are essential for this task.

**Step 3.** To win, the plaintiff must now prove either that the employer's reason is a *pretext* or that other, *less discriminatory* rules would achieve the same results. Chou Ping might suggest that all teachers could take a self-defense course or engage in martial arts training.

Note that the mere existence of a disparate impact does not *necessarily* mean that an employment practice violates the law. When the Illinois Law Enforcement Officers Training Board created an exam to test aspiring police officers, a higher percentage of minority applicants than white candidates failed the test. Some of the unsuccessful aspirants filed suit, alleging that the exam was illegal because it had a disparate impact. In response, the board presented evidence that the exam had been very carefully prepared by a consulting company that specialized in creating such exams. The court held that the exam was legal because it was "demonstrably a reasonable measure of job performance."

# COLOR

Title VII prohibits discrimination based on both race and color. Although many people assume that they are essentially the same, that is not necessarily the case. Dwight Burch's coworkers at an Applebee's restaurant called him names such as tar baby, porch monkey, and jig-a-boo. These colleagues were also African American but were lighter-skinned. Burch sued on the basis of "color discrimination."

Title VII prohibits the type of treatment that Burch allegedly suffered. While denying any wrongdoing, Applebee's settled the case by paying Burch $40,000 and agreeing to conduct anti-discrimination training.

## RELIGION

**Employers must make *reasonable accommodation* for a worker's religious beliefs unless the request would cause *undue hardship* for the business.** Scott Hamby told his manager at Wal-Mart that he could never work on Sunday because that was his Sabbath. It also happened to be one of the store's busiest days. When the manager forced Hamby to quit, he sued on the grounds of religious discrimination. Lawsuits such as his are on the rise as more businesses remain open on Sundays. Wal-Mart denied wrongdoing but settled the case with a cash payment of undisclosed amount. It also established a company-wide training program on religious accommodation.

## DEFENSES TO CHARGES OF DISCRIMINATION

Under Title VII, the defendant has three possible defenses.

### Merit

**A defendant is not liable if he shows that the person he favored was the most qualified.** Test results, education, or productivity can all be used to demonstrate merit, provided they relate to the job in question. Harry can show that he hired Bruce instead of Louisa because Bruce has a master's degree in physical education and seven years of coaching experience. On the other hand, the fact that Bruce scored higher on the National Latin Exam in the eighth grade is not a good reason to hire him over Louisa for a coaching job.

**ECONOMICS AND THE LAW** It is easy to say that the most qualified person should be hired or promoted. But how do you measure merit? For example, in Santa Clara, California, Paul Johnson scored higher on the dispatcher exam than Diane Joyce, but the county hired Joyce, in part, because no woman had ever held the job of radio dispatcher there. This case ultimately reached the U.S. Supreme Court on the issue of whether a less qualified woman could be promoted over a more qualified man. (The court ruled that she could.)

So do we feel sorry for Paul Johnson? Of course, we feel sorry for anyone who does not get the job of his dreams. It turns out, however, that his score on the dispatcher exam had been 75 out of 100; hers was 73. This two-point difference is not persuasive evidence that Johnson would be a better radio dispatcher than Joyce. Indeed, employment tests are typically not very good predictors of on-the-job performance. They are at best blunt instruments. Moreover, a 2-point differential on a 100-point test is meaningless. As an affirmative action case, *Johnson* was unusual only in that the court actually reported the test scores.

The moral of the story? Before concluding that a less qualified applicant has been promoted over a more qualified competitor, it is wise to ask about the validity of the test and the significance of the difference in scores.[1] ◆

[1] Michael Selmi, "Testing for Equality: Merit, Efficiency, and the Affirmative Action Debate," *UCLA Law Review*, June 1995, vol. 42, p. 1251.

## *Seniority*

**A legitimate seniority system is legal, even if it perpetuates past discrimination.** Suppose that Harry has always chosen the most senior assistant coach to take over as head coach when a vacancy occurs. Since the majority of the senior assistant coaches are male, most of the head coaches are, too. Such a system does not violate Title VII.

## *Bona Fide Occupational Qualification*

**An employer is permitted to establish discriminatory job requirements if they are *essential* to the position in question. Such a requirement is called a bona fide occupational qualification (BFOQ).** Catholic schools may, if they choose, refuse to hire non-Catholic teachers; mail order companies may refuse to hire men to model women's clothing. Generally, however, courts are not sympathetic to claims of BFOQ. They have, for example, almost always rejected BFOQ claims that are based on customer preference. Thus airlines could not refuse to hire male flight attendants even though travelers prefer female attendants. The major exception to this customer preference rule is sexual privacy: An employer may refuse to hire women to work in a men's bathroom and vice versa.

**Bona fide occupational qualification (BFOQ)**
An employer is permitted to establish discriminatory job requirements if they are *essential* to the position in question.

# AFFIRMATIVE ACTION

**Affirmative action is not required by Title VII, nor is it prohibited.** Affirmative action programs have three different sources:

- *Litigation.* Courts have the power under Title VII to order affirmative action to remedy the effects of past discrimination.

- *Voluntary Action.* Employers can voluntarily introduce an affirmative action plan to remedy the effects of past practices or to achieve equitable representation of minorities and women.

- *Government Contracts.* In 1965, President Lyndon Johnson signed Executive Order 11246, which prohibits discrimination by federal contractors. This order had a profound impact on the American workplace because one-third of all workers are employed by companies that do business with the federal government. If an employer found that women or minorities were underrepresented in its workplace, it was required to establish goals and timetables to correct the deficiency.

In 1995, however, the Supreme Court ruled that these affirmative action programs are permissible only if (1) the government can show that the programs are needed to overcome specific past discrimination; (2) they have time limits; and (3) nondiscriminatory alternatives are not available.

> Everyone has heard of sexual harassment, but few people know exactly what it is.

# SEXUAL HARASSMENT

Everyone has heard of sexual harassment, but few people know exactly what it is. Men fear that a casual comment or glance will be met with career-ruining charges; women claim that men "just don't get it." So what is sexual harassment, anyway? **Sexual harassment involves unwelcome sexual advances, requests for sexual favors, and other verbal or physical conduct of a sexual nature.** There are two major categories of sexual harassment:

- *Quid pro quo.* From a Latin phrase that means "one thing in return for another," ***quid pro quo*** harassment occurs if any aspect of a job is made contingent upon sexual activity. In other words, when a banker says to an assistant, "You can be promoted to teller if you sleep with me," that is *quid pro quo* sexual harassment.

**Sexual harassment**
Involves unwelcome sexual advances, requests for sexual favors, and other verbal or physical conduct of a sexual nature.

**Quid pro quo**
A Latin phrase that means "one thing in return for another."

- Hostile work environment. An employee has a valid claim of sexual harassment if sexual talk and innuendo are so pervasive that they interfere with her (or his) ability to work. Courts have found that offensive jokes, comments about clothes or body parts, and public displays of pornographic pictures create a hostile environment. In a landmark case, the Supreme Court found a company liable because its president frequently made inappropriate sexual comments to female employees. He called one worker "a dumb-ass woman" and suggested that the two of them "go to the Holiday Inn to negotiate her raise." He also insisted that women employees pick up objects he had thrown on the ground.[2]

Employees who commit sexual harassment are liable for their own wrongdoing. But is their company also liable? The Supreme Court has held that:

- If the victimized employee has suffered a "tangible employment action" such as firing, demotion, or reassignment, the company is liable to her for sexual harassment by a supervisor.
- Even if the victimized employee has *not* suffered a tangible employment action, the company is liable unless it can prove that (1) it used reasonable care to prevent and correct sexually harassing behavior; and (2) the employee unreasonably failed to take advantage of the company's complaint procedures.

Corning Consumer Products Co. asks its employees to apply four tests in judging whether their behavior constitutes sexual harassment:

- Would you say or do this in front of your spouse or parents?
- What about in front of a colleague of the opposite sex?
- Would you like your behavior reported in your local newspaper?
- Does it need to be said or done at all?

## PROCEDURES AND REMEDIES

Before a plaintiff in a Title VII case brings suit, she must first file a complaint with the federal Equal Employment Opportunity Commission (EEOC). The EEOC then has the right to sue on behalf of the plaintiff. This arrangement is favorable for the plaintiff because the government pays the legal bill. If the EEOC decides not to bring the case, or does not make a decision within six months, it issues a **right to sue letter,** and the plaintiff may proceed on her own in court. Many states also have their own version of the EEOC, but these state commissions are often understaffed.

Remedies available to the successful plaintiff include hiring, reinstatement, retroactive seniority, back pay, reasonable attorney's fees, and damages of up to $300,000. However, employers now often require new hires to agree in advance to arbitrate, not litigate, any future employment claims. Typically, employees receive worse results in the arbitrator's office than in the courtroom.

## PREGNANCY

Under the Pregnancy Discrimination Act of 1978, **an employer may not fire or refuse to hire a woman because she is pregnant.** An employer must also treat pregnancy as any other temporary disability. If, for example, employees are allowed time off from work for other medical disabilities, women must also be allowed a maternity leave. The United States is one of only four countries in the world (along with Liberia, Papua New Guinea, and Swaziland) that does not require paid maternity leave.

---

[2] *Harris v. Forklift Systems,* 510 U.S. 17, 114 S. Ct. 367, 1993 U.S. LEXIS 7155.

# · AGE DISCRIMINATION ·

**The Age Discrimination in Employment Act (ADEA) of 1967 prohibits age discrimination against employees or job applicants who are at least 40 years old.** An employer may not fire, refuse to hire, fail to promote, or otherwise reduce a person's employment opportunities because he is 40 or older. Employers may not require workers to retire at any age (with a few exceptions, such as police officers and top-level corporate executives).

The procedure for an age-bias claim is similar to that under Title VII—plaintiffs must first file a charge with the EEOC. If the EEOC does not take action, they can file suit themselves.

During tight economic times, companies often feel great pressure to lower costs. They are sometimes tempted to replace older, higher-paid workers with younger, less expensive employees. Courts traditionally held that replacing expensive, older workers with cheaper, younger ones was illegal discrimination under the ADEA. In some recent cases, however, courts have held that an employer is entitled to prefer *lower-paid* workers even if that preference results in the company also choosing *younger* workers. As the court put it in one case, "An action based on price differentials represents the very quintessence of a legitimate business decision."[3] The Supreme Court has suggested that the primary goal of the ADEA is to prevent employment decisions based on stereotypes about the productivity and competence of older workers.

As we have seen, Title VII permits employees to prove discrimination in two ways: *disparate treatment* and *disparate impact*. Disparate *treatment* has always been a violation of the ADEA, too, but it was not clear if disparate *impact* was as well. In the following case, the Supreme Court answers that question. The opinion in this case was written by the court's oldest member, 84-year-old Justice John Paul Stevens.

## SMITH v. CITY OF JACKSON

### 2005 U.S. LEXIS 2931
### SUPREME COURT OF THE UNITED STATES, 2005

## CASE SUMMARY

**Facts:** To attract new recruits, the city of Jackson, Mississippi (the City), granted pay raises to everyone on its police force. But to match the going rate in the market, officers with less than five years of service received proportionately greater raises than their more senior colleagues, who tended to be older. Some of these older officers filed suit under the ADEA claiming a disparate impact: that they were adversely affected by the plan because of their age.

**Issues: *Is disparate impact a violation of the ADEA? Were these police officers adversely affected because of their age?***

**Decision:** Disparate impact is a violation of the ADEA, but the police officers nonetheless lose as they were not adversely affected because of their age.

**Reasoning:** Disparate impact is a violation of the ADEA because the language of this statute is similar to that of Title VII (which the Court has interpreted to prohibit disparate impact). However, the ADEA has additional language that permits employment decisions based on "reasonable factors other than age" (RFOA). Congress added this language because age, unlike race or gender, may affect an individual's ability to perform a job. Moreover, age discrimination has not been as common as sexism or racism. Therefore, some employment plans may be acceptable, even if they adversely affect older workers.

To win a disparate impact case, it is not enough for the employees to point to some general policy. They must identify the specific employment practice that leads to the pay

---

[3] *Marks v. Loral Corp.*, 57 Cal. App. 4th 30, 1997 Cal. App. LEXIS 611 (Cal. Ct. App. 1997).

differences. The plaintiffs in this case have simply pointed out that the pay plan is less generous to older workers than to younger ones, but they have not identified any specific test or requirement that adversely affects older workers. Also, in this case, the plan was based on RFOA. When the City paid junior officers more, it was simply matching the market rate. There might have been other methods the City could have used to attract police officers, but this plan was reasonable.

## · AMERICANS WITH DISABILITIES ACT ·

Passed in 1990, the Americans with Disabilities Act (ADA) prohibits employers from discriminating on the basis of disability. As with Title VII, a plaintiff under the ADA must first file a charge with the EEOC. If the EEOC decides not to file suit, the individual may do so himself.

**Disabled person**

Someone with a physical or mental impairment that substantially limits a major life activity, or someone who is regarded as having such an impairment.

**A disabled person is someone with a physical or mental impairment that substantially limits a major life activity.** In 2008 amendments, Congress directed the EEOC to broaden its definition of major life activity. Now, this definition includes caring for oneself, performing manual tasks, seeing, hearing, eating, sleeping, walking, standing, lifting, bending, speaking, breathing, learning, reading, concentrating, thinking, communicating, and working. Cell growth and digestive, bowel, bladder, neurological, brain, respiratory, circulatory, endocrine, reproductive, and immune system functions are also considered major life activities. However, the definition does not include sexual disorders, pyromania, exhibitionism, or compulsive gambling.

**An employer may not refuse to hire or promote a disabled person as long as she can, with** *reasonable accommodation*, **perform the** *essential functions* **of the job. An accommodation is not reasonable if it would create** *undue hardship* **for the employer.**

- *Reasonable accommodation:* This includes buying necessary equipment, providing readers or interpreters, or permitting employees to work a part-time schedule.

- *Undue hardship:* In determining what this term means, relative cost, not absolute cost, is the issue. Even an expensive accommodation—such as hiring a full-time reader—is not considered an undue hardship unless it imposes a significant burden on the overall finances of the company.

- *Essential functions:* In one case, a court held that a welder who could perform 88 percent of a job was doing the essential functions.

**An employer may not ask about disabilities before making a job offer.** The interviewer may ask only whether an applicant can perform the work. **Before making a job offer, an employer cannot require applicants to take a medical exam** unless the exam is (1) job-related, and (2) required of all applicants for similar jobs. However, drug testing is permitted. **After a job offer has been made, an employer may require a medical test, but it must be related to the essential functions of the job.** For example, an employer could not test the cholesterol of someone applying for an accounting job, because high cholesterol is no impediment to good accounting.

**An employer may not discriminate against someone because of his relationship with a disabled person.** For example, an employer cannot refuse to hire an applicant because he has a child with Down's syndrome or a spouse with AIDS.

**Under EEOC rules, physical and mental disabilities are to be treated the same.** The difficulty is that physical ailments such as diabetes and deafness may be easy to diagnose, but what does a supervisor do when an employee is chronically late, rude, or impulsive? Does this mean the worker is mentally disabled or just a lazy, irresponsible jerk? Among other accommodations, the EEOC rules indicated that employers should be willing to put up barriers to isolate people who have difficulty concentrating, provide detailed day-to-day feedback to those who need greater structure in performing their jobs, or allow workers on antidepressants to come to work later if they are groggy in the morning.

While lauding the ADA's objectives, many managers have been apprehensive about its impact on the workplace. Most acknowledge, however, that society is clearly better off if every member has the opportunity to work. And as advocates for the disabled point out, we are all, at best, only temporarily able-bodied.

Every applicant feels slightly apprehensive before a job interview, but now the interviewer may be even more nervous—fearing that every question is a potential landmine of liability. Most interviewers (and students who have read this chapter) would know better than Delta Airlines interviewers, who allegedly asked applicants about their sexual preference, birth control methods, and abortion history. The following list provides guidelines for interviewers.

| Don't Even Consider Asking | Go Ahead and Ask |
|---|---|
| Can you perform this function with or without reasonable accommodation? | Would you need reasonable accommodation in this job? |
| How many days were you sick last year? | How many days were you absent from work last year? |
| What medications are you currently taking? | Are you currently using drugs illegally? |
| Where were you born? Are you a United States citizen? | Are you authorized to work in the United States? |
| How old are you? | What work experience have you had? |
| How tall are you? How much do you weigh? | Could you carry a 100-pound weight, as required by this job? |
| When did you graduate from college? | Where did you go to college? |
| How did you learn this language? | What languages do you speak and write fluently? |
| Have you ever been arrested? | Have you ever been convicted of a crime that would affect the performance of this job? |
| Do you plan to have children? How old are your children? What method of birth control do you use? | Can you work weekends? Travel extensively? Would you be willing to relocate? |
| What is your corrected vision? | Do you have 20/20 corrected vision? |
| Are you a man or a woman?<br>Are you single or married?<br>What does your spouse do?<br>What will happen if your spouse is transferred?<br>What clubs, societies, or lodges do you belong to? | Leave well enough alone! |

The most common gaffe on the part of interviewers? Asking women about their child care arrangements. That question assumes the woman is responsible for child care.

## EXAM *Strategy*

**Question:** For Michael, it was the job of his dreams—editor of *Literature* magazine. When Cyrus, the owner of the magazine, offered him the position, Michael accepted immediately. But he also revealed a secret few people knew—he had Parkinson's, a neurological disorder that affects the patient's ability to move. That part is controllable with medication, but about 40 percent of Parkinson's patients suffer severe dementia and become unable to work. Michael had no signs of dementia—he was the host of a popular television talk show. Fifteen minutes after Michael returned to his hotel room, Cyrus called to withdraw the job offer. He said he did not like some of Michael's ideas for changing the magazine. Has Cyrus violated the ADA? Could he fire Michael if dementia set in?

**Strategy:** Is Michael covered by the ADA? Can he perform the essential functions of the job?

**Result:** Michael is covered by the ADA. He has an impairment that substantially limits a major life activity—movement. But Michael is able to perform the essential functions of the job, so Cyrus is violating the law when he withdraws the offer. If Michael becomes demented and can no longer run a magazine, Cyrus could fire him.

## CHAPTER CONCLUSION

The statutes in this chapter have changed America—it is far different now than when Sandra Day O'Connor first looked for a job. People are more likely to be offered employment because of their efforts and talents rather than their age, appearance, faith, family background, or health.

## EXAM REVIEW

1. **EQUAL PAY ACT** Under the Equal Pay Act, an employee may not be paid for equal work at a lesser rate than employees of the opposite sex. (p. 295)

.........................................................................................................

2. **TITLE VII** Title VII of the Civil Rights Act of 1964 prohibits employers from discriminating on the basis of race, color, religion, sex, or national origin. (p. 295)

.........................................................................................................

3. **DISPARATE TREATMENT** To prove a disparate treatment case under Title VII, the plaintiff must show that she was treated differently because of her sex, race, color, religion, or national origin. (p. 295)

.........................................................................................................

4. **DISPARATE IMPACT** To prove disparate impact under Title VII, the plaintiff must show that the employer has a rule that, on its face, is not discriminatory, but in practice excludes too many people in a protected group. (p. 297)

**EXAM Strategy**

**Question:** The Duke Power Co. refused to transfer any employees at its generating plant to better jobs unless they had a high school diploma or could pass an intelligence test. The company was willing to pay two-thirds of the tuition for an employee's high school training. Neither a high school education nor the intelligence test was significantly related to successful job performance. Both requirements disqualified African Americans at a substantially higher rate than white applicants. Is the company in violation of Title VII?

**Strategy:** Was there evidence that blacks and whites were being treated differently? No, the same rules applied to both. But did the rules have a disparate impact? Yes, many more whites could pass the standard. Is race a protected category under Title VII? Yes. Were the standards essential for these jobs? Would other, less discriminatory rules have achieved the same result? (See the "Result" at the end of this section.)

**5.** **RELIGION** Employers must make reasonable accommodation for a worker's religious beliefs unless the request would cause undue hardship for the business. (p. 298)

**6.** **SENIORITY** A legitimate seniority system is legal, even if it perpetuates past discrimination. (p. 298)

**7.** **BONA FIDE OCCUPATIONAL QUALIFICATION (BFOQ)** An employer is permitted to establish discriminatory job requirements if they are *essential* to the position in question. (p. 299)

**EXAM Strategy**

**Question:** You are the vice president of administration at a hospital. You believe that both male and female patients prefer to have a male neurosurgeon, while men prefer male urologists and women prefer female gynecologists. Can you act on this information when hiring doctors?

**Strategy:** To hire based on sex would be a violation of Title VII, unless sex is a BFOQ for the job. (See the "Result" at the end of this section.)

**8.** **AFFIRMATIVE ACTION** Affirmative action is not required by Title VII, nor is it prohibited. (p. 299)

**9.** **SEXUAL HARASSMENT** Sexual harassment involves unwelcome sexual advances, requests for sexual favors, and other verbal or physical conduct of a sexual nature. (p. 299)

**10.** **PREGNANCY DISCRIMINATION** Under the Pregnancy Discrimination Act of 1978, an employer may not fire or refuse to hire a woman because she is pregnant. (p. 300)

**11.** **AGE DISCRIMINATION** The Age Discrimination in Employment Act (ADEA) of 1967 prohibits age discrimination against employees or job applicants who are at least 40 years old. (p. 301)

**12.** **AMERICANS WITH DISABILITIES ACT** Under the Americans with Disabilities Act an employer may not refuse to hire or promote a disabled person as long as she can, with reasonable accommodation, perform the essential functions of the job. A disabled person is someone with a physical or mental impairment that substantially limits a major life activity. An accommodation is not reasonable if it would create undue hardship for the employer. (p. 302)

**4. Result:** The Supreme Court held that Duke Power Co. was in violation of Title VII because the job requirements did not measure job performance. The Court stated that, "What Congress has commanded is that any tests used must measure the person for the job and not the person in the abstract."

**7. Result:** Customer preference does not justify discrimination, except in cases of sexual privacy. You cannot consider sex when hiring neurosurgeons, but you can when selecting urologists and gynecologists.

# PRACTICE EXAM

## MATCHING QUESTIONS

Match the following terms with their definitions:

___ A. Equal Pay Act

___ B. Right to sue letter

___ C. ADEA

___ D. Title VII

___ E. ADA

1. Statute that prohibits an employee from being paid at a lesser rate than employees of the opposite sex for equal work

2. Statute that prohibits discrimination on the basis of race, color, religion, sex, or national origin

3. Permission from the EEOC for a plaintiff to proceed with his case

4. Statute that prohibits age discrimination

5. Statute that prohibits discrimination against the disabled

## TRUE/FALSE QUESTIONS

Circle true or false:

1. T F In a disparate impact case, an employer may be liable for a rule that is not discriminatory on its face.
2. T F Title VII applies to all aspects of the employment relationship, including hiring, firing, and promotion.
3. T F If more whites than Native Americans pass an employment test, the test necessarily violates Title VII.
4. T F Employers that have contracts with the federal government are required to fill a quota of women and minority employees.
5. T F Employers do not have to accommodate an employee's religious beliefs if doing so would impose an undue hardship on the business.

## MULTIPLE-CHOICE QUESTIONS

6. Which of the following steps is *not* required in a disparate treatment case?
   A. The plaintiff must file with the EEOC.
   B. The plaintiff must submit to arbitration.
   C. The plaintiff must present evidence of a *prima facie* case.
   D. The defendant must show that its action had a nondiscriminatory reason.
   E. The plaintiff must show that the defendant's excuse was a pretext.

7. An employer can legally require all employees to have a high school diploma if:
   A. All of its competitors have such a requirement.
   B. Most of the applicants in the area have a high school diploma.
   C. Shareholders of the company are likely to pay a higher price for the company's stock if employees have at least a high school diploma.

   D. The company intends to branch out into the high-tech field, in which case a high school diploma would be needed by its employees.

   E. The nature of the job requires those skills.

8. Which of the following employers has violated Title VII?
   A. Carlos promoted the most qualified employee.
   B. Hans promoted five white males because they were the most senior.
   C. Luke refused to hire a Buddhist to work on a Christian Science newspaper.
   D. Max hired a male corporate lawyer because his clients had more confidence in male lawyers.
   E. Dylan hired a man to work as an attendant in the men's locker room.

9. Which of the following activities would *not* be considered sexual harassment?
   A. Shannon tells Connor she will promote him if he will sleep with her.
   B. Kailen has a screen saver that shows various people having sex.
   C. Paige says she wants "to negotiate Owen's raise at the Holiday Inn."
   D. Nancy yells "Crap!" at the top of her lungs every time her rotisserie baseball team loses.
   E. *Quid pro quo.*

10. Which of the following activities is *not* a violation of the law?
   A. When Taggart comes to a job interview, he has a white cane. Ann asks him if he is blind.
   B. Craig refuses to hire Ben, who is blind, to work as a playground supervisor because it is essential to the job that the supervisor be able to see what the children are doing.
   C. Concerned about his company's health insurance rates, Matt requires all job applicants to take a physical.
   D. Concerned about his company's health insurance rates, Josh requires all new hires to take a physical so that he can encourage them to join some of the preventive treatment programs available at the company.
   E. Jennifer refuses to hire Alexis because her child is ill and she frequently has to take him to the hospital.

## SHORT-ANSWER QUESTIONS

11. When Michelle told her boss that she was pregnant, his first comment was, "Congratulations on your pregnancy. My sister vomited for months." Then he refused to speak to her for a week. A month later, she was fired. Her boss told her the business was shifting away from her area of expertise. Does Michelle have a valid claim? Under what law?

12. ETHICS: John Mundorf hired three women to work for Gus Construction Co. as traffic controllers at road construction sites in Iowa. Male members of the construction crew incessantly referred to the women as "f—king flag girls." They repeatedly asked the women if they "wanted to f—k" or engage in oral sex. One crew member held a woman up to the cab window so other men could touch her. Another male employee exposed himself to the women. Male employees also urinated in a woman's water bottle and the gas tank of her car. Mundorf, the supervisor, was present during some of these incidents. He talked to crew members about their conduct, but the abuse continued until the women quit. What claim might the women make against their coworkers? Is Gus Construction Co. liable for the acts of its employees? What procedure must the women follow to pursue their claim? Why do you think these men behaved this way? Why did they want to humiliate their coworkers? What should the supervisor have done when he observed these incidents? What would you have done if you were the supervisor? Or a fellow employee?

13. Peter Oiler was a truck driver at the grocery chain Winn-Dixie. He was also a transvestite—he liked to dress as a woman. When his supervisor at Winn-Dixie found out about his cross-dressing, Oiler was fired. Is Winn-Dixie in violation of the law?

14. The Lillie Rubin boutique in Phoenix would not permit Dick Kovacic to apply for a job as a salesperson. It only hired women to work in sales because fittings and alterations took place in the dressing room or immediately outside. The customers were buying

expensive clothes and demanded a male-free dressing area. Has the Lillie Rubin store violated Title VII? What would its defense be?

15. When Thomas Lussier filled out a Postal Service employment application, he did not admit that he had twice pleaded guilty to charges of disorderly conduct. Lussier suffered from post-traumatic stress disorder (PTSD) acquired during military service in Vietnam. Because of this disorder, he sometimes had panic attacks that required him to leave meetings. He was also a recovered alcoholic and drug user. During his stint with the Postal Service, he had some personality conflicts with other employees. Once, another employee hit him. He also had one episode of "erratic emotional behavior and verbal outburst." In the meantime, a postal employee in Ridgewood, New Jersey, killed four colleagues. The Postmaster General encouraged all supervisors to identify workers who had dangerous propensities. Lussier's boss discovered that he had lied on his employment application about the disorderly conduct charges and fired him. Is the Postal Service in violation of the law?

16. ROLE REVERSAL: Write a multiple choice question that highlights the differences between a disparate treatment and a disparate impact case.

# INTERNET RESEARCH PROBLEM

Go to **http://www.eeoc.gov/facts/accommodation.html**. The EEOC offers advice on how to comply with some aspects of the Americans with Disabilities Act. Employers sometimes complain that the EEOC unfairly favors workers. What do you think of these EEOC guidelines? Are they fair and evenhanded? As an employee, would you like your company to follow these guidelines? If you were in a supervisory role, would your view of these guidelines be different?

**You can find further practice problems in the Online Quiz at www.cengage.com/blaw/beatty.**

# LABOR LAW

**A strike!** For five weeks, the union workers have been walking picket lines at JMJ, a manufacturer of small electrical engines. An entire town of 70,000 citizens, most of them blue-collar workers, is sharply divided, right down to the McNally kitchen table. Buddy, age 48, has worked on the assembly lines at JMJ for more than 25 years. Now he's sipping coffee in the house where he grew up. His sister Kristina, age 46, is a vice-president for personnel at JMJ. The two have always been close, but today, the conversation is halting.

"It's time to get back together, Buddy," Kristina murmurs. "The strike is hurting the whole company—and the town."

"Not the *whole* town, Kristina," he tries to quip lightly. "Your management pals still have fat incomes and nice houses."

"Oh yeah?" she attempts to joke, "you haven't seen our porch lately."

"Go talk to Tony Falcione," Buddy replies. "He can't pay his rent."

> **An entire town of 70,000 citizens, most of them blue-collar workers, is sharply divided, right down to the McNally kitchen table.**

"Talk to the Ericksons," Kristina snaps back, "they don't even work for JMJ. Their sandwich shop is going under because none of you guys stop in for lunch. Come back to work."

"Not with that clause on the table."

*That* clause is management's proposal for the new union contract—one that Kristina helped draft. The company officers want the right to subcontract work, that is, to send it out for other companies to perform.

"Buddy, we need the flexibility. K-Ball is underselling us by 35 percent. If we can't compete, there won't be *any* jobs or *any* contract!"

"The way to save money is not by sending our jobs overseas, where a bunch of foreigners will work for 50 bucks a month."

"OK, fine. Tell me how we *should* save money."

"Kristina, I really do not know how you can sit at this table and say these things—in this household. You never would have got a fancy college degree if Dad hadn't made union wages."

"If we can't sell motors to Latin America, we're out of business. All we're asking is the right to subcontract some of the smallest components. Everything else gets built here."

"Next it'll be the wiring, then you'll assemble the whole thing over there— and that'll be it for me. You take that clause off the table, we'll be back in 15 minutes."

"Never."

Buddy stands up. They stare silently, sadly, at each other, and then Kristina says, in a barely audible voice, "I have to tell you this. My boss is starting to talk about hiring replacement workers." Buddy walks out.

## · UNIONS DEVELOP ·

During the nineteenth century, as industrialization spread across America, workers found employment conditions unbearable and wages inadequate. In factories, workers, often women and children, worked 60 to 70 hours per week and sometimes more, standing at assembly lines in suffocating, dimly lit factories, performing monotonous yet dangerous work with heavy machinery for pennies a day. Mines were different—they were worse.

Workers began to band together into unions, but courts and Congress were hostile. From the 1800s through the 1920s, judges routinely issued injunctions against strikes, ruling that unions were either criminal conspiracies or illegal monopolies. With the economic collapse of 1929, however, and the vast suffering of the Great Depression, public sympathy shifted to the workers.

In 1932 Congress passed the **Norris-LaGuardia Act**, which prohibited federal court injunctions in nonviolent labor disputes. Congress was declaring that workers should be permitted to organize unions and to use their collective power to achieve legitimate economic ends.

In 1935 Congress passed the Wagner Act, generally known as the **National Labor Relations Act (NLRA)**. This is the most important of all labor laws. A fundamental aim of the NLRA is the establishment and maintenance of industrial peace, to preserve the flow of commerce. **Section 7 guarantees employees the right to organize and join unions, bargain collectively through representatives of their own choosing, and engage in other concerted activities.** Section 8 reinforces these rights by outlawing unfair labor practices.

**Section 8(a) makes it an unfair labor practice (ULP) for an employer:**

- To interfere with union organizing efforts;
- To dominate or interfere with any union;
- To discriminate against a union member; or
- To refuse to bargain collectively with a union.

The NLRA also established the **National Labor Relations Board (NLRB)** to administer and interpret the statute and to adjudicate labor cases. For example, when a union charges that an employer has committed an unfair labor practice—say, by refusing to bargain—the ULP charge goes first to the NLRB.

The Board, which sits in Washington, D.C., has five members, all appointed by the president. The NLRB makes final agency decisions about representation and ULP cases. But note that the Board has no power to *enforce* its orders. If it is evident that the losing party will not comply, the Board must petition a federal appeals court to enforce the order. Typically, the steps resulting in an appeal follow this pattern: The Board issues a decision, for example, finding that a company has unfairly refused to bargain with a union. The Board orders the company to bargain. The Board then appeals to the United States Court of Appeals to enforce its order, and the company cross-appeals, requesting the court not to enforce the Board's order. (The NLRB describes its mission and methods at **http://www.nlrb.gov/**.)

Throughout the 1930s and 1940s, unions grew in size and power, but employers complained of union abuse. In 1947 Congress responded with the Taft-Hartley Act, also known as the **Labor-Management Relations Act**. The statute amended Section 8 of the NLRA to outlaw certain unfair labor practices *by unions.*

**Section 8(b) makes it an unfair labor practice for a union:**

- To interfere with employees who are exercising their labor rights under Section 7;
- To encourage an employer to discriminate against a particular employee because of a union dispute;
- To refuse to bargain collectively; or
- To engage in an illegal strike or boycott, particularly secondary boycotts.

---

**Norris-LaGuardia Act**
Prohibits federal court injunctions in peaceful labor disputes.

**National Labor Relations Act (NLRA)**
Ensures the right of workers to form unions and encourages management and unions to bargain collectively.

**National Labor Relations Board (NLRB)**
Administers and interprets the NLRA and adjudicates labor cases.

**Labor-Management Relations Act**
is designed to curb union abuses.

Finally, in the 1950s the public became aware that certain labor leaders were corrupt. Some officers stole money from large union treasuries, rigged union elections, and stifled opposition within the organization. In response, in 1959 Congress passed the Landrum-Griffin Act, generally called the **Labor-Management Reporting and Disclosure Act (LMRDA).** The LMRDA requires union leadership to make certain financial disclosures and guarantees free speech and fair elections within a union.

These landmark federal labor laws are outlined below.

| Four Key Labor Statutes | |
| --- | --- |
| Norris-LaGuardia Act (1932) | Prohibits federal court injunctions in peaceful strikes. |
| National Labor Relations Act (1935) | Guarantees workers' right to organize unions and bargain collectively. Prohibits an employer from interfering with union organizing or discriminating against union members. Requires an employer to bargain collectively. |
| Labor-Management Relations Act (1947) | Prohibits union abuses such as coercing employees to join. Outlaws secondary boycotts. |
| Labor-Management Reporting and Disclosure Act (1959) | Requires financial disclosures by union leadership. Guarantees union members free speech and fair elections. |

## Labor Unions Today

In the 1950s, about 25 percent of the workforce belonged to a union. Today, only about 12.1 percent of all workers are union members, yet labor law still affects many. About 16 million workers are union members. The largest unions are national in scope, with hundreds of affiliated locals throughout the country. A local is the regional union, which represents workers at a particular company. For example, over 2.2 million teachers belong to the National Education Association, with thousands of locals spread throughout the nation.

Unions are much more common in government offices than private companies. Full-time workers who are union members average earnings of $863 per week, compared to $663 for their nonunionized counterparts. Union membership is highest in the Northeastern, North Central, and Pacific states, and lowest in the South. Half of all union members live in just six states: California, New York, Illinois, Michigan, Ohio, and Pennsylvania. (For the most recent union statistics, work your way to the Bureau of Labor Statistics Web site, at **http://www.bls.gov/**.)

## · ORGANIZING A UNION ·

## Exclusivity

**Under Section 9 of the NLRA, a validly recognized union is the exclusive representative of the employees.** This means that the union will represent all of the designated employees, regardless of whether a particular worker *wants* to be represented. The company may not bargain directly with any employee in the group, nor with any other organization representing the designated employees. A **collective bargaining unit** is the precisely defined group of employees who will be represented by a particular union.

**Collective bargaining unit**
The precisely defined group of employees represented by a particular union.

# ORGANIZING

A union organizing effort generally involves the following pattern.

## Campaign

Union organizers talk with employees—or attempt to talk—and interest them in forming a union. The organizers may be employees of the company, who simply chat with fellow workers about unsatisfactory conditions. Or a union may send nonemployees of the company to hand out union leaflets to workers as they arrive and depart from the factory.

## Authorization Cards

Union organizers ask workers to sign authorization cards, which state that the particular worker requests the specified union to act as her sole bargaining representative.

## Recognition

If a union obtains authorization cards from a sizable percentage of workers, it seeks recognition as the exclusive representative for the bargaining unit. The union may ask the employer to recognize it as the bargaining representative, but most of the time employers refuse to recognize the union voluntarily. The NLRA permits an employer to refuse recognition.

## Petition

Assuming that the employer does not voluntarily recognize a union, the union generally petitions the NLRB for an election. It must submit to the NLRB authorization cards signed by at least 30 percent of the workers. If the NLRB determines that the union has identified an appropriate bargaining unit and has enough valid cards, it orders an election.

If more than 50 percent of the workers vote for the union, the NLRB designates that union as the exclusive representative of all members of the bargaining unit. The issues that most commonly arise during an organizing effort are: (1) What may a union do during its organizing campaign? (2) What may the employer do to defeat the campaign? (3) What is an appropriate bargaining unit?

# WHAT WORKERS MAY DO

**The NLRA guarantees employees the right to talk among themselves about forming a union, to hand out literature, and ultimately to join a union.**[1] Workers may urge other employees to sign authorization cards and may vigorously push their cause. When employees hand out leaflets, the employer generally may not limit the content. In one case a union distributed leaflets urging workers to vote against political candidates who opposed minimum wage laws. The employer objected to the union using company property to distribute the information, but the Supreme Court upheld the union's right. Even though the content of the writing was not directly related to the union, the connection was close enough that the NLRA protected the union's activity.[2]

There are, of course, limits to what union organizers may do. The statute permits an employer to restrict organizing discussions if they interfere with discipline or production. A worker on a moving assembly line has no right to walk away from his task to talk with other employees about organizing a union.[3]

---

[1] NLRA §7.

[2] *Eastex, Inc. v. NLRB,* 434 U.S. 1045, 98 S. Ct. 888, 1978 U.S. LEXIS 547 (1978).

[3] *NLRB v. Babcock & Wilcox Co.,* 351 U.S. 105, 76 S. Ct. 679, 1956 U.S. LEXIS 1721 (1956).

# What Employers May Do

An employer may prohibit employees from organizing if the efforts interfere with the company's work. In a retail store, for example, management may prohibit union discussions in the presence of customers, because the discussions could harm business.

May the employer speak out against a union organizing drive? Yes. **Management is entitled to communicate to the employees why it believes a union will be harmful to the company.** But the employer's efforts must be limited to explanation and advocacy. The employer may not use either threats or promises of benefits to defeat a union drive.[4] The company is prohibited not only from threatening reprisals, such as firing a worker who favors the union, but also from offering benefits designed to defeat the union. A company that has vigorously rejected employee demands for higher wages may not suddenly grant a 10 percent pay increase in the midst of a union campaign.

It is an unfair labor practice for an employer to interfere with a union organizing effort. Normally, a union claiming such interference will file a ULP charge. If the Board upholds the union's claim, it will order the employer to stop its interference and permit a fair election.

Here is a case illustrating the tensions and crude language that so often arise during organizing efforts.

---

## Progressive Electric, Inc. v. National Labor Relations Board

### 453 F.3d 538, District of Columbia Court of Appeals, 2006

### CASE SUMMARY

**Facts:** Progressive Electric, Inc. was a non-union electrical contractor. The International Brotherhood of Electrical Workers (IBEW) targeted the company for organizing. Progressive did not go quietly.

Progressive advertised in the local paper that it was accepting applications for electrician/technicians. Without revealing his IBEW membership, David Cousins responded to the ad and was hired. A month later, eight more union members went as a group to Progressive to apply. They carried video and tape recording equipment. Randy Neeman, Progressive's president, realized that they were union members and told them, "You guys, we are not hiring. We are not taking no [sic] applications. We hired a couple of people and filled the spots. So I would love to put you all on and as soon as I get an opening, I will give you guys a call." The union members filled out job applications and Neeman said he would call when there was an opening. In fact, he immediately threw away the applications.

Don Hildreth, a Progressive foreman, told Cousins and one other employee that Neeman "didn't want any union crap around here." Hildreth continued, "If the unions got into Progressive, Progressive would lose contracts and would go out of business because Progressive couldn't afford the union wages and benefits."

Neeman held a company meeting, where he told the assembled employees: "All right, I've been quiet up 'til now, which is strange for me, I know. But now we're gonna talk about this dirty word—*union*." Neeman's presentation was punctuated by phrases such as "Mr. Asshole Union Rep" and "bunch of dummies." At some point in the presentation, Neeman wrote the word "union" on the board, drew a circle around it, and put a slash through it.

Progressive later filled various positions with non-union members, never advertising the jobs nor contacting the IBEW applicants.

The IBEW filed charges with the NLRB, which concluded that Progressive had committed an unfair labor practice by threatening job loss and plant closure if the union organized the company. The Board found in favor of the union, and Progressive appealed.

**Issue:** *Did the company commit a ULP?*

**Holding:** Yes, the company committed a ULP.

**Reasoning:** An employer may not use discriminatory hiring to discourage union membership. After Neeman accepted a sheet containing the union applicants' information, he lied to them, assuring them he would call them as soon as there

---

[4] *NLRB v. Gissel Packing Co.*, 395 U.S. 575, 89 S. Ct. 1918, 1969 U.S. LEXIS 3172 (1969).

was an opening, when in fact he had no such intention. The Board pointed to various other events over the next year indicating anti-union bias, including multiple union letters, which Progressive received but never responded to; the company's decision to use blind advertisements; and its failure to hire union applicants for any of the seven suitable positions. At the company meeting, Neeman showed overt hostility to the union, describing it in crude terms. Perhaps none of these actions in itself would be a ULP, but the Board reasonably found they were collectively part and parcel of Progressive's overall scheme to refuse to consider and hire the union applicants.

The Board's order is enforced.

## EXAM *Strategy*

**Question:** We Haul is a trucking company. The Teamsters Union is attempting to organize the drivers. Workers who favor a union have been using the lunchroom to hand out petitions and urge other drivers to sign authorization cards. The company posts a notice in the lunchroom: "No Union Discussions. Many employees do not want unions discussed in the lunchroom. Out of respect for them, we are prohibiting further union efforts in this lunchroom." Comment.

**Strategy:** The NLRA guarantees employees the right to talk among themselves about forming a union and to hand out literature. Union workers may vigorously push their cause. Management is entitled to communicate to the employees why it believes a union will be harmful to the company, but the employer's efforts must be limited to explanation and advocacy.

**Result:** We Haul has violated the NLRA. The company has the right to urge employees not to join the union. However, it is not entitled to block the union from its organizing campaign. Even assuming the company is correct that some employees do not want unions discussed, it has no right to prohibit such advocacy.

---

The employer in the following dispute admitted a glaring violation of labor law, yet claimed it should pay no damages because the injured worker was in the country illegally. What is your view?

## YOU *be the* JUDGE

### HOFFMAN PLASTIC COMPOUNDS, INC. v. NATIONAL LABOR RELATIONS BOARD

122 S. Ct. 1275, 152 L. Ed. 2d 271
United States Supreme Court, 2002

**Facts:** The United Rubber, Cork, Linoleum, and Plastic Workers of America began an organizing campaign at Hoffman Plastic Compounds, Inc. (Hoffman). Jose Castro and others supported this effort and, in retaliation, Hoffman fired them. Several years later (labor cases move very slowly), during hearings concerning his termination, Castro revealed for the first time that he was in the United States illegally. He had used false documents to obtain the job at Hoffman. Despite his illegal status, the NLRB found that Hoffman's retaliatory firing violated the NLRA and ordered the company to pay Castro $66,951, representing back pay from the date of firing until the employer learned that he was ineligible to work.

The company appealed and the issue reached the United States Supreme Court.

**You Be the Judge:** May an employer who has fired a worker for union organizing be ordered to pay back wages when the employee was illegally in the country?

**Argument for the Employer:** Any time an undocumented alien works in the United States, either he tenders fraudulent identification or the employer knowingly hires a worker in violation of its legal obligations. The Board ignored this fact and ordered back pay for wages that were illegally earned. There is simply no getting around the fact that the undocumented

*continued*

worker should not have had the job in the first place and should not have been paid at the time. Back pay for illegal work? It makes no sense.

**Argument for the Worker:** The employer in this case dismissed an employee for trying to organize a union—a gross violation of labor law. The company now wants a free pass on that illegal conduct. Further, any company that can avoid back wages will have an incentive to hire *additional* undocumented workers, knowing it can fire them on any pretext and avoid back pay. The company's position, if enforced, would undercut important goals of our labor *and* immigration laws. The men did the work—pay them.

### Appropriate Bargaining Unit

When a union petitions the NLRB for an election, the Board determines whether the proposed bargaining unit is appropriate. **The Board generally certifies a proposed bargaining unit if and only if the employees share a community of interest.** Employers frequently assert that the bargaining unit is inappropriate. If the Board agrees with the employer and rejects the proposed bargaining unit, it dismisses the union's request for an election.

**Managerial employees must be excluded from the bargaining unit.**[5] An employee is managerial if she is so closely aligned with management that her membership in the bargaining unit would create a conflict of interest between her union membership and her actual work. For example, a factory worker who spends one-third of his time performing assembly work but two-thirds of his time supervising a dozen other workers could not fairly be part of the bargaining unit.

Once the Board has excluded managerial employees, it looks at various criteria to decide whether the remaining employees should logically be grouped in one bargaining unit, that is, whether they share a **community of interest.** The Board looks for rough similarity of training, skills, hours of work, and pay. The Board either certifies the bargaining unit or rejects the unit and dismisses the union's petition.

## · COLLECTIVE BARGAINING ·

**Collective bargaining agreement (CBA)**
A contract between a union and management.

The goal of bargaining is a contract, which is called a **collective bargaining agreement (CBA).** Problems arise as union and employer advocate their respective positions. Three of the most common conflicts are (1) whether an issue is a mandatory subject of bargaining; (2) whether the parties are bargaining in good faith; and (3) how to enforce the agreement.

## SUBJECTS OF BARGAINING

The NLRA *permits* the parties to bargain almost any subject they wish, but *requires* them to bargain certain issues. **Mandatory subjects include wages, hours, and other terms and conditions of employment.** Either side may propose to bargain other subjects, but neither side may insist upon bargaining them.

Management and unions often disagree as to whether a particular topic is mandatory or not. Courts generally find these subjects to be mandatory: pay, benefits, order of layoffs and recalls, production quotas, work rules (such as safety practices), retirement benefits, and in-plant food service and prices (e.g., cafeteria food). Courts usually consider these subjects to be nonmandatory: product type and design, advertising, sales, financing, corporate organization, and location of plants.

Today, some of the angriest disputes between management and labor arise from a company's desire to subcontract work and/or to move plants to areas with cheaper costs. **Subcontracting** means that a manufacturer, rather than producing all parts of a product and then assembling

---

[5] *NLRB v. Bell Aerospace Co., Div. of Textron, Inc.*, 416 U.S. 267, 94 S. Ct. 1757, 1974 U.S. LEXIS 35 (1974).

them, contracts for other companies, frequently overseas, to make some of the parts. Is a business free to subcontract work? That depends on management's motive. A company that subcontracts in order to maintain its economic viability is probably not required to bargain first; however, **bargaining is mandatory if the subcontracting is designed to replace union workers with cheaper labor.**

### Employer and Union Security

Both the employer and the union will seek clauses making their positions more secure. Management, above all, wants to be sure that there will be no strikes during the course of the agreement. For its part, the union tries to ensure that its members cannot be turned away from work during the CBA's term, and that all newly hired workers will affiliate with the union. We look at several union security issues.

**No Strike/No Lockout**   Most agreements include some form of no-strike clause, meaning that the union promises not to strike during the term of the contract. In turn, unions insist on a no-lockout clause, meaning that in the event of a labor dispute, management will not prevent union members from working. No-strike and no-lockout clauses are both legal.

**Union Shop**   In a union shop, membership in the union becomes compulsory after the employee has been hired. Thus management retains an unfettered right to hire whom it pleases, but all new employees who fit into the bargaining unit must affiliate with the union. **A union shop is generally legal,** with two limitations. First, new members need not join the union for 30 days. Second, the new members, after joining the union, can only be required to pay initiation fees and union dues. If the new hire decides he does not want to participate in the union, the union may not compel him to do so.

## DUTY TO BARGAIN

**Both the union and the employer must bargain in good faith with an open mind. However, they are *not* obligated to reach an agreement.** This means that the two sides must meet and make a reasonable effort to reach a contract. Suppose a union proposes a 15 percent pay increase, and management offers a 1 percent raise. Each side is required to attend bargaining sessions, listen to the other side's proposal, and consider its supporting argument. But neither side has to agree.

Sometimes an employer will attempt to make changes without bargaining the issues at all. However, **management may not unilaterally change wages, hours, or terms and conditions of employment without bargaining the issues to impasse.** "Bargaining to impasse" means that both parties must continue to meet and bargain in good faith until it is clear that they cannot reach an agreement. The goal in requiring collective bargaining is to bring the parties together, to reach an agreement that brings labor peace. In one case, the union won an election, but before bargaining could begin, management changed the schedule from five 8-hour days to four 10-hour days a week. The company also changed its layoff policy from one of strict seniority to one based on ability and began laying off employees based on alleged poor performance. The court held that each of these acts violated the company's duty to bargain. The employer ultimately might be allowed to make every one of these changes, but first it had to bargain the issues to impasse.[6]

## ENFORCEMENT

Virtually all collective bargaining agreements provide for their own enforcement, typically through **grievance-arbitration.** Suppose a company transfers an employee from the day shift to the night shift, and the worker believes the contract prohibits such a transfer for any employee with her seniority. The employee complains to the union, which files a **grievance**, that is, a formal complaint with the company, notifying management that the union claims a contract violation.

**Grievance**
A formal complaint alleging a contract violation.

---

[6] *Adair Standish Corp. v. NLRB*, 912 F.2d 854, 1990 U.S. App. LEXIS 14670 (6th Cir. 1990).

Generally, the CBA establishes some kind of informal hearing, usually conducted by a member of management, at which the employee, represented by the union, may state her case.

After the manager's decision, if the employee is still dissatisfied, the union may file for **arbitration**, that is, a formal hearing before a neutral arbitrator. In the arbitration hearing, each side is represented by its lawyer. The arbitrator is required to decide the case based on the CBA. An arbitrator finds either for the employee, and orders the company to take certain corrective action, or for the employer, and dismisses the grievance.

In the vast majority of grievances, the arbitrator's decision is final. The following case demonstrates how reluctant courts are to interfere with an arbitrator's award.

**Arbitration**
A formal hearing before a neutral party to resolve a contract dispute between a union and a company.

## BRENTWOOD MEDICAL ASSOCIATES V. UNITED MINE WORKERS OF AMERICA

396 F.3d 237
United States Court of Appeals for the Third Circuit, 2005

### CASE SUMMARY

**Facts:** Brentwood Medical Associates operated a hospital. The United Mine Workers of America represented one unit of employees, which included Denise Cope, a phlebotomist (someone who draws blood). Exercising her seniority rights, Cope changed jobs to Charge Entry Associate. A year and a half later, BMA announced it was terminating the position. Cope asked to return to her old job. This would have required "bumping" the least senior phlebotomist out of a job. BMA refused, claiming that bumping was not allowed under the collective bargaining agreement (CBA). Cope filed a grievance, which an arbitrator heard.

The arbitrator ruled in Cope's favor. In his decision, he asked rhetorically why, if the CBA disallowed bumping, did it include the following language:

> . . . employees who exercise seniority rights and bump must have the skill to perform all of the work [in the new job].

The problem with the quoted language was that it did not in fact exist anywhere in the CBA. BMA filed suit, asking a federal court to overturn the arbitration decision. The trial court upheld the award and BMA appealed.

**Issue:** *Should the arbitration award be affirmed even though the arbitrator relied on language that cannot be found in the CBA?*

**Decision:** Yes, the decision is affirmed.

**Reasoning:** The parties wanted arbitration, bargained for it, and included it in their CBA. Full-blown judicial review of the arbitrator's decision would contravene their agreement, injecting a judicial interpretation that neither side expected.

Although the arbitrator did cite language he should not have, his decision relied on several provisions of the agreement. For example, Section 1 defines seniority as "bargaining unit-wide" and not within classification. Section 2 provides that the principle of seniority is a factor in layoffs and recalls. Section 5 specifies that in filling vacancies when the qualifications of two or more applicants are relatively equal, preference will be based on seniority.

The arbitrator's award does not rest solely upon the aberrant language that he unfortunately added. He attempted to give effect to all provisions of the agreement. His decision is affirmed.

## • CONCERTED ACTION •

**Concerted action**
Tactics taken by union members to gain bargaining advantage.

**Concerted action** refers to any tactics union members take in unison to gain some bargaining advantage. It is this power that gives a union strength. The NLRA guarantees the right of employees to engage in concerted action for mutual aid or protection.[7] The most common forms of concerted action are strikes and picketing.

---

[7] NLRA §7.

# STRIKES

**The NLRA guarantees employees the right to strike, but with some limitations.**[8] A union has a guaranteed right to call a strike if the parties are unable to reach a collective bargaining agreement. A union may call a strike to exert economic pressure on management, to protest an unfair labor practice, or to preserve work that the employer is considering sending elsewhere.

This right to strike can be waived. Management will generally insist that the CBA include a no-strike clause, which prohibits the union from striking while the CBA is in force. Other restrictions include a 60-day cooling-off period before many strikes, and in many states, a flat prohibition on strikes by public employees (police, teachers, and so forth). Violent strikes are always illegal.

**ETHICS**   Suppose state law prohibits teachers from striking, but the teachers' union is angry. Their contract expired a year ago, and the board of education has refused any pay raises. The teachers decide they will "work to rule," meaning they will teach classes, issues grades, and so forth . . . but will not write any college recommendations. What are the consequences? Is that just? What are the alternatives? ◆

# REPLACEMENT WORKERS

When employees go on strike, management generally wants to replace them to keep the company operating. Are replacement workers legal? Yes. **Management has the right to hire replacement workers during a strike.** May the employer offer the replacement workers permanent jobs, or must the company give union members their jobs back when the strike is over? It depends on the type of strike.

**After an *economic strike*, an employer may not discriminate against a striker, but the employer is not obligated to lay off a replacement worker to give a striker his job back.** An economic strike is one intended to gain wages or benefits. When a union bargains for a pay raise but fails to get it and walks off the job, that is an economic strike. During such a strike, an employer may hire permanent replacement workers. When the strike is over, the company has no obligation to lay off the replacement workers to make room for the strikers. However, if the company does hire more workers, it may not discriminate against the strikers.

**After a *ULP strike*, a union member is entitled to her job back, even if that means the employer must lay off a replacement worker.** Suppose management refuses to bargain in good faith by claiming poverty without producing records to substantiate its claim. The union strikes. Management's refusal to bargain was an unfair labor practice, and the strike is a ULP strike. When it ends, the striking workers must get their jobs back.

# PICKETING

**Picketing the employer's workplace in support of a strike is generally lawful.** Striking workers are permitted to establish picket lines at the employer's job site and to urge all others—employees, replacement workers, and customers—not to cross the line. But the picketers are not permitted to use physical force to prevent anyone from crossing the line.

---

[8] NLRA §13.

# LOCKOUTS

> **150 employees find the company's gate locked and armed guards standing on the other side.**

The workers have bargained with management for weeks, and discussions have turned belligerent. It is 6 a.m., the start of another day at the factory. But as 150 employees arrive for work, they are amazed to find the company's gate locked and armed guards standing on the other side. What is this? A lockout.

The power of a union comes ultimately from its potential to strike. But management, too, has weapons. In a lockout, management prohibits workers from entering the premises, denying the employees work and a chance to earn a paycheck.

**A lockout is legal if the parties have reached a bargaining impasse.** Management, bargaining a new CBA with a union, may wish to use a lockout to advance its position. It is allowed to do so provided the parties have reached an impasse. If there is no impasse, a lockout will probably be illegal. Most courts consider that a lockout before impasse indicates hostility to the union.

## EXAM *Strategy*

**Question:** Union workers are striking at Cheesey, a restaurant, forming picket lines in front of the restaurant during the lunch and dinner hours but at no other times. The union members chant slogans denouncing their wages and working conditions, urging diners not to enter. There is no violence, but the picketers cause many prospective customers to stay away, and Cheesey suffers a substantial drop in business. The restaurant files a charge with the NLRB, claiming that the union has committed a ULP by (1) deliberately harming its business and (2) engaging in a secondary boycott. Who will win?

**Strategy:** Striking workers are allowed to picket. May they *urge* non-union members to stay out of the business? May they *prohibit* others from entering? Secondary boycotts are illegal. Is this one?

**Result:** Striking workers may urge the public not to cross the picket line. The union may not use violence to keep people out, but this union has not done so. This is not a secondary boycott, which is a picket line established at a *different* company that does business with the employer. The company's loss of business is one possible—and legal—consequence of a strike. The union has committed no ULP.

# · REGULATING UNION AFFAIRS ·

Along with a union's exclusive bargaining power goes a duty of fairness to all of its members. The union's duty of fair representation was created by the NLRA and the Labor-Management Reporting and Disclosure Act. **The duty of fair representation requires that a union represent all members fairly, impartially, and in good faith.** A union is not entitled to favor some members over others. No union may discriminate against a member based on impermissible characteristics such as race or sex.

Unions must make reasonable decisions about whether to pursue an employee's grievance. A member may sue his union, claiming that the organization violated its duty of fair representation by deciding not to pursue a grievance on his behalf. But courts generally allow unions a wide range of latitude in deciding whether to pursue a grievance. A union's decision not to file a grievance is illegal only if it was arbitrary, discriminatory, or in bad faith.

## CHAPTER CONCLUSION

Contemporary clashes between union and management are less likely to stem from sweltering temperatures in a mine than from a management decision to subcontract work or from a teacher's refusal to write college recommendations. But although the flash points have changed, labor law is still dominated by issues of organizing, collective bargaining, and concerted action.

## EXAM REVIEW

1. **RIGHT TO ORGANIZE** Section 7 of the National Labor Relations Act (NLRA) guarantees employees the right to organize and join unions, bargain collectively, and engage in other concerted activities. (p. 311)

2. **INTERFERENCE WITH ORGANIZING** Section 8(a) of the NLRA makes it an unfair labor practice (ULP) for an employer to interfere with union organizing, discriminate against a union member, or refuse to bargain collectively. (p. 311)

3. **DISCRIMINATION** Section 8(b) of the NLRA makes it a ULP for a union to interfere with employees who are exercising their rights under Section 7 or to engage in an illegal strike or boycott. (p. 311)

4. **EXCLUSIVITY** Section 9 of the NLRA makes a validly recognized union the exclusive representative of the employees. (p. 312)

5. **EMPLOYER OPPOSITION** During a union organizing campaign, an employer may vigorously present anti-union views to its employees, but it may not use threats or promises of benefits to defeat the union effort. (p. 314)

**EXAM Strategy**

**Question:** Power, Inc., which operated a coal mine, suffered financial losses and had to lay off employees. The United Mine Workers of America (UMWA) began an organizing drive. Power's general manager warned miners that if the company was unionized, it would be shut down. An office manager told one of the miners that the company would get rid of union supporters. Shortly before the election was to take place, Power laid off 13 employees, all of whom had signed union cards. A low-seniority employee who had not signed a union card was not laid off. The union claimed that Power had committed ULPs. Comment.

**Strategy:** Section 7 of the NLRA guarantees employees the right to organize. An employer may vigorously advocate against a union organizing campaign. However, Section 8(a) makes it a ULP to interfere with union organizing or discriminate against a union member. (See the "Result" at the end of this section.)

6. **CERTIFICATION** The National Labor Relations Board (NLRB) will certify a proposed bargaining unit only if the employees share a community of interest. (p. 316)

7. **BARGAINING** The employer and the union must bargain over wages, hours, and other terms and conditions of employment. (p. 316)

**8.** **GOOD FAITH** The union and the employer must bargain in good faith, but they are not obligated to reach an agreement. (p. 317)

**Question:** Concrete Company was bargaining a CBA with the drivers' union. Negotiations went on for many months. Concrete made its final offer of $9.50 per hour, with step increases of $0.75 per hour in a year, and the same the following two years. The union refused to accept the offer and the two sides reached an impasse. Concrete then implemented its plan, minus the step increases. Was its implementation legal?

**Strategy:** Management may unilaterally change wages and so forth only if the parties have reached an impasse. At all stages, the two sides must bargain in good faith. The goal of the NLRA is to achieve labor peace through productive negotiations. (See the "Result" at the end of this section.)

**9.** **STRIKES** The NLRA guarantees employees the right to strike, with some limitations. (p. 319)

**10.** **REPLACEMENT WORKERS** During a strike, management may hire replacement workers. (p. 319)

**11.** **PICKETING** Picketing the employer's workplace in support of a strike is generally lawful. (p. 319)

**12.** **LOCKOUTS** Lockouts are lawful if the parties have bargained to impasse. (p. 320)

**13.** **FAIR REPRESENTATION** The duty of fair representation requires that a union represent all members fairly, impartially, and in good faith. (p. 320)

**5. Result:** Each of the acts described was a ULP. Threatening layoffs or company closure are classic examples of ULPs. Laying off those who had signed union cards but not those who refused was clear discrimination. The NLRB found the violations so extreme it certified the union and issued an order to bargain.

**8. Result:** The implementation was illegal. Because the parties had reached an impasse, the company was entitled to implement the last proposal it had made at the bargaining table. But it did not do so. By implementing a reduced plan, which it had never proposed, management showed bad faith. To allow the company to implement something that it had never offered would defeat the whole purpose of bargaining.

# PRACTICE EXAM

## MATCHING QUESTIONS

Match the following terms with their definitions:

___ A. ULP                              1. A specific group of employees that a union will represent

___ B. Exclusivity                      2. The union's right to be the sole representative of workers

___ C. Collective bargaining unit       3. Management interference with a union organizing effort

___ D. Union shop                       4. Picketing and strikes

___ E. Concerted action                 5. Workers within specified categories are required to join the union

## TRUE/FALSE QUESTIONS

Circle true or false:

1. T   F   The union and management are both obligated to bargain until they reach a CBA or a court declares the bargaining futile.

2. T   F   Health benefits are a mandatory subject of bargaining.

3. T   F   During the last two decades, labor unions have grown by about 15 percent in the United States.

4. T   F   Workers are entitled to form a union whether management wants them to or not.

5. T   F   While organizing, workers may not discuss union issues on company property but may do so off the premises.

## MULTIPLE-CHOICE QUESTIONS

6. During a union organizing drive, management urges workers not to join the union and discusses a competing company which lost business after a union was formed. Management

   A.  Committed a ULP by urging workers to reject the union, but did not do so by discussing a competing company
   B.  Committed a ULP by discussing a competing company, but did not do so by urging workers to reject the union
   C.  Committed a ULP both by urging workers to reject the union and by discussing a competitor
   D.  Committed no ULP
   E.  Has violated other sections of the NLRA

7. Which of these does the NLRA *not* protect?

   A.  Right to form a union
   B.  Right to picket
   C.  Right to strike
   D.  Right to block nonunion workers from company property
   E.  Right to bargain collectively

8. The CBA at Grey Corp. has expired, as has the CBA at Blue Corp. At Grey, union and management have bargained a new CBA to impasse. Suddenly, Grey locks out all union workers. The next day, during a bargaining session at Blue, management announces that it will not discuss pay increases.

   A.  Grey has committed a ULP but Blue has not.
   B.  Blue has committed a ULP but Grey has not.
   C.  Both Blue and Grey have committed ULPs.
   D.  Neither company has committed a ULP.
   E.  Grey and Blue have violated labor law, but not by committing ULPs.

9. When the union went on strike, the company replaced Ashley, a union member, with Ben, a nonunion member. The strike is now over, and a federal court has ruled that this was a ULP strike. Does Ashley get her job back?

   A.  The company is obligated to hire Ashley, even if that requires laying off Ben.
   B.  The company is obligated to hire Ashley *unless* that would require laying off Ben.
   C.  The company is obligated to hire Ashley only if Ben voluntarily leaves.
   D.  The company's only obligation is to notify Ashley of future job availability.
   E.  The company has no obligation at all to Ashley.

## SHORT-ANSWER QUESTIONS

10. Gibson Greetings, Inc., had a plant in Berea, Kentucky, where the workers belonged to the International Brotherhood of Firemen & Oilers. The old CBA expired, and the parties negotiated a new one, but were unable to reach an agreement on economic issues. The union struck. At the next bargaining session, the company claimed that the strike violated the old CBA, which had a no-strike clause and which stated that

the terms of the old CBA would continue in force as long as the parties were bargaining a new CBA. The company refused to bargain until the union at least agreed that by bargaining, the company was not giving up its claim of an illegal strike. The two sides returned to bargaining, but meanwhile the company hired replacement workers. Eventually, the striking workers offered to return to work, but Gibson refused to rehire many of them. In court, the union claimed that the company had committed a ULP by (1) insisting the strike was illegal; and (2) refusing to bargain until the union acknowledged the company's position. Why is it very important to the union to establish the company's act as a ULP? Was it a ULP?

11. Fred Schipul taught English at the Thomaston (Connecticut) High School for 18 years. When the position of English Department chairperson became vacant, Schipul applied, but the Board of Education appointed a less senior teacher. Schipul filed a grievance, based on a CBA provision that required the Board to promote the most senior teacher where two or more applicants were equal in qualification. Before the arbitrator ruled on the grievance, the Board eliminated all department chairpersons. The arbitrator ruled in Schipul's favor. The Board then reinstated all department chairs—all but the English Department. Comment.

12. ETHICS: This chapter refers in several places to the contentious issue of subcontracting. Make an argument for management in favor of a company's ethical right to subcontract, and one for unions in opposition.

13. ROLE REVERSAL: Write an essay question involving a union organizing campaign and a management response that includes both permissible advocacy and illegal conduct.

# INTERNET RESEARCH PROBLEM

Read about sweatshops. What are they? Do they exist in the United States? Describe a current student campaign about this issue. Do you agree or disagree with what the students are doing? Why?

You can find further practice problems in the Online Quiz at **www.cengage.com/blaw/beatty.**

# BUSINESS ORGANIZATIONS

<br>

# CHAPTER 20

## STARTING A BUSINESS: LLCs AND OTHER OPTIONS

**Poor Jeffrey Horning.** If only he had understood business law. Horning owned a thriving construction company—but it was so successful his workload was crushing. To lighten his burden, he brought in two partners to take on more of the day-to-day responsibilities. It seemed a good idea at the time.

> **Jeffrey Horning was stuck in purgatory, with two business partners he loathed and no way out.**

The business originally operated as a corporation—Horning Construction Company, Inc. He transferred it to Horning Construction, LLC and then gave one-third ownership each to two trusted employees, Klimowski and Holdsworth. But Horning did not pay enough attention to the legal formalities—the new LLC had no operating agreement.

Nothing worked out as he had planned. The two men did not take on extra work. Horning's relationship with them went from bad to worse, with the parties bickering over every petty detail and each man trying to sabotage the others. It got to the point that Klimowski sent Horning a letter full of curses. At his wit's end, Horning proposed that the LLC buy out his share of the business. Klimowski and Holdsworth refused. Really frustrated, Horning asked a court to dissolve the business on the grounds that Klimowski despised him, Holdsworth resented him, and neither of them trusted him. In his view, it was their goal "to make my remaining time with Horning, LLC so unbearable that I will relent and give them for a pittance the remainder of the company for which they have paid nothing to date."

Although the court was sympathetic, it refused to help. Because Horning, LLC did not have an operating agreement that provided for a buyout, it had to depend upon the LLC statute, which only permitted dissolution "whenever it is not reasonably practicable to carry on the business." Unfortunately, Horning, LLC was very successful, grossing over $25 million annually. Jeffrey Horning was stuck in purgatory, with two business partners he loathed and no way out.[1]

The law affects virtually every aspect of business. Wise (and successful) entrepreneurs know how to use the law to their advantage.

To begin, entrepreneurs must select a form of organization. The correct choice can reduce taxes, liability, and conflict while facilitating outside investment.

## · SOLE PROPRIETORSHIPS ·

**A sole proprietorship is an unincorporated business owned by a single person.** For example, Linda runs ExSciTe (which stands for Excellence in Science Teaching), a company that helps teachers prepare hands-on science experiments for the classroom.

Sole proprietorships are easy and inexpensive to create and operate. There is no need to hire a lawyer or register with the government. The company is not even required to file a separate tax return—all profits and losses are reported on the owner's personal return.

Sole proprietorships also have some serious disadvantages:

- The owner of the business is responsible for all of the business's debts. If ExSciTe cannot pay its suppliers or if a student is injured while doing an experiment, Linda is *personally* liable.
- The owner of a sole proprietorship has limited options for financing her business. Debt is generally her only source of working capital because she has no stock or memberships to sell.

**Sole proprietorship**
An unincorporated business owned by one person.

---

[1] *In the Matter of Jeffrey M. Horning*, 816 N.Y.S.2d 877; 2006 N.Y. Misc. LEXIS 555

If someone else brings in capital and helps with the management of the business, then it is a partnership, not a sole proprietorship. For this reason, sole proprietorships work best for small businesses without large capital needs.

## ▪ CORPORATIONS ▪

Corporations are the dominant form of organization for a simple reason—they have been around for a long time and, as a result, they are numerous and the law that regulates them is well developed.

## CORPORATIONS IN GENERAL

### Limited Liability

**Shareholders of a corporation have limited liability**, which means that if a corporation cannot pay its bills, shareholders lose their investment in the company, but not their other assets. Be aware, however, that individuals are always responsible for their *own* acts. Suppose that a careless employee who is also a company shareholder causes an accident at work. Being a shareholder does not protect him from liability for his own misdeeds. Both he and the company would be liable.

### Transferability of Interests

Ownership interests in a partnership are not transferable without the permission of the other partners, whereas corporate stock can be easily bought and sold.

### Duration

When a sole proprietor dies, legally so does the business. But corporations have perpetual existence: they can continue without their founders.

### Logistics

Corporations require substantial expense and effort to create and operate. The cost of establishing a corporation may exceed $1,000 in legal and filing fees, not to mention the cost of the annual filings that states require. Corporations must also hold annual meetings for both shareholders and directors. Minutes of these meetings must be kept indefinitely in the company minute book.

### Taxes

Because corporations are taxable entities, they must pay taxes and file returns. This is a simple sentence that requires a complex explanation. Originally, there were only three ways to do business: as a sole proprietorship, a partnership, or a corporation. The sole proprietor pays taxes on all of the business's profits. A partnership is not, as we say, a taxable entity, which means it does not pay taxes itself. All income and losses are passed through to the partners and reported on their personal income tax returns. Corporations, by contrast, are taxable entities and pay income tax on their profits. Shareholders must then pay tax on dividends from the corporation. Thus a dollar is taxed only once before it ends up in a partner's bank account, but twice before it is deposited by a shareholder.

Exhibit 20.1 compares the single taxation of partnerships with the double taxation of corporations. Suppose, as shown in the exhibit, that a corporation and a partnership each receive $10,000 in additional income. The corporation pays tax at a top rate of 35 percent.[2] Thus the corporation pays $3,500 of the $10,000 in tax. The corporation pays out the remaining $6,500 as a dividend

---

[2] This is the federal tax rate; most states also levy a corporate tax.

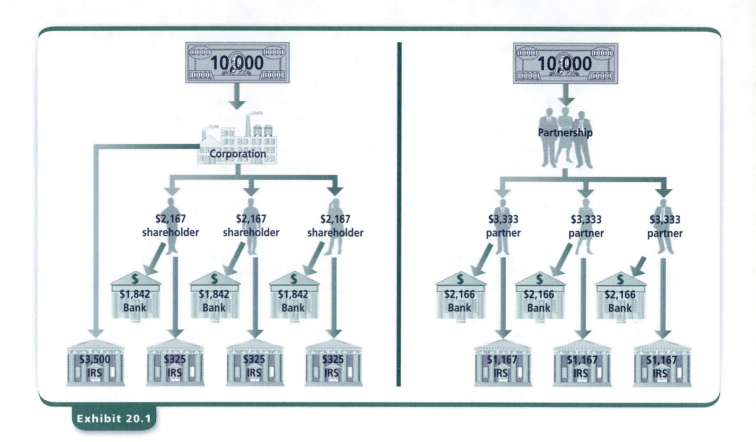

**Exhibit 20.1**

of $2,167 to each of its three shareholders. Then the shareholders are taxed at the special dividend rate of 15 percent, which means they each pay a tax of $325. They are each left with $1,842. Of the initial $10,000, almost 45 percent ($4,475) has gone to the Internal Revenue Service (IRS).

Compare the corporation to a partnership. The partnership itself pays no taxes, so it can pass on $3,333 to each of its partners. At a 35 percent individual rate, they will each pay an income tax of $1,167. As partners, they pocket $2,166, which is $324 more than they could keep as shareholders. Of the partnership's initial $10,000, 35 percent ($3,501) has gone to the IRS—compared with the corporation's 45 percent.

# CLOSE CORPORATIONS

A **close corporation** is a company whose stock is not publicly traded. Although the provisions of close corporation statutes vary from state to state, they tend to have certain common themes:

- **Protection of Minority Shareholders.** As there is no public market for the stock of a close corporation, a minority shareholder who is being mistreated by the majority cannot simply sell his shares and depart. Therefore, close corporation statutes often provide some protection for minority shareholders. For example, the charter of a close corporation could require a unanimous vote of all shareholders to choose officers, set salaries, or pay dividends. It could grant each shareholder veto power over all important corporate decisions.

- **Transfer Restrictions.** The shareholders of a close corporation often need to work closely together in the management of the company. Therefore, statutes typically permit the corporation to require that a shareholder first offer shares to the other owners before selling them to

**Close corporation**
A company whose stock is not publicly traded. Also known as a *closely held corporation.*

an outsider. In that way, the remaining shareholders have some control over who their new co-owners will be.

- **Flexibility.** Close corporations can typically operate without a board of directors, a formal set of bylaws, or annual shareholder meetings.
- **Dispute Resolution.** The shareholders are allowed to agree in advance that any one of them can dissolve the corporation if some particular event occurs or, if they choose, for any reason at all. If the shareholders are in a stalemate, the problem can be solved by dissolving the corporation. Even without such an agreement, a shareholder can ask a court to dissolve a close corporation if the other owners behave "oppressively" or "unfairly."

# S CORPORATIONS

The majority of new businesses lose money in their early years. Congress created S corporations (aka "S corps") to encourage entrepreneurship by offering tax breaks. **Shareholders of S corps have both the limited liability of a corporation and the tax status of a partnership.** Like a partnership, an S corp is not a taxable entity—all of the company's profits and losses pass through to the shareholders, who pay tax at their individual rates. It avoids the double taxation of a regular corporation (called a "C corporation"). If, as is often the case, the start-up loses money, investors can deduct these losses against their other income.

Note that state laws regulate corporations, while federal statutes determine their tax status. Thus *close corporations* are created by state law, while *S corporations* are a creation of federal statute. The two sets of statutes are completely independent. As a result, an S corporation can be either a close corporation or a (nonclose) corporation. Exhibit 20.2 illustrates the difference between state and IRS regulation of corporations.

S corps do face some major restrictions:

- There can be only one class of stock.
- There can be no more than 100 shareholders.
- Shareholders must be individuals, estates, charities, pension funds, or trusts, not partnerships or corporations.
- Shareholders must be citizens or residents of the United States, not non-resident aliens.
- All shareholders must agree that the company should be an S corporation.

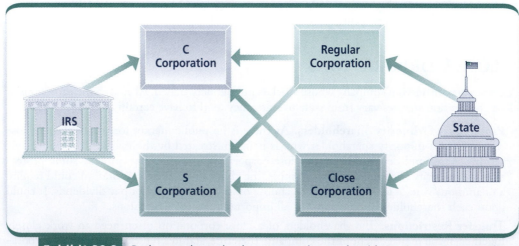

**Exhibit 20.2**   Both a regular and a close corporation can be either a C or an S corporation.

**EXAM** *Strategy*

**Question:** Consider these two entrepreneurs: Judith formed a corporation to publish a newsletter that will not generate substantial revenues. Drexel operated his construction and remodeling business as a sole proprietorship. Were these forms of organization right for these businesses?

**Strategy:** Prepare a list of the advantages and disadvantages for each form of organization. Sole proprietorships are best for businesses without substantial capital needs. Corporations can raise capital but are expensive to operate.

**Result:** Judith would be better off with a sole proprietorship—her revenues will not support the expenses of a corporation. Also, her debts are likely to be small, so she will not need the limited liability of a corporation. But for Drexel, a sole proprietorship could be disastrous because his construction company will have substantial expenses and a large number of employees. If an employee causes an injury, Drexel might be personally liable. And if his business ends up in bankruptcy, the court would liquidate his personal assets.

## · LIMITED LIABILITY COMPANIES ·

An LLC offers the limited liability of a corporation and the tax status of a partnership.

### Limited Liability

**Members are not personally liable for the debts of the company.** They risk only their investment, as if they were shareholders of a corporation. Are the members of the LLC liable in the following case? You be the judge.

### YOU *be the* JUDGE

**RIDGAWAY v. SILK**

2004 Conn. Super. LEXIS 548
Superior Court of Connecticut, 2004

**Facts:** Norman Costello and Joseph Ruggiero were members of Silk, LLC, which owned a bar and adult entertainment nightclub in Groton, Connecticut, called Silk Stockings. Anthony Sulls went drinking there one night—and drinking heavily. Although he was obviously drunk, employees at Silk Stockings continued to serve him. Giordano and Costello were working there that night. They both greeted customers (who numbered in the hundreds), supervised employees, and performed "other PR work." When Sulls left the nightclub at 1:45 A.M. with two friends, he drove off the highway at high speed, killing himself and one of his passengers, William Ridgaway, Jr.

Ridgaway's estate sued Costello and Giordano personally. The defendants filed a motion for summary judgment.

**You Be the Judge: Are Costello and Giordano personally liable to Ridgaway's estate?**

**Argument for Costello and Giordano:** The defendants did not own Silk Stockings, they were simply members of an LLC that owned the nightclub. The whole point of an LLC is to protect members against personal liability. The assets of Silk, LLC are at risk, but not the personal assets of Costello and Giordano.

**Argument for Ridgaway's Estate:** The defendants are not liable for being *members* of Silk, LLC, they are liable for their own misdeeds as *employees* of the LLC. They were both present at Silk Stockings on the night in question, meeting and greeting customers and supervising employees. It is possible that they might actually have served drinks to Sulls, but in

*continued*

any event they did not adequately supervise and train their employees so as to prevent them from serving alcohol to someone who was clearly drunk. The world would be an intolerable place to live if employees were free to be as careless as they wished, knowing that they were not liable because they were members of an LLC.

## Tax Status

As in a partnership, **income flows through the company to the individual members, avoiding the double taxation of a corporation.**

## Formation

**To organize an LLC, you must have a charter and you should have an operating agreement.** The charter contains basic information such as name and address. It must be filed with the Secretary of State in the jurisdiction in which it is being formed. An operating agreement sets out the rights and obligations of the owners, called members. Although some states do not require an operating agreement, lawyers recommend them as a way to avoid disputes. The Horning case that began the chapter illustrates one of the many things that can go wrong without an operating agreement.

On this issue, corporations have an advantage over LLCs. Corporations are so familiar that the standard documents (such as a charter, by-laws, and shareholder agreement) are well established and widely available. Lawyers can form a corporation easily and the Internet offers a host of free forms. This is not the case with LLCs. As yet, the law is so unsettled that standard forms may be dangerous, while customized forms can be expensive. Members of an LLC reside in foggy legal territory, as the following case illustrates.

# WYOMING.COM, LLC v. LIEBERMAN

2005 WY 42; 109 P.3D 883; 2005 WYO. LEXIS 48
SUPREME COURT OF WYOMING, 2005

## CASE SUMMARY

**Facts:** Lieberman was a member of an LLC, Wyoming.com. After he withdrew, he and the other members disagreed about what his membership was worth. Wyoming.com filed a lawsuit asking the court to determine the financial rights and obligations of the parties, if any, upon the withdrawal of a member.

The Supreme Court of Wyoming reached a decision that may have sounded logical but left Lieberman in a sad twilight zone—neither in nor out of the LLC. The court ruled that Lieberman still owned part of the business despite his withdrawal as a member. So far, so good. But neither the LLC statute nor the company's operating agreement required the LLC to pay a member the value of his share. In other words, Lieberman was still an owner, but he was not entitled to any payment for his ownership. Not quite understanding the implications of this ruling, Lieberman filed a motion seeking financial information about the company. The original trial court denied the request on the theory that, since Lieberman had no rights to a payout, the company had no obligation to give him financial data.

**Issue:** *Does Lieberman have a right to any financial data about Wyoming.com?*

**Decision:** Wyoming.com has no obligation to provide Lieberman with financial data about the company.

**Reasoning:** The court in the prior Lieberman case ruled that Lieberman was not entitled to any payment from Wyoming.com. Thus, there is no point in requiring the company to give him financial information. He still owns a share of the company, but he has no further rights.

## Flexibility

Unlike S corporations, LLCs can have members that are corporations, partnerships, or nonresident aliens. LLCs can also have different classes of membership. Unlike corporations, LLCs are not required to hold annual meetings or maintain a minute book.

## Transferability of Interests

Unless the operating agreement provides otherwise, the members of the LLC must obtain the unanimous permission of the remaining members before transferring their ownership rights. This is yet another reason to have an operating agreement.

## Duration

It used to be that LLCs automatically dissolved upon the withdrawal of a member (owing to, for example, death, resignation, or bankruptcy). The current trend in state laws, however, is to permit an LLC to continue in operation even after a member withdraws.

## Going Public

Once an LLC goes public, it loses its favorable tax status and is taxed as a corporation, not a partnership.[3] Thus, there is no advantage to using the LLC form of organization for a publicly traded company. And there are some disadvantages: unlike corporations, publicly traded LLCs do not enjoy a well-established set of statutory and case law that is relatively consistent across the many states. For this reason, privately held companies that begin as LLCs usually change to corporations when they go public.

## Piercing the LLC Veil

We end this section with a final cautionary note. It has long been the case that, if corporate shareholders do not comply with the technicalities of corporation law, they may be held personally liable for the debts of the organization. As the following case illustrates, under these circumstances, members of an LLC are also liable.

### BLD PRODUCTS, LTD. v. TECHNICAL PLASTICS OF OREGON, LLC

2006 U.S. DIST. LEXIS 89874
UNITED STATES DISTRICT COURT FOR THE DISTRICT OF OREGON, 2006

### CASE SUMMARY

**Facts:** Mark Hardie was the sole member of Technical Plastics of Oregon, LLC (TPO). The company operated out of an office in Hardie's home. He regularly used TPO's accounts to pay such expenses as landscaping and housecleaning. TPO also paid some of Hardie's personal credit card bills, loan payments on his Ford truck, the cost of constructing a deck on his house, his stepson's college bills and the expenses of family vacations to Disneyland. At the same time, Hardie deposited cash advances from his personal credit cards into the TPO checking account. Hardie did not take a salary from TPO. When TPO filed for bankruptcy, it owed BLD Products approximately $120,000.

In some cases, a court will "pierce the veil" of a corporation and hold its shareholders personally liable for the debts of the business. BLD argued that the same doctrine should apply to LLCs and the court should hold Hardie personally liable for TPO's debts.

**Issues:** *Does the doctrine of "piercing the veil" apply to LLCs? Is Hardy personally liable for TPO's debts?*

**Decision:** Yes, an LLC's veil can be pierced. Hardy is personally liable for TPO's debts.

---

[3] 26 U.S.C. §7704.

**Reasoning:** An LLC's veil can be pierced if the following three tests are met:

1. the member (that is, Hardie) controlled the LLC;

2. the member engaged in improper conduct; and

3. as a result of that improper conduct, the plaintiff was unable to collect on a debt against the insolvent LLC.

Hardie, as the sole member and manager of TPO, clearly controlled the company. In addition, he engaged in improper conduct when he paid his personal expenses from the TPO business account. These amounts were more than occasional dips into petty cash—they indicated a disregard of TPO's separate LLC identity. Moreover, he did not keep records of these personal payments.

It is not clear whether Hardie's improper conduct prevented BLD from collecting its entire $120,000 debt. A jury will have to determine the amount that Hardie owes BLD.

## Choices: LLC v. Corporation

When starting a business, which form makes the most sense—LLC or corporation? The tax status of an LLC is a major advantage over a corporation. Although an S corporation has the same tax status as an LLC, it also has all the annoying rules about classes of stock and number of shareholders. Once an LLC is established, it does not have as many housekeeping rules as corporations—it does not, for example, have to make annual filings or hold annual meetings. However, the LLC is not right for everyone. If done properly, an LLC is more expensive to set up than a corporation because it needs to have a thoughtfully crafted operating agreement. Also, venture capitalists almost always refuse to invest in LLCs, preferring C corporations instead. There are two reasons for this preference: (1) arcane tax issues and (2) C corporations are easier to merge, sell, or take public.

### EXAM *Strategy*

**Question:** Hortense and Gus are each starting a business. Hortense's business is an Internet start-up. Gus will be opening a yarn store. Hortense needs millions of dollars in venture capital and expects to go public soon. Gus has borrowed $10,000 from his girlfriend, which he hopes to pay back soon. Should either of these businesses organize as an LLC?

**Strategy:** Sole proprietorships may be best for businesses without substantial capital needs and without significant liability issues. Corporations are best for businesses that will need substantial outside capital and expect to go public shortly.

**Result:** An LLC is not the best choice for either of these businesses. Venture capitalists will insist that Hortense's business be a corporation, especially if it is going public soon. A yarn store has few liability issues and Gus does not expect to have any outside investors. Hence a sole proprietorship would be more appropriate.

## · GENERAL PARTNERSHIPS ·

Partnerships have two important advantages: They are *easy to form* and they do not pay *taxes*. Partnerships, however, also have some major disadvantages:

- *Liability.* Each partner is personally liable for the debts of the enterprise whether or not she caused them.

- *Funding.* Financing a partnership may be difficult because the firm cannot sell shares as a corporation does. The capital needs of the partnership must be met by contributions from partners or by borrowing.
- *Management.* Managing a partnership can also be difficult because, in the absence of an agreement to the contrary, all partners have an equal say in running the business.
- *Transferability.* A partner only has the right to transfer the *value* of her partnership interest, not the interest itself. Thus a mother who is a partner in a law firm can pass on to her son the value of her partnership interest, not the right to be a partner in the firm (or even the right to work there).

## FORMATION

A **partnership** is an association of two or more co-owners who carry on a business for profit. Each co-owner is called a *general partner.* Like sole proprietorships, partnerships are easy to form. Although, practically speaking, a partnership *should* have a written agreement, the law generally does not require anything in the way of forms or filings or agreements.

**Partnership**
An unincorporated association of two or more co-owners who operate a business for profit.

## TAXES

As we have seen above, a partnership is not a taxable entity, which means it does not pay taxes itself.

## LIABILITY

**Every partner is an agent of the partnership.** Thus, the entire partnership is liable for the act of one partner in, say, signing a contract. **A partnership is also liable for any torts that a partner commits in the ordinary course of the partnership's business.**

It gets worse. **If a partnership does not have enough assets to pay its debts, creditors may go after the personal property of individual partners, whether or not they were in any way responsible for the debt.** Because partners have **joint and several liability**, creditors can sue the partnership and the partners together or in separate lawsuits or in any combination. The partnership and the partners are all individually liable for the full amount of the debt, but, obviously, the creditor cannot keep collecting after he has already received the total amount owed. **Also note that, even if creditors have a judgment against an individual partner, they cannot go after that partner's assets until all the partnership's assets are exhausted.**

Letitia, one of the world's wealthiest people, enters into a partnership with penniless Harry to drill for oil on her estate. While driving on partnership business, Harry crashes into Rama, seriously injuring him. Rama can sue any combination of the partnership, Letitia, and Harry for the full amount, even though Letitia was 2,000 miles away on her Caribbean island when the accident occurred and she had many times cautioned Harry to drive carefully. Even if Rama obtains a judgment against Letitia, however, he cannot recover against her while the partnership still has assets. So, for all practical purposes, he must try to collect first against the partnership. If the partnership is bankrupt and he manages to collect the full amount from Letitia, he cannot then try to recover against Harry.

**Joint and several liability**
All members of a group are liable. They can be sued as a group, or any one of them can be sued individually for the full amount owing.

## MANAGEMENT

The management of a partnership can be a significant challenge.

### Management Rights
**Unless the partnership agrees otherwise, partners share both profits and losses equally, and each partner has an equal right to manage the business.**

In a large partnership, too many cooks can definitely spoil the firm's profitability.

In a large partnership, with hundreds of partners, too many cooks can definitely spoil the firm's profitability. That is why large partnerships are almost always run by one or a few partners who are designated as **managing partners** or **members of the executive committee.**

## Management Duties

Partners have a **fiduciary duty** to the partnership. This duty means that:

* *Partners are liable to the partnership for gross negligence or intentional misconduct.*
* *Partners cannot compete with the partnership.* Each partner must turn over to the partnership all earnings from any activity that is related to the partnership's business. Thus law firms would typically expect a partner to turn over any fees he earned as a director of a company, but he could keep royalties from his novel on scuba diving.
* *A partner may not take an opportunity away from the partnership unless the other partners consent.* If the partnership wants to buy a private plane and a partner hears of one for sale, she must give the partnership an opportunity to buy it before she purchases it herself.
* *If a partner engages in a conflict of interest, he must turn over to the partnership any profits he earned from that activity.* Thus, someone who bid on partnership assets at auction without telling his partner was in violation of his fiduciary duty to the partnership.

# Terminating a Partnership

A partnership begins with an *association* of two or more people. Appropriately, the end of a partnership begins with a *dissociation*. **A dissociation occurs when a partner quits.**

## Dissociation

**A partner always has the *power* to leave a partnership but may not have the *right*.** In other words, a partner can always dissociate, but she may have to pay damages for any harm that her departure causes.

A dissociation is a fork in the road: **The partnership can either buy out the departing partner(s) and continue in business or wind up the business and terminate the partnership.** If the partnership chooses to terminate the business, it must follow three steps: dissolution, winding up, and termination.

## Three Steps to Termination

**Dissolution**   The rules on dissolution depend, in part, on the type of partnership. If the partners have agreed in advance how long the partnership will last, it is a **term partnership.** At the end of the specified term, the partnership automatically ends. Otherwise, it is a **partnership at will**, which means that any of the partners can leave at any time, for any reason.

A partnership *automatically* dissolves:

* In a partnership at will, when a partner withdraws.
* In a term partnership when:
  a. A partner is dissociated and half of the remaining partners vote to wind up the partnership business.
  b. All the partners agree to dissolve.
  c. The term expires or the partnership achieves its goal.
* In any partnership when:
  a. An event occurs that the partners had agreed would cause dissolution.
  b. The partnership business becomes illegal.

c. A court determines that the partnership is unlikely to succeed. If the partners simply cannot get along or they cannot make a profit, any partner has the right to ask a court to dissolve the partnership.

**Winding Up**   During the winding up process, all debts of the partnership are paid, and the remaining proceeds are distributed to the partners.

**Termination**   Termination happens automatically once the winding up is finished. The partnership is not required to do anything official; it can go out of the world even more quietly and simply than it came in.

## ▪ LIMITED LIABILITY PARTNERSHIPS ▪

A limited liability partnership (LLP) is a type of general partnership that most states now permit. There is a very important distinction, however, between these two forms of organization: **in an LLP, the partners are not liable for the debts of the partnership.** They are, naturally, liable for their own misdeeds, just as if they were a member of an LLC or a shareholder of a corporation.

To form an LLP, the partners must file a statement of qualification with state officials. LLPs must also file annual reports. The other attributes of a partnership remain the same. Thus, an LLP is not a taxable entity.

Although an LLP can be much more advantageous for partners than a general partnership, the following case provides an important warning: it is essential to comply with all the technicalities of the LLP statute.

### APCAR v. GAUS

2005 TEX. APP. LEXIS 379
COURT OF APPEALS OF TEXAS, 2005

#### CASE SUMMARY

**Facts:** Smith & West, LLP had two partners: Michael L. Gaus and John C. West. The partnership registered in Texas as a limited liability partnership. The Texas statute requires LLPs to renew their registrations each year, but Smith & West never did so. Four years after its initial registration, the partnership entered into a lease with MF Partners, which subsequently assigned the lease to Apcar. Three years into the lease, Smith & West stopped paying rent and abandoned the premises. Apcar filed suit against the two partners individually and against the partnership. Gaus, West, and Apcar each filed a motion for summary judgment. The trial court granted Gaus and West's motions while denying Apcar's.

**Issue:** *Were Gaus and West personally liable for payments due under Smith & West's lease?*

**Decision:** Gaus and West were personally liable for the partnership's lease payments.

**Reasoning:** Under Texas law, a limited liability partnership must renew its registration within a year of making the initial application. Smith & West did not do so. Therefore, its status as a limited liability partnership expired on the first anniversary of its initial filing.

Smith & West signed a lease three years after its limited liability partnership status expired. Partners Gaus and West argue that they should be protected from personal liability on the lease even though the partnership had not strictly complied with the statute. But the statute makes no provision for substantial compliance, nor does it offer any grace period for filing a renewal application. Therefore, a partnership must comply with the precise terms of the statute for its partners to receive protection from individual liability. Smith and West failed to do that, and they are liable on the lease.

# ▪ LIMITED PARTNERSHIPS AND LIMITED LIABILITY LIMITED PARTNERSHIPS ▪

Although limited partnerships and limited liability limited partnerships sound confusingly similar to limited liability partnerships and general partnerships, like many siblings, they operate very differently. And truth to tell, limited partnerships and limited liability limited partnerships are relatively rare—they are generally only used for estate planning purposes (usually, to reduce estate taxes) and for highly sophisticated investment vehicles. You should be aware of their existence but you may not see them very often in your business life. Here are the major features:

## Structure

Limited partnerships must have at least one *limited* partner and one *general* partner.

## Liability

**Limited partners are not *personally* liable but general partners are.** Like corporate shareholders, limited partners risk only their investment in the partnership (which is called their "capital contribution"). In contrast, general partners of the limited partnership are personally liable for the debts of the organization.

However, the revised version of the Uniform Limited Partnership Act (ULPA) permits a limited partnership, in its certificate of formation and partnership agreement, simply to declare itself a *limited liability* limited partnership.[4] **In a limited liability limited partnership, the general partner is not personally liable for the debts of the partnership.** This provision effectively removes the major disadvantage of limited partnerships. Although, at this writing, fewer than 20 states have actually passed the revised version of the ULPA, this revision would seem to indicate the trend for the future.

## Taxes

Limited partnerships are not taxable entities. Income is taxed only once before landing in a partner's pocket.

## Formation

The general partners must file a **certificate of limited partnership** with their Secretary of State. Although most limited partnerships do have a partnership agreement, it is not required.

## Management

General partners have the right to manage a limited partnership. Limited partners are essentially passive investors with few management rights beyond the right to be informed about the partnership business.

## Transfer of Ownership

Limited partners have the right to transfer the *value* of their partnership interest, but they can only sell or give away the interest itself if the partnership agreement permits.

## Duration

Unless the partnership agreement provides otherwise, limited partnerships enjoy perpetual existence—they continue even as partners come and go.

---

[4] ULPA §102(9).

# · PROFESSIONAL CORPORATION ·

Traditionally, most professionals (such as lawyers and doctors) were not permitted to incorporate their businesses, so they organized as partnerships. Now professionals are allowed to incorporate in "professional corporations" or "PCs." **PCs provide more liability protection than a general partnership.** If a member of a PC commits malpractice, the corporation's assets are at risk but not the personal assets of the innocent members. If Drs. Sharp, Payne, and Graves form a *partnership,* all the partners will be personally liable when Dr. Payne accidentally leaves her scalpel inside a patient. If the three doctors have formed a *PC* instead, Dr. Payne's Aspen condo and the assets of the PC will be at risk, but not the personal assets of the two other doctors.

Generally, the shareholders of a PC are not personally liable for the contract debts of the organization, such as leases or bank loans. Thus, if Sharp, Payne, & Graves, P.C. is unable to pay its rent, the landlord cannot recover from the personal assets of any of the doctors.

PCs have some limitations:

- All shareholders of the corporation must be members of the same profession. For Sharp, Payne, & Graves, P.C., that means all shareholders must be licensed physicians.

- The required legal technicalities for forming and maintaining a PC are expensive and time-consuming.

- Tax issues can be complicated. A PC is a separate taxable entity, like any other corporation. It must pay tax on its profits, and then its shareholders pay tax on any dividends they receive. Salaries, however, are deductible from firm profits. Thus the PC can avoid paying taxes on its profits by paying out all the profits as salary. But any profits remaining in firm coffers at the end of the year are taxable. To avoid tax, PCs must be careful to calculate their profits accurately and pay them out before year's end. This chore can be time-consuming, and any error may cause unnecessary tax liability.

## CHAPTER CONCLUSION

The process of starting a business is immensely time-consuming. Not surprisingly, entrepreneurs are sometimes reluctant to spend their valuable time on legal issues that, after all, do not contribute directly to the bottom line. No customer buys more biscuits because the business is a limited liability company instead of a corporation. Wise entrepreneurs know, however, that careful attention to legal issues is an essential component of success. The idea for the business may come first, but legal considerations occupy a close second place.

## EXAM REVIEW

| | Separate Taxable Entity | Personal Liability for Owners | Ease of Formation | Transferable Interests (Easily Bought and Sold) | Perpetual Existence | Other Features |
|---|---|---|---|---|---|---|
| Sole Proprietorship | No | Yes | Very easy | No, can only sell entire business | No | |
| Corporation | Yes | No | Difficult | Yes | Yes | |

| | Separate Taxable Entity | Personal Liability for Owners | Ease of Formation | Transferable Interests (Easily Bought and Sold) | Perpetual Existence | Other Features |
|---|---|---|---|---|---|---|
| Close Corporation | Yes, for C corporation No, for S corporation | No | Difficult | Transfer restrictions | Yes | Protection of minority shareholders. No board of directors required |
| S Corporation | No | No | Difficult | Transfer restrictions | Yes | Only 100 shareholders. Only one class of stock. Shareholders must be individuals, estates, trusts, charities, or pension funds and be citizens or residents of the United States. All shareholders must agree to S status |
| Limited Liability Company | No | No | Difficult | Yes, if the operating agreement permits | Varies by state, but generally, yes | No limit on the number shareholders, the number of classes of stock, or the type of shareholder |
| General Partnership | No | Yes | Easy | No | Depends on the partnership agreement | Management can be difficult |
| Limited Liability Partnership | No | No | Difficult | No | Depends on the partnership agreement | |
| Limited Partnership | No | Yes, for general partner No, for limited partners | Difficult | Yes (for limited partners), if partnership agreement permits | Yes | |
| Limited Liability Limited Partnership | No | No | Difficult | Yes (for limited partners), if partnership agreement permits | Yes | |
| Professional Corporation | Yes | No | Difficult | Shareholders must all be members of same profession | Yes, as long as it has shareholders | Complex tax issues |

# PRACTICE EXAM

## MATCHING QUESTIONS

Match the following terms with their definitions:

___ A. S Corp

___ B. Dissociation

___ C. Close corp

___ D. Dissolution

___ E. Limited partnership

1. The first step in the process of terminating a partnership

2. Created by federal law

3. The general partner is liable

4. Created by state law

5. A partner leaves the partnership

# TRUE/FALSE QUESTIONS

Circle true or false:

1. T   F   Sole proprietorships must file a tax return.

2. T   F   Ownership in a partnership is not transferable.

3. T   F   Creditors of a partnership must first seek recovery from partnership assets before going after the personal assets of a partner.

4. T   F   In both a limited partnership and a limited liability limited partnership, the partners are not personally liable for the debts of the partnership.

5. T   F   Venture capitalists often require companies they own to become LLCs before going public.

# MULTIPLE-CHOICE QUESTIONS

6. CPA QUESTION: Assuming all other requirements are met, a corporation may elect to be treated as an S corporation under the Internal Revenue Code if it has:
   A. Both common and preferred stockholders
   B. A partnership as a stockholder
   C. 100 or fewer stockholders
   D. The consent of a majority of the stockholders

7. Which of the following statements is false:
   A. Partners are liable to the partnership for their own negligent conduct.
   B. Partners must turn over to the partnership any earnings from an activity that is related to the partnership's business.
   C. If a partner is offered an opportunity that is related to the partnership business, he must first seek permission of the other partners before accepting it.
   D. A partner must turn over any profits from an activity that is a conflict of interest with the partnership.
   E. Partners are personally liable for intentional misconduct.

8. The following event does *not* automatically dissolve a term partnership:
   A. The partnership achieves its goals.
   B. A partnership is dissociated and all of the remaining partners vote to wind up the business.
   C. A court determines the partnership cannot be run at a profit.
   D. A partner withdraws.
   E. The partners agree to dissolve before the end of the term.

9. Joint and several liability means that:
   A. A creditor of the partnership must sue all of the partners together.
   B. A creditor of the partnership must sue the partnership and all of the partners together.
   C. A creditor of the partnership can recover the full amount owed from the partnership or from any of the partners.
   D. A creditor of the partnership can recover the full amount owed from the partnership and from each partner, even if this results in the creditor receiving more than his original debt.
   E. A creditor of the partnership can recover from the partners individually, but not from the partnership.

10. While working part-time at a Supercorp restaurant, Jenna spills a bucket of hot French fries on a customer. Who is liable to the customer?

    A. Supercorp alone

    B. Jenna alone

    C. Both Jenna and Supercorp

    D. Jenna, Supercorp, and the president of Supercorp

    E. Jenna, Supercorp, and the shareholders of Supercorp

## SHORT-ANSWER QUESTIONS

11. Under Delaware law, a corporation cannot appear in court without a lawyer, but a partnership can. Fox Hollow Ventures, Ltd., was a limited liability company. One of its employees, who was not a lawyer, appeared in court to represent the company. Does an LLC more closely resemble a partnership, which may represent itself in court, or a corporation, which requires representation by a lawyer?

**EXAM Strategy**

12. **Question:** Alan Dershowitz, a law professor famous for his wealthy clients (O. J. Simpson, among others), joined with other lawyers to open a kosher delicatessen, Maven's Court. Dershowitz met with greater success at the bar than in the kitchen—the deli failed after barely a year in business. One supplier sued for overdue bills. What form of organization would have been the best choice for Maven's Court?

    **Strategy:** A sole proprietorship would not have worked, because there was more than one owner. A partnership would have been a disaster because of unlimited liability. They could have met all the requirements of an S Corporation or an LLC. (See the "Result" at the end of this section.)

**EXAM Strategy**

13. **Question:** Mrs. Meadows opened a biscuit shop called The Biscuit Bakery. The business was not incorporated. Whenever she ordered supplies, she was careful to sign the contract in the name of the business, not personally: The Biscuit Bakery by Daisy Meadows. Unfortunately, she had no money to pay her flour bill. When the vendor threatened to sue her, Mrs. Meadows told him that he could only sue the business, because all the contracts were in the business's name. Will Mrs. Meadows lose her dough?

    **Strategy:** The first step is to figure out what type of organization her business is. Then recall what liability protection that organization offers. (See the "Result" at the end of this section.)

14. The Logan Wright Foundation (LWF), an Oklahoma corporation, was a partner in a partnership formed to operate two Sonic Drive-In restaurants. LWF argued that it was not responsible for Sonic's taxes because LWF was merely a limited partner, with limited liability to the partnership's creditors, including the IRS. The partnership had never filed a certificate of limited partnership with the secretary of state. Is it a valid limited partnership?

15. ROLE REVERSAL: Write a multiple-choice question that focuses on the difference between an LLC and an S corporation.

**12. Result:** Maven's Court would have chosen an LLC or an S corporation.

**13. Result:** The Biscuit Bakery was a sole proprietorship. No matter how Mrs. Meadows signed the contracts, she is still personally liable for the debts of the business.

# INTERNET RESEARCH PROBLEM

Either go to **http://www.findlaw.com/casecode/#statelaw** or use Westlaw or LEXIS to find the statute on LLCs for your state. Fill out a sample certificate of organization for a business that you might like to start. Is an operating agreement required?

**You can find further practice problems in the Online Quiz at www.cengage.com/blaw/beatty.**

# CORPORATIONS

**On July 26, 2004,** Mark Zuckerberg signed a Certificate of Incorporation for his company, which he called TheFacebook, Inc. At 11:34 a.m. on July 29, 2004, that Certificate was filed with the Secretary of State for Delaware, and TheFacebook began its life as a corporation. Zuckerberg had started this social networking Internet site the previous February in his dorm room at Harvard. By December 2004, TheFacebook had almost 1 million users. By the beginning of 2006, the company was estimated to be worth between $750 million and $2 billion. As he built his company, what did Zuckerberg need to know about the law?

> **Zuckerberg started TheFacebook in his dorm room at Harvard. Within 10 months, it had almost 1 million users.**

## · PROMOTER'S LIABILITY ·

TheFacebook operated for five months before it was incorporated. During this period, Zuckerberg needed to be careful to avoid liability as a promoter. **A promoter is someone who organizes a corporation.**

Zuckerberg had moved company headquarters to Palo Alto, California, before the certificate of incorporation was filed. Suppose that he finds the perfect location for his headquarters. He is eager to sign the lease before someone else snatches the opportunity away, but TheFacebook does not yet legally exist—it is not incorporated. What would happen if he signed the lease anyway? **As promoter, he is personally liable on any contract he signs before the corporation is formed.** If Zuckerberg signs the lease before TheFacebook, Inc. legally exists, he is personally liable for the rent due. After formation, the corporation can **adopt** the contract, in which case, both it and the promoter are liable. Adoption means either that the board of directors approves the contract or the corporation accepts the benefits under the contract. The promoter can get off the hook personally only if the landlord agrees to a **novation**—that is, a new contract with the corporation alone.

**Promoter**
Someone who organizes a corporation.

**Novation**
A new contract with different parties.

### EXAM *Strategy*

**Question:** Warfield hired Wolfe, a young carpenter, to build his house. A week or so after they signed the contract, Wolfe filed Articles of Incorporation for Wolfe Construction, Inc. Warfield made payments to the corporation. Unfortunately, the work on the house was shoddy—the architect said he did not know whether to blow up the house or try to salvage what was there. Warfield sued Wolfe and Wolfe Construction, Inc. for damages. Wolfe argued that if he was liable as a promoter, then the corporation must be absolved and that, conversely, if the corporation was held liable he, as an individual, must not be. Who is liable to Warfield? Does it matter if Wolfe signed the contract in his own name or in the name of the corporation?

**Strategy:** Wolfe's argument is wrong—Warfield does not have to choose between suing him individually or suing the corporation. He can certainly sue both.

**Result:** Wolfe is personally liable on any contract signed before the corporation is filed, no matter whose name is on the contract. The corporation is liable only if it adopts the contract. Did it do so here? The fact that the corporation cashed checks that were made out to it means that the corporation is also liable. So Warfield can sue both Wolfe and the corporation.

## · INCORPORATION PROCESS ·

The mechanics of incorporation are easy: simply fill out the form online or mail or fax it to the Secretary of State for your state. But do not let this easy process fool you; the incorporation document needs to be completed with some care. The corporate charter defines the corporation, including everything from the company's name to the number of shares it will issue. States use different terms to refer to a charter; some call it the "articles of incorporation," others use "articles of organization," and still others say "certificate" instead of "articles." All these terms mean the same thing. Similarly, some states use the term "shareholders," and others use "stockholders"; they are both the same.

There is no federal corporation code, which means that a company can incorporate only under state, not federal, law. No matter where a company actually does business, it may incorporate in any state. This decision is important because the organization must live by the laws of whichever state it chooses for incorporation. To encourage similarity among state corporation statutes, the American Bar Association drafted the Model Business Corporation Act (the Model Act) as a guide. Many states do use the Model Act as a guide, although Delaware does not. Therefore, in this chapter we will give examples from both the Model Act and specific states, such as Delaware. Why Delaware? Despite its small size, it has a disproportionate influence on corporate law. Although only one-third of 1 percent of the U.S. population lives in Delaware, more than half of all public companies have incorporated there, including 58 percent of Fortune 500 companies.

# WHERE TO INCORPORATE?

A company is called a **domestic corporation** in the state where it incorporates and a **foreign corporation** everywhere else. Companies generally incorporate either in the state where they do most of their business or in Delaware. They typically must pay filing fees and franchise taxes in their state of incorporation, as well as in any state in which they do business. To avoid this double set of fees, a business that will be operating primarily in one state would probably select that state for incorporation rather than Delaware. But if a company is going to do business in several states, it might consider choosing Delaware (or, perhaps, Ohio, Pennsylvania, Nevada, or one of the other states with sophisticated corporate laws).

Delaware offers corporations several advantages:

- *Laws That Favor Management.* For example, if the shareholders want to take a vote in writing instead of holding a meeting, many other states require the vote to be unanimous; Delaware requires only a majority to agree.
- *An Efficient Court System.* Delaware has a special court (called "Chancery Court") that hears nothing but business cases and has judges who are experts in corporate law.
- *An Established Body of Precedent.* Because so many businesses incorporate in this state, its courts hear a vast number of corporate cases, creating a large body of precedent. This precedent makes the outcome of litigation more predictable.

# THE CHARTER

## Name

The Model Act imposes two requirements in selecting a name. First, all corporations must use one of the following words in their name: "corporation," "incorporated," "company," or "limited." Delaware also accepts some additional terms, such as "association" or "institute." Second, under both the Model Act and Delaware law, a new corporate name must be different from that of any corporation, limited liability company, or limited partnership that already exists in that state. If your name is Freddy Dupont, you cannot name your corporation "Freddy Dupont, Inc.," because Delaware already has a company named E. I. DuPont de Nemours & Co. It does not matter that Freddy Dupont is your real name or that the existing company is a large chemical business, whereas you want to open a video arcade. The names are too similar. "TheFacebook" was what Harvard students called their freshman directory.

## Address and Registered Agent

A company must have an official address in the state in which it is incorporated so that the Secretary of State knows where to contact it and so that anyone who wants to sue the corporation can serve the complaint in-state. Because most companies incorporated in Delaware do not actually have an office there, they hire a registered agent to serve as their official presence in the state.

## Incorporator

The incorporator signs the charter and delivers it to the Secretary of State for filing. Mark Zuckerberg was the incorporator for TheFacebook, but lawyers often serve this role.

## *Purpose*

The corporation is required to give its purpose for existence. Most companies use a very broad purpose clause, such as TheFacebook's:

> The purpose of the Corporation is to engage in any lawful act or activity for which corporations may be organized under the General Corporation Law of Delaware.

## *Stock*

The charter must provide three items of information about the company's stock.

**Par Value**   Par value does not relate to market value; it is usually some nominal figure such as 1¢ or $1 per share, or it is even common to have no par value stock. TheFacebook stock has a par value of $0.0001 per share.

**Number of Shares**   Before stock can be sold, it must first be authorized in the charter. The corporation can authorize as many shares as the incorporators choose, but the more shares, the higher the filing fee. The TheFacebook charter authorizes 10 million shares. After incorporation, a company can add authorized shares by simply amending its charter and paying the additional fee. Stock that the company has sold but later bought back is **treasury stock**.

**Classes of Stock**   Shareholders often make different contributions to a company. Some may be involved in management, whereas others may simply contribute financially. To reflect these varying contributions, a corporation can issue different classes of stock, such as preferred or common stock. Owners of **preferred stock** are in line before common shareholders to receive dividends and any liquidation payments after a company goes into bankruptcy.

> **Treasury stock**
> Stock that a company has sold, but later bought back.

> **Preferred stock**
> The owners of preferred stock have preference on dividends and also, typically, in liquidation.

## · AFTER INCORPORATION ·

## DIRECTORS AND OFFICERS

Under the Model Act, a corporation is required to have at least one director, unless (1) all the shareholders sign an agreement that eliminates the board, or (2) the corporation has 50 or fewer shareholders. To elect directors, the shareholders may hold a meeting, or, in the more typical case for a small company, they elect directors by **written consent.** A typical written consent looks like this:

---

Classic American Novels, Inc.

Written Consent

The undersigned shareholders of Classic American Novels, Inc., a corporation organized and existing under the General Corporation Law of the State of Wherever, hereby agree that the following action shall be taken with full force and effect as if voted at a validly called and held meeting of the shareholders of the corporation:

Agreed:   That the following people are elected to serve as directors for one year or until their successors have been duly elected and qualified:

Herman Melville

Louisa May Alcott

Mark Twain

Dated: _____   Signed: _____

Willa Cather

Dated: _____    Signed: _____
                                    Nathaniel Hawthorne

Dated: _____    Signed: _____
                                    Harriet Beecher Stowe

The directors then elect the officers of the corporation. They can use a consent form if they wish. The Model Act requires a corporation to have whatever officers are described in the bylaws. The same person can hold more than one office.

The written consents and any records of actual meetings are kept in a **minute book**, which is the official record of the corporation. Entrepreneurs sometimes feel they are too busy to bother with all these details, but if a corporation is ever sold, the lawyers for the buyers will *insist* on a well-organized and complete minute book.

**Minute book**
The official record of a corporation.

## BYLAWS

The **bylaws** list all the "housekeeping" details for the corporation. For example, bylaws set the date of the annual shareholders' meeting, define what a quorum is (i.e., what percentage of stock must be represented for a meeting to count), give titles to officers, set the number of directors, and establish the fiscal (i.e., tax) year of the corporation.

**Bylaws**
A document that specifies the organizational rules of a corporation such as the date of the annual meeting and the required number of directors.

## · DEATH OF THE CORPORATION ·

Sometimes, business ideas are not successful and the corporation fails. This death can be voluntary (the shareholders elect to terminate the corporation) or forced (by court order). Sometimes, a court takes a step that is much more damaging to shareholders than simply dissolving the corporation—it removes the shareholders' limited liability.

## PIERCING THE CORPORATE VEIL

One of the major purposes of a corporation is to protect its owners—the shareholders—from personal liability for the debts of the organization. Sometimes, however, a court will **pierce the corporate veil**; that is, the court will hold shareholders personally liable for the debts of the corporation. Courts generally pierce a corporate veil in four circumstances:

**Pierce the corporate veil**
A court holds shareholders personally liable for the debts of the corporation.

- *Failure to Observe Formalities.* If an organization does not act like a corporation, it will not be treated like one. It must, for example, hold required shareholders' and directors' meetings (or sign consents), keep a minute book as a record of these meetings, and make all the required state filings. In addition, officers must be careful to sign all corporate documents with a corporate title, not as an individual. An officer should sign like this:

   Classic American Novels, Inc.

   By: _*Stephen Crane*_

   Stephen Crane, President

- *Commingling of Assets.* Nothing makes a court more willing to pierce a corporate veil than evidence that shareholders have mixed their assets with those of the corporation. Sometimes, for example, shareholders may use corporate assets to pay their personal debts. If shareholders commingle assets, it is genuinely difficult for creditors to determine which assets belong to whom. This confusion is generally resolved in favor of the creditors—all assets are deemed to belong to the corporation.

- *Inadequate Capitalization.* If the founders of a corporation do not raise enough capital to give the business a fighting chance of paying its debts, courts may require shareholders to pay corporate obligations. For example, Oriental Fireworks Co. had hundreds of thousands of dollars in annual sales, but only $13,000 in assets. The company did not bother to obtain any liability insurance, keep a minute book, or defend lawsuits. There was no need because the company had no money. But then a court pierced the corporate veil and found the owner of the company personally liable.[1]

- *Fraud.* If fraud is committed in the name of a corporation, victims can make a claim against the personal assets of the shareholders who profited from the fraud.

## TERMINATION

Terminating a corporation is a three-step process:

- *Vote.* The directors recommend to the shareholders that the corporation be dissolved, and a majority of the shareholders agree.
- *Filing.* The corporation files "Articles of Dissolution" with the Secretary of State.
- *Winding Up.* The officers of the corporation pay its debts and distribute the remaining property to shareholders. When the winding up is completed, the corporation ceases to exist.

The Secretary of State may dissolve a corporation that violates state law by, for example, failing to pay the required annual fees. Indeed, many corporations, particularly small ones, do not bother with the formal dissolution process. They simply cease paying their required annual fees and let the Secretary of State act. In addition, a court may dissolve a corporation if it is insolvent or if its directors and shareholders cannot resolve conflict over how the corporation should be managed.

## · THE ROLE OF CORPORATE MANAGEMENT ·

Before the Industrial Revolution in the eighteenth and nineteenth centuries, a business owner typically supplied both capital and management. However, the capital needs of the great manufacturing enterprises spawned by the Industrial Revolution were larger than any small group of individuals could supply. To find capital, firms sought outside investors, who often had neither the knowledge nor the desire to manage the enterprise. Investors without management skills complemented managers without capital. ("Manager" includes both directors and officers.)

Modern businesses still have the same vast need for capital and the same division between managers and investors. As businesses grow, shareholders are too numerous and too uninformed to manage the enterprises they own. Therefore, they elect directors to manage for them. The directors set policy and then appoint officers to implement corporate goals.

**Managers have a fiduciary duty to act in the best interests of the corporation's shareholders.** Because shareholders are primarily concerned about their return on investment, managers must *maximize shareholder value,* which means providing shareholders with the highest possible financial return from dividends and stock price. However, reality is more complicated than this simple rule indicates. It is often difficult to determine which strategy will best maximize shareholder value. And what about other **stakeholders,** such as employees, customers, creditors, suppliers, and neighbors? A number of states have adopted statutes that permit directors to take into account the interests of stakeholders as well as stockholders.

---

[1] *Rice v. Oriental Fireworks Co.,* 75 Or. App. 627, 707 P.2d 1250, 1985 Ore. App. LEXIS 3928.

# · THE BUSINESS JUDGMENT RULE ·

Officers and directors have a fiduciary duty to act in the best interests of their stockholders, but under the **business judgment rule,** the courts allow managers great leeway in carrying out this responsibility. The business judgment rule is two shields in one: it protects both the manager and her decision. If a manager has complied with the rule, a court will not hold her personally liable for any harm her decision has caused the company, nor will the court rescind her decision. If the manager violates the business judgment rule, then she has the burden of proving that her decision was entirely fair to the shareholders. If it was not fair, she may be held personally liable, and the decision can be rescinded.

To be protected by the business judgment rule, managers must act in good faith:

| | |
|---|---|
| Duty of Loyalty | 1. Without a conflict of interest |
| Duty of Care | 2. With the care that an ordinarily prudent person would take in a similar situation, and |
| | 3. In a manner they reasonably believe to be in the best interests of the corporation. |

Analysis of the business judgment rule is divided into two parts. The obligation of a manager to act without a conflict of interest is called the **duty of loyalty**. The requirements that a manager act with care and in the best interests of the corporation are referred to as the **duty of care**.

**Duty of loyalty**
The obligation of a manager to act without a conflict of interest.

**Duty of care**
The requirement that a manager act with care and in the best interests of the corporation.

## Duty of Loyalty

**The duty of loyalty prohibits managers from making a decision that benefits them at the expense of the corporation.**

> Corporate officers sometimes forget that they do not have the right to do whatever they want.

### Self-Dealing

**Self-dealing means that a manager makes a decision benefiting either himself or another company with which he has a relationship.** While working at the Blue Moon restaurant, Zeke signs a contract on behalf of the restaurant to purchase bread from Rising Sun Bakery. Unbeknownst to anyone at Blue Moon, he is a part owner of Rising Sun. Zeke has engaged in self-dealing, which is a violation of the duty of loyalty.

Once a manager engages in self-dealing, the business judgment rule no longer applies. This does not mean the manager is automatically liable to the corporation or that his decision is automatically void. All it means is that the court will no longer presume that the transaction was acceptable. Instead, the court will scrutinize the deal more carefully. A self-dealing transaction is valid in any one of the following situations:

- **The disinterested members of the board of directors approve the transaction.** Disinterested directors are those who do not themselves benefit from the transaction.

- **The disinterested shareholders approve it.** The transaction is valid if the shareholders who do not benefit from it are willing to approve it.

- **The transaction was entirely fair to the corporation.** In determining fairness, the courts will consider the impact of the transaction on the corporation and whether the price was reasonable.

Exhibit 21.1 illustrates the rules on self-dealing.

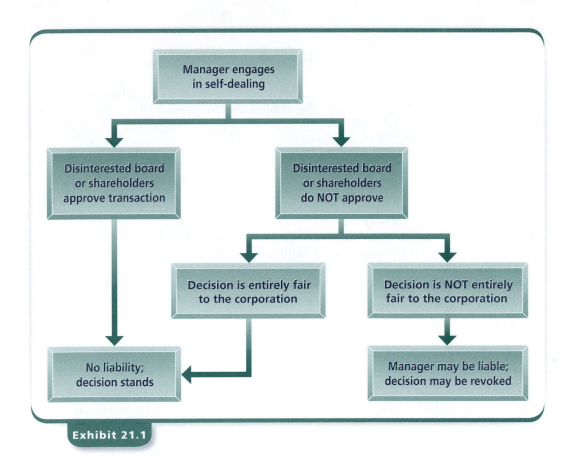

**Exhibit 21.1**

Corporate officers, especially in family businesses, sometimes forget that they do not have the right to do whatever they want. The following case illustrates the business judgment rule and also the enduring principle that litigation is a very sad method for resolving family disputes.

## LIPPMAN V. SHAFFER

15 MISC. 3D 705; 836 N.Y.S.2D 766; 2006 N.Y. MISC. LEXIS 4212
SUPREME COURT OF NEW YORK, 2006

### CASE SUMMARY

**Facts:** Harry Lippman's son, James, had two children, Wade and Amy. Years ago, Harry purchased Despatch Industries, Inc., which manufactured hardware for cabinets. James worked for the company until his retirement. In 1975, when Wade graduated from college, he joined the family business. Amy's husband, Alan Shaffer, went on the company payroll in 1982. In 1993, Wade and Alan both signed identical employment contracts with Despatch. In 1999, after Wade and his father, James, had a falling out, Wade quit his job with the company. The Despatch board (of which Alan was a member) agreed to pay $1.3 million to both Wade and

Alan. Company tax returns referred to these as "severance" payments, although Alan continued to work for the company and receive a salary.

Wade filed suit against Alan and Despatch, alleging that the payments to Alan were improper and should be returned. The defendants argued that the payments were protected by the business judgment rule. Wade filed a motion for summary judgment.

**Issue:** *Were the payments to Alan protected by the business judgment rule?*

**Decision:** No, these payments were not protected and Wade's motion was granted.

**Reasoning:** The purpose of the business judgment rule is to prevent courts from second-guessing corporate decision making. But that does not mean managers can do whatever they want. The business judgment rule does not apply if (1) the directors were self-dealing and (2) the decision was not entirely fair to the corporation. Here, Alan engaged in self-dealing: not only was he on the board that approved the payment to himself, he signed the check. The decision was not fair because Alan had no right to receive the money—it was a "severance" payment, but he still worked for the company. The payment to Wade, on the other hand, was fair because he had left the company. Alan received something he was not entitled to, while Wade simply got what he was owed under his contract.

### *Corporate Opportunity*

**Managers are in violation of the corporate opportunity doctrine if they compete against the corporation without its consent.** Charles Guth was president of Loft, Inc., which operated a chain of candy stores. These stores sold Coca-Cola. Guth purchased the Pepsi-Cola Co. personally, without offering the opportunity to Loft. The Delaware court found that Guth had violated the corporate opportunity doctrine and ordered him to transfer all his shares in Pepsi to Loft.[2] That was in 1939, and Pepsi-Cola was bankrupt; today, PepsiCo, Inc. is worth more than $100 billion.

## DUTY OF CARE

In addition to the *duty of loyalty*, managers also owe a *duty of care*. **The duty of care requires officers and directors to act in the best interests of the corporation and to use the same care that an ordinarily prudent person would in the management of her own assets.** To meet this duty of care:

- The decision must be legal;
- It must have a rational business purpose; and
- The manager must have made an informed decision.

Even if she violates the duty of care, a manager is not liable under the business judgment rule as long as the decision is entirely fair to the corporation. In the following case, the board of directors failed to hold meetings. Were these decisions informed?

## RSL COMMUNICATIONS V. BILDIRICI

2006 U.S. DIST. LEXIS 67548
UNITED STATES DISTRICT COURT FOR THE SOUTHERN DISTRICT OF NEW YORK, 2006

### CASE SUMMARY

**Facts:** RSL Plc (Plc) was a subsidiary of RSL Ltd., a multinational telecommunications corporation founded by Ronald S. Lauder. Plc issued $1.4 billion of bonds (that is, it borrowed money from investors). A few years later, in July, Lauder offered it a $100 million loan. Plc's board of directors did not hold a meeting to approve the Lauder loan. In August, Plc drew down $25 million from that loan. The following March, the company's directors held their first board meeting in a year. Five days later, Plc filed for bankruptcy.

---

[2] *Guth v. Loft,* 5 A2d 503, 1939 Del. Lexis 13 (Del. 1939).

**Issue:** *Did the directors of Plc violate their duty of care to the corporation?*

**Decision:** Yes, the directors were in violation of their duty of care.

**Reasoning:** The business judgment rule protects directors even if their *decisions* were stupid or irrational, as long as the *process* they used was rational and they acted in good faith. Where the directors' actions are so restricted in scope, so shallow in execution, or otherwise so halfhearted as to be a pretext or a sham, the business judgment rule offers no protection.

These directors did not meet during a time in which the company drew down $25 million from the Lauder loan. The board did not make a stupid decision—it failed to make any decision at all. The directors did not even consciously decide to skip a board meeting; they simply failed to discuss the company's business. It may be that decisions were being made by the parent company, but this is no excuse—the directors of the subsidiary owed a duty of care to that entity.

**EXAM** *Strategy*

**Question:** You are the CEO of a software company. You will only allow your engineers to create software for Apple computers, not for PCs, because you think Apple is cooler and you hate Microsoft. Some of your shareholders disagree with this policy. Is your decision protected by the business judgment rule?

**Strategy:** Remember that you owe a duty of care to the corporation. This means that you must have a rational business purpose for your decision.

**Result:** The courts are very generous in defining a rational business purpose. They would probably uphold your decision as long as it was not in some way personally benefiting you, e.g., as long as your name is not Steve Jobs (an Apple executive and major shareholder).

# · THE ROLE OF SHAREHOLDERS ·

As we have seen, *directors,* **not** *shareholders,* **have the right to manage the corporate business.** What rights do shareholders have?

## RIGHTS OF SHAREHOLDERS

**Shareholders have neither the right nor the obligation to manage the day-to-day business of the enterprise.** If you own stock in Starbucks Corp., your share of stock plus $3.83 entitles you to a cup of grande vanilla latte, the same as everyone else. By the same token, if the pipes freeze and the local Starbucks store floods, the manager has no right to call you, as a shareholder, to help clean up the mess.

## RIGHT TO INFORMATION

**Under the Model Act, shareholders acting in good faith and with a proper purpose have the right to inspect and copy the corporation's minute book, accounting records, and shareholder lists.** A proper purpose is one that aids the shareholder in managing and protecting her investment. If, for example, Celeste is convinced that the directors of Devil Desserts, Inc. are mismanaging the company, she might demand a list of other shareholders so that she can ask them to join her in a lawsuit. This purpose is proper—although the company may not like it—and the company is required to give her the list. If, however, Celeste wants to use the shareholder list as a potential source for her new mail-order catalog featuring exercise equipment, the company could legitimately turn her down.

# RIGHT TO VOTE

**A corporation must have at least one class of stock with voting rights.**

## Proxies

Shareholders who do not wish to attend a shareholders' meeting may appoint someone else to vote for them. Confusingly, both this person and the document the shareholder signs to appoint the substitute voter are called a **proxy.** Companies are not required to solicit proxies. However, a meeting is invalid without a certain percentage of shareholders in attendance, either in person or by proxy. This attendance requirement is referred to as a **quorum.** As a practical matter, if a public company with thousands of investors does not solicit proxies, it will not obtain a quorum. Therefore, virtually all public companies do solicit proxies. Along with the proxy, the company must also give shareholders a **proxy statement** and an **annual report.** The proxy statement provides information on everything from management compensation to a list of directors who miss too many meetings. The annual report contains detailed financial data.

## Shareholder Meetings

**Annual shareholder meetings are the norm for publicly traded companies.** (Although technically not all states require public companies to hold an annual meeting of shareholders, the New York Stock Exchange [NYSE] does.) Companies whose stock is not publicly traded can either hold an annual meeting or use written consents from their shareholders.

## Election and Removal of Directors

The process of electing directors of a publicly traded company is different from what most people think. The nominating committee of the board of directors produces a slate of directors, with one name per opening. This slate is then sent to shareholders whose only choice is to vote in favor of a nominee or to withhold their vote (i.e., not vote at all). If a large number of shareholders withhold their votes, the nominee may be embarrassed a little, but the reality is that as long as he receives at least one vote (which can be his own), he is elected because no one is running against him. If shareholders want to have a choice, they have to nominate their own slate, prepare and distribute a proxy statement to shareholders, and then communicate with shareholders why their slate is superior. This process is complex and expensive. Not surprisingly, each year only about one or two shareholder groups in the country undertake this effort.

## Compensation for Officers and Directors

Given that directors have little fear of being voted off the board by shareholders, it is not surprising that when the board sets the CEO's compensation, the results can sometimes appear to unfairly favor the CEO over the shareholders whose money is being used to compensate her. Between 2001 and 2003, public companies spent 9.8 percent of their net income on compensation for top executives. Although there is much talk about "pay for performance," the reality is that luck (such as a favorable movement in exchange rates) is as important a determinant of executive compensation as good performance.[3] Here are some examples of executive compensation that particularly agitated shareholders:

---

[3] See, for example, Marianne Bertrand and Sendhil Mullainathan, "Are CEOs Rewarded for Luck? The Ones Without Principals Are," *The Quarterly Journal of Economics,* August 2001.

- Michael Eisner was the head of Walt Disney Corporation for 20 years. At the beginning of his tenure, the company did very well, and few complained when he was exceedingly well paid. But for the final 13 years, he earned $800 million while the stock performed worse than government bonds (a low-risk, low-return investment).

- During a five-year period in which Pfizer stock lost 43 percent of its value, its CEO received $65 million in compensation. He was also entitled to a pension of $83 million when he retired.

- The CEO of Fannie Mae earned $90 million during a time when the company's accounting system was so flawed that it overstated its earnings by $11 billion.

There is little shareholders can do to challenge executive compensation. To be successful, they must prove that the board violated the business judgment rule either by making a decision that was *grossly uninformed* or by setting an amount so high that it had *no relation* to the value of the services performed and was really a gift.

## Fundamental Corporate Changes

A corporation must seek shareholder approval before undergoing any of the following fundamental changes: a merger, a sale of major assets, dissolution of the corporation, or an amendment to the charter or bylaws.

# CORPORATE GOVERNANCE IN PUBLICLY TRADED COMPANIES: SARBANES-OXLEY AND STOCK EXCHANGE RULES

A spate of corporate scandals, involving such high-flying companies as Enron Corp., revealed that some boards of directors have not provided adequate oversight of their companies. In response, Congress passed the Sarbanes-Oxley Act of 2002 (SOX). This statute applies to public companies as well as to all foreign companies listed on a U.S. stock exchange. Under SOX:

- Rule 404 requires each company to adopt effective financial controls.

- CEOs and CFOs must personally certify their company's financial statements. They are subject to criminal penalties for violations.

- All members of a board's audit committee must be independent.

- A company cannot make personal loans to its directors or officers.

- If a company has to restate its earnings, its chief executive officer and chief financial officer must reimburse the company for any bonus or profits they have received from selling company stock within a year of the release of the flawed financials.

- Each company must disclose if it has an ethics code and, if it does not, why not.

- It is a felony to interfere with a federal investigation into fraud.

- Whistleblowing employees are protected.

The NYSE and NASDAQ have also established a new role for independent directors at listed companies:

- Independent directors must comprise a majority of the board.

- They must meet regularly on their own without inside directors.

- Only independent directors can serve on compensation or nominating committees.

- Audit committees must have at least three independent directors who are financially literate.

## CHAPTER CONCLUSION

How can shareholders ensure that the corporation will operate in their best interest? How can managers make tough decisions without being second-guessed by shareholders? Balancing the interests of managers and shareholders is a complex problem the law struggles to resolve.

## EXAM REVIEW

1. **PROMOTERS** Promoters are personally liable for contracts they sign before the corporation is formed unless the corporation and the third party agree to a novation. (p. 345)

2. **STATE OF INCORPORATION** Companies generally incorporate in the state in which they will be doing business. However, if they intend to operate in several states, they may choose to incorporate in a jurisdiction known for its favorable corporate laws, such as Delaware or Nevada. (p. 345)

3. **CHARTER** A corporate charter must generally include the company's name, address, registered agent, purpose, and a description of its stock. (p. 346)

4. **PIERCING THE CORPORATE VEIL** A court may, under certain circumstances, pierce the corporate veil and hold shareholders personally liable for the debts of the corporation. (p. 348)

5. **TERMINATION** Termination of a corporation is a three-step process requiring a shareholder vote, the filing of Articles of Dissolution, and the winding up of the enterprise's business. (p. 349)

6. **FIDUCIARY DUTY** Officers and directors have a fiduciary duty to act in the best interests of the shareholders of the corporation. (p. 349)

7. **BUSINESS JUDGMENT RULE** The business judgment rule protects managers from liability for their decisions as long as the managers observe the duty of care and the duty of loyalty. (p. 350)

**EXAM Strategy**

**Question:** Employees of Exxon Corp. paid some $59 million in corporate funds as bribes to Italian political parties to secure special favors and other illegal commitments. Several Exxon directors were aware of these illegal payments. The board of directors decided not to sue the employees and directors who had committed the illegal acts. Were these decisions protected by the business judgment rule?

**Strategy:** Two decisions are at issue here: illegal payments and the decision not to sue. (See the "Result" at the end of this section.)

**8.** **DUTY OF LOYALTY: SELF-DEALING** Under the duty of loyalty, managers may not enter into an agreement on behalf of their corporation that benefits them personally, unless the disinterested directors or shareholders have first approved it. If the manager does not seek the necessary approval, the business judgment rule no longer applies, and the manager will be liable unless the transaction was entirely fair to the corporation. (p. 350)

**9.** **DUTY OF LOYALTY: CORPORATE OPPORTUNITY** Managers are in violation of the corporate opportunity doctrine if they compete against the corporation without its consent. (p. 352)

**EXAM Strategy**

**Question:** Vern Hayes owned 32 percent of Coast Oyster Co. and served as president and director. The company owned several large oyster beds, including two located in Washington State. Coast was struggling to pay its debts, so Hayes suggested that the company sell the Washington beds to Keypoint Co. After the sale, other officers at Coast discovered that Hayes owned 50 percent of Keypoint. They demanded that he give the Keypoint stock to Coast. Did Hayes violate his duty to Coast?

**Strategy:** Hayes has violated the duty of loyalty not once, but twice. (See the "Result" at the end of this section.)

**10.** **DUTY OF CARE** Under the duty of care, managers must make decisions that are legal, informed and have a rational business purpose. (p. 352)

**11.** **PROXY** Virtually all publicly held companies solicit proxies from their shareholders. A proxy authorizes someone else to vote in place of the shareholder. (p. 354)

**12.** **SHAREHOLDER RIGHTS** Shareholders have the right to:
- Receive annual financial statements;
- Inspect and copy the corporation's records (for a proper purpose);
- Elect and remove directors; and
- Approve fundamental corporate changes, such as a merger or a major sale of assets. (p. 354)

**13.** **PROTECTION AGAINST MANAGEMENT ABUSES** Congress, the NYSE, and NASDAQ have all taken steps to prevent management abuses. These new regulations require that companies adopt effective financial controls. They also require more independent directors on the board as a whole and on important subcommittees. (p. 355)

**7. Result:** The business judgment rule would not protect the underlying illegal payments, but it did protect the decision not to sue. In other words, anyone who *made* an illegal payment had violated the business judgment rule, but the people who had decided not to pursue the violators had not themselves breached the business judgment rule because they had not violated the duty of care or the duty of loyalty.

**9. Result:** If the shareholders and directors did not know of Hayes's interest in Keypoint, they could not properly evaluate the contract. By not telling them, he violated the rule against self-dealing. Also, by purchasing stock in Keypoint, Hayes took a corporate opportunity. He had to turn over to Coast any profits he had earned on the transaction, as well as his stock in Keypoint.

## PRACTICE EXAM

## MATCHING QUESTIONS

Match the following terms with their definitions:

___ A. Duty of loyalty
___ B. Duty of care
___ C. Promoter
___ D. Incorporator
___ E. Registered agent

1. Requires managers to act in the best interests of the corporation
2. The company's representative in its state of incorporation
3. Someone who organizes a corporation
4. The person who prepares and files the charter
5. Prohibits managers from making a decision that benefits them at the expense of the corporation

## TRUE/FALSE QUESTIONS

Circle true or false:

1. T   F   A corporation can be formed in any state or under the federal corporate code.

2. T   F   Shareholders and stockholders are the same thing.

3. T   F   Most companies use a very broad purpose clause in their charter.

4. T   F   Shareholders have the right to manage the corporate business.

5. T   F   To be elected to the board of directors, nominees must receive a majority of the votes cast.

## MULTIPLE-CHOICE QUESTIONS

6. A promoter is liable for any contract he signs on behalf of a corporation before it is formed, unless:
   A. The corporation adopts the contract.
   B. The promoter notifies the other party that the corporation has not yet been formed.
   C. The promoter signs the contract on behalf of the corporation.
   D. The promoter forms the corporation within 72 hours of signing the contract.
   E. The other party agrees to a novation.

7. CPA QUESTION: A corporate stockholder is entitled to which of the following rights?
   A. Elect officers
   B. Receive annual dividends
   C. Approve dissolution
   D. Prevent corporate borrowing

8. CPA QUESTION: Generally, a corporation's articles of incorporation must include all of the following except:
   A. The name of the corporation's registered agent
   B. The name of each incorporator
   C. The number of authorized shares
   D. Quorum requirements

9. Generally, a corporation's bylaws include all of the following except:
   A. Par value of the stock
   B. The date of the shareholders meeting
   C. The number of directors
   D. The titles of officers
   E. The date of the fiscal year

**10.** Under the duty of care, directors will be liable if they:

A.   Make a decision that has a rational business purpose

B.   Use the same care as an ordinarily prudent person

C.   Make informed decisions

D.   Engage in illegal behavior that is profitable to the company

E.   Make an informed decision that ultimately harms the company

## SHORT-ANSWER QUESTIONS

**11.** Michael Ferns incorporated Erin Homes, Inc., to manufacture mobile homes. He issued himself a stock certificate for 100 shares for which he made no payment. He and his wife served as officers and directors of the organization, but, during the eight years of its existence, the corporation held only one meeting. Erin always had its own checking account, and all proceeds from the sales of mobile homes were deposited there. It filed federal income tax returns each year, using its own federal identification number. John and Thelma Laya paid $17,500 to purchase a mobile home from Erin, but the company never delivered it to them. The Layas sued Erin Homes and Michael Ferns, individually. Should the court "pierce the corporate veil" and hold Ferns personally liable?

**12.** Davis Ajouelo signed an employment contract with William Wilkerson. The contract stated: ". . . whatever company, partnership, or corporation that Wilkerson may form for the purpose of manufacturing shall succeed Wilkerson and exercise the rights and assume all of Wilkerson's obligations as fixed by this contract." Two months later, Wilkerson formed Auto-Soler Company. Ajouelo entered into a new contract with Auto-Soler providing that the company was liable for Wilkerson's obligations under the old contract. Neither Wilkerson nor the company ever paid Ajouelo the sums owed him under the contracts. Ajouelo sued Wilkerson personally. Does Wilkerson have any obligations to Ajouelo?

**13.** ETHICS: Edgar Bronfman, Jr., dropped out of high school to go to Hollywood and write songs and produce movies. Eventually, he left Hollywood to work in the family business—the Bronfmans owned 36 percent of Seagram Co., a liquor and beverage conglomerate. Promoted to president of the company at the age of 32, Bronfman seized a second chance to live his dream. Seagram received 70 percent of its earnings from its 24 percent ownership of DuPont Co. Bronfman sold this stock at less than market value to purchase (at an inflated price) 80 percent of MCA, a movie and music company that had been a financial disaster for its prior owners. Some observers thought Bronfman had gone Hollywood, others that he had gone crazy. After the deal was announced, the price of Seagram shares fell 18 percent. Was there anything Seagram shareholders could have done to prevent what to them was not a dream but a nightmare? Apart from legal issues, was Bronfman's decision ethical? What ethical obligations did he owe Seagram's shareholders?

**14.** Angelica is planning to start a home security business in McGehee, Arkansas. She plans to start modestly but hopes to expand her business within 5 years to neighboring towns and, perhaps, within 10 years, to neighboring states. Her inclination is to incorporate her business in Delaware. Is her inclination correct?

**15.** ROLE REVERSAL: Write a multiple choice question that deals with the duty of care under the business judgment rule.

## INTERNET RESEARCH PROBLEM

Think of an idea for a new company and prepare a corporate charter for your business. You can find a sample Delaware charter at **http://www.state.de.us/corp**. For extra credit, find a sample charter for your own state.

**You can find further practice problems in the Online Quiz at www.cengage.com/blaw/beatty.**

# CHAPTER 22

# GOVERNMENT REGULATION: SECURITIES AND ANTITRUST

**Sandy is** a director of a public company. He tells his girlfriend, Carly, that the company is about to receive a takeover offer. Sandy does not buy any stock himself, but Carly does. When the offer is announced, the stock zooms up in price and Carly makes a tidy profit.

**Each of these people is about to find out, in a very unpleasant way, about government regulation.**

Steve and Joe coach college wrestling teams that are in the same league. Both men are also about to hire an assistant coach. And they have very tight budgets. One day at a meet, Steve suggests to Joe that they agree to limit their new coach's salary to $32,000. That way neither of them will break their budget and they might even have more money to give in athletic scholarships. Joe thinks this is a great plan and agrees on the spot.

360

Each of these people is about to find out, in a very unpleasant way, about government regulation. Sandy and Carly have violated securities laws on insider trading. Steve and Joe have engaged in price fixing that is illegal under antitrust laws. The moral of the story? It is important to be familiar with the most crucial government regulations. Ignorance can not only harm your business but also lead to fines and even imprisonment.

## · SECURITIES LAWS ·

There are two major securities laws: the Securities Act of 1933 (the 1933 Act) and the Securities Exchange Act of 1934 (the 1934 Act).

## WHAT IS A SECURITY?

Both the 1933 and the 1934 Acts regulate securities. **A security is any transaction in which the buyer (1) invests money in a common enterprise and (2) expects to earn a profit predominantly from the efforts of others.**

This definition covers investments that are not necessarily called *securities*. Besides the obvious stocks, bonds, or notes, the definition of security can even include items such as orange trees. W. J. Howey Co. owned large citrus groves in Florida. It sold these trees to investors, most of whom were from out of state and knew nothing about farming. Purchasers were expected to hire someone to take care of their trees. Someone like Howey-in-the-Hills, Inc., a related company that just happened to be in the service business. Customers were free to hire any service company, but 85 percent of the acreage was covered by service contracts with Howey-in-the-Hills. The court held that Howey was selling a security (no matter how orange or tart), because the purchaser was investing in a common enterprise (the orange grove) expecting to earn a profit from Howey's farmwork.

Other courts have interpreted the term "security" to include animal breeding arrangements (chinchillas, silver foxes, or beavers, take your pick); condominium purchases in which the developer promises the owner a certain level of income from rentals; and even investments in whiskey.

> **Security**
> Any transaction in which the buyer invests money in a common enterprise and expects to earn a profit predominantly from the efforts of others.

## SECURITIES ACT OF 1933

**The 1933 Act requires that, before offering or selling securities in a public offering, the issuer must register the securities with the Securities and Exchange Commission (SEC).** An **issuer** is the company that issues the stock.

It is important to remember that **when an issuer registers securities, the SEC does not investigate the quality of the offering.** Permission from the SEC to sell securities does not mean that the company has a good product or will be successful. SEC approval simply means that, on the surface, the company has answered all relevant questions about itself and its major products. For example, the Green Bay Packers football team sold an offering of stock to finance stadium improvements. The prospectus admitted:

> IT IS VIRTUALLY IMPOSSIBLE that any investor will ever make a profit on the stock purchase. The company will pay no dividends, and the shares cannot be sold.

This does not sound like a stock you want in your retirement fund; on the other hand, the SEC will not prevent Green Bay from selling it, or you from buying it, as long as you understand what the risks are.

One last point: **The 1933 Act prohibits fraud in any securities transaction.** Anyone who issues fraudulent securities is in violation of the 1933 Act, whether or not the securities are registered. Both the SEC and any purchasers of the stock can sue the issuer.

> **Issuer**
> Stock represents ownership in the issuer.

## Public Offerings

A company's first public sale of securities is called an **initial public offering** or an **IPO.** Any subsequent public sale is called a **secondary offering**.

**Registration Statement**   To do a public offering, the company must file a registration statement with the SEC. The **registration statement** has two purposes: to notify the SEC that a sale of securities is pending and to disclose information to prospective purchasers. The registration statement must include detailed information about the issuer and its business, a description of the stock, the proposed use of the proceeds from the offering, and audited balance sheets and income statements. Preparing a registration statement is neither quick nor inexpensive—it can cost as much as $1 million for an IPO.

**Prospectus**   Typically, buyers never see the registration statement; they are given the **prospectus** instead. (The prospectus is part of the registration statement that is sent to the SEC.) The prospectus includes all of the important disclosures about the company, while the registration statement includes additional information that is of interest to the SEC but not to the typical investor, such as the names and addresses of the lawyers for the issuer and underwriter. **All investors must receive a copy of the prospectus before purchasing the stock.**

**Sales Effort**   Even before the final Registration Statement and Prospectus are completed, the investment bank representing the issuer begins its sales effort. It cannot actually make sales during this period, but it can solicit offers. The SEC closely regulates an issuer's sales effort to ensure that it does not hype the stock by making public statements about the company before the stock is sold. For example, the SEC delayed an offering of stock by Google Inc. after *Playboy* magazine published an interview with its founders.

**Going Effective**   Once the SEC finishes its review of the registration statement, it sends the issuer a **comment letter,** listing required changes. An issuer almost always has to amend the registration statement at least once, and sometimes more than once. Remember that the SEC does not assess the value of the stock or the merit of the investment. Its role is to ensure that the company has disclosed enough information to enable investors to make an informed decision. After the SEC has approved a final registration statement (which includes, of course, the final prospectus), the issuer and underwriter agree on a price for the stock and the date to **go effective,** that is, to begin the sale.

Registering securities with the SEC for a public offering is very time-consuming and expensive, but the 1933 Act also permits issuers to sell stock in a private offering, which is much simpler (and cheaper).

## Private Offerings

**Under the 1933 Act, an issuer is not required to register securities that are sold in a private offering,** that is, an offering with a relatively small number of investors or a limited amount of money involved. There are many more private than public offerings each year. The most common and important type of private offering is under **Regulation D** (often referred to as Reg D). One provision of Reg D permits a company to sell up to $5 million of stock during each 12-month period, subject to the following restrictions:

- The company may not advertise the stock publicly.

- The issuer can sell to as many accredited investors as it wants, but is limited to only 35 uncredited investors. **Accredited investors** are institutions (such as banks and insurance companies) or wealthy individuals (with a net worth of more than $1 million or an annual income of more than $200,000).

- The company need not provide information to accredited investors but must make some disclosure to unaccredited investors.

## Securities Exchange Act of 1934

Most buyers do not purchase new securities from the issuer in an initial public offering. Rather, they buy stock that is publicly traded in the open market. This stock is, in a sense, secondhand because other people—perhaps many others—have already owned it. The purpose of the 1934 Act is to provide investors with ongoing information about public companies (that is, companies with publicly traded stock).

The 1934 Act requires public companies to file the following documents:

- **Annual reports** on Form 10-K, containing audited financial statements, a detailed analysis of the company's performance, and information about officers and directors. A public company must also send its annual report to shareholders.

- **Quarterly reports** on Form 10-Q, which are less detailed than 10-Ks and contain unaudited financials.

- **Form 8-K**s to report any significant developments, such as a change in control, the resignation of a director over a policy dispute, or a change in auditing firms.

## Insider Trading

Insider trading is immensely tempting. Anyone with reliable secret information can earn millions of dollars overnight. The downside? Insider trading is a crime punishable by fines and imprisonment. The guilty party may also be forced to turn over to the SEC three times the profit made. Ivan Boesky paid $100 million and spent two years in prison. Dennis Levine suffered an $11.6 million penalty and three years in prison.

Why is insider trading a crime? Who is harmed? Insider trading is illegal because:

- It offends our fundamental sense of fairness. No one wants to be in a poker game with marked cards.

- Investors will lose confidence in the market if they feel that insiders have an unfair advantage.

- Investment banks typically "make a market" in stocks, meaning that they hold extra shares so that orders can be filled smoothly. These marketmakers expect to earn a certain profit, but inside traders skim some of it off. So marketmakers simply raise the commission they charge. As a result, everyone who buys and sells stock pays a slightly higher price.

The rules on insider trading are as follows:

- *Fiduciaries.* Anyone who works for a company is a fiduciary. **A fiduciary may not trade stock of her company while in possession of important, secret information.** If the director of research for MediSearch learns of the promising new treatment for AIDS and buys stock in the company before the information is public, she is guilty of insider trading. But suppose that, while looking in a Dumpster, Harry finds correspondence indicating that MediSearch, will shortly announce a major breakthrough in the treatment of AIDS. Harry buys the stock, which promptly quadruples in value. Harry will be dining at the Ritz, not in the Dumpster nor in federal prison, because he has no fiduciary duty to MediSearch.

- *Temporary insiders.* Even outsiders who work for a company temporarily, such as lawyers and accountants, are considered to be fiduciaries.

- *Possession* versus *use* of information. Suppose that an insider sells stock just after learning that her company is about to report lower earnings but before this information is public. When challenged by the SEC, she argues that she sold her stock for other reasons—say, to buy a new house, or set her son up in business. To deal with this issue, the SEC ruled **that an insider may trade while in possession of material, nonpublic information, if she has committed in advance to a plan to sell those securities.** Thus, if an insider knows that she will want to sell stock to pay college tuition, she can establish such a sales plan in advance. (And, then, despite

**Material**
Important enough to affect an investor's decision.

any change in circumstances, she must sell according to the plan.) She will then not be liable for the sales, no matter what inside information she ultimately learns.

- *Tippers.* **Insiders who pass on important, secret information are liable, even if they do not trade themselves, as long as (1) they know the information is confidential; and (2) they expect some personal gain.** Personal gain is loosely defined. Essentially, any gift to a friend counts as personal gain. W. Paul Thayer was a corporate director, deputy secretary of defense, and former fighter pilot ace who gave stock tips to his girlfriend in lieu of paying her rent. That counted as personal gain, and he spent a year and a half in prison.

- *Tippees.* **Those who receive tips—tippees—are liable for trading on inside information,** even if they do not have a fiduciary relationship to the company, as long as (1) they know the information is confidential; (2) they know it came from an insider who was violating his fiduciary duty; and (3) the insider expected some personal gain. Barry Switzer, then head football coach at the University of Oklahoma, went to a track meet to see his son compete. While sunbathing on the bleachers, he overheard someone talking about a company that was going to be acquired. Switzer bought the stock but was acquitted of insider trading charges, because the insider had not breached his fiduciary duty. He had not tipped anyone on purpose—he had simply been careless. Also, Switzer did not know that the insider was breaching a fiduciary duty, and the insider expected no personal gain.[1]

- *Misappropriation.* A person is liable if he trades in securities (1) for personal profit; (2) using confidential information; and (3) in breach of a fiduciary duty to the *source of the information*. This rule applies even if that source was not the company whose stock was traded. In the following case, the lawyer should have known better.

# United States v. O'Hagan

521 U.S. 642, 117 S. Ct. 2199, 1997 U.S. LEXIS 4033
Supreme Court of the United States, 1997

## CASE SUMMARY

**Facts:** Grand Metropolitan PLC (Grand Met) hired the law firm of Dorsey & Whitney to represent it in a takeover of Pillsbury Co. James O'Hagan, a partner in Dorsey & Whitney, did not work for Grand Met, but he found out about the deal and purchased significant amounts of Pillsbury stock. After Grand Met publicly announced its takeover attempt, the price of Pillsbury stock rose dramatically. O'Hagan sold his stock at a profit of more than $4.3 million.

**Issue:** *Did O'Hagan violate insider trading laws?*

**Decision:** O'Hagan was guilty of misappropriation, which is illegal under insider trading laws.

**Reasoning:** Under the traditional law of insider trading, a corporate insider cannot use important, secret information to trade in the securities of his corporation. The traditional theory applies not only to officers, directors, and other employees of a corporation, but also to attorneys, accountants, and others who *temporarily* become fiduciaries of a corporation.

The misappropriation theory applies to someone who is not a corporate insider, but nonetheless owes a fiduciary duty to the source of the information. Thus, in this case, O'Hagan did not work for Pillsbury, the company whose stock he bought, but he did violate his fiduciary duty to his law firm. The theft of such information is the same thing as embezzlement. It makes no sense to find a lawyer like O'Hagan guilty if he works for a law firm representing the target of a tender offer, but not if he works for a law firm representing the bidder.

---

[1] *SEC v. Switzer,* 590 F. Supp. 756, 1984 U.S. Dist. LEXIS 15303 (W.D. Okla. 1984).

**EXAM** *Strategy*

**Question:** Paul was an investment banker who sometimes bragged about deals he was working on. One night he told a bartender, Ryanne, about an upcoming deal. Ryanne bought stock in the company Paul had mentioned. Both were prosecuted for insider trading. Ryanne was acquitted but Paul was convicted, even though Ryanne was the one who made money. How is that possible?

**Strategy:** Note that there are different standards for tippers and tippees.

**Result:** Paul is liable if he knew the information was confidential and he expected some personal gain. A gift counts as personal gain. (The courts have an expansive definition of gifts—practically anything counts. Here, the information could be interpreted as a tip to the bartender.) Ryanne would not be liable unless she knew the information was confidential and had come from an insider who was violating his fiduciary duty.

## FOREIGN CORRUPT PRACTICES ACT

In the 1970s, more than 450 major U.S. corporations paid millions of dollars in foreign bribes. The Japanese premier and the Italian president both resigned after it was revealed that Lockheed had paid them off. In response, Congress passed the Foreign Corrupt Practices Act as an amendment to the 1934 Act. **Under the Foreign Corrupt Practices Act, it is a crime for any American company to make or promise to make payments or gifts to foreign officials, political candidates, or parties in order to influence a governmental decision, even if the payment is legal under local law.** There is one exception: it is legal for a company to make payments to a foreign official to expedite a "routine governmental action." Anyone who violates the law is subject to fines and imprisonment.

## BLUE SKY LAWS

Currently, all states and the District of Columbia also regulate the sale of securities. These state statutes are called **blue sky laws** (because crooks were willing to sell naive investors a "piece of the great blue sky"). It can be an enormously complicated task for an issuer of securities to comply with federal securities laws and all the state laws as well.

## · ANTITRUST ·

Congress passed the Sherman Act in 1890 to prevent extreme concentrations of economic power. Because this statute was aimed at the Standard Oil Trust, which then controlled the oil industry throughout the country, it was termed **antitrust** legislation.

Violations of the antitrust laws are divided into two categories: *per se* and **rule of reason**. *Per se* violations are automatic. Defendants charged with this type of violation cannot defend themselves by saying, "But the impact wasn't so bad" or "No one was hurt." The court will not listen to excuses, and violators may be sent to prison.

Rule of reason violations, on the other hand, are illegal only if they have an anticompetitive impact on the market. For example, mergers are illegal only if they harm competition in their industry. Those who commit rule of reason violations are not sent to prison.

Both the Justice Department and the Federal Trade Commission (FTC) have authority to enforce the antitrust laws. In addition to the government, anyone injured by an antitrust violation has the right to sue for damages. The United States is unusual in this regard—in most other countries, only the government is able to sue antitrust violators. A successful plaintiff can recover treble (that is, triple) damages from the defendant.

**Per se violation**
An automatic breach of antitrust laws.

**Rule of reason violation**
An action that breaches antitrust laws only if it has an anticompetitive impact.

# THE SHERMAN ACT

## Price-Fixing

Section 1 of the Sherman Act prohibits all agreements "in restraint of trade." The most common, and one of the most serious, violations of this provision involves price-fixing. **When competitors agree on the prices at which they will buy or sell products, their price-fixing is a *per se* violation of §1 of the Sherman Act.**

In an early case, the defendants argued that price-fixing was only wrong if the prices were unfair. The Supreme Court disagreed. In its view, prices should be set by markets, not by competitors—or judges. Moreover, "The reasonable price fixed today may through economic and business changes become the unreasonable price of tomorrow."[2]

For a century, price-fixing has been illegal, yet it never seems to go away. Samsung Electronics Co. recently paid a $300 million fine for having conspired to fix prices of computer chips. Other companies engaged in the conspiracy have paid $346 million in fines. These fines were topped by F. Hoffmann-La Roche, which paid $500 million for conspiring to fix the prices of vitamins.

## Resale Price Maintenance

Resale price maintenance (RPM) means the manufacturer sets the minimum prices that retailers may charge. In other words, it prevents retailers from discounting. Why does the manufacturer care, though? After all, once the retailer purchases the item, the manufacturer has made its profit. The only way the manufacturer makes more money is to raise its wholesale price, not the retail price. RPM guarantees a profit margin for the retailer.

Manufacturers care about retail prices because pricing affects the product's image with consumers. If you go to the Armani Web site, you will see that the suits sell for around $1,000. What conclusion do you draw about the quality of those suits? Would your opinion change if you frequently saw Armani suits being sold in department stores at discounted prices? You can understand that Armani might want to prohibit retailers from lowering the prices on its suits. Consumer advocates contend, however, that manufacturers such as Armani are simply protecting dealers from competition. Discounting may or may not harm products, but, they insist, RPM certainly hurts consumers.

In 1911, the Supreme Court ruled that RPM was a *per se* violation of §1 of the Sherman Act.[3] However, what the Supreme Court giveth, it can also taketh away. In 2007, the Supreme Court overruled itself and held that RPM is a rule of reason violation. The following case explains why.

---

### LEEGIN CREATIVE LEATHER PRODUCTS, INC. v. PSKS, INC.

127 S. Ct. 2705, 2007 U.S. LEXIS 8668
SUPREME COURT OF THE UNITED STATES, 2007

#### CASE SUMMARY

**Facts:** Leegin manufactured belts and other women's fashion accessories under the brand name "Brighton." It sold these products only to small boutiques and specialty stores. The Brighton brand was important to Kay's Kloset, a boutique in Lewisville, Texas, because it accounted for 40 to 50 percent of the store's profits.

Leegin decided it would no longer sell to retailers who discounted Brighton prices. It wanted to ensure that stores

---

[2] *United States v. Trenton Potteries Co.*, 273 U.S. 392, 397, 1927 U.S. LEXIS 975 (1927).

[3] *Dr. Miles Medical Co. v. John D. Park & Sons*, 220 U.S. 373 (1911).

could afford to offer excellent service. It was also concerned that discounting harmed Brighton's image. Despite warnings from Leegin, Kay's Kloset persisted in marking down Brighton products by 20 percent. Leegin cut the store off.

Kay's sued Leegin, alleging that it had violated the *per se* rule against resale price maintenance. The trial court found for Kay's and entered judgment against Leegin for almost $4 million. The Court of Appeals affirmed. The Supreme Court granted *certiorari*. On appeal, Leegin did not dispute that it had entered into resale price maintenance agreements with retailers. Rather, it contended that the rule of reason should apply to those agreements.

**Issue:** *Is resale price maintenance a* **per se** *or rule of reason violation of the Sherman Act?*

**Decision:** RPM is a rule of reason violation of the Sherman Act.

**Reasoning:** To be a *per se* violation, an activity must not only be anticompetitive, it must also lack any redeeming virtue.

Recent research indicates that resale price maintenance may offer some benefits:

- Retailers can provide better service. Without RPM, consumers might go *look* at a product at the retailer who hires experienced sales help or offers product demonstrations but then go *buy* the item from a discounter who provides none of these services. In short order, the upscale retailer will either go out of business or cut back on service and consumers will have fewer options.

- If retailers do not have to compete with others who sell the same brand, they can focus instead on competing against other brands. For example, retailers selling the same brand may pool their marketing dollars to have greater impact.

It is worth noting, though, that RPM can have an anticompetitive effect. A manufacturer with market power could, for example, use resale price maintenance to give retailers an incentive not to sell the products of smaller rivals. Courts must be diligent in recognizing and preventing any RPM that has an anticompetitive impact.

## Monopolization

**Under §2 of the Sherman Act, it is illegal to monopolize or attempt to monopolize a market.** To monopolize means to acquire control over a market in the wrong way. *Having* a monopoly is legal unless it is *gained* or *maintained* by using wrongful tactics.

**ECONOMICS AND THE LAW**   What is so bad about a monopoly? Imagine, for example, that you owned the only movie theater in town. Although the price of movie tickets in other towns is $10, you are able to charge $20 or maybe even $30 (for *Star Wars,* Part XVII). Although fewer customers might buy tickets at this expensive price, your profits are still higher because you earn so much on each ticket. There are two things wrong with this picture: fewer people are able to afford the movies, and when they do attend, they have less choice about what to see. The owner of the only theater in town might not be in tune with the tastes of his audiences. Economists believe that it is harmful for the movie theater to have many buyers while the customers have only one seller. ◆

To determine if a defendant has illegally monopolized, we must ask two questions:

- **Does the company control the market?** No matter what its market share, a company does not have a monopoly unless it can exclude competitors or control prices. For example, the Justice Department sued a movie theater chain that possessed a 93 percent share of the box office in Las Vegas. But the court ruled against the Justice Department because the chain's market share decreased to 75 percent within three years. This decline indicated that the company did not control the market and that barriers to entry were low.[4]

> **Possessing a monopoly is not necessarily illegal; using "*bad acts*" to acquire or maintain one is.**

---

[4] *United States v. Syufy Enterprises,* 903 F.2d 659, 1990 U.S. App. LEXIS 7396, (9th Cir, 1990).

- **How did the company acquire or maintain its control?** If the law prohibited the mere possession of a monopoly, it might discourage companies from producing excellent products or offering low prices. So possessing a monopoly is not necessarily illegal; using *"bad acts"* to acquire or maintain one is. For example, Microsoft insisted that any computer manufacturer that wanted to install the Windows operating system on its computers had to purchase a license for every machine it made. This requirement meant that a manufacturer would not even consider offering consumers another operating system because it had already paid for Microsoft's on all of its machines. The Justice Department ordered Microsoft to halt this arrangement.

Predatory pricing is another example of a bad act.

## Predatory Pricing

**Predatory pricing occurs when a company lowers its prices below cost to drive competitors out of business.** Once the predator has the market to itself, it raises prices to make up lost profits—and more besides. Typically, the goal of a predatory pricing scheme is either to win control of a market or to maintain it. Therefore, it is illegal under §2 of the Sherman Act. **To win a predatory pricing case, the plaintiff must prove three elements:**

- The defendant is selling its products *below cost.*
- The defendant *intends* that the plaintiff go out of business.
- If the plaintiff does go out of business, the defendant will be able to earn sufficient profits to *recover* its prior losses.

The classic example of predatory pricing is a large grocery store that comes into a small town offering exceptionally low prices that are subsidized by profits from its other branches. Once all the "Ma and Pa" corner groceries go out of business, MegaGrocery raises its prices to much higher levels.

Predatory pricing cases can be difficult to win. It is, for example, hard for Ma and Pa to prove that MegaGrocery intended for them to go out of business. It is also difficult for Ma and Pa to show that MegaGrocery will be able to make up all its lost profits once the corner grocery is out of the way. They need to prove, for example, that no other grocery chain will come to town. It is difficult to prove a negative proposition like that, especially in the grocery business where barriers to entry are low.

# The Clayton Act

## Mergers

**The Clayton Act prohibits mergers that are anticompetitive.** Companies with substantial assets must notify the Federal Trade Commission (FTC) before undertaking a merger.[5] This notification gives the government an opportunity to prevent a merger ahead of time, rather than trying to untangle one after the fact.

## Tying Arrangements

**Tying arrangement**
An agreement to sell a product on the condition that a buyer also purchases another, usually less desirable, product.

**A tying arrangement is an agreement to sell a product on the condition that the buyer also purchases a different (or tied) product.** A tying arrangement is illegal under the Clayton Act if:

- The two products are clearly separate;
- The seller requires the buyer to purchase the two products together;

---

[5] For example, a notice must be filed if the acquiring company is purchasing stock or assets of the acquired company that are worth more than $212 million (adjusted annually for inflation).

- The seller has significant power in the market for the tying product; and
- The seller is shutting out a significant part of the market for the tied product.

Six movie distributors refused to sell individual films to television stations. Instead, they insisted that a station buy an entire package of movies. To obtain classics such as *Treasure of the Sierra Madre* and *Casablanca* (the **tying product**), the station also had to purchase such forgettable films as *Gorilla Man* and *Tugboat Annie Sails Again* (the **tied product**).[6] The distributors engaged in an illegal tying arrangement. These are the questions that the court asked:

- *Are the two products clearly separate?* A left and right shoe are not separate products, and a seller can legally require that they be purchased together. *Gorilla Man,* on the other hand, is a separate product from *Casablanca.*

- *Is the seller requiring the buyer to purchase the two products together?* Yes, that is the whole point of these "package deals."

- *Does the seller have significant power in the market for the tying product?* In this case, the tying products are the classic movies. Since they are copyrighted, no one else can show them without the distributor's permission. The six distributors controlled a great many classic movies. So, yes, they do have significant market power.

- *Is the seller shutting out a significant part of the market for the tied product?* In this case, the tied products are the undesirable films like *Tugboat Annie Sails Again.* Television stations forced to take the unwanted films did not buy "B" movies from other distributors. These other distributors were effectively foreclosed from a substantial part of the market.

> **Tying product**
> In a tying arrangement, the product offered for sale on the condition that another product be purchased as well.

> **Tied product**
> In a tying arrangement, the product that a buyer must purchase as the condition for being allowed to buy another product.

## EXAM *Strategy*

**Question:** Two medical supply companies in the San Francisco area provide oxygen to homes of patients. The companies are owned by the doctors who prescribe the oxygen. These doctors make up 60 percent of the lung specialists in the area. Does this arrangement create an antitrust problem?

**Strategy:** Does the seller have significant power in the market for the tying product (lung patients)? Is it shutting out a significant part of the market for the tied product (oxygen)?

**Result:** The FTC charged the doctors with an illegal tying arrangement. Because the doctors effectively controlled such a high percentage of the patients needing the service, other oxygen companies could not enter the market.

## THE ROBINSON-PATMAN ACT

**Under the Robinson-Patman Act (RPA), it is illegal to charge different prices to different purchasers if:**

- The items are the same; and
- The price discrimination lessens competition.

   **However, it is legal to charge a lower price to a particular buyer if:**

- The costs of serving this buyer are lower; or
- The seller is simply meeting competition.

---

[6] *United States v. Loew's Inc.,* 371 U.S. 38, 83 S. CT. 97, 1962 U.S. LEXIS 2332 (1962).

Congress passed the RPA in 1936 to prevent large chains from driving small, local stores out of business. Owners of these "Ma and Pa" stores complained that the large chains could sell goods cheaper because suppliers charged them lower prices. As a result of the RPA, managers who would otherwise like to develop different pricing strategies for specific customers or regions may hesitate to do so for fear of violating this statute. In reality, however, they have little to fear.

Under the RPA, a plaintiff must prove both that price discrimination occurred and that it lessened competition. It is perfectly permissible, for example, for a supplier to sell at a different price to its Texas and California distributors, or to its health care and educational distributors, as long as the distributors are not in competition with each other.

The RPA also permits price variations that are based on differences in cost. Thus Kosmo's Kitchen would be perfectly within its legal rights to sell its frozen cheese enchiladas to Giant at a lower price than to Corner Grocery if Kosmo's costs are lower to do so. Giant often buys shipments the size of railroad containers that cost less to deliver than smaller boxes.

## CHAPTER CONCLUSION

In this chapter, you have learned about some of the important government regulations that affect business. They can have a profound impact on your business—and on your life.

## EXAM REVIEW

1. **SECURITY** A security is any transaction in which the buyer (1) invests money in a common enterprise and (2) expects to earn a profit predominantly from the efforts of others. (p. 361)

**EXAM Strategy**

**Question:** As a pitcher for the Cleveland Indians farm team, Randy Newsom had dreams of glory but a paycheck that was a nightmare—$8,000 for the season. Newsom came up with a clever solution: He set up a Web site that offered fans the opportunity to buy a share of his future. For only $20, the buyer was entitled to .002 percent of his career pay. Any problems with this plan?

**Strategy:** Remember that even orange trees can be securities. (See the "Result" at the end of this section.)

2. **THE 1933 ACT** The 1933 Act requires that, before offering or selling securities in a public offering, the issuer must register the securities with the Securities and Exchange Commission (SEC). (p. 361)

3. **PROSPECTUS** All investors must receive a copy of the prospectus before purchasing stock in a public offering. (p. 362)

4. **PRIVATE OFFERING** Under the 1933 Act, an issuer is not required to register securities that are sold in a private offering. (p. 362)

**5.** **REGULATION D** The most common and important type of private offering is under Regulation D. (p. 362)

.....................................................................................................

**6.** **THE 1934 ACT** The 1934 Act requires public companies to make regular filings with the SEC, including annual reports, quarterly reports, and Form 8-Ks. (p. 363)

.....................................................................................................

**7.** **INSIDER TRADING** Insider trading is illegal. (p. 363)

.....................................................................................................

**8.** **FOREIGN CORRUPT PRACTICES ACT** Under the Foreign Corrupt Practices Act, it is a crime for any American company to make or promise to make payments or gifts to foreign officials, political candidates, or parties in order to influence a governmental decision, even if the payment is legal under local law. (p. 365)

.....................................................................................................

**9.** **BLUE SKY LAWS** State securities statutes are called blue sky laws. (p. 365)

.....................................................................................................

**10.** **PRICE-FIXING** When competitors agree on the prices at which they will buy or sell products, their price-fixing is a *per se* violation of §1 of the Sherman Act. (p. 366)

.....................................................................................................

**11.** **RESALE PRICE MAINTENANCE** RPM means the manufacturer sets minimum prices that retailers may charge. It is a rule of reason violation of §1 of the Sherman Act. (p. 366)

.....................................................................................................

**12.** **MONOPOLIZATION** Under §2 of the Sherman Act, it is illegal to monopolize or attempt to monopolize a market. (p. 367)

**EXAM Strategy**

**Question:** BAR/BRI is a company that prepares law students for bar exams. With branches in 45 states, it has the largest share of the bar review market in the country. Barpassers is a much smaller company located only in Arizona and California. BAR/BRI distributed pamphlets on campuses falsely suggesting Barpassers was near bankruptcy. Enrollments in Barpassers' courses dropped, and the company was forced to postpone plans for expansion. Does Barpassers have an antitrust claim against BAR/BRI?

**Strategy:** It does not matter if BAR/BRI *has* a monopoly. These "bad acts" could help the company *acquire* one. (See the "Result" at the end of this section.)

**13.** **PREDATORY PRICING** Predatory pricing occurs when a company lowers its prices below cost to drive competitors out of business. (p. 368)

.....................................................................................................

**14.** **THE CLAYTON ACT** The Clayton Act prohibits mergers that are anticompetitive. (p. 368)

.....................................................................................................

**15.** **TYING ARRANGEMENTS** A tying arrangement is an agreement to sell a product on the condition that the buyer also purchases a different (or tied) product. Certain tying arrangements are illegal under the Clayton Act. (p. 368)

.....................................................................................................

**16.**  **THE ROBINSON-PATMAN ACT** Under the Robinson-Patman Act, it is illegal to charge different prices to different purchasers if the items are the same and the price discrimination lessens competition. (p. 369)

**1. Result:** Newsom was selling securities: buyers were investing in him, hoping that they could earn a profit from his efforts. He needed to comply with the provisions of the 1933 Act.

**12. Result:** A jury found that BAR/BRI had violated §2 of the Sherman Act by attempting to create an illegal monopoly. The jury ordered BAR/BRI to pay Barpassers more than $3 million plus attorneys' fees.

# PRACTICE EXAM

## MATCHING QUESTIONS

Match the following terms with their definitions:

___ A. Securities Act of 1933
___ B. *Per se*
___ C. Misappropriation
___ D. Rule of reason
___ E. Securities Exchange Act of 1934

1. Only a violation if it has an anticompetitive impact
2. Regulates companies once they have gone public
3. Illegal insider trading
4. Regulates the issuance of securities
5. Automatic violation of the antitrust laws, punishable by imprisonment

## TRUE/FALSE QUESTIONS

Circle true or false:

**1.** T   F   Before permitting a company to issue new securities, the SEC investigates to ensure that the company has a promising future.

**2.** T   F   Small offerings of securities do not need to be registered with the SEC.

**3.** T   F   Price-fixing is legal as long as it does not have an anticompetitive impact.

**4.** T   F   Only the federal government regulates securities offerings; the states do not.

**5.** T   F   It is legal for a company to sell its product at a price below cost as long as it does not intend to drive competitors out of business.

## MULTIPLE-CHOICE QUESTIONS

**6.** Under Regulation D, an issuer:
  A. May not sell to a thousand accredited investors
  B. May not sell to 27 unaccredited investors
  C. Must make disclosure to accredited investors
  D. Must make disclosure to unaccredited investors
  E. May advertise the stock publicly

7. Which of the following statements is *not* true about a public offering?

   A. The issuer files a registration statement with the SEC.

   B. The issuer files a prospectus with the SEC.

   C. Company officers may make public statements about the offering before the stock is sold.

   D. Company officers may make public statements about the offering after the stock is sold.

   E. The issuer may solicit offers for the stock before the effective date.

8. To have an illegal monopoly, a company must:

   I. Control the market

   II. Maintain its control improperly

   III. Have a market share greater than 50 percent

   A. I, II, and III                  D. I and III

   B. I and II                        E. Neither I, II, nor III

   C. II and III

9. Lloyd sold car floor mats to Mercedes dealerships. Then Mercedes began to include floor mats as standard equipment. Mercedes has a 10 percent share of the luxury car market.

   A. Mercedes has created an illegal tying arrangement because floor mats and cars are separate products.

   B. Mercedes has not created an illegal tying arrangement because floor mats and cars are not separate products.

   C. Mercedes has created an illegal tying arrangement because its market share is 10 percent.

   D. Mercedes has not created an illegal tying arrangement because it is not tying the two products together.

   E. Mercedes has created an illegal tying arrangement because it controls the market in floor mats.

10. Mike is director of sales for his company. He negotiates prices with Paige and Lauren, who work for two of his biggest customers. Paige tells him that she can buy the same product cheaper elsewhere. He cuts the price for her, but not for his other customers. At the same time, he develops a crush on Lauren, so offers to sell her the product at a lower price. In subsequent months, these two customers come to dominate the market. Which statement is correct:

    A. Mike can charge whatever price he wants to any customer.

    B. Mike must charge all his customers the same price.

    C. The price cut to Paige, but not Lauren, is legal.

    D. The price cut to Lauren, but not Paige, is legal.

    E. Mike is not required to charge all his customers the same price, but neither of these price cuts is legal.

## SHORT-ANSWER QUESTIONS

11. Christopher Stenger bought 12 Impressionist paintings from R. H. Love Galleries for $1.5 million. Love told Stenger that art investment would produce a safe profit. The two men agreed that Stenger could exchange any painting within five years for any one or two other paintings with the same or greater value. When Stenger's paintings did not increase in value, he sued Love, arguing that the right to trade paintings made them securities. Is Stenger correct?

12. You're in line at the movie theater when you overhear a stranger say: "The FDA has just approved Hernstrom's new painkiller. When the announcement is made on Monday, Hernstrom stock will take off." What if you buy stock of the company before the announcement on Monday?

13. Fifty bakeries in New York agreed to raise the retail price of bread from 75¢ to 85¢. All the association's members printed the new price on their bread sleeves. Are the bakeries in violation of the antitrust laws?

14. Suppose that Disney insists that retailers cannot sell DVDs of the *High School Musical* series for less than

$14.95. The company threatens to cut off any retailers who discount that price. But video stores would like to use these movies as a loss leader—selling them at a very low price to lure customers. Is it legal for Disney to cut off retailers who discount prices?

15. Reserve Supply Corp., a cooperative of 379 lumber dealers, charged that Owens-Corning Fiberglass Corp. violated the Robinson-Patman Act by selling at lower prices to Reserve's competitors. Owens-Corning had granted lower prices to a number of Reserve's competitors to meet, but not beat, the prices of other insulation manufacturers. Is Owens-Corning in violation of the Robinson-Patman Act?

16. ROLE REVERSAL: Prepare a multiple-choice question that focuses on an issue involving insider trading.

# INTERNET RESEARCH PROBLEM

Go to the Internet and find an example of a price-fixing case that has arisen in the past year. What is it that the accused are alleged to have done? How were their misdeeds discovered? If there was a settlement, what were the terms? If they were convicted, what was the penalty?

**You can find further practice problems in the Online Quiz at www.cengage.com/blaw/beatty.**

# ACCOUNTANTS' LIABILITY

**The accounting** firm Arthur Andersen prided itself on its ethics. Old-timers would tell new recruits the legend of the firm's founder: how in 1914 the young Arthur Andersen had refused a client's request to certify a dubious earnings report. Although Andersen knew his firm would be fired, and he might not be able to meet payroll, he nonetheless stood on principle. He was vindicated a few months later when the client went bankrupt.

For its first 35 years, Andersen was primarily in the business of auditing public companies. Although its partners did not become rich, they made a good living. Then the firm entered the consulting business. Soon the consultants in the firm were generating much higher profits— and earning much higher salaries—than the auditors. Audits were fast becoming loss leaders to attract consulting business. Lower costs led to lower quality as Andersen (and other auditors) felt they could not afford to invest as many hours

> **The firm collapsed in disgrace, the first major accounting firm ever to be convicted of a crime.**

in their audits. And the audits were becoming less effective because partners were increasingly afraid to deliver bad news, for fear of losing both audit and consulting fees.

To save money, the firm began to force partners to retire at 56. This reduced the general level of experience and expertise. At the same time, accounting was becoming more complicated. Predictably, mistakes happened, lawsuits were filed, settlements were made.

Andersen's name was soiled by its role in a number of financial disasters such as Global Crossing and WorldCom. And then there was Enron. Andersen opened an office in Enron's headquarters staffed with more than 150 Andersen employees. When the federal government began investigating Enron's bankruptcy, panicked Andersen employees shredded documents, leading to the firm's conviction on a criminal charge of obstructing justice. And so, the firm that began as a model of ethics in the accounting profession collapsed in disgrace, the first major accounting firm ever to be convicted of a crime.[1] The conviction was ultimately overturned by the Supreme Court, but by then it was too late. Andersen was dead.

## · INTRODUCTION ·

To begin our study of the accounting industry, it is important to understand what accountants do.

## AUDITS

Accountants serve two masters—company management and the investing public. Management hires the accountants, but investors and creditors rely upon them to offer an independent evaluation of the financial statements that management issues.

---

[1] Based in part on information in Ken Brown and Ianthe Jeanne Dugan, "Andersen's Fall from Grace Is a Tale of Greed and Miscues," *The Wall Street Journal*, June 7, 2002, p. 1.

When conducting an audit, accountants verify information provided by management. Since it is impossible to check each and every transaction, they verify a *sample* of various types of transactions. If these are accurate, they assume all are. To verify transactions, accountants use two mirror image processes—vouching and tracing.

In **vouching**, accountants choose a transaction listed in the company's books and check backwards to make sure that there are original data to support it. They might, for example, find in accounts payable a bill for the purchase of 1,000 reams of photocopy paper. They would check to ensure that all the paper had actually arrived and that the receiving department had properly signed and dated the invoice. The auditors would also check the original purchase order to ensure the acquisition was properly authorized in the first place.

In **tracing**, the accountant begins with an item of original data and traces it forward to ensure that it has been properly recorded throughout the bookkeeping process. For example, the sales ledger might report that 1,000 copies of a software program were sold to a distributor. The accountant checks the information in the sales ledger against the original invoice to ensure that the date, price, quantity, and customer's name all match. The auditor then verifies each step along the paper trail until the software leaves the warehouse.

In performing their duties, accountants must follow two sets of rules: (1) generally accepted accounting principles (GAAP); and (2) generally accepted auditing standards (GAAS). **GAAP** are the rules for preparing financial statements, and **GAAS** are the rules for conducting audits. These two sets of standards include broadly phrased general principles as well as specific guidelines and illustrations. The application and interpretation of these rules require acute professional skill.

At this writing, the Securities and Exchange Commission (SEC) is proposing a set of rules that would ultimately require U.S. companies to use **international financial reporting standards (IFRS)** instead of GAAP.[2] In theory, as businesses become more international, there is something to be said for a worldwide, consistent set of accounting rules. If everyone used IFRS (as more than 100 countries now do), cross-country comparisons would be easier. For instance, IFRS and GAAP treat research and development costs differently, which affects a company's operating income and net profit. It may be, too, that foreign companies would be more willing to invest in the United States if they could use international accounting rules.

The downside? Some of the IRFS standards are weaker; for example, they provide less direction about the way in which companies report earnings. Generally, earnings under IFRS are 6 to 8 percent higher than under GAAP. Some experts worry that allowing the use of IFRS is the equivalent of outsourcing financial safety standards.

# OPINIONS

After an audit is complete, the accountant issues an opinion on the financial statements that indicates how accurately those statements reflect the company's true financial condition. The auditor has four choices:

- **Unqualified Opinion.** Also known as a **clean opinion,** this indicates that the company's financial statements fairly present its financial condition in accordance with GAAP. A less than clean opinion is a warning to potential investors and creditors that something may be wrong.

- **Qualified Opinion.** This opinion indicates that although the financial statements are generally accurate, there is nonetheless an outstanding, unresolved issue. For example, the company may face potential liability from environmental law violations, but the liability cannot yet be estimated accurately.

**Vouching**
Auditors choose a transaction listed in a company's books and check backwards for original data to support it.

**Tracing**
An auditor takes an item of original data and tracks it forward to ensure that it has been properly recorded throughout the bookkeeping process.

**GAAP**
"Generally accepted accounting principles" are the rules for preparing financial statements.

**GAAS**
"Generally accepted auditing standards" are the rules for conducting audits.

**IFRS**
"International financial reporting standards" are a set of international accounting principles that U.S. companies may ultimately be required to follow in preparing financial statements.

---

[2] IFRS are established by the International Accounting Standards Board, a privately funded organization located in London.

- **Adverse Opinion.** In the auditor's view, the company's financial statements do not accurately reflect its financial position. In other words, the company is being less than totally truthful about its finances.

- **Disclaimer of Opinion.** Although not as damning as an adverse opinion, a disclaimer is still not good news. It is issued when the auditor does not have enough information to form an opinion.

# CONGRESS RESPONDS TO ENRON: SARBANES-OXLEY

As the stock market tumbled after the Andersen verdict, Congress acted to restore investor confidence by passing the Sarbanes-Oxley Act of 2002 (SOX). The major provisions of this act as it relates to auditors are as follows.

## The Public Company Accounting Oversight Board

Congress established the Public Company Accounting Oversight Board (PCAOB) to ensure that investors receive accurate and complete financial information. The board has the authority to regulate public accounting firms, establishing everything from audit rules to ethics guidelines. All accounting firms that audit public companies must register with the board and the board must inspect them regularly. The PCAOB has the authority to revoke an accounting firm's registration or prohibit it from auditing public companies.

In an effort to keep the foxes out of the henhouse, the statute provides that no more than two of the five PCAOB board members may be certified public accountants. This board has the authority and, it is hoped, will have the political will to revise lax accounting rules that contributed to the Enron financial earthquake. The PCAOB's first inspection of the Big Four accounting firms found audit and accounting problems at all of them, but the board still expressed confidence in the general quality of their work.

## Reports to the Audit Committee

Traditionally, auditors reported to the senior management of a client. This reporting relationship created obvious conflicts of interest—the auditors were reporting concerns to the very people who could be causing, or at least benefiting from, these problems. Under SOX, auditors must report to the audit committee of the client's board of directors, not to senior management. The accountants must inform the audit committee of any: (1) significant flaws they find in the company's internal controls; (2) alternative options that the firm considered in preparing the financial statements; and (3) accounting disagreements with management.

## Consulting Services

For years, the SEC tried to restrict consulting by accounting firms, but the firms found powerful allies in Congress to protect them. SOX prohibits accounting firms that audit public companies from providing consulting services to their audit clients on topics such as bookkeeping, financial information systems, human resources, and legal issues (unrelated to the audit). Any consulting agreements must be approved by a client's audit committee. Auditing firms cannot base their employees' compensation on sales of consulting services to clients.

## Conflicts of Interest

An accounting firm cannot audit a company if one of the client's top officers has worked for that accounting firm within the prior year and was involved in the company's audit. In short, a client cannot hire one of its auditors to ensure a friendly attitude.

## Term Limits on Audit Partners

After five years with a client, the lead audit partner must rotate off the account for at least five years. Other partners must rotate off an account every seven years for at least two years.

## · LIABILITY TO CLIENTS ·

### CONTRACT

A written contract between accountants and their clients is called an **engagement letter**. The contract has both express and implied terms. The accountant *expressly* promises to perform a particular project by a given date. The accountant also *implies* that she will work as carefully as an ordinarily prudent accountant would under the circumstances. If she fails to do either, she has breached her contract and may be liable for any damages that result.

> **Engagement letter**
> A written contract by which a client hires an accountant.

### NEGLIGENCE

An accountant is liable for negligence to a client who can prove both of the following elements:

- **The accountant breached his duty to his client by failing to exercise the degree of skill and competence that an ordinarily prudent accountant would under the circumstances.** For example, if the accountant fails to follow GAAP or GAAS, he has almost certainly breached his duty.

- **The accountant's violation of duty caused harm to the client.** In the following case, the accounting firm had clearly breached its duty. But had this wrongdoing actually caused harm to the client?

## YOU *be the* JUDGE

### OREGON STEEL MILLS, INC. v. COOPERS & LYBRAND, LLP

336 Ore. 329, 83 P.3d 322, 2004 Ore. LEXIS 55
Supreme Court of Oregon, 2004

**Facts:** Oregon Steel Mills, Inc., was a publicly traded company whose financial statements were audited by Coopers & Lybrand, LLP. When Oregon sold the stock in one of its subsidiaries, Coopers advised Oregon that the transaction should be reported as a $1 million gain. This advice was wrong and Coopers was negligent in giving it.

Two years later, Oregon began a public offering of additional shares of stock. It intended to sell these shares to the public on May 2. Shortly before Oregon filed the stock offering with the SEC, it found out from Coopers that the sale of its subsidiary had been misreported and that it would have to revise its financial statements. As a result, the offering was delayed from May 2 to June 13. During this period of delay, the price of the stock fell.

Oregon filed suit against Coopers, seeking as damages the difference between what Oregon actually received for its stock and what it would have received if the offering had occurred on May 2—an amount equal to approximately $35 million.

**Issue:  Did Coopers' negligence cause the loss to Oregon?**

**Argument for Oregon:** Coopers was negligent in giving advice to Oregon. As a result, Oregon had to delay its securities offering for six weeks. During this time, the market price of Oregon stock fell so the company sold the new stock for $35 million less than it would have received on the original sale date. Someone is going to suffer a $35 million loss. It should be Coopers, which caused the loss, rather than Oregon, which was blameless.

**Argument for Coopers:** It is true that Coopers was negligent, the market price of the stock fell, and Oregon suffered a loss. However, to recover for negligence, the plaintiff must show that the loss was reasonably foreseeable.[3] When Coopers made its error, no one could foresee that, as a result, Oregon would suffer a loss two years later because its securities offering was delayed by six weeks. At the time of its mistake, Coopers did not know when the offering would take place, nor that one time would be more favorable than another. The decline in stock price was unrelated to Oregon's financial condition or Coopers' conduct. Coopers is not liable.

---

[3] See Chapter 6 for a discussion of negligence.

# FRAUD

**An accountant is liable for fraud if (1) she makes a false statement of fact; (2) she either knows it is not true or recklessly disregards the truth; and (3) the client justifiably relies on the statement.** William deliberately inflated numbers in the financials statements he prepared for Tess so that she would not discover that he had made some disastrous investments for her. Because of these errors, Tess did not realize her true financial position for some years. William committed fraud.

A fraud claim is an important weapon because it permits the client to ask for punitive damages. For example, the singer Billy Joel sued his business manager (and ex-wife's brother) for financial mismanagement. He claimed a mere $30 million on the negligence and breach of contract claims but asked for $60 million in punitive damages on a fraud claim.

# BREACH OF TRUST

> **Clients may put as much trust in their accountant as they do in their lawyer, clergy, or psychiatrist.**

Accountants occupy a position of enormous trust because financial information is often sensitive and confidential. Clients may put as much trust in their accountant as they do in their lawyer, clergy, or psychiatrist. Accountants have a legal obligation to (1) keep all client information confidential; and (2) use client information only for the benefit of the client. For example, Alexander Grant & Co. did accounting work for Consolidata Services, Inc. (CDS), a company that provided payroll services. The two firms had a number of clients in common. When Alexander Grant discovered discrepancies in CDS's client funds accounts, it notified those companies that were clients of both firms. Not surprisingly, these mutual clients fired CDS, which then went out of business. The court held that Alexander Grant had violated its duty of trust to CDS.[4]

## EXAM *Strategy*

**Question:** Zapper, Inc., hired the accounting firm PriceTouche to determine if building an apartment building was financially feasible. After PriceTouche determined that the building would be profitable, Zapper started construction. Before the structure was complete, it burned to the ground. Although Zapper rebuilt it, the apartment building turned out not to be profitable, at least in part because of the delay in construction. Is PriceTouche liable to Zapper?

**Strategy:** There are three potential bases for liability—contract, negligence, and breach of trust. Which apply here?

**Result:** If PriceTouche did not perform as carefully as an ordinarily prudent accountant would under the circumstances, then it has violated its contract with Zapper and would be liable under contract law. It would also be negligent. But it would only be liable if its negligence caused the harm. It might be that the apartment building was not profitable because it burned down during construction. If this is the case, PriceTouche would not be liable for negligence. There is no breach of trust because it has not violated client confidentiality.

---

[4] *Wagenheim v. Alexander Grant & Co.*, 19 Ohio App. 3d 7, 482 N.E.2d 955, 1983 Ohio App. LEXIS 11194 (App. Ct., Ohio, 1983).

# · LIABILITY TO THIRD PARTIES ·

No issue in the accounting field is more controversial than liability to third parties (those who are not clients, but nonetheless rely on audits). Plaintiffs argue that auditors owe an important duty to a trusting public. The job of the auditor, they say, is to provide an independent, professional source of assurance that a company's audited financial statements are accurate. If the auditors do their job properly, they have nothing to fear. The accounting profession says in response, however, that if everyone who has ever been harmed, even remotely, by a faulty audit can recover damages, there will soon be no auditors left.

## NEGLIGENCE

**Accountants who fail to exercise due care are liable to (1) anyone they knew would rely on the information; and (2) anyone else in the same class.** Suppose, for example, that Adrienne knows she is preparing financial statements for the BeachBall Corp. to use in obtaining a bank loan from the First National Bank of Tucson. If Adrienne is careless in preparing the statements and BeachBall bursts, she will be liable to First Bank. Suppose, however, that the company takes its financial statements to the Last National Bank of Tucson instead. She would also be liable, because the Last Bank is in the same class as the First Bank. Once Adrienne knows that a bank will rely on the statements she has prepared, the identity of the particular bank should not make any difference to her when doing her work.

Suppose, however, that BeachBall uses the financial statements to persuade a landlord to rent it a manufacturing facility. In this case, Adrienne would not be liable because the landlord is not in the same class as the First Bank, for whom Adrienne knew she was preparing the documents.

In the following case, a potential employee relied on audited financial statements that proved to be faulty. Was the accounting firm liable?

## ELLIS V. GRANT THORNTON

2008 U.S. APP. LEXIS 13379
UNITED STATES COURT OF APPEALS FOR THE FOURTH CIRCUIT

### CASE SUMMARY

**Facts:** For five years, the First National Bank of Keystone issued a lot of risky mortgage loans on which the borrowers defaulted. No situation is so bad it cannot be made worse. Keystone management lied about the value of the loans. When the Office of the Comptroller of the Currency (OCC) first began to smell trouble, it required Keystone to hire a nationally recognized independent accounting firm to audit its books. The bank hired Grant Thornton. Stan Quay was the lead partner on the account. On a theory of what can go wrong will go wrong, he was negligent in conducting the audit and failed to notice a discrepancy of $515 million between the reported and actual value of the loans.

As Quay was finishing his audit, the board began talking with Gary Ellis about becoming president of the bank. Ellis already had a perfectly good job, so he was understandably reluctant to move to a bank that the OCC was investigating. To reassure him, the Keystone board suggested he talk with Quay and look at the bank's financials. Quay told Ellis that Keystone would receive a clean, unqualified opinion. He did ultimately issue a clean opinion reporting shareholder's equity of $184 million when, in fact, the bank was insolvent. The first page of the report stated: "This report is intended for the information and use of the Board of Directors and Management of The First National Bank of Keystone and its regulatory agencies and should not be used by third parties for any other purpose." A week later, the Board voted to hire Ellis, who then quit his job elsewhere to come on board. Five months later, the OCC declared Keystone insolvent and shut it down. Ellis was out of work. He filed suit against Grant Thornton, seeking compensation for his lost wages. The district court ruled in favor of Ellis and granted him $2.5 million in damages. Grant Thornton appealed.

**Issue:** *Was Grant Thornton liable to Ellis for its negligence in preparing Keystone's financial statements?*

**Decision:** Grant Thornton was not liable.

**Reasoning:** Grant Thornton prepared its audit for the benefit of Keystone and the OCC. It did not know that Ellis or any other potential employee would be relying on the report. Keystone did not pay Grant Thornton to review the bank's financial position with potential employees and, indeed, the accountants did not know about Ellis' involvement until *after* it had decided to issue the clean opinion. Grant Thornton was not aware that it might be held liable for Ellis' lost wages. If the accountant is unaware of the risk, he cannot be held liable.

# FRAUD

Courts consider fraud to be much worse than negligence because it is *intentional*. Therefore, the penalty is heavier. **An accountant who commits fraud is liable to any foreseeable user of the work product who justifiably relied on it.** Take the example of TechDisk, a manufacturer of disk drives. Customers were buying disk drives faster than the company could make them. Afraid that the stock price would plummet if investors found out about the shortage, company officers helped their sales numbers by shipping out bricks wrapped up to look like disk drives. Company accountants altered the financial statements to pretend that the bricks were indeed computer parts. These accountants would be liable to any foreseeable users—including investors, creditors, and customers.

# SECURITIES ACT OF 1933

The Securities Act of 1933 (1933 Act) requires a company to register securities before offering them for sale to the public. To do this, the company files a registration statement with the SEC. This registration statement must include audited financial statements. **Auditors are liable for any important misstatement or omission in the financial statements that they prepare for a registration statement.**

The plaintiff must prove only that (1) the registration statement contained an important misstatement or omission; and (2) she lost money. Ernst & Young served as the auditor for FP Investments, Inc., a company that sold tax shelter partnerships. These partnerships were formed to cultivate tropical plants in Hawaii. The prospectus for this investment neglected to mention that the partnerships did not have enough cash on hand to grow the plants. The investors lost their money. A jury ordered Ernst & Young to pay damages of $18.9 million.[5]

**Due diligence**
An investigation of the registration statement by someone who signs it.

However, auditors can avoid liability by showing that they made a reasonable investigation of the financial statements. This investigation is called **due diligence**. Typically, auditors will not be liable if they can show that they complied with GAAP and GAAS.

# SECURITIES EXCHANGE ACT OF 1934

Under the Securities Exchange Act of 1934 (1934 Act), public companies must file an annual report containing audited financial statements and quarterly reports with unaudited financials.

## Fraud

**In these filings under the 1934 Act, an auditor is liable for making (1) a misstatement or omission of an important fact; (2) knowingly or recklessly; (3) that the plaintiff relies on in**

---

[5] *Hayes v. Haushalter*, 1994 U.S. App. LEXIS 23608 (9th Cir. 1994).

**purchasing or selling a security.** For example, when Price Waterhouse audited Altris Software, it failed to notice some obvious red flags: on the last day of the year, Altris recorded revenue from two customers that was more than 50 times greater than it had ever received from this type of transaction. The court held, however, that although Price Waterhouse may have been grossly negligent, it had not had actual knowledge of the falsehoods, nor had it been deliberately reckless.[6]

### Whistleblowing

**Auditors who suspect that a client has committed an illegal act must notify the client's board of directors.** If the board fails to take appropriate action, the auditors must issue an official report to the board. If the board receives such a report from its auditors, it must notify the SEC within one business day (and send a copy of this notice to its accountant). If the auditors do not receive this copy, they must notify the SEC themselves.

### Joint and Several Liability

Traditionally, liability under the 1934 Act was joint and several. When several different participants were potentially liable, a plaintiff could sue any one defendant or any group of defendants for the full amount of the damages. If a company committed fraud and then went bankrupt, its accounting firm might well be the only defendant with assets. Even if the accountants had caused only, say, 5 percent of the damages, they could be liable for the full amount.

Congress amended the 1934 Act to provide that accountants are **liable *jointly and severally*** only if they *knowingly* violate the law. Otherwise, the defendants are *proportionately* liable, meaning that they are liable only for the share of the damages that they themselves caused.

**Joint and several liability**
An injured third party has the right to recover the full amount of her damages from one, some, or all of those who caused her harm. She may not recover more than 100 percent of her damages.

## · CRIMINAL LIABILITY ·

Some violations by accountants are criminal acts for which the punishment may be a fine and imprisonment:

- The Justice Department has the right to prosecute **willful violations** under either the 1933 Act or the 1934 Act.

- The Internal Revenue Code imposes various criminal penalties on accountants for **wrongdoing in the preparation of tax returns.**

- Many states prosecute violations of their securities laws.

### EXAM *Strategy*

**Question:** When Benjamin hired Howard to prepare financial statements for American Equities, he gave Howard a handwritten sheet of paper entitled "Pro Forma Balance Sheet." It contained a list of real estate holdings and the balance sheets of two corporations that Benjamin claimed were owned by American Equities. From this one piece of paper and without any examination of books and records, Howard prepared an Auditor's Report for the company. Benjamin used the Auditor's Report to sell stock in American Equities. Has Howard committed a criminal offense?

**Strategy:** Willful violations of the securities laws are criminal offenses.

---

[6] *DSAM Global Value Fund v. Altris Software, Inc.* 288 F.3d 385, 2002 U.S. App. LEXIS 7213.

**Result:** A court held that Howard's actions were willful. He was found guilty of a criminal violation.

......................................................................................................................

## · OTHER ACCOUNTANT-CLIENT ISSUES ·

## THE ACCOUNTANT-CLIENT RELATIONSHIP

The SEC has long been concerned about the relationship between accountants and the companies they audit. Its rules require accountants to maintain independence from their clients. **An auditor or her family must not, for example, maintain a financial or business relationship with the client.**

**SEC rules on independence specifically prohibit accountants or their families from owning stock in a company that their firm audits.** To take one woeful example, the SEC discovered that most of PricewaterhouseCoopers's partners were in violation of this rule, including half of the partners who were charged with enforcing it. Even worse, the firm had been caught violating the same rule only a few years before. The SEC notified 52 of the firm's clients that there were potential concerns about the integrity of their financial statements and even requested that some of the companies select a new auditor.

SEC rules of practice specify that an accountant who engages in "unethical or improper professional conduct" may be banned from practice before the SEC. Auditors who are banned or suspended cannot perform the audits that are required by the 1933 and 1934 Acts—quite a professional blow.

## ACCOUNTANT-CLIENT PRIVILEGE

Traditionally, an accountant-client privilege did not exist under federal law. Accountants were under no obligation to keep confidential any information they received from their clients. In one notorious case, the IRS suspected that the owner of a chain of pizza parlors was underreporting his income. The agency persuaded the owner's CPA, James Checksfield, to spy on him for eight years. (The IRS agreed to drop charges against Checksfield, who had not paid his own taxes for three years.) Thanks to the information that Checksfield passed to the IRS, his client was indicted on criminal charges of evading taxes.

Congress passed the Internal Revenue Service Restructuring and Reform Act to reduce IRS abuse of taxpayers. This statute provides limited protection for tax advice that accountants give their clients. That is the good news. The bad news is the word "limited." **This new privilege applies only in civil cases involving the IRS or the U.S. government.** It does not apply to criminal cases, civil cases not involving the U.S. government, or cases with other federal agencies such as the SEC. Nor does it apply to advice about tax shelters. Thus, for example, this new accountant-client privilege would not have protected Checksfield's client because he was charged with a criminal offense.

### *Working Papers*

When working for a client, accountants use the client's own documents and also prepare working papers of their own—notes, memoranda, research. In theory, each party owns whatever it has prepared itself. Thus accountants own the working papers they have created. In practice, however, the client controls even the accountant's working papers. **The accountant (1) cannot show the working papers to anyone without the client's permission (or a valid court order); and (2) must allow the client access to the working papers.** Under the Sarbanes-Oxley Act, accountants for public companies must keep all audit work papers for at least seven years.

## CHAPTER CONCLUSION

Accountants serve many masters and, therefore, face numerous potential conflicts. Clients, third parties, and the government all rely on their work. Privy to clients' most intimate financial secrets, accountants must decide which of these secrets to reveal and which to keep confidential. The wrong decision may destroy the client, impoverish its shareholders, and subject its auditors to substantial penalties.

## EXAM REVIEW

**1.** **SARBANES-OXLEY** The Sarbanes-Oxley Act:
- Establishes the Public Company Accounting Oversight Board.
- Requires an accounting firm to make regular and complete reports to the audit committees of its clients.
- Prohibits accounting firms that audit public companies from providing consulting services to those companies on certain topics, such as bookkeeping, financial information systems, human resources, and legal issues (unrelated to the audit).
- Prohibits an accounting firm from auditing a company if one of the company's top officers has worked for the firm within the last year and was involved in the company's audit.
- Provides that a lead audit partner cannot work for a client in any auditing role for more than five years at a time. (p. 378)

**2.** **LIABILITY TO CLIENTS FOR NEGLIGENCE** Accountants are liable to their clients for negligence if:
- They breach their duty to their clients by failing to exercise the degree of skill and competence that an ordinarily prudent accountant would under the circumstances; and
- The violation of this duty causes harm to the client. (p. 379)

**CPA Question:** A CPA's duty of due care to a client most likely will be breached when a CPA:

    (a) Gives a client an oral instead of a written report

    (b) Gives a client incorrect advice based on an honest error judgment

    (c) Fails to give tax advice that saves the client money

    (d) Fails to follow generally accepted auditing standards

**Strategy:** Accountants are not liable for every error they make, only if they fail to act like an ordinarily prudent accountant. (See the "Result" at the end of this section.)

**3.** **LIABILITY TO CLIENTS FOR FRAUD** Accountants are liable for fraud if:
- They make a false statement of fact.
- They know it is not true or recklessly disregard the truth; and
- The client justifiably relies on the statement. (p. 380)

**4.** **BREACH OF TRUST** Accountants have a legal obligation to:
- Keep all client information confidential; and
- Use client information only for the benefit of the client. (p. 380)

5. **LIABILITY TO THIRD PARTIES FOR NEGLIGENCE** Accountants who fail to exercise due care are liable to (1) any third party they knew would rely on the information; and (2) anyone else in the same class. (p. 381)

6. **LIABILITY TO THIRD PARTIES FOR FRAUD** An accountant who commits fraud is liable to any foreseeable user of the work product who justifiably relies on it. (p. 382)

**EXAM Strategy**

**Question:** When Jeff Hall told one of the general partners of the Edge Energies limited partnerships that he did not wish to invest in these ventures, the general partner suggested he call Ronald W. Jackson, the partnerships' accountant. Jackson told Hall that Edge Energies partnerships were a "good deal," that they were "good moneymakers," and "they were expecting something like a two-year payoff." In fact, Jackson knew that the operators were mismanaging these ventures, and that the partnerships were bad investments. Hall relied on Jackson's recommendation and invested in Edge Energies. He subsequently lost his entire investment. Is Jackson liable to Hall?

**Strategy:** Whenever there is intentional wrongdoing—think fraud. (See the "Result" at the end of this section.)

7. **SECURITIES ACT OF 1933** Auditors are liable for any important misstatement or omission in the financial statements that they provide for a registration statement. (p. 382)

8. **SECURITIES EXCHANGE ACT OF 1934** Under the 1934 Act, an auditor is liable for making (1) any misstatement or omission of a material fact in financial statements; (2) knowingly or recklessly; (3) that the plaintiff relies on in purchasing or selling a security. (p. 382)

9. **WHISTLEBLOWING** Auditors who suspect that a client has committed an illegal act must notify the client's board of directors. (p. 383)

10. **JOINT AND SEVERAL LIABILITY** Under the 1934 Act, accountants are liable jointly and severally only if they knowingly violate the law. Otherwise, they are proportionately liable. (p. 383)

11. **CRIMINAL LIABILITY** The Justice Department has the right to prosecute willful violations under either the 1933 Act or the 1934 Act. The Internal Revenue Code imposes various criminal penalties on accountants for wrongdoing in the preparation of tax returns. (p. 383)

12. **AUDITOR INDEPENDENCE** Public accountants or their families may not own stock in a company that their firm audits. (p. 384)

13. **ACCOUNTANT-CLIENT PRIVILEGE** A limited accountant-client privilege exists under federal law. (p. 384)

14. **WORKING PAPERS** An accountant cannot show working papers to anyone without the client's permission (or a valid court order); and must allow the client access to the working papers. (p. 384)

**2. Result:** The correct answer is d because an ordinarily prudent accountant follows GAAS.

**6. Result:** Jackson was liable to Hall for fraud because Hall was a foreseeable user of the information and justifiably relied on it.

# PRACTICE EXAM

## MATCHING QUESTIONS

Match the following terms with their definitions:

___ A. GAAS

___ B. Tracing

___ C. Qualified opinion

___ D. GAAP

___ E. Vouching

___ F. Unqualified opinion

1. Rules for preparing financial statements
2. When accountants check backwards to ensure there are data to support a transaction
3. Clean opinion
4. Rules for conducting audits
5. When accountants check a transaction forward to ensure it has been properly recorded
6. When there is some uncertainty in the financial statements

## TRUE/FALSE QUESTIONS

Circle true or false:

1. T   F   Auditors are only liable under the 1933 Act if they intentionally misrepresent financial statements.

2. T   F   Auditors generally are not liable if they follow GAAP and GAAS.

3. T   F   Accountants are prohibited under federal law from disclosing a client's confidential information.

4. T   F   If auditors discover that company officers have committed an illegal act, they must immediately report this wrongdoing to the SEC.

5. T   F   Under federal law, accounting firms may not provide any consulting services to companies that they audit.

## MULTIPLE-CHOICE QUESTIONS

6. To be successful in a suit under the Securities Act of 1933, the plaintiff must prove

|     | Important Mistake in the Registration Statement | Plaintiff Lost Money |
| --- | --- | --- |
| A. | No | Yes |
| B. | No | No |
| C. | Yes | No |
| D. | Yes | Yes |

7. An accountant is liable to a client for conducting an audit negligently if the accountant:

   A. Acted with intent

   B. Was a fiduciary of the client

   C. Failed to exercise due care

   D. Executed an engagement letter

8. Which of the following statements about Sarbanes-Oxley is *not* true?

   A. All accounting firms that audit public companies must register with the PCAOB.

   B. Auditors must report to the CEO of the company they are auditing.

   C. Auditing firms cannot base their employees' compensation on sales of consulting services to clients.

   D. An accounting firm cannot audit a company if one of the client's top officers has worked for that firm within the prior year and was involved in the company's audit.

   E. Every five years, the lead audit partner must rotate off an audit account.

9. For a client to prove a case of fraud against an accountant, the following element is *not* required:

   A. The client lost money.

   B. The accountant made a false statement of fact.

   C. The client relied on the false statement.

   D. The accountant knew the statement was false.

   E. The accountant was reckless.

10. Dusty is trying to buy an office building to house his growing consulting firm. When Luke, a landlord, asks to see a set of financials, Dusty asks his accountant Ellen to prepare a set for Luke. Dusty shows these financials to a number of landlords, including Carter. Dusty rents from Carter. Ellen has been careless and the financials are inaccurate. Dusty cannot pay his rent and Carter files suit against Ellen. Which of the following statements is true?

    A. Carter will win because Ellen was careless.

    B. Carter will win because Ellen knew that landlords would see the financials.

    C. Carter will win because Ellen was careless and she knew that landlords would see the financials.

    D. Carter will lose because Ellen did not know that he would see the financials.

    E. Carter will lose because he had no contract with Ellen.

11. Ted prepared fraudulent financial statements for the Arbor Corp. Lacy read these statements before purchasing stock in the company. When Arbor goes bankrupt, Lacy sues Ted.

    A. Lacy will win because it was foreseeable that she would rely on these statements.

    B. Lacy will win because Ted was negligent.

    C. Lacy will lose because she did not rely on these statements.

    D. Lacy will lose because it was not foreseeable and she did not rely on these statements.

    E. Lacy will lose because it was not foreseeable that she would rely on these statements.

## SHORT-ANSWER QUESTIONS

12. Color-Dyne printed patterns on carpets. After reviewing the company's audited financial statements, the plaintiffs provided materials to Color-Dyne on credit. These financial statements showed that Color-Dyne owned $2 million in inventory. The audit failed to reveal, however, that various banks held secured interests in this inventory. The accountant did not know that the company intended to give the financial statements to plaintiffs or any other creditors. Color-Dyne went bankrupt. Is the accountant liable to plaintiffs?

13. James and Penelope Monroe purchased securities offered by Hughes Homes, Inc., a retailer of manufactured housing in Tacoma, Washington. During its audit, Deloitte & Touche found that Hughes Homes' internal controls had flaws. As a result, the accounting firm adjusted the scope of its audit to perform independent testing to verify the accuracy of the company's financial records. Satisfied that the internal controls were functional, Deloitte issued a clean opinion. After Hughes Homes went bankrupt, the Monroes sued

Deloitte for violating the 1933 Act. They alleged that Deloitte's failure to disclose that it had found flaws in Hughes's internal control system was a material omission. GAAS did not require disclosure. Is Deloitte liable?

14. The British Broadcasting Corp. (BBC) broadcast a TV program alleging that Terry Venables, a former professional soccer coach, had fraudulently obtained a £1 million loan by misrepresenting the value of his company. Venables had been a sportscaster for the BBC but had switched to a competing network. The source of the BBC's story was "confidential working papers" from Venables's accountant. According to the accountant, the papers had been stolen. Who owns these working papers? Does the accountant have the right to disclose the content of working papers?

15. Medtrans, an ambulance company, was unable to pay its bills. In need of cash, it signed an engagement letter with Deloitte & Touche to perform an audit that could be used to attract investors. Unfortunately, the audit had the opposite effect. The unaudited statements showed earnings of $1.9 million, but the accountants calculated that the company had actually lost about $500,000. While in the process of negotiating adjustments to the financials, Deloitte resigned. Some time passed before Medtrans found another auditor, and, in that interim, a potential investor withdrew its $10 million offer. Is Deloitte liable for breach of contract?

16. ROLE REVERSAL: Prepare a multiple-choice question like those found on the CPA exam. The earlier question in the exam review provides an example.

# INTERNET RESEARCH PROBLEM

Go to **http://sec.gov/** and find five examples of actions that the SEC has brought against accountants. (You might try typing the term "accounting violations" in the search box.) What does the SEC allege that the accountants have done?

**You can find further practice problems in the Online Quiz at www.cengage.com/blaw/beatty.**

# PROPERTY AND CONSUMER LAW

# CONSUMER LAW

**Three women** signed up for a lesson at the Arthur Murray dance studio in Washington, D.C. Expecting a session of quiet fun, they instead found themselves in a nightmare of humiliation and coercion:

> **I started crying and couldn't stop crying. All I thought of was getting out of there.**

- "I tried to say no and get out of it and I got very, very upset because I got frightened at paying out all that money and having nothing to fall back on. I remember I started crying and couldn't stop crying. All I thought of was getting out of there. So finally after—I don't know how much time, Mr. Mara said, well, I could sign up for 250 hours, which was half the 500 Club, which would amount to $4,300. So I finally signed it. After that, I tried to raise the money from the bank and found I couldn't get a loan for that amount and I didn't have any savings and I had to get a bank loan to pay for it. That was when I went back and asked him to cancel that contract. But Mr. Mara said that he couldn't cancel it."

- "I did not join the carnival. I did not wish to join the carnival, and while it was only an additional $55, I had no desire to join. [My instructor] asked everyone in the room to sit down in a circle around me and he stood me up in that circle, in the middle of the circle, and said, 'Everybody, I want you to look at this woman here who is too cheap to join the carnival. I just want you to look at a woman like that. Isn't it awful?'"

Because of abuses such as these, the Federal Trade Commission (FTC) ordered the Arthur Murray dance studio to halt its high-pressure sales techniques, limit each contract to no more than $1,500 in dance lessons, and permit all contracts to be canceled within seven days.[1]

## · INTRODUCTION ·

Years ago, consumers typically dealt with merchants they knew well. A dance instructor in a small town would not stay in business long if he tormented his elderly clients. As the population of the country grew and cities expanded, however, merchants became less and less subject to community pressure. The law has supplemented, if not replaced, these informal policing mechanisms. Both Congress and the states have passed statutes that protect consumers. But the legal system is generally too slow and expensive to handle small cases. The women who fell into the web of Arthur Murray had neither the wealth nor the energy to sue the studio themselves. To aid consumers such as these, Congress empowered federal agencies to enforce consumer laws. The FTC is the most important of these agencies.

## · SALES ·

Section 5 of the Federal Trade Commission Act (FTC Act) prohibits "unfair and deceptive acts or practices." You can report an unfair or deceptive practice to the FTC at its Web site (**http://www.ftc.gov**).

### DECEPTIVE ACTS OR PRACTICES

Many deceptive acts or practices involve advertisements. **Under the FTC Act, an advertisement is deceptive if it contains an important misrepresentation or omission that is likely to mislead a reasonable consumer.** A company advertised that a pain-relief ointment called "Aspercreme" provided "the strong relief of aspirin right where you hurt." From this ad and the

---

[1] *In re Arthur Murray Studio of Washington, Inc.*, 78 F.T.C. 401, 1971 FTC LEXIS 75 (1971).

name of the product, do you assume that the ointment contains aspirin? Are you a reasonable consumer? Consumers surveyed in a shopping mall believed the product contained aspirin. In fact, it does not. The FTC required the company to disclose that there is no aspirin in Aspercreme.[2]

Was the company in the following case deceptive about its business opportunity?

## YOU *be the* JUDGE

### FEDERAL TRADE COMMISSION v. BUSINESS CARD EXPERTS, INC.

2007 U.S. Dist. LEXIS 31366
United States District Court for the District
of Minnesota, 2007

**Facts:** Business Card Experts, Inc. (BCE) grossed over $16 million selling business-card dealerships. The prices of the dealerships ranged from $10,000 to $25,000—the higher the price, the lower the fee the dealers paid for each box of cards they ordered.

BCE ads claimed that dealers could earn $150,000 or more per year. In fact, no one ever earned $150,000; indeed, only one or two people even earned a third of that. Of the 1,300 people who purchased BCE dealerships; only about 300 were still ordering cards from BCE at the time of this case.

BCE sales representatives told potential dealers that, "there's no way in the world you could even lose a dime on this." Sales representatives also sometimes offered what they described as a "money-back guarantee"—which meant that dealers received a certain number of free boxes. Those who sold all of the free boxes at the suggested retail price of $49.95 would recoup their initial investment. But only a tiny percentage of dealers—something in the neighborhood of 3 percent—actually did recoup their investment.

When potential dealers asked for references, they were given the names of BCE sales reps, who lied and said that they were independent dealers earning a living selling business cards when instead all they sold were dealerships for the company. These reps would also offer prospective dealers exclusive territory, even if, in fact, there were other dealers in the same area. One salesperson told an FTC investigator posing as a potential dealer, "This is all we do. We make over $200,000 a year net profit doing this business." In reality, he had ordered only five boxes of cards in the prior three years.

On the other hand, dealers did testify that the BCE Web site for ordering cards was useful and that its cards were of good quality and its prices competitive.

The Court granted the FTC's motion for a temporary restraining order, enjoining BCE from selling dealerships. The FTC asked that the restraining order be made permanent.

**You Be the Judge:** Did BCE violate §5 of the FTC Act?

**Argument for the FTC:** BCE's actions were unfair and deceptive. Virtually no one made as much money as advertised. Salespeople openly lied to potential dealers. The so-called "money-back guarantee" was a fraud. This company should be shut down now.

**Argument for the Company:** BCE is a legitimate business. It has an excellent Web site and prints business cards that are high quality and reasonably priced. Able salespeople can earn a substantial income if they work hard enough. Not every business venture will work for every person, but this is a good opportunity for the right person. Prospective dealers bear the responsibility of weighing the risks and profit potential, and of following up their investment with the hard work and business savvy necessary to make the venture successful.

## UNFAIR PRACTICES

**The FTC Act also prohibits unfair acts or practices.** For example, a furnace repair company dismantled home furnaces for "inspection" and then refused to reassemble them until the consumers agreed to buy services or replacement parts.

---

[2] *In re Thompson Medical Co.*, 104 F.T.C. 648, 1984 LEXIS 6 (1984).

# Bait and Switch

**FTC rules prohibit bait and switch advertisements: A merchant may not advertise a product and then try to get consumers to buy a different (more expensive) item.** In addition, merchants must have enough stock on hand to meet reasonable demand for any advertised product.

Sears ran many advertisements like the following:

**Bait and switch**
A practice where sellers advertise products that are not generally available but are being used to draw interested parties in so that they will buy other items.

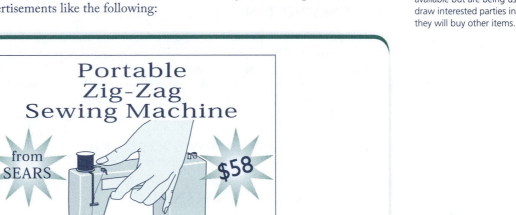

When eager customers went to buy this fabulous item, they were told that the machines were noisy, did not come with Sears's standard sewing machine guarantee, and could neither stitch in reverse nor do buttonholes. Also, the store was out of stock and would not be receiving any new machines for a long time.[3] Sears did not wish to sell the advertised merchandise; it wanted to switch consumers to another, higher-priced product. This practice violated FTC rules.

# Mail or Telephone Order Merchandise

**The FTC has established the following guidelines on mail or telephone order merchandise:**

- Mail-order companies must ship an item within the time stated or, if no time is given, within 30 days after receipt of the order.

- If a company cannot ship the product when promised, it must send the customer a notice with the new shipping date and an opportunity to cancel. If the new shipping date is within 30 days of the original one, and the customer does not cancel, the order is still on.

- If the company cannot ship within 30 days of the original date, it must send the customer another notice. This time, however, the company must cancel the order unless the customer returns the notice, indicating that he still wants the item.

---

[3] *In re Sears, Roebuck and Co.*, 89 F.T.C. 229, 1977 FTC LEXIS 225 (1977).

For example, Dell Computer Corp. advertised that its Dimension computer came with the "Dell Software Suite." In fact, the suite was not available for several months. Instead of the software, Dell sent customers a coupon for the suite "when available." Imagine having a coupon but no software. The FTC charged Dell with violations of the mail or telephone order rules.[4]

## TELEMARKETING

The telephone rings: "Could I speak with Alexander Johannson? This is Denise from Master Chimney Sweeps." It is 7:30 p.m.; you have just straggled in from work and are looking forward to a peaceful dinner of takeout cuisine. You are known as Sandy, your last name is pronounced Yohannson, and you live in a modern apartment without a chimney. A telemarketer has struck again! What can you do to protect your peace and quiet?

**The FTC prohibits telemarketers from calling any telephone number listed on its do-not-call registry.** You can register your telephone numbers with the FTC online at **http://www.donotcall.gov** or by telephone at (888) 382-1222. FTC rules also prohibit telemarketers from blocking their names and telephone numbers on Caller ID systems.

## UNORDERED MERCHANDISE

**Under §5 of the FTC Act, anyone who receives unordered merchandise in the mail can treat it as a gift.** She can use it, throw it away, or do whatever else she wants with it.

There you are, watching an infomercial for Anushka products, guaranteed to fight that scourge of modern life—cellulite! Rushing to your phone, you place an order. The Anushka cosmetics arrive, but for some odd reason, the cellulite remains. A month later another bottle arrives, like magic, in the mail. The magic spell is broken, however, when you get your credit card bill and see that, without your authorization, the company has charged you for the new supply of Anushka. This company was in violation of FTC rules because it did not notify customers that they were free to treat the unauthorized products as a gift, to use or throw out as they wished.[5]

## DOOR-TO-DOOR SALES

Consumers at home need special protection from salespeople. In a store, customers can simply walk out, but at home they may feel trapped. **Under the FTC door-to-door rules, a salesperson is required to notify the buyer that she has the right to cancel the transaction prior to midnight of the third business day thereafter.** This notice must be given both orally and in writing; the actual cancellation must be in writing. The seller must return the buyer's money within 10 days. For example, Tork & Associates violated FTC rules when it sold door-to-door magazine subscriptions. Customers were told that, to cancel, they had to submit a copy of the complete receipt, the canceled check, the salesperson's name, the magazine name, the date of the transaction, and the total cost. Salespeople never actually gave customers the complete receipt, so it was difficult for customers to comply with these requirements.

**EXAM** *Strategy*

**Question:** Mantra Films sold "Girls Gone Wild" DVDs on the Internet. When customers ordered one DVD, the company would automatically enroll them in a "continuity program" and send them unordered DVDs each month on a "negative-option" basis, charging consumers' credit cards for each DVD until consumers took action to stop the shipments. Is Mantra's marketing plan legal?

---

[4] *United States v. Dell Computer Corp.*, 1998 FTC LEXIS 30 (1998).

[5] *In the Matter of Synchronal Corp.*, 116 F.T.C. 1189, 1993 FTC LEXIS 280 (1993).

**Strategy:** Review the various sales regulations—more than one is involved in this case.

**Result:** This marketing plan was deceptive because customers were not told that they would be enrolled in the continuity program. Also, Mantra could not legally bill for the unordered DVDs. Under the unordered merchandise rule, consumers had the right to treat them as gifts.

·········································································································

# · CONSUMER CREDIT ·

Most states limit the maximum interest rate a lender may charge. These laws are called **usury statutes.** The penalty for violating usury statutes varies among the states. Depending upon the jurisdiction, the borrower may be allowed to keep (1) the interest above the usury limit; (2) all of the interest; or (3) all of the loan and the interest.

## Truth-in-Lending Act

The federal Truth-in-Lending Act (TILA) does not regulate interest rates or the terms of a loan; these are set by state law. It simply requires lenders to disclose the terms of a loan in an understandable and complete manner.

Under TILA:

- *The disclosure must be clear and in a sensible order.* A finance company violated TILA when it loaned money to Dorothy Allen. The company made all the required disclosures but scattered them throughout the loan document and intermixed them with confusing terms that were not required by TILA.[6] A TILA disclosure statement should not be a game of *Where's Waldo?*

- *The lender must disclose the finance charge.* The finance charge is the amount, in dollars, the consumer will pay in interest and fees over the life of the loan.

- *The creditor must disclose the annual percentage rate (APR).* This number is the actual rate of interest the consumer pays on an annual basis. Without this disclosure, it would be easy in a short-term loan to disguise a very high APR because the finance charge is low. Boris borrows $5 for lunch from his employer's credit union. Under the terms of the loan, he must repay $6 the following week. His finance charge is only $1, but his APR is astronomical—20 percent per week—which is over 1,000 percent for a year.

## Home Mortgage Loans

A new provision of TILA prohibits unfair, abusive or deceptive home mortgage lending practices. For example, lenders may not coerce an appraiser into misstating a home's value. Nor can they advertise a loan as "fixed" if in fact its rate or payments will change. This provision also regulates a new category of so-called **subprime loans** (also known as higher-priced mortgage loans). These are loans that have an above-market interest rate because they involve high-risk borrowers.[7] For subprime loans, a lender:

- Must verify the borrower's ability to repay the loan from income and assets other than the home's value

**Subprime loan**
A loan that has an above-market interest rate because the borrower is high-risk.

─────────

[6] *Allen v. Beneficial Fin. Co. of Gary,* 531 F.2d 797, 1976 U.S. App. LEXIS 12935 (7th Cir. 1976).

[7] In the official definition, subprime loans are first mortgages that have an APR 1.5 percentage points or more above the average prime offer rate or second mortgages that have an APR 3.5 percentage points or more above that index.

- May not charge a prepayment penalty if monthly payments can change in the first four years of the loan
- Must collect property taxes and homeowner's insurance for all first mortgages

# FAIR CREDIT BILLING ACT

Is there anyone in America who has not sometime or other discovered an error in a credit card bill? Before Congress passed the Fair Credit Billing Act (FCBA), a dispute with a credit card company often deteriorated into an avalanche of threatening form letters that ignored any response from the hapless cardholder. But under the FCBA:

- If, within 60 days of receipt of a bill, a consumer writes to a credit card company to complain about the bill, the company must acknowledge receipt of the complaint within 30 days.
- Within two billing cycles (but no more than 90 days) the credit card company must investigate the complaint and respond.
- The credit card company cannot try to collect the disputed debt or close or suspend the account until it has responded to the consumer complaint.
- The credit card company cannot report to credit agencies that the consumer has an unpaid bill until 10 days after the response. If the consumer still disputes the charge, the credit card company may report the amount to a credit agency but must disclose that it is disputed.

If you go to **http://www.ftc.gov** and search for "sample dispute letter fcba" you will see a form letter prepared by the FTC that you can send to a credit card company to dispute a bill.

# FAIR CREDIT REPORTING ACT

Most adults rely on credit—to acquire a house, credit cards, or overdraft privileges at the bank. A bad credit report makes life immensely more difficult. The goal of the Fair Credit Reporting Act (FCRA) is to ensure that consumer credit reports are accurate.

The FCRA regulates **consumer reporting agencies.** These are businesses that supply consumer reports to third parties such as credit card companies, banks, and employers. **Under the FCRA:**

- A consumer report can be used only for a legitimate business need. A nosy neighbor does not have the right to order a report.
- A consumer reporting agency cannot report information that is more than 7 years old. (In the case of bankruptcies, the limit is 10 years.)
- An employer cannot request a consumer report on an employee without the employee's permission.
- Anyone who penalizes a consumer because of a credit report must reveal the name and address of the reporting agency that supplied the information.
- Upon request from a consumer, a reporting agency must disclose all information in his file.
- If a consumer tells an agency that some of the information in his file is incorrect, the agency must investigate. The consumer also has the right to give the agency a short report telling his side of the story.

# FAIR AND ACCURATE CREDIT TRANSACTIONS ACT

In identity theft, a fraudster steals his victim's personal information, such as social security number, credit card information, or mother's maiden name, and uses it to obtain credit or goods in the victim's name—in short, to wreak havoc in the victim's life. The goal of the Fair and Accurate Credit Transactions Act (FACTA) is to reduce identity theft.

FACTA provides that consumers are entitled by law to one free credit report every year from each of the three major reporting agencies: Equifax, Experian, and TransUnion. You can order these reports at **https://www.annualcreditreport.com**. Consumer advocates recommend that you check your credit reports every year to make sure they are accurate and also that no one else has been obtaining credit in your name. If you find any errors, notify the agency in writing and warn it that failing to make corrections is a violation of the law. At **http://www.ftc.gov/bcp/edu/pubs/consumer/credit/cre21.shtm**, the FTC offers advice on how to dispute credit report errors.

FACTA also created the National Fraud Alert System which permits consumers who fear they may be the victim of identity theft to place an alert in their credit files, warning financial institutions to investigate carefully before issuing any new credit. It also requires credit bureaus to share information about identity theft.

## FAIR DEBT COLLECTION PRACTICES ACT

Debt collectors can be ruthless in tracking down their victims. Congress passed the Fair Debt Collection Practices Act (FDCPA) because it was concerned that abusive debt collection practices could contribute to the number of personal bankruptcies, to marital instability, to the loss of jobs, and to invasions of privacy. Debt collection practices can also disrupt Super Bowl Sunday. Debt collectors seek to catch their prey off guard, and what better time than when the entire nation is at home, glued to the television? If the phone rings, sports fans assume it is a friend calling to gab about the game.

Is that legal? It depends. **Under the FDCPA, collectors may not:**

- Call or write a debtor who has notified the collector in writing that he wishes no further contact;
- Call or write a debtor who is represented by an attorney;
- Call a debtor before 8 a.m. or after 9 p.m.;
- Threaten a debtor or use obscene or abusive language;
- Call or visit the debtor at work if the consumer's employer prohibits such contact;
- Threaten to arrest consumers who do not pay their debts;
- Make other false or deceptive threats, that is, threats that would be illegal if carried out or which the collector has no intention of doing—such as suing the debtor or seizing property;
- Contact acquaintances of the debtor for any reason other than to locate the debtor (and then only once); or
- Tell acquaintances that the consumer is in debt.

For example, after Sherri Gradisher bounced a check for $81.30 at Doug Born's Smokehouse, she received three notices on the letterhead of the local sheriff's department threatening to arrest her. It turns out that the notices were sent by a private company, not by the sheriff's department (although the sheriff's department had given its permission). These letters violated the FDCPA.[8]

> **After Sherri Gradisher bounced a check, she received three notices on the letterhead of the local sheriff's department threatening to arrest her.**

---

[8] *Gradisher v. Check Enforcement Unit, Inc.,* 2002 U.S. Dist. LEXIS 6003.

# EQUAL CREDIT OPPORTUNITY ACT

**The Equal Credit Opportunity Act (ECOA) prohibits any creditor from discriminating against a borrower because of race, color, religion, national origin, sex, marital status, age, or because the borrower is receiving welfare.** A lender must respond to a credit application within 30 days. If a lender rejects an application, it must either tell the applicant why or notify him that he has the right to a written explanation of the reasons for this adverse action.

As the following case illustrates, the ECOA protects against a broad range of wrongdoing.

## TREADWAY v. GATEWAY CHEVROLET OLDSMOBILE INC.

362 F.3d 971; 2004 U.S. App. LEXIS 6325
UNITED STATES COURT OF APPEALS FOR THE SEVENTH CIRCUIT, 2004

### CASE SUMMARY

**Facts:** Gateway Chevrolet Oldsmobile (Gateway), a car dealership, sent an unsolicited letter to Tonja Treadway notifying her that she was "pre-approved" for the financing to purchase a car. Gateway did not provide financing itself; instead, it arranged loans through banks or finance companies.

Treadway called the dealer to say that she was interested in purchasing a used car. She divulged her social security number so that Gateway could obtain her credit report. Based on this report, the dealer determined that Treadway was not eligible for financing. This was not surprising, given that Gateway had purchased Treadway's name from a list of people who had recently filed for bankruptcy.

Instead of applying for a loan on behalf of Treadway, Gateway called her and invited her to come to the dealership. There she was told that Gateway had found a bank that would finance her transaction, but only if she purchased a new car and provided a cosigner. Treadway agreed to purchase a new car and came up with Pearlie Smith, her godmother, to serve as a cosigner.

Concerned as it was with customer convenience, Gateway had an agent deliver papers directly to Smith's house to be signed immediately. If Smith had read the papers before she signed them, she might have realized that she had committed herself to be the sole purchaser and owner of the car. But she had no idea that she was the owner until she began receiving bills on the car loan. After Treadway made the first payment on behalf of Smith, both women refused to pay more—Smith because she did not want a new car; Treadway because the

car was not hers. The car was repossessed, but the financing company continued to demand payment.

It turned out that Gateway was running a scam. The dealership would lure desperate prospects off the bankruptcy rolls and into the showroom with promises of financing for a used car, and then sell a new car to their "cosigner" (who was, in fact, the sole signer). Instead of selling a used car to Tonja Treadway, Gateway sold a new car to Pearlie Smith.

Treadway filed suit against Gateway, alleging that it had violated the ECOA by not notifying her that it had taken an adverse action against her.

**Issue:** *Did Gateway violate the ECOA?*

**Decision:** Yes, Gateway's action was an adverse action under the ECOA.

**Reasoning:** The ECOA requires any lender who rejects a loan application to tell the applicant the reason or notify her that she has the right to a written explanation.

By deciding not to send Treadway's application to *any* lender, Gateway effectively rejected it. But because Gateway did not tell customers that it had done the rejecting, they would naturally assume that a bank or other lender had turned them down. If the dealership's role was secret, it would have no accountability—it could discriminate against any and all without getting caught. Gateway could simply throw the credit report of every minority applicant in the "circular file" and none would be the wiser.

---

## EXAM *Strategy*

**Question:** Clyde goes into a Tesla dealership to investigate buying an electric sports car. He does not look as if he can afford a six-figure purchase, so the sales staff order a credit report on him. After all, no point in wasting their time. Do they have the right to order a report on Clyde? Which consumer statute applies?

**Strategy:** The Fair Credit Reporting Act regulates the issuance of consumer reports. These reports can only be used for a legitimate business need.

**Result:** Generally, a car dealership cannot obtain a consumer report on someone who simply asks general questions about prices and financing or who wants to test-drive a car. Nor can the dealer order a report to use in negotiations. So the Tesla dealership does not have the right to order a report on Clyde. However, a dealer does have the right to a report if it is needed to arrange financing requested by the consumer or to verify a buyer's creditworthiness when he presents a personal check to pay for the vehicle.

....................................................................................................

## CONSUMER LEASING ACT

If you, like many other consumers, lease a car rather than buy it, you are protected under the Consumer Leasing Act (CLA). The CLA does not apply to the rental of real property—that is, to house or apartment leases. **Before a lease is signed, a lessor must disclose the following in writing:**

- The number and amount of all required payments
- The total amount the consumer will have paid by the end of the lease
- Maintenance requirements and a description of the lessor's wear and use standards
- The consumer's right to purchase the leased property and at what price
- The consumer's right to terminate a lease early

The government brochure "Keys to Vehicle Leasing" is available at **http://www.federalreserve.gov/pubs/leasing**. It lays out the lessor's rights and compares the advantages and disadvantages of leasing versus purchasing a car.

## ▪ MAGNUSON-MOSS WARRANTY ACT ▪

The Magnuson-Moss Warranty Act does not require manufacturers or sellers to provide a warranty on their products. **The Act does require any supplier that offers a written warranty on a consumer product that costs more than $15 to disclose the terms of the warranty in simple, understandable language before the sale.** Required disclosure includes the following:

- The name and address of the person the consumer should contact to obtain warranty service.
- The parts that are covered and those that are not.
- What services the warrantor will provide, at whose expense, and for what period of time.
- A statement of what the consumer must do and what expenses he must pay.

Although suppliers are not required to offer a warranty, if they do offer one, they must indicate whether it is *full* or *limited*. Under a **full warranty,** the warrantor must promise to fix a defective product for a reasonable time without charge; if, after a reasonable number of efforts to fix the defective product, it still does not work, the consumer must have the right to a refund or a replacement without charge; but the warrantor is not required to cover damage caused by the consumer's unreasonable use.

## · CONSUMER PRODUCT SAFETY ·

In 1969, the federal government estimated that consumer products caused 30,000 deaths, 110,000 disabling injuries, and 20 million trips to the doctor. Toys were among the worst offenders, injuring 700,000 children a year. Children were cut by Etch-a-Sketch glass panels, choked by Zulu gun darts, and burned by Little Lady toy ovens. Although injured consumers had the right to seek damages under tort law, the goal of the Consumer Product Safety Act (CPSA) was to prevent injuries in the first place. This act created the Consumer Product Safety Commission (CSPC) to evaluate consumer products and develop safety standards. Manufacturers must report all potentially hazardous product defects to the CSPC within 24 hours of discovery. The Commission can impose civil and criminal penalties on those who violate its standards. Individuals have the right to sue under the CPSA for damages, including attorney's fees, from anyone who knowingly violates a consumer product safety rule.

**ETHICS**   Defective toys are an obvious source of concern because their victims are so helpless. Mattel's Jeep Wrangler Power Wheels toys are used by children as young as two years old. Thousands of these toys had defective wiring and over 150 of them caught on fire. Mattel ended up paying a fine of $1.1 million for failing to report this fire hazard. It also recalled millions of the cars.

Legally, Mattel was required to report defects in the toy within 24 hours. Instead, the company delayed its reports for months or years. According to Mattel Chairman and CEO Robert Eckert, Mattel failed to comply because the law was unreasonable and the company was better than the CSPC at evaluating when a hazard should be reported and how it should be handled.

Is Mattel's stance ethical? What would the Ethics Checklist in Chapter 2 indicate? ◆

## CHAPTER CONCLUSION

Virtually no one will go through life without reading an advertisement, ordering from a catalog, borrowing money, needing a credit report, or using a consumer product. It is important to know your rights.

## EXAM REVIEW

1. **UNFAIR PRACTICES** The Federal Trade Commission (FTC) prohibits "unfair and deceptive acts or practices." (p. 393)

..................................................................................................

2. **DECEPTIVE ADVERTISEMENTS** The FTC considers an advertisement to be deceptive if it contains an important misrepresentation or omission that is likely to mislead a reasonable consumer. (p. 393)

..................................................................................................

3. **BAIT AND SWITCH** FTC rules prohibit bait and switch advertisements. A merchant may not advertise a product and then try to get consumers to buy a different (more expensive) item. (p. 395)

..................................................................................................

4. **MAIL ORDER RULES** Under FTC rules on mail or telephone order merchandise, mail-order companies must ship an item within the time stated or, if no time is given, within 30 days after receipt of the order. (p. 395)

5. **DO-NOT-CALL REGISTRY** The FTC prohibits telemarketers from calling telephone numbers listed on its do-not-call registry. (p. 396)

6. **UNORDERED MERCHANDISE** Consumers may keep as a gift any unordered merchandise that they receive in the mail. (p. 396)

7. **DOOR-TO-DOOR RULES** Under the FTC door-to-door rules, a salesperson is required to notify the buyer that she has the right to cancel the transaction prior to midnight of the third business day thereafter. (p. 396)

8. **TILA DISCLOSURE** In all loans regulated by the Truth-in-Lending Act, the disclosure must be clear and in a sensible order. The lender must disclose the finance charge and the annual percentage rate. (p. 397)

9. **SUBPRIME LOANS** For subprime loans, a lender:
   - Must verify the borrower's ability to repay the loan from income and assets other than the home's value
   - May not charge a prepayment penalty if monthly payments can change in the first four years of the loan
   - Must collect property taxes and homeowner's insurance for all first mortgages  (p. 397)

10. **FCBA** Under the Fair Credit Billing Act, a credit card company must promptly investigate and respond to any consumer complaints about a credit card bill. (p. 398)

11. **FCRA** Under the Fair Credit Reporting Act:
   - A consumer report can be used only for a legitimate business need;
   - A consumer reporting agency cannot report out-of-date information;
   - An employer cannot request a consumer report on an employee without the employee's permission; and
   - Anyone who penalizes a consumer because of a credit report must reveal the name and address of the reporting agency that supplied the information. (p. 398)

12. **FACTA** The Fair and Accurate Credit Transactions Act permits consumers to obtain one free credit report every year from each of the three major reporting agencies. (p. 399)

13. **FDCPA** Under the Fair Debt Collection Practices Act, a debt collector may not harass or abuse debtors. (p. 399)

14. **ECOA** The Equal Credit Opportunity Act prohibits any creditor from discriminating against a borrower on the basis of race, color, religion, national origin, sex, marital status, age, or because the borrower is receiving welfare. (p. 400)

**Question:** Kathleen Carroll, a single woman, applied for an Exxon credit card. Exxon rejected her application without giving any specific reason and without providing the name of the credit bureau it had used. When Carroll asked for a reason for the rejection, she was told that the credit bureau did not have enough information about her to establish creditworthiness. In fact, Exxon had denied her credit application because she did not have a major credit card or a savings account, she had been employed for only one year, and she had no dependents. Did Exxon violate the law?

**Strategy:** Exxon violated two laws. Review the statutes in the consumer credit section of the chapter. (See the "Result" at the end of this section.)

**15.** **WARRANTIES** The Magnuson-Moss Warranty Act requires any supplier that offers a written warranty on a consumer product costing more than $15 to disclose the terms of the warranty in simple and readily understandable language before the sale. (p. 401)

**16.** **CPSC** The Consumer Product Safety Commission evaluates consumer products and develops safety standards. Manufacturers must report all potentially hazardous product defects to the CSPC within 24 hours of discovery. (p. 402)

**Question:** Joel Curtis was two and his brother, Joshua, was three years old when their father left both children asleep in the rear seat of his automobile while visiting a friend. His cigarette lighter was on the dashboard of the car. After awaking, Joshua began playing with the lighter and set fire to Joel's diaper. Do the parents have a claim against the manufacturer of the lighter under the Consumer Product Safety Act?

**Strategy:** The CPSA regulates unsafe products. Was the cigarette lighter unsafe? (See the "Result" at the end of this section.)

**14. Result:** The court held that Exxon violated both the Fair Credit Reporting Act (FCRA) and the Equal Credit Opportunity Act (ECOA). The FCRA requires Exxon to tell Carroll the name of the credit bureau that it used. Under the ECOA, Exxon was required to tell Carroll the real reasons for the credit denial.

**16. Result:** The court held that the defendant did not have a claim because there was no evidence that the manufacturer had knowingly violated a consumer product safety rule.

# PRACTICE EXAM

## MATCHING QUESTIONS

Match the following terms with their definitions:

___ A. FCBA

___ B. FDCPA

1. Requires lenders to disclose the terms of a loan

2. Regulates credit reports

___ C. FCRA            3. Regulates debt collectors

___ D. ECOA            4. Prohibits lenders from discriminating based on race, religion, and sex

___ E. TILA            5. Regulates disputes between consumers and their credit card companies

## TRUE/FALSE QUESTIONS

Circle true or false:

**1.** T  F  If a store advertises a product, it must have enough stock on hand to fill every order.

**2.** T  F  The FTC has established a national do-not-call registry.

**3.** T  F  Under usury laws, lenders are limited in the amount of interest they may charge.

**4.** T  F  Under the Truth-in-Lending Act, it does not matter how the information is disclosed, as long as it is disclosed someplace on the first page of the loan document.

**5.** T  F  A consumer reporting agency has the right to keep information in its files secret.

## MULTIPLE-CHOICE QUESTIONS

**6.** Which of the following statements is *not* true?

A. Mail-order companies must ship a product within the time stated.

B. If no time is stated, the mail-order company must ship within 30 days.

C. If a company cannot ship a product when promised, the company must cancel the order unless the customer indicates he wants the item.

D. If a company cannot ship the product within 30 days of the original shipping date, the company must cancel the order unless the customer indicates he still wants the item.

E. Each time the shipping date changes, the company must notify the customer.

**7.** If you receive a product in the mail that you did not order:

A. You must pay for it or return it.

B. You must pay for it only if you use it.

C. You must throw it away.

D. It is a gift to you.

E. You must pay for it but the company must reimburse you for postage.

**8.** Zach sells Cutco Knives door to door. Which of the following statements is *not* true?

A. The buyer has three days to cancel the order.

B. Zach must tell the buyer of her rights.

C. Zach must give the buyer a written notice of her rights.

D. The seller can cancel orally or in writing.

E. If the seller cancels, Zach must return her money within 10 days.

**9.** Depending on state law, if a lender violates the usury laws, the borrower could possibly be allowed to keep:

I. The interest that exceeds the usury limit

II. All the interest

III. All of the loan and the interest

A. I, II, and III

B. Only I

C. Only II

D. Only III

E. Neither I, II, nor III

10. Jodie is upset because her credit card bill shows a charge of $39 to a pornographic Web site that she never visited. Under the FCBA:

    A. She should call the credit card company to tell them that this charge is wrong.

    B. She should call her parents to let them handle the problem.

    C. The credit card company has 90 days to respond to a complaint by Jodie.

    D. The credit card company has the right to close out her account until the dispute is resolved.

    E. The credit card company must investigate a complaint and respond within 90 days.

## SHORT-ANSWER QUESTIONS

11. Process cheese food slices must contain at least 51 percent natural cheese. Imitation cheese slices, by contrast, contain little or no natural cheese and consist primarily of water and vegetable oil. Kraft, Inc. makes Kraft Singles, which are individually wrapped process cheese food slices. When Kraft began losing market share to imitation slices that were advertised as both less expensive and equally nutritious as Singles, Kraft responded with a series of advertisements informing consumers that Kraft Singles cost more than imitation slices because they are made from five ounces of milk. Kraft does use five ounces of milk in making each Kraft Single, but 30 percent of the calcium contained in the milk is lost during processing. Imitation slices contain the same amount of calcium as Kraft Singles. Are the Kraft advertisements deceptive?

12. Josephine Rutyna was a 60-year-old widow who suffered from high blood pressure and epilepsy. A bill collector from Collections Accounts Terminal, Inc. called her and demanded that she pay $56 she owed to Cabrini Hospital Medical Group. She told him that Medicare was supposed to pay the bill. Shortly thereafter, Rutyna received a letter from Collections that stated:

    > You have shown that you are unwilling to work out a friendly settlement with us to clear the above debt. Our field investigator has now been instructed to make an investigation in your neighborhood and to personally call on your employer. The immediate payment of the full amount, or a personal visit to this office, will spare you this embarrassment.

    Has Collections violated the law?

13. 
    > GET ENOUGH BROADLOOM TO CARPET ANY AREA OF YOUR HOME OR APARTMENT UP TO 150 SQUARE FEET CUT, MEASURED, AND READY FOR INSTALLATION FOR ONLY $77. GET 100% DUPONT CONTINUOUS FILAMENT NYLON PILE BROADLOOM. CALL COLLECT

    When customers called the number provided, New Rapids Carpet Center, Inc. sent salespeople to visit them at home to sell them carpet that was not as advertised—it was not continuous filament nylon pile broadloom, and the price was not $77. Has New Rapids violated a consumer law?

14. ETHICS: After TNT Motor Express hired Joseph Bruce Drury as a truck driver, it ordered a background check from Robert Arden & Associates. TNT provided Drury's social security number and date of birth, but not his middle name. Arden discovered that a Joseph Thomas Drury, who coincidentally had the same birthdate as Joseph Bruce Drury, had served a prison sentence for drunk driving. Not knowing that it had the wrong Drury, Arden reported this information to TNT, which promptly fired Drury. When he asked why, the TNT executive merely stated, "We do not discuss these matters." Did TNT violate the law? Whether or not TNT was in violation, did its executives behave ethically? Who would have been harmed or helped if TNT managers had informed Drury of the Arden report?

15. Advertisements for Listerine mouthwash claimed that it was as effective as flossing in preventing tooth plaque and gum disease. This statement was true, but only if the flossing was done incorrectly. In fact, many consumers do floss incorrectly. However, if flossing is done right, it is more effective against plaque and gum disease than Listerine. Is this advertisement deceptive? Does it violate §5 of the FTC Act?

16. ROLE REVERSAL: Prepare a short-answer question that focuses on deceptive advertisements. Include a sample ad in the question (either a real ad or one that you have made up).

## INTERNET RESEARCH PROBLEM

The Consumer Product Safety Commission (**http://www.cpsc.gov**) lists products that have been recalled and provides consumers with a telephone number for contacting the manufacturer. Choose a recalled product and telephone the manufacturer to find out how it is handling the problem. Also see if you can find the manufacturer's Web site to learn if it has disclosed the recall there. What do you think of the manner in which the manufacturer has handled the recall? Is the manufacturer providing adequate protection to consumers?

**You can find further practice problems in the Online Quiz at www.cengage.com/blaw/beatty.**

**Michelle has** owned a building on Main Street for more than 20 years. At the beginning, one of the businesses in the building was a drycleaning shop. The operators of the shop disposed of the cleaning fluids legally. Recent testing of the groundwater in a nearby park revealed that it was contaminated by drycleaning chemicals from that shop. Michelle must pay the cost of cleaning up the chemicals, even though they were disposed of legally years ago. The cost of the cleanup will far exceed the value of the building she owns.

**The cost of the cleanup will far exceed the value of the building she owns.**

## · INTRODUCTION ·

This scenario is based on a true story. The environment is a complex issue. It is not enough simply to say, "We are against pollution." The question is: Who will pay? Who will pay for past damage inflicted before anyone understood the harm that pollutants cause? Who will pay for current changes necessary to prevent damage now and in the future? Are car owners willing to spend $100 or $1,000 more per car to prevent air pollution? Are easterners ready to ban oil drilling in the Arctic National Wildlife Refuge in Alaska if that means higher prices for heating oil? Will loggers in the West give up their jobs to protect endangered species?

The cost-benefit trade-off is particularly complex in environmental issues because those who pay the cost often do not receive the benefit. If a company dumps toxic wastes into a stream, its shareholders benefit by avoiding the expense of safe disposal. Those who fish or drink the waters pay the real costs without receiving any of the benefit. Economists use the term **externality** to describe the situation in which people do not bear the full cost of their decisions. Externalities prevent the market system from achieving a clean environment on its own. Only government involvement can realign costs and benefits.

As we begin our discussion of environmental law, please note that violations are a serious matter. Those who break environmental laws are liable not only for civil damages, but also for *criminal* penalties under some statutes such as the Clean Water Act, the Resource Conservation and Recovery Act, and the Endangered Species Act.

## · AIR POLLUTION ·

October 26, 1948, was the day on which many Americans first became aware of the real dangers of air pollution. Almost half of the 10,000 people in Donora, Pennsylvania, fell ill when a weather inversion trapped industrial pollutants in the air, creating a lethal smog. Twenty residents ultimately died. Although air pollution rarely causes this type of acute illness, it can cause diseases that are annoying, chronic, or even fatal—such as pneumonia, bronchitis, emphysema, and cancer.

There are three major sources of air pollution: coal-burning utility plants, factories, and motor vehicles. Local regulation is ineffective in controlling air pollution. For instance, when cities limited pollution from factory smokestacks, plants simply built taller stacks that sent the pollution hundreds, or even thousands, of miles away. Recognizing the national nature of the problem, Congress passed the Clean Air Act of 1970.

### The Clean Air Act

**The Clean Air Act of 1970 requires the Environmental Protection Agency (EPA) to establish national air quality standards.** These standards must protect public health *without regard to cost*. Once the EPA has established standards, states must develop so-called State Implementation Plans (**SIPs**) to meet them. The Clean Air Act is, however, a work in progress. More than 100 million Americans still live in areas that do not meet the EPA's national air quality standards.

In the following case, a power plant argued that the EPA had imposed a solution whose cost far outweighed its benefit. There is only one Grand Canyon. Should visibility there be preserved at any cost?

**SIPs**
The Clean Air Act requires states to develop State Implementation Plans (SIPs) for meeting air quality standards set by the EPA.

# YOU *be the* JUDGE

## CENTRAL ARIZONA WATER CONSERVATION DISTRICT v. EPA

990 F.2d 1531, 1993 U.S. App. LEXIS 5881
United States Court of Appeals for
the Ninth Circuit, 1993

**Facts:** The Navaho Generating Station (NGS) is a power plant 12 miles from the Grand Canyon. To protect the views of this national treasure, the EPA ordered NGS to reduce its sulfur dioxide emissions by 90 percent. To do so would cost NGS $430 million initially in capital expenditures and then $89.6 million annually. Average winter visibility in the Grand Canyon would be improved by at most 7 percent, but perhaps less. NGS sued to prevent implementation of the EPA's order. A court may nullify an EPA order if it determines that the agency action was arbitrary and capricious.

**You Be the Judge:** Did the EPA act arbitrarily and capriciously in requiring NGS to spend half a billion dollars to improve winter visibility at the Grand Canyon by at most 7 percent?

**Argument for NGS:** This case is a perfect example of environmentalism run amok. Half a billion dollars for the chance of increasing winter visibility at the Grand Canyon by 7 percent? Winter visitors to the Grand Canyon would undoubtedly prefer that NGS provide them with a free lunch rather than a 7 percent improvement in visibility. The EPA order is simply a waste of money.

**Argument for the EPA:** How can NGS, or anyone else, measure the benefit of protecting a national treasure like the Grand Canyon? Even people who never have and never will visit it during the winter sleep better at night knowing that the Canyon is protected. NGS has been causing harm to the Grand Canyon, and now it should remedy the damage.

## New Sources of Pollution

Some states had air so clean that they could have allowed air quality to decline and still have met EPA standards. However, the Clean Air Act declared that one of its purposes was to "protect and enhance" air quality. Using this phrase, the Sierra Club sued the EPA to prevent it from approving any SIPs that met EPA standards but nonetheless permitted a decline in air quality. As a result of this suit, the EPA developed a **prevention of significant deterioration (PSD) program**. **No one may undertake a building project that will cause a major increase in pollution without first obtaining a permit from the EPA.** The agency will grant permits only if an applicant can demonstrate that (1) its emissions will not cause an overall decline in air quality and (2) it has installed the **best available control technology** for every pollutant.

The PSD program prohibits any deterioration in current air quality, *regardless of health impact*. In essence, national policy values a clean environment for its own sake, apart from any health benefits.

**Prevention of significant deterioration (PSD) program**
No one may undertake a building project that will cause a major increase in pollution without first obtaining a permit from the EPA.

## · WATER POLLUTION ·

**Polluted water can cause a number of loathsome diseases.**

One day, thousands of Milwaukeeans began to suffer nausea, cramps, and diarrhea. The suspected culprit? Cryptosporidium, a tiny protozoan that usually resides in the intestines of cattle and other animals. Ironically, the parasite may have entered Milwaukee's water supply at a purification plant on Lake Michigan. Officials suspect that infected runoff from dairy farms spilled into Lake Michigan near the plant's intake pipe. Doctors advised those with a damaged immune system (such as AIDS patients) to avoid drinking municipal water. Most Milwaukeeans were taking no chances—more than 800,000 switched to boiled or bottled water.

Polluted water can cause a number of loathsome diseases, such as typhus and dysentery. But by 1930, most American cities had dramatically reduced outbreaks of waterborne diseases by chlorinating their water. (The parasite that caused the Milwaukee outbreak is relatively immune to chlorine.) However, industrial discharges into the water supply have increased rapidly, with a significant impact on water quality. These industrial wastes may not induce acute illnesses like typhus, but they can cause serious diseases such as cancer. There is more at stake than health alone; clean water is valued for esthetics, recreation, and fishing.

# The Clean Water Act

In 1972, Congress passed a statute, now called the Clean Water Act (CWA), with two ambitious goals: (1) to make all navigable water suitable for swimming and fishing; and (2) to eliminate the discharge of pollutants into navigable water. Like the Clean Air Act, the CWA sets goals without regard to cost. **In support of its goals, the CWA prohibits anyone from discharging pollution into water without a permit from the EPA.** However, like the Clean Air Act, the CWA's goals have not been met.

## Industrial Discharges

**The CWA prohibits any single producer from discharging pollution into water without a permit from the EPA.** Before granting a permit, the EPA must set limits, by industry, on the amount of each type of pollution any single producer (called a **point source**) can discharge. These limits must be based on the **best available technology.** The EPA faces a gargantuan task in determining the best available technology that each industry can use to reduce pollution. Furthermore, standards become obsolete quickly as technology changes.

**Point source**
A single producer of pollution.

## Water Quality Standards

The CWA requires states to set EPA-approved water quality standards and develop plans to achieve them. The first step in developing a plan is to determine how each body of water is used. Standards may vary depending upon the designated use—higher for recreational lakes than for a river used to irrigate farmland. No matter what the water's designated use, standards may not be set at a level lower than its current condition. Congress is not in the business of permitting more pollution.

# Wetlands

Wetlands are the transition areas between land and open water. They may look like swamps—they may even be swamps—but their unattractive appearance should not disguise their vital role in the aquatic world. They are natural habitats for many fish and wildlife. They also serve as a filter for neighboring bodies of water, trapping chemicals and sediments. Moreover, they are an important aid in flood control because they can absorb a high level of water and then release it slowly after the emergency is past.

**The CWA prohibits any discharge of dredge and fill material into wetlands without a permit.** Although filling in wetlands requires a permit, many other activities that harm wetlands, such as draining them, originally did not. (However, many states require permits for draining wetlands.) After some particularly egregious abuses, the EPA issued regulations to limit the destruction of wetlands. These new regulations were, however, successfully challenged in the courts.[1] The EPA then rewrote the regulations to accomplish the same goal within the parameters set out by the courts. These new regulations will certainly be challenged, too.

---

[1] *National Mining Ass'n v. U.S. Army Corps of Engineers,* 145 F.3d 1399 (D.C. Cir. 1998).

Although, in theory, the government's official policy is no net loss of wetlands, the reality has been different. Since the country was settled, about half of the original 230 million acres of wetlands in the continental United States have been destroyed. In 2002, the Bush administration amended the "no net loss" rule so that it could issue waivers in some cases. The Web site **http:// www.nwi.fws.gov** shows an inventory of wetlands in the United States.

## SEWAGE

Plumbing drains must be attached to either a septic system or a sewer line. A septic system is, in effect, a freestanding waste treatment plant. A sewer line, on the other hand, feeds into a publicly owned wastewater treatment plant, also known as a municipal sewage plant. **Under the CWA, a municipality must obtain a permit for any discharge from a wastewater treatment plant.** To obtain a permit, the municipality must first treat the waste to reduce its toxicity. However, taxpayers have stubbornly resisted the large increases in taxes or fees necessary to fund required treatments. Since the fines imposed by the EPA are almost always less than the cost of treatment, some cities have been slow to comply. There have, however, been some notable successes. For instance, the Charles River in Boston, which was the inspiration for the pop song "Love that Dirty Water," recently received a grade of B++ by the EPA. The river is now always safe for boating and is swimmable 63 percent of the time.

### EXAM *Strategy*

**Question:** Edward lives on a ranch near Wind River. He uses water from the river for irrigation. To divert more water to his ranch, he builds a dike in the river using scrap metal, cottonwood trees, car bodies, and a washing machine. This material does not harm downstream water. Has Edward violated the Clean Water Act?

**Strategy:** The CWA prohibits the discharge of pollution. Was this pollution?

**Result:** Yes, the court ruled that the material Edward placed in the water was pollution. It was irrelevant that the material did not flow downstream.

## ▪ WASTE DISPOSAL ▪

Do not be fooled by the name. Love Canal in Niagara Falls, New York, was decidedly an unlovely place after 1945, when Hooker Chemical Co. dumped 21,800 tons of chemicals into the Canal and on nearby land. Hooker then sold the land to the local school board to build an elementary school. Children swam in the Canal. They played with hot balls of chemical residue—what they called "fire stones"—that popped up through the ground. Cancer, epilepsy, respiratory problems, and skin diseases were common in the neighborhood. Finally, a national health emergency was declared, and 800 families were relocated.

In its time, what Hooker did was not unusual. Companies historically dumped waste in waterways, landfills, or open dumps. Out of sight was out of mind. Waste disposal continues to be a major problem in the United States. It has been estimated that the cost of cleaning up existing waste products will exceed $1 trillion. At the same time, the country continues to produce more than six billion tons of agricultural, commercial, industrial, and domestic waste each year.

Two major statutes regulate wastes. The Resource Conservation and Recovery Act (RCRA) focuses on preventing future Love Canals by regulating the production and disposal of solid wastes, both toxic and otherwise. The Comprehensive Environmental Response, Compensation, and Liability Act (CERCLA), also referred to as "Superfund," focuses on cleaning up existing hazardous waste sites.

# RESOURCE CONSERVATION AND RECOVERY ACT

The RCRA establishes rules for treating both hazardous wastes and other forms of solid waste (such as ordinary garbage). The disposal of nonhazardous solid waste has generally been left to the states, but they must follow guidelines set by the RCRA. The RCRA:

- Bans new open garbage dumps;
- Requires that garbage be sent to sanitary landfills;
- Sets minimum standards for landfills;
- Requires landfills to monitor nearby groundwater;
- Requires states to develop a permit program for landfills; and
- Provides some financial assistance to aid states in waste management.

**ECONOMICS AND THE LAW**   The federal Office of Management and Budget (OMB) objected to the solid waste regulations that the EPA intended to issue under the RCRA because, according to the OMB's calculations, complying with the proposed regulations would have cost more than $19 billion for every life saved. Not worth it, said the OMB. As a result, the EPA's revised regulations are more flexible than the original version.

This dispute typifies the ongoing conflict in environmental law. On the one hand, the EPA argues that scientific data are uncertain and the health risks of pollutants may be much worse than we realize. The EPA's goal is to stop pollution virtually without regard to cost. The OMB, on the other hand, prefers to base decisions on a numerical cost-benefit analysis. The OMB believes that a clean-air-and-water-for-its-own-sake approach makes little economic sense. Is a human life worth $19 billion? Is your life?  ◆

The RCRA also regulates hazardous wastes. **It provides that anyone who creates, transports, stores, treats, or disposes of more than a certain quantity of hazardous wastes must apply for an EPA permit.** All hazardous wastes must be tracked from creation to final disposal. They must be disposed of at a certified facility.

As the following case indicates, violating the RCRA is a serious matter.

## UNITED STATES OF AMERICA v. KELLY

### 1999 U.S. APP. LEXIS 2093
#### UNITED STATES COURT OF APPEALS FOR THE SEVENTH CIRCUIT, 1999

### CASE SUMMARY

**Facts:** Leo Kelly owned and operated a business that removed underground storage tanks. CCF, Inc. hired Kelly to remove six underground storage tanks from its property. Small amounts of hazardous waste—gasoline, heating oil, diesel fuel and sludge—remained in the tanks. Instead of taking the tanks to a licensed facility, Kelly sent them to Winter Auto Salvage, which does not sound like, and in fact was not, a licensed hazardous waste facility. A jury convicted Kelly of violating the

RCRA and the court sentenced him to 41 months in prison. Kelly appealed.

**Issue:** *Did Kelly violate the RCRA?*

**Decision:** The jury had sufficient facts to convict Kelly.

**Reasoning:** Kelly says he believed the substance in the barrels was nothing but gasoline. Although he admits gasoline is "hazardous," he alleges that it is not "waste" and, therefore, not subject to the RCRA. Kelly argues that the jury should have been instructed to consider "hazardous" and "waste" as two separate components, each with its own definition.

The jurors had to decide whether Kelly knowingly transported "hazardous waste," as defined by the RCRA. They heard conflicting testimony and, ultimately, did not believe Kelly. That was their right.

## SUPERFUND

**Superfund's** official name is the Comprehensive Environmental Response, Compensation, and Liability Act (CERCLA). Its goal is to clean up hazardous wastes that have been improperly dumped in the past.

The philosophy of Superfund is that "the polluter pays." **Therefore, anyone who has *ever* owned or operated a site on which hazardous wastes are found, or who has transported wastes to the site, or who has arranged for the disposal of wastes that were released at the site, is liable for (1) the cost of cleaning up the site; (2) any damage done to natural resources; and (3) any required health assessments.**

In a "shovels first, lawyers later" approach, Congress established a $15.2 billion revolving trust fund for the EPA to use in cleaning up sites even before obtaining reimbursement from those responsible for the damage. Any reimbursements go into the trust fund to be used to repair other sites. The trust fund was initially financed by a tax on the oil and chemical industries, which produce the bulk of hazardous waste. In 1995, however, the taxes expired, and Congress refused to renew them. Since then, the EPA has had to rely on reimbursements from polluters (which recently have been running $1 billion a year) and congressional appropriations of about $1.2 billion a year. That sounds like a lot of money but, according to the EPA, there could be as many as 355,000 hazardous waste sites that would require up to $250 billion to restore. Currently the EPA has a list of about 1,200 sites that represent a "significant risk to human health or the environment," but the agency spends about half of its annual Superfund budget on just 11 of these sites. Meanwhile, one in four Americans, including 10 million children below the age of 12, lives within four miles of a Superfund site. To find out about hazardous waste sites in your community, click on **http://www.epa.gov/oerrpage/superfund/sites.**

### EXAM *Strategy*

**Question:** In 1963, FMC Corp. purchased a manufacturing plant in Virginia from American Viscose Corp., the owner of the plant since 1937. During World War II, the government's War Production Board had commissioned American Viscose to make rayon for airplanes and truck tires. In 1982, inspections revealed carbon disulfide, a chemical used to manufacture this rayon, in groundwater near the plant. American Viscose was out of business by then. Who is responsible for cleaning up the carbon disulfide? Under what statute?

**Strategy:** Look at the statutes that govern waste disposal.

**Result:** Both FMC and the U.S. government are liable for clean-up under CERCLA.

## · NATURAL RESOURCES ·

Thus far, this chapter has focused on the regulation of pollution. Congress has also passed statutes whose purpose is to preserve the country's natural resources.

# NATIONAL ENVIRONMENTAL POLICY ACT

**The National Environmental Policy Act of 1969 (NEPA) requires all *federal agencies* to prepare an *environmental impact statement* (EIS) for every major federal action significantly affecting the quality of the human environment.** An EIS is a major undertaking—often hundreds, if not thousands, of pages long. It must discuss:

- Environmental consequences of the proposed action
- Available alternatives
- Direct and indirect effects
- Energy requirements
- Impact on urban quality, historic and cultural resources and
- Means to mitigate adverse environmental impacts

Once a draft report is ready, the federal agency must hold a hearing to allow for outside comments.

The EIS requirement applies not only to actions *undertaken* by the federal government, but also to activities *regulated* or *approved* by the government. For instance, the following projects required an EIS:

- Expanding the Snowmass ski area in Aspen, Colorado—because approval was required by the Forest Service
- Killing a herd of wild goats that was causing damage at the Olympic National Park (outside Seattle)
- Creating a golf course outside Los Angeles—because the project required a government permit to build in wetlands.

The EIS process is controversial. If a project is likely to have an important impact, environmentalists almost always litigate the adequacy of the EIS. Industry advocates argue that environmentalists are simply using the EIS process to delay—or halt—any projects they oppose. In 1976, seven years after NEPA was passed, a dam on the Teton River in Idaho burst, killing 17 people and causing $1 billion in property damage. The Department of the Interior had built the dam in the face of allegations that its EIS was incomplete; it did not, for example, confirm that a large earth-filled dam resting on a riverbed was safe. To environmentalists, this tragedy graphically illustrated the need for a thorough EIS.

Researchers have found that the EIS process generally has a beneficial impact on the environment. The mere prospect of preparing an EIS tends to eliminate the worst projects. Litigation over the EIS eliminates the next weakest group. If an agency does a good-faith EIS, honestly looking at the available alternatives, projects tend to be kinder to the environment, at little extra cost.

# ENDANGERED SPECIES ACT

**The Endangered Species Act (ESA):**

- Requires the Secretary of Commerce or the Secretary of the Interior to prepare a list of species that are in danger of becoming extinct;
- Requires the government to develop plans to revive these species;
- Requires all federal agencies to ensure that their actions will not jeopardize an endangered species;
- Prohibits any sale or transport of these species;

- Makes any taking of an endangered animal species unlawful—taking is defined as harassing, harming, killing, or capturing any endangered species or modifying its habitat in such a way that its population is likely to decline; and

- Prohibits the taking of any endangered plant species on federal property.

No environmental statute has been more controversial than the ESA. In theory, everyone is in favor of saving endangered species. In practice, however, the cost of saving a species can be astronomical. One of the earliest ESA battles involved the snail darter—a three-inch fish that lived in the Little Tennessee River. The Supreme Court upheld a decision under the ESA to halt work on a dam that would have blocked the river, flooding 16,500 acres of farmland and destroying the snail darter's habitat. To the dam's supporters, this decision was ludicrous: stopping a dam (on which $100 million in taxpayer money had already been spent) to save a little fish that no one had ever even thought of before the dam (or damn) controversy. The real agenda, they argued, was simply to halt development. Environmental advocates argued, however, that the wanton destruction of whole species will ultimately and inevitably lead to disaster for humankind. In the end, Congress overruled the Supreme Court and authorized completion of the dam. It turned out that the snail darter has survived in other rivers.

The snail darter was the first in a long line of ESA controversies that have included charismatic animals such as bald eagles, grizzly bears, and bighorn sheep but also more obscure fauna such as the Banbury Springs limpet and the triple-ribbed milkvetch. In 2007, a federal court moved to protect the delta smelt by ordering officials to shut down temporarily pumps that supplied as much as a third of southern California's water.[2] Opponents argue that too much time and money have been spent on litigation to save too few species of too little importance. Also, there is some evidence that the statute has a perverse impact—to avoid environmental regulation, landowners sometimes destroy a habitat to ensure that an endangered species will not occupy it. The following case, however, discusses the advantages of the ESA.

## GIBBS v. BABBITT

214 F.3d 483, 2000 U.S. App. LEXIS 12280
UNITED STATES COURT OF APPEALS FOR THE FOURTH CIRCUIT, 2000

### CASE SUMMARY

**Facts:** The red wolf used to roam throughout the southeastern United States. Owing to wetlands drainage, dam construction, and hunting, this wolf is now on the endangered species list. The Fish and Wildlife Service (FWS) trapped the remaining red wolves, placed them in a captive breeding program, and then reintroduced them into the wild in national wildlife refuges in North Carolina and Tennessee.

After reintroduction, about 41 red wolves wandered from federal refuges onto private property. Richard Mann shot a red wolf that he feared might threaten his cattle. Mann pled guilty to violating a provision of the ESA that prohibits the taking of any endangered species without a permit.

Under the commerce clause of the Constitution, Congress may only regulate commercial activity if it has an impact on interstate commerce. Plaintiffs filed suit against the U.S. government, alleging that the ESA was unconstitutional because it did not affect interstate commerce.

**Issue:** *Is the anti-taking provision of the ESA constitutional?*

**Decision:** The ESA is constitutional.

**Reasoning:** The red wolf has great impact on interstate commerce:

- Red wolves are part of the $29 billion national tourism industry. Many tourists travel each year to take part in "howling events"—evenings spent studying wolves and listening to their howls. It has been predicted that the wolves

---

[2] *Natural Resources Defense Council v. Kempthorne*, 2007 U.S. Dist. LEXIS 91968.

could contribute somewhere between $40 and $180 million per year to the economy of northeastern North Carolina.

- The red wolf is a subject of scientific research, which is an important industry on its own. And this research benefits us all—approximately 50 percent of all modern medicines are derived from wild plants or animals.

- It is also possible that if the red wolf thrives, it could be hunted for its pelt. The American alligator is a case in point. In 1975, the American alligator was nearing extinction and listed as endangered, but by 1987 conservation efforts restored the species. Now there is a vigorous trade in alligator hides.

- Mann shot a wolf that was threatening his livestock. Killing livestock also has an impact on interstate commerce. Under the commerce clause, any impact counts even if negative. It is also possible that red wolves help farms by preying on animals like raccoons, deer, and rabbits that destroy their crops.

Congress has the right to decide that protecting red wolves will one day produce a substantial commercial benefit to this country and that failure to preserve it may result in permanent, though unascertainable, loss. If a species becomes extinct, we are left to speculate forever on what we might have learned or what we may have realized. If we conserve the species, it will be available for study by and the benefit of future generations.

## CHAPTER CONCLUSION

**Environmental laws have a pervasive impact on our lives.** The cost has been great—whether it is the higher price for electricity produced in clean plants or the time spent filling out environmental impact statements. Some argue that cost is irrelevant, that a clean environment has incalculable value for its own sake. Others insist on a more pragmatic approach and want to know if the benefits outweigh the costs.

## EXAM REVIEW

1. **AIR** The Clean Air Act of 1970 requires the Environmental Protection Agency (EPA) to establish national air quality standards. (p. 409)

2. **WATER** The Clean Water Act prohibits anyone from discharging pollution into water without a permit from the EPA. (p. 411)

**EXAM Strategy**

**Question:** In theory, Astro Circuit Corp. in Lowell, Massachusetts, pretreated its industrial waste to remove toxic metals but, in practice, the factory was producing twice as much wastewater as the treatment facility could handle and, therefore, was dumping the surplus directly into the city sewer. It was David Boldt's job to keep the production line moving. Has Boldt violated the law by dumping polluted water into the city sewer? What penalties might he face?

**Strategy:** Whenever water is involved, look at the provisions of the Clean Water Act. (See the "Result" at the end of this section.)

**3.** **INDUSTRIAL DISCHARGES** The CWA prohibits any single producer from discharging pollution into water without a permit from the EPA. (p. 411)

**4.** **WATER QUALITY STANDARDS** The CWA requires states to set EPA-approved water quality standards and develop plans to achieve them. (p. 411)

**5.** **WETLANDS** The Clean Water Act prohibits any discharge of dredge and fill material into wetlands without a permit. (p. 411)

**6.** **SEWAGE** Under the Clean Water Act, a municipality must obtain a permit for any discharge from a wastewater treatment plant. (p. 412)

**7.** **RCRA** The Resource Conservation and Recovery Act establishes rules for treating hazardous wastes and other forms of solid waste. (p. 413)

**8.** **SUPERFUND** Under Superfund (CERCLA), anyone who has *ever* owned or operated a site on which hazardous wastes are found, or who has transported wastes to the site, or who has arranged for the disposal of wastes that were released at the site, is liable for (1) the cost of cleaning up the site, (2) any damage done to natural resources, and (3) any required health assessments. (p. 414)

**9.** **NEPA** The National Environmental Policy Act requires all federal agencies to prepare an environmental impact statement for every major federal action significantly affecting the quality of the environment. (p. 415)

**EXAM Strategy**

**Question:** The U.S. Forest Service planned to build a road in the Nez Perce National Forest in Idaho to provide access to loggers. The road was very narrow. Is the Forest Service required to prepare an environmental impact statement before building it?

**Strategy:** Will the road have a significant impact on the quality of the environment? (See the "Result" at the end of this section.)

**10.** **ESA** The Endangered Species Act prohibits activities that cause harm to endangered species. (p. 415)

**2. Result:** Although Boldt was in an unfortunate situation—he could have lost his job if he had not been willing to dump the industrial waste—he was found guilty of a criminal violation of the Clean Water Act. There are worse things than being fired—being fired *and* sent to prison.

**9. Result:** Although the road itself may not be significant enough to require an impact statement, its purpose was to provide access for logging, which did require an EIS.

## PRACTICE EXAM

### MATCHING QUESTIONS

___ A. EPA

___ B. ESA

___ C. NEPA

___ D. CERCLA

___ E. RCRA

1. Regulates the clean-up of hazardous wastes improperly dumped in the past
2. Establishes rules for treating newly created wastes
3. Protects red wolves
4. The agency that regulates environmental policy in the United States
5. Requires all federal agencies to prepare an environmental impact statement

### TRUE/FALSE QUESTIONS

1. T   F   In establishing national standards under the Clean Air Act, the EPA need not consider the cost of compliance.

2. T   F   The Clean Water Act requires anyone discharging pollution into water to obtain a permit from the EPA.

3. T   F   Any individual, business or federal agency that significantly affects the quality of the environment must file an environmental impact statement.

4. T   F   Since the United States was founded, about half of its existing wetlands have been destroyed.

5. T   F   Violating the environmental laws can be a criminal offense, punishable by a prison term.

### MULTIPLE-CHOICE QUESTIONS

6. Which of the following statements is true of Superfund?

   I. Anyone who has ever owned a site is liable for clean-up costs.

   II. Anyone who has ever transported waste to a site is liable for clean-up costs.

   III. Anyone who has ever disposed of waste at a site is liable for clean-up costs.

   A.  Neither I, II, nor III

   B.  I, II, and III

   C.  I and II

   D.  II and III

   E.  I and III

7. Which of the following statements is true?

   I. The EPA sets national air quality standards.

   II. The EPA develops plans to meet air quality standards.

   III. States set their own air quality standards.

   IV. The states develop plans to meet air quality standards.

   A.  II and III

   B.  III and IV

   C.  I and IV

   D.  I, III, and IV

   E.  I and II

8. Which of the following statements are true about the *Central Arizona* case? (There can be more than one correct answer.)

   A.  Emissions from the Navajo Generating Station (NGS) were greatly degrading the view of the Grand Canyon.

   B.  The cost of reducing emissions from the (NGS) was trivial.

   C.  The EPA performed a cost-benefit analysis before ordering the NGS to reduce its emissions.

D. Under the Clean Air Act, the cost of reducing the emissions was irrelevant.

E. A court may overturn an EPA order if it believes that the preponderance of the evidence is on the plaintiff's side.

9. The RCRA does *not:*

A. Ban new open garbage dumps

B. Require garbage to be treated before it is taken to an existing dump

C. Require landfills to monitor groundwater

D. Provide financial assistance to states

E. Require states to develop a permit program for landfills

10. An Environmental Impact Statement is *not* required to include a discussion of:

A. The commercial value of any threatened species

B. Available alternatives to the proposed actions

C. Direct impacts

D. Indirect impacts

E. Impact on cultural resources

## SHORT-ANSWER QUESTIONS

11. Tariq Ahmad owned Shankman Laboratories. He decided to dispose of some of the lab's hazardous chemicals by shipping them to his home in Pakistan. He sent the chemicals to Castelazo & Associates (in the United States) to prepare the materials for shipment. Ahmad did not tell the driver who picked up the chemicals that they were hazardous, nor did he give the driver any written documentation. Ahmad had packed the chemicals hurriedly in flimsy containers that were unsafe for transporting hazardous materials. He also grossly misrepresented to Castelazo the amount and type of hazardous material that he was shipping to Pakistan. Has Ahmad violated U.S. law? What penalties might he face?

12. The marbled murrelet is a rare seabird that nests only in old-growth forests on the West Coast. Logging has destroyed so much of its habitat that its numbers in California have declined from 60,000 to between 2,000 and 5,000. Pacific Lumber Co. wanted to harvest trees from 137 acres of land it owned in the Owl Creek forest in California. It originally received approval to log, on the condition that it would cooperate with regulators to protect the murrelet. But the company sneaked in one weekend and cut down trees before it had done anything for the murrelet. Caught in the act, it promised no more logging until it had a plan to protect the birds. This time it waited until the long weekend over Thanksgiving to take down some more trees. Finally, a federal court ordered a permanent halt to any further logging. There was no evidence that the company had harmed the murrelet. Had it violated the law?

13. YOU BE THE JUDGE WRITING PROBLEM: The Lordship Point Gun Club operated a trap and skeet shooting club in Stratford, Connecticut, for 70 years. During this time, customers deposited close to 5 million tons of lead shot and 11 million pounds of clay target fragments on land around the club and in Long Island Sound. Forty-five percent of sediment samples taken from the Sound exceeded the established limits for lead. Was the Gun Club in violation of the RCRA? **Argument for the Gun Club:** The Gun Club does not dispose of hazardous wastes, within the meaning of the RCRA. Congress meant the statute to apply only to companies in the business of manufacturing articles that produce hazardous waste. If the Gun Club happens to produce wastes, that is only incidental to the normal use of a product. **Argument for the plaintiff:** Under the RCRA, lead shot is hazardous waste. The law applies to anyone who produces hazardous waste, no matter how.

14. Suppose that you are the manager of the General Motors Hummer plant in Mishawaka, Indiana. Hummers are the successor to the U.S. Army jeep and have become popular recreational vehicles among the rich and famous. Arnold Schwarzenegger has several. The Hummer requires special protective paint that, as it turns out, reacts with other chemicals during the application process to create ozone, a pollutant. You want to increase production of Hummers. Are there any legal requirements you must observe?

15. Nucan Aluminum Corp. hired Mozart Co. to dispose of an emulsion it used during manufacturing. This

emulsion contained hazardous materials. Without Nucan's knowledge, Mozart dumped the emulsion into a borehole that connected to deep underground mines along the Susquehanna River in Pennsylvania. You can guess what happened next. Approximately 100,000 gallons of water contaminated with hazardous substances spilled from the borehole into the river. Is Nucan liable?

16. ROLE REVERSAL: Write a short-answer question that poses an ethics or economics question under the environmental laws.

# INTERNET RESEARCH PROBLEM

Chart the air quality in your area over the past decade. How does it compare with the national average? How many days a year is it unhealthy?

**You can find further practice problems in the Online Quiz at www.cengage.com/blaw/beatty.**

# CHAPTER 26

# CYBERLAW

**Garrett always** said that his computer was his best friend. He was online all the time, sending instant messages to his friends, listening to music, doing research for his courses, and, okay, maybe playing a few games now and again. Occasionally, the computer could be annoying. It would crash once in a while, trashing part of a paper he had forgotten to save. And there was the time that a copy of an e-mail he sent Lizzie complaining about Caroline somehow ended up in Caroline's mailbox. He was tired of all the spam advertising pornographic Web sites. But these things happen and, despite the petty annoyances, his computer was an important part of his life.

Then one day, Garrett received a panicked instant message from a teammate on the college wrestling squad telling him to click on a certain Web site pronto to see someone they knew. Garrett eagerly clicked on the Web site and discovered, to his horror, that *he* was featured—in the nude. The Web site was selling DVDs

> **Garrett eagerly clicked on the Web site and discovered, to his horror, that *he* was featured—in the nude.**

422

showing him and other members of the wrestling team in the locker room in various states of undress. Other DVDs, from other locker and shower rooms, were for sale, too, showing football players and wrestlers from dozens of universities. No longer trusting technology, Garrett pulled on his running shoes and dashed over to the office of his business law professor.

While the Internet has opened up enormous opportunities in both our business and personal lives, it has also created the need for new laws, both to pave the way for these opportunities and to limit their dangers. This chapter deals with issues that are unique to the cyberworld, such as online privacy, hacking, and spam.

Before beginning the chapter in earnest, let's return briefly to Garrett, the wrestler. What recourse does Garrett have for his Internet injuries? The nude video incident happened at Illinois State University and seven other colleges. Approximately thirty athletes filed suit against GTE and PSINet for selling the DVDs online, but the two Web hosts were found not liable under the Communications Decency Act because they had not produced the DVDs themselves; they had simply permitted the sale of someone else's content. What about Garrett's other computer injuries? Lizzie was not being a good friend, but it was perfectly legal for her to forward Garrett's e-mail to Caroline. The federal Can-Spam Act prohibits spam—unsolicited commercial e-mail—but a lawsuit is a slow and awkward tool for killing such a flourishing weed. Thus far, the available legal tools have been relatively ineffectual (as you can tell from your e-mail inbox).

## · PRIVACY ·

Computerized communication can be wonderfully efficient but also alarmingly dangerous. Consumers enter the most personal data—credit card numbers, bank accounts, lists of friends, medical information, product preferences—on the Internet. Who will have access to this data? Who can see it, use it, sell it? Many people fear that the Internet is a very large window through which the government, employers, business, and criminals can find out more than they should about you and your money, habits, beliefs, and health. Even e-mail has its dangers: Who has not been embarrassed by an e-mail that ended up in the wrong mailbox?

Many commentators argue that, without significant changes in the law, our privacy will be obliterated. At the moment, however, privacy on the Internet is very much like the weather—everyone talks about it, but (so far) no one has done much about it.

### OF COOKIES AND CACHES

If you order a book from Amazon.com, you may notice that the next time you log on, you will be greeted with the message, "Hello, [Your Name]. We have *recommendations* for you." Click on the link and you may find that, because you bought a GMAT study guide the first time, Amazon will entice you with other guides for standardized tests. However did Amazon know? Many Web sites automatically place a cookie on the hard drive of your computer when you visit them. **A cookie is a small file that includes an identification number and may also include personal data such as your address, phone and credit card numbers, and searches you have made or advertisements you have clicked on.**

**Personally identifiable information (PII)**
Data that identify a user of a Web site, such as name and address.

Cookies raise privacy issues. When you travel around the Internet, cookies create a file that could come back to haunt you. Although much of the information gathered is anonymous (that is, the consumer is identified only by a computer identification number), this anonymous information can be linked to **personally identifiable information (PII)**, such as name and address. One company markets a databank with the names of 150 million registered voters. Anyone can buy a list of voters that is sliced and diced however they want, say, Republicans between the ages of 45 and 60 with Hispanic surnames and incomes greater than $50,000.

If marketers can put together a databank of Hispanic Republican voters, they can also find out that you have visited a Web site for recovering alcoholics or unrecovered gamblers or Nazi sympathizers. Do you want information about every Web site you visit to be public? So far, consumers have not generally complained about Web data collection, because it all happens so secretly they are not aware of it. And besides, cookies make life easier. Who wants to have to enter a login name and password every time you return to your favorite sites?

Even without cookies, your computer creates a file about you. When you surf the Web, your computer stores a copy of the Web pages you visit in a cache file on your hard drive. Thus, anyone with access to your hard drive could get a good idea of your regular stopping places. Would you be concerned if your boss knew that you were visiting sites that specialized in job searches, cancer, or, for that matter, any non-job-related site? (For advice on how to protect your privacy, slip over to **http://www.consumerprivacyguide.org/topthings**. And for a list of privacy tools, see **http://epic.org/privacy/tools.html**.)

## Government Regulation of Online Privacy

Members of Congress have filed many bills to regulate online privacy. So intense, however, is the debate between industry and consumer advocates that no consensus—and little law—has emerged. There has, however, been some government regulation.

### The First Amendment

How would you like to be called cockroach, mega scumbag, and crook in front of thousands of people? What would you think if your ex-wife told 55,000 people that your insensitivity made her so sick she was throwing up every day? **The First Amendment to the Constitution protects free speech,** and that includes these postings and worse which have appeared on Internet message boards and blogs. As upsetting as they may be, they are protected as free speech under the First Amendment as long as the poster is not committing defamation. In these particular cases, the courts ruled that the statements were opinion, not fact, and therefore were not defamatory.

Explaining its ruling, one of the courts said:

> Users [of the Internet] are able to engage freely in informal debate and criticism, leading many to substitute gossip for accurate reporting and often to adopt a provocative, even combative tone. It hardly need be said that this [court does not] condone [these] rude and childish posts; indeed, [the] intemperate, insulting, and often disgusting remarks understandably offended plaintiff and possibly many other readers. Nevertheless, the fact that society may find speech offensive is not a sufficient reason for suppressing it. Indeed, if it is the speaker's opinion that gives offense, that consequence is a reason for according it constitutional protection.[1]

### The Fourth Amendment

**The Fourth Amendment to the Constitution prohibits unreasonable searches and seizures by the government.** In enforcing this provision of the Constitution, the courts ask: Did the person

---

[1] *Krinsky v. Doe,* 6159 Cal. App. 4th 1154, 2008 Cal. App. LEXIS 180.

being searched have a legitimate expectation of privacy in the place searched or the item seized? If yes, then the government must obtain a warrant from a court before conducting the search. The Fourth Amendment applies to computers.

The architecture professor in the following case would have benefited from a course in business law and perhaps in computer science, too.

## UNITED STATES OF AMERICA v. ANGEVINE

281 F.3D 1130, 2002 U.S. APP. LEXIS 2746
UNITED STATES COURT OF APPEALS FOR THE TENTH CIRCUIT, 2002

### CASE SUMMARY

**Facts:** Professor Eric Angevine taught architecture at Oklahoma State University. The university provided him with a computer that was linked to the university network, and through it to the Internet. Professor Angevine used this computer to download more than 3,000 pornographic images of young boys. After viewing the images and printing some of them, he deleted the files. Tipped off by Professor Angevine's wife, police officers seized the computer and turned it over to a police computer expert who retrieved the pornographic files that the professor had deleted. The police had not obtained a search warrant.

The Oklahoma State University computer policy states that:

- The contents of all storage media owned or stored on university computing facilities are the property of the university.

- Employees cannot use university computers to access obscene material.

- The university reserves the right to view or scan any file or software stored on a computer or passing through the network, and will do so periodically to audit the use of university resources. The university cannot guarantee confidentiality of stored data.

- System administrators keep logs of file names that may indicate why a particular data file is being erased, when it was erased, and what user identification has erased it.

The trial court held that federal agents did not need a warrant to search Professor Angevine's office computer because he had no expectation of privacy. He was sentenced to 51 months in prison for "knowing possession of child pornography." The professor appealed.

**Issue:** *Did Professor Angevine have a reasonable expectation of privacy in his office computer?*

**Decision:** Professor Angevine did not have a reasonable expectation of privacy.

**Reasoning:** The University's computer-use policy reserves the right to audit Internet use by employees and to monitor individuals suspected of misusing their computers. The policy explicitly cautions computer users that information flowing through the University network is not confidential either in transit or in storage on a computer. As a result, employees cannot have a reasonable expectation of privacy in downloaded data.

Professor Angevine made a careless effort to protect his privacy. Although he did attempt to erase the pornography, the University computer policy warned that system administrators kept logs recording when and by whom files were deleted. In any event, having transmitted pornographic data through a monitored University network, Professor Angevine could not create a reasonable expectation of privacy merely by deleting the files.

## The FTC

**Section 5 of the FTC Act prohibits unfair and deceptive acts or practices.** The FTC applies this statute to online privacy policies: It does not require Web sites to have a privacy policy, but if they do have one, they must follow it. For example, Gateway Learning Corporation sold *Hooked on Phonics* products online. The privacy policy on its Web site sounded good: it promised that the company would not give PII to third parties without the customer's consent and would not change its privacy policy without first notifying customers. Wrong on both counts—the company changed its policy, gave PII to third parties, and never told its customers. Gateway admitted that it was in violation of the FTC Act and agreed to discontinue its illegal practices.

## Electronic Communications Privacy Act of 1986

**The Electronic Communications Privacy Act of 1986 (ECPA) is a federal statute that prohibits unauthorized interception or disclosure of wire and electronic communications or unauthorized access to stored communications.** The definition of electronic communication includes e-mail and transmissions from pagers and cellular phones. Violators are subject to both criminal and civil penalties. An action does not violate the ECPA if it is unintentional or if either party consents. Also, the USA Patriot Act, passed after the September 11th attacks, has broadened the *government's* right to monitor electronic communications.

Under the ECPA:

1. **Any intended recipient of an electronic communication has the right to disclose it.** Thus, if you sound off in an e-mail to a friend about your boss, the (erstwhile) friend may legally forward that e-mail to the boss or anyone else.

2. **Internet service providers (ISPs) are generally prohibited from disclosing electronic messages to anyone other than the addressee,** unless this disclosure is necessary for the performance of their service or for the protection of their own rights or property.

3. **An employer has the right to monitor workers' electronic communications if (1) the employee consents, (2) the monitoring occurs in the ordinary course of business, or (3) the employer provides the computer system (in the case of e-mail).** Note that an employer has the right to monitor electronic communication even if it does not relate to work activities.

4. **To access electronic communications that have been stored for 180 days or less, the government must obtain a search warrant. Once the communications have been stored for more than 180 days, the government can access it by obtaining a search warrant, subpoena or court order.**

One lesson from the ECPA: e-mail is not private and it is dangerous. The majority of employers monitor their employees' e-mail. In the event of litigation, the opposing party can access e-mail, even messages that have in theory been deleted. Many people who should have known better have been caught in the e-mail trap. Merrill Lynch stock analyst Henry Blodget praised stocks to the public even was he was referring to them in e-mails as a "piece of s***." He has been banned for life from the securities industry. Then there was Harry Stonecipher, the CEO of Boeing, who sent explicit e-mails to the employee with whom he was having an extra-marital affair. When copies of the e-mails were sent to the board of directors, he was fired.

In the following case, two important principles are at stake. Which one should win?

# YOU *be the* JUDGE

## SCOTT v. BETH ISRAEL MEDICAL CENTER INC.

2007 N.Y. Misc. LEXIS 7114
Supreme Court of New York, 2007

**Facts:** Beth Israel Medical Center (BI)'s e-mail policy stated:

All information and documents created, received, saved, or sent on the Medical Center's computer or communications systems are the property of the Medical Center.

"Employees have no personal privacy right in any material created, received, saved or sent using Medical Center communication or computer systems. The Medical Center reserves the right to access and disclose such material at any time without prior notice."

*continued*

Dr. Norman Scott was head of the orthopedics department at BI. His contract with the hospital provided for $14 million in severance pay if he was fired without cause. BI did fire him and the question was whether it was for cause or not. In preparation for a lawsuit against BI, Scott used the hospital's computer system to send e-mails to his lawyer. Each of these e-mails included the following notice:

> This message is intended only for the use of the Addressee and may contain information that is privileged and confidential. If you are not the intended recipient, you are hereby notified that any dissemination of this communication is strictly prohibited. If you have received this communication in error, please erase all copies of the message and its attachments and notify us immediately.

BI obtained copies of all of Scott's e-mails. It notified him that it had copies of the e-mails to his lawyer. No one at BI had read the e-mails yet, but they intended to do so.

Communications between a client and lawyer are generally protected, but a client waives this privilege if he publicly discloses the information. When Scott requested that the e-mails be returned to him unread, BI refused. Scott filed a motion seeking the return of the documents.

**You Be the Judge: Did Scott have a right to privacy in e-mails he sent to his lawyer using the BI system?**

**Argument for Scott:** Despite BI's policy, all the e-mails Scott sent asserted that they were confidential. That should be enough to protect them. The attorney-client privilege is a foundation of our legal system. It is absolutely crucial for justice that clients be able to communicate with their lawyers in confidence. In a test between a core principle such as attorney-client privilege and a private entity's e-mail policy, the privilege must win. The hospital should not be allowed to read Scott's e-mails.

**Argument for BI:** Scott was aware of BI's policy and knew that e-mails were property of the hospital. Therefore, when he sent the e-mails, he was disclosing them publicly. If the communications were that important, he should have made a greater effort to protect them. BI has the right to read them.

## Children's Online Privacy Protection Act of 1998

**The Children's Online Privacy Protection Act of 1998 (COPPA) prohibits Internet operators from collecting information from children under 13 without parental permission. It also requires sites to disclose how they will use any information they acquire.** The FTC is charged with enforcing COPPA. The Web site for Mrs. Fields cookies offered birthday coupons for free cookies to children under 13. Although the company did not share information with outsiders, it did collect PII without parental consent from 84,000 children. This information included name, home address, and birthdate. Mrs. Fields paid a penalty of $100,000 and agreed not to violate the law again.

## Gramm-Leach-Bliley Privacy Act of 1999

**The Gramm-Leach-Bliley Privacy Act of 1999 (GLB) requires banks and other financial institutions to tell a consumer if they plan to reveal any of her nonpublic information to third parties.** A financial institution cannot disclose this private information if the consumer opts out (that is, denies permission). Advice on how to opt out is available at **http://www.privacyrights .org/fs/fs24a-optout.htm**.

## State Regulation

A few states have passed their own online privacy statutes. For instance, the California Online Privacy Act of 2003 requires any Web site that collects PII from California residents to post a privacy policy conspicuously and then abide by its terms.

## · SPAM ·

> **As much as 62 percent of all e-mail is spam.**

Spam is officially known as *unsolicited commercial e-mail (UCE)* or *unsolicited bulk e-mail (UBE)*. As much as 62 percent of all e-mail is spam. **The Controlling the Assault of Non-Solicited Pornography and Marketing Act (Can-Spam) prohibits spammers from using false or misleading return addresses and headers in their e-mail.** Also, spammers must provide a valid method for unsubscribing from their e-mail lists.

Although one can only applaud the effort, in truth, the Can-Spam Act has not noticeably decreased the amount of spam. Spammers operate in the netherworld of cyberspace where they are difficult to identify and locate.

### EXAM *Strategy*

**Question:** Cruise.com operated a website selling cruise vacations. It sent unsolicited e-mail advertisements—dubbed "E-deals"—to prospective customers. Eleven of these "E-deals" went to **inbox@webguy.net**. Each message offered the recipient an opportunity to be removed from the mailing list by clicking on a line of text or by writing to a specific postal address. Has cruise.com violated the Can-Spam Act?

**Strategy:** Remember that this Act does not prohibit all unsolicited e-mails.

**Result:** Cruise.com was not in violation because it offered the recipients a way to unsubscribe.

## · INTERNET SERVICE PROVIDERS AND WEB HOSTS: COMMUNICATIONS DECENCY ACT OF 1996 ·

ISPs are companies, such as Earthlink, that provide connection to the Internet. Web hosts post Web pages on the Internet.

The Internet is an enormously powerful tool for disseminating information. But what if some of this information happens to be false or in violation of our privacy rights? Is an ISP liable for transmitting it to the world? In 1995, a trial judge in New York held that an ISP, Prodigy Services Company, was potentially liable for defamatory statements that an unidentified person posted on one of its bulletin boards.[2] The message alleged that the president of an investment bank had committed "criminal and fraudulent acts." It was not only a false statement, it was posted on the most widely read financial computer bulletin board in the country. Although one can only feel sympathy for the target of this slur, the decision nonetheless alarmed many observers who argued that there was no way ISPs could review every piece of information that hurtles through their portals. The next year, Congress overruled the *Prodigy* case by passing the Communications Decency Act of 1996 (CDA).[3] **Under the CDA, ISPs and Web hosts are not liable for information that is provided by someone else. Only content providers are liable.** The following case lays out the arguments in favor of the CDA, but also illustrates some of the costs of the statute (and of the Internet).

---

[2] *Stratton Oakmont, Inc. v. Prodigy Services Company*, 1995 N.Y. Misc. LEXIS 229.
[3] 47 U.S.C. 230.

## CARAFANO v. METROSPLASH.COM, INC.

339 F.3D 1119, 2003 U.S. APP. LEXIS 16548
UNITED STATES COURT OF APPEALS FOR THE NINTH CIRCUIT, 2003

### CASE SUMMARY

**Facts:** Matchmaker.com is an Internet dating service that permits members to post profiles of themselves and to view the profiles of other members. Matchmaker reviews photos for impropriety before posting them but does not examine the profiles themselves.

Christianne Carafano is an actor who uses the stage name Chase Masterson. She has appeared in numerous films and television shows, such as *Star Trek: Deep Space Nine* and *General Hospital.* Without her knowledge or consent, someone in Berlin posted a profile of her in the Los Angeles section of Matchmaker. In answer to the question "Main source of current events?" the person posting the profile put "*Playboy Playgirl*" and for "Why did you call?" responded "Looking for a one-night stand." In addition, the essays indicated that she was looking for a "hard and dominant" man with "a strong sexual appetite" and that she "liked sort of being controlled by a man, in and out of bed." Pictures of the actor taken off the Internet were included with the profile. The profile also provided her home address and an e-mail address, which, when contacted, produced an automatic e-mail reply stating, "You think you are the right one? Proof it !!" [sic], and providing Carafano's home address and telephone number.

Unaware of the improper posting, Carafano began receiving sexually explicit messages on her home voice mail as well as a sexually explicit fax that threatened her and her son. She received numerous phone calls, letters, and e-mail from male fans, expressing concern that she had given out her address and phone number (but simultaneously indicating an interest in meeting her). Feeling unsafe, Carafano and her son stayed in hotels or away from Los Angeles for several months.

One Saturday a week or two after the profile was first posted, Carafano's assistant, Siouxzan Perry, learned of the false profile through a message from "Jeff." Acting on Carafano's instructions, Perry contacted Matchmaker,

demanding that the profile be removed immediately. The Matchmaker employee did not remove it then because Perry herself had not posted it, but on Monday morning the company blocked the profile from public view and then deleted it the following day.

Carafano filed suit against Matchmaker alleging invasion of privacy, misappropriation of the right of publicity, defamation, and negligence. The district court rejected Matchmaker's argument for immunity under the CDA on the grounds that the company provided part of the profile content.

**Issue:** *Does the CDA protect Matchmaker from liability?*

**Decision:** Matchmaker is not liable.

**Reasoning:** Under the CDA, Internet publishers are not liable for false or defamatory material if someone else provided the information. In this way, Internet publishers are different from print, television, and radio publishers.

Interactive computer services have millions of users. It would be impossible for these services to screen each of their millions of postings. If they were liable for content, they might choose to severely limit the number and type of messages. To avoid any restriction on free speech, Congress chose to protect computer services from liability if someone else provided the content.

The fact that some of the content in Carafano's fake profile was provided in response to Matchmaker's questionnaire does not make the company liable. The answers to the questions were provided exclusively by the user. No profile has any content until a user actively creates it. In this case, Carafano's home address and the e-mail address that revealed her phone number were transmitted unaltered to profile viewers. Thus, Matchmaker did not play a significant role in creating, developing, or transforming the relevant information.

Despite the serious and utterly deplorable consequences in this case, Matchmaker cannot be sued under the CDA.

### EXAM *Strategy*

**Question:** Craigslist, Inc. runs a Web site for classified ads, including ads for the sale and rental of houses and apartments. Some of the posted ads were discriminatory (although not consistent), containing text such as: "Neighborhood is predominantly Caucasian, Polish, and Hispanic," "NO MINORITIES," "Non-Women of Color NEED NOT APPLY." Was Craigslist liable for these ads?

**Strategy:**  Remember that only content providers are liable.

**Result:**  Craigslist was not liable because it was only a conduit for information, not a provider itself.

---

## · CRIME ON THE INTERNET ·

Despite its great benefits, the Internet has also opened new frontiers in crime.

## HACKING

**Gaining unauthorized access to a computer system is called** *hacking*. The goal of hackers is varied; some do it for little more than the thrill of the challenge. The objective for other hackers may be industrial espionage, extortion, or theft of credit card information. Whatever the motive, hacking is a major crime. The Federal Bureau of Investigation ranks cybercrime as its third highest priority, right behind terrorism and spying.

Hacking is a crime under the federal Computer Fraud and Abuse Act of 1986 (CFAA). **The CFAA prohibits:**

- Theft of financial information
- Theft of information from the U.S. government
- Theft from a computer
- Computer trespass
- Computer fraud
- Intentional, reckless, and negligent damage to a computer
- Computer extortion

## FRAUD

**Fraud is the deception of another person for the purpose of obtaining money or property from him.** Common scams include the sale of merchandise that is either defective or nonexistent; the so-called Nigerian letter scam;[4] billing for services that are touted as "free"; fraudulent stock offers; fake scholarship search services; business opportunity scams (for a small investment, you will get rich); romance fraud (you meet someone online who wants to visit you but needs money for "travel expenses"); and credit card scams (for a fee, you can get a credit card, even with a poor credit rating). One new scam involves *over*payment. You are renting out a house, selling a pet, accepting a job, and, "by accident" are sent too much money. You wire the excess back, only to find out that the initial check or fund transfer was no good. To protect yourself from Internet fraud, steal over to **http://www.lookstoogoodtobetrue.com**.

---

[4] Victims receive an e-mail from someone alleging to be a Nigerian government official who has stolen money from the government. He needs some place safe to park the money for a short time. The official promises that, if the victim will permit her account to be used for this purpose, she will be allowed to keep a percentage of the stolen money. Instead, of course, once the "official" has the victim's bank information, he cleans out the account.

Fraud can be prosecuted under state law or the Computer Fraud and Abuse Act. In addition, federal mail and wire fraud statutes prohibit the use of mail or wire communication in furtherance of a fraudulent scheme. The FTC can bring civil cases under §5 of the FTC Act.

## Identity Theft

Identity theft is one of the scariest crimes against property. Thieves steal the victim's social security number and other personal information such as bank account numbers and mother's maiden name, which they use to obtain loans and credit cards. The money owed is never repaid, leaving victims to prove that they were not responsible for the debts. The thieves may even commit (additional) crimes under their new identities. Meanwhile, the victim may find himself unable to obtain a credit card, loan, or job. One victim spent several nights in jail after he was arrested for a crime that his alter ego had committed.

Although identity fraud existed before computers, the Internet has made it much easier. For example, consumer activists were able to purchase the social security numbers of the director of the CIA, the Attorney General of the United States, and other top administration officials. The cost? $26 each. No surprise then that 8 million Americans are victims of this crime each year.

Responding to these concerns, Congress passed the Identity Theft and Assumption Deterrence Act of 1998.[5] **This statute prohibits the use of false identification to commit fraud or other crime and it also permits the victim to seek restitution in court.** In addition, the owner of a credit card must generally pay only the first $50 that is stolen. Nonetheless, the time and effort required to undo the damage can be substantial.

What can you do to prevent the theft of your identity?

1. Check your credit reports at least once a year. (Consumers are entitled by law to one free credit report every year from each of the three major reporting agencies. You can order these reports at **https://www.annualcreditreport.com.**)

2. Place a freeze on your credit report so that anyone who is about to issue a loan or credit card will double-check with you first.

3. If you suspect that your identity has been stolen, contact the FTC at 877-IDTHEFT, 877-438-4338, or **http://www.consumer.gov/idtheft**. Also, file a police report immediately and keep a copy to show creditors. Notify the three credit agencies.

## Phishing

Have you ever received an e-mail like this:

> We regret to inform you that your eBay account could be suspended if you don't re-update your account information. To resolve this problems [sic] please use the link below and re-enter your account information. If your problems could not be resolved your account will be suspended for a period of 24 hours, after this period your account will be terminated.

This e-mail is not from eBay, but rather from a fraudster hoping to lure the recipient into revealing her eBay account information, including credit card numbers and passwords. It is part of one of the most rapidly growing areas of Internet fraud: **phishing. In this crime, a fraudster sends an e-mail directing the recipient to enter personal information on a Web site that is an illegal imitation of a legitimate site.** Prosecutors can bring criminal charges against phishers for fraud. The targeted companies have sued these criminals for fraud, trademark infringement, false advertising, and cybersquatting.

No reputable company will ask customers to respond to an e-mail with personal information. When in doubt, close down the suspicious e-mail, re-launch your Web browser and then go to the company's main Web site. If the legitimate company needs information from you, it will so indicate on the site.

---

[5] 18 U.S. §1028.

## CHAPTER CONCLUSION

The Internet has changed our lives in ways that were inconceivable a generation ago. Like a racer coming off a delayed start, the law is rushing to catch up. Not only will laws change, as legislators and courts learn from experience, but new laws will inevitably be needed.

## EXAM REVIEW

1. **THE FIRST AMENDMENT** The First Amendment to the Constitution protects speech on the Internet as long as the speech is not defamatory. (p. 424)

2. **THE FOURTH AMENDMENT** The Fourth Amendment to the Constitution prohibits unreasonable searches and seizures by government agents. This provision applies to computers. (p. 424)

**EXAM Strategy**

**Question:** Three travel agents used fictitious accounts to steal 61 million frequent flyer miles from American Airlines. As evidence in the criminal trial, prosecutors used electronic communications from the agents on SABRE, American's computerized travel reservations system. The agents alleged that this search was illegal. Do you agree?

**Strategy:** There are two laws that are relevant to this case: the ECPA and the Fourth Amendment. (See the "Result" at the end of this section.)

3. **THE FTC ACT** Section 5 of the FTC Act prohibits unfair and deceptive practices. (p. 425)

4. **THE ECPA** The Electronic Communications Privacy Act of 1986 is a federal statute that prohibits unauthorized interception or disclosure of wire and electronic communications or unauthorized access to stored communications. Under this statute:
   - Any intended recipient of an e-mail has the right to disclose it.
   - An employer has the right to monitor workers' e-mail messages if (1) the employee consents; (2) the monitoring occurs in the ordinary course of business; or (3) the employer provides the e-mail system.
   - The government has the right to access e-mail messages if it first obtains a search warrant or court order. (p. 426)

5. **COPPA** The Children's Online Privacy Protection Act of 1998 prohibits Internet operators from collecting information from children under 13 without parental permission. It also requires sites to disclose how they will use any information they acquire. (p. 427)

6. **GLB** The Gramm-Leach-Bliley Privacy Act of 1999 requires banks and other financial institutions to tell a consumer if they plan to reveal any of her nonpublic information to third parties.

The financial institution cannot disclose this private information if the consumer opts out. (p. 427)

.................................................................................

7.  **CAN-SPAM**  The Controlling the Assault of Non-Solicited Pornography and Marketing Act prohibits spammers from using false or misleading return addresses and headers in their e-mail. Also, spammers must provide a valid method for unsubscribing from their e-mail lists. (p. 428)

.................................................................................

8.  **THE CDA**  Under the Communications Decency Act of 1996, ISPs and Web hosts are not liable for information that is provided by someone else. (p. 428)

**Question:**  Ton Cremers was the director of security at Amsterdam's famous Rijksmuseum and the operator of the Museum Security Network (the Network) Web site. Robert Smith, a handyman working for Ellen Batzel in North Carolina, sent an e-mail to the Network alleging that Batzel was the granddaughter of Heinrich Himmler (one of Hitler's henchmen) and that she had art that Himmler had stolen. These allegations were completely untrue. Cremers posted Smith's e-mail on the Network's Web site and sent it to the Network's subscribers. Cremers exercised some editorial discretion in choosing which e-mails to send to subscribers, generally omitting any that were unrelated to stolen art. Is Cremers liable to Batzel for the harm that this inaccurate information caused?

**Strategy:**  Cremers is only liable if he is a content provider. (See the "Result" at the end of this section.)

.................................................................................

9.  **THE CFAA**  Hacking is illegal under the federal Computer Fraud and Abuse Act of 1986. The CFAA prohibits:
    *   Theft of financial information
    *   Theft of information from the U.S. government
    *   Theft from a computer
    *   Computer trespass
    *   Computer fraud
    *   Intentional, reckless, and negligent damage to a computer
    *   Computer extortion (p. 430)

.................................................................................

10. **FRAUD**  Fraud is the deception of another person for the purpose of obtaining money or property from him. (p. 430)

.................................................................................

11. **IDENTITY THEFT**  The Identity Theft and Assumption Deterrence Act of 1998 prohibits the use of false identification to commit fraud or other crime. (p. 431)

.................................................................................

**2. Result:**  Under the ECPA, American had a right to disclose any electronic communications sent on its system (it owned SABRE). The agents did not have a reasonable expectation of privacy on the American system.

**8. Result:**  The court found that he was not liable.

# PRACTICE EXAM

## MATCHING QUESTIONS

Match the following terms with their definitions:

___ A. ECPA

___ B. Fourth Amendment to the Constitution

___ C. CFAA

___ D. COPPA

___ E. CDA

1. Regulates access to e-mail
2. Regulates Internet service providers
3. Regulates collection of information from children
4. Prohibits unreasonable searches and seizures of computers
5. Regulates computer hacking

## TRUE/FALSE QUESTIONS

Circle true or false:

**1.** T  F  The First Amendment to the Constitution protects bloggers who post insults about other people.

**2.** T  F  Under the Gramm-Leach-Bliley Act, a financial institution cannot disclose private information about consumers unless the consumers give permission.

**3.** T  F  The FTC requires Web sites to establish a privacy policy and then abide by it.

**4.** T  F  Any intended recipient of an e-mail may forward it to whomever she wishes.

**5.** T  F  The police can read anyone's e-mail anytime as long as they have probable cause to believe that the e-mail will reveal evidence of a crime.

## MULTIPLE-CHOICE QUESTIONS

**6.** Rory is concerned that the employees in her division are wasting too much time on personal matters. She would like to monitor them. Which of the following activities is she *not* allowed to do?

A. Ask key employees to forward to her any e-mails they receive from their colleagues that contain jokes or other silly content

B. Read all messages sent to employee pagers

C. Read all employee e-mails sent through the office system

D. Read employees' private e-mail accounts

E. Read all e-mails sent in the ordinary course of business

**7.** Three terrorists are plotting to blow up a high-rise office building, which could lead to thousands of deaths. The police capture their computers and read the files before obtaining a warrant. Which of the following searches would be illegal?

I. Marshall has written elaborate plans, which are stored on the hard drive of his laptop.

II. Winston has violated school policies by downloading plans for bombs from the Internet through his school's network.

III. Montgomery has made rental car reservations over the Internet in a cybercafe.

A. I, II, and III

B. Neither I, II, nor III

C. Just I

D. Just II

E. Just III

8. The Computer Fraud and Abuse Act prohibits all of the following activities except:

   A. Theft of financial information

   B. Illegal file sharing over the Internet

   C. Theft of information from the U.S. government

   D. Negligent damage to a computer

   E. Computer extortion

9. Under the Can-Spam Act, it is legal to:

   A. Send out advertisements for sexually explicit Web sites

   B. Send e-mails with false return addresses

   C. Send e-mails with fake headers

   D. Refuse to unsubscribe recipients

   E. Send out e-mails with headers that, while technically accurate, are in fact misleading

10. Your novel has just been published and is now for sale on Amazon.com. You access Amazon via Earthlink one day and are horrified to see that a reader (or alleged reader) has posted a bad review that is not only totally unfair but also totally inaccurate. (You did not plagiarize portions of the book!) Which of the following would be liable to you:

    I. Amazon.com

    II. Earthlink

    III. The person who wrote the review

    A. I, II, and III

    B. Neither I, II, nor III

    C. I and III

    D. Just I

    E. Just III

## SHORT-ANSWER QUESTIONS

11. ETHICS: Matt Drudge published a report on his Web site (**http://www.drudgereport.com**) that White House aide Sidney Blumenthal "has a spousal abuse past that has been effectively covered up. . . . There are court records of Blumenthal's violence against his wife." The Drudge Report is an electronic publication focusing on Hollywood and Washington gossip. AOL paid Drudge $3,000 a month to make the Drudge Report available to AOL subscribers. Drudge e-mailed his reports to AOL, which then posted them. Before posting, however, AOL had the right to edit content. Drudge ultimately retracted his allegations against Blumenthal, who sued AOL. He alleged that under the Communications Decency Act of 1996, AOL was a "content provider" because it paid Drudge and edited what he wrote. Do you agree? Putting liability aside, what moral obligation did AOL have to its members? To Blumenthal? Should AOL be liable for content it bought and provided to its members?

12. To demonstrate the inadequacies of existing computer security systems, Cornell student Robert Morris created a computer virus. His plan, however, went awry, as plans sometimes do. He thought his virus would be relatively harmless but it ran amok, crashing scores of computers at universities, military sites, and medical research sites. Under what statute might Morris be charged? Does it matter that he did not intend to cause damage?

13. Nancy Garrity and Joanne Clark worked for John Hancock Mutual Life Insurance Company. On their office computers they regularly received sexually explicit e-mails from friends and from Internet joke sites, which they then sent to coworkers. When a fellow employee complained, Hancock searched their e-mail folders and, finding inappropriate e-mails, fired the two women. The Hancock e-mail policy states: "Messages that are defamatory, abusive, obscene, profane, sexually oriented, threatening or racially offensive are prohibited. Company management reserves the right to access all e-mail files." The two employees filed suit against Hancock, alleging that the company had invaded their privacy. How would you rule as judge?

14. What can you do to protect your privacy online? Draw up a concrete list of steps that you might reasonably consider. Are there some actions that you would not be willing to take, either because they are not worth the effort or because they are too sneaky?

**15.** During the course of 10 months, Joseph Melle sent more than 60 million unsolicited e-mail advertisements to AOL members. What charges could be brought against him?

**16.** ROLE REVERSAL: Write a multiple-choice question that deals with an issue involving crime in cyberspace.

## INTERNET RESEARCH PROBLEMS

The FTC provides an online brochure entitled *Site Seeing on the Internet* (at **http://www.ftc.gov/bcp/edu/pubs/consumer/tech/tec04.shtm**) that offers suggestions for safe travel on the Internet. Have you ever violated the FTC's advice on how to protect yourself in cyberspace?

**You can find further practice problems in the Online Quiz at www.cengage.com/blaw/beatty.**

# INTELLECTUAL PROPERTY

**Jason is** a college student who fervently believes that he has the right to use any and all intellectual property for free. With this principle in mind, he downloads music, movies, television shows, and books from the Internet with never a thought of paying for them. Indeed, he has never paid for any of the music on his iPod.

This belief is not, however, shared by those who produce intellectual property. And these producers have the law on their side. Thus, the Recording Industry Association of America (RIAA) has sued more than 25,000 people (particularly students) who download music from illegal sites. Jason was horrified to receive a complaint from the RIAA seeking $750 in damages for *each* song he downloaded "for free." The total damages exceed $750,000. Jason is afraid he will be in debt for the rest of his life. How can he even afford a lawyer? What is he to do?

> Jason is afraid he will be in debt for the rest of his life.

437

## · INTRODUCTION ·

For much of history, land was the most valuable form of property. It was the primary source of wealth and social status. Today, intellectual property is a major source of wealth. New ideas—for manufacturing processes, computer programs, medicines, books—bring both affluence and influence.

**ECONOMICS AND THE LAW** Although both can be valuable assets, land and intellectual property are fundamentally different. The value of land lies in the owner's right to exclude, to prevent others from entering it. Intellectual property, however, has little economic value unless others use it. This ability to share intellectual property is both good news and bad. On the one hand, the owner can produce and sell unlimited copies of, say, a software program, but, on the other hand, the owner has no easy way to determine if someone is using the program for free. The high cost of developing intellectual property, combined with the low cost of reproducing it, makes it particularly vulnerable to theft.

Because intellectual property is nonexclusive, many people see no problem in using it for free. For example, students often argue that it is okay to copy CDs for their friends. How can copying a few CDs hurt a big recording studio? But if record companies earn lower royalties, they will produce fewer songs and music lovers everywhere will suffer. Some commentators suggest that the United States has been a technological leader partly because its laws have always provided strong protection for intellectual property. The Constitution provided for patent protection early in the country's history. In contrast, one of the oldest civilizations in the world, China, has been relatively slow in developing new technology. It did not institute a patent system until 1985. ◆

## · PATENTS ·

**Patent**
A grant by the government permitting the inventor exclusive use of an invention for a specified period.

**A patent is a grant by the government permitting the inventor exclusive use of an invention for 20 years.** During this period, no one may make, use, or sell the invention without permission. In return, the inventor publicly discloses information about the invention that anyone can use upon expiration of the patent.

**A patent is not available solely for an idea, but only for its tangible application.** Thus patents are available for:

| Type of Invention | Example |
|---|---|
| Mechanical invention | A hydraulic jack used to lift heavy aircraft |
| Chemical invention | The chemical 2-chloroethylphosphonic acid used as a plant growth regulator |
| Process | A method for applying a chemical to a plant—such as a process for applying a weed killer to rice |

Patents are not available for laws of nature, scientific principles, mathematical algorithms, or formulas such as $a^2 + b^2 = c^2$.

In recent years, so-called "business method patents" have been controversial. These patents involve data processing or mathematical calculations used in business. For instance, a patent has been issued on a type of trust that reduces taxes on stock options. Business method patents have been particularly common in e-commerce. For example, Amazon.com patented its One-Click method of instant ordering. The company then obtained an injunction to prevent Barnesandnoble.com from using its Express Lane service that was similar to One-Click. The judge directed Barnesandnoble.com to add an additional step to its ordering process.

However, the law changed recently when the United States Court of Appeals for the Federal Circuit ruled that, to be patentable, a process must either be tied to a particular machine, or it must transform an article. This standard is called the "machine-or-transformation test."[1]

In the case before the Court, the applicants had tried to patent a method of hedging risk in commodities trading. For example, coal power plants purchase coal to produce electricity. The plants could suffer financial disaster if the market price of coal increased dramatically. Conversely, coal mining companies would be harmed financially if coal prices fell. The patent involved a process whereby an intermediary would buy and sell coal at fixed prices, thereby protecting the power plants and the mining companies from market fluctuations. The intermediary would manage its risk, and earn profits, by buying and selling options to purchase coal. The Court ruled that this process was not patentable because options are simply legal rights and do not transform any physical object. In short, it seems that inventors cannot patent a process that simply involves ideas. The impact of this ruling on the Amazon case in particular, and e-commerce in general, is yet to be determined.

## REQUIREMENTS FOR A PATENT

To obtain a patent, the inventor must show that her invention meets all of the following tests:

- **Novel.** An invention is not patentable if it (1) is known or has already been used in this country; or (2) has been described in a publication here or overseas. For example, an inventor discovered a new use for existing chemical compounds but was not permitted to patent it because the chemicals had already been described in prior publications, though the new use had not.[2]

- **Nonobvious.** An invention is not patentable if it is obvious to a person with ordinary skill in that particular area. An inventor was not allowed to patent a waterflush system designed to remove cow manure from the floor of a barn because it was obvious.[3]

- **Useful.** To be patented, an invention must be useful. It need not necessarily be commercially valuable, but it must have some current use. Being merely of scientific interest is not enough. Thus a company was denied a patent for a novel process for making steroids because they had no therapeutic value.[4]

### EXAM *Strategy*

**Question:** In 1572, during the reign of Queen Elizabeth I of England, a patent application was filed for a knife with a bone rather than a wooden handle. Would this patent be granted under current U.S. law?

**Strategy:** Was a bone handle novel, nonobvious, and useful?

---

[1] *In re Bilski,* 2008 U.S. App. LEXIS 22479 (2008).

[2] *In re Schoenwald,* 964 F.2d 1122, 1992 U.S. App. LEXIS 10181 (Fed. Cir. 1992).

[3] *Sakraida v. Ag Pro, Inc.,* 425 U.S. 273, 96 S. Ct. 1532, 1976 U.S. LEXIS 146 (1976).

[4] *Brenner v. Manson,* 383 U.S. 519, 86 S. Ct. 1033, 1966 U.S. LEXIS 2907 (1966).

**Result:** It was useful—no splinters from a bone handle. It was novel—no one had ever done it before. But the patent was denied because it was obvious.

---

# PATENT APPLICATION AND ISSUANCE

To obtain a patent, the inventor must file a complex application with the Patent and Trademark Office (PTO) in Washington, D.C. If a patent examiner determines that the application meets all legal requirements, the PTO will issue the patent. Traditionally, patent examiners relied on their (often substantial) expertise, their reading of scientific papers, and database searches to evaluate patents. More complex technology and a huge increase in the number of applications have challenged the ability of any one human being to keep up with latest developments. The PTO has begun a pilot project—called Peer to Patent—it hopes will make the approval process quicker and more accurate. Taking a page from Wikipedia, the online encyclopedia, the PTO will post selected applications on the Web. Anyone may participate in the review process, but participants will rate contributions and only the most valuable will go to the patent examiner.

If an examiner denies a patent application for any reason, the inventor can appeal that decision to the PTO Board of Appeals and from there to the Court of Appeals for the Federal Circuit in Washington. Alternatively, upon denial of the application, the inventor can file suit against the PTO in the federal district court in Washington.

### Priority Between Two Inventors

When two people invent the same product, who is entitled to a patent—the first to invent or the first to file an application? Generally, the person who invents and *puts the invention into practice* has priority over the first filer. Having the idea is not enough—the inventor must actually use the product.

### Prior Sale

An inventor must apply for a patent within one year of selling the product commercially. The purpose of this rule is to encourage prompt disclosure of inventions. It prevents someone from inventing a product, selling it for years, and then obtaining a 20-year monopoly with a patent.

### Provisional Patent Application

Inventors who are unable to assess the market value of their ideas sometimes hesitate to file a patent application because the process is expensive and cumbersome. To solve this problem, the PTO now permits inventors to file a **provisional patent application (PPA).** The PPA is a simpler, shorter, cheaper application that gives inventors the opportunity to show their ideas to potential investors without incurring the full expense of a patent application. **PPA protection lasts only one year.** To maintain protection after that time, the inventor must file a regular patent application.

### International Patent Treaties

Suppose you have a great idea that you want to protect around the world. **The Paris Convention for the Protection of Industrial Property requires each member country to grant to citizens of other member countries the same rights under patent law as its own citizens enjoy.** Thus, the patent office in each member country must accept and recognize all patent and trademark applications filed with it by anyone who lives in any member country. For example, the French patent office cannot refuse to accept an application from an American, as long as the American has complied with French law. Still to be worked out, however, is an international standard for patent laws.

## · COPYRIGHTS ·

**The holder of a copyright owns the *particular expression* of an idea, but not the underlying idea or method of operation.** Abner Doubleday could copyright a book setting out his particular version of the rules of baseball, but he could not copyright the rules themselves, nor could he require players to pay him a royalty.

Unlike patents, the ideas underlying copyrighted material need not be novel. For example, three movies—*Like Father Like Son, Vice Versa,* and *Freaky Friday*—were about a parent and child who switch bodies. The movies all had the same plot, but there was no copyright violation because their *expressions* of the basic idea were different.

Originally, copyrights lasted only 14 years, with the right to one 14-year extension. But copyright holders have aggressively fought to lengthen the copyright period. These efforts have been led by the Walt Disney Company, which wants to protect its rights in Mickey Mouse. Now, a copyright is valid until 70 years after the death of the work's last living author or, in the case of works owned by a corporation, the copyright lasts 95 years from publication or 120 years from creation. Once a copyright expires, anyone may use the material. Mark Twain died in 1910, so anyone may now publish *Tom Sawyer* without permission and without paying a copyright fee.

A work is automatically copyrighted once it is in tangible form. For example, when a songwriter puts notes on paper, the work is copyrighted without further ado. But if she whistles a happy tune without writing it down, the song is not copyrighted, and anyone else can use it without permission. Registration with the Copyright Office of the Library of Congress is necessary only if the holder wishes to bring suit to enforce the copyright. Although authors still routinely place the copyright symbol (©) on their works, such a precaution is not necessary in the United States. However, some lawyers still recommend using the copyright symbol because other countries recognize it. Also, the penalties for intentional copyright infringement are heavier than for unintentional violations, and the presence of a copyright notice is evidence that the infringer's actions were intentional.

### INFRINGEMENT

Anyone who uses copyrighted material without permission is violating the Copyright Act. **To prove a violation, the plaintiff must present evidence that the work was original and that either:**

- The infringer actually copied the work; or
- The infringer had access to the original and the two works are substantially similar.

### FIRST SALE DOCTRINE

Suppose you buy a CD that, in the end, you do not like. Under the **first sale doctrine,** you have the legal right to sell that CD. **The first sale doctrine permits a person who owns a lawfully made copy of a copyrighted work to sell or otherwise dispose of that copy.** Note, however, that the first sale doctrine does not permit the owner to *make a copy*. If you listen to a CD and then decide to sell it, that is legal. But it is not legal to copy the CD onto your iPod and then dispose of the original or any copy of it.

### FAIR USE

Because the period of copyright protection is so long, it has become even more important to uphold the exceptions to the law. Bear in mind that the point of copyright laws is to encourage creative work. A writer who can control, and profit from, artistic work will be inclined to produce more. If enforced oppressively, however, the copyright laws could stifle creativity by denying

**Fair use doctrine**
Permits limited use of copyrighted material without permission of the author.

access to copyrighted work. **The doctrine of fair use permits limited use of copyrighted material without permission of the author for purposes such as criticism, news reporting, scholarship, or research.** Courts generally do not permit a use that will decrease revenues from the original work by, say, competing with it. A reviewer is permitted, for example, to quote from a book without the author's permission, but could not reproduce so much that the review was competing with the book itself.

Also under the fair use doctrine, faculty members are permitted to photocopy and distribute copyrighted materials to students, as long as the materials are brief and the teacher's action is spontaneous. If, over his breakfast coffee one morning, Professor Learned spots a terrific article in *Mad Magazine* that perfectly illustrates a point he intends to make in class that day, the fair use doctrine permits him to photocopy the page and distribute it to his class. However, when professors put together course packets, they (or the copy shop) must obtain permission and pay a royalty for the use of copyrighted material. Likewise, it is illegal for students to make photocopies of a classmate's course packet or textbook.

### Internet Searching

Internet searching has created a new issue of copyright law and fair use. In the following case, the court is asked to decide if the mighty Google search engine violates copyright law.

## YOU *be the* JUDGE

### PERFECT 10, INC. v. GOOGLE INC.
487 F.3d 701; 2007 U.S. App. LEXIS 11420
United States Court of Appeals for the Ninth Circuit, 2007

**Facts:** Perfect 10, Inc. has a Web site on which it sells copyrighted images of nude models. Subscribers pay a monthly fee to view these photos. Perfect 10 also sells smaller images for use on cell phones. Sometimes, Google's image search engine displays thumbnails of Perfect 10's photos. (Thumbnails are low-resolution images roughly 2 inches × 1.5 inches.) In theory, these thumbnails could also be used on cell phones, although there was no evidence that they had been so far.

Perfect 10 filed suit alleging that Google was violating copyright law by reproducing the thumbnail images. The district court issued an injunction prohibiting Google from displaying Perfect 10's photos. Google appealed, alleging that the thumbnails were a fair use.

**You Be the Judge:** Do Google's thumbnail displays of Perfect 10's photos violate copyright law? Are they a fair use?

**Argument for Perfect 10:** When Google makes and displays copies of Perfect 10's photographs, it is in direct violation of copyright law. Perfect 10 owns the images, and Google is displaying them without permission. Although the photos are small, they can be enlarged. They can also be used on cell phones in direct competition with Perfect 10's own business. The fact that these thumbnails have not yet been downloaded to cell phones does not mean that it will not happen in the future.

Google is not some charitable organization doing searches for the public good. It is a hugely profitable business. If it wants to make a profit from copyrighted works, it should pay for the privilege.

**Argument for Google:** The goal of the copyright law is to protect original work but also to support the development of new ideas that build on earlier ones. Courts have long acknowledged that they must avoid an application of this statute that is so rigid it would stifle the very creativity the law is designed to foster. Hence the fair use exception. These thumbnails are a fair use.

Although the images were created originally to serve an entertainment or aesthetic function, a search engine transforms them into a research tool, directing users to a source of information. As an electronic reference tool, search engines provide an enormous social benefit. They are a crucial part of the way we all live and work. If Perfect 10 prevails in this case, and search engines either cannot display copyrighted material or have to pay for it, Internet searching will be crippled. It is more important that the public have access to information on the Internet than it is to protect Perfect 10's right to its images.

In short, Google's search engine promotes the purposes of copyright and serves the interests of the public.

# DIGITAL MUSIC AND MOVIES

One of the major challenges in regulating copyrights is simply that modern intellectual property is so easy to copy. The entertainment world used to turn a blind eye to illegal copying, but recording companies and movie studios have come to believe that illegal downloading is hurting their profits. For the first time, CD sales actually declined nationally. One study found that the decline was particularly sharp in areas around college campuses. But whether or not free downloading has harmed record companies, they have the legal right to determine how their property will be distributed.

As the chapter opener illustrates, the RIAA is aggressively suing those who download illegally. And a coalition of entertainment businesses sued two companies that distributed the software used by many consumers to violate copyright law. So important was this issue that the Supreme Court waded into these murky waters.

## METRO-GOLDWYN-MAYER STUDIOS INC. v. GROKSTER, LTD.

125 S. CT. 2764, 2005 U.S. LEXIS 5212
SUPREME COURT OF THE UNITED STATES, 2005

### CASE SUMMARY

**Facts:** Grokster, Ltd., and StreamCast Networks, Inc., distributed free software that allowed computer users to share electronic files through peer-to-peer networks, so called because users' computers communicated directly with each other, not through central servers. The Grokster and StreamCast software could be used for legal purposes. Indeed, peer-to-peer networks were utilized by universities, government agencies, and libraries, among others. Even the briefs in this very case could be downloaded legally with the StreamCast software.

Nonetheless, nearly 90 percent of the files available for download through Grokster or StreamCast were copyrighted. Billions of files were shared each month—the scope of copyright infringement was staggering. The two companies even encouraged the illegal uses of their software. For example, the chief technology officer of StreamCast said that "the goal is to get in trouble with the law and get sued. It's the best way to get in the news."

A group of copyright holders (MGM and others) sued Grokster and StreamCast alleging that they were violating the copyright law by knowingly and intentionally distributing their software to users who would reproduce and distribute copyrighted works illegally. Both parties moved for summary judgment. The trial court held for Grokster and StreamCast; the appeals court affirmed. The Supreme Court granted *certiorari*.

**Issue:** *Were Grokster and StreamCast violating copyright law?*

**Decision:** Grokster and StreamCast did violate copyright law.

**Reasoning:** This case presents a trade-off between protecting artistic expression and inhibiting technological innovation. It is important not to discourage the development of technologies that could have both lawful and unlawful potential. Accordingly, mere knowledge that a product *could be* used to infringe copyrights is not enough to create liability. But when users can use Grokster software to copy songs or movies easily, they develop a disdain for copyright protection. If a product is widely used to commit infringement, copyright holders may not be able to enforce their rights effectively unless they go against the distributor of the copying device. To balance these competing interests, we hold that distributors are only liable if they deliberately encourage copyright violation.

Grokster distributed an electronic newsletter containing links to articles promoting its software's ability to access popular copyrighted music. Both Grokster and StreamCast helped customers locate and play copyrighted materials. Neither company attempted to develop filtering tools or other mechanisms to diminish the illegal use of their software. There is evidence of infringement on a gigantic scale.

These companies made money by selling advertisements that were sent to the screens of computers using their software. The more the software was used, the more ads they could send out and the greater their advertising revenue became. The success of the defendant's business model hinged on high-volume use, which infringed copyrights. The unlawful objective is unmistakable.

Anyone who distributes a product or software and then promotes its use for the purpose of infringing copyrights is liable for the resulting acts of infringement by third parties.

### The Digital Millennium Copyright Act

Tom Tomorrow drew a cartoon that was syndicated to 100 newspapers, but, by the time the last papers received it, the cartoon had already gone zapping around cyberspace. Because his name had been deleted, some editors thought he had plagiarized it.

In response to incidents such as this, Congress passed the **Digital Millennium Copyright Act (DMCA),** which provides that:

- **It is illegal to delete copyright information, such as the name of the author or the title of the article.** It is also illegal to distribute false copyright information. Thus, anyone who e-mailed Tom Tomorrow's cartoon without his name on it, or who claimed it was his own work, would be violating the law.

- **It is illegal to circumvent encryption or scrambling devices that protect copyrighted works.** For example, some software programs are designed so that they can only be copied once. Anyone who overrides this protective device to make another copy is violating the law.

- **It is illegal to distribute tools and technologies used to circumvent encryption devices.** If you help others to copy that software program, you have violated the statute.

## INTERNATIONAL COPYRIGHT TREATIES

**The Berne Convention requires member countries to provide automatic copyright protection to any works created in another member country.** The protection expires 50 years after the death of the author.

## · TRADEMARKS ·

**Trademark**
Any combination of words and symbols that a business uses to identify its products or services and distinguish them from others.

**A trademark is any combination of words and symbols that a business uses to identify its products or services and distinguish them from others.** Trademarks are important to both consumers and businesses. Consumers use trademarks to distinguish between competing products. People who feel that Nike shoes fit their feet best can rely on the Nike trademark to know they are buying the shoe they want. A business with a high-quality product can use a trademark to develop a loyal base of customers who are able to distinguish its product from another.

## OWNERSHIP AND REGISTRATION

Under common law, the first person to use a mark in trade owns it. Registration under the federal Lanham Act is not necessary. However, registration has several advantages:

- Even if a mark has been used in only one or two states, registration makes it valid nationally.

- Registration notifies the public that a mark is in use, because anyone who applies for registration first searches the Public Register to ensure that no one else has rights to the mark.

- The holder of a registered trademark generally has the right to use it as an Internet domain name.

Under the Lanham Act, the owner files an application with the PTO in Washington, D.C. The PTO will accept an application only if the owner has already used the mark attached to a product in interstate commerce or promises to use the mark within six months after the filing. In addition, the applicant must be the first to use the mark in interstate commerce. Initially, the trademark is valid for 10 years, but the owner can renew it for an unlimited number of 10-year terms as long as the mark is still in use.

## VALID TRADEMARKS

Words (Reebok); symbols (Microsoft's flying window logo); phrases (Nike's "Just do it"); shapes (Apple's iPod); sounds (NBC's three chimes); colors (Owens Corning's pink insulation); and even scents (plumeria blossoms on sewing thread) can be trademarked. To be valid, a trademark must be distinctive—that is, the mark must clearly distinguish one product from another.

The following categories are not distinctive and *cannot* be trademarked:

- **Similar to an existing mark.** To avoid confusion, the PTO will not grant a trademark that is similar to one already in existence on a similar product. Once the PTO had granted a trademark for "Pledge" furniture polish, it refused to trademark "Promise" for the same product.

- **Generic trademarks.** No one is permitted to trademark an item's ordinary name—"shoe" or "book," for example. Sometimes, however, a word begins as a trademark and later becomes a generic name. Zipper, escalator, aspirin, linoleum, thermos, yo-yo, band-aid, ping-pong, and nylon all started out as trademarks, but became generic. Once a name is generic, the owner loses the trademark because the name can no longer be used to distinguish one product from another—all products are called the same thing. That is why Xerox Corp. encourages people to say, "I'll photocopy this document," rather than "I'll xerox it."

- **Descriptive marks.** Words cannot be trademarked if they simply describe the product—such as "low-fat," "green," or "crunchy." Descriptive words can, however, be trademarked if they do not describe that particular product because they then become distinctive rather than descriptive. "Blue Diamond" is an acceptable trademark for nuts as long as the nuts are neither blue nor diamond shaped.

- **Names.** The PTO generally will not grant a trademark in a surname because other people are already using it and have the right to continue. No one could register "Jefferson" as a trademark.

- **Scandalous or immoral trademarks.** The PTO refused to register a mark that featured a nude man and woman embracing.[5]

## DOMAIN NAMES

Internet addresses, known as domain names, can be immensely valuable. Suppose you want to buy a new pair of jeans. Without thinking twice, you type in **http://www.jcrew.com** and there you are, ready to order. What if that address took you to a different site altogether, say, the personal site of one Jackie Crew? The store might lose out on a sale. Companies not only want to own their own domain name, they want to prevent complaint sites such as **http://www.untied .com** (about United Airlines) or **http://www.ihatestarbucks.com**. Generic domain names can be valuable, too. Shopping.com paid $750,000 to acquire its domain name from the previous (lucky) owner.

**The Anticybersquatting Consumer Protection Act permits both trademark owners and famous people to sue anyone who registers their name as a domain name in "bad faith."** The rightful owner of a trademark is entitled to damages of up to $100,000.

The good news about this statute is that it prevents Princeton Review from keeping the name kaplan.com, which the company acquired simply to inconvenience its archrival in the test preparation business. The bad news is that some businesses have used the law to threaten innocent holders of domain names. The maker of Pokey toys threatened a boy who had registered his nickname, Pokey, and Archie Comics went after a girl named Veronica. The Web site **http://www .chillingeffects.org** maintains a database of so-called "cease and desist" letters sent to holders of domain names.

---

[5] *In re McGinley,* 660 F.2d 481, 211 U.S.P.Q. (BNA) 668, 1981 CCPA LEXIS 177 (C.C.P.A. 1981).

## INTERNATIONAL TRADEMARK TREATIES

Under the **Paris Convention,** if someone registers a trademark in one country, then he has a grace period of six months during which he can file in any other country using the same original filing date. Under the **Madrid Agreement,** any trademark registered with the international registry is valid in all signatory countries. (The United States is a signatory.) The **Trademark Law Treaty** simplifies and harmonizes the process of applying for trademarks around the world. Now, a U.S. firm seeking international trademark protection need only file one application, in English, with the PTO, which sends the application to the World Intellectual Property Organization, which transmits it to each country in which the applicant would like trademark protection.

### EXAM *Strategy*

**Question:** Jerry Falwell was a nationally known Baptist minister. You can read about him on falwell.com. You can read about his views on homosexuality at fallwell.com—a site critical of his views. This site has a disclaimer indicating that it is not affiliated with Reverend Falwell. The minister sued fallwell.com, alleging a violation of trademark law and the anticybersquatting statute. Is there a violation?

**Strategy:** To win a trademark claim, the reverend must show that there was some confusion between the two sites. To win the cybersquatting claim, he must show bad faith on the part of fallwell.com.

**Result:** The reverend lost on both counts. The court ruled that there was no confusion—fallwell. com had a clear disclaimer. Also there was no indication of bad faith. The court was reluctant to censor political commentary.

## • TRADE SECRETS •

**Trade secret**
A formula, device, process, method, or compilation of information that, when used in business, gives the owner an advantage over competitors.

Trade secrets—such as the formula for Coca-Cola—can be a company's most valuable asset. It has been estimated that the theft of trade secrets costs U.S. businesses $100 billion a year. Under the Uniform Trade Secrets Act (UTSA), **a trade secret is a formula, device, process, method, or compilation of information that, when used in business, gives the owner an advantage over competitors who do not know it.** In determining if information is a trade secret, courts consider:

- How difficult (and expensive) was the information to obtain? Was it readily available from other sources?
- Does the information create an important competitive advantage?
- Did the company make a reasonable effort to protect it?

Although a company can patent some types of trade secrets, it may be reluctant to do so because patent registration requires that the formula be disclosed publicly. In addition, patent protection expires after 20 years. Some types of trade secrets cannot be patented—customer lists, business plans, manufacturing processes, and marketing strategies.

The following case deals with a typical issue: How much information can employees take with them when they start their own, competing business?

## POLLACK v. SKINSMART DERMATOLOGY AND AESTHETIC CENTER P.C.

2004 PA. DIST. & CNTY. DEC. LEXIS 214
COMMON PLEAS COURT OF PHILADELPHIA COUNTY, PENNSYLVANIA, 2004

### CASE SUMMARY

**Facts:** Dr. Andrew Pollack owned the Philadelphia Institute of Dermatology (PID), a dermatology practice. Drs. Toby Shawe and Samy Badawy worked for PID as independent contractors, receiving a certain percentage of the revenues from each patient they treated. Natalie Wilson was Dr. Pollack's medical assistant.

Pollack tentatively agreed to sell the practice to Shawe and Badawy. But instead of buying his practice, the two doctors decided to start their own, which they called Skinsmart. They executed a lease for the Skinsmart office space, offered Wilson a job, and instructed PID staff members to make copies of their appointment books and printouts of the patient list. Then they abruptly resigned from PID. Wilson called PID patients to reschedule procedures at Skinsmart. The two doctors also called patients and sent out a mailing to patients and referring physicians to tell them about Skinsmart.

Pollack filed suit, alleging that the two doctors had misappropriated trade secrets.

**Issue:** *Did Shawe and Badawy misappropriate trade secrets from PID?*

**Decision:** The two doctors did misappropriate trade secrets.

**Reasoning:** The right to protect trade secrets must be balanced against the right of individuals to pursue whatever occupation they choose. For this reason, secrets will only be protected if they are the particular information of the employer, not general secrets of the trade. Pollack must also demonstrate that the trade secret has value and importance to his business and that he either discovered or owned the secret.

Against this backdrop, it is clear the patient list is a trade secret, worthy of protection. Patient information is confidential and is not known to anyone outside the practice. Pollack relied upon the patient list as the core component of his practice. For this reason, it is valuable. He made substantial effort to compile the list over a number of years. It contained 20,000 names with related information. He spent money on computers, software, and employees to keep and maintain the list. He also sought to protect the secrecy of the information. Within PID's offices, the information was not universally known or accessible. Not every staff member, including the practicing physicians, could pull the records. Wilson did not have access to them, and the doctors relied on other PID employees to access the patient list.

## CHAPTER CONCLUSION

For many individuals and companies, intellectual property is the most valuable asset they will ever own. As its economic value increases, so does the need to understand the rules of intellectual property law.

## EXAM REVIEW

|  | Patent | Copyright | Trademark | Trade Secrets |
|---|---|---|---|---|
| Protects: | An invention that is the tangible application of an idea | The tangible expression of an idea, but not the idea itself | Words and symbols that a business uses to identify its products or services | Information that, when used in business, gives its owner an advantage over competitors |
| Requirements for protections: | Application approved by the PTO | Automatic once it is in tangible form | Must be used on the product in interstate commerce | Must be kept confidential |
| Duration: | 20 years | 70 years after death of the author or, for a corporation, 95 years from publication | 10 years, but can be renewed an unlimited number of times | As long as it is kept confidential |

## PRACTICE EXAM

### MATCHING QUESTIONS

Match the following terms with their definitions:

___ A. Patent

___ B. Copyright

___ C. Trade secrets

___ D. Trademark

___ E. Paris Convention

1. Protects the particular expression of an idea
2. Words that a business uses to identify its products
3. Extends patent protection overseas
4. Grants the inventor exclusive use of an invention
5. Compilation of information that would give its owner an advantage in business

### TRUE/FALSE QUESTIONS

Circle true or false:

**1.** T   F   Once you have purchased a CD and copied it onto your iPod, it is legal to give the CD to a friend.

**2.** T   F   A provisional patent lasts until the product is used in interstate commerce.

**3.** T   F   In the case of corporations, copyright protection lasts 120 years from the product's creation.

**4.** T   F   Under the fair use doctrine, you have the right to make a photocopy of a chapter of this textbook for a classmate.

**5.** T   F   The first person to file the application is entitled to a patent over someone else who invented the product first.

### MULTIPLE-CHOICE QUESTIONS

**6.** To obtain a patent, an inventor must show that her invention meets all of the following tests, except:

A. It has not ever been used anyplace in the world.

B. It is a new idea.

C. It has never been described in a publication.

D. It is nonobvious.

E. It is useful.

**7.** After the death of Babe Ruth, one of the most famous baseball players of all time, his daughters registered the name "Babe Ruth" as a trademark. Which of the following uses would be legal without the daughters' permission?

I. Publication of a baseball calendar with photos of Ruth

II. Sales of a "Babe Ruth" bat

III. Sales of Babe Ruth autographs

A. Neither I, II, nor III

B. Just I

C. Just II

D. Just III

E. I and III

8. To prove a violation of copyright law, the plaintiff does not need to prove that the infringer actually copied the work, but she does need to prove:

   I. The item has a © symbol on it.

   II. The infringer had access to the original.

   III. The two works are similar.

   A. I, II, and III

   B. II and III

   C. I and II

   D. I and III

   E. Neither I, II, nor III

9. Eric is a clever fellow who knows all about computers. He:

   I. Removed the author's name from an article he found on the Internet and sent it via e-mail to his lacrosse team, telling them he wrote it

   II. Figured out how to unscramble his roommate's cable signal so they could watch cable on a second TV

   III. Taught the rest of his lacrosse team how to unscramble cable signals

   Which of these activities is legal under the Digital Millennium Copyright Act?

   A. I, II, and III

   B. Neither I, II, nor III

   C. II and III

   D. Just III

   E. Just I

10. Which of the following items *cannot* be trademarked?

    A. Color

    B. Symbol

    C. Phrase

    D. Surname

    E. Shape

## SHORT-ANSWER QUESTIONS

11. Rebecca Reyher wrote (and copyrighted) a children's book entitled *My Mother Is the Most Beautiful Woman in the World*. The story was based on a Russian folktale told to her by her own mother. Years later, the children's TV show *Sesame Street* televised a skit entitled "The Most Beautiful Woman in the World." The *Sesame Street* version took place in a different locale and had fewer frills, but the sequence of events in both stories was identical. The author of the *Sesame Street* script denied he had ever seen Reyher's book but said his skit was based on a story told to his sister some 20 years before. Has *Sesame Street* infringed Reyher's copyright?

12. **Question:** A man asked a question of the advice columnist at his local newspaper. His wife had thought of a clever name for an automobile. He wanted to know if there was any way they could own or register the name so that no one else could use it. If you were the columnist, how would you respond?

    **Strategy:** The couple want to trademark this name. Can they do so? (See the "Result" at the end of this section.)

**EXAM Strategy**

13. **Question:** Frank B. McMahon wrote one of the first psychology textbooks to feature a light and easily readable style. He also included slang and examples that appealed to a youthful student market. Charles G. Morris wrote a psychology textbook that copied McMahon's style. Has Morris infringed McMahon's copyright?

    **Strategy:** McMahon cannot copyright an idea, only the *expression* of an idea. (See the "Result" at the end of this section.)

14. ETHICS: After Edward Miller left his job as a salesperson at the New England Insurance Agency, Inc., he took some of his New England customers to his new employer. At New England, the customer lists had been kept in file cabinets. Although the company did not restrict access to these files, it said there was a "you do not peruse my files and I do not peruse yours" understanding. The lists were not marked "confidential" or "not to be disclosed." Did Miller steal New England's trade secrets? Whether or not he violated the law, was it ethical for him to use this information at his new job?

15. In the documentary movie, *Expelled: No Intelligence Allowed*, there is a 15-second clip of "Imagine," a song by John Lennon. His wife and sons, who held the copyright, sued to block this use of the song. The movie is sympathetic to "intelligent design"—the theory that the universe is too complex to have been created by evolution alone, and there must have been a god involved. Who will win this suit?

16. ROLE REVERSAL: Draft a multiple-choice question that focuses on an issue of copyright law.

**12. Result:** The couple could not trademark the name unless they had already or were intending to attach it to a product used in interstate commerce. So unless they had plans to manufacture a car, they could not trademark the name.

**13. Result:** The style of a textbook is an idea and not copyrightable. Thus, Morris could write a book with funny stories, just not the same stories told in the same way as in McMahon's book. Morris did not infringe McMahon's copyright.

# INTERNET RESEARCH PROBLEM

Think of a name for an interesting new product. Click on TESS (Trademark Electronic Search System) at **http://www.uspto.gov/main/trademarks.htm** to see if this name is available as a trademark. Also look at **http://www.verisign.com** to see if it is available as an Internet domain name.

You can find further practice problems in the Online Quiz at **www.cengage.com/blaw/beatty.**

# REAL PROPERTY

**Some men** have staked claims to land for its oil, others for its gold. But Paul Termarco and Gene Murdoch are staking their claim to an island using . . . hot dogs. Their quest to market frankfurters in the New Jersey wilderness has made their children blush with embarrassment, their wives shrug in bewilderment, and strangers burst into laughter. But for three years, the two friends from West Milford have sold chili dogs, cheese dogs, and the ever-traditional, hold-everything-but-the-mustard hot dogs from a tiny island in Greenwood Lake. Now it seems as though everyone knows about "Hot Dog Island."

> **Paul Termarco and Gene Murdoch are staking their claim to an island using . . . hot dogs.**

"People love it," said Termarco. "They say, 'Thank you for being here.' I always say, 'No. Thank you.'" The personalized service and the inexpensive prices (hot dogs cost $1.75, chili dogs, cheese dogs, and sauerkraut $2) have cultivated a base of regulars. "I think it's great. It's better than going to a restaurant for two hours and spending a lot of money," said Joan Vaillant, who frequently jet-skis to the island for hot dogs slathered in mustard.

At two-eighths of an acre, the island's pile of craggy rocks, scrubby bushes, and a few ash trees are difficult to spot. Termarco doesn't mind. "Not everyone can say they own an island," he boasted. Termarco and Murdoch decided to claim the slip of land after chatting with a local restaurateur a few years ago. Termarco had just finished suggesting that the man expand his lakeside business to the island when Murdoch kicked his friend under the table.

"We left thinking, 'We can do this ourselves,'" said Murdoch, who rushed to the township offices the following day to see who owned the island. Property records showed that the state owned the lake and lake floor, but nobody owned the island. An attorney told them about the law of adverse possession written in the 1820s. If Murdoch and Termarco could show that they used the island for five years, it would be theirs. As crazy as the scheme sounded, Murdoch figured it was worth trying.[1]

Can two friends acquire an island simply by pretending they own it? Possibly. The law of adverse possession permits people to obtain title to land by using it if they meet certain criteria, which we examine later in the chapter. Real property law can provide surprises.

## · NATURE OF REAL PROPERTY ·

**Grantor**
An owner who conveys an interest in his property to someone else.

**Grantee**
A person who receives an interest in property from a grantor.

We need to define a few terms. A **grantor** is an owner who conveys his property, or some interest in it, to someone else, called the **grantee**. If you sell your house to Veronica, you are the grantor and she is the grantee. Real property may be any of the following:

- **Land.** Land is the most common and important form of real property. In England, land was historically the greatest source of wealth, and so the law of real property has been of paramount importance for nearly 1,000 years.
- **Buildings.** Buildings are real property. Houses, office buildings, and factories all fall (or stand) in this category.
- **Subsurface Rights.** In most states, the owner of the land also owns anything under the surface, down to the center of the earth. The subsurface rights may be worth far more than the surface land, for example, if there is oil or gold underfoot. Although the landowner generally owns these rights, she may sell them, while retaining ownership of the surface land.

---

[1] Leslie Haggin, "Pair Stake Their Claim to Hot Dog Island," *Record* (Bergen, NJ), Sept. 5, 1994, p. A12. Excerpted with permission of the *Record,* Hackensack, NJ.

- **Air Rights.** The owner of land owns the airspace above the land. Suppose you own an urban parking lot. If the owner of an adjacent office building wishes to build a walkway across your property to join his building with a neighboring skyscraper, he needs your permission and will expect to pay handsomely for it.

- **Plant Life.** Plant life growing on land is real property, whether the plants are naturally occurring, such as trees, or cultivated crops. When a landowner sells his property, plant life is automatically included in the sale, unless the parties agree otherwise.

- **Fixtures.** Fixtures are goods that have become attached to real property. A house (which is real property) contains many fixtures. The furnace and heating ducts were goods when they were manufactured and when they were sold to the builder, because they were movable. But when the builder attached them to the house, the items became fixtures. By contrast, neither the refrigerator nor the grand piano is a fixture.

When an owner sells real property, the buyer normally takes the fixtures, unless the parties specify otherwise. Sometimes it is difficult to determine whether something is a fixture. The general rule is this: an object is a fixture if a reasonable person would consider the item to be a permanent part of the property. To decide the issue, courts look at:

*Attachment.* If an object is attached to property in such a way that removing it would damage the property, it is probably a fixture.

*Adaptation.* Something that is made or adapted especially for attachment to the particular property is probably a fixture, such as custom-made bookshelves fitted in a library.

*Other manifestations of permanence.* If the owner of the property clearly intends the item to remain permanently, it is probably a fixture. A homeowner who builds a large concrete platform in his backyard, then bolts a heavy metal shed to it, has created a fixture. For many, beef is a dietary fixture. Is this cattle scale a fixture?

## FREEMAN V. BARRS

237 S.W.3D 285, MISSOURI COURT OF APPEALS, 2007

### CASE SUMMARY

**Facts:** Mary Ann Barrs paid $3.5 million to Francis Freeman for 4,000 acres of ranch land, including a covered "pole-barn," which had open sides, a large cattle scale, and an enclosed veterinarian's office. The parties used a form contract, which stated that all fixtures were included with the sale. The document offered space for the parties to specify items that were included or excluded with the sale, but neither party listed the cattle scale as either in or out of the deal. After the agreement went through, Barrs and Freeman got into a beef over who owned the scale. The trial judge grilled numerous witnesses and ultimately weighed in on the side of Barrs, declaring the scale a fixture that belonged to the real estate. Broiling, Freeman appealed.

**Issue:** *Was the cattle scale a fixture?*

**Decision:** Yes, the scale was a fixture.

**Reasoning:** The scale's maker testified that it was designed to be portable. It would only take him an hour to cut away a welded metal fence and then quickly move the scale itself.

On the other hand, the scale weighs approximately 6,500 pounds. It could not be installed until a fence and gates within the barn were cut off. Concrete ramps and fencing were installed on two sides of the scale to direct cattle onto it. The metal posts for the fence were set in the concrete. The scale has remained in place since its installation.

A 6,500-pound scale placed on a specially sized concrete pad and surrounded by metal pole fencing is annexed to the real estate. The permanency of the installation is emphasized by the fact the barn is covered and includes a veterinary office. The scale was a fixture, and was included in the sale of the real estate.

Affirmed.

# · ESTATES IN REAL PROPERTY ·

Use and ownership of real estate can take many different legal forms. A person may own property outright, having the unrestricted use of the land and an unlimited right to sell it. However, someone may also own a lesser interest in real property. For example, you could inherit the use of a parcel of land during your lifetime, but have no power to leave the land to your heirs. The different rights that someone can hold in real property are known as **estates or interests.**

## FREEHOLD ESTATES

**Freehold estate**
gives the owner the right to possess the property and use it in any lawful way she wants.

**The owner of a freehold estate has the present right to possess the property and to use it in any lawful way she wants.** The three most important freehold estates are (1) fee simple absolute; (2) fee simple defeasible; and (3) life estate.

## FEE SIMPLE ABSOLUTE

**Fee simple absolute**
provides the owner with the greatest possible control of the property.

**A fee simple absolute provides the owner with the greatest possible control of the property.** This is the most common form of land ownership. Suppose Cecily inherits a fee simple interest in a 30-acre vineyard. She may use the land for any purpose that the law allows. She may continue to raise grapes, or she may rip up the vines and build a bowling alley. Although zoning laws may regulate her use, nothing in Cecily's estate itself limits her use of the land. Cecily may pass on to her heirs her entire estate, that is, her full fee simple absolute.

## FEE SIMPLE DEFEASIBLE

Other estates contain more limited rights than the fee simple absolute. Wily establishes the Wily Church of Perfection. Upon his death, Wily leaves a 100-acre estate to the church for as long as it keeps the name "Wily Church of Perfection." Wily has included a significant limitation in the church's ownership. The church has a fee simple defeasible.

**Fee simple defeasible**
may terminate upon the occurrence of some limiting event.

   **A fee simple defeasible may terminate upon the occurrence of some limiting event.** If the congregation decides to rename itself the Happy Valley Church of Perfection, the church automatically loses its estate in the 100 acres. Ownership of the land then **reverts** to Wily's heirs, meaning title goes back to them. Because the heirs might someday inherit the land, they are said to have a future interest in the 100 acres. A landowner may create a fee simple defeasible to ensure that property is used in a particular way, or is not used in a specified manner (for example, as a casino).

## LIFE ESTATE

**Life estate**
Ownership of property for the lifetime of a particular person.

A **life estate** is exactly what you would think: **an estate for the life of some named person.** Aretha owns Respect Farm, and in her will she leaves it to Max, for his lifetime. Max is the **life tenant**. He is entitled to live on the property and work it as a normal farm during his lifetime, though he is obligated to maintain it properly. The moment Max dies, the farm reverts to Aretha or her heirs.

**Life tenant**
A person who has the use of a property during his lifetime only.

## CONCURRENT ESTATES

**Concurrent estate**
Two or more people owning property at the same time.

When two or more people own real property at the same time, they have **concurrent estates**. In a **tenancy in common**, the owners have an equal interest in the entire property. Each co-tenant has the right to sell her interest to someone else, or to leave it to her heirs upon her death. A **joint tenancy** is similar, except that upon the death of one joint tenant (owner), his interest passes to the surviving joint tenants, not to his heirs.

**Tenancy in common**
Two or more people holding equal interest in a property, but with no right of survivorship.

**Joint tenancy**
Two or more people holding equal interest in a property, with the right of survivorship.

## EXAM *Strategy*

**Question:** Thomas, aged 80, has spent a lifetime accumulating unspoiled land in Oregon. He owns 16,000 acres, which he plans to leave to his five children, aged 48 to 60, all of whom he adores. He is not so crazy about his grandchildren, many of whom dislike each other and squabble with their aunts and uncles. Thomas cringes at the problems the grandchildren would cause if some of them inherited an interest in the land and became part-owners along with Thomas's own children. Should Thomas leave his land to his children as tenants in common or joint tenants?

**Strategy:** When a co-tenant dies, her interest in property passes to her heirs. When a joint tenant dies, his interest in the property passes to the surviving joint tenants.

**Result:** Thomas is better off leaving the land to his children as joint tenants. That way, when one of his children dies, that child's interest in the land will go to Thomas's surviving children, not to his grandchildren. (There are other approaches Thomas could take, such as creation of a trust, and they are discussed in Chapter 31 on estate planning.)

To provide special rights for married couples, some states have created **tenancy by the entirety** and **community property.** These forms of ownership allow one spouse to protect some property from the other, and from the other's creditors.

Condominiums and cooperatives are most common in apartment buildings with multiple units, though they can be used in other settings, such as a cluster of houses on a single parcel of land. In a **condominium,** the owner of the apartment typically has a fee simple absolute in his particular unit. He is normally entitled to sell or lease the unit, must pay taxes on it, and may receive the normal tax deduction if he is carrying a mortgage. All unit owners belong to a condominium association, which manages the common areas. In a **cooperative,** the residents generally do not own their particular unit. Instead, they are shareholders in a corporation that owns the building and leases specified units to the shareholders.

## · NONPOSSESSORY INTERESTS ·

All of the estates and interests that we have examined thus far focused on one thing: possession of the land. Now we look at interests that *never* involve possession. These interests may be very valuable, even though the holder never lives on the land.

## EASEMENTS

The Alabama Power Co. drove a flatbed truck over land owned by Thomas Burgess, damaging the property. The power company did this to reach its power lines and wooden transmission poles. Burgess had never given Alabama Power permission to enter his land, and he sued for the damage that the heavy trucks caused. He recovered—nothing. Alabama Power had an easement to use Burgess's land.

**An easement gives one person the right to enter land belonging to another and make a limited use of it, without taking anything away.** Burgess had bought his land from a man named Denton, who years earlier had sold an easement to Alabama Power. The easement gave the power company the right to construct several transmission poles on one section of Denton's land and to use reasonable means to reach the poles. Alabama Power owned that easement forever, and when Burgess bought the land, he took it subject to the easement. Alabama Power drove its trucks

**Easement**
The right to enter land belonging to another and make limited use of it.

across a section of land where the power company had never gone before, and the easement did not explicitly give the company this right. But the court found that the company had no other way to reach its poles, and therefore the easement allowed this use. Burgess is stuck with his uninvited guest as long as he owns the land.

Property owners normally create easements in one of two ways. A **grant** occurs when a landowner expressly intends to convey an easement to someone else. This is how Alabama Power acquired its easement. A **reservation** occurs when an owner sells land but keeps some right to enter the property. A farmer might sell 40 acres to a developer but reserve an easement giving him the right to drive his equipment across a specified strip of the land.

The following case demonstrates the potential power of easements. *Too* powerful?

## YOU *be the* JUDGE

### CARVIN v. ARKANSAS POWER AND LIGHT

14 F.3d 399, 1993 U.S. App. LEXIS 33986
United States Court of Appeals for
the Eighth Circuit, 1993

**Facts:** Between 1923 and 1947, Arkansas Power & Light (AP&L) constructed several dams on two Arkansas lakes, Hamilton and Catherine. The company then obtained "flood easements" on property adjoining the lakes. AP&L obtained some of the easements by grant and others by reservation, selling lakeside property and keeping the easement. These flood easements permitted AP&L to "clear of trees, brush, and other obstructions and to submerge by water" certain acreage, which was described exactly. AP&L properly recorded the easements, and when the current landowners bought lakeside property, they were aware of the documents.

During one 12-hour period in May 1990, extraordinarily heavy rains fell in the Ouachita River Basin, including both lakes. In some areas, over 10 inches of rain fell, causing the water to reach the highest levels ever recorded. To avoid flooding Lake Hamilton, AP&L opened the gates of a dam called Carpenter. This caused Lake Catherine to flood, with water in some places rising 25 feet. This flood caused massive damage to the plaintiffs' houses, with water in some cases rising to the roof level.

Several dozen landowners sued, claiming that AP&L was negligent in opening one dam without simultaneously opening another and also in failing to warn homeowners of the intended action. The federal district court granted summary judgment for AP&L, based on the flood easements, and the landowners appealed.

**You Be the Judge:** Did the easements relieve AP&L from liability for flooding?

**Argument for the Landowners:** No sane homeowner would give a power company the right to do what this company has done. AP&L has destroyed land, demolished houses, and ruined lives. AP&L opened a dam knowing that this would flood the shores of Lake Catherine and inundate dozens of properties.

These flood easements were many years old, created long before many of the present owners bought their property. None of them ever dreamed something like this could happen. Even if the easements were once valid, they should not be enforced any longer.

Further, no easement authorizes negligence. At most the easements would permit some minimal flooding by a carefully controlled process, after adequate notice to everyone concerned. Here there was no notice, no care, no decency. AP&L should not be allowed to rely on ancient pieces of paper to wash away land and ruin lives.

**Argument for AP&L:** The flooding was caused by an act of God, not by anything AP&L did. The company opened the dam without notice because there was no time to give notice. AP&L had the duty to act quickly, to protect residents of a much wider area.

A flood easement exists for one reason: to allow a company, when necessary, to flood land. Although some of these owners did not grant the easements, their predecessors did. The value of the property would naturally decline somewhat with a flood easement attached, and as a result these owners paid less for their property. All of the owners made calculated decisions to accept the risk, and they must now live with their choices.

## PROFIT

**A profit gives one person the right to enter land belonging to another and take something away.** You own 100 acres of vacation property, and suddenly a mining company informs you that the land contains valuable nickel deposits. You may choose to sell a profit to the mining company, allowing it to enter your land and take away the nickel. You receive cash up front, and the company earns money from the sale of the mineral.

**Profit**
gives one person the right to enter land belonging to another and take something away.

## LICENSE

**A license gives the holder temporary permission to enter upon another's property.** Unlike an easement or profit, a license is a temporary right. When you attend a basketball game by buying a ticket, the basketball club that sells you the ticket is the licensor and you are the licensee. You are entitled to enter the licensor's premises, namely the basketball arena, and to remain during the game, though the club can revoke the license if you behave unacceptably.

**License**
gives the holder temporary permission to enter upon another's property.

## MORTGAGE

Generally, in order to buy a house, a prospective owner must borrow money. The bank or other lender will require security before it hands over its money, and the most common form of security for a real estate loan is a mortgage. **A mortgage is a security interest in real property.** The homeowner who borrows money is the **mortgagor,** because she is giving the mortgage to the lender. The lender, in turn, is the **mortgagee,** the party acquiring a security interest. The mortgagee in most cases obtains a lien on the house, meaning the right to foreclose on the property if the mortgagor fails to pay back the money borrowed.

**Mortgage**
A security interest in real property.

### EXAM *Strategy*

**Question:** Madison owns 160 acres of unused land in Montana. To make some money from the property, she has recently sold an easement, a profit, and a license. Give examples that show how Madison might have done that, and how the three interests differ from each other.

**Strategy:** An easement gives someone the right to enter land belonging to another and make a limited use of it, without taking anything away. A profit gives a person the right to enter land belonging to another and take something away. A license gives the holder temporary permission to enter upon another's property.

**Result:** Madison sold an easement to an adjacent property owner, allowing him to drive "all farm equipment" straight across her property on a designated road. To a mineral company, she sold the right to extract silver from 80 specified acres. For a local Fourth of July celebration, she charged a hot-air balloon company a one-time fee, allowing the outfit to give rides from her property, at the same time selling tickets to park on the land.

## · SALE OF REAL PROPERTY ·

For most people, buying or selling a house is the biggest, most important financial transaction they will make. Here we consider several of the key issues that may arise.

# Seller's Obligations Concerning the Property

Historically, the common law recognized the rule of caveat emptor in the sale of real property—that is, let the buyer beware. If a buyer walked into his new living room and fell through the floor into a lake of toxic waste, it was his tough luck. But the common law changes, and today courts place an increasing burden of fairness on sellers. Two significant obligations are the implied warranty of habitability and the duty to disclose defects.

## Implied Warranty of Habitability

**Most states now impose an implied warranty of habitability on a builder who sells a new home.** This means that, whether he wants to or not, the builder is guaranteeing that the new house contains **adequate materials** and **good workmanship.** The law implies this warranty because of the inherently unequal position of builder and buyer. Some defects might be obvious to a lay observer, such as a room with no roof or a front porch that sways whenever the neighbors sneeze. But only the builder will know if he made the frame with proper wood or if the heating system was second-rate. In most states the law implies this warranty to protect buyers of residential, but not commercial, property.

## Duty to Disclose Defects

**The seller of a home must disclose facts that a buyer does not know and cannot readily observe if they materially affect the property's value.** Roy and Charlyne Terrell owned a house in the Florida Keys, where zoning codes required all living areas to be 15 feet above sea level. They knew that their house violated the code because a bedroom and bathroom were on the ground floor. They offered to sell the house to Robert Revitz, assuring him that the property complied with all codes and that flood insurance would cost about $350 per year. Revitz bought the house, moved in, and later learned that because of the code violations, flood insurance would be slightly more expensive—costing just over $36,000 per year. He sued and won. The court declared that the Terrells had a duty to disclose the code violations; it ordered a rescission of the contract, meaning that Revitz got his money back. The court mentioned that the duty to disclose was wide-ranging and included leaking roofs, insect infestation, cracks in walls and foundations, and any other problems that a buyer might be unable to discern.

> Revitz learned flood insurance would be slightly more expensive than $350 per year—it would cost just over $36,000.

# Sales Contract and Title Examination

The statute of frauds requires that an agreement to sell real property must be in writing to be enforceable. A contract for the sale of a house is often several pages of dense legal reading, in which the lawyers for the buyer and seller attempt to allocate risks for every problem that might go wrong. Once the parties have agreed to the terms and signed a contract, the buyer's lawyer performs a **title examination,** that is, a search through the local land registry for all documents relating to the property. The purpose is to ensure that the seller actually has valid title to this land. Even if the seller owns the land, his title may be subject to other claims, such as an easement or a mortgage.

# Closing and Deeds

While the buyer is checking the seller's title, she also probably needs to arrange financing, as described earlier in the section on mortgages. When the title work is complete and the buyer has arranged financing, the parties arrange a **closing,** a meeting at which the property is actually sold. The seller brings to the closing a **deed**, which is the document proving ownership of the land. The seller signs the deed over to the buyer in exchange for the purchase price. The buyer pays the price either with a certified check and/or by having her lender pay. If a lender pays part or all of the price, the buyer executes a mortgage to the lender as part of the closing.

**Deed**
A document that proves ownership of property.

# RECORDING

**Recording** the deed means filing it with the official state registry. The registry clerk places a photocopy of the deed in the agency's bound volumes and indexes the deed by the name of the grantor and the grantee. Recording is a critical step in the sale of land, because it puts all the world on notice that the grantor has sold the land.

## ▪ ADVERSE POSSESSION ▪

Recall Paul Termarco and Gene Murdoch, who opened this chapter by trying to sell us a hot dog from the middle of a New Jersey lake. The pair had their sights set on more than mustard and relish: They hoped that by using the island as if they owned it, they *would* own it. They were relying on the doctrine of adverse possession. **Adverse possession allows someone to take title to land if she demonstrates possession that is (1) exclusive; (2) notorious; (3) adverse to all others; and (4) continuous.**

**Adverse possession** allows someone to take title to land without paying for it, if she meets four specific standards.

### ENTRY AND EXCLUSIVE POSSESSION

The user must take physical possession of the land and must be the only one to do so. If the owner is still occupying the land, or if other members of the public share its use, there can be no adverse possession.

### OPEN AND NOTORIOUS POSSESSION

The user's presence must be visible and generally known in the area, so that the owner is on notice that his title is contested. This ensures that the owner can protect his property by ejecting the user. Someone making secret use of the land gives the owner no opportunity to do this, and hence acquires no rights in the land.

### A CLAIM ADVERSE TO THE OWNER

The user must clearly assert that the land is his. He does not need to register a deed or take other legal steps, but he must act as though he is the sole owner. If the user occupies the land with the owner's permission, there is no adverse claim and the user acquires no rights in the property.

### CONTINUOUS POSSESSION FOR THE STATUTORY PERIOD

State statutes on adverse possession prescribe a period of years for continuous use of the land. Originally, most states required about 20 years to gain adverse possession, but the trend has been to shorten this period. Many states now demand 10 years, but a few require only 5 years' use. The reason for shortening the period is to reward those who make use of land.

Regardless of the length required, the use must be continuous. In a residential area, the user would have to occupy the land year round for the prescribed period. In a wilderness area generally used only in the summer, a user could gain ownership by seasonal use.

How did Murdoch and Termarco fare? They certainly entered on the land and established themselves as the exclusive occupants. Their use has been open and notorious, allowing anyone who claimed ownership to take steps to eject them from the property. Their actions have been adverse to anyone else's claim. If the two hot dog entrepreneurs have grilled those dogs for the full statutory period, they should take title to the island.

In the following case, the couple claiming adverse possession have taken up residence in a ghost town.

## RAY V. BEACON HUDSON MOUNTAIN CORP.

88 N.Y.2D 154, 666 N.E.2D 532, 1996 N.Y. LEXIS 676
COURT OF APPEALS OF NEW YORK, 1996

### CASE SUMMARY

**Facts:** In 1931, Rose Ray purchased a cottage in a mountain-top resort town in the Adirondacks, at the same time agreeing to rent the land on which the structure stood. The long-term lease required her to pay the real estate taxes and provided that when the tenancy ended, the landlord would buy back the cottage at fair market value. In 1960, the landlord terminated the lease of everyone in the town, so Ray and all other residents packed up and left. She died in 1962, without ever getting a penny for the cottage. The next year, Mt. Beacon Incline Lands, Inc., bought all rights to the abandoned 156-acre resort.

Robert and Margaret Ray, the son and daughter-in-law of Rose Ray, reentered the cottage and began to use it one month per year, every summer from 1963 to 1988. They paid taxes, insured the property, installed utilities, and posted "no trespassing" signs.

In 1978, Beacon Hudson bought the resort in a tax foreclosure sale. Finally, in 1988, the Rays filed suit, claiming title to the cottage by adverse possession. Beacon Hudson counterclaimed, seeking to eject the Rays. The trial court ruled for the couple. The appellate court reversed, stating that the Rays had been absent too frequently to achieve adverse possession. The Rays appealed to New York's highest court.

**Issue:** *Did the Rays acquire title by adverse possession?*

**Decision:** The Rays acquired title by adverse possession. Reversed.

**Reasoning:** To obtain property by adverse possession, the claiming party must prove continuous possession, among other elements. However, the actual occupancy need not be constant. The claimant must simply use the land as ordinary owners would.

Beacon Hudson argues that the Rays cannot demonstrate continuous possession because they only occupied the property one month per year. However, that argument fails to consider the Rays' other acts of control over the premises. The couple maintained and improved the cottage and installed utilities. They also repelled trespassers, posted the land, and padlocked the cottage. These acts demonstrated continuous control of the property.

The Rays' seasonal use of the cottage, along with the improvements described, put the owner on notice of the couple's hostile and exclusive claim of ownership, especially considering that all neighboring structures had collapsed due to vandalism and neglect. The Rays have obtained title by adverse possession.

## · LAND USE REGULATION ·

### ZONING

**Zoning statutes**
State laws that permit local communities to regulate land use.

**Zoning statutes are state laws that permit local communities to regulate building and land use.** The local communities, whether cities, towns, or counties, then pass zoning ordinances that control many aspects of land development. For example, a town's zoning ordinance may divide the community into an industrial zone where factories may be built, a commercial zone in which stores of a certain size are allowed, and several residential zones in which only houses may be constructed. Within the residential zones, there may be further divisions, for example, permitting two-family houses in certain areas and requiring larger lots in others.

**ETHICS** Many people abhor "adult" businesses, such as strip clubs and pornography shops. Urban experts agree that a large number of these concerns in a neighborhood often causes crime to increase and property values to drop. Nonetheless, many people patronize such businesses, which can earn a good profit. Should a city have the right to restrict adult businesses? Some cities have passed zoning ordinances that prohibit adult businesses from all residential neighborhoods, from some commercial districts, or from being within 500 feet of schools, houses of worship, daycare centers, or other sex shops (to avoid clustering). Owners and patrons of these shops have protested, claiming the restrictions unfairly deny access to a form of entertainment that the public obviously desires. From the Chapter 2 Ethics Checklist: Who are the stakeholders? What are the consequences of these restrictions? Are there any superior alternatives? ◆

# EMINENT DOMAIN

**Eminent domain is the power of the government to take private property for public use.** A government may need land to construct a highway, an airport, a university, or public housing. All levels of government—federal, state, and local—have this power. But the Fifth Amendment to the United States Constitution states: ". . . nor shall private property be taken for public use, without just compensation." The Supreme Court has held that this clause, the Takings Clause, applies not only to the federal government but also to state and local governments. So, although all levels of government have the power to take property, they must pay the owner a fair price.

A "fair price" generally means the reasonable market value of the land. Generally, if the property owner refuses the government's offer, the government will file suit seeking **condemnation** of the land, that is, a court order specifying what compensation is just and awarding title to the government.

> **Eminent domain**
> The power of the government to take private property for public use.

## CHAPTER CONCLUSION

**Real property law is ancient but forceful,** as waterfront property owners discovered when a power company flooded their land and an old-fashioned easement deprived them of compensation. Had the owners truly understood nonpossessory interests when they bought their property, they would have realized the risk the investment represented. Although real property today is not the dominant source of wealth that it was in medieval England, it is still the greatest asset that most people will ever possess—and is worth understanding.

## EXAM REVIEW

1.  **REAL PROPERTY** Real property includes land, buildings, air and subsurface rights, plant life, and fixtures. A fixture is any good that has become attached to other real property. (p. 452)

**EXAM Strategy**

**Question:** Paul and Shelly Higgins had two wood stoves in their home. Each rested on, but was not attached to, a built-in brick platform. The downstairs wood stove was connected to the chimney flue and was used as part of the main heating system for the house. The upstairs stove, in the master bedroom, was purely decorative. It had no stovepipe connecting it to the chimney. The Higginses sold their house to Jack Everitt, and neither party said anything about the two stoves. Is Everitt entitled to either stove? Both stoves?

**Strategy:** An object is a fixture if a reasonable person would consider the item to be a permanent part of the property, taking into account attachment, adaptation, and other objective manifestations of permanence. (See the "Result" at the end of this section.)

2.  **FEE SIMPLE ABSOLUTE** A fee simple absolute provides the owner with the greatest possible control of the property, including the right to make any lawful use of it and to sell it. (p. 454)

3. **FEE SIMPLE DEFEASIBLE** A fee simple defeasible may terminate upon the occurrence of some limiting event. (p. 454)

4. **LIFE ESTATE** A life estate permits the owner to possess the property during her life, but not to sell it or leave it to heirs. (p. 454)

5. **CONCURRENT ESTATES** When two or more people own real property at the same time, they have a concurrent estate. (p. 454)

6. **EASEMENTS** An easement gives a person the right to enter land belonging to another and make a limited use of it, without taking anything away. (p. 455)

7. **IMPLIED WARRANTY OF HABITABILITY** The implied warranty of habitability means that a builder selling a new home guarantees the adequacy of materials and workmanship. (p. 458)

8. **DISCLOSURE** The seller of a home must disclose facts that a buyer does not know and cannot readily observe, if they materially affect the property's value. (p. 458)

9. **ADVERSE POSSESSION** Adverse possession permits the user of land to gain title if he can prove entry and exclusive possession, open and notorious possession, a claim adverse to the owner, and continuous possession for the required statutory period. (p. 459)

**EXAM Strategy**

**Question:** In 1966, Arketex Ceramic Corp. sold land in rural Indiana to Malcolm Aukerman. The deed described the southern boundary as the section line between sections 11 and 14 of the land. Farther south of this section line stood a dilapidated fence running east to west. Aukerman and Arketex both believed that this fence was the actual southern boundary of his new land, though in fact it lay on Arketex's property.

Aukerman installed a new electrified fence, cleared the land on "his" side of the new fence, and began to graze cattle there. In 1974, Harold Clark bought the land that bordered Aukerman's fence, assuming that the fence was the correct boundary. In 1989, Clark had his land surveyed and discovered that the true property line lay north of the electric fence. Aukerman filed suit, seeking a court order that he had acquired the disputed land by adverse possession. The statutory period in Indiana is 20 years. Who wins?

**Strategy:** There are four elements to adverse possession. Has Aukerman proved them? (See the "Result" at the end of this section.)

10. **REGULATION** Nuisance law, zoning ordinances, and eminent domain all permit a government to regulate property and in some cases to take it for public use. (p. 460)

**1. Result:** A buyer normally takes all fixtures. The downstairs stove was permanently attached to the house and used as part of the heating system. The owner who installed it *intended* that it remain, and it was a fixture; Everitt got it. The upstairs stove was not permanently attached and was not a fixture; the sellers could take it with them.

**9. Result:** Aukerman wins. He considered himself to be the owner, as had Arketex for eight years and Clark for 15. All the owners had maintained the land and kept everyone else off for more than 20 years.

# PRACTICE EXAM

## MATCHING QUESTIONS

Match the following terms with their definitions:

___ A. Easement

___ B. Fee simple defeasible

___ C. Adverse possession

___ D. Fixture

___ E. License

1. Temporary permission to enter upon another's property, for example, to attend a concert

2. Gives one person the right to enter land belonging to another and make a limited use of it

3. Goods that have become attached to real property

4. A type of ownership that may terminate upon the occurrence of some limiting event

5. A chance to own land without ever paying for it

## TRUE/FALSE QUESTIONS

Circle true or false:

1. T   F   The owner of a fee simple absolute could lose the property if she uses it in a prohibited manner.

2. T   F   If one joint tenant dies, his interest in the property passes to surviving joint tenants, not to his heirs.

3. T   F   If you sell the oil rights in your property while keeping the surface rights, the oil company has purchased a profit.

4. T   F   In the sale of a house, a seller may not make false statements about conditions, but is under no obligation to mention defective conditions unless the buyer asks about them.

5. T   F   The federal government has the power to take private property for public use, but local governments have no such power.

## MULTIPLE-CHOICE QUESTIONS

6. CPA QUESTION: On July 1, 1992, Quick, Onyx, and Nash were deeded a piece of land as tenants in common. The deed provided that Quick owned one half the property and Onyx and Nash owned one quarter each. If Nash dies, the property will be owned as follows:

   A.  Quick $\frac{1}{2}$, Onyx $\frac{1}{2}$

   B.  Quick $\frac{5}{8}$, Onyx $\frac{3}{8}$

   C.  Quick $\frac{1}{3}$, Onyx $\frac{1}{3}$, Nash's heirs $\frac{1}{3}$

   D.  Quick $\frac{1}{2}$, Onyx $\frac{1}{4}$, Nash's heirs $\frac{1}{4}$

7. Marta places a large, prefabricated plastic greenhouse in her backyard, with the steel frame bolted into concrete that she poured specially for that purpose. She attaches gas heating ducts and builds a brick walkway around the greenhouse. Now the town wants to raise her real property taxes, claiming that her property has been improved. Marta argues that the greenhouse is not part of the real property. Is it?

   A.  The greenhouse is not part of the real property because it was prefabricated.

   B.  The greenhouse is not part of the real property because it could be removed.

   C.  The greenhouse cannot be part of the real property if Marta owns a fee simple absolute.

   D.  The greenhouse is a fixture and is part of the real property.

   E.  The greenhouse is an easement, and is part of the real property.

8. A pro football team ejects five fans for rowdy behavior. The team is

   A. Revoking an easement
   B. Reserving an easement
   C. Terminating a profit
   D. Revoking a license
   E. Condemning certain use

9. Takeoff Construction is struggling financially, and to save money, has "cut corners" in two construction projects: a three-story office building and a large house. In both buildings, the company used cheap structural supports, pipes, and insulation, which it knows will not last long. Both properties sell, and neither buyer asks about those specific materials. Six months later, both buyers sue, based on Takeoff's shabby material and workmanship.

   A. The homeowner will win but the office buyer will lose.

   B. The office buyer will win but the homeowner will lose.

   C. Both the homeowner and office buyer will win.

   D. Both the homeowner and office buyer will lose.

   E. In both cases, a jury will decide whether Takeoff "adequately responded to all questions the buyer posed."

10. A common security interest in real property is

   A. A profit
   B. A license
   C. An easement
   D. A mortgage
   E. A warranty

## SHORT-ANSWER QUESTIONS

11. In 1944, W. E. Collins conveyed land to the Church of God of Prophecy. The deed said: "This deed is made with the full understanding that should the property fail to be used for the Church of God, it is to be null and void and property to revert to W. E. Collins or heirs." In the late 1980s, the church wished to move to another property and sought a judicial ruling that it had the right to sell the land. The trial court ruled that the church owned a fee simple absolute and had the right to sell the property. Comment.

12. ETHICS: Mark Wasser negotiated to purchase a 67-year-old apartment building from Michael and Anna Sasoni. The Sasonis told Wasser that the building was "a very good building" and "an excellent deal." The contract stated that the Wassers took the building "as is" and that there were no express or implied warranties or representations. After Wasser took over the building, he discovered that it needed major structural repairs. He sued the Sasonis, claiming that they had failed to disclose defects. Who wins? (Slow down before answering.) Ethically, who should win? Why?

13. ROLE REVERSAL: Write a short-answer question focusing on one of these issues: a fixture, an easement, or adverse possession.

## INTERNET RESEARCH PROBLEM

A client interested in buying a condominium wants your advice on how that form of ownership differs from others, what problems might arise, and how he should protect himself. Read at least three articles on condominium disputes, and then write a short memo explaining advantages and disadvantages of condominium ownership.

**You can find further practice problems in the Online Quiz at www.cengage.com/blaw/beatty.**

# LANDLORD-TENANT LAW

**On a January** morning in Studio City, California, Alpha Donchin took her small Shih-Tzu for a walk. Suddenly, less than a block from her house, two large Rottweilers attacked Donchin and her pet. The heavy animals mauled the 14-pound Shih-Tzu, and when Donchin picked her dog up, the Rottweilers knocked her down, breaking her hip and causing other serious injuries.

Ubaldo Guerrero, who lived in a rented house nearby, owned the two Rottweilers, and Donchin sued him. But she also sued Guerrero's landlord, David Swift, who lived four blocks away from the rental property. Donchin claimed that the landlord was liable for her injuries, because he knew of the dogs' vicious nature and permitted them to escape from the property he rented to Guerrero. Should the landlord be liable for injuries caused by his tenant's dogs?

As is typical of many landlord-tenant issues, the law in this area is in flux. Under the common law, a landlord had no liability for injuries caused by animals

> **Suddenly, less than a block from her house, two large Rottweilers attacked Donchin and her pet.**

belonging to a tenant, and many states adhere to that rule. But some states are expanding the landlord's liability for injuries caused on or near his property. The California court ruled that Donchin could maintain her suit against Swift. If Donchin could prove that Swift knew the dogs were dangerous and allowed them to escape through a defective fence, the landlord would be liable for her injuries.[1]

One reason for the erratic evolution of landlord-tenant law is that it is really a combination of three venerable areas of law: property, contract, and negligence. The confluence of these legal theories produces results that are unpredictable but interesting and important. (To survey a variety of articles and laws in this rapidly evolving area, visit **http://topics.law.cornell.edu/**.) We begin our examination of landlord-tenant law with an analysis of the different types of tenancy.

Recall that a freehold estate is the right to possess real property and use it in any lawful manner. **When an owner of a freehold estate allows another person temporary, exclusive possession of the property, the parties have created a landlord-tenant relationship.** The freehold owner is the **landlord**, and the person allowed to possess the property is the **tenant**. The landlord has conveyed a **leasehold** interest to the tenant, meaning the right to temporary possession. Courts also use the word "tenancy" to describe the tenant's right to possession. A leasehold may be commercial or residential.

**Landlord**
The owner of a freehold estate who allows another person temporarily to live on his property.

**Tenant**
A person given temporary possession of a landlord's property.

**Lease**
A contract that creates a landlord-tenant relationship.

## THREE LEGAL AREAS COMBINED

Property law influences landlord-tenant cases because the landlord is conveying rights in real property to the tenant. She is also keeping a reversionary interest in the property, meaning the right to possess the property when the lease ends. Contract law plays a role because the basic agreement between the landlord and tenant is a contract. **A lease is a contract that creates a landlord-tenant relationship.** And negligence law increasingly determines the liability of landlord and tenant when there is an injury to a person or property. Many states have combined these three legal issues into landlord-tenant statutes. You can find your state's statute at **www.rentlaw.com**.

## LEASE

**The statute of frauds generally requires that a lease be in writing.** Some states will enforce an oral lease if it is for a short term, such as one year or less, but even when an oral lease is permitted, it is wiser for the parties to put their agreement in writing, because a written lease avoids many misunderstandings. At a minimum, a lease must state the names of the parties, the premises being leased, the duration of the agreement, and the rent. But a well-drafted lease generally includes many provisions, called covenants. A **covenant** is simply a promise by either the landlord or the tenant to do something or refrain from doing something. For example, most leases include a covenant concerning the tenant's payment of a security deposit and the landlord's return of the

---

[1] *Donchin v. Guerrero,* 34 Cal. App. 4th 1832, 1995 Cal. App. LEXIS 462 (Cal. Ct. App. 1995).

deposit, a covenant describing how the tenant may use the premises, and several covenants about who must maintain and repair the property, who is liable for damage, and so forth. The parties should also agree about how the lease may be terminated and whether the parties have the right to renew it.

## ▪ TYPES OF TENANCY ▪

There are four types of tenancy: a tenancy for years, a periodic tenancy, a tenancy at will, and a tenancy at sufferance. The most important feature distinguishing one from the other is how each tenancy terminates. In some cases, a tenancy terminates automatically, while in others, one party must take certain steps to end the agreement.

### TENANCY FOR YEARS

**Any lease for a stated, fixed period is a tenancy for years**. If a landlord rents a summer apartment for the months of June, July, and August of next year, that is a tenancy for years. A company that rents retail space in a mall beginning January 1, 2009, and ending December 31, 2012, also has a tenancy for years. A tenancy for years terminates automatically when the agreed period ends.

**Tenancy for years**
A lease for a stated, fixed period.

### PERIODIC TENANCY

**A periodic tenancy is created for a fixed period and then automatically continues for additional periods until either party notifies the other of termination.** This is probably the most common variety of tenancy, and the parties may create one in either of two ways. Suppose a landlord agrees to rent you an apartment "from month to month, rent payable on the first." That is a periodic tenancy. The tenancy automatically renews itself every month, unless either party gives adequate notice to the other that she wishes to terminate. A periodic tenancy could also be for one-year periods—in which case it automatically renews for an additional year if neither party terminates—or for any other period.

**Periodic tenancy**
A lease for a fixed period, automatically renewable unless terminated.

### TENANCY AT WILL

**A tenancy at will has no fixed duration and may be terminated by either party at any time.**[2] Tenancies at will are unusual tenancies. Typically, the agreement is vague, with no specified rental period and with payment, perhaps, to be made in kind. The parties might agree, for example, that a tenant farmer could use a portion of his crop as rent. Since either party can end the agreement at any time, it provides no security for either landlord or tenant.

**Tenancy at will**
A tenancy with no fixed duration, which may be terminated by either party at any time.

### TENANCY AT SUFFERANCE

**A tenancy at sufferance occurs when a tenant remains on the premises, against the wishes of the landlord, after the expiration of a true tenancy.** Thus a tenancy at sufferance is not a true tenancy because the tenant is staying without the landlord's agreement. The landlord has the option of seeking to evict the tenant or of forcing the tenant to pay rent for a new rental period.

**Tenancy at sufferance**
A tenancy that exists without the permission of the landlord, after the expiration of a true tenancy.

---

[2] The courts of some states, annoyingly, use the term "tenancy at will" for what are, in reality, periodic tenancies. They do this to bewilder law students and even lawyers, a goal at which they are quite successful. This text uses "tenancy at will" in its more widely known sense, meaning a tenancy terminable at any time.

## · LANDLORD'S DUTIES ·

### DUTY TO DELIVER POSSESSION

The landlord's first important duty is to **deliver possession** of the premises at the beginning of the tenancy, that is, to make the rented space available to the tenant. In most cases, this presents no problems and the new tenant moves in. But what happens if the previous tenant has refused to leave when the new tenancy begins? In most states, the landlord is legally required to remove the previous tenant. In some states, it is up to the new tenant either to evict the existing occupant or begin charging him rent.

### QUIET ENJOYMENT

**Quiet enjoyment**
The right to use the property without interference from the landlord.

**All tenants are entitled to quiet enjoyment of the premises,** meaning the right to use the property without the interference of the landlord. Most leases expressly state this covenant of quiet enjoyment. And if a lease includes no such covenant, the law implies the right of quiet enjoyment anyway, so all tenants are protected. If a landlord interferes with the tenant's quiet enjoyment, he has breached the lease, entitling the tenant to damages.

The most common interference with quiet enjoyment is an eviction, meaning some act that forces the tenant to abandon the premises. Of course, some evictions are legal, as when a tenant fails to pay the rent. But some evictions are illegal. There are two types of eviction: actual and constructive.

### ACTUAL EVICTION

**Eviction**
means that the landlord has prevented the tenant from possessing the premises.

**If a landlord prevents the tenant from possessing the premises, he has actually evicted her.** Suppose a landlord decides that a group of students are "troublemakers." Without going through lawful eviction procedures in court, the landlord simply waits until the students are out of the apartment and changes the locks. By denying the students access to the premises, the landlord has actually evicted them and has breached their right of quiet enjoyment.

### CONSTRUCTIVE EVICTION

**Constructive eviction**
refers to a landlord's substantial interference with the tenant's use and enjoyment.

**If a landlord substantially interferes with the tenant's use and enjoyment of the premises, he has constructively evicted her.** Courts construe certain behavior as the equivalent of an eviction. In these cases, the landlord has not actually prevented the tenant from possessing the premises, but has instead interfered so greatly with her use and enjoyment that the law regards the landlord's actions as equivalent to an eviction. Suppose the heating system in an apartment house in Juneau, Alaska, fails during January. The landlord, an avid sled-dog racer, tells the tenants he is too busy to fix the problem. If the tenants move out, the landlord has constructively evicted them and is liable for all expenses they suffer.

To claim a constructive eviction, the tenant must vacate the premises. The tenant must also prove that the interference was sufficiently serious and lasted long enough that she was forced to move out. A lack of hot water for two days is not fatal, but lack of any water for two weeks creates a constructive eviction.

### DUTY TO MAINTAIN PREMISES

In most states, a landlord has a **duty to deliver the premises in a habitable condition** and a continuing duty to maintain the habitable condition. This duty overlaps with the quiet enjoyment obligation, but it is not identical. The tenant's right to quiet enjoyment focuses primarily on the tenant's ability to use the rented property. The landlord's duty to maintain the property focuses on whether the property meets a particular legal standard. The required standard may be stated in the lease, created by a state statute, or implied by law.

## Lease
The lease itself generally obligates the landlord to maintain the exterior of any buildings and the common areas. If a lease does not do so, state law may imply the obligation.

## Building Codes
Many state and local governments have passed building codes, which mandate minimum standards for commercial and/or residential property. The codes are likely to be stricter for residential property and may demand such things as minimum room size, sufficient hot water, secure locks, proper working kitchens and bathrooms, absence of insects and rodents, and other basics of decent housing. Generally, all rental property must comply with the building code, whether the lease mentions the code or not.

## Implied Warranty of Habitability
Students Maria Ivanow, Thomas Tecza, and Kenneth Gearin rented a house from Les and Martha Vanlandingham. The monthly rent was $900. But the roommates failed to pay any rent for the final five months of the tenancy. After they moved out, the Vanlandinghams sued. How much did the landlords recover? Nothing. The landlords had breached the implied warranty of habitability.

**The implied warranty of habitability requires that a landlord meet all standards set by the local building code, or that the premises be fit for human habitation.** Most states, though not all, imply this warranty of habitability, meaning that the landlord must meet this standard whether the lease includes it or not.

The Vanlandinghams breached the implied warranty. The students had complained repeatedly about a variety of problems. The washer and dryer, which were included in the lease, frequently failed. A severe roof leak caused water damage in one of the bedrooms. Defective pipes flooded the bathroom. The refrigerator frequently malfunctioned, and the roommates repaired it several times. The basement often flooded, and when it was dry, rats and opossums lived in it. The heat sometimes failed.

In warranty of habitability cases, a court normally considers the severity of the problems and their duration. In the case of Maria Ivanow and friends, the court abated (reduced) the rent 50 percent. The students had already paid more than the abated rent to the landlord, so they owed nothing for the last five months.[3]

## Tenant Remedies for Defective Conditions
Different states allow various remedies for defective conditions. For tenant rights in your state, go to **http://worldtenant.com** and click on your state. Many states allow a tenant to withhold rent, representing the decreased value of the premises. In some states, if a tenant notifies the landlord of a serious defect and the landlord fails to remedy the problem, the tenant may deduct a reasonable amount of money from the rental payment and have the repair made himself. Also, a landlord who refuses to repair significant defects is breaching the lease and/or state law, and the tenant may simply sue for damages.

---

[3] *Vanlandingham v. Ivanow,* 246 Ill. App. 3d 348, 615 N.E.2d 1361, 1993 Ill. App. LEXIS 985 (Ill. Ct. App. 1993).

> One tenant slept with blankets over her head, to keep heat in and bugs out.

## Duty to Return Security Deposit

Most landlords require tenants to pay a security deposit, in case the tenant damages the premises. In many states, a landlord must either return the security deposit soon after the tenant has moved out or notify the tenant of the damage and the cost of the repairs. A landlord who fails to do so may owe the tenant damages of two or even three times the deposit.

Your authors are always grateful when a litigant volunteers to illustrate half a dozen legal issues in one lawsuit. The landlord in the following case demonstrates problems of security deposit, quiet enjoyment, constructive eviction, and . . . well, see how many you can count.

### HARRIS v. SOLEY

2000 ME. 150, 756 A.2D 499, SUPREME JUDICIAL COURT OF MAINE, 2000

### CASE SUMMARY

**Facts:** Near Labor Day, Andrea Harris, Kimberly Nightingale, Karen Simard, and Michelle Dussault moved into a large apartment in the Old Port section of Portland, Maine. The apartment had been condemned by the city of Portland, but Joseph Soley, the landlord, assured the tenants that all problems would be repaired before they moved in. Not quite. When the women arrived, they found the condemnation notice still on the door, and the apartment an uninhabitable mess. Soley's agent told the tenants that if they cleaned the unit themselves, they would receive a $750 credit on their first month's rent of $1,000. So the four rented a steam cleaner, bought supplies, and cleaned the entire apartment. Unfortunately, their problems had only begun.

The tenants suffered a continuous problem with mice and cockroaches, along with a persistent odor of cat urine. They ultimately discovered a dead cat beneath the floorboards. During October, the apartment had no heat. One tenant slept with blankets over her head, to keep heat in and bugs out. In November, the women submitted a list of complaints to Soley, including a broken toilet, inoperable garbage disposal, and shattered skylight, as well as a leaking roof and cockroach infestation. Snow began to fall into the living room through the skylight.

Soley made no repairs and the women stopped paying the rent. He phoned them several times, aggressively demanding payments. The tenants found another place to live but before they had moved, Soley's agents broke into the apartment and took many of their belongings. The tenants located Soley at the restaurant he owned and asked for their possessions back, but he refused to return the belongings unless they paid him $3,000. He threatened them by saying that he knew where their families lived.

The tenants sued, claiming breach of contract, conversion [wrongful taking of property], intentional infliction of emotional distress, wrongful eviction, and wrongful retention of a security deposit. Soley refused to respond to discovery requests, and eventually the trial court gave a default judgment for the plaintiffs. The judge instructed the jury that all allegations were deemed true, and their job was to award damages. The jury awarded damages for each of the claims, including $15,000 to each tenant for emotional distress and a total of *$1 million* in punitive damages. Soley appealed.

**Issue:** *Are the tenants entitled to such large damages?*

**Decision:** The tenants are entitled to all damages. Affirmed.

**Reasoning:** Soley argues that the identical awards to all four tenants indicates the verdict is a result of irrational thinking, passion, and prejudice. However, the jury could reasonably have found that the emotional distress suffered by each tenant deserved comparable compensation, even if the harm was not identical to each. Among the factual findings from the trial court was this statement:

> The plaintiffs were shaken up, infuriated, violated, intimidated, and in fear for their physical safety. The conduct of [Soley] was so extreme and outrageous as to exceed all possible bounds of decency. Defendant acted intentionally, knowingly, willfully, wantonly, and with malice.

The jury was entirely justified in awarding substantial punitive damages. The tenants had to endure insect and rodent infestation, dead animals, and falling snow. Soley refused to repair conditions that made the apartment unfit for human habitation, violently removed the tenants' property, destroyed some of their belongings, and threatened the young women. His conduct was utterly intolerable and the verdict is reasonable.

## · TENANT'S DUTIES ·

### DUTY TO PAY RENT

> My landlord said he's gonna raise the rent. "Good," I said, "'cause I can't raise it."
> *Slappy White,* comedian (1921–1995)

**Rent** is the compensation the tenant pays the landlord for use of the premises, and paying the rent, despite Mr. White's wistful hope, is the tenant's foremost obligation. The lease normally specifies the amount of rent and when it must be paid. Typically, the landlord requires that rent be paid at the beginning of each rental period, whether that is monthly, annually, or otherwise.

If the tenant fails to pay rent on time, the landlord has several remedies. She is entitled to apply the security deposit to the unpaid rent. She may also sue the tenant for nonpayment of rent, demanding the unpaid sums, cost of collection, and interest. Finally, the landlord may evict a tenant who has failed to pay rent.

State statutes prescribe the steps a landlord must take to evict a tenant for nonpayment. Typically, the landlord must serve a termination notice on the tenant and wait for a court hearing. At the hearing, the landlord must prove that the tenant has failed to pay rent on time. If the tenant has no excuse for the nonpayment, the court grants an order evicting him. The order authorizes a sheriff to remove the tenant's goods and place them in storage, at the tenant's expense. However, if the tenant was withholding rent because of unlivable conditions, the court may refuse to evict.

**Rent**
Compensation paid by a tenant to a landlord.

### EXAM *Strategy*

**Question:** Leo rents an apartment from Donna for $900 per month, both parties signing a lease. After six months, Leo complains about defects, including bugs, inadequate heat, and window leaks. He asks Donna to fix the problems, but she responds that the heat is fine and that Leo caused the insects and leaks. Leo begins to send in only $700 for the monthly rent. Donna repeatedly phones Leo, asking for the remaining rent. When he refuses to pay, she waits until he leaves for the day, then has a moving company place his belongings in storage. She changes the locks, making it impossible for him to re-enter. Leo sues. What is the likely outcome?

**Strategy:** A landlord is entitled to begin proper eviction proceedings against a tenant who has not paid rent. However, the landlord must follow specified steps, including a termination notice and a court hearing. Review the consequences for actual eviction, described in the section "Quiet Enjoyment."

**Result:** Donna has ignored the legal procedures for evicting a tenant. Instead, she engaged in *actual eviction*, which is quick and, in the short term, effective. However, by breaking the law, Donna has ensured that Leo will win his lawsuit. He is entitled to possession of the apartment, as well as damages for rent he may have been forced to pay elsewhere, injury to his possessions, and the cost of retrieving them. He may receive punitive damages as well. Bad strategy, Donna.

### DUTY TO MITIGATE

Pickwick & Perkins, Ltd., was a store in the Burlington Square Mall in Burlington, Vermont. Pickwick had a five-year lease, but abandoned the space almost two years early and ceased paying rent. The landlord waited eight months before renting the space to a new tenant and then sued, seeking the unpaid rent. Pickwick defended on the grounds that Burlington had failed to **mitigate damages,** that is, to keep its losses to a minimum by promptly seeking another tenant. The winner? Pickwick, the tenant. Today, most (but not all) courts rule that **when a tenant breaches the lease, the landlord must make a reasonable effort to mitigate damages.** Burlington failed to mitigate, so it also failed to recover its losses.

## DUTY TO USE PREMISES PROPERLY

A lease normally lists what a tenant may do in the premises and prohibits other activities. For example, a residential lease allows the tenant to use the property for normal living purposes, but not for any retail, commercial, or industrial purpose. A tenant may never use the premises for an illegal activity, such as gambling or selling drugs, whether or not the lease mentions the issue. A tenant may not disturb other tenants, and a landlord has the right to evict anyone who unreasonably disturbs neighbors.

    **A tenant is liable to the landlord for any significant damage he causes to the property.** The tenant is not liable for normal wear and tear. If, however, he knocks a hole in a wall or damages the plumbing, the landlord may collect the cost of repairs, either by using the security deposit or by suing if necessary.

# · CHANGE IN THE PARTIES ·

Sometimes the parties to a lease change. This can happen when the landlord sells the property or when a tenant wants to turn the leased property over to another tenant.

## SALE OF THE PROPERTY

**Generally, the sale of leased property does not affect the lease but merely substitutes one landlord, the purchaser, for another, the seller.** The lease remains valid, and the tenant enjoys all rights and obligations until the end of the term. The new landlord may not raise the rent during the period of the existing lease or make any other changes in the tenant's rights.

### EXAM *Strategy*

**Question:** Julie, an MBA student, rents an apartment from Marshall for $1,500 a month. The written lease will last for two years, until Julie graduates. Julie moves in and enjoys the apartment. However, after 10 months, Marshall sells the building to Alexia, who notifies Julie that the new rent will be $1,750, effective immediately. If Julie objects, Alexia will give her one month to leave the apartment. Julie comes to you for advice. What are her options?

**Strategy:** What effect does the sale of leased property have on existing leases?

**Result:** Generally, the sale of leased property does not affect the lease but merely substitutes one landlord, the purchaser, for another, the seller. Alexia has no right to raise the rent during Julie's tenancy. Julie is entitled to the apartment, for $1,500 per month, until the lease expires.

## ASSIGNMENT AND SUBLEASE

**Assignment**
A tenant's transfer of all legal interest in a property to another party.

A tenant who wishes to turn the property over to another tenant will attempt to assign the lease or to sublet it. In an **assignment**, the tenant transfers all of his legal interest to the other party.

If a tenant validly assigns a lease, the new tenant obtains all rights and liabilities under the lease. The new tenant is permitted to use and enjoy the property and must pay the rent. **However, the original tenant remains liable to the landlord unless the landlord explicitly releases him, which the landlord is unlikely to do.** This means that if the new tenant fails to pay the rent on time, the landlord can sue *both* parties, old and new, seeking to evict both and to recover the unpaid rent from both.

A landlord generally insists on a covenant in the lease prohibiting the tenant from assigning without the landlord's written permission. Some states permit a landlord to deny permission for any reason at all, but a growing number of courts insist that a landlord act reasonably and grant permission to sublease unless he has a valid objection to the new tenant.

## · INJURIES ·

### TENANT'S LIABILITY

**A tenant is generally liable for injuries occurring within the premises she is leasing, whether that is an apartment, a store, or otherwise.** If a tenant permits grease to accumulate on a kitchen floor and a guest slips and falls, the tenant is liable. If a merchant negligently installs display shelving that tips onto a customer, the merchant pays for the harm. Generally, a tenant is not liable for injuries occurring in common areas over which she has no control, such as exterior walkways. If a tenant's dinner guest falls because the building's common stairway has loose steps, the landlord is probably liable.

### LANDLORD'S LIABILITY

Historically, the common law held a landlord responsible only for injuries that occurred in the common areas, or due to the landlord's negligent maintenance of the property. Increasingly, though, the law holds landlords liable under the normal rules of negligence law. In many states, a landlord must use reasonable care to maintain safe premises and is liable for foreseeable harm. For example, most states now have building codes that require a landlord to maintain structural elements in safe condition. States further imply a warranty of habitability, which mandates reasonably safe living conditions.

### CRIME

Landlords may be liable in negligence to tenants or their guests for criminal attacks that occur on the premises. Courts have struggled with this issue and have reached opposing results in similar cases. The very prevalence of crime sharpens the debate. What must a landlord do to protect a tenant? Courts typically answer the question by looking at four factors.

- *Nature of the crime.* How did the crime occur? Could the landlord have prevented it?
- *Reasonable person standard.* What would a reasonable landlord have done to prevent this type of crime? What did the landlord actually do?
- *Foreseeability.* Was it reasonably foreseeable that such a crime might occur? Were there earlier incidents or warnings?
- *Prevalence of crime in the area.* If the general area, or the particular premises, has a high crime rate, courts are more likely to hold that the crime was foreseeable and the landlord responsible.

The following case highlights one issue that courts face as they apply changing mores to a tragic loss. Should the landlord be responsible?

# YOU *be the* JUDGE

### DICKINSON ARMS-REO, L.P. v. CAMPBELL

4 S.W.3d 333
Texas Court of Appeals, 1999

**Facts:** About midnight, Joe Campbell and his girlfriend, Jenny Cady, left a club in separate cars, agreeing to meet at her apartment. Campbell parked his pickup truck in a space at the Dickinson Arms Apartments, where Cady lived.

Meanwhile, two 16-year-olds, Jeremy Gartrell and Donald Nichols, members of the Assassins, were visiting a fellow gang member who lived at the apartments. Gartrell approached Campbell, demanded the truck, and shot Campbell, killing him. Gartrell was convicted of murder and sentenced to 50 years.

Campbell's parents sued the Dickinson Arms, claiming that the landlord's neglect of security had permitted the killing. Testimony indicated as follows. Over a three-year period at the Dickinson Arms, there had been 184 reported criminal offenses at the apartments, including 20 burglaries, 13 auto thefts, 11 assaults, and 8 thefts.

Gartrell had wanted to do a carjacking throughout much of the day. But at a nearby Taco Bell, and then at a different apartment complex, the security and bright lighting deterred him.

The plaintiffs' expert witness stated that because of the high crime rates, the Dickinson Arms should have been protected with a perimeter fence, gates, and a security guard. With such precautions, the crime would likely not have occurred.

The Dickinson Arms' expert witness testified that a security guard, perimeter fencing, and limited access gates would not have stopped an offender like Gartrell, who was an impulsive, explosive individual—a ticking time bomb. Teachers and peers testified that Gartrell was violent and could not be deterred.

A resident stated that the lighting in the parking lot was good enough for her to see Campbell's body and truck from her apartment window. But Nichols testified it was dark in the parking lot, with no working lights.

The jury found that the landlord failed to provide adequate security, and awarded $341,000 to the plaintiffs. The Dickinson Arms appealed.

**You Be the Judge: Was the landlord liable for the death?**

**Argument for the Dickinson Arms:** This family tragedy has nothing to do with the landlord. Yes, an apartment complex is an easy target for liability, but this court should not hold the Dickinson Arms responsible for a murder it did not commit and did not want.

What good would a fence have done? Gartrell would have been free to enter through the main gate. He was a lawful visitor to the apartments. If there had been a security guard, he would have—should have—admitted Gartrell. The lower court decision imposes an unfair punishment on an inexpensive apartment complex. The result will be greater expense to the owner, higher rents for tenants—and no more security for anyone. Those who commit terrible crimes should pay the price—but injured plaintiffs should not be allowed to go where they think the money is.

**Argument for the Campbells:** The 184 crimes at the complex had all been dangerous, and many violent. The owner could not only *foresee* a more serious crime, it could confidently *predict* such a tragedy. The Dickinson Arms was a land mine, waiting to destroy innocent life.

Yes, Gartrell was an impulsive young man, but despite his eagerness for violence, he refused to commit a carjacking at two locations earlier in the day, because they had proper security and lighting. If a Taco Bell can light its parking lot and deter crime, then the Dickinson Arms can do so as well—and should have.

The defendant's argument about higher costs is a phony one. In fact, the Dickinson Arms has increased its profits at the expense of law-abiding tenants and guests, one of whom has paid the ultimate price. The landlord should pay for its terrible negligence in this case—and then make improvements so this does not happen again.

## CHAPTER CONCLUSION

A century ago, no plaintiff would even have argued that a landlord was responsible for bites inflicted by a tenant's dog. But living patterns alter, social mores reflect the change, and the law—in theory—responds to both. The current trend is clearly for expanded landlord liability, but how far that will continue is impossible to divine.

# EXAM REVIEW

1. **LANDLORD-TENANT RELATIONSHIP** When an owner of a freehold estate allows another person temporary, exclusive possession of the property, the parties have created a landlord-tenant relationship. (p. 466)

......................................................................................................

2. **TENANCIES** Any lease for a stated, fixed period is a tenancy for years. A periodic tenancy is created for a fixed period and then automatically continues for additional periods until either party notifies the other of termination. A tenancy at will has no fixed duration and may be terminated by either party at any time. A tenancy at sufferance occurs when a tenant remains, against the wishes of the landlord, after the expiration of a true tenancy. (p. 467)

......................................................................................................

3. **QUIET ENJOYMENT** All tenants are entitled to the quiet enjoyment of the premises, without the interference of the landlord. (p. 468)

......................................................................................................

4. **CONSTRUCTIVE EVICTION** A landlord may be liable for constructive eviction if he substantially interferes with the tenant's use and enjoyment of the premises. (p. 468)

......................................................................................................

5. **IMPLIED WARRANTY OF HABITABILITY** The implied warranty of habitability requires that a landlord meet all standards set by the local building code and/or that the premises be fit for human habitation. (p. 469)

......................................................................................................

6. **RENT** The tenant is obligated to pay the rent, and the landlord may evict for nonpayment. The modern trend is to require a landlord to mitigate damages caused by a tenant who abandons the premises before the lease expires. (p. 471)

**EXAM Strategy**

**Question:** Loren Andreo leased retail space in his shopping plaza to Tropical Isle Pet Shop for five years, at a monthly rent of $2,100. Tropical Isle vacated the premises 18 months early, turned in the key to Andreo, and acknowledged liability for the unpaid rent. Andreo placed a "for rent" sign in the store window and spoke to a commercial real estate broker about the space. But he did not enter into a formal listing agreement with the broker, or take any other steps to rent the space, for about nine months. With approximately nine months remaining on the unused part of Tropical's lease, Andreo hired a commercial broker to rent the space. He also sued Tropical for 18 months' rent. Comment.

**Strategy:** When a tenant abandons leased property early, the landlord is obligated to mitigate damages. Did Andreo? (See the "Result" at the end of this section.)

7. **DAMAGES TO PROPERTY** A tenant is liable to the landlord for any significant damage he causes to the property. (p. 472)

......................................................................................................

8. **ASSIGNMENT** A tenant typically may assign a lease or sublet the premises only with the landlord's permission, but the current trend is to prohibit a landlord from unreasonably withholding permission. (p. 472)

......................................................................................................

**EXAM Strategy**

**Question:** Doris Rowley rented space from the city of Mobile, Alabama, to run the Back Porch Restaurant. Her lease prohibited assignment or subletting without the landlord's permission. Rowley's business became unprofitable, and she asked the city's real estate officer for permission to assign her lease. She told the officer that she had "someone who would accept if the lease was assigned." Rowley provided no other information about the assignee. The city refused permission. Rowley repeated her requests several times without success, and finally she sued. Rowley alleged that the city had unreasonably withheld permission to assign and had caused her serious financial losses as a result. Comment.

**Strategy:** A landlord may not unreasonably refuse permission to assign a lease. Was the city's refusal unreasonable? (See the "Result" at the end of this section.)

9. **MAINTENANCE OF THE PROPERTY** Many courts require a landlord to use reasonable care in maintaining the premises, and hold her liable for injuries that were foreseeable. (p. 473)

10. **CRIME** Landlords may be liable in negligence to tenants or their guests for criminal attacks on the premises. Courts determine liability by looking at factors such as the nature of the crime, what a reasonable landlord would have done to prevent it, and the foreseeability of the attack. (p. 473)

**6. Result:** For about nine months, Andreo made no serious effort to lease the store. The court rejected his rent claim for that period, permitting him to recover unpaid money only for the period he made a genuine effort to lease the space.

**8. Result:** A landlord is allowed to evaluate a prospective assignee, including its financial stability and intended use of the property. Mobile could not do that because Rowley provided no information about the proposed assignee. Mobile wins.

# PRACTICE EXAM

## MATCHING QUESTIONS

Match the following terms with their definitions:

___ A. Warranty of habitability

___ B. Tenancy at sufferance

___ C. Periodic tenancy

___ D. Constructive eviction

___ E. Tenancy at will

1. Landlord's substantial interference with a tenant's use and enjoyment of the premises

2. A tenancy without fixed duration, which either party may terminate at any time

3. Tenant remains on premises after expiration of true tenancy

4. A tenancy that automatically renews unless one party terminates it

5. Requires a landlord to meet state building code standards

## TRUE/FALSE QUESTIONS

Circle true or false:

**1.** T  F  A landlord must maintain an apartment in compliance with the state's building code, unless the lease specifically exempts that particular unit.

**2.** T  F  A landlord could be liable for a constructive eviction even if he never asked the tenant to leave.

**3.** T  F  A nonrenewable lease of a store, for six months, establishes a tenancy for years.

**4.** T  F  A landlord may charge a tenant for normal wear and tear on an apartment, but the charges must be reasonable.

**5.** T  F  A landlord is generally liable for personal injuries sustained within an apartment, but cannot be liable for criminal attacks that occur there.

## MULTIPLE-CHOICE QUESTIONS

**6.** CPA QUESTION: Which of the following forms of tenancy will be created if a tenant stays in possession of the leased premises without the landlord's consent, after the tenant's one-year written lease expires?

A.  Tenancy at will
B.  Tenancy for years
C.  Tenancy from period to period
D.  Tenancy at sufferance

**7.** CPA QUESTION: To be enforceable, a residential real estate lease must:

A.  Require the tenant to obtain liability insurance
B.  Entitle the tenant to exclusive possession of the leased property
C.  Specify a due date for rent
D.  Be in writing

**8.** CPA QUESTION: A tenant renting an apartment under a three-year written lease that does not contain any specific restrictions may be evicted for:

A.  Counterfeiting money in the apartment
B.  Keeping a dog in the apartment
C.  Failing to maintain a liability insurance policy on the apartment
D.  Making structural repairs to the apartment

**9.** In May, Sharon and Joanne, both sophomores, are looking for an apartment to share beginning in September. They find the perfect unit which Ralph, the landlord, is working on right then. The parties agree on a rent of $1,000 per month, for 12 months. "Come back in late August, when I'm finished working," says Ralph. "I'll have a lease ready, I'll take your deposit, and you can move right in." The young women return in August to discover that Ralph has rented the apartment for $1,500 to other students. When they sue Ralph, Sharon and Joanne will

A.  Win $12,000
B.  Win $18,000
C.  Win possession of the apartment
D.  Win the difference between $12,000 and whatever they are forced to spend for a similar apartment
E.  Lose

**10.** Michael signs a lease for an apartment. The lease establishes a periodic tenancy for one year, starting September 1 and ending the following August 31. Rent is $800 per month. As August 31 approaches, Michael decides he would like to stay another year. He phones the landlord to tell him this, but the landlord is on holiday and Michael leaves a message. Michael sends in the September rent, but on September 15, the landlord tells him the rent is going up to $900 per month. He gives Michael the choice of paying the higher rent or leaving. Michael refuses to leave and continues to send checks for $800. The landlord sues. Landlord will

A.  Win possession of the apartment because the lease expired
B.  Win possession of the apartment because Michael did not renew it in writing
C.  Win possession of the apartment because he has the right to evict Michael at any time, for any reason
D.  Win $1,200 (12 months times $100)
E.  Lose

## SHORT-ANSWER QUESTIONS

**11.** ETHICS: Lisa Preece rented an apartment from Turman Realty, paying a $300 security deposit. Georgia law states: "Any landlord who fails to return any part of a security deposit which is required to be returned to a tenant pursuant to this article shall be liable to the tenant in the amount of three times the sum improperly withheld plus reasonable attorney's fees." When Preece moved out, Turman did not return her security deposit, and she sued for triple damages plus attorney's fees, totaling $1,800. Turman offered evidence that its failure to return the deposit was inadvertent and that it had procedures reasonably designed to avoid such errors. Is Preece entitled to triple damages? Attorney's fees? What is the rationale behind a statute that requires triple damages? Is it ethical to force a landlord to pay $1,800 for a $300 debt?

**12.** Philip Schwachman owned a commercial building and leased space to Davis Radio Corp. for use as a retail store. In the same building, Schwachman leased other retail space to Pampered Pet, a dog grooming shop. Davis Radio complained repeatedly to Schwachman that foul odors from Pampered Pet entered its store and drove away customers and workers. Davis abandoned the premises, leaving many months' rent unpaid. Schwachman sued for unpaid rent and moved for summary judgment. What ruling would you make on the summary judgment motion?

**13.** ROLE REVERSAL: Write a multiple-choice question concerning one of these issues: tenancy for years, security deposit, or sublease.

# INTERNET RESEARCH PROBLEM

Search for the law of your state concerning a landlord's obligation to provide a habitable apartment. Now assume that you are living in a rental unit with serious defects. Draft a letter to the landlord asking for prompt repairs.

**You can find further practice problems in the Online Quiz at www.cengage.com/blaw/beatty.**

# PERSONAL PROPERTY AND BAILMENT

"**My only child** is a no-good thief," Riley murmurs sadly to his visitors. "He has always treated me contemptuously. Now he's been sentenced to five years for stealing from a children's charity. He is my only heir, but why should I leave him everything?" Riley continues talking to his three guests: a bishop, a rabbi, and Earnest, a Boy Scout leader. "I have $500,000 in stocks in my bank deposit box. Tomorrow morning I'm going to the bank and hand the shares to the Boy Scouts so that other kids won't turn out so bad." Everyone applauds. But the following morning, on his way to the bank, Riley is struck by an ambulance and killed. A dispute arises over the money. The three witnesses assure the court that Riley was on his way to give the money to the Boy Scouts. From prison, the ne'er-do-well son demands the money as Riley's sole heir. Who wins? This is a typical issue of personal property law.

> My only child is a no-good thief. He is my only heir, but why should I leave him everything?

**Personal property**
All property other than real property.

**Personal property means all property other than real property.** In Chapter 28, we saw that real property means land and things firmly attached to it, such as buildings, crops, and minerals. All other property is personal property—a bus, a toothbrush, a share of stock. In this chapter, we look at several ways in which personal property can be acquired, including gifts and found property. In the section on gifts we learn that Riley's no-good son gets the money. Riley intended to give the stocks and bonds to the Boy Scouts the following day, but he never completed a valid gift because he failed to deliver the papers. Then we turn to disputes over found property. And finally we examine bailments, which occur when the owner of personal property permits another to possess it.

## · GIFTS ·

**Gift**
A voluntary transfer of property from one person to another, without consideration.

**Donor**
A person who gives property away.

**Donee**
A person who receives a gift of property.

**A gift is a voluntary transfer of property from one person to another without any consideration.** It is the lack of consideration that distinguishes a gift from a contract. Contracts usually consist of mutual promises to do something in the future. Each promise is consideration for the other one, and the mutual consideration makes each promise enforceable. But a gift is a one-way transaction, without consideration. The person who gives property away is the **donor** and the one who receives it is the **donee**.

A gift involves three elements:

- The donor intends to transfer ownership of the property to the donee immediately.
- The donor delivers the property to the donee.
- The donee accepts the property.

## INTENTION TO TRANSFER OWNERSHIP

The donor must intend to transfer ownership to the property right away, immediately giving up all control of the item. Notice that the donor's intention must be to give title to the donee. Merely proving that the owner handed you property does not guarantee that you have received a gift; if the owner only intended that you use the item, there is no gift and she can demand it back.

The donor must also intend the property to transfer immediately. A promise to make a gift in the future is unenforceable. Promises about future behavior are governed by contract law, and a contract is unenforceable without consideration. That is why the Boy Scouts will never touch the promised stocks. If Riley had handed Earnest the shares as he spoke, the gift would have been complete. However, the promise to make a gift the next day is legally worthless. Nor does Earnest have an enforceable contract, since there was no consideration for Riley's promise.

A *revocable gift* is a contradiction in terms, because it violates the rule just discussed. It is not a gift and the donee keeps nothing.[1] Suppose Harold tells his daughter Faith, "The mule is yours from now on, but if you start acting stupid again, I'm taking her back." Harold has retained some control over the animal, which means he has not intended to transfer ownership. There is no gift, and Harold still owns the mule.

## DELIVERY

### *Physical Delivery*
**The donor must deliver the property to the donee.** Generally, this involves physical delivery. If Anna hands Eddie a Rembrandt drawing, saying, "I want you to have this forever," she has satisfied the delivery requirement.

---

[1] The only exception to this rule is a gift *causa mortis,* discussed later in the chapter.

### Constructive Delivery

Physical delivery is the most common and the surest way to make a gift, but it is not always necessary. **A donor makes constructive delivery by transferring ownership without a physical delivery.** Most courts permit constructive delivery only when physical delivery is impossible or extremely inconvenient. Suppose Anna wants to give her niece Jen a blimp, which is parked in a hangar at the airport. The blimp will not fit through the doorway of Jen's dorm. Anna may simply deliver to Jen the certificate of title and the keys to the blimp.

## Inter Vivos Gifts and Gifts Causa Mortis

A gift can be either *inter vivos* or *causa mortis*. An **inter vivos gift** means a gift made during life, that is, when the donor is not under any fear of impending death. The vast majority of gifts are *inter vivos*, involving a healthy donor and donee. Shirley, age 30 and in good health, gives her husband Terry an eraser for his birthday. This is an *inter vivos* gift, which is absolute. The gift becomes final upon delivery, and the donor may not revoke it. If Shirley and Terry have a fight the next day, Shirley has no power to erase her gift.

A **gift causa mortis** is one made in contemplation of approaching death. The gift is valid if the donor dies as expected, but is revoked if he recovers. Suppose Lance's doctors have told him he will probably die of a liver ailment within a month. Lance calls Jane to his bedside and hands her a fistful of emeralds, saying, "I'm dying; these are yours." Jane sheds a tear, then sprints to the bank. If Lance dies of the liver ailment within a few weeks, Jane gets to keep the emeralds. But note that this gift is revocable. Since a gift *causa mortis* is conditional (upon the donor's death), the donor has the right to revoke it at any time before he dies. If Lance telephones Jane the next day and says that he has changed his mind, he gets the jewels back. Further, if the donor recovers and does not die as expected, the gift is automatically revoked.

*Inter vivos* **gift**
A gift made during the donor's life, with no fear of impending death.

*Gift causa mortis*
A gift made in contemplation of approaching death.

### EXAM *Strategy*

**Question:** Julie does good deeds for countless people, and many are deeply grateful. On Monday, Wilson tells Julie, "You are a wonderful person, and I have a present for you. I am giving you this baseball, which was the 500th home run hit by one of the great players of all time." He hands her the ball, which is in fact worth nearly half a million dollars. On Tuesday, Cassandra tells Julie, "I only have a few weeks to live. I want you to have this signed first edition of *Ulysses*. It is priceless and it is yours." The book is worth about $200,000. On Wednesday, both Wilson and Cassandra decide they have been foolhardy, and demand that Julie return the items. Must she do so?

**Strategy:** Both of these donors are attempting to revoke their gifts. An *inter vivos* gift cannot be revoked, but a gift *causa mortis* can be. To answer the question, you must know what kind of gifts these were.

**Result:** A gift *causa mortis* is one made in fear of approaching death, and this rule applies to Cassandra. Such a gift is revocable any time before the donor dies, so Cassandra gets her book back. A gift *inter vivos* is one made without any such fear of death. Most gifts fall in this category, and they are irrevocable. Wilson was not anticipating his demise, so his was a gift *inter vivos*. Julie keeps the baseball.

## Acceptance

**The donee must accept the gift.** This rarely leads to disputes, but if a donee should refuse a gift and then change her mind, she is out of luck. Her repudiation of the donor's offer means there is no gift, and she has no rights in the property.

The following case offers a combination of love and anger, alcohol and diamonds—always a volatile mix.

# YOU *be the* JUDGE

## ALBINGER v. HARRIS
2002 Mont. 118, 2002 WL 1226858
Montana Supreme Court, 2002

**Facts:** Michelle Harris and Michael Albinger lived together, on and off, for three years. Their roller-coaster relationship was marred by alcohol abuse and violence. When they announced their engagement, Albinger gave Harris a $29,000 diamond ring, but the couple broke off their wedding plans because of emotional and physical turmoil. Harris returned the ring. Later, they reconciled and resumed their marriage plans, and Albinger gave his fiancée the ring again. This cycle repeated several times over the three years. Each time they broke off their relationship, Harris returned the ring to Albinger, and each time they made up, he gave it back to her.

On one occasion Albinger held a knife over Harris as she lay in bed, threatening to chop off her finger if she didn't remove the ring. He beat her and forcibly removed the ring. Criminal charges were brought but then dropped when, inevitably, the couple reconciled. Another time, Albinger told her to "take the car, the horse, the dog, and the ring and get the hell out." Finally, mercifully, they ended their stormy affair, and Harris moved to Kentucky—keeping the ring.

Albinger sued for the value of the ring. The trial court found that the ring was a conditional gift, made in contemplation of marriage, and ordered Harris to pay its full value. She appealed. The Montana Supreme Court had to decide, in a case of first impression, whether an engagement ring was given in contemplation of marriage. (In Montana and in many states, neither party to a broken engagement may sue for breach of contract, because it is impossible to determine who is responsible for ending the relationship.)

**You Be the Judge: Who owns the ring?**

**Argument for Harris:** The problem with calling the ring a "conditional gift" is that there is no such thing. The elements of a gift are intent, delivery, and acceptance, and Harris has proven all three. Once a gift has been accepted, the donor has no more rights in the property and may not demand its return. Hundreds of years of litigation have resulted in only one exception to this rule—a gift *causa mortis*—and despite some cynical claims to the contrary, marriage is not death. What is more, to create a special rule for engagement rings would be blatant gender bias, because the exception would only benefit men. This court should stick to settled law and permit the recipient of a gift to keep it.

**Argument for Albinger:** The symbolism of an engagement ring is not exactly news. For decades, Americans have given rings—frequently diamond—in contemplation of marriage. All parties understand why the gift is made and what is expected if the engagement is called off: The ring must be returned. Albinger's intent, to focus on one element, was conditional—and Michelle Harris understood that. Each time the couple separated, she gave the ring back. She knew that she could wear this beautiful ring in anticipation of their marriage, but that custom and decency required its return if the wedding was off. We are not asking for new law, but for confirmation of what everyone has known for generations: There is no wedding ring when there is no wedding.

The following chart distinguishes between a contract and a gift.

### A CONTRACT AND A GIFT DISTINGUISHED

**A Contract:**

Lou: I will pay you $2,000 to paint the house, if you promise to finish by July 3.

Abby: I agree to paint the house by July 3, for $2,000.

Lou and Abby have a contract. Each promise is consideration in support of the other promise. Lou and Abby can each enforce the other's promise.

**A Gift:**

Lou hands Phil two opera tickets, while saying:
I want you to have these two tickets to *Rigoletto*. — Phil: Hey, thanks.

This is a valid *inter vivos* gift. Lou intended to transfer ownership immediately and delivered the property to Phil, who now owns the tickets.

---

**Neither Contract nor Gift:**

Lou: You're a great guy. Next week, I'm going to give you two tickets to *Rigoletto*. — Jason: Hey, thanks.

There is no gift because Lou did not intend to transfer ownership immediately, and he did not deliver the tickets. There is no contract because Jason has given no consideration to support Lou's promise.

## FOUND PROPERTY

As you stagger to your 8 a.m. class, there is a gleam of light, not in your mind (which is vacant), but right there on the sidewalk. A ring! You stop in at the local jewelry shop, where you learn this ruby marvel is worth just over $700,000. Is it yours to keep?

**The primary goal of the common law has been to get found property back to its proper owner.** The finder must make a good-faith effort to locate the owner. In some states, the finder is obligated to notify the police of what she has found and entrust the property to them until the owner can be located or a stated period has passed. A second policy has been to reward the finder if no owner can be located. But courts are loath to encourage trespassing, so finders who discover personal property on someone else's land generally cannot keep it. Those basic policies yield various outcomes, depending on the nature of the property. The common-law principles follow, although some states have modified them by statute.

- **Abandoned property** is something that the owner has knowingly discarded because she no longer wants it. A vase thrown into a garbage can is abandoned. Generally, the finder is permitted to keep abandoned property, provided he can prove that the owner intended to relinquish all rights.
- **Lost property** is something accidentally given up. A ring that falls off a finger into the street is lost property. Usually, the finder of lost property has rights superior to all the world except the true owner. If the true owner comes forward, he gets his property back; otherwise, the finder may keep it. However, if the finder has discovered the item on land belonging to another, the landowner is probably entitled to keep it.
- **Mislaid property** is something the owner has intentionally placed somewhere and then forgotten. A book deliberately placed on a bus seat by an owner who forgets to take it with her is mislaid property. Generally, the finder gets no rights in property that has simply been mislaid. If the true owner cannot be located, the mislaid item belongs to the owner of the premises where the item was found.

**Abandoned property**
is something that the owner has knowingly discarded because she no longer wants it.

**Lost property**
is something accidentally given up.

**Mislaid property**
is something the owner has intentionally placed somewhere and then forgotten.

## BAILMENT

**A bailment is the rightful possession of goods by one who is not the owner.** The one who delivers the goods is the **bailor** and the one in possession is the **bailee**. Bailments are common. Suppose you are going out of town for the weekend and lend your motorcycle to Stan. You are the

**Bailment**
The rightful possession of goods by one who is not the owner, usually by mutual agreement between the bailor and bailee.

**Bailor**
The one who delivers the goods.

**Bailee**
The one who possesses the goods.

bailor and your friend is the bailee. When you check your suitcase with the airline, you are again the bailor and the airline is the bailee. If you rent a car at your destination, you become the bailee while the rental agency is the bailor. In each case, someone other than the true owner has rightful, temporary possession of personal property.

**The parties generally create a bailment by agreement.** In each of the examples, the parties agreed to the bailment. In two cases, the agreement included payment, which is common but not essential. When you buy your airline ticket, you pay for your ticket, and the price includes the airline's agreement, as bailee, to transport your suitcase. When you rent a car, you pay the bailor for the privilege of using it. By loaning your motorcycle, you engage in a bailment without either party paying compensation.

**A bailment without any agreement is called a constructive, or involuntary, bailment.** Suppose you find a wristwatch in your house that you know belongs to a friend. You are obligated to return the watch to the true owner, and until you do so, you are the bailee, liable for harm to the property. This is called a constructive bailment because, with no agreement between the parties, the law is construing a bailment.

**Involuntary bailment**
A bailment that occurs without an agreement between the bailor and bailee.

# CONTROL

**To create a bailment, the bailee must assume physical control with intent to possess.** A bailee may be liable for loss or damage to the property. But it is not fair to hold him liable unless he has taken physical control of the goods, intending to possess them.

Disputes about whether someone has taken control often arise in parking lot cases. When a car is damaged or stolen, the lot's owner may try to avoid liability by claiming it lacked control of the parked auto and therefore was not a bailee. If the lot is a "park and lock" facility, where the car's owner retains the key and the lot owner exercises *no control at all*, there is probably no bailment and no liability for damage.

By contrast, when a driver leaves her keys with a parking attendant, the lot clearly is exercising control of the auto, and the parties have created a bailment. The lot is probably liable for loss or damage in that case.

**EXAM** *Strategy*

**Question:** Jack arrives at Airport Hotel's valet parking area in a 40-foot customized coach, just as Kim drives up in her rustbucket car. A valet drives Kim's car away, but the supervisor asks Jack to park the coach himself, in the hotel's lot across the street. Jack parks as instructed, locking the coach and keeping the keys. During the night, both vehicles are stolen. The owners sue for the value of their vehicles—about $2,000 for Kim's clunker and $350,000 for Jack's coach. Each owner will win if there was a bailment but lose if there was not. Can either or both prove a bailment?

**Strategy:** To create a bailment, the bailee must assume physical control with intent to possess.

**Result:** When the valet drove Kim's car away, the hotel assumed control with intent to possess. The parties created a bailment and the hotel is liable. But Jack loses. The hotel never had physical control of the coach. Employees did not park the vehicle, and Jack kept the keys. Jack's coach was a "park and lock" case, with no bailment.

**ETHICS** Many companies post their parking policies on the Internet, often including a disclaimer stating that use of their facility creates no bailment or liability. Find such a statement and analyze it. Why does the owner claim (or hope) that no bailment exists? If a parked car is damaged, will a court honor the disclaimer? Does the facility operator have any control of the cars as they enter, or while parked, or as they leave? Do you consider the facility's policy fair, or is it an unjust effort to escape responsibility? ◆

## RIGHTS OF THE BAILEE

The bailee's primary right is possession of the property. **Anyone who interferes with the bailee's rightful possession is liable to her.** The bailee is typically, though not always, permitted to use the property. When a farmer loans his tractor to a neighbor, the bailee is entitled to use the machine for normal farm purposes. But some bailees have no authority to use the goods. If you store your furniture in a warehouse, the storage company is your bailee, but it has no right to curl up in your bed.

A bailee may or may not be entitled to compensation, depending on the parties' agreement. A warehouse will not store your furniture for free, but a friend might.

> **If you store your furniture in a warehouse, the storage company is your bailee, but it has no right to curl up in your bed.**

## DUTIES OF THE BAILEE

**The bailee is strictly liable to redeliver the goods on time to the bailor or to whomever the bailor designates.** Strict liability means there are virtually no exceptions. Rudy stores his $6,000 drum set with Melissa's Warehouse while he is on vacation. Blake arrives at the warehouse and shows a forged letter, supposedly from Rudy, granting Blake permission to remove the drums. If Melissa permits Blake to take the drums, she will owe Rudy $6,000, even if the forgery was a high-quality job.

### Due Care

The bailee is obligated to exercise due care. **The level of care required depends upon who receives the benefit of the bailment.** There are three possibilities:

- *Sole benefit of bailee.* If the bailment is for the sole benefit of the bailee, the bailee is required to use **extraordinary care** with the property. Generally, in these cases, the bailor loans something for free to the bailee. Since the bailee is paying nothing for the use of the goods, most courts consider her the only one to benefit from the bailment. If your neighbor loans you a power lawn mower, the bailment is probably for your sole benefit. You are liable if you are even slightly inattentive in handling the lawn mower and can expect to pay for virtually any harm done.

- *Mutual benefit.* When the bailment is for the mutual benefit of bailor and bailee, the bailee must use **ordinary care** with the property. Ordinary care is what a reasonably prudent person would use under the circumstances. When you rent a car, you benefit from the use of the car, and the agency profits from the fee you pay. When the airline hauls your suitcase to your destination, both parties benefit. Most bailments benefit both parties, and courts decide the majority of bailment disputes under this standard.

- *Sole benefit of bailor.* When the bailment benefits only the bailor, the bailee must use only **slight care.** This kind of bailment is called a gratuitous bailment, and the bailee is liable only for gross negligence. Sheila enters a greased-pig contest and asks you to hold her $140,000 diamond engagement ring while she competes. You put the ring in your pocket. Sheila wins the $20 first prize, but the ring has disappeared. This was a gratuitous bailment, and you are not liable to Sheila unless she can prove gross negligence on your part. If the ring dropped from your pocket or was stolen, you are not liable. If you used the ring to play catch with friends, you are liable.

### Burden of Proof

In an ordinary negligence case, the plaintiff has the burden of proof to demonstrate that the defendant was negligent and caused the harm alleged. In bailment cases, the burden of proof is reversed. **Once the bailor has proven the existence of a bailment and loss or harm to the goods, a presumption of negligence arises,** and the burden shifts to the bailee to prove adequate care. This is a major change from ordinary negligence cases. Georgina rents Sam her sailboat for a month. At the end of the month, Sam announces that the boat is at the bottom of Lake Michigan. If Georgina sues Sam, she only needs to demonstrate that the parties had a bailment and that he failed to return the boat. The burden then shifts to Sam to prove that the boat was lost through no fault of his own. If he cannot meet that burden, Georgina recovers the full value of the boat.

The parties may use a contract to specify whether they have created a bailment, hoping to protect their rights. But even then things do not always go smoothly, as the following case demonstrates.

## MITCHELL v. BANK OF AMERICA NATIONAL ASSOCIATION

2002 WL 31139375, COURT OF APPEALS OF TEXAS, 2002

### CASE SUMMARY

**Facts:** Donna and Timothy Mitchell rented a safe deposit box from a Dallas branch of the Bank of America. The lease agreement stated that the bank "had no possession or custody of, nor control over, the contents of the Box, and the Lessee [the couple] assumes all risks in connection with the depositing of such content." The lease also permitted the bank to remove the box's contents if the rental fee went unpaid.

Bank officers, believing the Mitchells were behind in their rental fees, drilled into the box and removed the contents, which they inventoried and sent to a central vault elsewhere. When the Mitchells learned of this, they were very upset, and "loudly discussed the value of the contents" in the lobby of the Dallas branch.

A week later, the bank informed the Mitchells the contents were back at the Dallas branch. The couple placed the contents into a bag, which they put under the front seat of their car. Shortly after leaving the bank, the Mitchells had a flat tire. A stranger offered assistance. While they were all changing the tire, the bag disappeared.

The Mitchells sued the bank, claiming that its negligence enabled bank employees to learn of the box's contents. In a well-prepared scam, an employee or his accomplice let the air out of the couple's tire, offered roadside assistance, and stole the bag.

The trial court gave summary judgment for the bank, finding that the contract language quoted above meant that there was no bailment, and no possible negligence. The Mitchells appealed.

**Issue:** *Was there a bailment?*

**Decision:** Yes, there was a bailment.

**Reasoning:** The common law establishes rules for liability in bailments, but the parties can use an express written contract to change legal responsibility. Here, the parties signed a lease for the safe deposit box, and to the extent it applies, the lease controls the bank's liability.

The lease stated that as long as the Mitchells' property was in the box, there was no delivery to the Bank. That provision is valid, and it means that when the Mitchells placed their possessions in the safe deposit box, the parties created no bailment.

However, the lease also authorized the Bank to remove the contents of the box if the Mitchells failed to pay the rental fee. The parties thus contemplated a delivery of the property to the Bank under certain circumstances, and they did *not* change the common law duties once the Bank took control of the box's contents.

The trial court granted summary judgment for the Bank on the grounds that the contract precluded a bailment, and hence liability. That was error. Once the Bank took the property, the contract by its own terms no longer applied. The parties had entered into a bailment, and the common law rules of liability controlled their conduct.

Reversed.

## RIGHTS AND DUTIES OF THE BAILOR

The bailor's rights and duties are the reverse of the bailee's. The bailor is entitled to the return of his property on the agreed-upon date. He is also entitled to receive the property in good condition and to recover damages for harm to the property if the bailee failed to use adequate care.

## LIABILITY FOR DEFECTS

Depending upon the type of bailment, the bailor is potentially liable for known or even unknown defects in the property. **If the bailment is for the sole benefit of the bailee, the bailor must notify the bailee of any known defects.** Suppose Megan lends her stepladder to Dave. The top rung is loose and Megan knows it, but forgets to tell Dave. The top rung crumbles and Dave falls onto his girlfriend's iguana. Megan is liable to Dave and the girlfriend unless the defect in the ladder was obvious. Notice that Megan's liability is not only to the bailee, but also to any others injured by the defects. Megan would not be liable if she had notified Dave of the defective rung.

**In a mutual-benefit bailment, the bailor is liable not only for known defects but also for unknown defects that the bailor could have discovered with reasonable diligence.** Suppose RentaLot rents a power sander to Dan. RentaLot does not realize that the sander has faulty wiring, but a reasonable inspection would have revealed the problem. When Dan suffers a serious shock from the defect, RentaLot is liable to him, even though it was unaware of the problem.

## COMMON CARRIERS AND CONTRACT CARRIERS

A carrier is a company that transports goods for others. It is a bailee of every shipment entrusted to it. There are two kinds of carriers: common carriers and contract carriers. The distinction is important because each type of company has a different level of liability.

A **common carrier** makes its services available on a regular basis to the general public. For example, a trucking company located in St. Louis that is willing to haul freight for anyone, to any destination in the country, is a common carrier. **Generally, a common carrier is strictly liable for harm to the bailor's goods.** A bailor needs only to establish that it delivered property to the carrier in good condition and that the cargo arrived damaged. The carrier is then liable unless it can show that it was not negligent *and* that the loss was caused by an act of God (such as a hurricane) or some other extraordinary event, such as war. These are hard defenses to prove, and in most cases a common carrier is liable for harm to the property.

A common carrier is, however, allowed to limit its liability by contract. For example, a common carrier might offer the bailor the choice of two shipping rates: a low rate, with a maximum liability, say, of $10,000, or a higher shipping rate, with full liability for any harm to the goods. In that case, if the bailor chooses the lower rate, the limitation on liability is enforceable. Even if the bailor proves a loss of $300,000, the carrier owes merely $10,000.

A **contract carrier** does not make its services available to the general public, but engages in continuing agreements with particular customers. Assume that Steel Curtain Shipping is a trucking company in Pittsburgh that hauls cargo to California for two or three steel producers and carries manufactured goods from California to Pennsylvania and New York for a few West Coast companies. Steel Curtain is a contract carrier. **A contract carrier does not incur strict liability.** The normal bailment rules apply, and a contract carrier can escape liability by demonstrating that it exercised due care of the property.

**Common carrier**
A company that transports goods and makes its services regularly available to the general public.

**Contract carrier**
A company that transports goods for particular customers.

## INNKEEPERS

Hotels, motels, and inns frequently act as bailees of their guests' property. Most states have special innkeeper statutes that regulate liability.

Hotel patrons often assume that anything they bring to a hotel is safe. But some state innkeeper statutes impose an absolute limit on a hotel's liability. Other statutes require guests to leave valuables in the inn's safe deposit box. And even that may not be enough to protect them fully. For example, a state statute might require the guest to register the nature and value of the goods with the hotel. If a guest fails to follow the statutory requirements, he receives no compensation for any losses suffered.

## CHAPTER CONCLUSION

**Personal property law plays an almost daily role in all of our lives.** The manager of a parking lot, the finder of lost property, and the operator of an airport security system must all realize that they may incur substantial liability for personal property, whether they intend to accept that obligation or not. Understanding personal property can be worth a lot of chips—but do not leave them lying around your hotel room.

# EXAM REVIEW

**1.** **GIFTS** A gift is a voluntary transfer of property from one person to another without consideration. The elements of a gift are intention to transfer ownership immediately, delivery, and acceptance. (p. 480)

..................................................................................................................................

**2.** **FOUND PROPERTY** The finder of property must attempt to locate the true owner, unless the property was abandoned. The following principles generally govern:
- Abandoned property—the finder may keep it.
- Lost property—the finder generally has rights superior to everyone but the true owner, except that if she found it on land belonging to another, the property owner generally is entitled to it.
- Mislaid property—generally, the finder has no rights in the property. (p. 483)

**EXAM Strategy**

**Question:** The government accused Carlo Francia and another person of stealing a purse belonging to Frances Bainlardi. A policeman saw Francia sorting through the contents of the purse, which included a photo identification of Bainlardi. Francia kept some items, such as cash, while discarding others. At trial, Francia claimed that he had thought the purse was lost or abandoned. Besides the fact that Francia's accomplice was holding burglary tools, what is the weakness in Francia's defense?

**Strategy:** The finder of property must attempt to locate the true owner unless the property was abandoned. Is there any likelihood that the purse was abandoned? If it was not abandoned, did Francia attempt to locate the owner? (See the "Result" at the end of this section.)

**3.** **BAILMENT** A bailment is the rightful possession of goods by one who is not the owner. The one who delivers the goods is the bailor and the one in possession is the bailee. To create a bailment, the bailee must assume physical control with intent to possess. (p. 483)

..................................................................................................................................

**4.** **BAILEE'S RIGHTS** The bailee is always entitled to possess the property, is frequently allowed to use it, and may be entitled to compensation. (p. 485)

..................................................................................................................................

**5.** **REDELIVERY** The bailee is strictly liable to redeliver the goods to the bailor. (p. 485)

..................................................................................................................................

**6.** **DUE CARE** The bailee is obligated to exercise due care. The level of care required depends upon who receives the benefit of the bailment: If the bailee is the sole beneficiary, she must use extraordinary care; if the parties mutually benefit, the bailee must use ordinary care; and if the bailor is the sole beneficiary of the bailment, the bailee must use only slight care. (p. 485)

..................................................................................................................................

**7.** **PRESUMPTION OF NEGLIGENCE** Once the bailor has proven the existence of a bailment and loss, a presumption of negligence arises, and the burden shifts to the bailee to prove adequate care. (p. 485)

..................................................................................................................................

**Question:** Lonny Joe owned two rare 1955 Ford Thunderbird automobiles, one red and one green, both in mint condition. He stored the cars in his garage. His friend Stephanie wanted to use the red car in a music video, so Lonny Joe rented it to her for two days, for $300 per day. When she returned the red car, Lonny Joe discovered a long scratch along one side. That same day, he noticed a long scratch along the side of the green car. He sued Stephanie for harm to the red car. Lonny Joe sued an electrician for damage to the green car, claiming that the scratch occurred while the electrician was fixing a heater in the garage. Explain the different burdens of proof in the two cases.

**Strategy:** In an ordinary negligence case, the plaintiff must prove all elements by a preponderance of the evidence. However, in a bailment, a *presumption* of negligence arises. To answer this question, you need to know whether Lonny Joe established a bailment with either or both defendants. (See the "Result" at the end of this section.)

**8. BAILOR'S RESPONSIBILITY** The bailor must keep the property in suitable repair, free of any hidden defects. If the bailor is in the business of renting property, the bailment is probably subject to implied warranties. (p. 486)

**9. COMMON CARRIERS** Generally, a common carrier is strictly liable for harm to the bailor's goods. A contract carrier incurs only normal bailment liability. (p. 487)

**10. INNKEEPER LIABILITY** The liability of an innkeeper is regulated by state statute. A guest intending to store valuables with an innkeeper must follow the statute to the letter. (p. 487)

**2. Result:** Abandoned property is something that the owner has knowingly discarded because she no longer wants it. The burden is on the finder to prove that the property was abandoned, which will be impossible in this case, since no one would throw away cash and credit cards. Because the purse contained photo identification, Francia could easily have located its owner. He made no attempt to do so and his defense is unpersuasive.

**7. Results:** Lonny Joe had no bailment with the electrician because the electrician never assumed control of the car. To win that case, Lonny Joe must prove that the electrician behaved unreasonably and caused the scratch. However, when Lonny Joe rented Stephanie the red car, the parties created a bailment, and the law *presumes* Stephanie caused the damage unless she can prove otherwise. That is a hard burden, and Stephanie will likely lose.

# PRACTICE EXAM

## MATCHING QUESTIONS

Match the following terms with their definitions:

____ A. Extraordinary care

____ B. *Inter vivos* gift

____ C. Ordinary care

____ D. Gift *causa mortis*

____ E. Slight care

1. Cannot be revoked

2. Required in a bailment for the sole benefit of the bailee

3. Can be revoked

4. Required in a bailment for the mutual benefit of bailor and bailee

5. Required in a bailment for the sole benefit of the bailor

## TRUE/FALSE QUESTIONS

Circle true or false:

**1.** T   F   A gift is unenforceable unless both parties give consideration.

**2.** T   F   A gift *causa mortis* is automatically revoked if the donor dies shortly after making it.

**3.** T   F   A bailee always has the right to possess the property.

**4.** T   F   A finder of lost property generally may keep the property unless the true owner comes forward.

**5.** T   F   A common carrier is strictly liable for harm to the bailor's goods.

## MULTIPLE-CHOICE QUESTIONS

**6.** CPA QUESTION: Which of the following requirements must be met to create a bailment?

  I. Delivery of personal property to the intended bailee

  II. Possession by the intended bailee

  III. An absolute duty on the intended bailee to return or dispose of the property according to the bailor's directions

  A.  I and II only                              C.  II and III only

  B.  I and III only                             D.  I, II, and III

**7.** Martin is a rich businessman in perfect health. Monday morning he tells his niece, Stephanie, "Tomorrow I'm going to give you my brand new Ferrari." Stephanie is ecstatic. That afternoon, Martin is killed in a car accident. Does Stephanie get the car?

  A.  Stephanie gets the car because this is a valid *inter vivos* gift.

  B.  Stephanie gets the car because this is a valid gift *causa mortis*.

  C.  Stephanie gets the car because there is no reason to dispute that Martin made the promise.

  D.  Stephanie gets the car unless Martin left a wife or children.

  E.  Stephanie does not get the car.

**8.** Margie has dinner at Bill's house. While helping with the dishes, she takes off her Rolex watch, and forgets to put it back on when she leaves for the night. Bill finds the watch in the morning and decides to keep it.

  A.  This is abandoned property and Bill is entitled to it.

  B.  This is lost property and Bill is entitled to it.

  C.  This is lost property and Margie is entitled to it.

  D.  This is mislaid property and Bill is entitled to it.

  E.  This is mislaid property and Margie is entitled to it.

**9.** Arriving at a restaurant, Max gives his car keys to the valet. When the valet returns the car three hours later, it has a large, new dent. The valet says he did not cause it. Max sues the valet service.

  A.  The burden is on the valet service to prove it did not cause the dent.

  B.  The burden is on Max to prove that the valet service caused the dent.

  C.  The valet service is strictly liable for harm to Max's car.

  D.  The valet service has no liability to Max, regardless of how the dent was caused.

  E.  The valet service is only liable for gross negligence.

**10.** Car Moves hauls autos anywhere in the country. Valerie hires Car Moves to take her Porsche from Chicago to Los Angeles. The Porsche arrives badly damaged because the Car Moves truck was hit by a bus. The accident was caused by the bus driver's negligence. If Valerie sues Car Moves for the cost of repairs

A. Valerie will win.

B. Valerie will win only if she can prove Car Moves was partly negligent.

C. Valerie will win only if she can prove that Car Moves agreed to strict liability.

D. Valerie will lose because Car Moves did not cause the accident.

E. Valerie will lose because this was a bailment for mutual benefit.

## SHORT-ANSWER QUESTIONS

**11.** While in her second year at the Juilliard School of Music in New York City, Ann Rylands had a chance to borrow for one month a rare Guadagnini violin, made in 1768. She returned the violin to the owner in Philadelphia, but telephoned her father to ask if he would buy it for her. He borrowed money from his pension fund and paid the owner. Ann traveled to Philadelphia to pick up the violin. She had exclusive possession of the violin for the next 20 years, using it in her professional career. Unfortunately, she became an alcoholic, and during one period when she was in a treatment center, she entrusted the violin to her mother for safekeeping. At about that time, her father died. When Ann was released from the center, she requested return of the violin, but her mother refused. Who owns the violin?

**12.** Ronald Armstead worked for First American Bank as a courier. His duties included making deliveries between the bank's branches in Washington, D.C. Armstead parked the bank's station wagon near the entrance of one branch in violation of a sign saying: "No Parking Rush Hour Zone." In the rear luggage section of the station wagon were four locked bank dispatch bags, containing checks and other valuable documents. Armstead had received tickets for illegal parking at this spot on five occasions. Shortly after Armstead entered the bank, a tow truck arrived and its operator prepared to tow the station wagon. Transportation Management, Inc., operated the towing service on behalf of the District of Columbia. Armstead

ran out to the vehicle and told the tow truck operator that he was prepared to drive the vehicle away immediately. But the operator drove away with the station wagon in tow. One and one-half hours later, a bank employee paid for the car's release, but one dispatch bag, containing documents worth $107,000, was missing. First American sued Transportation Management and the District of Columbia. The defendants sought summary judgment, claiming they could not be liable. Were they correct?

**13.** Eileen Murphy often cared for her elderly neighbor, Thomas Kenney. He paid her $25 per day for her help and once gave her a bank certificate of deposit worth $25,000. She spent the money. Murphy alleged that shortly before his death, Kenney gave her a large block of shares in three corporations. He called his broker, intending to instruct him to transfer the shares to Murphy's name, but the broker was ill and unavailable. So Kenney told Murphy to write her name on the shares and keep them, which she did. Two weeks later Kenney died. When Murphy presented the shares to Kenney's broker to transfer ownership to her, the broker refused because Kenney had never endorsed the shares as the law requires, that is, signed them over to Murphy. Was Murphy entitled to the $25,000? To the shares?

**14.** ROLE REVERSAL: Write a multiple-choice question focusing on one of these topics: a gift *causa mortis*, lost property, or a bailment.

## INTERNET RESEARCH PROBLEM

You own a helicopter worth $250,000. A business associate wishes to use it for one week to show prospective clients around various islands in the Caribbean. You are willing to let him use it, for a fee of $15,000. Draft a bailment agreement. For help, find a sample agreement online.

**You can find further practice problems in the Online Quiz at www.cengage.com/blaw/beatty.**

# ESTATE PLANNING

**Pablo Picasso,** the renowned artist, created hundreds of paintings and sculptures as well as thousands of drawings and sketches. His personal life was unconventional, featuring a series of wives, mistresses, and children, both legitimate and illegitimate. Despite this large group of feuding heirs, he died in France without a will.

> **Despite having a large group of feuding heirs, Picasso died without a will.**

After four years of litigation, the French court decided that his estate would be shared by his widow, Jacqueline (who later committed suicide); two grandchildren by his legitimate child, Paulo (who died of cirrhosis of the liver); and his three illegitimate children, Maya, Claude, and Paloma. But by the time the decision was reached, legal fees had swallowed up all the cash in the estate.[1]

---

[1] Adapted from Barber, Lynn, "A Perfectly Packaged Picasso," *The Independent,* Dec. 9, 1990, p. 8.

## · INTRODUCTION ·

There is one immutable law of the universe: "You can't take it with you." But you can control where your assets go after your death. Or you can decide not to bother with an estate plan and leave all in chaos behind you.

## DEFINITIONS

Like many areas of the law, estate planning uses its own terminology:

- **Estate Planning.** The process of giving away property after (or in anticipation of) death.
- **Estate.** The legal entity that holds title to assets after the owner dies and before the property is distributed.
- **Decedent.** The person who has died.
- **Testator or Testatrix.** Someone who has signed a valid will. Testatrix is the female version (from the Latin).
- **Intestate.** To die without a will.
- **Heir.** Technically, the term "heir" refers to someone who inherits from a decedent who died intestate. **Devisee** means someone who inherits under a will. However, many courts use "heir" to refer to anyone who inherits property, and we follow that usage in this chapter.
- **Probate.** The process of carrying out the terms of a will.
- **Executor or Executrix.** A personal representative chosen by the decedent to carry out the terms of the will. An executrix is a female executor.
- **Administrator or Administratrix.** A personal representative appointed by the probate court to oversee the probate process for someone who has died intestate. As you can guess, an administratrix is a female administrator.
- **Grantor or Settlor.** Someone who creates a trust.
- **Donor.** Someone who makes a gift or creates a trust.

## PURPOSE

**Estate planning has two primary goals: to ensure that property is distributed as the owner desires and to minimize estate taxes.** Although tax issues are beyond the scope of this chapter, they are an important element of estate planning, often affecting not only how people transfer their property but, in some cases, to whom. For instance, wealthy people may give money to charity, at least in part, to minimize the taxes on the rest of their estate.

## PROBATE LAW

The federal government and many states levy estate taxes (although traditionally, state taxes have been much lower). Under current law, federal estate taxes will be eliminated in 2010 and then revived in 2011. Most analysts predict that Congress will not allow either event to occur, but the actual result is anyone's guess.

Only the states, and not the federal government, have probate codes to regulate the creation and implementation of wills and trusts. These codes vary from state to state. This chapter, therefore, speaks only of general trends among the states. Certainly, anyone who is preparing a will must consult the laws of the relevant state. To make probate law more consistent, the National Conference of Commissioners on Uniform State Laws issued a Uniform Probate Code (UPC). However, fewer than half of the states have adopted it.

## · WILLS ·

**Will**
A legal document that disposes of the testator's property after death.

**A will is a legal document that disposes of the testator's property after death.** It can be revoked or altered at any time until death. Virtually every adult, even those with only modest assets, should have a will to:

- Ensure that their assets (modest though they may be) are distributed in accordance with their wishes.
- Select a personal representative to oversee the estate. If the decedent does not name an executor in a will, the court will appoint an administrator. Generally, people prefer to have a friend, rather than a court, in charge of their property.
- Avoid unnecessary expenses. Those who die intestate often leave behind issues for lawyers to resolve. A properly drafted will can also reduce the estate tax bill.
- Provide guardians for minor children. If parents do not appoint a guardian before they die, a court will. Presumably, the parents are best able to make this choice.

## REQUIREMENTS FOR A VALID WILL

**Generally speaking, a person may leave his assets to whomever he wants.** However, the testatrix must be:

- Of **legal age** (which is 18).
- Of **sound mind.** That is, she must be able to understand what a will is, more or less what she owns, who her relatives are, and how she is disposing of her property.
- Acting without **undue influence.** Undue influence means that one person has enough power over another to force him to do something against his free will.

## LEGAL TECHNICALITIES

A testator must comply with the legal requirements for executing a will: It must be in writing, and the testator must sign it or direct someone else to sign it for him, if he is too weak. Generally, two witnesses must also sign the will. No one named in a will should also serve as a witness because, in many states, a witness may not inherit under a will. The importance of abiding by the legal technicalities cannot be overstated. No matter what the testator's intent, courts will not enforce a will unless each requirement of the law has been fully met.

### *Holographic Will*

**Holographic will**
A will that is handwritten and signed by the testator, but not witnessed.

Sometimes courts will accept a **holographic will: a will that is handwritten and signed by the testatrix, but not witnessed.** Suppose Rowena is on a plane that suffers engine trouble. For 15 minutes, the pilot struggles to control the plane. Despite his efforts, it crashes, killing everyone aboard. During those 15 minutes, Rowena writes on a Post-it note, "This is my last will and testament. I leave all my assets to the National Gallery of Art in Washington, D.C." She signs her name, but her fellow passengers are too frantic to witness it. This note is found in the wreckage of the plane. Her previous will, signed and witnessed in a lawyer's office, left everything to her friend, Ivan. If Rowena resides in one of the majority of states that accepts a holographic will, then Ivan is out of luck and the National Gallery will inherit all. One court has, indeed, accepted as a will a handwritten Post-it note that had not been witnessed.

### *Nuncupative Will*

**Nuncupative will**
An oral will.

Some states will also accept a **nuncupative will**. This is the formal term for an oral will. For a nuncupative will to be valid, the testatrix must know she is dying, there must be three witnesses, and these witnesses must know that they are listening to her will. Suppose that Rowena survives the airplane crash for a few hours. Instead of writing a will on the plane, she whispers to a nurse in the hospital, "I'd like all my property to go to the Angell Memorial Cat Hospital." This oral will is valid if there are two other witnesses and Rowena also says, "I'm dying. Please witness my oral will."

## SPOUSE'S SHARE

In community property states, no matter what the decedent's will says, a spouse can override it and claim one half of all marital property acquired during the marriage, except property that the testator inherited or received as a gift.[2]

In most non-community property states, a spouse can override the will and claim some percentage (usually one third to one half) of the decedent's probate estate (unless she has waived that right by written contract). Under the UPC, a surviving spouse is entitled to whichever is greater: $50,000, or a percentage of the decedent's assets. The percentage depends upon how long the couple was married. At 5 years, a spouse is entitled to 15 percent; at 10 years, 30 percent; and at 15 years, 50 percent. Suppose that, when Drew and Sandy marry, Drew has assets of $500,000 while Sandy has virtually nothing. If Drew dies anytime during the first 5 years of their marriage, Sandy is entitled to $50,000. At 5 years, the share automatically goes up to $75,000. After 15 years, it reaches the maximum of $250,000.

## CHILDREN'S SHARE

**Parents are not required to leave assets to their children.** They may disinherit their children for any reason.[3] However, the law presumes that a **pretermitted child** (that is, a child left nothing in the parent's will) was omitted by accident, unless the parent clearly indicates in the will that he has omitted the child on purpose. To do so, he must either leave her some nominal amount, such as $1, or specifically write in the will that the omission was intentional: "I am making no bequest to my daughter because she has chosen a religion of which I disapprove."

If a pretermitted child is left out by accident, she is generally entitled to the same share she would have received if her parent had died intestate. How likely is it that a parent would *forget* a child? Do you think the father in the following case simply forgot?

> **Pretermitted child**
> A child who is left nothing under the parent's will.

## *IN RE* ESTATE OF JOSIAH JAMES TRELOAR, JR.

151 N.H. 460; 859 A.2D 1162; 2004 N.H. LEXIS 177
SUPREME COURT OF NEW HAMPSHIRE, 2004

### CASE SUMMARY

**Facts:** Josiah James Treloar, Jr.'s first will left his estate to his wife unless she died before he did, in which case one piece of land was to go to his daughter Evelyn, another to his son, Rodney, and the rest of his estate was to be divided equally among Evelyn, Rodney, and another daughter, Beverly.

After his daughter Evelyn died, Josiah executed a new will. To help his lawyer in preparing this document, Josiah gave him a copy of the old will with handwritten changes, including Evelyn's name crossed out. The new will left all the assets to Rodney and Beverly. Evelyn's husband and children

---

[2] Arizona, California, Idaho, Louisiana, Nevada, New Mexico, Texas, and Washington all have community property laws; Wisconsin's system is a variation of the same principle.

[3] Except in Louisiana, whose laws are based on the French model.

got nothing, although Evelyn's husband, Leon, was named as executor. The will stated: "I hereby nominate and so far as I legally may appoint as Executor of this will, my son-in-law, Leon Merrill of Concord, New Hampshire."

Under New Hampshire law, all **issue** (including children and grandchildren) can qualify as pretermitted heirs. The law assumes that if the testator does not leave anything to his issue or does not refer to them in his will, it is because he has forgotten them. They are therefore entitled to a share of his estate. If Josiah had mentioned Evelyn, then the assumption would be that he had not forgotten her or her children. Evelyn's children argued that they were entitled to a share of Josiah's estate because he had not left her or them out on purpose. Josiah's attorney was serving as executor (not Leon). When he refused to pay the children, they sued.

**Issue:** *Are Evelyn's children entitled to a share of Josiah's estate?*

**Decision:** Evelyn's children are entitled to a share of the estate.

**Reasoning:** Most people leave their money to their children and grandchildren. Therefore, when a parent omits one or more of these heirs from his will, the law in New Hampshire assumes that it was a mistake unless he clearly specifies *in the will* that he had left them out on purpose. In this case, it seemed from circumstantial evidence that Josiah had not forgotten Evelyn or her children. After all, he had crossed her name out of the old will he had given his lawyer to use as a basis for the new document. He also listed her husband, Leon, as executor. Presumably he remembered that Leon was married to Evelyn.

Nonetheless, it is not the court's job to try to figure out what Josiah did or did not remember. The law is clear—indirectly alluding to the children or grandchildren is not sufficient. Because Josiah did not specifically refer to Evelyn or her children within the four corners of the will, it is presumed he forgot them and they are therefore entitled to a share of his estate.

---

**Issue**
A person's direct descendants, such as children and grandchildren.

**Per stirpes** distribution
Under a will, each branch of a family receives an equal share.

**Per capita** distribution
Under a will, each heir receives the same amount.

In drafting a will, lawyers almost always use the term **issue** instead of *children*. Issue means all descendants such as children, grandchildren, and so on. If a will left property just to "my children" and one child died before the testator, that child's children would not inherit their parent's share.

The will must also indicate whether issue are to inherit *per stirpes* or *per capita*. **Per stirpes** means that each *branch* of the family receives an equal share. Each child of the deceased receives the same amount, and, if a child has already died, her heirs inherit her share. **Per capita** means that each *heir* receives the same amount. If the children have died, then each grandchild inherits the same amount.

Suppose that Gwendolyn has two children, Lance and Arthur. Lance has one child, Arthur has four. Both sons predecease their mother. If Gwendolyn's will says *"per stirpes,"* Lance's child will inherit her father's entire share, which is half of Gwendolyn's estate. Arthur's four children will share their father's portion, so each will receive one eighth $\left(\frac{1}{4} \times \frac{1}{2}\right)$. If Gwendolyn's will says *"per capita,"* each of her grandchildren will inherit one fifth of her estate. Although it might sound fairer to give all grandchildren the same inheritance, most people choose a *per stirpes* distribution, on the theory that they are treating their children equally. The chart on the next page illustrates the difference between *per stirpes* and *per capita*.

## AMENDING A WILL

**Codicil**
An amendment to a will.

**A testator can generally revoke or alter a will at any time prior to death.** In most states, he can revoke a will by destroying it, putting an X through it, writing "revoked" (or some synonym) on it, or signing a new will. He can also execute an amendment—called a **codicil**—to change specific terms of the will, while keeping the rest of it intact. A codicil must meet all the requirements of a will, such as two witnesses. Suppose that Uncle Herman, who has a long and elaborate will, now wants his sterling silver Swiss Army knife to go to Cousin Larry rather than Niece Shannon. Instead of redoing his whole will, he can ask his lawyer to draw up a codicil changing only that one provision.

## INTESTACY

When singer John Denver died unexpectedly in a plane accident, he had had several marriages, children, and platinum albums. His estate was worth $20 million. What he did not have was a

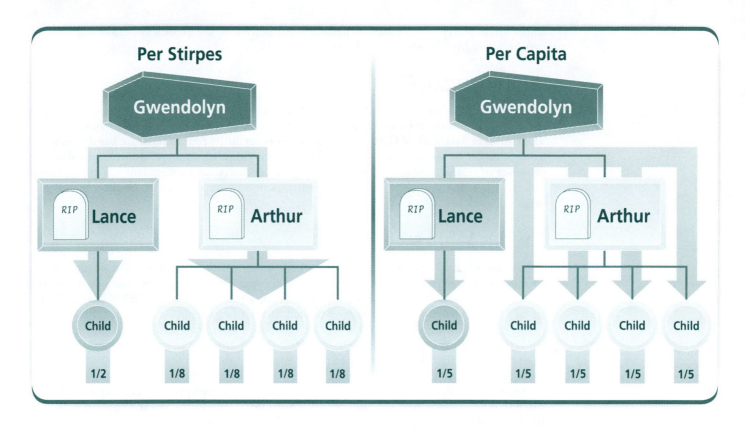

will. He was in good company—almost three quarters of Americans die intestate, that is, without a will. In this event, the law steps in and determines how to distribute the decedent's property. Although, in theory, intestacy laws are supposed to be based on what most people would prefer, in practice, they are not. The vast majority of married people, for instance, leave all their assets to their surviving spouse. Most intestacy laws do not. In some states, if a married person dies intestate, some portion of her property (one half or two thirds) goes to her spouse, and the remainder to her issue (including grandchildren). Few people would actually want grandchildren to take a share of their estate in preference to their spouse.

## POWER OF ATTORNEY

A **durable power of attorney** is a document that permits the **attorney-in-fact** to act for the principal. (An attorney-in-fact need not be a lawyer.) The power of attorney is effective until the principal dies or revokes it.

Lawyers generally recommend that their clients execute a durable power of attorney, particularly if they are elderly or in poor health. The power of attorney permits the client not only to choose the person who will act for him, but also to give advance instructions, such as "loan money to my son, Billy, if ever he needs it." If a client becomes incompetent and has no power of attorney, a court will appoint a guardian.

**Durable power of attorney**
Grants someone the authority to act for another person.

## PROBATE

The testatrix cannot implement the terms of the will from beyond the grave, so she appoints an executor for this task. Typically, the executor is a family member, lawyer, or close friend. If the decedent does not select an executor, the probate court appoints an administrator to fulfill the same functions. Both the executor and the administrator are entitled to reasonable compensation—typically between 1 percent and 5 percent of the estate's value, although family members and friends often waive the fee.

## ANATOMICAL GIFTS

Doctors have become increasingly successful at transplanting human organs. The demand for these organs—hearts, corneas, kidneys, pituitary glands, skin—is much greater than the supply. **The Uniform Anatomical Gift Act (UAGA) allows an individual to indicate her desire to be a donor either by putting a provision in her will or by signing an organ donation card in the presence of two witnesses.** The UAGA also provides that, unless a decedent has affirmatively indicated her desire not to be a donor, family members have the right to make a gift of her organs after death.

## LIVING WILLS

At the age of 25, Nancy Cruzan was in a devastating car accident. Deprived of oxygen for 14 minutes, a large part of her brain was destroyed. No one in her condition had ever recovered, but she could have continued to live for 25 years. In a rehabilitation hospital in Missouri, she lay in a fetal position, with her hands so twisted that her fingernails cut her wrists. She seemed to feel pain, and a nurse claimed that Cruzan cried once when read a Valentine's Day card. She seemed to sleep. When her eyes were open, they gazed around the room randomly. Cruzan's parents believed that their daughter would rather be dead than live this way. They went to court to obtain permission to stop feeding her.

Nancy Cruzan's tragedy led to a national debate over the right to die. **The Supreme Court ruled that family members can choose to discontinue treatment for an incompetent person if there is evidence the patient would have made that choice herself.**[4] After the Supreme Court decision, the probate court in Missouri heard new witnesses testify that Cruzan had said she would not want to live "like a vegetable." The lower court considered this clear and convincing evidence of Cruzan's wishes and granted the family permission to withhold feeding.

Spurred by the Cruzan case, many people executed so-called **living wills** or **advance directives.** Living wills permit adults to refuse extreme medical treatment that would prolong their lives, such as artificial feeding or cardiac resuscitation. In addition, a living will can be used to appoint a **health care proxy** to make decisions for a person who has become incompetent.

Living wills become particularly important if family members disagree about appropriate treatment. Terri Schiavo was only 26 years old when her heart stopped beating one evening, causing brain damage that put her in a persistent vegetative state. Her husband said she would not have wanted to live that way and asked to have her feeding tube removed; her parents disagreed and fought him through the courts. Even Congress intervened to try to keep the tube in place. Her husband ultimately prevailed and the tube was removed, but only after 15 years of litigation and public uproar. If Schiavo had had a living will, her family would have had more privacy, fewer legal bills, and, perhaps, greater peace. Information about living wills and samples are available at **http://www.partnershipforcaring.org** and **http://abalawinfo.org**.

Doctors are permitted to shorten a patient's life by withholding medical treatment. Can they go the next step and prescribe medication to end the life of a terminal patient who is suffering intolerably? In most states, the answer is no—**assisted suicide** is a felony. The following case explains the legal basis for these felony statutes.

---

**Living will**
In the event that a person is unable to make medical decisions, this document indicates her preferences and may also appoint someone else to makes these decisions for her. Also known as an *advance directive*.

**Health care proxy**
Someone who is authorized to make health care decisions for a person who is incompetent.

**Assisted suicide**
The process of hastening death for a terminally ill patient at the request of this patient.

> **If Schiavo had had a living will, her family would have had more privacy, fewer legal bills, and, perhaps, greater peace.**

---

[4] *Cruzan v. Director, Missouri Department of Health,* 497 U.S. 261, 110 S. Ct. 2841, 1990 U.S. LEXIS 3301 (1990).

## WASHINGTON V. GLUCKSBERG

521 U.S. 702, 117 S. CT. 2258, 1997 U.S. LEXIS 4039
UNITED STATES SUPREME COURT, 1997

### CASE SUMMARY

**Facts:** The plaintiffs are five physicians who treat terminally ill patients, three patients in the terminal stage of excruciatingly painful illnesses, and Compassion in Dying (an organization that provides support to mentally competent, fatally ill adults considering suicide). The defendant is the state of Washington, which passed a statute making assisted suicide a felony punishable by up to five years in prison and a $10,000 fine. Plaintiffs argued that this statute was unconstitutional.

**Issue:** *Does a state have the right to punish those who assist the terminally ill to commit suicide?*

**Decision:** Yes, the state has the right to regulate assisted suicide.

**Reasoning:** In the *Cruzan* case, this court suggested that an individual has the right to refuse life-saving treatment. However, there is an enormous difference between withholding aid and actively killing someone.

For over 700 years, Anglo-American common law has punished those who help suicides. Most states that have considered this issue have decided that assisted suicide should be illegal. Given this history, it is difficult to argue that the Constitution somehow protects, as a fundamental liberty, the right to assisted suicide.

The American Medical Association is concerned that physicians would be less diligent in fighting disease if killing patients were as acceptable an option as curing them.

Without an anti-suicide statute, the ill, the elderly, minorities, and the poor would all be pressured to consent to their own deaths. Pain is a significant factor in creating a desire for assisted suicide, and doctors are notoriously less aggressive in providing pain relief to the underprivileged.

For all these reasons, laws that treat assisted suicides as felonies are constitutional.

---

It is important to note the limits to this ruling. The court is only saying that a state *may* punish those who assist suicide, not that a state *must* do so. Indeed, voters in Washington ultimately passed a statute that permits doctor-assisted suicide, within strict limits. That statute is valid. The state of Oregon also permits assisted suicide.

### EXAM *Strategy*

**Question:** Tim's will provides that all of his money will go to his cat, Princess Ida. After he dies, his widow and children claim that they are entitled to a share of his estate. Is this true? Will Princess Ida be living like royalty?

**Strategy:** The answer is different for his wife and children.

**Result:** Tim's wife is entitled to a share of his assets unless she signed a contract waiving that right. His children are entitled to a share of his assets unless he clearly indicated in his will that he intended to leave them out.

---

## · TRUSTS ·

Trusts are an increasingly popular method for managing assets, both during life and after death. **A trust is an entity that separates legal and beneficial ownership.** It involves three people: the **grantor** (also called the **settlor** or **donor**), who creates and funds it; the **trustee**, who manages the assets; and the **beneficiary,** who receives the financial proceeds. A grantor can create a trust during her lifetime or after her death through her will.

**Trust**
An entity that separates the legal and beneficial ownership of assets.

**Grantor**
Someone who creates and funds a trust. Also called a *settler* or *donor*.

**Trustee**
Someone who manages the assets of a trust.

**Beneficiary**
Someone who receives the financial proceeds of a trust.

## ADVANTAGES AND DISADVANTAGES

Why do people use trusts? These are among the advantages:

- **Control.** The grantor can control her assets after her death. In the trust document, she can direct the trustees to follow a specific investment strategy, and she can determine how much income the beneficiaries receive. As an example, suppose the grantor has a husband and children. She wants to provide her husband with adequate income after her death, but she does not want him to spend so lavishly that nothing is left for the children. Nor does she want him to spend all her money on his second wife. The grantor could create a trust in her will that allows her husband to spend the income and, upon his death, gives the principal to their children.

- **Caring for children.** Minor children cannot legally manage property on their own, so parents or grandparents often establish trusts to take care of these assets until the children grow up.

- **Tax savings.** Although tax issues are beyond the scope of this chapter, it is worth noting that many married couples use a so-called **marital trust** to minimize their estate taxes.

- **Privacy.** A will is filed in probate court and becomes a matter of public record. Anyone can obtain a copy of it. Some companies are even in the business of providing copies to celebrity hounds. Jacqueline Kennedy Onassis's will is particularly popular. Trusts, however, are private documents and are not available to the public.

- **Probate.** Because a will must go through the often lengthy probate process, the heirs may not receive assets for some time. Assets that are put into a trust *before the grantor dies* do not go through probate; the beneficiaries have immediate access to them.

The major *disadvantage* of a trust is expense. Although it is always possible for the grantor to establish a trust himself with the aid of software or form books, trusts are complex instruments with many potential pitfalls. Do-it-yourself trusts are a recipe for disaster. In addition to the legal fees required to establish a trust, the trustees may have to be paid. Professional trustees typically charge an annual fee of about one percent of the trust's assets. Family members usually do not expect payment.

## TYPES OF TRUSTS

Depending upon the goal in establishing a trust, a grantor has two choices.

### Living Trust

**Also known as an *inter vivos* trust, a living trust is established while the grantor is still alive.** In the typical living trust, the grantor serves as trustee during his lifetime. He maintains total control over the assets and avoids a trustee's fee. If the grantor becomes disabled or dies, the successor trustee, who is named in the trust instrument, takes over automatically. All of the assets stay in the trust and avoid probate. Most living trusts are **revocable**, meaning that the grantor can undo the trust or change it at any time.

### Testamentary Trust

**A testamentary trust is created by a will.** It goes into effect when the grantor dies. Naturally, it is **irrevocable** because the grantor is dead. The grantor's property must first go through probate, on its way to the trust.

Living trusts are particularly popular with older people because they want to ensure that their assets will be properly managed if they become disabled. Younger people typically opt for a testamentary trust because the probability they will become disabled anytime soon is remote. Also they want to avoid the effort of transferring their assets to the trust.

**Marital trust**
A legal entity created for the purpose of reducing a married couple's estate taxes.

**Living trust**
A trust established while the grantor is still alive.

**Revocable trust**
A trust that can be undone or changed at any time.

**Testamentary trust**
A trust that goes into effect when a grantor dies.

# TRUST ADMINISTRATION

The primary obligation of trustees is to carry out the terms of the trust. They may exercise any powers expressly granted to them in the trust instrument and any implied powers reasonably necessary to implement the terms of the trust. In carrying out the terms of the trust, the trustees have a fiduciary duty to the beneficiary. This fiduciary duty includes:

- **A duty of loyalty.** In managing the trust, the trustees must put the interests of the beneficiaries first. They must disclose any relevant information to the beneficiaries. They may not mix their own assets with those of the trust; do business with the trust (unless expressly permitted by the terms of the trust); or favor one beneficiary over another.

- **A duty of care.** The trustee must act as a reasonable person would when managing the assets of another. The trustee must make careful investments, keep accurate records, and collect debts owed the trust.

A trustee is liable to the beneficiaries of the trust if she breaches her duty. W. Averell Harriman was a member of a wealthy New York family. When he died, he left half of his $65 million estate outright to his wife, Pamela Harriman, and half in trust for his two daughters from an earlier marriage (who were in their 70s). Pamela was a trustee and had the right to appoint the other trustees. She had been married twice before, to Winston Churchill's son and to Hollywood producer Leland Hayward. After Averell's death, she became ambassador to France, partly because of her generous contributions to the Democratic Party.

Under Pamela's care, the trust assets were invested in a series of risky real estate deals, including a seedy conference center in New Jersey that had once been a Playboy Club. The beneficiaries filed suit against her when they discovered that trust assets had declined in value from $30 million to $3 million. She and the children ultimately settled their litigation for an undisclosed sum, and then both sides filed suit against the two other trustees. This litigation also was settled.

# TERMINATION

A trust ends upon the occurrence of any of these events:

- On the date indicated by the grantor.
- If the trust is revocable, when revoked by the grantor. Even if the trust is irrevocable, the grantor and all the beneficiaries can agree to revoke it.
- When the purpose of the trust has been fulfilled. If the grantor established the trust to pay college tuition for his grandchildren, the trust ends when the last grandchild graduates.

## EXAM *Strategy*

**Question:** Maddie set up a trust for her children, with Blair as trustee. Blair decided to sell a piece of trust real estate to his wife without obtaining an appraisal, attempting to market the property, or consulting a real estate agent. Maddie was furious and ordered him not to make the sale. Can she stop him? Would she have to go to court?

**Strategy:** The answer depends upon what type of trust she has established.

**Result:** If the trust is revocable, Maddie can simply undo it and take the property back. If it is irrevocable, she could still prevent the sale by going to court because Blair has violated the duties he owes to the beneficiaries. He has violated the duty of loyalty by selling trust property to his wife. He has violated the duty of care by failing to act as a reasonable seller would.

## CHAPTER CONCLUSION

Attitudes toward inherited money vary greatly. Self-made Warren Buffet, whose holdings in Berkshire Hathaway Inc. are worth billions of dollars, disapproves of inherited wealth. His children have occasionally borrowed money from him, but he insists that they sign formal loan documents and repay the loans. Other wealthy, and not so wealthy, people spend considerable time and effort minimizing their estate taxes and maximizing their children's inheritance. Neither view is right or wrong. People are perfectly entitled to dispose of their money as they see fit. The only wrong is in not deciding.

## EXAM REVIEW

1. **WILL** A will is a legal document that disposes of the testator's property after death. (p. 494)

2. **HOLOGRAPHIC WILL** A holographic will is handwritten by the testator but not witnessed. (p. 494)

3. **NUNCUPATIVE WILL** An oral will. For a nuncupative will to be valid, the testatrix must know she is dying, there must be three witnesses, and these witnesses must know that they are listening to her will. (p. 494)

4. **SURVIVING SPOUSE AND CHILDREN** A spouse is entitled to a certain share of the decedent's estate, but children have no automatic right to share in a parent's estate as long as the parent indicates in his will that the pretermitted child has been left out on purpose. (p. 495)

**EXAM Strategy**

**Question:** Josh was a crotchety fellow, often at outs with his family. In his will, he left his son an autographed copy of his book, *A Guide to Federal Prisons*. He completely omitted his wife of 35 years and his daughter, instead leaving the rest of his substantial estate to the Society for the Assistance of Convicted Felons. Under the UPC, which member of his family fared best?

**Strategy:** Children and spouses are treated differently. Pretermitted children fare differently from those named in the will. (See the "Result" at the end of this section.)

5. **PER STIRPES V. PER CAPITA** In a will, a *per stirpes* distribution means that each branch of the family receives an equal share. *Per capita* means that each heir receives the same amount. (p. 496)

**EXAM** *Strategy*

**CPA QUESTION**  A decedent's will provided that the estate was to be divided among the decedent's issue, *per capita* and not *per stirpes*. If there are two surviving children and three grandchildren who are children of a predeceased child at the time the will is probated, how will the estate be divided?

(a)  1/2 to each surviving child

(b)  1/3 to each surviving child and 1/9 to each grandchild

(c)  1/4 to each surviving child and 1/6 to each grandchild

(d)  1/5 to each surviving child and grandchild

**Strategy:**  Remember that *per stirpes* divides equally among the children, *per capita* equally among the issue.

6.  **REVOCATION OF A WILL**  A testator may generally revoke or alter a will at any time prior to death. (p. 496)

7.  **INTESTACY**  Dying without a will. In this event, the law determines how the decedent's property will be distributed. (p. 496)

8.  **DURABLE POWER OF ATTORNEY**  A durable power of attorney is a document that permits the attorney-in-fact to act for the principal. (p. 497)

9.  **ANATOMICAL GIFTS**  The Uniform Anatomical Gift Act (UAGA) allows an individual to indicate her desire to be an organ donor either by putting a provision in her will or by signing an organ donation card in the presence of two witnesses. (p. 498)

10.  **LIVING WILL**  A living will permits an adult to refuse medical treatment that would prolong life. (p. 498)

11.  **TRUST**  A trust is an entity that separates legal and beneficial ownership. (p. 499)

12.  **LIVING TRUST**  Also known as an *inter vivos* trust, a living trust is established while the grantor is still alive. (p. 500)

13.  **TESTAMENTARY TRUST**  A testamentary trust is created by a will. (p. 500)

14.  **TRUSTEE'S DUTY**  In carrying out the terms of a trust, a trustee has a fiduciary duty to the beneficiary, which includes a duty of loyalty and a duty of care. (p. 501)

**4. Result:**  Under the UPC, his wife is entitled to the greater of $50,000 or 50 percent of his assets. His daughter, as a pretermitted child, is entitled to whatever she would have received if he had died intestate. Because his son received something in the will, he is entitled to nothing more than the book.

**5. Result:**  There are five surviving issue (two children and three grandchildren), so they each get one-fifth. D is the correct answer.

# PRACTICE EXAM

## MATCHING QUESTIONS

Match the following terms with their definitions:

___ A. Executor

___ B. Intestate

___ C. Testator

___ D. Administrator

___ E. Testatrix

1. Woman who has signed a valid will
2. Man who has signed a valid will
3. Personal representative chosen by the decedent to carry out the terms of a will
4. To die without a will
5. Personal representative appointed by the probate court to oversee the probate process

## TRUE/FALSE QUESTIONS

Circle true or false:

1. T  F  Under the Uniform Probate Code, one spouse is not required to leave any money to the other spouse.

2. T  F  A holographic will does not need to be witnessed.

3. T  F  A nuncupative will does not need to be witnessed.

4. T  F  A principal may not revoke a durable power of attorney.

5. T  F  A grantor may not be the trustee of a trust.

## MULTIPLE-CHOICE QUESTIONS

6. CPA QUESTION: A personal representative of an estate would breach her fiduciary duties if she:
   A. Combined personal funds with funds of the estate so that both could purchase Treasury bills
   B. Represented the estate in a lawsuit brought against it by a disgruntled relative of the decedent
   C. Distributed property in satisfaction of the decedent's debts
   D. Engaged a non-CPA to prepare the records for the estate's final accounting

7. Hallie is telling her cousin Anne about the will she has just executed. "Because of my broken arm, I couldn't sign my name, so I just told Bertrand, the lawyer, to sign it for me. Bertrand also witnessed the will." Anne said, "You made a big mistake:
   I. You should have at least made some sort of mark on the paper yourself."
   II. The lawyer is not permitted to witness the will."
   III. You did not have enough witnesses."

   Which of Anne's statements is true?
   A. I, II, and III
   B. Neither I, II, nor III
   C. Just I
   D. Just II
   E. Just III

**8.** Owen does not want to leave any money to his son, Kevin. What must he do to achieve this goal?

   I. Nothing. If he dies without a will, Kevin will inherit nothing.

  II. Make a will that leaves nothing to Kevin.

 III. Leave Kevin $1 in his will.

  A.  I, II, or III                         D.  Just II

  B.  II or III                             E.  Just III

  C.  Just I

**9.** Lauren is a resident of Kansas who has signed a living will directing her husband to make medical decisions for her. Now that she is dying of cancer and suffering terribly, she is begging her husband and her doctors to kill her. Which of the following statements is true?

   I. If she goes into a coma, her husband has the right to direct her doctors to withhold treatment.

  II. Her doctor has the right to give her an overdose of pills that will kill her.

 III. Her husband has the right to give her an overdose of pills that will kill her.

  A.  I, II, and III                       D.  Just II

  B.  Neither I, II, nor III             E.  Just III

  C.  Just I

**10.** Blake tells his client that there are five good reasons to set up a trust. Which of the following is *not* a good reason?

  A.  To pay his grandchildren's college tuition if they go to the same college he attended

  B.  To save money, since a trust is cheaper than a will

  C.  To make sure the money is properly invested

  D.  To avoid probate

  E.  To safeguard his privacy

## SHORT-ANSWER QUESTIONS

**11.** William Cook was a very successful undertaker. When he died, his will left all of his property to his brother Eugene. There were two other pieces of paper in the safe with the will. One said that that his stamp collection should go to his housekeeper, Bertha. This document was signed by two witnesses—the gardener and the cook. There was also a piece of paper stating that he would like all of his assets to go to his sister's daughter, Evangeline. Who will get what?

**12.** Kevin Fitzgerald represented the down-and-out Mission Hill and Roxbury Districts in the Massachusetts House of Representatives. A priest alerted him that Mary Guzelian, a street person who roamed his district, had trash bags in her ghetto apartment stuffed with cash, bonds, and bank books. Fitzgerald visited the apartment with his top aide, Patricia McDermott. Two weeks later, Guzelian signed a will, drafted by one of Fitzgerald's acquaintances, that left Guzelian's $400,000 estate to Fitzgerald and McDermott. Fitzgerald claimed not to know about the will until Guzelian's death four years later. Guzelian, 64, suffered from chronic paranoid schizophrenia and severe health problems. Would Guzelian's sister have a claim on Guzelian's estate?

**13.** When Bill died, he left all of his property in a trust to take care of his wife, Dorris, for the rest of her life. On her death, the money would go to their son, Rob. The Bank of Tulsa was the trustee of this trust. Fifty years later, Rob needed money, so he began writing checks out of Dorris's checking account. She knew about the checks but could never say no to him. At the rate at which Rob was spending her money, the trust funds would all be gone within a couple of years. What was the bank's responsibility? Was it obligated to let Dorris have as much money as she wanted?

**14.** After nearly 40 years of marriage, Frank Honigman executed a new will that left his wife only the minimum required by law. The balance went to his brothers and sisters (the couple had no children). For some time before his death, Honigman had repeatedly told both friends and strangers, using obscene and abusive language, that his wife was unfaithful. Honigman was normal and rational in other respects but, by all evidence, his suspicions were untrue. They were based on such evidence as the fact that, when he left the house, his wife would ask him when he planned to return. Also, whenever the telephone rang, Mrs. Honigman answered it. For the last two years of his life he positively forbade her to answer the telephone. Is Mr. Honigman's will valid?

15. When Gregg died, his will left his money equally to his two children, Max and Alison. Max had died a few years earlier, leaving behind a widow and four children. Who will get Gregg's money?

16. ROLE REVERSAL: Draft a multiple-choice question that compares *per stirpes* with *per capita*.

# INTERNET RESEARCH PROBLEM

Fill out your own organ donor card (available at **http://www.delafe.com/form/frmdonor.htm**) or advance directive (see **http://www.partnershipforcaring.org**).

**You can find further practice problems in the Online Quiz at www.cengage.com/blaw/beatty.**

# INSURANCE

**What insurance** policies are right for Jamie? When he bought a high-definition television at Shopping World for $1,000, the salesperson offered him a two-year service plan for $80. Should he buy it? He has moved out of a dorm and is renting an apartment. Does he need rental insurance? And then his mother suggested he get a term life insurance policy while he is young and the rates are low. He applied for health insurance. Should he admit to being a smoker? And then there is travel insurance available at the airport in case his flight home crashes. Is that a good deal?

> **He applied for health insurance. Should he admit to being a smoker?**

How does he evaluate his options? To answer these questions, it is important to understand the economics of the insurance industry. Suppose that you have recently purchased a $500,000 house. The probability your house will burn down in the next year is 1 in 1,000. That is a low risk, but the consequences would be devastating, especially since you could not afford to rebuild. Instead of bearing that risk yourself, you take out a fire insurance policy. You pay an insurance company $1,200 in return for a promise that, if your house burns down in the next 12 months, the company will pay you $500,000. The insurance company sells the same policy to 1,000 similar homeowners, expecting that on average one of these houses will burn down. If all 1,000 policyholders pay $1,200, the insurance company takes in $1.2 million each year, but expects to pay out only $500,000. It will put some money aside in case two houses burn down, or even worse, a major forest fire guts a whole tract of houses. It must also pay overhead expenses such as marketing and administration. And, of course, shareholders expect profits.

When purchasing insurance, it is important to remember that insurance companies have a lot of data on people like you so they can predict accurately the probability that a calamity will befall you. They then price their premiums so that they will make a profit. For that reason, most people who buy insurance pay out more in premiums than they take in from the policy. So why do they buy insurance? To protect themselves from disasters—no matter how improbable—that they simply cannot afford.

To review Jamie's situation: high-definition televisions are reliable and unlikely to need repairs in the first two years. These service plans are remarkably profitable—for the seller. Stores often make a larger profit from the insurance than from the product itself. Does Jamie need rental insurance? Not to replace the $10 couch he bought off Craigslist, but he should consider buying a policy that would protect him from liability if someone is injured in his apartment. If he buys life insurance, term is the cheapest form, but does he need it? Whom is he protecting? He has no spouse or children. He is not supporting his mother. It seems that he does not need life insurance now. When applying for health insurance, he must admit that he is a smoker—otherwise the health insurance company can cancel his policy if he becomes ill. There is no point in lying on *any* insurance application because then the policy is voidable. As for travel insurance, those last-minute policies are almost always a bad deal. And if Jamie needs to protect someone, he should have life insurance that covers him all the time, not just on his trip home.

## · INTRODUCTION ·

Insurance has its own terminology, so it is important to understand key terms:

- **Person.** An individual, corporation, partnership, or any other legal entity
- **Insurance.** A contract in which one person, in return for a fee, agrees to guarantee another against loss caused by a specific type of danger
- **Insurer.** The person who issues the insurance policy and serves as guarantor
- **Insured.** The person whose loss is the subject of the insurance policy
- **Owner.** The person who enters into the insurance contract and pays the premiums
- **Premium.** The consideration that the owner pays under the policy
- **Beneficiary.** The person who receives the proceeds from the insurance policy

The beneficiary, the insured, and the owner can be, but are not necessarily, the same person. If a homeowner buys fire insurance for her house, she is the insured, the owner, and the beneficiary because she bought the policy and receives the proceeds if her house burns down. If a mother buys a life insurance policy on her son that is payable to his children in the event of his death, then the mother is the owner, the son is the insured, and the grandchildren are the beneficiaries.

## · INSURANCE CONTRACT ·

**An insurance policy must meet all the common law requirements for a contract.** There must be an offer, acceptance, and consideration. The owner must have legal capacity; that is, he must be an adult of sound mind. Fraud, duress, or undue influence invalidates a policy. In theory, insurance contracts need not be in writing because the statute of frauds does not apply to any contract that can be performed within one year and it is possible that the house may burn down or the car may crash within a year. Some states, however, specifically require insurance contracts to be in writing.

## OFFER AND ACCEPTANCE

**The purchaser of a policy makes an offer by delivering an application and a premium to the insurer.** The insurance company then has the option of either accepting or rejecting the offer. **It can accept by oral notice, by written notice, or by delivery of the policy.** It also has a fourth option—a written binder. A binder is a short document acknowledging receipt of the application and premium. It indicates that a policy is *temporarily* in effect but does not constitute *final* acceptance. The insurer still has the right to reject the offer once it has examined the application carefully. Kyle buys a house on April 1 and wants insurance right away. The insurance company issues a binder to him the same day. If Kyle's house burns down on May 1, the insurer must pay, even though it has not yet issued the final policy. If, however, there is no fire, but on May 1 the company decides Kyle is a bad risk, it has the right to reject his application at that time because it has not yet issued the policy.

## LIMITING CLAIMS BY THE INSURED

Insurance policies can sometimes look like a quick way to make easy money. More than one person suffering from overwhelming financial pressure has insured a building to the hilt and then burned it down for the insurance money. Unbelievably, more than one parent has killed a child to collect the proceeds of a life insurance policy. Therefore, the law has created a number of rules to protect insurance companies from fraud and bad faith on the part of insureds.

### Insurable Interest

**An insurance contract is not valid unless the owner has an *insurable interest* in the subject matter of the policy.** To understand why an insurable interest is important, read this tragic story. Twenty-year-old Deana Wild was thrilled when James Coates proposed to her. To celebrate their engagement, they took a sightseeing trip along the California coast with Coates's mother, Virginia Rearden. They seemed to be just one big happy family. Only one problem: Wild slipped while walking along the edge of a cliff at Big Sur and fell to her death. That would have been the end of the story except that, the day before, Rearden had taken out a $35,000 life insurance policy on Wild, naming Coates and Rearden as beneficiaries. When the insurance company investigated, it learned that Coates was married to someone else. Therefore, he could not be Wild's fiancé, and neither he nor Rearden had an insurable interest in Wild. It also turned out that Rearden had taken out the policy without Wild's knowledge. Rearden was convicted of first-degree murder and sentenced to life in prison without parole.

These are the rules on insurable interest:

**Insurable interest**
means that someone would suffer a loss if the insured event occurs.

- **Definition.** A person has an insurable interest if she would be harmed by the danger that she has insured against. If Jessica takes out a fire insurance policy on her own barn, she will presumably be reluctant to burn it down. However, if she buys a policy on Nathan's barn, she will not mind, she may even be delighted, when fire sweeps through the building. It is a small step to saying that she might even burn the barn down herself.

- **Amount of loss.** The insurable interest can be no greater than the actual amount of loss suffered. If the barn is worth $50,000, but Jessica insures it (and pays premiums) for $100,000, she will recover only $50,000 when it burns down. Nor is she entitled to a refund of the excess premiums she has paid. The goal is to make sure that Jessica does not profit from the policy.
- **Life insurance.** A person always has an insurable interest in his own life and the life of his spouse or fiancée. Parents and minor children also have an insurable interest in each other.
- **Work relationships.** Business partners, employers, and employees have an insurable interest in each other if they would suffer some financial harm from the death of the insured. For example, a start-up company will often buy **key person life insurance** on its officers to compensate the company if an important person dies.

# MISREPRESENTATION

**Material**

Important to the insurer's decision to issue a policy or set a premium amount.

**Insurers have the right to void a policy if, during the application process, the insured makes a material misstatement or conceals a material fact.** The policy is voidable whether the misstatement was oral or in writing, intentional or unintentional. **Material** means that the misstatement or omission affected the insurer's willingness to issue the policy or the amount of the premium. In the following case, the applicant lied about his health. Were his misstatements material?

## GOLDEN RULE INSURANCE CO. v. HOPKINS

788 F. SUPP. 295, 1991 U.S. DIST. LEXIS 19970
UNITED STATES DISTRICT COURT FOR THE SOUTHERN DISTRICT OF MISSISSIPPI, 1991

### CASE SUMMARY

**Facts:** Brian Hopkins submitted an application to Golden Rule Insurance Co. for medical and life insurance. In filling out the application, he answered "no" to questions asking whether he had had any of the following conditions: heart murmur, growths, skin disorders, immune deficiencies, sexually transmitted diseases, or any disorders of the glands. In fact, he had had all of the above. In response to questions about past surgery, Hopkins reported that he had had tonsils and hemorrhoids removed, failing to reveal that he had also had rectal warts excised.

A year later, Hopkins was hospitalized. While in the hospital, he was diagnosed with AIDS. In his discharge summary, Dr. William A. Causey stated that Hopkins had known that he was HIV-positive for three years. (HIV is the virus that causes AIDS.) Shortly thereafter, Dr. Causey wrote to Golden Rule to say that he was mistaken and that Hopkins was not HIV-positive. During the trial, however, Dr. Causey admitted that he was reluctant to tell insurance companies information that would harm his patients. The following year, Hopkins died of AIDS. Golden Rule rescinded Hopkins's policies, contending that his application contained material misrepresentations.

**Issues:** *Did Hopkins materially misrepresent his health when applying for insurance? Does Golden Rule have the right to rescind his insurance policies?*

**Decision:** Golden Rule had the right to rescind Hopkins's insurance policies because he made material misrepresentations in his application.

**Reasoning:** An insurer has the right to rescind an insurance policy if the application contains a false statement that affects the insurer's risk. When Hopkins filled out the Golden Rule application, he knew that he was HIV-positive and had a heart murmur as well as a history of skin disorders, swollen lymph glands, and rectal warts. All of these conditions were material and would have affected Golden Rule's decision to issue the policy.

Golden Rule is entitled to rescind Hopkins's policies. The company is not obligated to pay any of his medical costs, but must refund the premiums it received from him.

### **EXAM** *Strategy*

**Question:** During a visit to a hospital emergency room for treatment of a gunshot wound to his chest, John Cummings tested positive for cocaine. Six months later, he applied for a life insurance policy, which was to benefit his mother. The application asked if he had, within the prior five years, used any controlled drugs without a prescription by a physician. Cummings answered, "No." A year after the policy was issued, Cummings died of a gunshot wound. Was the policy valid?

**Strategy:** If the insured makes a material misstatement during the application process, the insurer has the right to void a policy, whether or not the misstatement relates to the cause of death.

**Result:** Cummings's mother argued that the policy was valid because her son had not died from taking drugs. The gunshot wound was unrelated to his cocaine use. However, an insurer has a right to void a policy if the insured makes *any* material misstatement. Here the misstatement was material because the insurance company would not have issued the policy if it had known about the cocaine. As a result, the policy is voidable.

## BAD FAITH BY THE INSURER

**Insurance policies often contain a covenant of *good faith and fair dealing*.** Even if the policy itself does not *explicitly* include such a provision, an increasing number of courts (but not all) *imply* this covenant. An insurance company can violate the covenant of good faith and fair dealing by (1) fraudulently inducing someone to buy a policy; (2) unreasonably refusing to pay a valid claim; or (3) refusing to accept a reasonable settlement offer that has been made to an insured. When an insurance company violates the covenant of good faith and fair dealing, it becomes liable for both compensatory and punitive damages.

### Fraud

In recent years, a number of insurance companies have paid substantial damages to settle fraud charges involving the sale of life insurance. For example, agents for Prudential Insurance Company of America tricked customers into trading in existing policies for new ones with higher coverage and bigger premiums. Sales agents promised the customers that their premiums would not increase, but that was not true. The higher premiums were disguised at the beginning because the company used cash reserves that had built up in the original policy to pay the premiums on the new policy. Eventually, however, all the cash in the old policy was used up and the customers began to receive bills for much higher premiums. In many cases, they could not afford to pay the premiums, so their policy lapsed. This meant that Prudential received premiums for years, but never had to pay benefits because the policies lapsed before anyone died.

> In short, Prudential had trained its agents to commit fraud.

In short, Prudential had trained its agents to commit fraud. Agents were also trained to target the elderly. The state of Florida found that Prudential had deliberately cheated its customers for more than 10 years. Prudential agreed to pay as much as $2 billion in refunds. In a similar case, State Farm Insurance agreed to pay its customers $200 million.

### Refusing to Pay a Valid Claim

Perhaps because juries feel sympathy for those who must deal with an immovable bureaucracy, damage awards are often sizeable when an insurance company unreasonably refuses to pay a legitimate claim. For example, a jury in Ohio entered a $13 million verdict against Buckeye Union Insurance Co. for its bad-faith refusal to pay a claim. An Ohio sheriff stopped the automobile of 19-year-old Eugene Leber. As the sheriff approached Leber's car, he slipped on ice and his gun discharged. By incredible bad luck, the bullet struck Leber, permanently paralyzing him from the rib cage down. The insurance company recognized that it was liable under the policy, but it nonetheless fought the case for *16 years*.

Consumers complain that insurance companies often "low-ball"—that is, they make an unreasonably low offer to settle a claim. Some insurance companies even set claims quotas that limit how much their adjusters can pay out each year, regardless of the merits of each individual claim. If juries continue to award multimillion-dollar verdicts, insurance companies may decide simply to pay the claims.

In the following case, the insurance company ultimately paid the claim, but not fast enough to satisfy the jury.

## GOODSON V. AMERICAN STANDARD INSURANCE COMPANY OF WISCONSIN

89 P.3d 409, 2004 Colo. LEXIS 388
SUPREME COURT OF COLORADO, 2004

### CASE SUMMARY

**Facts:** Dawn Goodson and her two children were in an automobile accident while driving a car owned by Chet Weber. He was insured by American Standard Insurance Company of Wisconsin.

To treat injuries that she and her children suffered in the accident, Goodson sought care from a chiropractor. She submitted these bills, totaling about $8,000, to American Standard. The insurance company offered a number of erroneous reasons why it should not pay the claims: that the chiropractor was not a member of American Standard's preferred provider organization; that Weber's policy was not in effect at the time of the accident; that Goodson and her children needed to undergo an independent medical evaluation to determine whether their injuries were related to the accident and whether their medical treatment was reasonable and necessary. In the end, American Standard did pay Goodson's bills, but it took 18 months to do so.

Goodson filed suit against American Standard, alleging that it had engaged in a bad-faith breach of the insurance contract. Although the company's delay in payment had not caused Goodson any economic damage, it had caused her substantial emotional distress. The jury awarded Goodson and her children $75,000 in actual damages and an additional $75,000

in punitive damages. The appeals court overturned the verdict. Goodson appealed to the state Supreme Court.

**Issue:** *Can Goodson recover damages for the emotional distress caused by American Standard's delay in paying her claim?*

**Decision:** Yes, Goodson can recover for emotional distress.

**Reasoning:** An insurer that violates its duties of good faith and fair dealing is liable for both compensatory and punitive damages. Compensatory damages include emotional distress; pain and suffering; inconvenience; fear and anxiety; and impairment of the quality of life. The goal of punitive damages is to punish the insurer and deter wrongful conduct by other companies. To recover punitive damages, the insured must show that the insurer acted with fraud, malice, or willful and wanton conduct.

Goodson suffered emotional distress as a result of the company's delay. Her worries about the medical bills left her anxious, fearful, stressed, and worried about whether she would have to pay the bills herself.

The whole point of buying insurance is to enjoy peace of mind. The fact that the company finally paid the bill after 18 months of unreasonable delays does not undo the distress caused by the bad faith conduct.

## Refusing to Accept a Settlement Offer

An insurer also violates the covenant of good faith and fair dealing when it *wrongfully* refuses to settle a claim. An insurance company is supposed to negotiate a settlement as if the policy had no limits. Suppose that Dmitri has a $1 million liability policy on his house. When Tanya slips on his icy front walk, she breaks her back and ends up paralyzed. She sues him for $5 million. As provided in the policy, Dmitri's insurance company defends him against Tanya's claim. She offers to settle for $1 million, but the insurance company refuses because it only has $1 million at risk anyway. It may get lucky with the jury. Instead, a jury comes in with a $3 million verdict. The insurance company is liable for only $1 million, but Dmitri must pay $2 million. In this instance, a court might well find that the insurance company had violated its covenant of good faith and fair dealing.

**EXAM** *Strategy*

**Question:** Geoff takes out renter's insurance with Fastball Insurance Co. On the application where it asks if he has any pets, he fills in "poodle." Although he does not know it, his "poodle" is really a Portuguese water dog. The two breeds look a lot alike. A month later, his apartment is robbed. Fastball investigates and discovers that Geoff does not have a poodle, after all. It denies his claim. Geoff files suit. What result?

**Strategy:** There are two issues here: Was Geoff's answer on the application a material misstatement? Was Fastball's denial in bad faith?

**Result:** Geoff's misrepresentation was not material—the breed of dog does not affect liability on the renter's policy. If he said he had an attack dog such as a Doberman, perhaps the premium would have been lower because the dog would scare off intruders (or higher because the dog would also attack friends and neighbors), but poodles and Portuguese water dogs are equally friendly. Fastball would be liable for refusing to pay the claim.

## · TYPES OF INSURANCE ·

Insurance is available for virtually any risk. Bruce Springsteen, Michael Jackson, Billy Joel, and the Rolling Stones have insured their voices. When Kerry Wallace shaved her head in the Star Trek films, she bought insurance in case her hair failed to grow back. Food critic Egon Ronay insured his taste buds. And an amateur dramatics group took out insurance to protect against the risk that a member of the audience might die laughing. Most people, however, get by with six different types of insurance: property, life, health, disability, liability, and automobile.

## PROPERTY INSURANCE

**Property insurance** (also known as **casualty insurance**) covers physical damage to real estate, personal property (boats, furnishings), or inventory, from causes such as fire, smoke, lightning, wind, riot, vandalism, or theft.

> **Property insurance**
> covers physical damage to real estate, personal property, or inventory from causes such as fire, smoke, lightning, wind, riot, vandalism, or theft.

## LIFE INSURANCE

**Life insurance** is really death insurance—it provides for payments to a beneficiary upon the death of the insured. The purpose is to replace at least some of the insured's income so that her family will not be financially devastated.

> **Life insurance**
> provides for payments to a beneficiary upon the death of the insured.

### Term Insurance
Term insurance is the simplest, cheapest life insurance option. It is purchased for a specific period, such as 1, 5, or 20 years. If the insured dies during the period of the policy, the insurance company pays the policy amount to the beneficiary. If the owner stops paying premiums, the policy terminates and the beneficiary receives nothing. As the probability of death rises with age, so do the premiums. A $200,000 policy on a 25-year-old nonsmoking woman costs as little as $100 annually; at age 60, the same policy costs $612. Term insurance is the best choice for a person who simply wants to protect his family by replacing his income if he dies young.

### Whole Life Insurance
**Whole life** or **straight life** insurance is designed to cover the insured for his entire life. A portion of the premiums pays for insurance, and the remainder goes into savings. This savings portion is

called the cash value of the policy. The company pays dividends on this cash value and typically, after some years, the dividends are large enough to cover the premium so that the owner does not have to pay any more. The cash value accrues without being taxed until the policy is cashed in. The owner can borrow against the cash value, in many cases at a below-market rate. In addition, if the owner cancels the policy, the insurance company will pay her the policy's cash value. When the owner purchases the policy, the company typically sets a premium that stays constant over the life of the policy. A healthy 25-year-old nonsmoker pays annual premiums of roughly $1,300 per year on a $200,000 policy.

The advantage of a whole life policy is that it forces people to save. It also has some significant disadvantages:

- The investment returns from the savings portion of whole life insurance have traditionally been mediocre. Mutual funds may offer better investment opportunities.

- A significant portion of the premium for the first year goes to pay overhead and commissions. Agents have a great incentive to sell whole life policies, rather than term, because their commissions are much higher.

- Unless the customer holds a policy for about 20 years, it will typically generate little cash value. Half of all whole life policyholders drop their policies in the first seven or eight years. At that point, the policy has generated little more than commissions for the agent.

- Whole life insurance provides the same amount of insurance throughout the insured's life. In contrast, most people need more insurance when they have young children and less as they approach retirement age.

### Universal Life

Universal life insurance is a flexible combination of whole life and term. The owner can adjust the premiums over the life of the policy and also adjust the allocation of the premiums between insurance and savings. The options are complex and often difficult for the customer to understand.

### Annuities

**Annuity**
Payment to a beneficiary during his lifetime.

As life expectancy has increased, people have begun to worry as much about supporting themselves in their old age as they do about dying young. **Annuities are the reverse of life insurance—they make payments *until* death whereas life insurance pays *after* death.** In the basic annuity contract, the owner makes a lump-sum payment to an insurance company in return for a fixed annual income for the rest of her life, no matter how long she lives. If she dies tomorrow, the insurance company makes a huge profit. If she lives to be 95, the company loses money. But whatever happens, she knows she will have an income until the day she dies.

In a **deferred annuity contract,** the owner makes a lump-sum payment but receives no income until some later date, say, in 10 or 20 years when he retires. From that date forward, he will receive payments for the rest of his life.

# HEALTH INSURANCE

Traditional health insurance plans are **pay for service.** The insurer pays for virtually any treatment that any doctor orders. The good news under this system is that policyholders have the largest possible choice of doctor and treatment. The bad news is that doctors and patients have an incentive to overspend on health care because the insurance company picks up the tab. It has been estimated that as many as one-third of the medical procedures performed in pay for service plans have little medical justification, which in the end is not good for the patient.

Instead of, or in addition to, pay for service plans, many insurers offer **managed care plans.** There are many variations on this theme, but they all work to limit treatment choices. In some plans, the patient has a primary care physician who must approve all visits to specialists. In **health maintenance organizations,** known as **HMOs,** the patient can be treated only by doctors in the organization, unless there is some extraordinary need for an outside specialist.

Neither type of plan is perfect. In pay for service plans, doctors have an incentive to over-treat. In managed care plans, they may have an incentive to under-treat. For example, a recent study revealed that managed care plans tend to treat mental illness primarily with drugs. A combination of drugs and therapy is more successful but also more expensive.

# DISABILITY INSURANCE

**Disability insurance** replaces the insured's income if he becomes unable to work because of illness or injury. "Ah!" you think, "that will never happen to me." In fact, the average person is seven times more likely to be disabled for at least 90 days than she is to die before age 65. A significant percentage of all mortgage foreclosures are caused by an owner's disability. Everyone should have disability insurance to replace between 60% percent and 75% percent of their income. (There is no need for 100% percent replacement because expenses while unemployed are lower.) Many employers provide some disability protection.

**Disability insurance**
replaces the insured's income if he becomes unable to work because of illness or injury.

# LIABILITY INSURANCE

Most insurance—property, life, health, disability—is designed to reimburse the insured (or her family) for any harm she suffers. **Liability insurance** is different. **Its purpose is to reimburse the insured for any liability she incurs by (*accidentally*) harming someone else.** (Note that this insurance does not cover any *intentional* torts the insured commits.) This type of insurance covers tort claims by:

**Liability insurance**
reimburses the insured for any liability she incurs by accidentally harming someone else.

- Those injured on property owned by the insured—the mail carrier who slips and falls on the front sidewalk, or the parents of the child who drowns in the pool;
- Those injured by the insured away from his home or business—the jogger crushed by an insured who loses control of his rollerblades; and
- Those whose property is damaged by the insured—the owner whose stone wall is pulverized by the insured's swerving car.

These are the types of claims covered in a *personal* liability policy. *Business* liability policies may also protect against other sorts of claims:

- Professional malpractice on the part of an accountant, architect, doctor, engineer, or lawyer.
- Product liability for any injuries caused by the company's products.
- Employment practices liability insurance to protect employers against claims of sexual harassment, discrimination, and wrongful termination. About 30 percent of American firms carry this type of insurance. Note that this insurance typically does not protect the person who actually commits the wrongdoing—the sexual harasser, for instance—but it does protect the innocent insureds, such as the company itself.

# AUTOMOBILE INSURANCE

An automobile insurance policy is a combination of several different types of coverage that, depending on state law, are either mandatory or optional. These are the basic types of coverage:

- **Collision** covers the cost of repairing or replacing a car that is damaged in an accident.
- **Comprehensive** covers fire, theft, and vandalism—but not collision.
- **Liability** covers harm the owner causes to other people or their property—their body, car, or stone wall. Most states require drivers to carry liability insurance.
- **Uninsured motorist** covers the owner and anyone else in the car who is injured by an uninsured motorist.

Most Americans spend a considerable percentage of their disposable income on insurance. What can you do to reduce this expense?

- **Do not insure against every risk.** If you can afford the loss yourself, it is better not to purchase insurance. For example, Jamie from the opening scenario did not need to buy an insurance plan on his big-screen television.

- **Do not buy "special occasion" insurance.** After a major plane crash, sales of flight accident insurance jump. If you need life insurance, you should have it, no matter how you die. Your family does not need more money because you die in a plane crash rather than a car accident. The same rule holds true for other special occasion policies such as cancer insurance. You need health insurance regardless of your illness.

- **Select as high a deductible as you can afford.** The higher the deductible, the lower the premium. Over the lifetime of your house or car, you can save thousands of dollars by self-insuring the small losses and buying insurance to protect only against major catastrophes.

- **Shop for the best price.** The lowest-cost company may charge as little as two thirds as much as its highest-price competitor. The Internet offers a great opportunity to compare prices for different types of insurance.

- **Shop for quality.** An insurance company can fail as easily as any other business. What a disaster to pay premiums, only to discover later that you are not in safe hands after all.

## CHAPTER CONCLUSION

**Life is a risky business.** Cars crash, people die, houses burn. So what can we do? Buy insurance, and get on with our lives, knowing that we have prepared as best we can.

## EXAM REVIEW

1. **CONTRACT** An insurance policy must meet all the common-law requirements for a contract—offer, acceptance, and consideration. (p. 509)

.................................................................................................................................

2. **INSURABLE INTEREST** A person has an insurable interest if she would be harmed by the danger that she has insured against. (p. 509)

.................................................................................................................................

3. **MATERIAL MISREPRESENTATION** Insurers have the right to void a policy if the insured makes a material misstatement or conceals a material fact. (p. 510)

**EXAM Strategy**

**Question:** When Mark applied for life insurance with Farmstead, he indicated on the application that he had not received any traffic tickets in the preceding five years. In fact, he had received several such citations for driving while intoxicated. Two years later, Mark was shot to death. When Farmstead discovered the traffic tickets, it denied coverage to his beneficiary. Was Farmstead in the right?

**Strategy:** A misrepresentation is material if it affects the insurer's decision to issue a policy or the amount of the premium. (See the "Result" at the end of this section.)

4. **BAD FAITH BY INSURER** Many courts have held that insurance policies contain a covenant of good faith and fair dealing and have found insurance companies liable for compensatory and punitive damages if they commit fraud, unreasonably refuse to pay legitimate claims in a timely manner, or reject reasonable settlement offers. (p. 511)

**EXAM Strategy**

**Question:** Pamela Stone was in a car accident. Her policy did not cover any damages she suffered if she was more than 50 percent to blame. The insurance company investigated and determined that the accident was at least 60 percent her fault, so it refused to pay her claim. When Stone sued the company, the jury determined she was only 45 percent at fault. Did the insurance company violate its covenant of good faith and fair dealing?

**Strategy:** The insurance company violated its covenant of good faith and fair dealing if it was unreasonable when it failed to pay Stone's claim. Was it unreasonable? (See the "Result" at the end of this section.)

5. **PROPERTY INSURANCE** Property insurance covers physical damage to real estate, personal property (boats, furnishings), or inventory from causes such as fire, smoke, lightning, wind, riot, vandalism, or theft. (p. 513)

6. **LIFE INSURANCE** Life insurance is really death insurance—it provides for payments to a beneficiary upon the death of the insured. (p. 513)

7. **ANNUITIES** Annuities are the reverse of life insurance policies; they make payments until death. (p. 514)

8. **HEALTH INSURANCE** Health insurance is available in pay for service plans, managed care plans, or HMOs. (p. 514)

9. **DISABILITY INSURANCE** Disability insurance replaces the insured's income if he becomes unable to work because of illness or injury. (p. 515)

10. **LIABILITY INSURANCE** Liability insurance reimburses the insured for any liability she incurs by accidentally harming someone else. (p. 515)

**3. Result:** If Mark had told the truth, Farmstead still would have issued the policy, but the premium would have been higher. It can deny coverage even though his lie was not a factor in his death.

**4. Result:** No, it was not unreasonable. The two parties had a good faith disagreement about the validity of the claim. The insurance company had to pay the claim but not any penalty for violating the covenant of good faith and fair dealing.

# PRACTICE EXAM

## MATCHING QUESTIONS

Match the following terms with their definitions:

___ A. Insured

___ B. Insurer

___ C. Owner

___ D. Beneficiary

___ E. Insurable interest

1. The person who issues the insurance policy
2. The person who receives the proceeds from the insurance policy
3. The person who takes out the policy would be harmed by the danger that she has insured against
4. The person who enters into the policy and pays the premiums
5. The person whose loss is the subject of an insurance policy

## TRUE/FALSE QUESTIONS

Circle true or false:

**1.** T   F   If the insured makes any false statement in the application process, the insurance policy is voidable.

**2.** T   F   Once an insurance company issues a binder, the policy is irrevocable.

**3.** T   F   Although whole life insurance is more expensive than term, it is the best choice because it forces the customer to save money.

**4.** T   F   You are more likely to die before 65 than to become disabled before 65.

**5.** T   F   An annuity is simply a type of life insurance.

## MULTIPLE-CHOICE QUESTIONS

**6.** Lucas has bought the following insurance this week:

   I. A life insurance policy on his brother

   II. A life insurance policy on the partner in his accounting practice

   III. A fire insurance policy on the fitness club he belongs to so that if it burns down, he will receive a large enough payment to enable him to join a different club

   In which of these policies does he have an insurable interest?

   A. I, II, and III

   B. Neither I, II, nor III

   C. I and II

   D. I and III

   E. II and III

**7.** An insurance company does *not* violate its covenant of good faith and fair dealing if it:

   A. Charges elderly customers higher premiums than it charges younger customers

   B. Tells potential customers that their premiums will decline when that is not true

   C. Tells potential customers that their returns on a whole life policy are certain to be higher than an equivalent amount invested in the stock market

   D. Refuses to pay a valid claim until after four years of litigation

   E. Refuses to accept a settlement offer on behalf of an insured that was reasonable, but not in the company's best interest

8. If you are a smart consumer, you will:

   I. Insure against as many different kinds of risks as you can so that no matter what happens, you will be protected

   II. Select as low a deductible as possible so that no matter what happens, you will not have to pay large sums out of pocket

   III. Buy flight insurance when you take long airplane flights so that your family will be protected if your plane crashes

   A. I, II, and III                      D. Just I
   B. Neither I, II, nor III              E. Just II
   C. I and II

9. Hamish owned an office building with a fair market value of $250,000. He insured it for $300,000. When it burned down, he was entitled to:

   A. Nothing                                      C. $250,000
   B. $250,000 and a return of the excess premiums  D. $300,000
      he paid on the $300,000 policy

10. Which of the following policies are you likely to need in your lifetime?

    I. Service plan on an appliance

    II. Whole life insurance

    III. Disability insurance

    IV. Health insurance

    A. All of the above          D. III and IV
    B. None of the above         E. IV
    C. II, III, and IV

## SHORT-ANSWER QUESTIONS

11. Linda Richmond and Eddie Durham had two children before they were divorced. Under the terms of their divorce decree, Durham obtained title to their house. When he died suddenly of a heart attack, the children inherited the house. Richmond moved into the house with the children and began paying the mortgage that was in Durham's name. She also took out fire insurance. Ten months later, fire totally destroyed the house. The insurance company refused to pay a benefit under the policy because Richmond did not have an insurable interest in the property. Do you agree?

12. Armeen ran a stop sign and hit the Smiths' car, killing their child. He had $1.5 million in insurance. The Smiths offered to settle the case for that amount, but Liberty State, Armeen's insurance company, refused and proposed $300,000 instead. At trial, the jury awarded the Smith's $1.9 million, which meant that Armeen was liable for $400,000 rather than the zero dollars he would have had to pay if Liberty had accepted the Smiths' offer. What is Liberty's liability? Under what theory?

13. Dannie Harvey sued her employer, O. R. Whitaker, for sexual harassment, discrimination, and defamation. Whitaker counterclaimed for libel and slander, requesting $1 million in punitive damages. Both Whitaker and Harvey were insured by Allstate, under identical homeowner's policies. This policy explicitly promised to defend Harvey against the exact claim Whitaker had made against her. Harvey's Allstate agent, however, told her that she was not covered. Because the agent kept all copies of Harvey's insurance policies in his office, she took him at his word. She had no choice but to defend against the claim on her own. Whitaker mounted an exceedingly hostile litigation attack, taking 80 depositions. After a year, Allstate agreed to defend Harvey. However, instead of hiring the lawyer who had been representing her, it chose another lawyer who had no expertise in this type of case and was a close friend of Whitaker's

attorney. Harvey's new lawyer refused to meet her or to attend any depositions. Harvey and Whitaker finally settled. Whitaker had spent $1 million in legal fees, Harvey $169,000, and Allstate $2,513. Does Harvey have a claim against Allstate?

14. Clyde Anderson received a letter from his automobile insurance company notifying him that it would not renew his policy that was set to expire on February 28. Anderson did not obtain another policy, and, on March 1, at 2:30 a.m., he struck another vehicle, killing two men. Later that day, Anderson applied for insurance coverage. As part of this application, he indicated that he had not been involved in any accident in the last three years. The new policy was effective as of 12:01 a.m. on March 1. Will the estates of the two dead men be able to recover under this policy?

15. Jason lived in an apartment with Miri, to whom he was not married. When he applied for homeowner's insurance, the form asked their marital status. He checked the box that said "married." Later, the apartment was robbed and Jason filed a claim with his insurance company. When the company discovered that Jason and Miri were not married, it refused to pay the claim on the grounds that he had made a material misrepresentation. Jason argued that the misrepresentation was not material because the insurance company would have issued the policy no matter how he answered that question. Is Jason's policy valid?

16. ROLE REVERSAL: Write a short-answer question dealing with either misrepresentation on the part of an applicant for insurance or bad faith by an insurer.

## INTERNET RESEARCH PROBLEM

Go online and see which you can find first: an example of insurance fraud or bad faith by an insurer.

**You can find further practice problems in the Online Quiz at www.cengage.com/blaw/beatty.**

# APPENDIX A

## THE CONSTITUTION OF THE UNITED STATES

**Preamble**

We the People of the United States, in Order to form a more perfect Union, establish Justice, insure domestic Tranquility, provide for the common defense, promote the general Welfare, and secure the Blessings of Liberty to ourselves and our Posterity, do ordain and establish this Constitution for the United States of America.

### ARTICLE I

**Section 1.**

All legislative Powers herein granted shall be vested in a Congress of the United States, which shall consist of a Senate and House of Representatives.

**Section 2.**

The House of Representatives shall be composed of Members chosen every second Year by the People of the several States, and the Electors in each State shall have the Qualifications requisite for Electors of the most numerous Branch of the State Legislature.

No Person shall be a Representative who shall not have attained to the Age of twenty five Years, and been seven Years a Citizen of the United States, and who shall not, when elected, be an Inhabitant of that State in which he shall be chosen.

Representatives and direct Taxes shall be apportioned among the several States which may be included within this Union, according to their respective Numbers, which shall be determined by adding to the whole Number of free Persons, including those bound to Service for a Term of Years, and excluding Indians not taxed, three fifths of all other Persons. The actual Enumeration shall be made within three Years after the first Meeting of the Congress of the United States, and within every subsequent Term of ten Years, in such Manner as they shall by Law direct. The number of Representatives shall not exceed one for every thirty Thousand, but each State shall have at Least one Representative; and until such enumeration shall be made, the State of New Hampshire shall be entitled to chuse three, Massachusetts eight, Rhode Island and Providence Plantations one, Connecticut five, New-York six, New Jersey four, Pennsylvania eight, Delaware one, Maryland six, Virginia ten, North Carolina five, South Carolina five, and Georgia three.

When vacancies happen in the Representation from any State, the Executive Authority thereof shall issue Writs of Election to fill such vacancies.

The House of Representatives shall chuse their Speaker and other Officers; and shall have the sole Power of Impeachment.

**Section 3.**    The Senate of the United States shall be composed of two Senators from each State, chosen by the Legislature thereof, for six Years; and each Senator shall have one Vote.

Immediately after they shall be assembled in Consequence of the first Election, they shall be divided as equally as may be into three Classes. The Seats of the Senators of the first Class shall be vacated at the Expiration of the second Year, of the second Class at the Expiration of the fourth Year, and of the third Class at the Expiration of the sixth Year, so that one third may be chosen every second Year; and if Vacancies happen by Resignation or otherwise, during the Recess of the Legislature of any State, the Executive thereof may make temporary Appointments until the next Meeting of the Legislature, which shall then fill such Vacancies.

No Person shall be a Senator who shall not have attained to the Age of thirty Years, and been nine Years a Citizen of the United States, and who shall not, when elected, be an Inhabitant of that State for which he shall be chosen.

The Vice President of the United States shall be President of the Senate, but shall have no Vote, unless they be equally divided.

The Senate shall chuse their other Officers, and also a President pro tempore, in the Absence of the Vice President, or when he shall exercise the Office of President of the United States.

The Senate shall have the sole power to try all Impeachments. When sitting for that Purpose, they shall be on Oath or Affirmation. When the President of the United States is tried, the Chief Justice shall preside: And no Person shall be convicted without the Concurrence of two thirds of the Members present.

Judgment in Cases of Impeachment shall not extend further than to removal from Office, and disqualification to hold and enjoy any Office of honor, Trust or Profit under the United States: but the Party convicted shall nevertheless be liable and subject to Indictment, Trial, Judgment and Punishment, according to Law.

**Section 4.**    The Times, Places and Manner of holding Elections for Senators and Representatives, shall be prescribed in each State by the Legislature thereof: but the Congress may at any time by Law make or alter such Regulations, except as to the Places of chusing Senators.

The Congress shall assemble at least once in every Year, and such Meeting shall be on the first Monday in December, unless they shall by Law appoint a different Day.

**Section 5.**    Each House shall be the Judge of the Elections, Returns and Qualifications of its own Members, and a Majority of each shall constitute a Quorum to do Business; but a smaller Number may adjourn from day to day, and may be authorized to compel the Attendance of absent Members, in such Manner, and under such Penalties as each House may provide.

Each House may determine the Rules of its Proceedings, punish its Members for disorderly Behaviour, and, with the Concurrence of two thirds, expel a Member.

Each House shall keep a Journal of its Proceedings, and from time to time publish the same, excepting such Parts as may in their Judgment require Secrecy; and the Yeas and Nays of the Members of either House on any question shall, at the Desire of one fifth of those Present, be entered on the Journal.

Neither House, during the Session of Congress, shall, without the Consent of the other, adjourn for more than three days, nor to any other Place than that in which the two Houses shall be sitting.

**Section 6.**    The Senators and Representatives shall receive a Compensation for their Services, to be ascertained by Law, and paid out of the Treasury of the United States. They shall in all Cases, except Treason, Felony and Breach of the Peace, be privileged from Arrest during their Attendance at the Session of their respective Houses, and in going to and returning from the same; and for any Speech or Debate in either House, they shall not be questioned in any other Place.

No Senator or Representative shall, during the Time for which he was elected, be appointed to any civil Office under the Authority of the United States, which shall have been created, or the Emoluments whereof shall have been encreased during such time; and no Person holding any Office under the United States, shall be a Member of either House during his Continuance in Office.

**Section 7.**   All Bills for raising Revenue shall originate in the House of Representatives; but the Senate may propose or concur with Amendments as on other Bills.

Every Bill which shall have passed the House of Representatives and the Senate, shall, before it become a Law, be presented to the President of the United States; If he approve he shall sign it, but if not he shall return it, with his Objections to that House in which it shall have originated, who shall enter the Objections at large on their Journal, and proceed to reconsider it. If after such Reconsideration two thirds of that House shall agree to pass the Bill, it shall be sent, together with the Objections, to the other House, by which it shall likewise be reconsidered, and if approved by two thirds of that House, it shall become a Law. But in all such Cases the Votes of both Houses shall be determined by Yeas and Nays, and the Names of the Persons voting for and against the Bill shall be entered on the Journal of each House respectively. If any Bill shall not be returned by the President within ten Days (Sundays excepted) after it shall have been presented to him, the Same shall be a Law, in like Manner as if he had signed it, unless the Congress by their Adjournment prevent its Return, in which Case it shall not be a Law.

Every Order, Resolution, or Vote to which the Concurrence of the Senate and House of Representatives may be necessary (except on a question of Adjournment) shall be presented to the President of the United States; and before the Same shall take Effect, shall be approved by him, or being disapproved by him, shall be repassed by two thirds of the Senate and House of Representatives, according to the Rules and Limitations prescribed in the Case of a Bill.

**Section 8.**   The Congress shall have Power to lay and collect Taxes, Duties, Imposts and Excises, to pay the Debts and provide for the common Defence and general Welfare of the United States; but all Duties, Imposts and Excises shall be uniform throughout the United States;

To borrow Money on the credit of the United States;

To regulate Commerce with foreign Nations, and among the several States, and with the Indian Tribes;

To establish an uniform Rule of Naturalization, and uniform Laws on the subject of Bankruptcies throughout the United States;

To coin Money, regulate the Value thereof, and of foreign Coin, and fix the Standard of Weights and Measures;

To provide for the Punishment of counterfeiting the Securities and current Coin of the United States;

To establish Post Offices and post Roads;

To promote the Progress of Science and useful Arts, by securing for limited Times to Authors and Inventors the exclusive Right to their respective Writings and Discoveries;

To constitute Tribunals inferior to the supreme Court;

To define and punish Piracies and Felonies committed on the high Seas, and Offenses against the Law of Nations;

To declare War, grant Letters of Marque and Reprisal, and make Rules concerning Captures on Land and Water;

To raise and support Armies, but no Appropriation of Money to that Use shall be for a longer Term than two Years;

To provide and maintain a Navy;

To make Rules for the Government and Regulation of the land and naval Forces;

To provide for calling forth the Militia to execute the Laws of the Union, suppress Insurrections and repel Invasions;

To provide for organizing, arming, and disciplining, the Militia, and for governing such Part of them as may be employed in the Service of the United States, reserving to the States respectively, the Appointment of the Officers, and the Authority of training the Militia according to the discipline described by Congress;

To exercise exclusive Legislation in all Cases whatsoever, over such District (not exceeding ten Miles square) as may, by Cession of particular States, and the Acceptance of Congress, become the Seat of the Government of the United States, and to exercise like Authority over all Places purchased by the Consent of the Legislature of the State in which the Same shall be, for the Erection of Forts, Magazines, Arsenals, dock-Yards, and other needful Buildings;—And

To make all Laws which shall be necessary and proper for carrying into Execution the foregoing Powers, and all other Powers vested by this Constitution in the Government of the United States, or in any Department or Officer thereof.

**Section 9.**

The Migration or Importation of such Persons as any of the States now existing shall think proper to admit, shall not be prohibited by the Congress prior to the Year one thousand eight hundred and eight, but a Tax or Duty may be imposed on such Importation, not exceeding ten dollars for each Person.

The Privilege of the Writ of Habeas Corpus shall not be suspended, unless when in Cases of Rebellion or Invasion the public Safety may require it.

No Bill of Attainder or ex post facto Law shall be passed.

No Capitation, or other direct, Tax shall be laid, unless in Proportion to the Census or Enumeration herein before directed to be taken.

No Tax or Duty shall be laid on Articles exported from any State.

No Preference shall be given by any Regulation of Commerce or Revenue to the Ports of one State over those of another; nor shall Vessels bound to, or from, one State, be obliged to enter, clear, or pay Duties in another.

No Money shall be drawn from the Treasury, but in Consequence of Appropriations made by Laws; and a regular Statement and Account of the Receipts and Expenditures of all public Money shall be published from time to time.

No Title of Nobility shall be granted by the United States: And no Person holding any Office of Profit or Trust under them, shall, without the Consent of the Congress, accept of any present, Emolument, Office, or Title, of any kind whatever, from any King, Prince, or foreign State.

**Section 10.**

No State shall enter into any Treaty, Alliance, or Confederation; grant Letters of Marque and Reprisal; coin Money; emit Bills of Credit; make any Thing but gold and silver Coin a Tender in Payment of Debts; pass any Bill of Attainder, ex post facto Law, or Law impairing the Obligation of Contracts, or grant any Title of Nobility.

No State shall, without the Consent of the Congress, lay any Imposts or Duties on Imports or Exports, except what may be absolutely necessary for executing its inspection Laws: and the net Produce of all Duties and Imposts, laid by any State on

Imports or Exports, shall be for the Use of the Treasury of the United States; and all such Laws shall be subject to the Revision and Controul of the Congress.

No State shall, without the Consent of Congress, lay any Duty of Tonnage, keep Troops, or Ships of War in time of Peace, enter into any Agreement or Compact with another State, or with a foreign Power, or engage in War, unless actually invaded, or in such imminent Danger as will not admit of delay.

## ARTICLE II

**Section 1.**

The executive Power shall be vested in a President of the United States of America. He shall hold his Office during the Term of four Years, and, together with the Vice President, chosen for the same Term, be elected, as follows:

Each State shall appoint, in such Manner as the Legislature thereof may direct, a Number of Electors, equal to the whole Number of Senators and Representatives to which the State may be entitled in the Congress: but no Senator or Representative, or Person holding an Office of Trust or Profit under the United States, shall be appointed an Elector.

The Electors shall meet in their respective States, and vote by Ballot for two Persons, of whom one at least shall not be an Inhabitant of the same State with themselves. And they shall make a list of all the Persons voted for, and of the Number of Votes for each; which List they shall sign and certify, and transmit sealed to the Seat of the Government of the United States, directed to the President of the Senate. The President of the Senate shall, in the presence of the Senate and House of Representatives, open all the Certificates, and the Votes shall be counted. The Person having the greatest Number of Votes shall be the President, if such Number be a Majority of the whole Number of Electors appointed; and if there be more than one who have such Majority, and have an equal Number of Votes, then the House of Representatives shall immediately chuse by Ballot one of them for President; and if no Person have a Majority, then from the five highest on the List the said House shall in like Manner chuse the President. But in chusing the President, the Votes shall be taken by States, the Representation from each State having one Vote; A quorum for this Purpose shall consist of a Member or Members from two thirds of the States, and a Majority of all the States shall be necessary to a Choice. In every Case, after the Choice of the President, the Person having the greatest Number of Votes of the Electors shall be the Vice President. But if there should remain two or more who have equal Votes, the Senate shall chuse from them by Ballot the Vice President.

The Congress may determine the Time of Chusing the Electors, and the Day on which they shall give their Votes; which Day shall be the same throughout the United States.

No Person except a natural born Citizen, or a Citizen of the United States, at the time of the Adoption of this Constitution, shall be eligible to the Office of President; neither shall any Person be eligible to that Office who shall not have attained to the Age of thirty five Years, and been fourteen Years a Resident within the United States.

In Case of the Removal of the President from Office, or of his Death, Resignation, or Inability to discharge the Powers and Duties of the said Office, the Same shall devolve on the Vice President, and the Congress may by Law provide for the Case of Removal, Death, Resignation or Inability, both of the President and Vice President, declaring what Officer shall then act as President, and such Officer shall act accordingly, until the Disability be removed, or a President shall be elected.

The President shall, at stated Times, receive for his Services, a Compensation, which shall neither be increased nor diminished during the Period for which he shall have been elected, and he shall not receive within that Period any other Emolument from the United States, or any of them.

Before he enter on the Execution of his Office, he shall take the following Oath or Affirmation:—"I do solemnly swear (or affirm) that I will faithfully execute the

Office of President of the United States, and will to the best of my Ability, preserve, protect and defend the Constitution of the United States."

**Section 2.**    The President shall be Commander in Chief of the Army and Navy of the United States, and of the Militia of the several States, when called into the actual Service of the United States; he may require the Opinion, in writing, of the principal Officer in each of the executive Departments, upon any Subject relating to the Duties of their respective Offices, and he shall have Power to grant Reprieves and Pardons for Offenses against the United States, except in Cases of Impeachment.

He shall have Power, by and with the Advice and Consent of the Senate, to make Treaties, providing two thirds of the Senators present concur; and he shall nominate, and by and with the Advice and Consent of the Senate, shall appoint Ambassadors, other public Ministers and Consuls, Judges of the supreme Court, and all other Officers of the United States, whose Appointments are not herein otherwise provided for, and which shall be established by Law: but the Congress may by Law vest the Appointment of such inferior Officers, as they think proper, in the President alone, in the Courts of Law, or in the Heads of Departments.

The President shall have Power to fill up all Vacancies that may happen during the Recess of the Senate, by granting Commissions which shall expire at the End of their next Session.

**Section 3.**    He shall from time to time give to the Congress Information of the State of the Union, and recommend to their Consideration such Measures as he shall judge necessary and expedient; he may, on extraordinary Occasions, convene both Houses, or either of them, and in Case of Disagreement between them, with Respect to the Time of Adjournment, he may adjourn them to such Time as he shall think proper, he shall receive Ambassadors and other public Ministers; he shall take Care that the Laws be faithfully executed, and shall Commission all the Officers of the United States.

**Section 4.**    The President, Vice President and all civil Officers of the United States, shall be removed from Office on Impeachment for, and Conviction of, Treason, Bribery, or other high Crimes and Misdemeanors.

## ARTICLE III

**Section 1.**    The judicial Power of the United States, shall be vested in one supreme Court, and in such inferior Courts as the Congress may from time to time ordain and establish. The Judges, both of the supreme and inferior Courts, shall hold their Offices during good Behaviour, and shall, at Times, receive for their Services, a Compensation, which shall not be diminished during their Continuance in Office.

**Section 2.**    The judicial Power shall extend to all Cases, in Law and Equity, arising under this Constitution, the Laws of the United States, and Treaties made, or which shall be made, under their Authority;—to all Cases affecting Ambassadors, other public Ministers and Consuls;—to all Cases of admiralty and maritime Jurisdiction;—to Controversies to which the United States shall be a Party;—to controversies between two or more States;—between a State and Citizens of another State;—between Citizens of different States;—between Citizens of the same State claiming Lands under Grants of different States; and between a State, or the Citizens thereof, and foreign States, Citizens or Subjects.

In all Cases affecting Ambassadors, other public Ministers and Consuls, and those in which a State shall be Party, the supreme Court shall have original Jurisdiction.

In all the other Cases before mentioned, the supreme Court shall have appellate Jurisdiction, both as to Law and Fact, with such Exceptions, and under such Regulations as the Congress shall make.

The Trial of all Crimes, except in Cases of Impeachment, shall be by Jury; and such Trial shall be held in the State where the said Crimes shall have been committed; but when not committed within any State, the Trial shall be at such Place or Places as the Congress may by Law have directed.

**Section 3.**   Treason against the United States, shall consist only in levying War against them, or in adhering to their Enemies, giving them Aid and Comfort. No Person shall be convicted of Treason unless on the Testimony of two Witnesses to the same overt Act, or on Confession in open Court.

The Congress shall have Power to declare the Punishment of Treason, but no Attainder of Treason shall work Corruption of Blood, or Forfeiture except during the Life of the Person attainted.

## ARTICLE IV

**Section 1.**   Full Faith and Credit shall be given in each State to the public Acts, Records, and judicial Proceedings of every other State. And the Congress may by general Laws prescribe the Manner in which such Acts, Records and Proceedings shall be proved, and the Effect thereof.

**Section 2.**   The Citizens of each State shall be entitled to all Privileges and Immunities of Citizens in the several States.

A Person charged in any State with Treason, Felony, or other Crime, who shall flee from Justice, and be found in another State, shall on Demand of the executive Authority of the State from which he fled, be delivered up, to be removed to the State having Jurisdiction of the Crime.

No Person held to Service or Labour in one State, under the Laws thereof, escaping into another, shall, in Consequence of any Law or Regulation therein, be discharged from such Service or Labour, but shall be delivered up on Claim of the Party to whom such Service or Labour may be due.

**Section 3.**   New States may be admitted by the Congress into this Union; but no new State shall be formed or erected within the Jurisdiction of any other State; nor any State be formed by the Junction of two or more States, or Parts of States, without the Consent of the Legislatures of the States concerned as well as the Congress.

The Congress shall have Power to dispose of and make all needful Rules and Regulations respecting the Territory or other Property belonging to the United States; and nothing in this Constitution shall be so construed as to Prejudice any Claims of the United States, or of any particular State.

**Section 4.**   The United States shall guarantee to every State in this Union a Republican Form of Government, and shall protect each of them against Invasion; and on Application of the Legislature, or of the Executive (when the Legislature cannot be convened) against domestic Violence.

## ARTICLE V

The Congress, whenever two thirds of both Houses shall deem it necessary, shall propose Amendments to this Constitution, or, on the Application of the Legislatures of two thirds of the several States, shall call a Convention for proposing

Amendments, which, in either Case, shall be valid to all Intents and Purposes, as Part of this Constitution, when ratified by the Legislatures of three fourths of the several States, or by Conventions in three fourths thereof, as the one or the other Mode of Ratification may be proposed by the Congress; Provided that no Amendment which may be made prior to the Year One thousand eight hundred and eight shall in any Manner affect the first and fourth Clauses in the Ninth Section of the first Article; and that no State, without its Consent, shall be deprived of its equal Suffrage in the Senate.

## ARTICLE VI

All Debts contracted and Engagements entered into, before the Adoption of this Constitution, shall be as valid against the United States under this Constitution, as under the Confederation.

This Constitution, and the Laws of the United States which shall be made in Pursuance thereof; and all Treaties made, or which shall be made, under the Authority of the United States, shall be the supreme Law of the Land; and the Judges in every State shall be bound thereby, any Thing in the Constitution or Laws of any State to the Contrary notwithstanding.

The Senators and Representatives before mentioned, and the Members of the several State Legislatures, and all executive and judicial Officers, both of the United States and of the Several States, shall be bound by Oath or Affirmation, to support this Constitution; but no religious Test shall ever be required as a Qualification to any Office or public Trust under the United States.

## ARTICLE VII

The Ratification of the Conventions of nine States, shall be sufficient for the Establishment of this Constitution between the States so ratifying the Same.

**Amendment I [1791].**

Congress shall make no law respecting an establishment of religion, or prohibiting the free exercise thereof; or abridging the freedom of speech, or the press; or the right of the people peaceably to assemble, and to petition the Government for a redress of grievances.

**Amendment II [1791].**

A well regulated Militia, being necessary to the security for a free State, the right of the people to keep and bear Arms, shall not be infringed.

**Amendment III [1791].**

No Soldier shall, in time of peace be quartered in any house, without the consent of the Owner, nor in time of war, but in a manner to be prescribed by law.

**Amendment IV [1791].**

The right of the people to be secure in their persons, houses, papers, and effects, against unreasonable searches and seizures, shall not be violated, and no Warrants shall issue, but upon probable cause, supported by Oath or Affirmation, and particularly describing the place to be searched, and the persons or things to be seized.

**Amendment V [1791].**

No person shall be held to answer for a capital, or otherwise infamous crime, unless on a presentment or indictment of a Grand Jury, except in cases arising in the land or naval forces, or in the Militia, when in actual service in time of War or public danger; nor shall any person be subject for the same offense to be twice put in jeopardy of life or limb; nor shall be compelled in any criminal case to be a witness against himself, nor be deprived of life, liberty, or property, without due process of law; nor shall private property be taken for public use, without just compensation.

**Amendment VI [1791].**

In all criminal prosecutions, the accused shall enjoy the right to a speedy and public trial, by an impartial jury of the State and district wherein the crime shall have been committed, which district shall have been previously ascertained by law, and to be informed of the nature and cause of the accusation; to be confronted with the Witnesses against him; to have compulsory process for obtaining witnesses in his favor, and to have the Assistance of counsel for his defence.

**Amendment VII [1791].**

In suits at common law, where the value in controversy shall exceed twenty dollars, the right of trial by jury shall be preserved, and no fact tried by a jury, shall be otherwise re-examined in any Court of the United States, than according to the rules of the common law.

**Amendment VIII [1791].**

Excessive bail shall not be required, no excessive fines imposed, nor cruel and unusual punishments inflicted.

**Amendment IX [1791].**

The enumeration in the Constitution, of certain rights, shall not be construed to deny or disparage others retained by the people.

**Amendment X [1791].**

The powers not delegated to the United States by the Constitution, nor prohibited by it to the States, are reserved to the States respectively, or to the people.

**Amendment XI [1798].**

The judicial power of the United States shall not be construed to extend to any suit in law or equity, commenced or prosecuted against one of the United States by Citizens of another State, or by Citizens or Subjects of any Foreign State.

**Amendment XII [1804].**

The Electors shall meet in their respective states and vote by ballot for President and Vice-President, one of whom, at least, shall not be an inhabitant of the same state with themselves; they shall name in their ballots the person voted for as President, and in distinct ballots the person voted for as Vice-President, and they shall make distinct lists of all persons voted for as President, and of all persons voted for as Vice-President, and of the number of votes for each, which lists they shall sign and certify, and transmit sealed to the seat of the government of the United States, directed to the President of the Senate;—The President of the Senate shall, in the presence of the Senate and House of Representatives, open all the certificates and the votes shall then be counted;—The person having the greatest number of votes for President, shall be the President, if such number be a majority of the whole number of Electors appointed; and if no person have such majority, then from the persons having the highest numbers not exceeding three on the list of those voted for as President, the House of Representatives shall choose immediately, by ballot, the President. But in choosing the President, the votes shall be taken by states, the representation from each state having one vote; a quorum for this purpose shall consist of a member or members from two-thirds of the states, and a majority of all the states shall be necessary to a choice. And if the House of Representatives shall not choose a President whenever the right of choice shall devolve upon them, before the fourth day of March next following, then the Vice-President shall act as President, as in the case of the death or other constitutional disability of the President. The person having the greatest number of votes as Vice-President, shall be the Vice-President, if such number be a majority of the whole number of Electors appointed, and if no person have a majority, then from the two highest numbers on the list, the Senate shall choose the Vice-President; a quorum for the purpose shall consist of two-thirds of the whole number of Senators, and a majority of the whole number shall be necessary to a choice. But no person constitutionally ineligible to the office of President shall be eligible to that of the Vice-President of the United States.

**Amendment XIII [1865].**

**Section 1.** Neither slavery nor involuntary servitude, except as a punishment for crime whereof the party shall have been duly convicted, shall exist within the United States, or any place subject to their jurisdiction.

**Section 2.** Congress shall have power to enforce this article by appropriate legislation.

**Amendment XIV [1868].**

**Section 1.** All persons born or naturalized in the United States, and subject to the jurisdiction thereof, are citizens of the United States and of the State wherein they reside. No State shall make or enforce any law which shall abridge the privileges or immunities of citizens of the United States; nor shall any State deprive any person of life, liberty, or property, without due process of law; nor deny to any person within its jurisdiction the equal protection of the laws.

**Section 2.** Representatives shall be apportioned among the several States according to their respective numbers, counting the whole number of persons in each State, excluding Indians not taxed. But when the right to vote at any election for the choice of electors for President and Vice President of the United States, Representatives in Congress, the Executive and Judicial officers of a State, or the members of the Legislature thereof, is denied to any of the male inhabitants of such State, being twenty-one years of age, and citizens of the United States, or in any way abridged, except for participation in rebellion, or other crime, the basis of representation therein shall be reduced in the proportion which the number of such male citizens shall bear the whole number of male citizens twenty-one years of age in such State.

**Section 3.** No person shall be a Senator or Representative in Congress, or elector of President and Vice President, or hold any office, civil or military, under the United States, or under any State, who, having previously taken an oath, as a member of Congress, or as an officer of the United States, or as a member of any State legislature, or as an executive or judicial officer of any State, to support the Constitution of the United States, shall have engaged in insurrection or rebellion against the same, or given aid or comfort to the enemies thereof. But Congress may by a vote of two-thirds of each House, remove such disability.

**Section 4.** The validity of the public debt of the United States, authorized by law, including debts incurred for payment of pensions and bounties for services in suppressing insurrection or rebellion, shall not be questioned. But neither the United States nor any State shall assume or pay any debt or obligation incurred in aid of insurrection or rebellion against the United States, or any claim for the loss or emancipation of any slave; but all such debts, obligations and claims shall be held illegal and void.

**Section 5.** The Congress shall have power to enforce, by appropriate legislation, the provisions of this article.

**Amendment XV [1870].**

**Section 1.** The right of citizens of the United States to vote shall not be denied or abridged by the United States or by any State on account of race, color, or previous condition of servitude.

**Section 2.** The Congress shall have power to enforce this article by appropriate legislation.

**Amendment XVI [1913].**

The Congress shall have power to lay and collect taxes on incomes, from whatever source derived, without apportionment among the several States, and without regard to any census or enumeration.

**Amendment XVII [1913].**

The Senate of the United States shall be composed of two Senators from each State, elected by the people thereof, for six years; and each Senator shall have one vote. The electors in each State shall have the qualifications requisite for electors of the most numerous branch of the State legislatures.

When vacancies happen in the representation of any State in the Senate, the executive authority of each State shall issue writs of election to fill such vacancies; *Provided,* That the legislature of any State may empower the executive thereof to make temporary appointments until the people fill the vacancies by election as the legislature may direct.

This amendment shall not be construed as to affect the election or term of any Senator chosen before it becomes valid as part of the Constitution.

**Amendment XVIII [1919].**

**Section 1.** After one year from the ratification of this article the manufacture, sale, or transportation of intoxicating liquors within, the importation thereof into, or the exportation thereof from the United States and all territory subject to the jurisdiction thereof for beverage purposes is hereby prohibited.

**Section 2.** The Congress and the several States shall have concurrent power to enforce this article by appropriate legislation.

**Section 3.** This article shall be inoperative unless it shall have been ratified as an amendment to the Constitution by the legislatures of the several States, as provided in the Constitution, within seven years from the date of the submission hereof to the States by the Congress.

**Amendment XIX [1920].**

The right of citizens of the United States to vote shall not be denied or abridged by the United States or by any State on account of sex.

Congress shall have power to enforce this article by appropriate legislation.

**Amendment XX [1933].**

**Section 1.** The terms of the President and Vice President shall end at noon on the 20th day of January, and the terms of Senators and Representatives at noon on the 3d day of January, of the years in which such terms would have ended if this article had not been ratified; and the terms of their successors shall then begin.

**Section 2.** The Congress shall assemble at least once in every year, and such meeting shall begin at noon on the 3d day of January, unless they shall by law appoint a different day.

**Section 3.** If, at the time fixed for the beginning of the term of the President, the President elect shall have died, the Vice President elect shall become President. If a President shall not have been chosen before the time fixed for the beginning of his term, or if the President elect shall have failed to qualify, then the Vice President elect shall act as President until a President shall have qualified; and the Congress may by law provide for the case wherein neither a President elect nor a Vice President elect shall have qualified, declaring who shall then act as President, or the manner in which one who is to act shall be selected, and such person shall act accordingly until a President or Vice President shall have qualified.

**Section 4.** The Congress may by law provide for the case of the death of any of the persons from whom the House of Representatives may choose a President whenever the right of choice shall have devolved upon them, and for the case of the death of any of the persons from whom the Senate may choose a Vice President whenever the right of choice shall have devolved upon them.

**Section 5.** Sections 1 and 2 shall take effect on the 15th day of October following the ratification of this article.

**Section 6.** This article shall be inoperative unless it shall have been ratified as an amendment to the Constitution by the legislatures of three-fourths of the several States within seven years from the date of its submission.

**Amendment XXI [1933].**

**Section 1.** The eighteenth article of amendment to the Constitution of the United States is hereby repealed.

**Section 2.** The transportation or importation into any State, Territory, or possession of the United States for delivery or use therein of intoxicating liquors, in violation of the laws thereof, is hereby prohibited.

**Section 3.** This article shall be inoperative unless it shall have been ratified as an amendment to the Constitution by conventions in the several States, as provided in the Constitution, within seven years from the date of the submission hereof to the States by the Congress.

**Amendment XXII [1951].**

**Section 1.** No person shall be elected to the office of the President more than twice, and no person who has held the office of President, or acted as President, for more than two years of a term to which some other person was elected President shall be elected to the office of the President more than once. But this Article shall not apply to any person holding the office of President when this Article was proposed by the Congress, and shall not prevent any person who may be holding the office of President, or acting as President, during the term within which this Article becomes operative from holding the office of President, or acting as President during the remainder of such term.

**Section 2.** This article shall be inoperative unless it shall have been ratified as an amendment to the Constitution by the legislatures of three-fourths of the several States within seven years from the date of its submission to the States by the Congress.

**Amendment XXIII [1961].**

**Section 1.** The District constituting the seat of Government of the United States shall appoint in such manner as the Congress may direct:

A number of electors of President and Vice President equal to the whole number of Senators and Representatives in Congress to which the District would be entitled if it were a State, but in no event more than the least populous State; they shall be in addition to those appointed by the States, but they shall be considered, for the purposes of the election of President and Vice President, to be electors appointed by a State; and they shall meet in the District and perform such duties as provided by the twelfth article of amendment.

**Section 2.** The Congress shall have power to enforce this article by appropriate legislation.

**Amendment XXIV [1964].**

**Section 1.** The right of citizens of the United States to vote in any primary or other election for President or Vice President, for electors for President or Vice President, or for Senator or Representative in Congress, shall not be denied or abridged by the United States or any State by reason of failure to pay any poll tax or other tax.

**Section 2.** The Congress shall have power to enforce this article by appropriate legislation.

**Amendment XXV [1967].**

**Section 1.** In case of the removal of the President from office or of his death or resignation, the Vice President shall become President.

**Section 2.** Whenever there is a vacancy in the office of the Vice President, the President shall nominate a Vice President who shall take office upon confirmation by a majority vote of both Houses of Congress.

**Section 3.** Whenever the President transmits to the President pro tempore of the Senate and the Speaker of the House of Representatives his written declaration that he is unable to discharge the powers and duties of his office, and until he transmits to them a written declaration to the contrary, such powers and duties shall be discharged by the Vice President as Acting President.

**Section 4.** Whenever the Vice President and a majority of either the principal officers of the executive departments or of such other body as Congress may by law provide, transmit to the President pro tempore of the Senate and the Speaker of the House of Representatives their written declaration that the President is unable to discharge the powers and duties of his office, the Vice President shall immediately assume the powers and duties of the office as Acting President.

Thereafter, when the President transmits to the President pro tempore of the Senate and the Speaker of the House of Representatives his written declaration that no inability exists, he shall resume the powers and duties of his office unless the Vice President and a majority of either the principal officers of the executive department or of such other body as Congress may by law provide, transmit within four days to the President pro tempore of the Senate and the Speaker of the House of Representatives their written declaration that the President is unable to discharge the powers and duties of his office. Thereupon Congress shall decide the issue, assembling within forty-eight hours for that purpose if not in session. If the Congress, within twenty-one days after receipt of the latter written declaration, or, if Congress is not in session, within twenty-one days after Congress is required to assemble, determines by two-thirds vote of both Houses that the President is unable to discharge the powers and duties of his office, the Vice President shall continue to discharge the same as Acting President; otherwise, the President shall resume the powers and duties of his office.

**Amendment XXVI [1971].**

**Section 1.** The right of citizens of the United States, who are eighteen years of age or older, to vote shall not be denied or abridged by the United States or by any State on account of age.

**Section 2.** The Congress shall have power to enforce this article by appropriate legislation.

**Amendment XXVII [1992].**

No law, varying the compensation for the services of the Senators and Representatives, shall take effect, until an election of Representatives shall have intervened.

# APPENDIX B

## UNIFORM COMMERCIAL CODE

The Uniform Commercial code can be found at
**http://www.law.cornell.edu/ucc/ucc.table.html** or **http://www.law.cornell.edu**

# GLOSSARY

## A

**Abandoned property** Something that the owner has knowingly discarded because she no longer wants it. (Chapter 30)

**Accession** The use of labor and/or materials to add value to the personal property of another. (Chapter 28)

**Accord and satisfaction** An agreement to settle a debt for less than the sum claimed. (Chapter 11)

**Accounts** Any right to receive payment for goods sold or leased, other than rights covered by chattel paper or instruments. (Chapter 14)

**Accredited investor** Under the Securities Act of 1933, an accredited investor is an institution (such as a bank or insurance company) or any individual with a net worth of more than $1 million or an annual income of more than $200,000. (Chapter 22)

**Acquit** To find the defendant not guilty of the crime for which he was tried. (Chapter 7)

**Act of State doctrine** A rule requiring American courts to abstain from cases if a court order would interfere with the ability of the president or Congress to conduct foreign policy. (Chapter 8)

**Actual malice** The defendant in a defamation suit knew that his or her statement was false or acted with reckless disregard of the truth. (Chapter 5)

***Actus reus*** The guilty act. The prosecution must show that a criminal defendant committed some proscribed act. In a murder prosecution, taking another person's life is the *actus reus*. (Chapter 7)

**Additional terms** Raise issues not covered in an offer. (Chapter 9)

**Adhesion contract** A standard form contract prepared by one party and presented to the other on a "take it or leave it" basis. (Chapter 9)

**Adjudicate** To hold a formal hearing in a disputed matter and issue an official decision. (Chapter 4)

**Administrative law** Concerns all agencies, boards, commissions, and other entities created by a federal or state legislature and charged with investigating, regulating, and adjudicating a particular industry or issue. (Chapter 1)

**Administrative law judge** An agency employee who acts as an impartial decision maker. (Chapter 4)

**Administrator** A person appointed by the court to oversee the probate process for someone who has died intestate (that is, without a will). (Chapter 31)

**Administratrix** A female administrator. (Chapter 31)

**Adversary system** A system based on the assumption that if two sides present their best case before a neutral party, the truth will be established. (Chapter 3)

**Adverse possession** A means of gaining ownership of land belonging to another by entering upon the property, openly and notoriously, and claiming exclusive use of it for a period of years. (Chapter 28)

**Affidavit** A written statement signed under oath. (Chapter 7)

**Affirm** A decision by an appellate court to uphold the judgment of a lower court. (Chapters 1, 3)

**Affirmative action** A plan introduced in a workplace for the purpose of either remedying the effects of past discrimination or achieving equitable representation of minorities and women. (Chapter 18)

**After-acquired property** Items that a debtor obtains after making a security agreement with the secured party. (Chapter 14)

**Agent** A person who acts for a principal. (Chapter 16)

**Alternative dispute resolution** Any method of resolving a legal conflict other than litigation, such as negotiation, arbitration, mediation, mini-trials, and summary jury trials. (Chapter 3)

**Amendment** Any addition to a legal document. The constitutional amendments, the first ten of which are known collectively as the Bill of Rights, secure numerous liberties and protections directly for the people. (Chapter 1)

**Annual report** Each year, public companies must send their shareholders an annual report that contains detailed financial data. (Chapter 21)

**Annuity** A policy that makes payments to a beneficiary during his lifetime. (Chapter 32)

**Answer** The pleading, filed by the defendant in court and served on the plaintiff, which responds to each allegation in the plaintiff's complaint. (Chapter 3)

**Apparent authority** A situation in which conduct of a principal causes a third party to believe that the principal consents to have an act done on his behalf by a person purporting to act for him when, in fact, that person is not acting for the principal. (Chapter 16)

**Appellant** The party who appeals a lower court decision to a higher court. (Chapter 3)

**Appellate court** Any court in a state or federal system that reviews cases that have already been tried. (Chapter 3)

**Appellee** The party opposing an appeal from a lower court to a higher court. (Chapter 3)

**Arbitration** A form of alternative dispute resolution in which the parties hire a neutral third party to hear their respective arguments, receive evidence, and then make a binding decision. (Chapters 3, 19)

**Arms Export Control Act** Prohibits the export of specific weapons. (Chapter 8)

**Arson** Malicious use of fire or explosives to damage or destroy real estate or personal property. (Chapter 7)

**Assault** An intentional act that causes the plaintiff to fear an imminent battery. (Chapter 5)

**Assignee** The party who receives an assignment of contract rights from a party to the contract. (Chapter 11)

**Assignment** A tenant's transfer of all legal interest in a property to another party. (Chapter 29)

**Assignment of rights** A contracting party transfers his rights under a contract to someone else. (Chapter 11)

**Assignor** The party who assigns contract rights to a third person. (Chapter 11)

**Assisted suicide** The process of hastening death for a terminally ill patient at the request of the patient. (Chapter 31)

**Assumption of the risk** The principle that a person who voluntarily enters a situation of obvious danger cannot complain if she is injured. (Chapter 6)

**Attachment** A court order seizing property of a party to a civil action, so that there will be sufficient assets available to pay the judgment. (Chapter 4)

**Authenticate** To sign a document or use any symbol or encryption method that identifies the person and clearly indicates she is adopting the record as her own. (Chapter 14)

**Authorized and issued stock** Stock that has been approved by the corporation's charter and subsequently sold. (Chapter 21)

**Authorized and unissued stock** Stock that has been approved by the corporation's charter but has not yet been sold. (Chapter 21)

**Automatic stay** Prohibits creditors from collecting debts that the bankrupt incurred before the petition was filed. (Chapter 15)

# B

**Bailee** A person who rightfully possesses goods belonging to another. (Chapter 30)

**Bailment** Giving possession and control of personal property to another person. (Chapter 30)

**Bailor** One who creates a bailment by delivering goods to another. (Chapter 30)

**Bait and switch** A practice where sellers advertise products that are not generally available but are being used to draw interested parties in so that they will buy other items. (Chapter 24)

**Bank fraud** Using deceit to obtain money, assets, securities, or other property under the control of any financial institution. (Chapter 7)

**Bankrupt** Someone who files for protection under the bankruptcy code. Another term for *debtor*. (Chapter 15)

**Bankruptcy estate** The new legal entity created when a debtor files a bankruptcy petition. All the debtor's existing assets pass into the estate. (Chapter 15)

**Battery** The intentional touching of another person in a way that is unwanted or offensive. (Chapter 5)

**Bearer paper** An instrument payable "to bearer." Any holder in due course can demand payment from the issuer. (Chapter 13)

**Beneficiary** Someone who receives the financial proceeds of a trust. (Chapter 31)

**Beyond a reasonable doubt** The government's burden in a criminal prosecution; the case against the defendant must be proved to such an extent that no reasonable person would doubt it. (Chapters 3, 7)

**BFOQ** See *Bona fide occupational qualification (BFOQ)*.

**Bilateral contract** A binding agreement in which each party has made a promise to the other. (Chapter 9)

**Bilateral mistake** Occurs when both parties negotiate based on the same factual error. (Chapter 10)

**Bill** A proposed statute that has been submitted for consideration to Congress or a state legislature. (Chapter 4)

**Bill of lading** A receipt for goods, given by a carrier such as a ship, that minutely describes the merchandise being shipped. A negotiable bill of lading may be transferred to other parties and entitles any holder to collect the goods. (Chapter 8)

**Bill of Rights** The first ten amendments to the Constitution. (Chapter 4)

**BIOC** See *Buyer in ordinary course of business (BIOC)*.

**Blue sky laws** State securities laws. (Chapter 22)

**Bona fide occupational qualification (BFOQ)** A job requirement that would otherwise be discriminatory is permitted in situations in which it is *essential* to the position in question. (Chapter 18)

**Bona fide purchaser** Someone who buys goods in good faith, for value, typically from a seller who has merely voidable title. (Chapter 12)

**Breach of duty** A defendant breaches his duty of due care by failing to behave the way a reasonable person would under similar circumstances. (Chapter 6)

**Brief** The written legal argument that an attorney files with an appeal court. (Chapter 3)

**Bulk sale** A transfer of most or all of a merchant's assets. (Chapter 12)

**Burden of proof** The allocation of which party must prove its case. In a civil case, the plaintiff has the burden of proof to persuade the fact finder of every element of her case. In a criminal case, the government has the burden of proof. (Chapter 3)

**Business judgment rule** A common law rule that protects managers from liability if they are acting without a conflict of interest and make informed decisions that have a rational business purpose. (Chapter 21)

**Buyer in ordinary course of business (BIOC)** Someone who buys goods in good faith from a seller who routinely deals in such goods. (Chapter 14)

**Bylaws** A document that specifies the organizational rules of a corporation or other organization, such as the date of the annual meeting and the required number of directors. (Chapter 21)

# C

**Capacity** The legal ability to enter into a contract. (Chapter 10)

**Certiorari, writ of** Formal notice from the U.S. Supreme Court that it will accept a case for review. (Chapter 3)

**Challenge for cause** An attorney's request, during *voir dire,* to excuse a prospective juror because of apparent bias. (Chapter 3)

**Chancery, court of** In medieval England, the court originally operated by the Chancellor. (Chapter 1)

**Chattel paper** Any writing that indicates two things: (1) a debtor owes money; and (2) a secured party has a security interest in specific goods. The most common chattel paper is a document indicating a consumer sale on credit. (Chapter 14)

**Check** An instrument in which the drawer orders the drawee bank to pay money to the payee. (Chapter 13)

**Civil law** The large body of law concerning the rights and duties between parties. It is distinguished from criminal law, which concerns behavior outlawed by a government. (Chapter 1)

**Class action** A method of litigating a civil lawsuit in which one or more plaintiffs (or occasionally defendants) seek to represent an entire group of people with similar claims against a common opponent. (Chapter 3)

**Classification** The process by which the Customs Service decides what label to attach to imported merchandise, and therefore what level of tariff to impose. (Chapter 8)

**Close corporation** A company whose stock is not publicly traded. Also known as a *closely held corporation.* (Chapter 20)

**Codicil** An amendment to a will. (Chapter 31)

**Collateral** The property subject to a security interest. (Chapter 14)

**Collateral promises** A promise to pay the debt of another person, as a favor to the debtor. (Chapter 14)

**Collective bargaining** Contract negotiations between an employer and a union. (Chapter 19)

**Collective bargaining agreement** A contract between a union and management. (Chapter 19)

**Collective bargaining unit** The precisely defined group of employees who are represented by a particular union. (Chapter 19)

**Comity** A doctrine that requires a court to abstain from hearing a case out of respect for another court that also has jurisdiction. *International comity* demands that an American court refuse to hear a case in which a foreign court shares jurisdiction if there is a conflict between the laws and if it is more logical for the foreign court to take the case. (Chapter 8)

**Commerce Clause** One of the powers granted by Article I, section 8 of the U.S. Constitution, it gives Congress exclusive power to regulate international commerce and concurrent power with the states to regulate domestic commerce. (Chapter 4)

**Commercial exploitation** Prohibits the unauthorized use of another person's likeness or voice for business purposes. (Chapter 5)

**Commercial impracticability** When, after the creation of a contract, an entirely unforeseen event occurs that makes enforcement of the contract extraordinarily unfair. (Chapter 11)

**Commercial paper** Instruments such as checks and promissory notes that contain a promise to pay money. Commercial paper includes both negotiable and non-negotiable instruments. (Chapter 13)

**Commercial speech** Communication, such as television advertisements, that has the dominant theme of proposing a commercial transaction. (Chapter 4)

**Common carrier** A transportation company that makes its services available on a regular basis to the general public. (Chapter 30)

**Common law** Judge-made law, that is, the body of all decisions made by appellate courts over the years. (Chapters 1, 4)

**Common stock** Certificates that reflect ownership in a corporation. Owners of this equity security are last in line for corporate payouts such as dividends and liquidation proceeds. (Chapter 21)

**Comparative negligence** A rule of tort law that permits a plaintiff to recover even when the defendant can show that the plaintiff's own conduct contributed in some way to her harm. (Chapter 6)

**Compensatory damages** Damages that flow directly from the contract. (Chapters 5, 11)

**Complaint** A pleading, filed by the plaintiff, providing a short statement of the claim. (Chapter 3)

**Concerted action** Tactics, such as a strike, used by a union to gain a bargaining advantage. (Chapter 19)

**Concurrent estate** Two or more people owning property at the same time. (Chapter 28)

**Condition** An event that must occur in order for a party to be obligated under a contract. (Chapter 11)

**Condition precedent** A condition that must occur before a particular contract duty arises. (Chapter 11)

**Condition subsequent** A condition that must occur after a particular contract duty arises, or the duty will be discharged. (Chapter 11)

**Confirmed irrevocable line of credit** A promise made by the seller's bank to pay for goods, and then guaranteed by the buyer's bank. (Chapter 8)

**Confiscation** Expropriation without adequate compensation of property owned by foreigners. (Chapter 8)

**Conforming goods** Items that satisfy the contract terms. If a contract calls for blue sailboats, then green sailboats are non-conforming. (Chapter 12)

**Consequential damages** Damages resulting from the unique circumstances of *this injured party*. (Chapters 11, 12)

**Consideration** In contract law, something of legal value that has been bargained for and given in exchange by the parties. (Chapter 9)

**Constitutional rights** Protect against government acts. (Chapter 4)

**Constructive eviction** When a landlord substantively interferes with the tenant's use and enjoyment of his property. (Chapter 29)

**Consumer credit contract** A contract in which a consumer borrows money from a lender to purchase goods and services from a seller who is affiliated with the lender. (Chapter 13)

**Contract** A legally enforceable promise or set of promises. (Chapter 9)

**Contract carrier** A transportation company that does not make its services available to the general public but engages in continuing agreements with particular customers. (Chapter 30)

**Contributory negligence** A rule of tort law that permits a negligent defendant to escape liability if she can demonstrate that the plaintiff's own conduct contributed in any way to the plaintiff's harm. (Chapter 6)

**Conversion** A tort committed by taking or using someone else's personal property without his permission. (Chapter 5)

**Cookie** A small computer file that identifies the user of a computer. Internet sites typically place cookies on a computer's hard drive to track visitors to their site. (Chapter 26)

**Copyright** Under federal law, the holder of a copyright owns a particular expression of an idea, but not the idea itself. This ownership right applies to creative activities such as literature, music, drama, and software. (Chapter 27)

**Counterclaim** A claim made by the defendant against the plaintiff. (Chapter 3)

**Cover** The buyer's right to obtain substitute goods when a seller has breached a contract. (Chapter 12)

**Creditor beneficiary** When one party to a contract intends to benefit a third party to whom he owes a debt, that third party is referred to as a *creditor beneficiary*. (Chapter 12)

**Criminal law** Rules that permit a government to punish certain behavior by fine or imprisonment. (Chapter 1)

**Cross-examination** When a lawyer questions an opposing witness during a hearing. (Chapter 3)

**Cure** The seller's right to respond to a buyer's rejection of non-conforming goods; the seller accomplishes this by delivering conforming goods before the contract deadline. (Chapter 12)

# D

**Damages** (1) The harm that a plaintiff complains of at trial, such as an injury to her person, or money lost because of a contract breach. (2) Money awarded by a trial court for injury suffered. (Chapter 5)

**De novo** The power of an appellate court or appellate agency to make a new decision in a matter under appeal, entirely ignoring the findings and conclusions of the lower court or agency official. (Chapter 3)

**Debtor** (1) A person who owes money or some other obligation to another party. (2) Someone who files for protection under the bankruptcy code. (Chapters 14, 15)

**Decedent** A person who has died. (Chapter 31)

**Deed** A document that proves ownership of property. (Chapter 28)

**Defamation** The act of injuring someone's reputation by stating something false about her to a third person. *Libel* is defamation done either in writing or by broadcast. *Slander* is defamation done orally. (Chapter 5)

**Default** The failure to perform an obligation, such as the failure to pay money when due. (Chapter 14)

**Default judgment** A court order awarding one party everything it requested because the opposing party failed to respond in time. (Chapter 3)

**Defective products** Generally lead to strict liability. (Chapter 6)

**Defendant** The person being sued. (Chapter 1)

**Definiteness** A doctrine holding that a contract will only be enforced if its terms are sufficiently precise that a court can determine what the parties meant. (Chapter 10)

**Delegatee** A person who receives an obligation under a contract to someone else. (Chapter 11)

**Delegation of duties** A contracting party transfers her duties pursuant to a contract to someone else. (Chapter 11)

**Delegator** A person who gives his obligation under a contract to someone else. (Chapter 11)

**Deponent** The person being questioned in a deposition. (Chapter 3)

**Deposition** A form of discovery in which a party's attorney has the right to ask oral questions of the other party or of a witness. Answers are given under oath. (Chapter 3)

**Deterrence** Using punishment, such as imprisonment, to discourage criminal behavior. (Chapter 7)

**Devisee** Someone who inherits under a will. (Chapter 31)

**Different terms** Contradict the terms of an offer. (Chapter 12)

**Direct examination** During a hearing, for a lawyer to question his own witness. (Chapter 3)

**Directed verdict** The decision by a court to instruct a jury that it must find in favor of a particular party because, in the judge's opinion, no reasonable person could disagree on the outcome. (Chapter 3)

**Disabled person** Someone with a physical or mental impairment that substantially limits a major life activity, or someone who is regarded as having such an impairment. (Chapter 18)

**Disability insurance** Replaces the insured's income if she becomes unable to work because of illness or injury. (Chapter 32)

**Disaffirm** To give notice of refusal to be bound by an agreement. (Chapter 11)

**Discharge** (1) A party to a contract has no more duties. (2) A party to an instrument is released from liability. (Chapter 11)

**Disclaimer** A statement that a particular warranty does not apply. (Chapter 12)

**Discovery** A stage in litigation, after all pleadings have been served, in which each party seeks as much relevant information as possible about the opposing party's case. (Chapter 3)

**Dishonor** An obligor refuses to pay an instrument that is due. (Chapter 24)

**Dismiss** To terminate a lawsuit, often on procedural grounds, without reaching the merits of the case. (Chapter 3)

**Dissociation** A dissociation occurs when a partner leaves a partnership. (Chapter 20)

**Diversity case** A lawsuit in which the plaintiff and defendant are citizens of different states *and* the amount in dispute exceeds $75,000. (Chapter 3)

**Domestic corporation** A corporation is considered a domestic corporation in the state in which it was formed. (Chapter 21)

**Donee** A person who receives a gift. (Chapter 30)

**Donee beneficiary** When one party to a contract intends to make a gift to a third party, that third party is referred to as a *donee beneficiary*. (Chapter 11)

**Donor** A person who makes a gift to another or creates a trust. (Chapters 30, 31)

**Draft** The drawer of this instrument orders someone else to pay money. Checks are the most common form of draft. The drawer of a check orders a bank to pay money. (Chapter 13)

**Drawee** The person who pays a draft. In the case of a check, the bank is the drawee. (Chapter 13)

**Drawer** The person who issues a draft. (Chapter 13)

**Due diligence** An investigation of the registration statement by someone who signs it. (Chapter 23)

**Due Process Clause** Part of the Fifth Amendment. *Procedural due process* ensures that before depriving anyone of liberty or property, the government must go through procedures that ensure that the deprivation is fair. *Substantive due process* holds that certain rights, such as privacy, are so fundamental that the government may not eliminate them. (Chapter 4)

**Dumping** Selling merchandise at one price in the domestic market and at a cheaper, unfair price in an international market. (Chapter 8)

**Durable power of attorney** An instrument that permits an attorney-in-fact to act for a principal. A durable power is effective until the principal revokes it or dies. It continues in effect even if the principal becomes incapacitated. (Chapter 31)

**Duress** (1) A criminal defense in which the defendant shows that she committed the wrongful act because a third person threatened her with imminent physical harm. (2) An improper threat made to force another party to enter into a contract. (Chapter 7)

**Duty** (1) If a defendant can foresee injury to a particular person, she has a duty to him. (Chapter 6) (2) A tax imposed on imported items. (Chapter 8)

**Duty of care** The requirement under the business judgment rule that a manager act with care and in the best interests of the corporation. (Chapter 21)

**Duty of loyalty** The obligation of a manager under the business judgment rule to act without a conflict of interest. (Chapter 21)

# E

**Easement** The right to enter land belonging to another and make a limited use of it, without taking anything away. (Chapter 28)

**Economic loss doctrine** A common law rule holding that when an injury is purely economic and arises from a contract made between two businesses, the injured party may sue only under the Uniform Commercial Code. (Chapter 12)

**Element** A fact that a plaintiff to a lawsuit must prove in order to prevail. (Chapter 5)

**Embezzlement** Fraudulent conversion of property already in the defendant's possession. (Chapter 7)

**Eminent domain** The power of the government to take private property for public use. (Chapter 28)

**Employee at will** A worker who does not have a contract specifying the duration of employment. (Chapter 17)

**Enabling legislation** A statute authorizing the creation of a new administrative agency and specifying its powers and duties. (Chapter 4)

**Engagement letter** A written contract by which a client hires an accountant. (Chapter 23)

**Equal Protection Clause** Part of the Fourteenth Amendment, it generally requires the government to treat equally situated people the same. (Chapter 4)

**Equity** The broad powers of a court to fashion a remedy where justice demands it and no common law remedy exists. An injunction is an example of an equitable remedy. (Chapter 1)

**Error of law** A mistake made by a trial judge that concerns a legal issue as opposed to a factual matter. Permitting too many leading questions is a legal error; choosing to believe one witness rather than another is a factual matter. (Chapter 3)

**Estate** The legal entity that holds title to assets after the owner dies and before the property is distributed. (Chapter 31)

**Estoppel** Out of fairness, a person is denied the right to assert a claim. (Chapter 29)

**Ethics** The study of how people ought to act. (Chapter 2)

**European Union** An association of 27 European countries joined together for the purpose of facilitating trade, free movement between nations, and setting economic and foreign policy. (Chapter 8)

**Eviction** When a landlord prevents a tenant from possessing the premises. (Chapter 29)

**Evidence, rules of** Law governing the proof offered during a trial or formal hearing. These rules limit the questions that may be asked of witnesses and the introduction of physical objects. (Chapter 3)

**Exclusionary rule** In a criminal trial, a ban on the use of evidence obtained in violation of the U.S. Constitution. (Chapter 7)

**Exculpatory clause** A contract provision that attempts to release one party from liability in the event the other party is injured. (Chapter 10)

**Executed contract** A binding agreement in which all parties have fulfilled all obligations. (Chapter 9)

**Executive agency** An administrative agency within the executive branch of government. (Chapter 4)

**Executive order** An order by a president or governor, having the full force of law. (Chapter 1)

**Executor** A person chosen by the decedent to oversee the probate process. (Chapter 31)

**Executory contract** A binding agreement in which one or more of the parties has not fulfilled its obligations. (Chapter 9)

**Executrix** A female executor. (Chapter 31)

**Exhaustion of remedies** A principle of administrative law that no party may appeal an agency action to a court until she has utilized all available appeals within the agency itself. (Chapter 4)

**Expectation interest** A remedy in a contract case that puts the injured party in the position he would have been in had both sides fully performed. (Chapter 11)

**Expert witness** A witness in a court case who has special training or qualifications to discuss a specific issue, and who is generally permitted to state an opinion. (Chapter 3)

**Export** To transport goods or services out of a country. (Chapter 8)

**Express authority** Words or conduct of a principal that, reasonably interpreted, cause the agent to believe that the principal desires him to do a specific act. (Chapter 16)

**Express contract** A binding agreement in which the parties explicitly state all important terms. (Chapter 9)

**Express warranty** A guarantee, created by the words or actions of the seller, that goods will meet certain standards. (Chapter 12)

**Expropriation** A government's seizure of property or companies owned by foreigners. (Chapter 8)

**Extraterritoriality** The power of one nation to impose its laws in other countries. (Chapter 8)

# F

**Fact finder** The one responsible, during a trial, for deciding what occurred, that is, who did what to whom, when, how, and why. It is either the jury or, in a jury-waived case, the judge. (Chapter 4)

**Factual cause** The defendant's breach led to the ultimate harm. (Chapter 6)

**Fair representation, duty of** The union's obligation to act on behalf of all members impartially and in good faith. (Chapter 19)

**Fair use doctrine** Permits limited use of copyrighted material without permission from the author. (Chapter 27)

**False imprisonment** The intentional restraint of another person without reasonable cause and without her consent. (Chapter 5)

**Federalism** A double-layered system of government, with the national and state governments each exercising important but limited powers. (Chapter 1)

**Federal question case** A claim based on the U.S. Constitution, a federal statute, or a federal treaty. (Chapter 3)

**Federal sentencing guidelines** The detailed rules that judges follow when sentencing defendants in federal court. (Chapter 7)

**Fee simple absolute** The greatest possible ownership right in real property, including the right to possess, use, and dispose of the property in any lawful manner. (Chapter 28)

**Fee simple defeasible** Ownership interest in real property that may terminate upon the occurrence of some limiting event. (Chapter 28)

**Felony** The most serious crimes, typically those for which the defendant could be imprisoned for more than a year. (Chapter 7)

**Fiduciary duty** An obligation to behave in a trustworthy and confidential fashion toward the object of that duty. (Chapter 16)

**Fifth Amendment** The amendment to the U.S. Constitution that prohibits self-incrimination. (Chapter 7)

**Financing statement** A document that a secured party files to give the general public notice that the secured party has a secured interest in the collateral. (Chapter 14)

**Firm offer** A contract offer that cannot be withdrawn during a stated period. (Chapter 10)

**First Amendment** The amendment to the U.S. Constitution that protects freedom of speech. (Chapter 4)

**Fixtures** Goods that are attached to real estate. (Chapter 14)

**FOIA** See *Freedom of Information Act (FOIA).*

**Foreign corporation** A corporation formed in another state. (Chapter 21)

**Foreign Corrupt Practices Act** A federal statute that prohibits an American businessperson from giving anything of value to a foreign official to influence an official decision. (Chapter 8)

**Foreign Sovereign Immunity Act** A federal statute that protects other nations from suit in courts of the United States, except under specified circumstances. (Chapter 8)

**Foreseeable type of harm** Refers to injury that a reasonable person could anticipate. (Chapter 6)

**Formal rulemaking** The process whereby an administrative agency notifies the public of a proposed new rule and then permits a formal hearing, with opportunity for evidence and cross-examination, before promulgating the final rule. (Chapter 4)

**Founding Fathers** The authors of the U.S. Constitution, who participated in the Constitutional Convention in Philadelphia in 1787. (Chapter 1)

**Fourth Amendment** The amendment to the U.S. Constitution that prohibits the government from making illegal searches and seizures. (Chapter 7)

**Framers** See *Founding Fathers.*

**Fraud** Deception of another person to obtain money or property from her. (Chapters 5, 7, 10)

**Freedom of Information Act (FOIA)** A federal statute giving private citizens and corporations access to many of the documents possessed by an administrative agency. (Chapter 4)

**Freehold estate** The present right to possess property and to use it in any lawful manner. (Chapter 28)

**Fresh start** After the termination of a bankruptcy case, creditors cannot make a claim against a debtor for money owed before the initial bankruptcy petition was filed. (Chapter 15)

**Frustration of purpose** After the creation of a contract, an entirely unforeseen event occurs that eliminates the value of the contract for one of the parties. (Chapter 11)

**Fully disclosed principal** If the third party in an agency relationship knows the identity of the principal, that principal is fully disclosed. (Chapter 16)

**Fundamental rights** In constitutional law, those rights that are so basic that any governmental interference with them is suspect and likely to be unconstitutional. (Chapter 4)

**GAAP** See *Generally accepted accounting principles (GAAP).*

**GAAS** See *Generally accepted auditing standards (GAAS).*

**Gap fillers** Rules set by the Uniform Commercial Code for supplying missing terms. (Chapter 12)

**GATT** See *General Agreement on Tariffs and Trade (GATT).*

**General Agreement on Tariffs and Trade (GATT)** An international treaty designed to eliminate trade barriers and bolster international commerce, negotiated in stages between the 1940s and 1994 and signed by over 130 nations. (Chapter 8)

**General deterrence** See *Deterrence.*

**General intangibles** Potential sources of income such as copyrights, patents, trademarks, goodwill and certain other rights to payment. (Chapter 14)

**General intent** Means that the defendant intended to do the prohibited physical act. (Chapter 7)

**Generally accepted accounting principles (GAAP)** Rules set by the Financial Accounting Standards Board to be used in preparing financial statements. (Chapter 23)

**Generally accepted auditing standards (GAAS)** Rules set by the American Institute of Certified Public Accountants (AICPA) to be used in conducting audits. (Chapter 23)

**Gift** A voluntary transfer of property from one person to another without consideration. (Chapter 30)

**Gift *causa mortis*** A gift made in contemplation of approaching death. (Chapter 30)

**Goods** Anything movable, except for money, securities, and certain legal rights. (Chapters 9, 12)

**Grantee** The person who receives property, or some interest in it, from the owner. (Chapter 28)

**Grantor** (1) An owner who conveys property, or some interest in it. (2) Someone who creates a trust. (Chapters 28, 31)

**Grievance** A formal complaint alleging a contract violation. (Chapter 19)

# H

**Hacking** Gaining unauthorized access to a computer system. (Chapter 26)

**Harmless error** A ruling made by a trial court which an appeals court determines was legally wrong but not fatal to the decision. (Chapter 3)

**Health care proxy** Someone who is authorized to make health care decisions for a person who is incompetent. (Chapter 31)

**Heir** Technically, someone who inherits from a decedent who died intestate (that is, without a will). However, this term is often used more broadly to indicate anyone who inherits, even under a will. (Chapter 31)

**Holder** For order paper, anyone in possession of the instrument if it is payable to or indorsed to her. For bearer paper, anyone in possession. (Chapter 13)

**Holder in due course** Someone who has given value for an instrument, in good faith, without notice of outstanding claims or other defenses. (Chapter 13)

**Holding** A court's decision. (Chapter 1)

**Holographic will** A handwritten and signed will that has not been witnessed. (Chapter 31)

**Hybrid rulemaking** A method of administrative agency procedure incorporating some elements of formal and some elements of informal rulemaking, typically involving a limited public hearing with restricted rights of testimony and cross-examination. (Chapter 4)

# I

**Identify** In sales law, to designate the specific goods that are the subject of a contract. (Chapter 12)

**IFRS** See *International financial reporting standards (IFRS)*.

**Illegal contract** An agreement that is void because it violates a statute or public policy. (Chapter 10)

**Illusory promise** An apparent promise that is unenforceable because the promisor makes no firm commitment. (Chapter 10)

**Implied authority** When a principal directs an agent to undertake a transaction, the agent has the right to do acts that are incidental to it, usually accompany it, or are reasonably necessary to accomplish it. (Chapter 16)

**Implied contract** A binding agreement created not by explicit language but by the informal words and conduct of the parties. (Chapter 9)

**Implied warranty** Guarantees created by the Uniform Commercial Code and imposed on the seller of goods. (Chapter 12)

**Implied warranty of fitness for a particular purpose** If the seller knows that the buyer plans to use goods for a particular purpose, the seller generally is held to warrant that the goods are in fact fit for that purpose. Also known as *warranty of fitness*. (Chapter 12)

**Implied warranty of habitability** A landlord must meet all standards set by the local building code or otherwise ensure that the premises are fit for human habitation. (Chapter 30)

**Implied warranty of merchantability** Goods must be of at least average, passable quality in the trade. (Chapter 12)

**Import** To transport goods or services into a country. (Chapter 8)

***In camera*** "In the judge's chambers," meaning that the judge does something out of view of the jury and the public. (Chapter 3)

**Incidental damages** The relatively minor costs, such as storage and advertising, that the injured party suffered when responding to a contract breach. (Chapter 11)

**Incorporator** The person who signs a corporate charter. (Chapter 21)

**Independent agency** An administrative agency outside the executive branch of government, such as the Interstate Commerce Commission. (Chapter 4)

**Independent contractor** Someone who undertakes tasks for others but whose work is not closely controlled. (Chapter 16)

**Indictment** The government's formal charge that a defendant has committed a crime and must stand trial. (Chapter 7)

**Indorsement** The signature of the payee. (Chapter 13)

**Infliction of emotional distress** A tort. It can be the *intentional infliction of emotional distress*, meaning that the defendant behaved outrageously and deliberately caused the plaintiff severe psychological injury, or it can be the *negligent infliction of emotional distress*, meaning that the defendant's conduct violated the rules of negligence. (Chapter 5)

**Informal rulemaking** The process whereby an administrative agency notifies the public of a proposed new rule and permits comment but is then free to promulgate the final rule without a public hearing. (Chapter 4)

**Initial public offering (IPO)** A company's first public sale of securities. (Chapter 22)

**Injunction** A court order that a person either do or stop doing something. (Chapters 1, 11)

**Injury** Must be genuine, not speculative. (Chapter 6)

**Instructions or charge** The explanation given by a judge to a jury, outlining the jury's task in deciding a lawsuit and the underlying rules of law the jury should use in reaching its decision. (Chapter 3)

**Instruments** Drafts, checks and notes. (Chapter 13)

**Insurable interest** A person has an insurable interest if she would be harmed by the danger that she has insured against. (Chapter 32)

**Insured** A person whose loss is the subject of an insurance policy. (Chapter 32)

**Insurer** The person who issues an insurance policy. (Chapter 32)

**Integrated contract** A writing that the parties intend as the complete and final expression of their agreement. (Chapter 10)

**Intentional tort** An act deliberately performed that violates a legally imposed duty and injures someone. (Chapter 5)

**International financial reporting standards (IFRS)** A set of rules for preparing financial statements that international companies follow. The Securities and Exchange Commission is proposing that U.S. companies follow these rules as well. (Chapter 23)

**Interest** A legal right in something, such as ownership or a mortgage or a tenancy. (Chapter 28)

**Interference with a contract** See *Tortious interference with a contract.*

**Interference with a prospective advantage** See *Tortious interference with a prospective advantage.*

**Interpretive rules** A formal statement by an administrative agency expressing its view of what existing statutes or regulations mean. (Chapter 4)

**Interrogatory** A form of discovery in which one party sends to an opposing party written questions that must be answered under oath. (Chapter 3)

*Inter vivos* **gift** A gift made "during life," that is, when the donor is not under any fear of impending death. (Chapter 30)

*Inter vivos* **trust** A trust established while the grantor is still living. (Chapter 31)

**Intestate** To die without a will. (Chapter 31)

**Intrusion** Interfering in someone's life in a way that a reasonable person would find offensive. (Chapter 5)

**Inventory** Goods that the seller is holding for sale or lease in the ordinary course of its business. (Chapter 14)

**Invitee** Someone who has the right to be on property, such as a customer in a shop. (Chapter 6)

**Involuntary bailment** A bailment that occurs without an agreement between the bailor and bailee. (Chapter 30)

**IPO** See *Initial public offering (IPO).*

**Issue** All direct descendants such as children and grandchildren. (Chapter 31)

**Issuer** (1) The maker of a promissory note or the drawer of a draft. (2) A company that issues stock. (Chapters 13, 22)

# J

**Joint and several liability** All members of a group are liable. They can be sued as a group, or any one of them can be sued individually for the full amount owing. (Chapters 16, 20, 23)

**Joint tenancy** Two or more people holding equal interest in a property, with the right of survivorship. (Chapter 28)

**Judgment** *non obstante verdicto* **(n.o.v.)** "Judgment notwithstanding the verdict," when a trial judge overturns the verdict of the jury and enters a judgment in favor of the opposing party. (Chapter 3)

**Judicial activism** The willingness shown by certain courts (and not by others) to decide issues of public policy, such as constitutional questions (free speech, equal protection, etc.) and matters of contract fairness (promissory estoppel, unconscionability, etc.). (Chapter 4)

**Judicial restraint** A court's preference to abstain from adjudicating major social issues and to leave such matters to legislatures. (Chapter 4)

**Judicial review** The power of the judicial system to examine, interpret, and even nullify actions taken by another branch of government. (Chapter 4)

**Jurisdiction** The power of a court to hear a particular dispute, civil or criminal, and to make a binding decision. (Chapter 3)

**Jurisprudence** The study of the purposes and philosophies of the law, as opposed to particular provisions of the law. (Chapter 1)

**Justification** A criminal defense in which the defendant establishes that he broke the law to avoid a greater harm. (Chapter 7)

# L

**Labor-Management Relations Act** Designed to curb union abuses. (Chapter 19)

**Landlord** The owner of a freehold estate who allows another person to live on his property temporarily. (Chapter 29)

**Larceny** Taking personal property with the intention of preventing the owner from ever using it. (Chapter 7)

**Law case** The decision a court has made in a civil lawsuit or criminal prosecution. (Chapter 1)

**Law merchant** The body of rules and customs developed by traders and businesspersons throughout Europe from roughly the fifteenth to the eighteenth centuries. (Chapter 12)

**Lease** A contract creating a landlord-tenant relationship. (Chapter 29)

**Legal positivism** The legal philosophy holding that law is what the sovereign says it is, regardless of its moral content. (Chapter 1)

**Legal realism** The legal philosophy holding that what really influences law is who makes and enforces it, not what is put in writing. (Chapter 1)

**Legal remedy** Generally, money damages. It is distinguished from equitable remedy, which includes injunctions and other non-monetary relief. (Chapter 11)

**Legislative history** Used by courts to interpret the meaning of a statute, this is the record of hearings, speeches, and explanations that accompanied a statute as it made its way from newly proposed bill to final law. (Chapter 4)

**Legislative rules** Regulations issued by an administrative agency. (Chapter 4)

**Letter of credit** A commercial device used to guarantee payment in international trade, usually between parties that have not previously worked together. (Chapter 8)

**Liability insurance** Reimburses the insured for any liability she incurs by accidentally harming someone else. (Chapter 32)

**Libel** See *Defamation*.

**License** To grant permission to another person (1) to make or sell something or (2) to enter on property. (Chapter 28)

**Licensee** A person who is on the property of another for her own purposes but with the owner's permission. A social guest is a typical licensee. (Chapter 6)

**Lien** A security interest created by rule of law, often based on labor that the secured party has expended on the collateral. (Chapter 14)

**Life estate** An ownership interest in real property entitling the holder to use the property during his lifetime, but which terminates upon his death. (Chapter 28)

**Life insurance** Provides for payments to a beneficiary upon the death of the insured. (Chapter 32)

**Life tenant** A person who has the use of a property during his lifetime only. (Chapter 28)

**Limited liability company** An organization that has the limited liability of a corporation but is not a taxable entity. (Chapter 20)

**Limited liability limited partnership** In a limited liability limited partnership, the general partner is not personally liable for the debts of the partnership. (Chapter 21)

**Limited partnership** A partnership with two types of partners: (1) limited partners, who have no personal liability for the debts of the enterprise nor any right to manage the business; and (2) general partners, who are responsible for management and personally liable for all debts. (Chapter 21)

**Liquidated damages** A contract clause specifying how much a party must pay upon breach. (Chapter 11)

**Liquidated debt** The amount of the indebtedness that is not in dispute. (Chapter 11)

**Litigation** The process of resolving disputes through formal court proceedings. (Chapter 3)

**Living trust** A trust established while the grantor is alive. See also inter vivos *trust*. (Chapter 31)

**Living will** An instrument that permits adults to refuse medical treatment. It can also appoint a health care proxy to make medical decisions for a person who has become incompetent. Also called an *advance directive*. (Chapter 31)

**Lockout** A management tactic, designed to gain a bargaining advantage, in which the company refuses to allow union members to work (and hence deprives them of their pay). (Chapter 19)

**Lost property** Something that is given up accidentally. (Chapter 30)

# M

**Mailbox rule** A contract doctrine holding that acceptance is effective upon dispatch, that is, when it is mailed or otherwise taken out of the control of the offeree. (Chapter 10)

**Maker** The issuer of a promissory note. (Chapter 13)

**Marital trust** A legal entity created for the purpose of reducing a married couple's estate taxes. (Chapter 31)

**Material** (1) Meaning that the maker of an agreement expected the other party to rely on her words. (2) Important enough to affect the decision of an investor or a life insurance company. (Chapters 10, 22, 32)

**Mediation** The process of using a neutral person to aid in the settlement of a legal dispute. A mediator's decision is non-binding. (Chapter 3)

**Medicare fraud** Using false statements, bribes, or kickbacks to obtain Medicare payments from the federal or state government. (Chapter 7)

***Mens rea*** "Guilty state of mind," what the defendant was thinking or intended when she committed the crime in question. (Chapter 7)

**Merchant** Someone who routinely deals in a particular good. (Chapter 12)

**Merger** An acquisition of one company by another. (Chapter 22)

**Mini-trial** A form of alternative dispute resolution in which the parties present short versions of their cases to a panel of three "judges." (Chapter 3)

**Minor** A person under the age of 18. (Chapter 10)

**Minute book** Records of shareholder meetings and directors' meetings are kept in the corporation's minute book. (Chapter 21)

**Mirror image rule** A contract doctrine that requires acceptance to be on exactly the same terms as the offer. (Chapter 9)

**Misdemeanor** A less serious crime, typically one for which the maximum penalty is incarceration for less than a year, often in a jail, as opposed to a prison. (Chapter 7)

**Mislaid property** Something that the owner intentionally placed somewhere and then forgot about. (Chapter 30)

**Misrepresentation** A factually incorrect statement made during contract negotiations. (Chapter 10)

**Mitigation** One party acts to minimize its losses when the other party breaches a contract. (Chapter 11)

**M'Naghten Rule** A test to gauge sanity that evaluates whether a criminal suffered a serious, identifiable mental disease that kept him from understanding the nature of his act or know that it was wrong. (Chapter 7)

**Modify** An appellate court order changing a lower court ruling. (Chapter 3)

**Money laundering** Taking the profits of criminal acts and either (1) using the money to promote more crime or (2) attempting to conceal the money's source. (Chapter 7)

**Monopolization** When a company acquires or maintains a monopoly through the commission of unacceptably aggressive acts. A violation of §2 of the Sherman Act. (Chapter 22)

**Mortgage** A security interest in real property. (Chapter 28)

**Mortgagee** A creditor who obtains a security interest in real property, typically in exchange for money given to the mortgagor to buy the property. (Chapter 28)

**Mortgagor** A debtor who gives a mortgage (security interest) in real property to a creditor, typically in exchange for money used to buy the property. (Chapter 28)

**Motion** A formal request that a court take some specified step during litigation. For example, a motion to compel discovery is a request that a trial judge order the other party to respond to discovery. (Chapter 3)

**Motion to suppress** A request that the court exclude evidence because it was obtained in violation of the U.S. Constitution. (Chapter 7)

**Multinational enterprise (MNE)** A corporation that is doing business in more than one country simultaneously. (Chapter 8)

# N

**NAFTA** See *North American Free Trade Agreement (NAFTA).*

**National Labor Relations Act (NLRA)** A law that ensures the right of workers to form unions and encourages management and unions to bargain collectively. (Chapter 19)

**National Labor Relations Board (NLRB)** The administrative agency charged with overseeing labor law. (Chapter 19)

**Nationalization** A government's seizure of property or companies. (Chapter 8)

**Natural law** The theory that an unjust law is no law at all, and that a rule is legitimate only if based on an immutable morality. (Chapter 1)

**Negative or dormant aspect of the Commerce Clause** The doctrine that prohibits a state from any action that interferes with or discriminates against interstate commerce. (Chapter 4)

**Negligence *per se*** Violation of a standard of care set by statute. Driving while intoxicated is illegal; thus, if a drunk driver injures a pedestrian, he has committed negligence *per se*. (Chapter 6)

**Negotiable instrument** A type of commercial paper that is freely transferable. (Chapter 13)

**Negotiation** The transfer of an instrument by someone other than the issuer. To be negotiated, order paper must be indorsed and then delivered to the transferee. For bearer paper, no indorsement is required—it must simply be delivered to the transferee. (Chapter 13)

**NLRA** See *National Labor Relations Act (NLRA).*

**NLRB** See *National Labor Relations Board (NLRB).*

**Nominal damages** A token sum, such as $1, given to an injured plaintiff who cannot prove damages. (Chapter 11)

**Noncompetition agreement** A contract in which one party agrees not to compete with another in a stated type of business. (Chapter 10

**North American Free Trade Agreement (NAFTA)** A commercial association among Canada, the United States, and Mexico designed to eliminate almost all trade barriers. (Chapter 8)

**Note** An unconditional, written promise that the maker of the instrument will pay a specific amount of money on demand or at a definite time. (Chapter 13)

**Novation** If there is an existing contract between *A* and *B*, a novation occurs when *A* agrees to release *B* from all liability on the contract in return for *C*'s willingness to accept *B*'s liability. (Chapter 10)

**Nuncupative will** An oral will. (Chapter 31)

# O

**Obligee** The party to a contract who is entitled to receive performance from the other party. (Chapter 11)

**Obligor** The party to a contract who is required to do something for the benefit of the other party. (Chapter 11)

**Obscenity** Constitutional law doctrine holding that some works will receive no First Amendment protection because a court determines they depict sexual matters in an offensive way. (Chapter 4)

**Offer** In contract law, an act or statement that proposes definite terms and permits the other party to create a contract by accepting those terms. (Chapter 9)

**Offeree** The party in contract negotiations who receives the first offer. (Chapter 9)

**Offeror** The party in contract negotiations who makes the first offer. (Chapter 9)

**Oppression** When one party uses superior power to force a contract on another party. (Chapter 10)

**Order for relief** An official acknowledgment that a debtor is under the jurisdiction of the bankruptcy court. (Chapter 15)

**Order paper** An instrument that includes the words "pay to the order of" or their equivalent. (Chapter 13)

**Output contract** An agreement that obligates the seller of goods to sell everything he produces during a stated period to a particular buyer. (Chapter 10)

**Override** The power of Congress or a state legislature to pass legislation despite a veto by a president or governor. A congressional override requires a two-thirds vote in each house. (Chapter 4)

# P

**Parol evidence** Written or oral evidence, outside the language of a contract, offered by one party to clarify interpretation of the agreement. (Chapter 11)

**Parol evidence rule** In the case of an integrated contract, neither party may use evidence outside the writing to contradict, vary, or add to its terms. (Chapter 11)

**Part performance** An exception to the statute of frauds permitting a buyer of real estate to enforce an oral contract if she paid part of the price, entered the property, and made improvements, with the owner's knowledge. (Chapter 10)

**Partnership** An unincorporated association of two or more persons to carry on as co-owners of a business for profit. (Chapter 20)

**Partnership at will** A partnership that has no fixed duration. Any partner has the right to resign from the partnership at any time and for any reason. (Chapter 20)

**Patent** A grant by the government permitting the inventor the exclusive use of an invention. (Chapter 27)

**Payable on demand** The holder of an instrument is entitled to be paid whenever she asks. (Chapter 13)

**Payee** Someone who is owed money under the terms of an instrument. (Chapter 13)

***Per capita* distribution** Under a will, each heir receives the same amount. (Chapter 31)

**Peremptory challenge** During *voir dire*, a request by one attorney that a prospective juror be excused for an unstated reason. (Chapter 3)

**Perfection** A series of steps a secured party must take to protect its rights in collateral against people other than the debtor. (Chapter 14)

**Perfect tender rule** A rule permitting the buyer to reject goods if they fail in any respect to conform to the contract. (Chapter 21)

**Periodic tenancy** A lease for a fixed period, automatically renewable unless terminated. (Chapter 29)

***Per se* violation of an antitrust law** An automatic breach. Courts will generally not consider mitigating factors. (Chapter 22)

**Personally identifiable information (PII)** Data that identify a user of a Web site, such as name and address. (Chapter 26)

**Personal property** All property other than real property. (Chapter 30)

***Per stirpes* distribution** Under a will, each branch of a family receives an equal share. (Chapter 31)

**Pierce the veil** When a court holds shareholders personally liable for the debts of a corporation, or members personally liable for the debts of an LLC. (Chapters 20, 21)

**PII** See *Personally identifiable information (PII)*.

**Plain meaning rule** In statutory interpretation, the premise that words with an ordinary, everyday significance will be so interpreted unless there is some apparent reason not to. (Chapter 4)

**Plaintiff** The person who is suing. (Chapter 1)

**Plea bargain** An agreement between prosecution and defense that the defendant will plead guilty to a reduced charge in exchange for a reduced sentence. (Chapter 7)

**Pleadings** The documents that begin a lawsuit: the complaint, the answer, the counterclaim, and the reply. (Chapter 3)

**PMSI** See *Purchase money security interest (PMSI)*.

**Point source** A single producer of pollution. (Chapter 25)

**Positive aspect of the Commerce Clause** The power granted to Congress to regulate commerce between the states. (Chapter 4)

**Precedent** An earlier case that decided the same legal issue as that presently in dispute and which therefore will control the outcome of the current case. (Chapters 1, 3)

**Predatory pricing** A violation of §2 of the Sherman Act, in which a company lowers its prices below cost to drive competitors out of business. (Chapter 22)

**Preemption** The doctrine, based on the Supremacy Clause, by which any federal statute takes priority whenever (1) a state statute conflicts or (2) there is no conflict, but Congress indicated an intention to control the issue involved. (Chapter 4)

**Preferred stock** Owners of preferred stock have a right to receive dividends and liquidation proceeds of the company before common shareholders. (Chapter 21)

**Preference** When a debtor unfairly pays creditors immediately before filing a bankruptcy petition. (Chapter 15)

**Preponderance of the evidence** The level of proof that a plaintiff must meet to prevail in a civil lawsuit, it means that the plaintiff must offer evidence that, in sum, is slightly more persuasive than the defendant's evidence. (Chapter 3)

**Pretermitted child** A child omitted from a parent's will. (Chapter 31)

**Prevention of significant deterioration (PSD) program** Stipulates that no one may undertake a building project that will cause a major increase in pollution without first obtaining a permit from the Environmental Protection Agency. (Chapter 25)

*Prima facie* "At first sight," a fact or conclusion that is presumed to be true unless someone presents evidence to disprove it. (Chapter 18)

**Principal** In an agency relationship, the principal is the person for whom the agent is acting. (Chapter 16)

**Privacy Act** A federal statute prohibiting federal agencies from divulging to other agencies or organizations information about private citizens. (Chapter 4)

**Privity** The relationship that exists between two parties who make a contract, as opposed to a third party who, though affected by the contract, is not a party to it. (Chapter 12)

**Probable cause** In a search and seizure case, it means that the information available indicates that it is more likely than not that a search will uncover particular criminal evidence. (Chapter 7)

**Probate** The process of carrying out the terms of a will. (Chapter 31)

**Procedural due process** See *Due Process Clause*.

**Procedural law** The rules establishing how the legal system itself is to operate in a particular kind of case. (Chapter 1)

**Proceeds** Anything that a debtor obtains from the sale or disposition of collateral. Normally, the term *proceeds* refers to cash obtained from the sale of the secured property. (Chapter 14)

**Production of documents and things** A form of discovery in which one party demands that the other furnish original documents or physical things, relating to the suit, for inspection and copying. (Chapter 3)

**Product liability** The potential responsibility that a manufacturer or seller has for injuries caused by defective goods. (Chapter 12)

**Professional corporation** A form of organization that permits professionals (such as doctors, lawyers, and accountants) to incorporate. Shareholders are not personally liable for the torts of other shareholders or for the contract debts of the organization. (Chapter 20)

**Profit** The right to enter land belonging to another and take something away, such as minerals or timber. (Chapter 28)

**Promisee** The person to whom a promise is made. (Chapter 11)

**Promisor** The person who makes the promise that a third party beneficiary benefits from. (Chapter 11)

**Promissory estoppel** A doctrine in which a court may enforce a promise made by the defendant even when there is no contract, if the defendant knew that the plaintiff was likely to rely on the promise, the plaintiff did in fact rely, and enforcement of it is the only way to avoid injustice. (Chapter 9)

**Promissory note** The maker of the instrument promises to pay a specific amount of money. (Chapter 13)

**Promoter** The person who organizes a corporation. (Chapter 21)

**Promulgate** To issue a new rule. (Chapter 4)

**Proof of claim** A form stating the name of an unsecured creditor and the amount of the claim against the debtor. (Chapter 15)

**Property insurance** Covers physical damage to real estate, personal property, or inventory from causes such as fire, smoke, lightning, wind, riot, vandalism, or theft. (Chapter 32)

**Prosecution** The government's attempt to convict a defendant of a crime by charging him, trying the case, and forcing him to defend himself. (Chapter 7)

**Prospectus** Under the Securities Act of 1933, an issuer must provide this document to anyone who purchases a security in a public transaction. The prospectus contains detailed information about the issuer and its business, a description of the stock, and audited financial statements. (Chapter 22)

**Protective order** A court order limiting one party's discovery. (Chapter 3)

**Proxy** (1) A person whom the shareholder designates to vote in his place. (2) The written form (typically a card) that the shareholder uses to appoint a designated voter. (Chapter 21)

**Proxy statement** When a public company seeks proxy votes from its shareholders, it must include a proxy statement. This statement contains information about the company, such as a detailed description of management compensation. (Chapter 21)

**Publicly traded corporation** A company that (1) has completed a public offering under the Securities Act of 1933, (2) has securities traded on a national exchange, or (3) has 500 shareholders and $10 million in assets. (Chapter 21)

**Punitive damages** Money awarded at trial not to compensate the plaintiff for harm but to punish the defendant for conduct that the fact finder considers extreme and outrageous. (Chapter 5)

**Purchase money security interest (PMSI)** A security interest taken by the person who sells the collateral to the debtor or by a person who advances money so that the debtor may buy the collateral. (Chapter 14)

**Qualified privilege** The principle that employers are liable only for false statements that they know to be false or that are primarily motivated by ill will. (Chapter 17)

*Quantum meruit* "As much as she deserves," the damages awarded in a quasi-contract case. (Chapter 9)

**Quasi-contract** A legal fiction in which, to avoid injustice, the court awards damages as if a contract had existed, although one did not. (Chapter 9)

*Quid pro quo* A Latin phrase meaning "one thing in return for another," it refers to a form of sexual harassment in which some aspect of a job is made contingent upon sexual activity. (Chapter 18)

**Quiet enjoyment** A tenant's right to use property without the interference of the landlord. (Chapter 29)

**Quorum** The number of voters that must be present for a meeting to count. (Chapter 21)

**Quota** A limit on the quantity of a particular good that may enter a nation. (Chapter 8)

**Racketeer Influenced and Corrupt Organizations Act (RICO)** Prohibits using two or more racketeering acts to accomplish certain specified goals connected to criminal activity. (Chapter 7)

**Ratification** (1) When someone accepts the benefit of an unauthorized transaction or fails to repudiate it once he has learned of it, he is then bound by it. (2) The vote by a nation's legislature to honor an international agreement. (Chapter 8)

**Reaffirm** To promise to pay a debt even after it is discharged. (Chapter 15)

**Real property** Land, together with certain things associated with it, such as buildings, subsurface rights, air rights, plant life, and fixtures. (Chapter 28)

**Reasonable doubt** The level of proof that the government must meet to convict the defendant in a criminal case. The fact finder must be persuaded to a very high degree of certainty that the defendant did what the government alleges. (Chapter 3)

**Reciprocal dealing agreement** An agreement under which Company *A* will purchase from Company *B* only if Company *B* also buys from Company *A*. These agreements are rule of reason violations of the Sherman Act. (Chapter 22)

**Record** Information written on paper or stored in an electronic or other medium. (Chapter 14)

**Reformation** The process by which a court rewrites a contract to ensure its accuracy or viability. (Chapter 11)

**Registration statement** A document filed with the Securities and Exchange Commission under the Securities Act of 1933 by an issuer seeking to sell securities in a public transaction. (Chapter 22)

**Reliance interest** A remedy in a contract case that puts the injured party in the position he would have been in had the parties never entered into a contract. (Chapter 11)

**Remand** The power of an appellate court to return a case to a lower court for additional action. (Chapter 1)

**Rent** Compensation paid by a tenant to a landlord. (Chapter 29)

**Reply** A pleading filed by the plaintiff in response to a defendant's counterclaim. (Chapter 3)

**Repossess** A secured party takes collateral because the debtor has defaulted on payments. (Chapter 14)

**Repudiation** An indication made by one contracting party to the other that it will not perform. (Chapter 21)

**Request for admission** A form of discovery in which one party demands that the opposing party either admit or deny particular factual or legal allegations. (Chapter 3)

**Requirements contract** An agreement that obligates a buyer of specified goods to purchase all of the goods she needs during a stated period from a particular seller. (Chapter 10)

**Resale price maintenance** A rule of reason violation of the Sherman Act, in which a manufacturer enters into an agreement with retailers setting the minimum prices they may charge. (Chapter 22)

**Rescind** To cancel a contract by mutual agreement. (Chapters 10, 11)

*Res ipsa loquitur* A doctrine of tort law holding that the facts may imply negligence when the defendant had exclusive control of the thing that caused the harm, the accident would not normally have occurred without negligence, and the plaintiff played no role in causing the injury. (Chapter 6)

**Respondeat superior** A rule of agency law holding that an employer is liable for a tort committed by his employee acting within the scope of employment or acting with apparent authority. (Chapter 16)

**Restitution** Restoring an injured party to its original position. (Chapter 10)

**Restitution interest** A remedy in a contract case that returns to the injured party a benefit that he has conferred on the other party, which it would be unjust to leave with that person. (Chapter 11)

**Reverse** The power of an appellate court to overrule a lower court and grant judgment for the party that had lost in the lower court. (Chapters 1, 3)

**Reverse and remand** To nullify a lower court's decision and return a case to trial. (Chapter 3)

**Revocable trust** A trust that can be undone or changed at any time. (Chapter 31)

**Revocation** The act of disavowing a contract offer so that the offeree no longer has the power to accept it. (Chapter 10)

**RICO** See *Racketeer Influenced and Corrupt Organizations Act (RICO).*

**Rulemaking** The power of an administrative agency to issue regulations. (Chapter 4)

**Rule of reason violation** An action that breaches the antitrust laws only if it has an anticompetitive impact. (Chapter 22)

# S

**Sale on approval** A transfer in which a buyer takes goods, intending to use them herself, but has the right to return the goods to the seller. (Chapter 12)

**Sale or return** A transfer in which the buyer takes goods, intending to resell them, but has the right to return the goods to the original owner. (Chapter 12)

**S corporation** An organization that provides both the limited liability of a corporation and the tax status of a partnership. (Chapter 20)

**Search warrant** Written permission to conduct a search, given by a neutral official. (Chapter 7)

**Secondary boycott** Picketing, directed by a union against a company, designed to force that company to stop doing business with the union's employer. (Chapter 19)

**Secondary offering** Any public sale of securities by a company after the initial public offering. (Chapter 22)

**Secured party** A person or company that holds a security interest. (Chapter 14)

**Security** Any purchase in which the buyer invests money in a common enterprise and expects to earn a profit predominantly from the efforts of others. (Chapter 22)

**Security agreement** A contract in which the debtor gives a security interest to the secured party. (Chapter 14)

**Security interest** An interest in personal property or fixtures that secures the performance of some obligation. (Chapter 14)

**Separation of powers** The principle, established by the first three articles of the U.S. Constitution, that authority should be divided among the legislative, executive, and judicial branches. (Chapter 4)

**Settlor** Someone who creates a trust. Also called a *grantor* or *donor*. (Chapter 31)

**Sexual harassment** Unwelcome sexual advances, requests for sexual favors, and other verbal or physical conduct of a sexual nature that violates Title VII of the 1964 Civil Rights Act. (Chapter 18)

**Signatory** A person, company, or nation that has signed a legal document, such as a contract, agreement, or treaty. (Chapter 8)

**Single recovery principle** A rule of tort litigation that requires a plaintiff to claim all damages, present and future, at the time of trial, not afterwards. (Chapter 5)

**SIP** See *State Implementation Plan (SIP).*

**Slander** See *Defamation.*

**Sole proprietorship** An unincorporated business owned by a single person. (Chapter 20)

**Sovereign immunity** The right of a national government to be free of lawsuits brought in foreign courts. (Chapter 8)

**Spam** Unsolicited commercial or bulk e-mail. ("To spam" is to send such e-mail.) (Chapter 26)

**Specific deterrence** See *Deterrence.* (Chapter 7)

**Specific intent** Means that the defendant intended to do something beyond the mere prohibited physical act. (Chapter 7)

**Specific performance** A contract remedy requiring the breaching party to perform the contract by conveying land or some unique asset, rather than by paying money damages. (Chapter 11)

**Stakeholders** Anyone who is affected by the activities of a corporation, such as employees, customers, creditors, suppliers, shareholders, and neighbors. (Chapter 21)

**Stale check** A check presented more than six months after its due date. (Chapter 25)

**Stare decisis** "Let the decision stand," a basic principle of the common law that precedent is usually binding. (Chapters 1, 4)

**State Implementation Plan (SIP)** Under the Clean Air Act, states must establish a plan for meeting the air quality standards set by the Environmental Protection Agency. (Chapter 25)

**Statute** A law passed by a legislative body, such as Congress. (Chapters 1, 4)

**Statute of frauds** This law provides that certain contracts are not enforceable unless in writing. (Chapter 10)

**Statute of limitations** A statute that determines the period within which a lawsuit must be filed. (Chapter 11)

**Statute of repose** A law that places an absolute limit on when a lawsuit may be filed, regardless of when the defect was discovered. (Chapter 12)

**Statutory interpretation** A court's power to give meaning to new legislation by clarifying ambiguities, providing limits, and ultimately applying it to a specific fact pattern in litigation. (Chapter 4)

**Straight bankruptcy** Also known as "liquidation," this form of bankruptcy mandates that the bankrupt's assets be sold to pay creditors but the bankrupt has no obligation to share future earnings. (Chapter 15)

**Strict liability** A tort doctrine holding to a very high standard all those who engage in ultrahazardous activity (e.g., using explosives) or who manufacture certain products. (Chapter 6)

**Strike** The ultimate weapon of a labor union, it occurs when all or most employees of a particular plant or employer walk off the job and refuse to work. (Chapter 19)

**Strike suit** A lawsuit without merit that defendants sometimes settle simply to avoid the nuisance of litigation. (Chapter 19)

**Subpoena** An order to appear, issued by a court or government body. (Chapter 4)

**Subpoena *duces tecum*** An order to produce certain documents or items before a court or government body. (Chapter 4)

**Subprime loan** A loan that has an above-market interest rate because the borrower is high-risk. (Chapter 24)

**Subsidiary** A company controlled by a foreign company. (Chapter 8)

**Substantial performance** The promisor performs contract duties well enough to be entitled to his full contract price, minus the value of any defects. (Chapter 11)

**Substantive due process** See *Due Process Clause.* (Chapter 4)

**Substantive law** Rules that establish the rights of parties. For example, the prohibition against slander is substantive law, as opposed to procedural law. (Chapter 1)

**Summary judgment** The power of a trial court to terminate a lawsuit before a trial has begun, on the grounds that no essential facts are in dispute. (Chapter 3)

**Summary jury trial** A form of alternative dispute resolution in which a small panel of jurors hears shortened, summarized versions of the evidence. (Chapter 3)

**Superseding cause** An event that interrupts the chain of causation and relieves a defendant from liability based on her own act. (Chapter 6)

**Supremacy Clause** From Article VI of the U.S. Constitution, it declares that federal statutes and treaties take priority over any state law if there is a conflict between the two or, even absent a conflict, if Congress manifests an intent to preempt the field. (Chapter 4)

**Surprise** When a party does not fully understand the consequences of its agreement to a contract. (Chapter 10)

# T

**Takings Clause** Part of the Fifth Amendment, it ensures that when any governmental unit takes private property for public use, it must compensate the owner. (Chapter 4)

**Tariff** A duty imposed on imported goods by the government of the importing nation. (Chapter 8)

**Tenancy at sufferance** A tenancy that exists without the permission of the landlord, after the expiration of a true tenancy. (Chapter 29)

**Tenancy at will** A tenancy of no fixed duration, which may be terminated by either party at any time. (Chapter 29)

**Tenancy by the entirety** A form of joint ownership available only to married couples. If one member of the couple dies, the property goes automatically to the survivor. Creditors cannot attach the property, nor can one owner sell the property without the other's permission. (Chapter 28)

**Tenancy for years** A lease for a stated, fixed period. (Chapter 29)

**Tenancy in common** Two or more people holding equal interest in a property, but with no right of survivorship. (Chapter 28)

**Tenant** A person given temporary possession of a landlord's property. (Chapter 29)

**Tender** To make conforming goods available to the buyer. (Chapter 12)

**Term partnership** When the partners agree in advance on the duration of a partnership. (Chapter 20)

**Testamentary trust** A trust created by the grantor's will that goes into effect when the grantor dies. (Chapter 31)

**Testator** Someone who dies having executed a will. (Chapter 31)

**Testatrix** A female testator. (Chapter 31)

**Third party beneficiary** Someone who stands to benefit from a contract to which she is not a party. An *intended* beneficiary may enforce such a contract; an *incidental* beneficiary may not. (Chapter 11)

**Three-Fifths Clause** A clause in Article 1, section 2 of the U.S. Constitution, now void and regarded as racist, which required that for purposes of taxation and representation, a slave should be counted as three-fifths of a person. (Chapter 4)

**Tied product** In a tying arrangement, the product that a buyer must purchase as the condition for being allowed to buy another product. (Chapter 22)

**Tort** A civil wrong, committed in violation of a duty that the law imposes. (Chapter 5)

**Tortious interference with a contract** A tort in which the defendant deliberately impedes an existing contract between the plaintiff and another. (Chapter 5)

**Tortious interference with a prospective advantage** A tort in which the defendant deliberately obstructs a developing venture or advantage that the plaintiff has created. (Chapter 5)

**Tracing** When an auditor takes an item of original data and tracks it forward to ensure that it has been properly recorded throughout the bookkeeping process. (Chapter 23)

**Trade acceptance** A draft drawn by a seller of goods on the buyer and payable to the seller or some third party. (Chapter 22)

**Trademark** Any combination of words and symbols that a business uses to identify and distinguish its products or services and that federal law will protect. (Chapter 27)

**Trade secret** A formula, device, process, method, or compilation of information that, when used in business, gives the owner an advantage over competitors who do not know it. (Chapter 27)

**Treasury stock** Stock that has been bought back by its issuing corporation. (Chapter 21)

**Trespass** A tort committed by intentionally entering land that belongs to someone else, or remaining on the land after being asked to leave. (Chapter 5)

**Trespasser** A person on someone else's property without consent. (Chapter 6)

**Trial court** Any court in a state or federal system that holds formal hearings to determine the facts in a civil or criminal case. (Chapter 3)

**Trust** An entity that separates legal and beneficial ownership of assets. (Chapter 31)

**Trustee** Someone who manages the assets of a trust. (Chapter 31)

**Tying arrangement** An agreement to sell a product on the condition that the buyer also purchases a different (or tied) product. This arrangement is illegal under the Clayton Act if the seller uses significant power in the market for the tying product to shut out a substantial part of the market for the tied product. (Chapter 22)

**Tying product** In a tying arrangement, the product offered for sale on the condition that another product be purchased as well. (Chapter 22)

**Ultrahazardous activity** Conduct that is lawful yet unusual and much more likely to cause injury than normal commercial activity. (Chapter 6)

**Unconscionable contract** An agreement that a court refuses to enforce because it is fundamentally unfair as a result of unequal bargaining power by one party. (Chapter 10)

**Undisclosed principal** If a third party in an agency relationship does not know that the agent is acting for a principal, that principal is undisclosed. (Chapter 16)

**Undue influence** One party so dominates the thinking of another party to a contract that the dominant party cannot truly consent to the agreement. (Chapter 10)

**Unenforceable agreement** A contract where the parties intend to form a valid bargain but a court declares that some rule of law prevents enforcing it. (Chapter 9)

**Unfair labor practice** An act, committed by either a union or an employer, that violates the National Labor Relations Act, such as failing to bargain in good faith. (Chapter 19)

**Unidentified principal** If the third party in an agency relationship knows that the agent is acting for a principal but does not know the identity of the principal, that principal is unidentified. Formerly referred to as a *partially disclosed principal*. (Chapter 16)

**Unilateral contract** A binding agreement in which one party has made an offer that the other can accept only by action, not words. (Chapter 9)

**Unilateral mistake** Occurs when only one party negotiates based on a factual error. (Chapter 10)

**United Nations Convention on Contracts for the International Sale of Goods** A uniform, international law on trade that has been adopted by the United States and most of its principal trading partners. (Chapter 8)

**Unliquidated debt** A claimed debt that is disputed, either because the parties disagree over whether there is in fact a debt or because they disagree over the amount. (Chapter 11)

**U.S. Constitution** The supreme law of the United States. (Chapter 1)

**U.S. Trustee** Oversees the administration of bankruptcy law in a region. (Chapter 15)

**Usury** Charging interest at a rate that exceeds legal limits. (Chapter 10)

**Valid contract** A contract that satisfies all the law's requirements. (Chapter 9)

**Valuation** A process by which the Customs Service determines the fair value of goods being imported, for purposes of imposing a duty. (Chapter 8)

**Value** When a holder has already done something in exchange for an instrument. (Chapter 13)

# TABLE OF CASES

## A

Abkco Music v. Harrisongs Music, Ltd., 265n.7
Adair Standish Corp. v. NLRB, 317n.6
Albinger v. Harris, 482
Allen v. Beneficial Fin. Co. of Gary, 397n.6
Andreason v. Aetna Casualty & Surety Co., 134n.1
Apcar v. Gaus, 337
Arthur Murray Studio of Washington, Inc., *In re,* 392–393
Avenues in Leather, Inc. v. U. S., 114–115

## B

Baer v. Chase, 138
Baker v. Daves, 161–162
Bi-Economy Market, Inc. v. Harleysville Ins. Co. of New York, 182
Bieber v. People, 97–98
Bilski, *In re,* 439n.1
Blasco v. Money Services Center, 216–217
BLD Products, Ltd. v. Technical Plastics of Oregon, LLC, 333–334
Boeken v. Philip Morris, Incorporated, 73
Brenner v. Manson, 439n.4
Brentwood Medical Associates v. United Mine Workers of America, 318
Brunswick Hills Racquet Club Inc. v. Route 18 Shopping Center Associates, 178

## C

Carafano v. Metrosplash.com, Inc., 429–430
Carey v. Davis, 58n.4
Carnero v. Boston Scientific Corporation, 121–122
Carvin v. Arkansas Power and Light, 456
Central Arizona Water Conservation District v. EPA, 410
Centrifugal Casting Machine Co., Inc. v. American Bank & Trust Co., 120–121
Colby v. Burnham, 180, 180n.6, 181
Commonwealth v. Angelo Todesca Corp., 101
Commonwealth v. James, 263n.3

Conseco Finance Servicing Corp. v. Lee, 237
Corona Fruits & Veggies, Inc. v. Frozsun Foods, Inc., 233
Cruzan v. Director, Missouri Department of Health, 498, 498n.4
Culbertson v. Brodsky, 142–143

## D

Dacor Corporation v. Sierra Precision, 201n.14
Demasse v. ITT Corporation, 132
Detroit Institute of Arts Founders Society v. Rose, The, 171–173, 173n.2
Dickinson Arms-REO, L.P. v. Campbell, 474
Doe v. Gonzalez, 107n.2
Doe v. Liberatore, 272–273
Donchin v. Guerrero, 465–466, 466n.1
Dr. Miles Medical Co. v. John D. Park & Sons, 366n.3
DSAM Global Value Fund v. Altris Software, Inc., 383n.6

## E

Earl of Chesterfield v. Janssen, 154n.4
Eastex, Inc. v. NLRB, 313n.2
Ellis v. Grant Thornton, 381–382
Estate of Claussen, *In re,* 183–184
Estate of Josiah James Treloar Jr., *In re,* 495–496

## F

Federal Trade Commission v. Business Card Experts, Inc., 394
Fimbel v. DeClark, 158
Fleming v. Benzaquin, 76n.5
Ford Motor Credit Co. v. Sheehan, 71n.2
Foster v. Ohio State University, 140n.2
Freeman v. Barrs, 453

## G

Galella v. Onassis, 75n.4
George Grubbs Enterprises v. Bien, 72n.3

**Verdict** The decision of the fact finder in a case. (Chapter 3)

**Veto** The power of the president to reject legislation passed by Congress, terminating the bill unless Congress votes by a majority to override. (Chapter 4)

**Void agreement** An agreement that neither party may legally enforce, usually because the purpose of the bargain was illegal or because one of the parties lacked capacity to make it. (Chapter 9)

**Voidable contract** An agreement that, because of some defect, may be terminated by one party, such as a minor, but not by both parties. (Chapter 9)

**Voir dire** The process of selecting a jury. Attorneys for the parties and the judge may inquire of prospective jurors whether they are biased or incapable of rendering a fair and impartial verdict. (Chapter 3)

**Vouching** When an auditor chooses a transaction listed in the company's books and checks backwards for original data to support it. (Chapter 23)

# W

**Warranty** A guarantee that goods will meet certain standards. (Chapter 12)

**Warranty of fitness for a particular purpose** An assurance under the Uniform Commercial Code that the goods are fit for the special purpose for which the buyer intends them and of which the seller is aware. (Chapter 12)

**Warranty of merchantability** An assurance under the Uniform Commercial Code that the goods are fit for their ordinary purpose. (Chapter 12)

**Whistleblower** Someone who discloses illegal behavior. (Chapter 17)

**Will** A legal document that disposes of a testator's property after death. (Chapter 31)

**Winding up** The process whereby the debts of a partnership are paid and the remaining assets are distributed to the partners. (Chapter 20)

**Wire fraud and mail fraud** Involve the use of mail, telegram, telephone, radio, or television to obtain property by deceit. (Chapter 7)

**World Trade Organization** A group created by the General Agreement on Tariffs and Trade to resolve trade disputes. (Chapter 8)

**Writ** An order from a government compelling someone to do a particular thing. (Chapter 1)

**Wrongful discharge** The principle that an employer may not fire a worker for any reason that violates basic social rights, duties, or responsibilities. (Chapter 17)

# Z

**Zoning statutes** State laws that permit local communities to regulate land use. (Chapter 28)

Gibbs v. Babbitt, 416–417

Golden Rule Insurance Co. v. Hopkins, 510

Goodman v. Wenco Foods, Inc., 202

Goodson v. American Standard Insurance Company of Wisconsin, 512

Gradisher v. Check Enforcement Unit, Inc., 399, 399n.8

Guth v. Loft, 352n.2

### H

Hadley v. Baxendale, 181

Harris v. Forklift Systems, 300n.2

Harris v. Soley, 470

Hayes v. Haushalter, 382n.5

Hebert v. Enos, 86n.2

Hernandez v. Arizona Board of Regents, 82

Hoffman Plastic Compounds, Inc. v. National Labor Relations Board, 315–316

Hoffman, *In re,* 253

Hume v. United States, 154n.4

Hyler v. Garner, 183n.7

### I

In the Matter of Jeffrey M. Horning, 327n.1

In the Matter of Synchronal Corp., 396n.5

### J

Jackson v. Holiday Furniture, 248–249

James v. Meow Media, 10–11

Jane Doe and Nancy Roe v. Lynn Mills, 71

Jannusch v. Naffziger, 195–196

Jespersen v. Harrah's, 296

Jones v. Clinton, 38

### K

Keller v. Inland Metals All Weather Conditioning, Inc., 200–201

Kelsoe v. International Wood Products, Inc., 141n.3

Kennedy v. Louisiana, 50

King v. Head Start Family Hair Salons, Inc., 151–152

Kozloski v. American Tissue Services Foundation, 282–283

Krinsky v. Doe, 424n.1

Kuehn v. Pub Zone, 8–9

### L

Leegin Creative Leather Products, Inc. v. PSKS, Inc., 366–367

Lippman v. Shaffer, 351–352

### M

Marbury v. Madison, 51

Marks v. Local Corp., 301n.3

Mashburn v. Collins, 67n.1, 68

McGinley, *In re,* 445n.5

McInerney v. Charter Golf, Inc., 162n.8

Metro-Goldwyn-Mayer Studios Inc. v. Grokster, Ltd., 443

Metropolitan Creditors Service of Sacramento v. Sadri, 148–149, 149n.1

Michael A. Smyth v. The Pillsbury Co., 287

Milicic v. Basketball Marketing Company, Inc., 185

Mitchell v. Bank of America National Association, 486

### N

National Mining Ass'n v. U.S. Army Corps of Engineers, 411n.1

Natural Resources Defense Council v. Kempthorne, 416n.2

New Jersey Department of Environmental Protection v. Alden Leeds, Inc., 89–90

New York Times Co. v. Sullivan, 69–70

NLRB v. Babcock & Wilcox Co., 313n.3

NLRB v. Bell Aerospace Co., Div. of Textron, Inc., 316n.5

NLRB v. Gissel Packing Co., 314n.4

Novak v. Credit Bureau Collection Service, 135

### O

Oregon Steel Mills, Inc. v. Coopers & Lybrand, LLP, 379

Otsuka v. Polo Ralph Lauren Corporation, 262–264

### P

Palsgraf v. Long Island Railroad, 81

Pando v. Fernandez, 161n.7

Perfect 10, Inc. v. Google Inc., 442

Pollack v. Skinsmart Dermatology and Aesthetic Center, P.C., 447

Progressive Electric, Inc. v. National Labor Relations Board, 314–315

# R

Ra v. Superior Court, 87
Ray v. Beacon Hudson Mountain Corp., 460
Rice v. Oriental Fireworks Co., 349n.1
Ridgaway v. Silk, 331–332
RSL Communications v. Bildirici, 352–353

# S

Sakraida v. Ag Pro, Inc., 439n.3
Sawyer v. Mills, 163
Schauer v. Mandarin Gems of California, Inc., 173–174
Schoenwald, *In re,* 439n.2
Scott v. Beth Israel Medical Center, Inc., 426–427
Scott v. Mayflower Home Improvement Corp., 220–221
Sears, Roebuck and Co., *In re,* 395n.3
SEC v. Switzer, 364n.1
Smith v. City of Jackson, 301–302
Stanford v. Kuwait Airways Corp., 264n.4
Stinton v. Robin's Wood, Inc., 37
Stratton Oakmont, Inc. v. Prodigy Services Company, 428n.2

# T

Tarasoff v. Regents of the University of California, 58
Texas v. Johnson, 52
Thompson Medical Co., *In re,* 394n.2
Treadway v. Gateway Chevrolet Oldsmobile Inc., 400

# U

Union Pacific Railway Co. v. Cappier, 57–58
Uniroyal Goodrich Tire Company v. Martinez, 205–206
United States of America v. Angevine, 425
United States of America v. Kelly, 413–414
United States v. Dell Computer Corp., 396n.4
United States v. Dorsey, 99n.1
United States v. Dragon, 99
United States v. Kennard, 103
United States v. Loew's Inc., 369n.6
United States v. O'Hagen, 364
United States v. Syufy Enterprises, 367n.4
United States v. Trenton Potteries Co., 366n.2
Universal Services Fund Telephone Billing Litigation, 36n.1

# V

Vanlandingham v. Ivanow, 469n.3

# W

Wagenheim v. Alexander Grant & Co., 380n.4
Washington v. Glucksberg, 499
Waters v. Min Ltd., 154n.5
Wiener v. Southcoast Childcare Centers, Inc., 83
Wightman v. Consolidated Rail Corporation, 89n.3
Williams, *In re,* 250n.3
Wyoming.com, LLC v. Lieberman, 332

# Y

Yeagle v. Collegiate Times, 69

# INDEX

## A

Abandoned property, 483
Abandonment, scope of employment and, 272
Acceptance
   contract law, 139
   insurance contracts, 509
   of private property, 481–482
Access Device Fraud Act, 98
Accountant-client privilege, 384
Accountants' liability
   accountant-client relationship, 384
   audits, 376–377
   to clients, 379–380
   criminal liability, 383–384
   example, 375–376
   opinions, 377–378
   Sarbanes-Oxley provisions, 377
   to third parties, 380–383
Accredited investors, 362
Achievement of purpose, termination of agency
      relationships and, 267
Actual malice, 69–70
*Actus reus,* criminal law, 96
Adaptation, as real property, 453
Additional terms, in sales agreements, 197
Address, for corporation, 346
Adequate materials, implied warranty of
      habitability, 458
Adjudication, administrative law and, 60
Administrative agencies, federal government, 6
Administrative law, basic principles of, 6–7, 59–60
Administrative law judge, 60
Administrator/administratrix, defined, 493
Adversary system, trial proceedings, 39
Adverse opinion, 378
Adverse possession, real property law, 459–460
Affidavit, 104–105
Affirm
   in appeals, 42
   defined, 9
Affirmative action, employment discrimination
      laws, 299
Age discrimination, 301–302
Age Discrimination in Employment Act
      (ADEA), 301
Agency at will, termination of agency relationships
      and, 268

Agency relationships
   agent duties, 266
   breach of duty in, 267
   confidential information, 265
   control in, 264
   creation of, 263–264
   duty to principals, 264–267
   example of, 262–263
   fiduciary relations, 264
   liability in, 268–274
   outside benefits, 265
   principal's duties to, 267
   termination of, 267–268
Agent
   in agency relationship, 263
   contract liability for, 269–270
   tort liability of, 273–274
Agreement
   attachment of security interest, 229–230
   in contracts, 137–141
   duration of, 162–163
   written contracts, 160–161
Air pollution, government regulations on, 409–410
Air rights, as real property, 453
Akers, John, 17
Alcohol and drug testing, employee privacy, 286
Alternative dispute resolution
   arbitration, 29
   litigation *vs.,* 28–29
   mediation, 29
Altris Software, 383
Ambiguities, interpretation of, in negotiable
      instruments, 216–217
Amendments to U.S. Constitution, 5. *See also* specific
      amendments, e.g., First Amendment
Amendments to wills, 496
American Law Institute (ALI)
   Restatement (Second) of Contracts, 136
   UCC development, 192
Americans with Disabilities Act (ADA), employment
      discrimination and, 302–304
Amount of loss, insurable interest, 510
Anatomical gifts, 498
Ancillary agreements, restraint of trade, 150
Annual percentage rate (APR), consumer credit
      regulations concerning, 397
Annual reports
   corporate shareholders' right to, 354
   Form 10-K for securities, 363

Annuities, 514
Answer, in litigation, 33–34
Anticybersquatting Consumer Protection Act, 445
Antitrust regulations, 365–370
Apparent authority, principal's contract liability, 269
Appeal courts, 31
   options in, 42–43
Appeals, criminal law, 106–107
Appellant, 31
Appellate courts
   common law and, 56–57
   federal courts, 32–33
   state courts, 31
Appellee, 31
Appointments, executive powers for, 49
Appropriate behavior, between agency and
     principal, 265
Arbitration, 29
   collective bargaining agreement, 317–318
Arms Export Control Act, 113–114
Arraignment, 106
Arrest, 105
Arson, 99–100
Arthur Andersen, 375–376
Assault, as intentional tort, 70
Assignee, 174
Assignment of leased property, 473–474
Assignment of rights, 174–176
Assignor, 174
Assisted suicide, 498–499
Assumption of risk, 87
Attachment
   to future property, 230–231
   as real property, 453
   of security interest, 229–231
Audit committee, reports to, 378
Audit partners, term limits for, 378
Audits, accountants' liability and, 376–377
Authorization, scope of employment and, 272
Authorization cards, union organization, 313
Automatic stay, Chapter 7 bankruptcy, 248
Automobile insurance, 515–516

# B

Bad acts principle, monopoly regulations, 367–368
Bad-faith behavior, nondischargeable debts, 252–253
Bad faith principle
   domain name protection and, 445
   insurers, 511
Bailee, 483–485
Bailment, private property and, 483–487
Bailor, 483–484
   rights and duties of, 486
Bait and switch sales practices, 395
Bank fraud, 99–100

Bank privacy, online privacy regulations, 427
Bankruptcy
   bankruptcy estate, 249
   chapter 7 liquidation, 246–253
   chapter 11 liquidation, 253–255
   chapter 13 consumer reorganizations, 255–256
   examples of, 244–245
   overview of, 245–246
   payment of claims, 250
Bargaining
   collective bargaining agreement, 316–317
   consideration and, 141–142
   invitation to, 137
Bargaining unit, union organization and, 316
Baskin, Sheldon, 15–16, 22
Battery, as intentional tort, 70
Battles of the form, UCC Section 2-207 and, 197
Bearer payer, as negotiable instrument, 215
Beneficiaries
   incidental beneficiaries, 172
   insurance, 508
   third party beneficiary, 171–173
   in trusts, 499
Berne Convention, 444
Best available technology principle, water pollution
     standards, 411
Beyond a reasonable doubt standard, criminal law, 96
Bilateral contracts, 131
Bilateral mistake, 159
Bill, defined, 55
Blodget, Henry, 426
Blue sky laws, 365
Boards of directors, corporations, 347–348,
     350–353
Body of precedent, incorporation process and, 346
Boesky, Ivan, 363
Bona fide occupational qualification, defenses to
     discrimination charges and, 299
Breach
   of contract, 179
   of duty, 84
   negligence and, 81
   of trust, accountants' liability for, 380
Breach of duty by agents, 267
Bribery, international law and, 122–123
Buckeye Union Insurance Co., 511
Building codes, 469
Buildings, as real property, 452
Burden of proof
   bailment and, 485–486
   criminal law, 96
   trial proceedings, 40
Burnham, Alexander, 180–181
Business judgment rule, 350–353
"Business method patents," 439
Business organizations
   corporations, 328–331, 344–355
   crimes against, 98–100

crimes committed by, 101–104
example of, 326–327
general partnerships, 334–337
law and, 16–17
limited liability companies, 331–334
limited liability partnerships, 337
limited partnerships and limited liability
    partnerships, 338–339
LLC *versus* corporate structures, 334
nondischargeable debts of, 252
professional corporation, 339
sole proprietorships, 327–328
tort law in, 74–75
Buyer in ordinary course of business (BIOC), secured
    transaction, 236–237
Buyers
past performance, in land contracts, 161
protection of, 236–237
remedies in sales agreements, 198
Bylaws, for corporation, 348
Bystander cases, 57–58

## C

Caches, cyberlaw and, 423–424
Campaign rules, union organization, 313
Capacity, in contract law, 154–155
Cardozo, Benjamin, 81
Case adjudication, constitutional law concerning, 49
Casualty insurance, 513
*Causa mortis,* 480n.1, 481
C corporations, 330
Certainty
reasonable certainty, 164–165, 181
in written contracts, 164–165
Certificate of limited partnership, 338
Changing parties, landlord-tenant laws, 472–473
Chapter 7 bankruptcy liquidation, 246–253
automatic stay, 248
creditors, 247
involuntary petition, 247
petition filing, 246
trustee responsibility, 247
voluntary petition, 246–247
Chapter 11 bankruptcy reorganization, 253–255
Chapter 13 consumer reorganization
    bankruptcy, 255–256
Charter
of incorporation, 346–347
for limited liability companies, 332
Check, as negotiable instrument, 213
Checks and balances, constitutional guarantee of, 50–51
Checksfield, James, 384
Chief executive officers (CEOs)
compensation for, 354–355
ethical issues facing, 22

Child labor, international law
    and, 117
Children, trusts for, 500
Children's Online Privacy Protection Act of 1998
    (COPPA), 427
Children's share of will, 495
Children's television advertising, ethical
    issues in, 21
Civil law
basic principles of, 7–8
criminal law comparisons, 95–97
torts under, 67
Claim adverse to owner, real property law, 459
Claims payments
bankruptcy, 250–251
insurance contracts limitations, 509–510
Class action, in litigation, 35
Classes of stock, 347
Classification, tariffs, 114
Clayton Act, 368–369
Clean Air Act of 1970, 60, 409–410
Clean opinion, 377
Clean Water Act (CWA), 411–412
Clients, accountants' liability to, 379–380, 384
Close corporations, 329–330
Closing arguments, trial proceedings and, 41
Closing procedures, real property sale, 458
Codicils to wills, 496
Colby, William, 180–181
Collateral, possession and disposition, 238–239
Collateral promise, contract law, 164
Collective bargaining agreement, 316–317
duty to bargain and, 317
enforcement, 317–318
strikes and lockouts, 319–320
Collective bargaining unit, union organization
    and, 312
Collision insurance, 515
Color discrimination. *See* race discrimination
Comment letter, securities offerings, 362
Commerce Clause (U.S. Constitution), 49
Commercial exploitation, tort law and, 75
Commercial paper
fundamental "rule" of, 213–216
negotiability of, 214–216
as negotiable instruments, 212, 214–215
Commingling of assets, piercing the corporate veil
    principle and, 348
Committee work, statutory law and, 55–56
Common carriers, bailment proceedings and, 487
Common law
basic principles, 56–57
contract law and, 135–136
defined, 5
employment security protections in, 281–285, 285
found property and, 483
insurance contracts, 509–513
*Stare decisis* and, 57

Communication of false statement, intentional
    tort and, 68
Communications Decency Act of 1996, 428–430
Community of interest, bargaining unit as, 316
Community property, 455
    spouse's share of will, 495
Comparative negligence, 88–89
Compensation for corporate officers and directors,
    354–355
Compensatory damages, 71–72, 87, 181
Competition, between agent and principal, 265
Complaint, in litigation, 33–34
Compliance programs, 102
Comprehensive auto insurance, 515
Comprehensive Environmental Response,
    Compensation, and Liability Act (CERCLA),
    412–414
Computer crime, 95, 98–99
Computer Fraud and Abuse Act (CFAA), 98,
    430–431
Concerted action, unions and,
    318–320
Concurrent estate, 454–454
Condemnation, eminent domain and, 461
Conduct outlawed
    criminal law, 96
    off-duty conduct, employee privacy and, 286
Conference of Commissioners on Uniform
    State Laws, 493
Confirmation of Chapter 11 bankruptcy plan, 254
Confirmed irrevocable letter of credit, 119–121
Conflict of interest
    accounting regulations and, 378
    between agency principals, 265
Conforming goods, sales agreements, 198
Congressional powers
    committee work and, 55–56
    under constitutional law, 48–49
Conscious uncertainty, contract law, 159
Consent
    in agency relationship, 263–264
    in contract law, 155–159
Consequential damages, as contract remedy, 181–182
Consideration, contract law, 141–143
Consideration of marriage, promise made in, 164
Consolidated Omnibus Budget Reconciliation Act
    (COBRA), 281
Constitutional law, 48–54
    powers granted under, 48–49
Constitutional rights, 50–51
Constitutions, as contemporary law source, 4–5
Constructive delivery, transfer of personal property
    through, 481
Constructive eviction, 468
Consulting services, regulation of, 378
Consumer credit
    contract, as negotiable instrument, 220
    regulations concerning, 397–401

Consumer exception, negotiable
    instruments, 220
Consumer expectation test, strict liability
    and, 205
Consumer goods, perfection of, 234–236
Consumer law
    consumer credit, 397–401
    deceptive acts or practices, 393–394
    example of, 392–393
    insurance claims and, 511–512
    product safety, 402
    sales, 393–397
    warranty protections, 401
Consumer Leasing Act (CLA), 401
Consumer Product Safety Act (CPSA), 402
Consumer reporting agencies, regulations
    concerning, 398
Consumer sales
    strict liability and, 204–206
    warranties and product liability, 202–203
Contemporary Books, 180–181
Contemporary law, sources of, 4–7
Continuous possession for statutory period, 459
Contract carriers, bailment proceedings and, 487
Contract law. See also bankruptcy
    acceptance, 139
    accountants' liability to clients, 379
    agent liability in, 269–270
    agreements, 137–141
    assignment and delegation, 174–176
    breach in, 179
    capacity, 154–155
    collective bargaining agreements, 316–317
    conscious uncertainty, 159
    consent issues, 155–159
    consideration, 141–143
    consideration of marriage promise, 164
    consumer credit contract, 220
    counteroffers, 139
    defined, 131
    electronic contracts and signatures, 165–166
    elements of, 131
    employment issues in, 150–151, 283
    estate executor promises, 164
    examples of, 129–130
    exculpatory clauses, 152–153
    expiration, 139
    gambling and, 148–149
    illusory promise, 142
    impossibility in, 179
    insurance contracts, 509–513
    judicial activism, remedies by, 133–135
    judicial activism vs. judicial restraint, 130
    leases, 466–467
    legality issues, 150–153
    mirror image rule, 139–140
    misrepresentation and fraud in, 156–158
    mistakes in, 159

noncompete clauses, 151–152
noncompetition agreements, 129
novation contract, 345
performance and discharge under, 176–179
principal's liability in, 268–269
promise to pay debt of another, 164
promissory estoppel and, 133–134
purpose of, 130
real property sales contract and title
    examination, 458
rejection, 139
remedies in, 133–135, 179–186
rescinding in, 155
restatement (second) of, 136
restraint of trade and, 150
revocation, 139
sale of business, 150
sales agreements, 194–196
sources of, 135–136
statute of limitations, 179
subject matter destruction, 139
termination of offers
third party claims, 170–171
tortious interference with, 74
type of, 131–133
unconscionable contracts, 153–154
written contracts, 160–165
Contract prohibition
    assignment of rights and, 174
    delegation of duties and, 176
Contractual relations, strict liability and,
    204–206
Contract *vs.* gift, 482–483
Contributory negligence, 88–89
Control
    in agency relationship, 264
    in trusts, 500
Controlling the Assault of Non-Solicited Pornography
    and Marketing Act, 428
Control of bailment, 484
Cookie files, cyberlaw and, 423–424
Copyright law, 441–444
Corporate opportunity doctrine, 352
Corporations
    business judgment rule, 350–353
    bylaws, 348
    close corporations, 329–330
    corporate management of, 349
    death of, 348–349
    directors and officers, 347–348
    duration of, 328
    example of, 344
    generally, 328–329
    governance rules, 355
    incorporation process, 345–347
    limited liability company structure *vs.*, 334
    limited liability of, 328
    logistics of, 328

promoter's liability, 345
S corporations, 330–331
shareholders in, 353–355
tax issues, 328–329
termination, 349
transferability of ownership interest, 328
Corruption perception index, 123
Cost-benefit analysis, environmental law and, 409
Costs of unethical behavior, 18
Counteroffer, contract law, 139
Court systems, 29–33
    federal courts, 31–32
    incorporation process and, 346–347
    state courts, 29–31
Covenant
    insurance policies, 511
    leases, 466–467
Cover, sales agreements, 198
Creditor beneficiary, 172
Creditors
    Chapter 7 bankruptcy, 247
    secured transactions, priorities of, 237–238
Creditors' committee, Chapter 11 bankruptcy, 254
Credit reports, regulations concerning, 398–399
Criminal law
    basic principles of, 7–8
    crimes against businesses, 98–100
    crimes by businesses, 101–104
    example of, 94–95
    Internet regulations, 430–431
    landlord-tenant law and, 473–474
    landowner's liability and, 83
    social costs of, 95–97
    statutory law and, 55
Criminal liability, accountants' liability as,
    383–384
Criminal process, 104–107
Cruzan, Nancy, 498
Customers, organization's responsibility to, 22
Cyberlaw
    copyright issues and, 442
    domain name regulations, 445
    example of, 422–423
    Internet crime, 430–431
    Internet service providers and web hosts,
        428–430
    patent issues and, 439
    privacy issues, 423–427
    spam regulations, 428

## D

Damages
    agent's breach of duty, 267
    compensatory damages, 71–72, 87, 181
    consequential damages, 181–182, 198–199

Damages (*continued*)
  duty to mitigate, 472
  duty to use premises properly, 472
  incidental damages, 182, 198–199
  mitigation of, 186
  punitive damages, 72–73, 87
  in sales agreements, 198–199
  tort law on, 71–74
Debt
  nondischargeable, 251–252
  reaffirmation of, 252–253
Debtor
  in bankruptcy, 246
  Chapter 13 bankruptcy reorganization, 255–256
  in possession, Chapter 11 bankruptcy, 254–255
  rights of, in secured transactions, 230
Debt payments, promise to pay debt of
    another, 164
Decedent, defined, 493
Deceptive sales acts or practices, 393–394
Deductibles on insurance, 516
Deeds, real property sale, 458–459
Defamation
  employers' liability for, 283
  as intentional tort, 68–69
Defamatory statement, 68
Default, in secured transactions, 238–239
Default judgment, in litigation, 34
Defective products
  bailment liability issues, 486–487
  duty to disclose, real property law, 458
  liability law and, 89
  negotiable instruments, 219
  tenant remedies for defective conditions, 469
Defendant
  comparative and contributory negligence, 88–89
  criminal law, 95
  defined, 9
  trial proceedings and case of, 41
Defense
  assumption of risk, 87
  criminal law, 97
  against negligence, 87–89
Deferred annuity contract, 514
Definiteness, in contract law, 137–138
Delaware, incorporation process in, 345–347
Delegatee, delegation of duties
    and, 175
Delegation of duties, 174–176
Delegator, delegation of duties and, 175
Delivery, personal property transfer, 480–481
Dell Computer Corporation, 396
Deponent, in litigation, 35
Depositions, in litigation, 35
Detroit Institute of Arts, 170–173
Developing countries, organizational responsibilities
    in, 23–24
Devisee, defined, 493

Different terms, in sales agreements, 197–198
Digital Millennium Copyright Act, 444
Digital music and movies, copyright law and, 437,
    443–444
Directors, of corporations, 347–348
  compensation for, 354–355
  election and removal of, 354
Disability insurance, 515
Disabled person, employment discrimination
    against, 302–304
Disaffirmance, capacity in contract law and, 155
Discharge
  Chapter 7 bankruptcy, 251–253
  Chapter 11 bankruptcy, 254
  Chapter 13 bankruptcy reorganization, 256
  in contract law, 176–179
Disclaimers
  express warranties, 200
  of opinion, 378
Disclosure provisions, Truth-in-Lending
    Act (TILA), 397
Discovery
  e-discovery, 36
  in litigation, 35–36
  motion to compel, 36
Dishonesty, nondischargeable debts and, 252
Disinterested directors and shareholders, business
    judgment rule and, 350
Disparate impact principle
  age discrimination law, 301
  employment discrimination laws, 296
Disparate treatment principle
  age discrimination law, 301
  employment discrimination laws, 295–296
Disposition, of collateral, 239
Dispute resolution, close corporations, 330
Dissociation, of partnership, 336
Dissolution, of partnership, 336–337
Diversity cases, 31
Documentation, in litigation, 35
Domain names, trademark law concerning, 445
Domestic corporation, 346
Donee, personal property gifts, 480
Donor
  defined, 493
  personal property gifts, 480
Door-to-door sales, FTC regulations concerning,
    396–397
Draft, as negotiable instrument, 213
Drawee, drafts paid by, 213
Drawor, drafts issued by, 213
Due care, duty of, 81
  of bailee, 485
Due diligence, accountants' liability and, 382
Due process
  Fifth Amendment right to, 52–53
  procedural due process, 53
Dumping, import controls, 115

Durable power of attorney, 497
Duration
    of corporations, 328
    of limited liability companies, 333
    of limited partnerships, 338
Duty, breach of, 84
Duty in agency relationships, 264–266
Duty of care, 81
    agency relationships, 266
    business judgment rule, 350, 352–353
    trust administration, 501
Duty of loyalty
    business judgment rule, 350–352
    trust administration, 501
Duty to bargain, union organization and, 317
Duty to deliver possession, 468
Duty to disclose defects, 458
Duty to maintain premises, landlord-tenant
    laws, 468–469
Duty to mitigate, 471–472
Duty to pay rent, 471
Duty to return security deposit, 470
Duty to use premises properly, 472

# E

Easements, 455
E-commerce, business method patents and, 439
Economics
    employment discrimination law and, 298
    environmental law and, 413
    intellectual property law and, 438
    monopolies and, 367
Economic strike, 319
E-discovery, 36
Eisner, Michael, 355
Electronic Communications Privacy Act (ECPA)
    employee privacy and, 286–287
    online privacy provisions, 426
Electronic contracts and signatures, contract law and,
    165–166
Electronic Signatures in Global and National
    Commerce Act (E-Sign), 165–166
Electronic workplace monitoring, employee
    privacy and, 286–287
Element, defined, 68
E-mail privacy
    government regulations and, 423–427
    Internet fraud and, 430–431
    phishing and, 431
    spam regulations, 428
Embezzlement, 100
Eminent domain, 461
Emotional distress, infliction of
    employers' liability for, 284
    as intentional tort, 70–71

Employee handbook, as contract, 283
Employees
    online privacy issues for, 426
    organization's responsibility to, 22
    principal's tort liability, 270–271
    safety and privacy rights, 285–287
    union organization and rights of, 313–314
Employers
    liability of, 283–284
    union organization and rights of, 314–315, 317
Employment, scope of, 271–272
Employment contracts, 129,
    150–151. See also labor law
Employment discrimination laws. See also labor law
    affirmative action, 299
    age discrimination, 301–302
    Americans with Disabilities Act, 302–304
    defenses to discrimination charges,
        298–299
    Equal Pay Act of 1963, 295
    example of, 294–295
    pregnancy and, 300
    procedures and remedies, 300
    proof of discrimination, 295–297
    race discrimination, 297–298
    religious discrimination, 298
    sexual harassment, 299–300
    Title VII, 295–300
Employment law
    employment security provisions, 280–285
    example of, 279
    financial protection, 287–288
    history of, 280
    whistleblowing, 284–285
    workplace safety and privacy, 285–287
Endangered Species Act (ESA), 415–416
Engagement letter, accountant to client, 379
Enron Corporation, 355, 376
Entry, adverse possession and, 459
Environment
    air pollution laws, 409–410
    laws and regulations concerning, 408–417
    natural resources laws, 414–417
    waste disposal, 412–414
    water pollution laws, 410–412
    World Trade Organization and, 116–117
Environmental impact statement (EIS)
    requirements, 415
Environmental Protection Agency (EPA)
    as administrative law, 60
    air quality standards, 409–410
    waste disposal regulations and, 412–413
    water pollution standards, 411–412
Equal Credit Opportunity Act (ECOA), 400
Equal Employment Opportunity Commission (EEOC),
    300–301
    disabled persons employment discrimination,
        302–304

Equal Pay Act of 1963, 295
Equal protection clause (Fourteenth Amendment), 50–51, 54
Equitable interests, as contract remedies, 183–184
Equity, common law and, 5
Ernst & Young, 382
Error of law, appellate courts and, 31
Essential functions principle, disabled persons employment discrimination, 302–304
Estate
  bankruptcy estate, 249
  defined, 493
  as real property, 454–455
Estate executor, promises made by, 164
Estate planning
  definitions, 493
  example, 492
  probate law, 493
  purpose and goals, 493
  trusts, 499–501
  wills, 494–499
Ethical behavior
  bailment and, 483
  bankruptcies and, 252
  basic principles of, 18–19
  benefits of, 17–18
  consumer product safety, 402
  contracts, 133
  disclosure and, 158
  employment security and, 282, 284
  international law and, 117
  land use regulations, 460–461
  strike activity and, 319
Ethics
  checklist for, 19–24
  decision-making checklist for, 20–24
  defined, 16
  importance of, 17–18
  social benefits of, 17
European Union (EU), 117–118
Eviction proceedings, landlord-tenant laws, 468
Exclusionary rule, 105
Exclusive possession, real property law, 459
Exclusivity, union organization and, 312
Exculpatory clauses, contract law, 152–153
Executed contracts, 133
Executive committee, in partnerships, 335–336
Executive Order 11246 (affirmative action), 299
Executive powers, under constitutional law, 49
Executor/executrix, defined, 493
Executory contracts, 133
Exempt property, bankruptcy estate, 249
Expectation interest, as contract remedy, 180–181
Expiration, contract law, 139
Export controls, 113–114
Express authority, principal's contract liability, 268
Express contracts, 132
Express warranties, 200

Externality, environmental law and, 409
Extraordinary care, duty of bailee to use, 485
Extraterritoriality, 121
*Exxon Valdez* case, tort reform and, 74

# F

Facebook, The, Inc., 344–347
Factual cause, negligence and, 81, 84–85
Failure to observe formalities, piercing the corporate veil principle and, 348
Failure to warn
  negligence and, 203
  strict liability and, 204–205
Fair and Accurate Credit Transactions Act (FACTA), 398–399
Fair Credit Billing Act (FCBA), 398
Fair Credit Reporting Act (FCRA), 398, 401
Fair dealing, insurance policies, 511
Fair Debt Collection Practices Act (FDCPA), 399
Fair Labor Standards Act, 287–288
Fair representation, duty of, 320
Fair use doctrine, copyright law, 441–442
False Claims Act, 284
False imprisonment, 70
False statements, 68
  contract law, 156
Family and Medical Leave Act (FMLA), 281
Fannie Mae, 355
Federal courts, 31–32
  constitutional law concerning, 49
Federal government
  checks and balances in, 50–51
  organizational structure of, 6
Federalism
  constitutional law and, 48
  defined, 4
Federal question cases, 31
Federal sentencing guidelines, 102
Federal Trade Commission Act (FTC Act), 393–397
Federal Trade Commission (FTC)
  consumer law provisions, 393–397
  Internet fraud policies, 430–431
  online privacy policies and, 425–427
  securities transactions, 365, 368
Federal Unemployment Tax Act (FUTA), 288
Fee simple absolute, 454
Fee simple defeasible, 454
Felony, criminal law, 96
Feuerstein, Aaron, 17
Fiduciaries, securities transactions, 363
Fiduciary duty
  corporate management, 349
  insider trading as breach of, 363–364
  partnerships, 336
  trust administration, 501

Fiduciary relationship, agency and, 264
Fifth Amendment
  eminent domain and, 461
  guarantees in, 5
  protected rights under, 50–51, 52–53
  self-incrimination protections under, 105
Filing procedures
  for corporate termination, 349
  financial statements, perfection in, 231–232
Finance charges, consumer credit regulations
    concerning, 397
Financial protection of employees, 287–288
Financing for partnerships, 335
Financing statement
  contents, 232–233
  filing place and duration, 233–234
  perfection in, 231–236
First Amendment
  examples of protection under, 47–48
  guarantees in, 5
  online privacy and, 424
  protected rights under, 50–52
First sale doctrine, copyright law, 441
Fixtures, as real property, 453
Flag burning, as First Amendment right, 48–49, 52
Flexibility
  close corporations, 330
  common law and, 57
  for limited liability companies, 333
Foreign corporation, 346
Foreign Corrupt Practices Act (FCPA),
    122–123, 365
Foreign policy, constitutional law and, 49
Foreseeable harm
  crime provisions, landlord-tenant law and,
    473–474
  negligence and, 81, 84–86
Form 8-K for securities, 363
Form 10-K for securities, 363
Form 10-Q for securities, 363
Found property, 483
Fourteenth Amendment
  protected rights under, 50–51, 54
  search and seizure protections, 105
Fourth Amendment
  guarantees in, 5
  online privacy and, 424–425
  protected rights under, 50–51
FP Investments, Inc., 382
Fraud
  accountants' liability for, 380
  accountants' third party liability, 382
  contract law, 156–158
  criminal fraud, 99–100
  insurance policies, 511
  as intentional tort, 70
  Internet fraud, 430–431
  materiality and, 156–157

  piercing the corporate veil principle and, 349
  Securities Exchange Act provisions concerning,
    382–383
  UCC statutes of, 196
Fraudulent transfers, bankruptcy estate, 249
Freehold estate, 454
Free speech
  First Amendment right of, 50–52
  online privacy and, 424
Fresh start, bankruptcy proceedings, 251
Friedman, Milton, 22–23
Full performance by seller, written contract
    agreements, 161
Full warranty, regulations concerning, 401
Fully disclosed principal, agent liability and, 269

## G

Gambling, contract law and, 148–149
Gap fillers, sales agreements, 198
Gateway Learning Corporation, 425–426
Gender issues, equal protection clause (Fourteenth
    Amendment), 54
General Agreement on Tariffs and Trade (GATT), 116
General Electric Co. (GE), ultrasound screening
    controversy and, 21
General intent, criminal law, 96
Generally accepted accounting principles
    (GAAP), 377
Generally accepted auditing standards (GAAS), 377
General partnerships, 334–337
Generic trademarks, 445
Gifts
  anatomical gifts, 498
  contracts vs., 482–483
  inter vivos and causa mortis gifts, 481
  as personal property, 480–483
Gillette Co., 22
Global Crossing, 376
Globalization, international law and, 111–112
Going effective, securities transactions, 362
Good faith
  in contract law, 177–178
  employment security and, 280
  found property and, 483
  insurance policies, 511
  negotiable instruments, 218
  union duty of fair representation and, 320
Goods
  bailment and loss or harm to, 485–486
  conforming goods, 198
  contract for sale of, 165
  perfection of consumer goods, 234–236
  as real property, 453
  UCC provisions concerning, 136, 194
  warranties and product liability, 199–206

Good workmanship, implied warranty of
    habitability, 458
Government contracts, affirmative action, 299
Government powers, constitutional law and, 48
Government regulations
    accounting laws, 378–384
    air pollution laws, 409–410
    antitrust act, 365–370
    cyberlaw regulations, 424–427
    example of, 360–361
    patents, 438–440
    securities laws, 361–365
    spam regulations, 428
    water pollution laws, 410–412
Gramm-Leach-Bliley Privacy Act of 1999
    (GLB), 427
Grant, easements and, 456
Grantee, in real property law, 452
Grantor
    defined, 493
    in real property law, 452
    in trusts, 499
Grievance, collective bargaining agreement, 317–318
Gross negligence, exculpatory clauses, 152–153

# H

Habitability
    duty to maintain premises, 468–469
    implied warranty of, 458, 469
Hacking, cyberlaw concerning, 430
Happiness, money and, 17
Harm
    accountants' harm to client, 379–380
    nonphysical, tort liability and, 273
Harriman, Pamela, 501
Harriman, W. Averell, 501
Haupt, Arthur, 15–16
Health care proxy, 498
Health insurance, 514–515
Health maintenance organizations (HMOs),
    514–515
"Hedonic treadmill," 17
Heir, defined, 493
Hiring, negligence in, principal's tort liability, 271
Hiring, truth in, 283
Holder, for order paper, 218
Holder in due course
    defenses against, 219–220
    negotiable instruments and, 218–220
Holding, defined, 9
Holographic will, 494
Home mortgage loans, consumer credit regulations
    concerning, 397–398
Hooker Chemical Company, 412–413
Hostile work environment, sexual harassment laws, 300

# I

Identity theft, 98–99
    cyberlaw concerning, 431
Identity Theft and Assumption Deterrence Act,
    99, 431
Illegality, impossibility in contract and, 179
Illusory promise, contract law, 142
Implied authority, principal's contract liability, 268
Implied contracts, 132
Implied warranties, 201–203
    of fitness, 202
    of habitability, real property law, 458, 469
Import controls, 113–116
Impossibility, in contract law, 179
Inadequate capitalization, piercing the corporate veil
    principle and, 349
Incidental beneficiaries, 172
Incidental damages
    as contract remedy, 182
    sales agreements, 198–199
Incorporation process, 345–347
Incorporator, duties of, 346
Independent contractors, principal's tort liability,
    270–271
Indictment, 106
Indorsement (payee's signature), 217–218
Industrial discharges, water pollution standards,
    411–412
Informant, 104–105
Information
    agent's duty to provide, 266
    shareholders' right to, 353–354
Infringement, copyright law, 441
Initial public offering (IPO), 362
Injunction
    as contract remedy, 184–185
    defined, 5
Injury
    intentional tort and, 68
    landlord-tenant laws and, 473–474
    negligence and, 81, 86–87
Innkeepers, bailment policies and, 487
Insanity defense, criminal law, 97
Insider trading, securities transactions, 363–364
Instructions, agent's duty to obey, 266
Insurable interest, 509–510
Insurance, defined, 508
Insurance claims
    limitations on, 509–510
    litigation concerning, 27–28
    refusal to pay valid claims, 511–512
Insurance policies
    automobile insurance, 515–516
    contract, 509–513
    disability insurance, 515

example, 507–508
health insurance, 514–515
liability insurance, 515
life insurance, 513–514
property insurance, 513
terminology, 508
Insured, defined, 508
Insurer
bad faith by, 511
defined, 508
refusal to accept settlement offer by, 512
Intellectual property law
copyrights, 441–444
example, 437
historical background, 438
patents, 438–440
trademarks, 444–446
trade secrets, 446–447
Intentional torts, 68–71
battery and assault, 70
defamation, 68–69
emotional distress, infliction of, 70–71
exculpatory clauses, 152–153
false imprisonment, 70
fraud, 70
infliction of emotional distress, 284
principal's liability in, 272
public personalities and, 69–70
Intent to create contract, UCC Section 2-207
provision on, 197
Interest. *See also* transferability of interest
equitable interests, 180, 183–184
expectation interest, 180
insurable interest, 509–510
purchase money security interest (PMSI),
234–236
reliance interest, 180, 183
remedies in contract law and, 179–181
restitution interest, 180, 183
Internal Revenue Service (IRS), accountant-client
privilege, 384
International copyright treaties, 444
International financial reporting standards
(IFRS), 377
International law
example, 111–112
foreign investment, 122–123
regional agreements, 117–118
sales agreements, 118–121
trade regulation and, 112–117
International patent treaties,
440–441
International trademark treaties, 446
Internet domain names, regulations concerning, 445
Internet searching, copyright law, 442
Internet service providers (ISPs), government
regulation of, 426, 428–430
Interpretive rules, administrative law and, 60

Interrogatories, in litigation, 35
Interstate commerce, under constitutional law, 49
Interview guidelines, disabled persons employment
discrimination, 303–304
*Inter vivos* gifts, 482
Intestacy, wills and, 496–497
Intestate, defined, 493
Intrusion, tort law and, 74–75
Investigation, administrative law and, 60
Invitees, liability of, 82
Involuntary bailment, 484
Involuntary petition, Chapter 7 bankruptcy, 247
Irrevocable trust, 500
Issue, in wills, 496
Issuer
of promissory notes and drafts, 213
securities transactions, 361

# J

Joint and several liability
accountants' liability, 383
agency liability, 269
partnerships, 335
Joint tenancy, 454
Judicial activism, contract remedies and,
133–135
Judicial power, constitutional law and, 49
Judicial review, constitutional law
concerning, 49
Judicial rulings, statutory law and, 55
Jurisdiction, trial courts, 31
Jury right
criminal law, 95
trial proceedings, 39–40
Justifiable reliance, misrepresentation and
fraud, 156

# K

Key person life insurance, 510
Kilts, James, 22
King, Martin Luther Jur., 16

# L

Labor law. *See also* employment contracts; employment
discrimination law
collective bargaining, 316–318
concerted action, 318–320
duty to bargain and, 317
online privacy issues in, 426

Labor law (*continued*)
  strike actions, 309–310
  union history, 311–312
  union organization, 312–316
  union regulation, 320
Labor-Management Relations Act, 311–313
Labor-Management Reporting and Disclosure
    Act, 312, 320
Land, as real property, 452
Land interests, written contract agreements, 161
Landlord
  defined, 466
  duty to mitigate, 471–472
  liability for injury, 473–474
Landlord-tenant law
  change in parties, 472–473
  examples, 465–466
  injuries, 473–474
  landlord's duties, 468–470
  lease provisions, 466–467
  tenancy categories, 467
  tenant's duties, 471–472
Landowner's duty, negligence and, 82
Land use regulation, 460–461
Lanham Act, 444–445
Larceny, 98
Law
  fascination with, 4
  importance of, 4
  morality and, 7–8
  power and, 3
  sources of, 5–6
Law case, defined, 8
Lease
  consumer leases, 401
  landlord's duties in, 469
  landlord-tenant law, 466–467
Leber, Eugene, 511
Legal age, in wills, 494
Legal cause, defined, 84n.1
Legal duty, employee performance of, 282
Legal rights, employment security
    and, 282
Legislation, constitutional law
    and, 49
Legislative rules, administrative law and, 60
Letter of credit, 119–121
Levine, Dennis, 363
Liability
  accountants' liability, 375–384
  agency relationships, 268–274
  automobile insurance, 515
  bailment provision, 485–487
  common carriers and contract
    carriers, 487
  of corporations, 328–331
  exculpatory clauses, 152–153
  insider trading, 363–364

invitees, 82
joint and several liability, 269, 335
landlord, 473–474
of landowner's, criminal and tort law, 83
licensees, 82
in limited liability companies, 331–334
of limited liability companies, 333–334
limited liability partnerships, 337–338
partnerships, 334–335, 335–336
product liability, 199–206
professional corporations, 339
promoter's liability, 345
sales agreements, 192–199
in sole proprietorships, 327–328
strict liability, 89–90
tenants, 471–472, 473
trespassers, 82
warranties and products, 199–205
Liability insurance, 515
Libel, defined, 68
Library of Congress, Copyright Office, 441
License, real property and, 457
Licensee, 82
Lie detector tests, employee privacy, 286
Life estate, 454
Life insurance, 513–514
  insurable interest, 510
  key person life insurance, 510
Life tenant, 454
Limited liability
  of corporations, 328
  S corporations, 330
Limited liability company (LLC), 331–334
  corporate structure *vs.*, 334
Limited liability partnerships (LLPs),
    337–338
  limited partnerships *vs.*, 338
Limited partnerships, 338
Limited warranty, regulations concerning, 401
Litigation
  affirmative action, 299
  alternative dispute resolution *vs.*, 28–29
  complaint, 33–34
  defined, 28
  out-of-court settlements, prevalence of, 39
  pleadings, 33
  summary judgment and, 37–38
  of trusts, 501
Living trust, 500
Living wills, 498
Lockouts
  labor law and, 320
  no strike/no lockout agreements, 317
Logistics, of corporations, 328
Lost property, 483
*Lost Victory,* 180–181
Love Canal disaster, 412–413
Lowest liability taxpayer, 82

# M

Madrid Agreement, 446
Magnuson-Moss Warranty Act, 401
Mail fraud, 100
Mail order sales regulations,
    395–396
Majority rule, contract agreements, 162–163
Maker, of promissory note, 213
Malden Mills factory fire, 17
Malice, actual malice, 69
Managed care health plans, 514–515
Management issues
    corporate management, 349
    corporate opportunity and, 352
    limited partnerships, 338
    partnerships, 335–336
    self-dealing and, 350–353
Managerial employees, bargaining unit, exclusion
        from, 316
Marital trust, 500
Material
    insurance contracts, 510
    in securities transactions, 363
Materiality, fraud and, 156–157
McCarger, James, 180–181
Mediation, defined, 29
Medicare fraud, 94–95, 100
Meeting of the minds principle, contract agreement, 137
Meetings, of shareholders, 354
Mens rea, criminal law, 96
Mental examination, in litigation, 35–36
Mentally impaired persons, 155
Merchantability, implied warranty of, 201–203
Merchants, sales agreements and, 194
Mergers, antitrust regulations and, 365, 368–379
Merit, defenses to discrimination charges and, 298
Merrill Lynch Corporation, 426
Minority shareholders, close corporations, 329–330
Minors, capacity in contract law and, 155
Minute book, for corporation, 348
Mirror image rule
    contract law, 139–140
    UCC Section 2-207, 197
Misappropriation, in securities transactions, 364
Misdemeanor, criminal law, 96
Mislaid property, 483
Misrepresentation
    contract law, 156–158
    insurance contracts, 510
    nondisclosure of facts as, 158
Mistake, in contract law, 159
Mitigation of damages, as contract remedy, 186
M'Naghten Rule, insanity defense, 97
Model Business Corporation Act, 346–348, 353–354
Money laundering, 102, 104

Monopolization, antitrust laws, 367–368
Morality
    contract law and, 148–149
    law and, 7–8
Mortgage, on real property, 457
Mortgagee, on real property, 457
Mortgagor, on real property, 457
Motions, in litigation, 36
Multinational enterprises (MNEs)
    growth of, 111–112
    power of, 113
Mutual agreements, termination of agency
        relationships and, 267–268
Mutual benefit, bailee duties regarding, 485

# N

Names, on trademarks, 445
National Conference of Commissioners on Uniform
        State Laws (NCCUSL), 192
National Environmental Policy Act (NEPA), 415
National Labor Relations Act, 280, 311–312, 316–320
National Labor Relations Board, 311–315
National security letter (NSL), 106–107
Natural resources, government regulations protecting,
        414–417
NBC Television, 170–173
Negligence
    accountants' liability to clients, 379
    accountants' third party liability, 381
    bailment and, 485–486
    basic principles, 81
    breach of duty, 84
    case study of, 10–11
    contributory and comparative negligence, 88–89
    damages and, 87
    elements of, 81
    example of, 80
    factual cause and foreseeable harm, 84–85
    in hiring, principal's tort
        liability, 271
    injury and, 86
    landowner's duty, 82
    landowner's liability, 83–84
    res ipsa loquitur, 86
    street crime case study, 2–3
    warranties and product liability, 199, 203
Negligent design, 203
Negligent manufacture, 203
Negligent torts, principal's liability in, 272
Negotiable instruments
    ambiguities in, 216–217
    categories of, 212–218
    commercial paper, 212, 214–215
    consumer credit contract, 220
    consumer exception, 220–221

Negotiable instruments (*continued*)
 defense against holder in due course, 219–220
 fundamental "rule" of commercial paper, 213–216
 good faith in, 218
 holder in due course, 218–220
 outstanding claims and other defects, 219
 value in, 218–219
Negotiation, of negotiable instruments, 217–218
New issues, statutory law concerning, 55
Noncompete agreement
 employment contracts, 150–151
 examples of, 129
 legality of, 152
 sale of business, 150
Nonconforming goods, sales agreements, 198
Nondischargeable debts, 251–252
Nondisclosure of facts, misrepresentation as, 158
Nonobvious test, patent law, 439
Nonphysical harm, tort liability, 273
Nonpossessory interests, 455–457
Norris-LaGuardia Act, 311–312
North American Free Trade Agreement
  (NAFTA), 118
No strike/no lockout agreements, 317
Novation, 345
Novel test, patent law, 439
Number of shares, corporate
  stock, 347
Nuncupative will, 494–495

Obligee, assignment of rights
  and, 174
Obligor, assignment of rights and, 174–175
Occupational Safety and Health Act (OSHA),
  285–286
Off-duty conduct
 agency-principal relationships, 265
 employee privacy and, 286
Offer
 in contract law, 137
 insurance contracts, 509
 termination of, 139
Offeree
 additional or different terms from, 197
 in contract law, 137
Offeror, in contract law, 137
Office of Management and Budget (OMB),
  environmental law and, 413
Officers of corporation, 347–348
 compensation for, 354–355
Online privacy, cyberlaw regulations, 423–427
Open and notorious possession, 459
Opening agreement, for limited liability
  companies, 332

Opening statements, trial proceedings, 40
Opinions
 accountants' liability for, 377–378
 false statements and, 156
 intentional torts and, 68–69
Oppression, unconscionable contracts, 154
Oral will, 494–495
Order for relief, Chapter 7 bankruptcy, 247
Order paper
 holder for, 218
 as negotiable instrument, 215
Ordinary care, bailee duties regarding, 485
Organizational responsibility
 to customers, 22
 to employees, 22
 ethics and, 20–21
 overseas responsibilities, 23–24
 to shareholders, 22–23
Outside benefits, in agency relationships, 265
Outstanding claims, negotiable instruments, 219
Owner, defined, 508
Ownership interest. *See also* real property
 close corporations, transfer restrictions,
   329–330
 limited liability companies, transferability
   of, 333
 limited partnerships, transferability, 338
 partnerships, transferability issues, 335
 personal property, intention to transfer,
   480–483
 transferability of, 328
Ownership of trademarks, 444–445

Paris Convention for the Protection of
  Industrial Property
 patent provisions, 440
 trademark provisions, 446
Partnerships
 benefits and limitations of, 334–337
 example of, 326–327
 formation of, 335
 liability of, 334–335
 limited liability partnerships, 337–339
 limited partnerships and limited liability
   partnerships, 337–339
 management of, 335–336
 ownership interests of, 328
 professional corporations *vs.*, 339
 tax issues for, 328–329, 335
 termination of, 336–337
Part performance by buyer, land contracts, 161
Par value, corporate stock, 347
Patent and Trademark Office (PTO),
  440, 444–446

Patents, 438–440

Payee, of promissory note, 213

Pay for service, in health
insurance, 514

Payment of claims, bankruptcy, 250

Payment plan, Chapter 13 bankruptcy
reorganization, 256

*Per capita* distribution in wills, 496

Perfection
by possession, 234
in secured transactions, 231–236

Performance
in contract law, 176–179
in sales agreements, 198–199

Periodic tenancy, 467

Permanence, manifestation of, real property
law and, 453

*Per se* violations, antitrust laws, 365–366

Person, defined, 508

Personally identifiable information (PII),
cyberlaw regulations, 424

Personal property law
bailment, 483–487
defined, 480
example of, 479
found property, 483
gifts, 480–483

Personal services contract, promisor's
death in, 179

*Per stirpes* distribution in wills, 496

Petitions
bankruptcy filings, 246
Chapter 13 bankruptcy reorganization,
255–256
union organization, 313

Pfizer Corporation, 355

Phishing, as Internet crime, 431

Physical delivery, personal property transfer,
480–481

Physical examination, in litigation, 35–36

Picasso, Pablo, 492

Picketing, during strikes, 319–320

Piercing the corporate veil principle, 348

Plaintiff
comparative and contributory
negligence, 88–89
defined, 9
misrepresentation and fraud remedies,
156–157
in negligence suits, 81
trial proceedings and case of, 40–41

Plant life, as real property, 453

Plea bargain, 106

Point source, water pollution standards, 411

Pollution sources, air pollution, 410

Possession
attachment of security interest, 230
bailment and, 483–487

of collateral, 238
duty to deliver, 468
perfection by, 234
securities transactions, 363

Power of attorney, wills and, 497

Precedent
appeals courts and, 42
defined, 5

Predatory pricing, antitrust laws, 368

Predictability, common law and, 57

Preferences, voidable preferences, bankruptcy
estate, 249

Preferred stock, 347

Pregnancy, employment discrimination laws
and, 300

Premium, defined, 508

Pretermitted child, wills and, 495

Prevention of significant deterioration (PSD)
program, 410

Price-fixing. *See also* predatory pricing
antitrust regulations, 366, 369–370

Price Waterhouse, 383

Principal
agency competition with, 265
in agency relationship, 263
agents' duties to, 264–267
conflict of interest with, 265
contract liability of, 268–269
duties to agents of, 267
fully disclosed principal, 269
remedies for agent's breach of duty, 267
secret dealings with, 265
tort liability, 270–273
undisclosed principal, 269–270
unidentified principal, 269

Priority claims
bankruptcy, 251
patent law, 440

Prior sale principle, patent law, 440

Privacy law
cyberlaw, 423–427
employee privacy, 286–287
trusts and, 500

Private offerings, securities transactions, 362

Probable cause, 105

Probate
defined, 493
estate planning and, 493
trusts and, 500
wills and, 497–498

Procedural due process, 53

Procter & Gamble Co., 22

Product liability
negligence and, 203
strict liability, 199, 203–206
warranties and, 199–206

Product safety, consumer product safety
regulations, 402

Professional corporations (PCs), 339
Profit, real property and, 457
Promisee, third party claims, 172
Promisor
  death of, in personal services contract, 179
  third party claims, 172
Promissory estoppel, contract remedy and, 133–134
Promissory note, as negotiable instrument, 212–213
Promoter's liability, 345
Proof of claim, Chapter 7 bankruptcy, 247
Proof of discrimination, employment discrimination
    law, 295–297
Property insurance, 513
Property law. *See* personal property law;
    real property law
Prosecution, criminal law, 95–96
Prospectus, securities offerings, 362
Protected rights, under constitutional law, 50–51
Protective order, motions for, 36
Provisional patent application, 440
Proxies
  health care proxy, 498
  shareholders, 354
Proximate cause, defined, 84n.1
Proxy statement, 354
Public companies
  corporate governance in, 355
  employees of, 285
  limited liability companies changeover to, 333
Public Company Accounting Oversight Board
    (PCAOB), 378
Public offerings, securities, 362
Public personalities, intentional tort law and, 69–70
Public policy doctrine
  assignment of rights and, 174
  delegation of duties and, 175–176
  employment security and, 282–283
Puffery, false statements as, 156
Punishment, criminal law, 95–96
Punitive damages, 72–73, 87
Purchase money security interest (PMSI),
    perfection of consumer goods, 234–236
Purpose of corporation, 347

# Q

Qualified opinion, 377
Qualified privilege, employer's liability for, 283–284
*Quantum meruit*, quasi-contract cases, 134–135
Quarterly reports, for securities offerings, 363
Quasi-contract cases, 133–135
*Quid pro quo*, sexual harassment laws, 299–300
Quiet enjoyment principle, landlord-tenant
    laws, 468
Quorum, 354
Quotas, import and export controls, 116

# R

R. J. Reynolds Tobacco Company, 20
Race discrimination
  employment discrimination laws, 297–298
  equal protection clause (Fourteenth Amendment), 54
Racketeer Influenced and Corruption Organizations
    Act (RICO), 102
Ratification, of international treaties, 116
Reaffirmation of debt, bankruptcies and, 252–253
Real property
  adverse possession, 459–460
  estates in, 454–455
  example of claim on, 451–452
  land use regulation, 460–461
  nature of, 452–453
  nonpossessory interests, 455–457
  sale of, 457–459
Reasonable accommodation principle, disabled persons
    employment discrimination, 302–304
Reasonable care
  agent's duty of, 266
  sexual harassment laws, 300
Reasonable certainty
  compensatory damages, 181
  in written contracts, 164–165
"Reasonable factors other than age" (RFOA) principle,
    age discrimination law, 301–302
Reasonable person standard, 84
  crime provisions, landlord-tenant law
    and, 473–474
Recognition principle, union organization, 313
Recording Industry Association
    of America (RIAA), 437, 443–444
Recording of deed, real property sale, 459
Record keeping, international law and, 122–123
Refusal to violate law, employment security and,
    281–282
Registered agent, for corporation, 346
Registration of trademarks, 444–445
Registration statement, securities offerings, 362
Regulation D (Securities Act of 1933), 362
Rejection, contract law, 139
Reliance interest, as contract remedy, 183
Religious discrimination, employment
    discrimination laws, 298
Remand
  in appeals, 42
  defined, 9
Remedies
  buyer's remedies, 198–199
  compensatory damages, 181
  consequential damages, 181–182
  in contract law, 179–186
  employment discrimination laws, 300
  incidental damages, 182

injunction, 184–185
interest remedies, 179–181
in sales agreements, 198–199
seller's remedies, 199
tenant remedies for defective
conditions, 469
Rent, duty to pay, 471
Reorganization plan
Chapter 11 bankruptcy, 254
Chapter 13 bankruptcy, 255–256
Repeated bankruptcy filings, 252
Replacement workers, strikes and, 319
Resale price maintenance (RPM), antitrust
laws, 366–367
Rescind
agent's breach of duty as grounds for, 267
in contract law, 155, 176
Rescission, restitution and, 183
Reservation, easements and, 456
*Res ipsa loquitur,* negligence and, 86
Resource Conservation and Recovery Act
(RCRA), 413
*Respondeat superior,* principal's tort liability,
270–273
Restatement (Second) of Contracts, 136
assignment and delegation in, 174
good faith in, 177–178
strict liability in, 203–206
third party beneficiaries, 172
Restatement (Third) of Torts
negligent and intentional torts,
272nn.13–14
principal's contract liability, 268–269
principal's tort liability, 270n.11–12
strict liability and, 204–206
unidentified principal in, 269
Restitution, capacity in contract law
and, 155
Restitution interest, as contract remedy, 183
Restraint of trade, contract law, 150
"Restraint of trade" prohibitions, antitrust
regulations, 366
Reverse
in appeals, 42
defined, 9
Revised Patriot Act, 106–107
Revocable gift, 480
Revocable trust, 500
Revocation
contract law, 139
nondischargeable debts, 252
Rienzi Plaza, 16, 22
Risk, assumption of, 87
Risk-utility test, strict liability and, 205
Robinson-Patman Act (RPA), 369–370
Rockefeller, John D., 17
Rose, Christopher, 171–173
Rose, Rufus, 170–173

Rule making, administrative law and, 59–60
Rule of reason violations, antitrust laws, 365

# S

Sachs, Jeffrey, 23
Safety and privacy issues
consumer product safety, 402
employment law, 285–287
Sale of business, contract law
and, 150
Sale of real property, 457–459, 473–474
Sales agreements
additional and different terms, 197
contract formation, 194–196
fraud statutes, 196–198
gap fillers, 198
goods contracts, 165, 194
international law, 118–121
merchants, 194
mirror image rule, 197
performance and remedies,
198–199
real property sales contract and title
examination, 458
UCC development, 192–194
"Sales clerks don't count" defense, agency
relationships and, 262–263
Sales efforts, securities offerings, 362
Sales regulations
bait and switch, 395
consumer law, 393–397
deceptive acts or practices,
393–394
door-to-door sales, 396–397
mail or telephone order merchandise, 395–396
telemarketing, 396
unfair practices, 394
unordered merchandise, 396
Sarbanes-Oxley Act, 285
accountant-client privilege, 384
accounting regulations, 378
securities regulations, 355
Schiavo, Terri, 498
Scope of employment, principal's tort
liability, 271–272
S corporations, 330
Search and seizure, 105
online privacy and, 424–425
Search engines, copyright issues, 442–444
Search warrant, 105
Secondary offering, securities, 362
Secured claims, bankruptcy, 251
Secured transactions
buyer transactions, 236–237
components of, 228–229

Secured transactions (*continued*)
  creditors' priorities, 237–238
  debtor rights in collateral, 230
  default and termination, 238–239
  example of, 226–227
  future property attachments, 230–231
  perfection in, 231–236
  security interest attachment, 229–231
  termination of, 239
  value in, 230
Securities Act of 1933
  accountants' liability provisions, 382
  criminal liability provisions, 383
  securities transactions, 361–362
Securities and Exchange Commission (SEC)
  accountant-client provisions, 384
  accounting regulations, 377
  securities regulations of, 361–362
Securities Exchange Act of 1934
  criminal liability provisions, 383
  fraud provisions, 382–383
  joint and several liability provisions, 383
  securities regulations, 363
  whistleblowing provisions, 383
Securities laws, 361–365
Security deposit, duty to return, 470
Security issues, union organization, 317
Security transactions, regulation of, 361–365
Self-dealing, duty of loyalty and, 350–351
Self-incrimination, 105
Seller
  full performance requirements, land
    contracts, 161
  real property, obligations of, 458
  remedies for, 199
  strict liability of, 204–206
Seniority, defenses to discrimination charges
    and, 299
Separation of powers, constitutional law and, 48
Settlement offer, refusal to accept, 512
Settlor, defined, 493
Sewage, government regulations concerning, 412
Sexual harassment laws, 299–300
Shareholders
  business judgment rule and, 350
  close corporations, 329–330
  corporate management duty to, 349
  meetings, 354
  organization's responsibility to, 22–23
  as preferred stockholders, 347
  rights of, 353–355
  S corporations, 330
Sherman Act of 1890, 365–368
Signatory nations, 116
Signatures, in written contracts, 164
Silence, misrepresentation and fraud and, 157–158
Single recovery principle, compensatory
    damages, 72

Sixth Amendment
  guarantees in, 5
  protected rights under Fifth Amendment, 50–51
Slander, defined, 68
Slight care, duties of bailee regarding, 485
Small-business bankruptcy,
    254–255
Social Security, financial protection for employees
    and, 288
Society
  ethical behavior as benefit to, 17
  organizations' responsibility to, 20–21
Sole benefit
  of bailee, 485
  of bailor, 485
Sole proprietorships, 327–328
Sound mind principle, in wills, 494
Spam, government regulations concerning, 428
Special damages, as contract remedy, 181–182
"Special occasion" insurance, 516
Specific intent, criminal law, 96
Specific performance, as contract remedy, 183–184
Spouse's share of will, 495
Stakeholders
  corporate management duty to, 349
  ethics and identification of, 19–24
Standard Oil Trust, 365
Staples, Inc., 22–23
*Stare decisis*
  basic principles, 57
  defined, 5
State constitutions, purposes of, 5
State courts, 29–30
State governments
  organizational structure, 6
  zoning regulations, 460–461
State Implementation Plans (SIPS), air quality
    standards, 409–410
State legislatures, statutes passed by, 5
State online privacy regulations, 427
Statute of frauds, lease provisions, 466–467
Statute of limitations, contract
    law, 179
Statutes, defined, 5, 54
Statutory law, 54–56
  continuous possession for statutory period, 459
Stock, in corporation, 347
Stock exchange, rules of, 355
Stonecipher, Harry, 426
Straight bankruptcy, 246
Straight life insurance, 513–514
Strict liability, 89–90
  of bailee, 485
  warranties and product liability, 199, 203–206
Strict performance, in contract law, 176–177
Strike activity, labor law and, 309–310
  no strike/no lockout agreements, 317
  picketing and, 319–320

replacement workers, 319
rights and limitations, 319
Subcontracting, collective bargaining agreements and, 316–317
Subject matter destruction
contract law, 139
impossibility in contract law and, 179
Sublease, landlord-tenant laws and, 473–474
Subpoena, investigations and, 60
Subpoena *duces tecum,* investigations and, 60
Subprime loans, consumer credit regulations concerning, 397–398
Subsidiaries, 121
Substantial change, assignment of rights and, 174
Substantial interest in personal performance, delegation of duties and, 176
Substantial performance, in contract law, 176–177
Subsurface rights, as real property, 452
Sullivan, Louis W., 20
Summary judgment, 37–38
Superfund regulations, 412–414
Surprise, unconscionable contracts, 154

# T

Takings clause, in Fifth Amendment, 52–54
Tangible application principle, patent law and, 438–440
"Tangible employment action" principle, sexual harassment laws, 300
Tariffs, international law and, 114–116
Taxes
of corporations, 328–329
criminal liability of accountants and preparation of, 383
estate taxes, 493
in limited liability companies, 331–334
limited partnerships, 338
partnerships, 335
S corporations, 330
trust planning and, 500
Telemarketing regulations, 396
Telephone order sales regulations, 395–396
Temporary insiders, securities transactions, 363
Tenancy
categories of, 467
in common, 454
by the entirety, 455
at sufferance, 467
at will, 467
for years, 467
Tenant
defined, 466
duties of, 471–472
liability for injury, 473

Tenant remedies for defective conditions, 469
Term agreement, in agency relationships, 267
Termination
of agency relationships, 267–268
of corporation, 349
of partnership, 336
of secured transactions, 239
of trusts, 501
Term insurance, 513
Term limits for audit partners, 378
Term partnership, 336–337
Testamentary trust, 500
Testator/testatrix
amendments to wills and, 496
defined, 493
holographic will, 494
probate proceedings and, 497–498
Third party beneficiary, 171–173
Third party claims
accountants' liability for, 381–383
contract law and, 171
Tied product, 369
Tippees, in securities transactions, 364
Tippers, in securities transactions, 364
Title, real property, examination of, 458
Title VII of the Civil Rights Act of 1964, 295–300
Tortious interference with contracts, 74
Tort law. *See also* negligence
agent's liability, 273–274
business torts, 74–75
damages, 71–74
defamation, 283–284
employment security and, 283
example of, 66–67
*Exxon Valdez* and reform of, 74
infliction of emotional distress, 284
intentional torts, 68–71, 272
intrusion and, 74–75
landowner's liability and, 83
liability insurance and, 515
negligent torts, 272
nonphysical harm, 273
principal's liability in, 270–273
strict liability and, 204–206
Torts, defined, 67
Tracing, in audits, 377
Trademark law, 444–446
Trademark Law Treaty, 446
Trade regulation, international law and, 112–116
Trade secrets regulations, 446–447
Transactions in goods, UCC provisions on, 194n.1
Transferability of ownership interest
close corporations, 329–330
corporations, 328
limited liability companies, 333
limited partnerships, 338
partnerships, 335
personal property, intention to transfer, 480–483

Treasury stock, in corporation, 347
Trespasser, negligence, 82
Trial courts
    federal courts, 32–33
    state courts, 30–31
Trial proceedings
    adversary system, 39
    burden of proof, 40
    closing argument, 41
    criminal law, 106–107
    defendant's case, 41
    opening statements, 40
    plaintiff's case, 40–41
    right to jury, 39–40
    verdict, 41
Trustee, in trusts, 499
Trusts, planning for, 499–501
Truth in hiring, contract law and, 283
Truth-in-Lending Act (TILA), 397–398
Tying arrangements, 368–369
Tying product, 369

# U

U.S. Bankruptcy Code, 245
    discharge provisions, 251–253
    exempt property provision, 249
U.S. Trustee, Chapter 7 bankruptcy, 247
Ultrahazardous products, strict liability, 89–90
Ultrasound screenings, ethical issues concerning, 21
Uncertainty, conscious uncertainty, 159
Unconscionable contracts, 153–154
Undisclosed principal, agent liability and, 269–270
Undue hardship principle, disabled persons
        employment discrimination, 302–304
Undue influence, in wills, 494
Unenforceable agreement, 133
    longer than one year, 162–163
Unfair labor practices, 311–312
    strike as result of, 319
Unfair sales practices, 394
Unidentified principal, agent liability and, 269
Uniform Commercial Code (UCC)
    Article 2A, 194n.2
    Article 2 of, 194
    assignment and delegation in, 174
    buyer in ordinary course of business transactions,
        236–237
    consumer sales provisions, 202–203
    contract law and, 136, 194–196
    development of, 192
    filing perfection, 231–233
    gap fillers in, 198
    good faith in, 177–178
    interpretation of ambiguities, 216–217
    key elements of, 193

merchants' provisions, 194
    mirror image rule, 140
    perfection of consumer goods, 234–236
    performance and remedies in, 198–199
    sale of goods under, 165
    Section 2-201, 196
    Section 2-204, 195–196
    Section 2-207, 197
    warranties and product liability, 199–206
Uniform Electronic Transaction Act (UETA),
        165–166
Uniform Probate Code (UPC), 493, 495
Uniform Trade Secrets Act (UTSA), 446
Unilateral contracts, 131
Unilateral mistake, contract law, 159
Unincorporated businesses, sole proprietorships
        as, 327–328
Uninsured motorists, 515
Unions
    bargaining units and, 316
    collective bargaining agreements, 316–317
    employer and union security, 317
    historical development of,
        311–312
    organization of, 312–316
    regulation of, 320
    union shop provisions, 317
United Nations Convention on Contracts for the
        International Sale of Goods (CISG), 119
United States Constitution. *See also* specific
        amendments, e.g. First Amendment
    amendments to, 5
    Commerce Clause, 49
    government power in, 48
    protected rights under, 50–51
    as supreme law, 4–5
United States Courts of Appeals, 32
United States Custom Service, 114–115
United States District Courts, 32
United States Supreme Court, 32–33
    constitutional law concerning, 49
Universal life insurance, 514
Unordered merchandise, FTC regulations
        concerning, 396
Unqualified opinion, 377
Unsecured claims, bankruptcy, 251
USA Patriot Act, online privacy provisions, 426
Usefulness test, patent law, 439
Usury statutes, 397–401

# V

Valid contracts, 133
    refusal to pay valid insurance claims, 511–512
Valid trademarks, 445–446
Valuation, import controls, 115

Value
in negotiable instruments, 218
in secured transactions, 230
Values, ethics and, 20–24
Verdict, in trial proceedings, 41
Voidable contract, 133
Voidable preferences, bankruptcy estate, 249
Void agreement, 133
Voluntary action, affirmative action, 299
Voluntary petition
Chapter 7 bankruptcy, 246–247
Chapter 13 bankruptcy reorganization, 255–256
Voting
for corporate termination, 349
shareholders' right to, 354
Vouching, in audits, 377

# W

*Wall Street Journal, The,* 16, 22
Warranties, 199–206
consumer sales, 202–203
express warranties, 200
implied warranties, 201–203, 458
negligence and, 203
regulations concerning, 401
strict liability, 199, 203–206
Warranty of fitness, 202
Waste disposal, government regulations
concerning, 412–414
Wastewater treatment plants, government
regulations concerning, 412
Water pollution, government regulations on, 410–412
Water quality standards, 411
Wealth, happiness and, 17
Web sites
corruption perception index, 123
hosting regulations for, 428–430
House of Representatives, 5, 55
Senate, 55
state courts, 29–30
U.S. Appeals Courts, 32
U.S. Supreme Court, 32
Wetlands protection, government regulations
on, 411–412
Whistleblowing
accountants' liability and, 383
employment law and, 284–285

White collar crime, example of, 94–95
Whole life insurance, 513–514
Willful violations, criminal liability of
accountants, 383
Wills, 494–499
amendments to, 496
anatomical gifts, 498
children's share, 495–496
holographic will, 494
intestacy, 496–497
living wills, 498
nuncupative will, 494–495
power of attorney, 497
probate, 497–498
requirements for, 494–495
spouse's share, 495
testamentary trusts, 500
Winding up process
corporate termination, 349
partnership termination, 337
Wire and Electronic Communications
Interception Act, 99
Wire fraud, 100
Working papers, accountant-client
privilege, 384
Workmen's compensation claims
employment security and, 282
financial protection for employees
and, 288
Workplace monitoring
employee privacy and, 286–287
sexual harassment laws, 300
Workplace safety laws, 285–286
Work relationships, insurable interest, 510
WorldCom, 376
World Intellectual Property Organization, 446
World Trade Organization, 116–117
Written consent, corporate officers and directors
election, 347–348
Written contracts, requirements for, 160–165
Wrongful discharge, employment security
law, 281–283
Wrongful termination, agency relationships, 268

# Z

Zoning statutes, 460–461
Zuckerberg, Mark, 344–346